Lecture Notes in Computer Science 3845

Commenced Publication in 1973
Founding and Former Series Editors:
Gerhard Goos, Juris Hartmanis, and Jan van Leeuwen

Jacques Farré   Igor Litovsky
Sylvain Schmitz (Eds.)

Implementation and Application of Automata

10th International Conference, CIAA 2005
Sophia Antipolis, France, June 27-29, 2005
Revised Selected Papers

 Springer

Volume Editors

Jacques Farré
Sylvain Schmitz
Université de Nice - Sophia Antipolis
Laboratoire I3S, Les Algorithmes - bât. Euclide B
2000, route des lucioles, BP 121, 06903 Sophia Antipolis - Cedex, France
E-mail: Jacques.Farre@unice.fr;schmitz@i3s.unice.fr

Igor Litovsky
Université de Nice - Sophia Antipolis
Ecole Polytechnique
930, route des colles, BP 145, 06903 Sophia Antipolis - Cedex, France
E-mail: lito@essi.fr

Library of Congress Control Number: 2006920773

CR Subject Classification (1998): F.1.1, F.1.2, F.4.2, F.4.3, F.2

LNCS Sublibrary: SL 1 – Theoretical Computer Science and General Issues

ISSN   0302-9743
ISBN-10   3-540-31023-1 Springer Berlin Heidelberg New York
ISBN-13   978-3-540-31023-5 Springer Berlin Heidelberg New York

Springer is a part of Springer Science+Business Media

springer.com

© Springer-Verlag Berlin Heidelberg 2006
Printed in Germany

Typesetting: Camera-ready by author, data conversion by Scientific Publishing Services, Chennai, India
Printed on acid-free paper   SPIN: 11605157   06/3142   5 4 3 2 1 0

Preface

The 10th International Conference on Implementation and Application of Automata (CIAA 2005) was held in the Technopole of Sophia Antipolis, France, on June 27–29, 2005.

This volume of the *Lecture Notes in Computer Science* series contains the notes of the two invited lectures, the 26 papers selected for presentation at the conference, and the abstracts of the eight posters that were displayed.

The papers and posters were selected amongst 87 submitted papers. The submissions came from countries in five continents. They show applications of automata in many fields, including mathematics, linguistics, networks, XML processing, biology and music. The elderly lady of automata is alive and kicking, ready to face the new challenges of computer science.

Based on the reviews, the Best Paper Award was given to Markus Lohrey and Sebastian Maneth for their excellent article on Tree Automata and XPath on Compressed Trees (see page 225). This award was generously sponsored by the University of California at Santa Barbara.

We wish to thank all the Program Committee members and the additional referees for their efforts in refereeing and selecting papers, and maintaining the high standard of CIAA conferences. We are grateful to all the contributors to the conference, in particular to the invited speakers, for making CIAA 2005 a scientific success.

We also thank the Computer Science Department of the École Polytechnique Universitaire of the University of Nice - Sophia Antipolis for accommodating CIAA in its buildings and providing the logistical support.

October 2005

J. Farré
I. Litovsky
S. Schmitz

Organization

Program Committee

Olivier Carton	LIAFA, Paris, France
Jean-Marc Champarnaud	Université de Rouen, France
Maxime Crochemore	Université de Marne-la-Vallée, France
Jürgen Dassow	University of Magdeburg, Germany
Jacques Farré (Co-chair)	Université de Nice - Sophia Antipolis, France
José Fortes Gálvez	Universidad de Las Palmas de Gran Canaria, Spain
Jozef Gruska	Masaryk University, Brno, Czech Republic
Tero Harju	University of Turku, Finland
Oscar Ibarra	University of California at Santa Barbara, USA
Balázs Imreh	University of Szeged, Hungary
Masami Ito	Kyoto Sangyo University, Japan
Lauri Karttunen	PARC, California, USA
Nils Klarlund	Lucent Bell Labs, USA
Bertrand Le Saëc	LaBRI, Bordeaux, France
Igor Litovsky (Co-chair)	Université de Nice - Sophia Antipolis, France
Do Long Van	Institute of Mathematics, Hanoi, Vietnam
Carlos Martín Vide	Universitat Rovira i Virgili, Tarragona, Spain
Denis Maurel	Université de Tours, France
Filippo Mignosi	Università degli Studi di Palermo, Italy
Victor Mitrana	University of Bucharest, Romania
Mehryar Mohri	New York University, USA
Jean-Éric Pin	LIAFA, Paris, France
Jacques Sakarovitch	ENST, Paris, France
Kai T. Salomaa	Queen's University, Kingston, Canada
Pierluigi San Pietro	Politecnico di Milano, Italy
Bruce W. Watson	University of Eindhoven, The Netherlands
	University of Pretoria, South Africa
Thomas Wilke	Christian-Albrechts-Universität zu Kiel, Germany
Pierre Wolper	Université de Liège, Belgium
Derick Wood	Hong Kong University, China
Hsu-Chun Yen	National Taiwan University, Taipei, Taiwan
Sheng Yu	University of Western Ontario, London, Canada

Additional Referees

Cyril Allauzen	Marcella Anselmo	Constantinos Bartzi
Yongbo An	Ricardo Baeza-Yates	Marie-Pierre Béal

Gary Benson	Sándor Horváth	Andrei Păun
Vilmos Bilicki	Lucian Ilie	Radek Pélanek
Zoltán Blázsik	Csanád Imreh	Dominique Perrin
Luc Boasson	Tatiana B. Jajcayova	Lubos Popelínsky
Bernard Boigelot	Tao Jiang	Marc Pouzet
Béatrice Bouchou	Sandrine Julia	Matteo Pradella
Lubos Brim	Jarkko Kari	Christophe Prieur
Tevfik Bultan	André Kempe	Ashish Rastogi
Pascal Caron	Ernest Ketcha Ngassam	Bala Ravikumar
Didier Caucal	Daniel Kirsten	Chloe Rispal
Christian Choffrut	Felix Klaedtke	Eric Rivals
Loek Cleophas	Ines Klimann	Nicoletta Sabadini
Stefano Crespi Reghizzi	Hirotada Kobayashi	Nicolae Sântean
Mark Daley	Satoshi Kobayashi	Sylvain Schmitz
Zhe Dang	Mojmír Křetínský	Patrice Séébold
Pál Dömösi	Antonín Kucera	Olivier Serre
Michael Domaratzki	Grégory Kucherov	Petr Sosík
J.-Ph. Dubernard	Olivier Lecarme	Paola Spoletini
Chiara Epifanio	Sylvain Lombardy	Ralf Stiebe
Berndt Farwert	Jean Mairesse	Samuel Tardieu
Rūsiņš Freivalds	Nicolas Markey	Marc Tommasi
Dora Giammarresi	Ian Mcquillan	Nicholas Tran
Irène Guessarian	Christophe Morvan	Szilvia Varró-Gyapay
Peter Habermehl	Angelo Morzenti	Misha Volkov
Jan Holub	Christopher Nehaniv	François Yvon
Andrew Horner	Alexander Okhotin	Marc Zeitoun
Géza Horváth	Michael Palis	Gilles Zémor

Steering Committee

Jean-Marc Champarnaud	Université de Rouen, France
Oscar Ibarra	University of California at Santa Barbara, USA
Denis Maurel	Université de Tours, France
Derick Wood	Hong Kong University, China
Sheng Yu	University of Western Ontario, London, Canada

Organizing Committee

Jacques Farré (Co-chair)	Micheline Hagneré	Igor Litovsky (Co-chair)
Carine Fédèle	Corinne Julien	Sylvain Schmitz

Sponsoring Institutions

Université de Nice - Sophia Antipolis (UNSA)
Centre National de la Recherche Scientifique (CNRS)

Institut National de Recherche en Informatique et en Automatique (INRIA
Sophia Antipolis)
European Association for Theoretical Computer Science (EATCS)

Ministère de l'Éducation Nationale, de l'Enseignement Supérieur et de la Recherche
(direction des relations internationales et de la coopération)
Conseil Régional Provence-Alpes-Côte d'Azur
Conseil Général des Alpes Maritimes
Communauté d'Agglomération de Sophia Antipolis
SAEM Sophia Antipolis Côte d'Azur

Table of Contents

Invited Lectures

Technical Contributions

Poster Abstracts

Languages Recognizable by Quantum Finite Automata*

Rūsiņš Freivalds

Institute of Mathematics and Computer Science,
University of Latvia, Raiņa bulv. 29, Rīga, Latvia
Rusins.Freivalds@mii.lu.lv

Abstract. There are several nonequivalent definitions of quantum finite automata. Nearly all of them recognize only regular languages but not all regular languages. On the other hand, for all these definitions there is a result showing that there is a language l such that the size of the quantum automaton recognizing L is essentially smaller than the size of the minimal deterministic automaton recognizing L.

For most of the definitions of quantum finite automata the problem to describe the class of the languages recognizable by the quantum automata is still open. The partial results are surveyed in this paper. Moreover, for the most popular definition of the QFA, the class of languages recognizable by a QFA is not closed under union or any other binary Boolean operation where both arguments are significant.

The end of the paper is devoted to unpublished results of the description of the class of the recognizable languages in terms of the second order predicate logics. This research is influenced by the results of Büchi [1, 2], Elgot [3], Trakhtenbrot [4] (description of regular languages in terms of MSO), R.Fagin [5, 6] (description of NP in terms of ESO), von Neumann [7] (quantum logics), Barenco, Bennett et al. [8] (universal quantum gates).

1 Introduction

A quantum finite automaton (QFA) is a theoretical model for a quantum computer with a finite memory.

If we compare them with their classical (non-quantum) counterparts, QFAs have both strengths and weaknesses. The strength of QFAs is shown by the fact that quantum automata can be exponentially more space efficient than deterministic or probabilistic automata [9]. The weakness of QFAs is caused by the fact that any quantum process has to be reversible (unitary). This makes quantum automata unable to recognize some regular languages.

2 Definitions

Quantum finite automata (QFA) were introduced independently by Moore and Crutchfield [10] and Kondacs and Watrous [11]. They differ in a seemingly small

---

* Research supported by Grant No.05.1528 from the Latvian Council of Science and European Commission, contract IST-1999-11234.

J. Farré, I. Litovsky, and S. Schmitz (Eds.): CIAA 2005, LNCS 3845, pp. 1–14, 2006.

detail. The first definition allows the measurement only at the very end of the computation process. Hence the computation is performed on the quantum information only. The second definition allows the measurement at every step of the computation. In the process of the measurement the quantum information (or rather, a part of it) is transformed into the classical information. The classical information is not processed in the subsequent steps of the computation. However, we add the classical probabilities obtained during these many measurements. There is something not 100 percent natural in this definition. We will see below that this leads to unusual properties of the quantum automata and the languages recognized by these automata.

To distinguish these quantum automata, we call them, correspondingly, MO-QFA (measure-once) and MM-QFA (measure-many).

Definition 1. *An MM-QFA is a tuple $M = (Q; \Sigma; V; q_0; Q_{acc}; Q_{rej})$ where Q is a finite set of states, Σ is an input alphabet, V is a transition function, $q_0 \in Q$ is a starting state, and $Q_{acc} \subseteq Q$ and $Q_{rej} \subseteq Q$ are sets of accepting and rejecting states $(Q_{acc} \cap Q_{rej} = \emptyset)$. The states in Q_{acc} and Q_{rej}, are called halting states and the states in $Q_{non} = Q - (Q_{acc} \cup Q_{rej})$ are called non halting states. κ and $\$$ are symbols that do not belong to Σ. We use κ and $\$$ as the left and the right endmarker, respectively. The working alphabet of M is $\Gamma = \Sigma \cup \{\kappa; \$\}$.*

The state of M can be any superposition of states in Q (i. e., any linear combination of them with complex coefficients). We use $|q\rangle$ to denote the superposition consisting of state q only. $l_2(Q)$ denotes the linear space consisting of all superpositions, with l_2-distance on this linear space.

The transition function V is a mapping from $\Gamma \times l_2(Q)$ to $l_2(Q)$ such that, for every $a \in \Gamma$, the function $V_a : l_2(Q) \to l_2(Q)$ defined by $V_a(x) = V(a, x)$ is a unitary transformation (a linear transformation on $l_2(Q)$ that preserves l_2 norm).

The computation of a MM-QFA starts in the superposition $|q_0\rangle$. Then transformations corresponding to the left endmarker κ, the letters of the input word x and the right endmarker $\$$ are applied. The transformation corresponding to $a \in \Gamma$ consists of two steps.

1. First, V_a is applied. The new superposition ψ' is $V_a(\psi)$ where ψ is the superposition before this step.
2. Then, ψ' is observed with respect to $E_{acc}, E_{rej}, E_{non}$ where $E_{acc} = span\{|q\rangle : q \in Q_{acc}\}$, $E_{rej} = span\{|q\rangle : q \in Q_{rej}\}$, $E_{non} = span\{|q\rangle : q \in Q_{non}\}$. It means that if the system's state before the measurement was

$$\psi' = \sum_{q_i \in Q_{acc}} \alpha_i |q_i\rangle + \sum_{q_j \in Q_{rej}} \beta_j |q_j\rangle + \sum_{q_k \in Q_{non}} \gamma_k |q_k\rangle$$

then the measurement accepts ψ' with probability $\Sigma \alpha_i^2$, rejects with probability $\Sigma \beta_j^2$ and continues the computation (applies transformations corresponding to next letters) with probability $\Sigma \gamma_k^2$ with the system having state $\psi = \Sigma \gamma_k |q_k\rangle$.

We regard these two transformations as reading a letter a. We use V'_a to denote the transformation consisting of V_a followed by projection to E_{non}. This is the transformation mapping ψ to the non-halting part of $V_a(\psi)$. We use V'_w to denote the product of transformations $V'_w = V'_{a_n} V'_{a_{n-1}} \ldots V'_{a_2} V'_{a_1}$, where a_i is the i-th letter of the word w. We also use ψ_y to denote the non-halting part of QFA's state after reading the left endmarker κ and the word $y \in \Sigma^*$. From the notation it follows that $\psi_w = V'_{\kappa w}(|q_0\rangle)$.

We will say that an automaton recognizes a language L with probability p $(p > \frac{1}{2})$ if it accepts any word $x \in L$ with probability $\geq p$ and rejects any word $x \notin L$ with probability $\geq p$.

The MO-QFA differ from MM-QFA only in the additional requirement demanding that non-zero amplitudes can be obtained by the accepting and rejecting states no earlier than on reading the end-marker of the input word.

A probability distribution $\{(p_i, \phi_i) | 1 \leq i \leq k\}$ on pure states $\{\phi_i\}_{i=1}$ with probabilities $0 \leq p_i \leq 1$ ($\sum_{i=1}^{k}(p_i) = 1$), is called a mixed state or mixture.

A quantum finite automaton with mixed states is a tuple

$$(Q, \Sigma, \phi_{init}, \{T_\delta\}, Q_a, Q_r, Q_{non}),$$

where Q is finite a set of states, Σ is an input alphabet, ϕ_{init} is a initial mixed state, $\{T_\delta\}$ is a set of quantum transformations, which consists of defined sequence of measurements and unitary transformations, $Q_a \sqsubseteq Q$, $Q_r \sqsubseteq Q$ and $Q_{non} \sqsubseteq Q$ are sets of accepting, rejecting and non-halting states.

3 MO-Quantum Finite Automata

Sometimes even MO-QFA can be size-efficient compared with the classical FA.

Theorem 1. *[9]*

1. *For every prime p the language $L_p = \{$ the length of the input word is a multiple of p $\}$ can be recognized by a MO-QFA with no more than $const \log p$ states.*
2. *For every p a deterministic FA recognizing L_p needs at least p states.*
3. *For every p a probabilistic FA with a bounded error recognizing L_p needs at least p states.*

4 MM-Quantum Finite Automata

4.1 First Results

The previous work on 1-way quantum finite automata (QFAs) has mainly considered 3 questions:

1. What is the class of languages recognized by QFAs?
2. What accepting probabilities can be achieved?
3. How does the size of QFAs (the number of states) compare to the size of deterministic (probabilistic) automata?

In this paper, we consider the first question. The first results in this direction were obtained by Kondacs and Watrous [11].

Theorem 2. *[11]*

1. *All languages recognized by 1-way MM-QFAs are regular.*
2. *There is a regular language that cannot be recognized by a 1-way MM-QFA with probability $\frac{1}{2} + \epsilon$ for any $\epsilon > 0$.*

Brodsky and Pippenger [12] generalized the second part of Theorem 2 by showing that any language satisfying a certain property is not recognizable by an MM-QFA.

Theorem 3. *[12] Let L be a language and M be its minimal automaton (the smallest DFA recognizing L). Assume that there is a word x such that M contains states q_1, q_2 satisfying:*

1. *$q_1 \neq q_2$,*
2. *If M starts in the state q_1 and reads x, it passes to q_2,*
3. *If M starts in the state q_2 and reads x, it passes to q_2, and*
4. *There is a word y such that if M starts in q_2 and reads y, it passes to q_1,*

then L cannot be recognized by any 1-way quantum finite automaton (Fig.1).

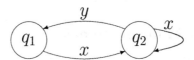

Fig. 1. Conditions of theorem 3

A language L with the minimal automaton not containing a fragment of Theorem 3 is called *satisfying the partial order condition* [13]. [12] conjectured that any language satisfying the partial order condition is recognizable by a 1-way QFA. In this paper, we disprove this conjecture.

Another direction of research is studying the accepting probabilities of QFAs.

Theorem 4. *[9] The language a^*b^* is recognizable by an MM-QFA with probability 0.68... but not with probability $7/9 + \epsilon$ for any $\epsilon > 0$.*

This shows that the classes of languages recognizable with different probabilities are different. Next results in this direction were obtained by [14] where the probabilities with which the languages $a_1^* \ldots a_n^*$ can be recognized are studied.

There is also a lot of results about the number of states needed for QFA to recognize different languages. In some cases, it can be exponentially less than for deterministic or even for probabilistic automata [9, 15]. In other cases, it can be exponentially bigger than for deterministic automata [16, 17].

A good survey on early results on quantum automata is Gruska [18].

4.2 Necessary Condition

First, we give the new condition which implies that the language is not recognizable by an MM-QFA. Similarly to the previous condition (Theorems 3), it can be formulated as a condition about the minimal deterministic automaton of a language. This condition is visualized in Figure 2.

Theorem 5. *[19] Let L be a language. Assume that there are words x, y, z_1, z_2 such that its minimal automaton M contains states q_1, q_2, q_3 satisfying:*

1. *$q_2 \neq q_3$,*
2. *if M starts in the state q_1 and reads x, it passes to q_2,*
3. *if M starts in the state q_2 and reads x, it passes to q_2,*
4. *if M starts in the state q_1 and reads y, it passes to q_3,*
5. *if M starts in the state q_3 and reads y, it passes to q_3,*
6. *for all words $t \in (x|y)^*$ there exists a word $t_1 \in (x|y)^*$ such that if M starts in the state q_2 and reads tt_1, it passes to q_2,*
7. *for all words $t \in (x|y)^*$ there exists a word $t_1 \in (x|y)^*$ such that if M starts in the state q_3 and reads tt_1, it passes to q_3,*
8. *if M starts in the state q_2 and reads z_1, it passes to an accepting state,*
9. *if M starts in the state q_2 and reads z_2, it passes to a rejecting state,*
10. *if M starts in the state q_3 and reads z_1, it passes to a rejecting state,*
11. *if M starts in the state q_3 and reads z_2, it passes to an accepting state.*

Then L cannot be recognized by a 1-way MM-QFA.

For languages whose minimal automaton does not contain the construction of Figure 3, this condition (together with Theorem 3) is necessary and sufficient.

Theorem 6. *[19] Let U be the class of languages whose minimal automaton does not contain "two cycles in a row" (Fig. 3). A language that belongs to U can be recognized by a 1-way MM-QFA if and only if its minimal deterministic automaton does not contain the "forbidden construction" from Theorem 3 and the "forbidden construction" from Theorem 5.*

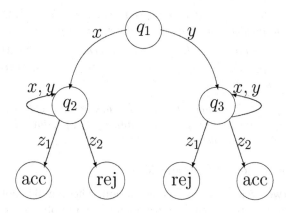

Fig. 2. Conditions of theorem 5, conditions 6 and 7 are shown symbolically

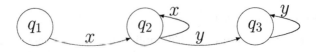

Fig. 3. Conditions of theorem 6

4.3 Non-closure Under Union

Let L_1 be the language consisting of all words that start with any number of letters a and after first letter b (if there is one) there is an odd number of letters a.

This language satisfies the conditions of Theorem 5. (q_1, q_2 and q_3 of Theorem 5 are just q_1, q_2 and q_3 of G_1. x, y, z_1 and z_2 are b, aba, ab and b.) Hence, it cannot be recognized by a QFA.

Consider 2 other languages L_2 and L_3 defined as follows.

L_2 consists of all words which start with an even number of letters a and after first letter b (if there is one) there is an odd number of letters a.

L_3 consists of all words which start with an odd number of letters a and after first letter b (if there is one) there is an odd number of letters a.

It is easy to see that $L_1 = L_2 \bigcup L_3$.

These languages (or rather their minimal automata) do not contain any of the "forbidden constructions" of Theorem 6. Therefore, L_2 and L_3 can be recognized by a MM-QFA and we get

Theorem 7. *[20] There are two languages L_2 and L_3 which are recognizable by a MM-QFA but the union of them $L_1 = L_2 \bigcup L_3$ is not recognizable by a MM-QFA.*

Corollary 1. *[20] The class of languages recognizable by a MM-QFA is not closed under union.*

As $L_2 \bigcap L_3 = \emptyset$ then also $L_1 = L_2 \Delta L_3$. So the class of languages recognizable by MM-QFA is not closed under symmetric difference. From this and from the fact that this class is closed under complement, it easily follows:

Corollary 2. *[20] The class of languages recognizable by a MM-QFA is not closed under any binary boolean operation where both arguments are significant.*

Theorem 8. *[19] If 2 languages L_1 and L_2 are recognizable by a MM-QFA with probabilities p_1 and p_2 and $\frac{1}{p_1} + \frac{1}{p_2} < 3$ then $L = L_1 \bigcup L_2$ is also recognizable by QFA with probability $\frac{2p_1 p_2}{p_1 + p_2 + p_1 p_2}$.*

Theorem 9. *[19] If 2 languages L_1 and L_2 are recognizable by a MM-QFA with probabilities p_1 and p_2 and $p_1 > 2/3$ and $p_2 > 2/3$, then $L = L_1 \bigcup L_2$ is recognizable by QFA with probability $p_3 > 1/2$.*

4.4 More "Forbidden" Constructions

If we allow the "two cycles in a row" construction, Theorem 6 is not longer true. More and more complicated "forbidden fragments" that imply non-recognizability by an MM-QFA are possible.

Theorem 10. *[19] Let L be a language and M be its minimal automaton. If M contains a fragment of the form shown in Figure 4 where $a, b, c, d, e, f, g, h, i \in \Sigma^*$ are words and $q_0, q_a, q_b, q_c, q_{ad}, q_{ae}, q_{bd}, q_{bf}, q_{ce}, q_{cf}$ are states of M and*

1. *If M reads $x \in \{a, b, c\}$ in the state q_0, its state changes to q_x.*
2. *If M reads $x \in \{a, b, c\}$ in the state q_x, its state again becomes q_x.*
3. *If M reads any string consisting of a, b and c in a state q_x ($x \in \{a, b, c\}$), it moves to a state from which it can return to the same state q_x by reading some (possibly, different) string consisting of a, b and c.*
4. *If M reads $y \in \{d, e, f\}$ in the state q_x ($x \in \{a, b, c\}$), it moves to the state q_{xy}.[1]*
5. *If M reads $y \in \{a, b, c\}$ in a state q_{xy}, its state again becomes q_{xy}.*
6. *If M reads any string consisting of d, e and f in the state q_{xy} it moves to a state from which it can return to the same state q_{xy} by reading some (possibly, different) string consisting of d, e and f.*
7. *Reading g in the state q_{ad}, h in the state q_{bf} and i in the state q_{ce} leads to accepting states. Reading h in the state q_{ae}, i in the state q_{bd}, g in the state q_{cf} leads to rejecting states.*

then L is not recognizable by an MM-QFA.

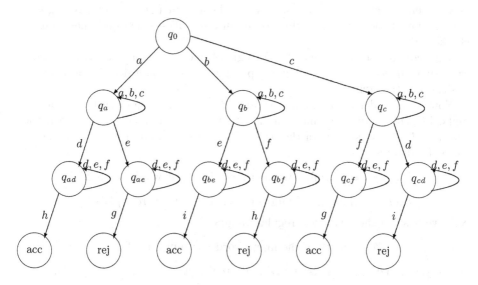

Fig. 4. Conditions of theorem 10

---

[1] Note: We do not have this constraint (and the next two constraints) for pairs $x = a, y = f$, $x = b$, $y = e$ and $x = c$, $y = d$ for which the state q_{xy} is not defined.

5 Descriptive Complexity

Deterministic finite automata can be regarded as a special type of Turing machines working real-time. Deterministic finite automata can also be regarded as a special type of Turing machines working in small space. Hence theory of finite automata is a part of computational coplexity theory. However, computational complexity theory was soon followed by descriptive complexity theory. The origins and the first impressive results of the decsriptive complexity theory is described by N.Immerman [21, 22].

Computational complexity began with the natural physical notions of time and space. Given a property, S, an important issue is the computational complexity of checking whether or not an input satisfies S. For a long time, the notion of complexity referred to the time or space used in the computation. A mathematician might ask, "What is the complexity of *expressing* the property S?" It should not be surprising that these two questions - that of cheching and that of expressing - are related. However, it is startling how tied they are when the second question refers to expressing the property in first-order logic. Many complexity classes originally defined in terms of time or space resources have precise definitions in first-order or second-order logic. At first, this was discovered for finite automata.

In early sixties Büchi [1, 2], Elgot [3] and Trakhtenbrot [4] showed how a logical formula may effectively be transformed into a finite state automaton accepting the language specified by the formula, and *vice versa*. It demonstrates how to relate the specification of a system behaviour (the formula) to a possible implementation (the behaviour of an automaton) - which underlies modern checking tools.

The monadic second-order (MSO) logic of one successor is a logical framework that allows one to specify string prperties using quantification over sets of positions in the string.

Now we consider an example how an automaton can be described by a formula. Let the input word have the length n in the alphabet $\{a, b\}$. Then the considered sets are subsets of the set $\{1, 2, \ldots, n\}$. $P_a(x)$ and $P_b(x)$ are, respectively, predicates

$$P_a(x) = \{\text{the symbol number } x \text{ in the input word equals } a\}$$

$$P_b(x) = \{\text{the symbol number } x \text{ in the input word equals } b\}$$

Now we wish to show how the regular language

$$\{\text{the length of the input word is a multiple of 3}\}$$

can be described. We use also individual predicates

$$S(x, y) = \{y = x + 1\}$$
$$first(x) = \{x = 1\}$$
$$last(x) = \{x = n\}$$

We use in our example three set-variables having the following meaning:

$$X_1 = \{\text{all the positions } i \text{ such that } i \equiv 1(\text{mod}3)\}$$

$$X_2 = \{\text{all the positions } i \text{ such that } i \equiv 2(\text{mod}3)\}$$

$$X_0 = \{\text{all the positions } i \text{ such that } i \equiv 0(\text{mod}3)\}$$

The MSO formula is as follows.

$$\exists X_1 X_2 X_0 ((X_1 \cap X_2 = \phi) \wedge (X_1 \cap X_2 = \phi) \wedge (X_1 \cap X_2 = \phi) \wedge$$

$$\wedge \forall (first(x) \Rightarrow X_1(x)) \wedge$$

$$\wedge \forall xy (S(x,y) \wedge ((X_1 \wedge X_2(y)) \vee (X_2(x) \wedge X_0(y)) \vee (X_0(x) \wedge X_1(y)) \wedge$$

$$\wedge \forall x (last(x) \Rightarrow X_0(x)))$$

It needs to be reminded that Büchi [1] considers description of automata on infinite strings. On the other hand, up to now quantum automata have been considered as processing finite words only. Perhaps there is some quantum mechanics based motivation behind this restriction.

As for classical Büchi automata, in the 1970's there was relatively little interest in these automata. There was some theoretical work on automata with infinite state spaces such as pushdown tree automata. However, the decision problems usually became undecidable. Thus, while of some theoretical interest, it did not appear to have major impact on Computing Science. The situation changed on 1977 when Pnueli's paper [23] appeared. Pnueli proposed the use of Temporal Logic for reasoning about continuously operating concurrent programs. Temporal Logic is a type of modal logic that provides a formalism for describing how the truth values of assertions vary over time. While there are a variety of different systems of Temporal Logic, typical temporal operators or modalities include Fp ("sometimes p") which is true now provided there is a future moment where p holds, and Gp ("always p) which is true now provided that p holds at all future moments. As Pnueli argued, Temporal Logic seems particularly well-suited to describing correct behaviour of continuously operating concurrent programs.

Automata provide strictly more expressive power than (ordinary) Temporal Logic. The property G_2p, meaning that at all even moments p holds, is easily described by an automaton, but not in Temporal Logic. Today Büchi and related automata are studied both from theoretical and practical viewpoint. The central technical use of automata by Büchi - to provide a decision procedure for a logical theory by reduction to the emptiness problem for the automata - remains today the main use of such automata in connection with logical theories, such as Temporal Logic, for reasoning about program correctness.

Many automata classes are now described in terms of logics. For instance, Engelfriet and Hoogeboom [24] equated 2DGSM, the family of string transductions realized by deterministic two-way finite state transducers (i.e. finite state automata equiped with a two-way input tape and a one-way output tape) and MSOS, the family obtained by restricting monadic second-order definable graph transductions to strings. Thus, string transductions that are specified in

MSO logic can be implemented on two-way finite state transducers, and vice versa.

In 1974 Fagin gave a characterization of nondeterministic polynomial time (NP) as the set of properties expressible in second-order existential logic. Some the results arising from this approach include characterizing polynomial time (P) as the set of properties expressible in first-order logic plus a least fixed point operator, and showing that the set of first-order inductive definitions for finite structures is closed under complementation.

It is well known that second-order formulas may be transformed into prenex form, with all second-order quantifiers in front. Let SO be the set of second-order expressible properties, and let ESO be the set of second-order properties that may be written in prenex form with no universal second-order quantifiers.

We consider the following example. Let the structure $G = (\{1, 2, \cdots, n\}, E)$ represent a graph of n vertices, and E be a single binary relation representing the edges of the graph. We say that the graph G is 3-colourable (in colors Red, Yellow, Blue) iff its vertices may be coloured with one of three colours such that no two adjacent vertices are the same colour. Three colourability is an NP-complete property. Consider the following ESO-formula α where R, Y, B are set-variables expressing the set of the vertices coloured correspondingly.

$$\alpha = (\exists R)(\exists Y)(\exists B)((R(x) \vee Y(x) \vee B(x)) \wedge (\forall y)(E(x, y) \Rightarrow$$

$$\neg(R(x) \wedge R(y)) \wedge \neg(Y(x) \wedge Y(y)) \wedge \neg(B(x) \wedge B(y))))$$

Observe that a graph G satisfies α iff G is 3-colourable. Fagin [5] proves that all NP-properties and only these properties are ESO-expressible.

Theorem 11. *[5] (ESO) = NP.*

Stockmeyer [25] followed this theorem by a nice characterization of the polynomial-time hierarchy.

Theorem 12. *[25] (SO) = PH.*

Definition 2. *We now define (FO + LFP) to be the set of first-order inductive definitions. We do this by adding a least fixed point operator (LFP) to first-order logic. If $\phi(R^k, x_1, \cdots, x_k)$ is an R^k -positive formula (i.e. R does not occure within any negation signs) in (FO + LFP) then $(LFP_{R^k_{x_1, \cdots, x_k}} \phi)$ is a formula in (FO + LFP) denoting the least fixed point of ϕ. We also define $IND[f(n)]$ to be the sublanguage of (FO + LFP) in which we only include least fixed points of first-order formulas ϕ for which $|\phi|$ is $O[f(n)]$. For example, the reflexive, transitive closure of E is expressible as $(LFP_{Rxy}\beta)$ and is thus in $IND[\log n]$. Note also that,*

$$(FO + LFP) = \cup_{k=1}^{\infty} IND[n^k].$$

Immerman [26] and Vardi [27] characterized the complexity of (FO + LFP) as follows,

Theorem 13. *[26, 27] (FO + LFP) = P.*

Immerman [28] characterized the complexity of PSPACE similar way,

Theorem 14. *[28] $PSPACE = \cup_{k=1}^{\infty} FO[2^{n^k}]$.*

These theorems are most exciting. Indeed, Theorem 13 says that if we add to first-order logic the power to define new relations by induction, then we can express exactly the properties that are checkabale in polynomial time. Polynomial time is characterized using only basic logical notions and no mention of computation. The famous open problems in Theory of Computation turn out to be equivalent to purely logical problems. For instance, $P =?NP$ is equivalent to whether or not every second-order expressible property over finite ordered structures is already expressible in first-order logic using inductive definitions.

6   Description of Languages Recognized by QFA

We noted in Section 4 (Theorem 2) that QFA recognize only regular languages but not all regular languages. Hence the logical description of these languages should be weaker that MSO considered by Büchi. The first intension is to consider "natural" subclasses of MSO. However, Theorem 7 shows that even the most popular logical operations conjunctions and disjunctions cannot be present in the logics we are seeking for. The only way out is to consider less standard logics, like Quantum Logics introduced by von Neumann[7].

Instead of $\vee, \wedge, \neg$ we use only unitary operations. However, von Neumann's quantum logics turns out to be very far removed from qubits, discrete unitary transformations and all the usual machinery of quantum finite automata. Next ideas come from fuzzy logics by L.Zadeh [29]. Predicates $P_a(x)$ were replaced by distributions of probabilities in [29]. Following this line, I constructed a logic allowing distributions of amplitudes with amplitudes being complex numbers [where *distribution* means that the total of square moduli of these values equals 1]. Finally, I use a result by D. P. DiVincenzo [30] who proved that two-bit quantum gates are universal for quantum computation. I use also a result by A.Barenco et al. [8] where the authors prove that all one-bit quantum gates $(U(2))$ and the two-bit exclusive-or gate (that maps Boolean values (x, y) to $(x, x \oplus y))$ is universal in the sense that all unitary operations on arbitrarily many bits n $(U(2^n))$ can be expressed as compositions of these gates. This allows to use in this new logics only a logical operation *exclusive-or* and arbitrary *rotations* of one qbit.

However, I do not describe here the details of this logics because in June 2005 Ilze Dzelme defended in the University of Latvia her Master thesis [31] containing the theorem 15 (below).

Generalized quantifiers were introduced by Mostowski [32]. This theorem uses the notion of *Lindström quantifiers*. [We take the definition of these quantifiers from [33]].

Consider the classical first-order existential quantifier applied to some quantifier-free formula ψ with free variable x, i.e. consider the formula $\Psi = \exists x \psi(x)$. Given an ordered structure A, we can associate a binary (i.e., 0-1) sequence a_ψ with ψ by evaluating ψ for every possible value of x from U^A and then adding 0 for false and 1 for true to a_ψ. To be more formal: If n is assigned to x then $a_{\psi(n)=1}$ iff $\psi(x)$ evaluates to true. The formula Ψ evaluates to true in A if the above defined sequence a_ψ is such that it has at least one position with the value 1. It is immediate to give a condition for sequences corresponding to a universal quantifier (all positions must be 1), or for the $\exists!$ quantifier (exactly one position must be 1), or for modular quantifiers $\exists_{\equiv k}$ (the number of 1 positions must be equivalent to 0 mod k).

Thus, it is very natural to define generalized quantifiers by considering arbitrary conditions on binary sequences (which we will call logical acceptance types). Let us give a formal definition.

Let τ be a set of s-tuples of binary sequences, i.e., τ consists of tuples $(a_1, \cdots, a_s)$ where for every $i(1 \leq i \leq s), a_i$ is a mapping from $\{1, \cdots k\}$ to $\{0, 1\}$ for some k. We call such a τ a *logical acceptance type*. The set of all s-tuples of finite binary sequences will in the following be denoted by $\tau(s)$.

Then we denote the Lindström quantifier given by τ by Q_τ. By $Q_\tau \Sigma_k - FO$ we denote the set of formulae built as follows: If $\psi_1, \cdots, \psi_s$ are $\Sigma_k - FO$ formulae, each over r free variables.

Let A be a finite structure over the corresponding signature.. Then $A \models Q_\tau \overrightarrow{x}[\psi_1(\overrightarrow{x}), \cdots, \psi_s(\overrightarrow{x})]$ if the tuple $(a_1, \cdots, a_s)$ is in τ, where the sequences a_i are defined as follows: For $1 \leq n \leq |U^A|^r$, $a_i(n) = 1$ if and only if $A \models \psi_i(\overrightarrow{x})$ where n is the rank of $\overrightarrow{x}$ on the order of r-tuples over $A(1 \leq i \leq s)$. $Q_\tau \Sigma_k - FO$ is defined analogously. We write $Q_\tau^0 \Sigma_k^0$ for $Mod(Q_\tau^0 \Sigma_k^0)$ and $Q_\tau^0 \Pi_k^0$ for $Mod(Q_\tau^0 \Pi_k^0)$.

Given a Lindström quantifier Q_τ, define Q_τ^+ to be the set of first-order formulae in prenex normal form that starts with one quantifier Q_τ followed by arbitrary first-order formulae.

Second-order Lindström quantifiers are defined as follows. Let $\tau \in \tau(s)$ be a logical acceptance type as above. By $Q_\tau \Sigma_k - SO$ we denote the set of formulae built as follows: If $\psi_1, \cdots, \psi_s$ are $\Sigma_k - SO$ formulae, each over q free predicates $\overrightarrow{R} = R_1, R_2, \cdots, R_r$, then $Q_\tau \overrightarrow{R}[\psi_1(\overrightarrow{R}), \cdots, \psi_s(\overrightarrow{R})]$ is a $Q_\tau \Sigma_k - SO$ formula. The semantics of such a formula is defined as follows: Let r the sum of arities of all predicate symbols in $\overrightarrow{R}$. Then we can identify one possible assigment of $\overrightarrow{R}$ over a set U_A with its characteristic sequence $c_{\overrightarrow{R}}$ which is a binary string of length $|U^A|^r$.

Based on the lexicographical ordering of these strings, we define an ordering on assignments of $\overrightarrow{R}$. Let now A be a finite structure over the corresponding signature. Then $A \models Q_\tau \overrightarrow{R}[\psi_1(\overrightarrow{R}), \cdots, \psi_s(\overrightarrow{R})]$ if the tuple $(a_1, \cdots, a_s)$ is in τ, where the sequences a_i are defined as follows: For $1 \leq n \leq |U^A|^r$, $a_i(n) = 1$ if and only if $A \models \psi_i(\overrightarrow{x})$ where n is the rank of $\overrightarrow{x}$ in the above-sketched order of assignments of $\overrightarrow{R}(1 \leq i \leq s)$. Analogously to the first-order case, we can also define $Q_\tau \Pi_k - SO$. We use $Q_\tau - FO$ and $Q_\tau - SO$ as abbreviations for $Q_\tau \Sigma_0 - SO$ and $Q_\tau \Sigma_0 - SO$, resp.

Theorem 15. *[31] A language can be recognized by a MO-QFA if and only if this language can be described by a second-order Lindström quantifier formula corresponding to group languages.*

References

1. Büchi, J.R.: Weak second-order arithmetic and finite automata. Zeitschrift für Mathematische Logik und Grundlagen der Mathematik **6** (1960) 66–92
2. Büchi, J.R.: On a decision method in restricted second order arithmetic. In Nagel, E., ed.: Proceeding of the International Congress on Logic, Methodology and Philosophy of Science, Stanford, CA, Stanford University Press (1960) 1–11
3. Elgot, C.C.: Decision problems of finite automata design and related arithmetics. Trans. Amer. Math. Soc. **98** (1961) 21–51
4. Trakhtenbrot, B.A.: Finite automata and the logic of one-place predicates. Siberian Mathematical Journal **3** (1962) 103–131 (in Russian), English translation: American Mathematical Society Translations **59** (1966) 23–55.
5. Fagin, R.: Generalized first-order spectra and polynomial-time recognizable sets. In Karp, R.M., ed.: Complexity of Computation. Volume 7 of SIAM-AMS Proceedings. (1974) 43–73
6. Fagin, R.: Monadic generalized spectra. Zeitschrift für Mathematische Logik und Grundlagen der Mathematik **21** (1975) 89–96
7. von Neumann, J.: Mathematical Foundations of Quantum Mechanics. Princeton University Press, Princeton, NJ (1932)
8. Barenco, A., Bennett, C.H., Cleve, R., DiVincenzo, D.P., Margolus, N.H., Shor, P.W., Sleator, T., Smolin, J.A., Weinfurter, H.: Elementary gates for quantum computation. Physical Review A **52** (1995) 3457–3467
9. Ambainis, A., Freivalds, R.: 1-way quantum finite automata: Strengths, weaknesses and generalizations. In: Proc. FOCS'98. (1998) 332–341 also quant-ph/9802062[2].
10. Moore, C., Crutchfield, J.P.: Quantum automata and quantum grammars. Theor. Comput. Sci. **237** (2000) 275–306 also quant-ph/9707031.
11. Kondacs, A., Watrous, J.: On the power of quantum finite state automata. In: Proc. FOCS'97. (1997) 66–75
12. Brodsky, A., Pippenger, N.: Characterizations of 1-way quantum finite automata. SIAM J. Comput. **31** (2002) 1456–1478 also quant-ph/9903014.
13. Meyer, A.R., Thompson, C.: Remarks on algebraic decomposition of automata. Mathematical Systems Theory **3** (1969) 110–118
14. Ambainis, A., Bonner, R.F., Freivalds, R., Kikusts, A.: Probabilities to accept languages by quantum finite automata. In: Proc. COCOON'99. (1999) 174–183 also quant-ph/9904066.
15. Kikusts, A.: A small 1-way quantum finite automaton (1998) quant-ph/9810065.
16. Ambainis, A., Nayak, A., Ta-Shma, A., Vazirani, U.: Dense quantum coding and quantum finite automata. J. ACM **49** (2002) 496–511 also quant-ph/9804043.
17. Nayak, A.: Optimal lower bounds for quantum automata and random access codes. In: Proc. FOCS'99. (1999) 369–377 also quant-ph/9904093.
18. Gruska, J.: Descriptional complexity issues in quantum computing. Journal of Automata, Languages and Combinatorics **5** (2000) 191–218

---

[2] Quant-ph preprints are available at http://www.arxiv.org/abs/quant-ph/preprint-number.

19. Ambainis, A., Kikusts, A., Valdats, M.: On the class of languages recognizable by 1-way quantum finite automata. In Ferreira, A., Reichel, H., eds.: Proc. STACS'01. Volume 2010 of Lecture Notes in Computer Science., Springer (2001) 75–86

20. Valdats, M.: The class of languages recognizable by 1-way quantum finite automata is not closed under union. In: Proc. Int. Workshop Quantum Computation and Learning, Sundbyholm Slott, Sweden (2000) 52–64

21. Immerman, N.: Descriptive and computational complexity. In Csirik, J., Demetrovics, J., Gécseg, F., eds.: Proc. FCT'89. Volume 380 of Lecture Notes in Computer Science., Springer (1989) 244–245

22. Immerman, N.: Descriptive complexity: A logician's approach to computation. Notices of the AMS **42** (1995) 1127–1133

23. Pnueli, A.: The temporal logic of programs. In: Proc. FOCS'77. (1977) 1–14

24. Engelfriet, J., Hoogeboom, H.J.: MSO definable string transductions and two-way finite-state transducers. ACM Trans. Comput. Logic **2** (2001) 216–254

25. Stockmeyer, L.: The polynomial-time hierarchy. Theoretical Computer Science **3** (1977) 1–22

26. Immerman, N.: Relational queries computable in polynomial time (extended abstract). In: Proc. STOC '82, New York, NY, USA, ACM Press (1982) 147–152

27. Vardi, M.Y.: Complexity of relational query languages. In: Proc. STOC'82. (1982) 137–146

28. Immerman, N.: Upper and lower bounds for first order expressibility. J. Comput. Syst. Sci. **25** (1982) 76–98

29. Zadeh, L.A.: Fuzzy sets. Information and Control **8** (1965) 338–353

30. Vincenzo, D.P.D.: Two-bit gates are universal for quantum computation. Physical Review A **51** (1995) 1015–1022

31. Dzelme, I.: Quantum finite automata and logics. Master's thesis, University of Latvia (2005) Advisor: Freivalds, R.

32. Mostowski, A.: On a generalization of quantifiers. Fundamenta Mathematicae **44** (1957) 12–36

33. Burtschik, H.J., Vollmer, H.: Lindström quantifiers and leaf language definability. In: Electronic Colloquium on Computational Complexity. (1996) TR96–005

The Language, the Expression, and the (Small) Automaton

Jacques Sakarovitch

LTCI, CNRS/ENST,
46 rue Barrault, F-75634 Paris Cedex 13, France
sakarovitch@enst.fr

Abstract. This survey paper reviews the means that allow to go from one representation of the languages to the other and how, and to what extend, one can keep them small. Some emphasis is put on the comparison between the expressions that can be computed from a given automaton and on the construction of the derived term automaton of an expression.

1 Plato's Cave

Formal language theory, especially that part which consists in the study of the so-called *regular* or *recognisable* languages, is a model instance of Plato's myth of the cavern. The real objects are the languages – or the power series – potentially *infinite* and what we, poor computer scientists bound to manipulate *finite* objects, can only see are the expressions that denote, or the automata that recognize them. Hopefully, these expressions and automata are fairly faithful descriptions of the languages (or of the series) they stand for and all the more effective that one can take advantage of this double light.

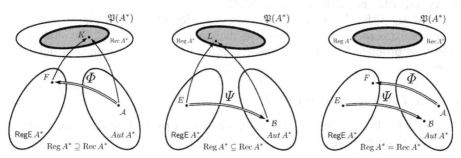

Fig. 1. The Φ and Ψ algorithms

It is the idea I have tried to illustrate with Figure 1 in the case of Kleene's Theorem. Kleene's Theorem states the equality of two classes of languages: the class of recognisable languages, that is those languages recognised by a finite

J. Farré, I. Litovsky, and S. Schmitz (Eds.): CIAA 2005, LNCS 3845, pp. 15–30, 2006.

automaton, and the class of regular languages, that is those languages denoted by a regular expression. A closer look *at the proof* allows to argue that Kleene's Theorem is indeed the combination of two classes of algorithms: one that transform an automaton into an expression and one that build an automaton from an expression. In this setting, the real languages — or series — almost disappear: only exist their symbolic (and finitary) representations.

In this talk, mostly a survey, I review the means that allow to go from one representation of the languages to the other and how, and to what extend, one can keep them small.

The first section presents the classical methods of computing an expression from an automaton and of computing an automaton from an expression. We discuss the relationships between the different expressions obtained from a given automaton and the ways of reaching a compact one. In the second section, I classify the methods that build an automaton from an expression and describe with more details the one which is probably the lesser known: Antimirov's construction of *derived term automaton*.

As a conclusion, I mention the problem of finding an algorithm that is inverse to those which compute an expression from an automaton, hence taming the combinatorial explosion induced by the latter ones, and sketch a first attempt to solve it.

2   The Φ Algorithms

We use mostly classical notation ([1, 2]). In particular we denote an automaton as $\mathcal{A} = \langle Q, A, E, I, T \rangle$ where I and T are subsets of the set Q of states, and E is the set of transitions labeled by letters of the alphabet A, or equivalently as $\mathcal{A} = \langle I, E, T \rangle$ where E is the square matrix of dimension Q whose entry (p, q) is the set of letters that label the transitions from p to q, and where I and T are Boolean vectors of dimension Q. The language accepted by $\mathcal{A}$ is denoted by $L(\mathcal{A})$ and with the latter notation, $L(\mathcal{A}) = I \cdot E^* \cdot T$.

A "Φ algorithms", computes an expression for $L(\mathcal{A})$ and thus amounts to compute expressions for the entries of the star of the matrix E. We shall consider this problem both from a theoretical and from an experimental point of view.

2.1   A Theoretical Point of View

There are (at least) four methods or algorithms for computing a regular expression that denotes $L(\mathcal{A})$:

1. Iterative computation of E^*: known as *McNaughton–Yamada algorithm* after their seminal paper ([3]) and probably the most popular among textbooks on automata theory. Called algorithm MNY here.
2. Direct computation of the entries of E^*: the so-called *state elimination method* ([4, 5]) looks more elementary and is indeed the easiest for hand computation as well as for computer implementation (*cf.* Figure 2).

3. Computation of $E^* \cdot T$ as a solution of a system of linear equations. Based on Arden's Lemma, it also allows to consider $E^* \cdot T$ as a fixed point.
4. Recursive computation of E^*: based on Arden's Lemma as well, this algorithm appeared first in Conway's book ([6]) conjugates mathematical elegance and computational inefficiency.

Fig. 2. One step in the state elimination method

The first three algorithms rely on a total order ω on Q, the fourth on a recursive division τ of the same set Q. All these algorithms, and for each algorithm all orders on Q will give by definition equivalent, but likely distinct, expressions. It is thus a natural problem that to compare these expressions; but this raise the question: 'what does it mean *to compare* expressions'? A possible answer — the one we choose here — consists in the characterisation of which of the *basic identities* are necessary to transform one into another. We thus first begin with a presentation of those identities which roughly follows that that Krob ([7]) gave of Conway's system ([6]).

Trivial and natural identities

$$\mathsf{E + 0 \equiv 0 + E \equiv E} \quad, \quad \mathsf{E \cdot 0 \equiv 0 \cdot E \equiv 0} \quad, \quad \mathsf{E \cdot 1 \equiv 1 \cdot E \equiv E} \quad \textbf{(T)}$$
$$\mathsf{(E + F) + G \equiv E + (F + G)} \quad, \quad \mathsf{(E \cdot F) \cdot G \equiv E \cdot (F \cdot G)} \quad \textbf{(A)}$$
$$\mathsf{E \cdot (F + G) \equiv E \cdot F + E \cdot G} \quad, \quad \mathsf{(E + F) \cdot G \equiv E \cdot G + F \cdot G} \quad \textbf{(D)}$$
$$\mathsf{E + F \equiv F + E} \quad \textbf{(C)}$$

Aperiodic identities

$$\mathsf{E^* \equiv 1 + E \cdot E^*} \quad, \quad \mathsf{E^* \equiv 1 + E^* \cdot E} \quad \textbf{(U)}$$
$$\mathsf{(E + F)^* \equiv E^* \cdot (F \cdot E^*)^*} \quad, \quad \mathsf{(E + F)^* \equiv (E^* \cdot F)^* \cdot E^*} \quad \textbf{(S)}$$
$$\mathsf{(E \cdot F)^* \equiv 1 + E \cdot (F \cdot E)^* \cdot F} \quad \textbf{(P)}$$

Cyclic identities

$$\mathsf{E^* \equiv E^{<n} \cdot (E^n)^*} \quad \textbf{(Z)}_n$$

Idempotency identities

$$\mathsf{E + E \;\equiv\; E} \quad \textbf{(I)} \qquad\qquad \mathsf{(E^*)^* \;\equiv\; E^*} \quad \textbf{(J)}$$

The State Elimination and Equation Solution Methods

Proposition 1 ([8]). *The state elimination method and the solution (by Gaussian elimination) of a system of linear equations taken from an automaton give the same regular expression (assuming that the same order in elimination is used in both cases).*

Proof. For p and q in Q, the *set of words* which are the label of a computation which goes from p to a final state of $\mathcal{A}$ is written: $L_p = \{f \mid \exists t \in T \quad p \xrightarrow{f}_{\mathcal{A}} t\}$ and we write $E_{p,q}$ for the *set of labels of transitions* which go from p to q and the symbol $\delta_{p,R}$ for a subset R of Q, which is 1_{A^*} if p is in R and $\emptyset$ if not. The system of equations associated with $\mathcal{A}$ is written:

$$L(\mathcal{A}) = \sum_{p \in I} L_p \quad = \sum_{p \in Q} \delta_{p,I} L_p \tag{1}$$

$$\forall p \in Q \quad L_p = \sum_{q \in Q} E_{p,q} L_q + \delta_{p,T} \tag{2}$$

After the elimination of a certain number of unknowns L_p – we write Q' for the set of indices of those which have not been eliminated – we obtain a system of the form:

$$L(\mathcal{A}) = \sum_{p \in Q'} G_p L_p + H \tag{3}$$

$$\forall p \in Q' \quad L_p = \sum_{q \in Q'} F_{p,q} L_q + K_p \tag{4}$$

We can make a generalised automaton $\mathcal{B}'$ corresponding to such a system, whose set of states is $Q' \cup \{i, t\}$, where i and t do not belong to Q', and such that, for all p and q in Q': (i) the transition from p to q is labelled $F_{p,q}$; (ii) the transition from p to t is labelled K_p; (iii) the transition from i to p is labelled G_p; and (iv) the transition from i to t is labelled H.

Note that this definition applied to the system (1)–(2) characterises the automaton constructed in the first phase of the state elimination method applied to $\mathcal{A}$.

The elimination in the system (3)–(4) of the unknown L_p by substitutions and the application of Arden's Lemma give the system:

$$L(\mathcal{A}) = \sum_{r \in Q' \backslash p} \left[G_r + G_p F_{p,p}^* F_{p,r} \right] L_r + \left[H + G_p F_{p,p}^* K_p \right] \tag{5}$$

$$\forall r \in Q' \backslash p \quad L_r = \sum_{q \in Q' \backslash p} \left[F_{r,q} + F_{r,p} F_{p,p}^* F_{r,q} \right] L_q + \left[K_r + F_{r,p} F_{p,p}^* K_p \right] \tag{6}$$

whose coefficients are exactly the transition labels of the generalised automaton obtained by removing the state p from $\mathcal{B}'$.

Thus, since the starting points correspond and since each step maintains the correspondence, the expression obtained for $L(\mathcal{A})$ by the state elimination method is the same as that obtained by the solution of the system (1)–(2).

More precisely, we can say that the state elimination method reproduces in the automaton $\mathcal{A}$ the computations corresponding to the solution of the system.

The State Elimination and MNY Algorithms, Identical Orders

The order ω fixes the operation of the state elimination method whose result is a rational expression over A^*, written[1] $\mathsf{E}_{BMC}(\mathcal{A},\omega)$. For greater precision, we write the result of this algorithm $\mathsf{E}_{BMC}(\mathcal{A},\omega,(p,q))$ when we take p as the initial state and q as the final state.

On the other hand, we will write $\mathsf{M}_{MNY}(\mathcal{A},\omega)$ for the matrix of rational expressions obtained when we apply the McNaughton–Yamada algorithm to the automaton $\mathcal{A}$ whose states are ordered by ω. It then follows that:

Proposition 2 ([8]). *Let $\mathcal{A} = \langle Q, A, E, I, T \rangle$ an automaton over A^*. For every (total) order ω on Q and all p and q in Q, we have:*

$$(\mathbf{U}) \vdash \qquad [\mathsf{M}_{MNY}(\mathcal{A},\omega)]_{p,q} \quad \equiv \quad \mathsf{E}_{BMC}(\mathcal{A},\omega,(p,q))\,.$$

Proof. To prove this result we will show a correspondence between the operations performed by the two algorithms. The difficulty, if it can be called that, is that we have to compare two objects whose form and mode of construction are rather different: on one hand a $Q \times Q$ matrix obtained by successive transformations, from which we choose one entry, and on the other an expression obtained by repeated modification of an automaton, hence of a matrix, but one whose size decreases at each step.

In the following, $\mathcal{A}$ and ω are fixed and remain implicit. The automaton $\mathcal{A}$ has n states, identified with the integers from 1 to n; the two algorithms perform n steps starting in a situation called 'step 0', the kth step of the state elimination method consisting of the removal of state k, and that of algorithm MNY consisting of calculating the labels of paths that do not include nodes (strictly) greater than k. We write:

$$\mathsf{E}^{(k)}(r,s)$$

for the label of the transition from r to s in the automaton obtained from $\mathcal{A}$ (and ω) at the kth step of the state elimination method; necessarily, in this notation, $k+1 \leqslant r$ and $k+1 \leqslant s$ (abbreviated to $k+1 \leqslant r, s$). We write:

$$\mathsf{M}^{(k)}_{r,s}$$

for the entry r, s of the $n \times n$ matrix computed by the kth step of algorithm MNY. At step 0, the automaton $\mathcal{A}$ has not been modified and we have:

$$\forall r, s,\ 1 \leqslant r, s \leqslant n \qquad \mathsf{M}^{(0)}_{r,s} = \mathsf{E}^{(0)}(r, s)\,, \tag{7}$$

which will be the base case of the inductions to come. Algorithm MNY is written:

$$\forall k,\ 0 < k \leqslant n,\ \forall r, s,\ 1 \leqslant r, s \leqslant n$$

$$\mathsf{M}^{(k)}_{r,s} = \mathsf{M}^{(k-1)}_{r,s} + \mathsf{M}^{(k-1)}_{r,k} \cdot [\mathsf{M}^{(k-1)}_{k,k}]^* \cdot \mathsf{M}^{(k-1)}_{k,s}\,. \tag{8}$$

---

[1] A reminder that this algorithm is due to J. Brzozowski and E. McCluskey ([9]).

The state elimination algorithm is written:

$$\forall k,\, 0 < k \leqslant n,\, \forall r, s,\, k < r, s \leqslant n$$
$$E^{(k)}(r, s) = E^{(k-1)}(r, s) + E^{(k-1)}(r, k) \cdot [E^{(k-1)}(k, k)]^* \cdot E^{(k-1)}(k, s) \quad (9)$$

Hence we conclude, for given r and s and by induction on k:

$$\forall r, s,\, 1 \leqslant r, s \leqslant n,\, \forall k,\, 0 \leqslant k < \min(r, s) \qquad M_{r,s}^{(k)} = E^{(k)}(r, s) \quad (10)$$

We see in fact (as there is even so something to see) that if $k < \min(r, s)$ then all integer triples (l, u, v) such that $M_{u,v}^{(l)}$ occurs in the computation of $M_{r,s}^{(k)}$ by the (recursive) use of (8), are such that $l < \min(u, v)$.

Suppose now that we have p and q, also fixed, such that $1 \leqslant p < q \leqslant n$ (the other cases are dealt with similarly). We call the initial and final states added to $\mathcal{A}$ in the first phase of the state elimination method i and t respectively; i and t are not integers between 1 and n. The transition from i to p and that from q to t are labelled 1_{A^*}. Now let us consider step p of each algorithm. For every state s, $p < s$, $M_{p,s}^{(p)}$ is given by (8):

$$M_{p,s}^{(p)} = M_{p,s}^{(p-1)} + M_{p,p}^{(p-1)} \cdot [M_{p,p}^{(p-1)}]^* \cdot M_{p,s}^{(p-1)}$$

and $E^{(p)}(i, s)$ by:

$$E^{(p)}(i, s) = [E^{(p-1)}(p, p)]^* \cdot E^{(p-1)}(p, s)$$

and hence, by (10):

$$\forall s,\, p < s \leqslant n \qquad (\mathbf{U}) \vdash \qquad M_{p,s}^{(p)} \equiv E^{(p)}(i, s). \quad (11)$$

Next we consider the steps following p (and row p of the matrices $M^{(k)}$). For all k, $p < k$, and all s, $k < s \leqslant n$, $M_{p,s}^{(k)}$ is always computed by (8) and $E^{(k)}(i, s)$ by:

$$E^{(k)}(i, s) = E^{(k-1)}(i, s) + E^{(k-1)}(i, k) \cdot [E^{(k-1)}(k, k)]^* \cdot E^{(k-1)}(k, s). \quad (12)$$

From (11), and based on an observation analogous to the previous one, we conclude from the term-by-term correspondence of (8) and (12) that:

$$\forall k,\, p < k,\, \forall s,\, p < s \leqslant n \qquad (\mathbf{U}) \vdash \qquad M_{p,s}^{(k)} \equiv E^{(k)}(i, s). \quad (13)$$

The analysis of step q gives a similar, and symmetric, result to that which we have just obtained from the analysis of step p: for all r, $q < r$, we have:

$$M_{r,q}^{(q)} = M_{r,q}^{(q-1)} + M_{r,q}^{(q-1)} \cdot [M_{q,q}^{(q-1)}]^* \cdot M_{q,q}^{(q-1)}$$

and $$E^{(q)}(r, t) = E^{(q-1)}(r, q) \cdot [E^{(q-1)}(q, q)]^*$$

and hence

$$\forall r,\, q < r \leqslant n \qquad (\mathbf{U}) \vdash \qquad M_{r,q}^{(q)} \equiv E^{(q)}(r, t). \quad (14)$$

The steps following q give rise to an equation symmetric to (13) (for column q of the matrices $M^{(k)}$):

$$\forall k,\, q < k,\, \forall r,\, q < r \leqslant n \qquad (\mathbf{U}) \vdash \qquad M^{(k)}_{r,q} \equiv E^{(k)}(r,t). \qquad (15)$$

Finally, from:

$$M^{(k)}_{p,q} = M^{(k-1)}_{p,q} + M^{(k-1)}_{p,k} \cdot [M^{(k-1)}_{k,k}]^* \cdot M^{(k-1)}_{k,q}$$

and $\quad E^{(k)}(i,t) = E^{(k-1)}(i,t) + E^{(k-1)}(i,k) \cdot [E^{(k-1)}(k,k)]^* \cdot E^{(k-1)}(k,t)$

Equations (10), (13) and (15) together allow us to conclude, by induction on k, that:

$$\forall k,\, q \leqslant k \leqslant n \qquad (\mathbf{U}) \vdash \qquad M^{(k)}_{p,q} \equiv E^{(k)}(i,t). \qquad (16)$$

When we reach $k = n$ in this equation we obtain the identity we want.

The State Elimination and MNY Algorithms, Distinct Orders

Having compared the state elimination and MNYalgorithms under the same order, that is the same execution conditions, we can compare the results of these algorithms for different execution conditions.

Theorem 1 (Conway [6], Krob [7]). *Let $\mathcal{A} = \langle Q, A, E, I, T \rangle$ be an automaton over A^*. The expressions denoting $L(\mathcal{A})$ computed by the McNaughton–Yamada algorithm, like those computed by the state elimination method or the solution of a system of equations, are all equivalent modulo* (**S**) *and* (**P**), *i.e., for all orders ω and ω' on Q and all p and q in Q:*

$$(\mathbf{S}) \wedge (\mathbf{P}) \quad \vdash \quad [M_{MNY}(\mathcal{A},\omega)]_{p,q} \quad \equiv \quad [M_{MNY}(\mathcal{A},\omega')]_{p,q}\,,$$

$$(\mathbf{S}) \wedge (\mathbf{P}) \quad \vdash \quad E_{BMC}(\mathcal{A},\omega,(p,q)) \quad \equiv \quad E_{BMC}(\mathcal{A},\omega',(p,q)).$$

Proof. The previous proposition allows us to show the property for expressions computed by the state elimination method, which is easier to deal with (remembering that (**P**) 'contains' (**U**)). Furthermore, we can go from an order ω to any other order ω', a permutation of Q, by a series of transpositions.

We therefore arrive at the situation illustrated in Figure 3 (left) and need to show that the expressions obtained by the state elimination method when we first remove the state r and then r' are equivalent to those obtained from removing first r' and then r, modulo (**S**) $\wedge$ (**P**).

The removal of state r gives the expressions in Figure 3 (right). The removal of state r' gives the expression:

$$E = K L^* H + (K L^* G + K') [G' L^* G + L']^* (G' L^* H + H')\,,$$

which using (**S**) (and the natural identities) becomes:

$$\begin{aligned}
E \equiv\ & K L^* H + K L^* G \left[L'^* G' L^* G\right]^* L'^* G' L^* H \\
& + K' \left[L'^* G' L^* G\right]^* L'^* G' L^* H + K L^* G \left[L'^* G' L^* G\right]^* L'^* H' \\
& \qquad\qquad\qquad + K' \left[L'^* G' L^* G\right]^* L'^* H'.
\end{aligned}$$

We write:

$$K' \left[L'^* G' L^* G \right]^* L'^* H' \equiv K' L'^* H' + K' L'^* G' L^* \left[G L'^* G' L^* \right]^* G L'^* H'$$

by using (**P**) then, by 'switching the brackets' (using the identity $(XY)^* X \equiv X(YX)^*$ which is also a consequence of (**P**)), we obtain:

$$\begin{aligned} \mathsf{E} \equiv\ & K L^* H \\ &+ K L^* G \left[L'^* G' L^* G \right]^* L'^* G' L^* H + K' L'^* G' \left[L^* G L'^* G' \right]^* L^* H \\ &+ K L^* G \left[L'^* G' L^* G \right]^* L'^* H' + K' L'^* G' \left[L^* G L'^* G' \right]^* L^* G L'^* H' \\ &\hspace{7cm} + K' L'^* H' \end{aligned}$$

an expression that is perfectly symmetric in the letters with and without ticks, which shows that we would have obtained the same result if we had started by removing r' then r.

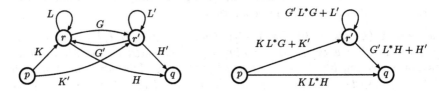

Fig. 3. First step of two in the state elimination method

Remark 1. It is known that the Φ-algorithms described above are valid for automata with multiplicity. It is thus not surprising that the idempotency identities are not used to pass from an expression to another one. On the other hand, it is also known ([6]) that an infinite number of identities (among which the cyclic identities $(\mathbf{Z})_n$ for all *prime numbers* n) are necessary to derive all possible equivalence among epressions. Taking this into account, the above results show that all expressions computed from a given automaton can be considered as 'close' since only the two identities (**S**) and (**P**) are necessary to derive one from another.

The State Elimination and the Recursive Methods

Finally, it remains to compare the matrices obtained by the algorithm MNY and the recursive algorithm. A simple two state automaton is sufficient for observing that there is no hope for a global comparison of the entries of the two matrices. We can however state the following conjecture.

Conjecture 1. For every recursive division τ of Q and for every pair (p, q) of states, there exists an ordering ω' of Q such that

$$(\mathbf{U}) \quad \vdash \quad [C(\tau)]_{p,q} \equiv E(\omega', p, q).$$

2.2   An Experimental Point of View

It is easily seen that the size of a regular expression E computed from an automaton $\mathcal{A}$ may be exponential in the number of states of $\mathcal{A}$. A complete graph shows that this combinatorial explosion is unavoidable.

But most of the interesting automata are not complete graph. Basic examples show how different the size of expressions computed from a same automaton can be: in Figure 4, E_1 is obtained by eliminating the states in the order 1–2–3 whereas E_2 is obtained with the reverse order 3–2–1.

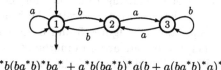

$$E_1 = a^* + a^*b(ba^*b)^*ba^* + a^*b(ba^*b)^*a(b + a(ba^*b)^*a)^*a(ba^*b)^*ba^*$$
$$E_2 = (a + b(ab^*a)^*b)^*$$

Fig. 4. Two results of the state elimination method

Finding the ordering of states that yields the shortest expression for a given automaton is probably a hard combinatorial problem. On the other hand, it is not too difficult to design heuristics which do not imply heavy computations and prove to be pretty efficient.

In order to create as few transitions as possible at a given step (*cf.* Figure 2), one associates to every state q an index which is the product of the in-degree of q by its out-degree (once the possible loop on q is discarded); one then choose to eliminate among those states with smallest index a state without loop, if any; the index is then recomputed at each step.

This rather naive heuristic had been implemented in VAUCANSON ([10]). Delgado and Morais ([11]) have proposed a heuristic which is based on the same principle, but in which the length of the expressions that label the transitions is also taken into account in the computation of the index. This other heuristic has also been implemented in the newer version of VAUCANSON ([12]). First experiments show that it might be better (on a first set of "random" automata, it outperforms the naive one in 55% of the cases). More experiments on much larger sets of automata need certainly to be done: *the proof of a heuristic is in the computing.*

3   The Ψ Algorithms

We call "Ψ algorithm" an algorithm that is given a regular expression E and computes an automaton which accepts the language denoted by E. As for the Φ algorithms, there is no much mystery left in this question. But not all aspects are equally well-known.

3.1   A Theoretical Point of View

Although there are numerous ways to present them, there are *two* main distinct constructions of an automaton from a regular expression: the *standard automaton* and the *derived term automaton*. Automata are compared via *morphisms*.

The Standard Automaton

We say that an automaton is *standard* if it has only one initial state and if this initial state is not the end of any transition (and if the automaton is accessible). We call *standard automaton* of an expression E *the* automaton $\mathcal{S}_E$ build by induction on the depth of E, starting from the (unique possible) standard automata for 0, 1, and every letter a in A, and with the "natural" constructions for the union, product and star: *cf.* Figures 5 and 6. Of course, any standard automaton is not, in general, the standard automaton of an expression.

Let us denote by $\ell(E)$ the *literal length* of the expression E — that is the number of occurrences of letters in E.

Proposition 3 (Glushkov [13]). *The standard automaton $\mathcal{S}_E$ of the expression* E *has* $\ell(E)+1$ *states.*

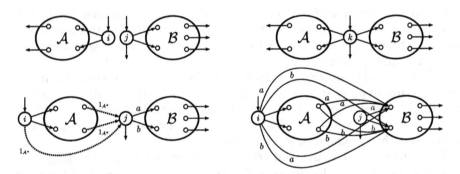

Fig. 5. Construction of the standard automaton for the union and the product

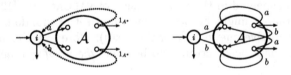

Fig. 6. Construction of the standard automaton for the star

The 'standard automaton of an expression' is usually attributed to Glushkov [13] and hence often called *Glushkov's automaton*. It is also called *position* automaton of E as the original method of construction somehow starts from the occurrences of letters in E, taken as states, and then computes the transitions — also by induction on the depth of E. A characteristic feature of $\mathcal{S}_E$ is that it is *small* in terms of the 'input' E: linear for the states, quadratic for the transitions and it is so because it is *non deterministic*. In [3], McNaughton and Yamada already had the idea of using the positions of letters in the expression in order to define an automaton but they computed directly[2] its determinised version and thus lost any property on the size of the result. The mode of construction given here is adapted from [14]; it is well suited to the generalisation to automata with multiplicity ([14, 8, 15]).

Another method for building an automaton from an expression was given by Thompson ([16]). It amounts to recursive connection via spontaneous transitions (*i.e.* ε-moves) of 'atomic' automata that recognise letters and it was designed for a direct array implementation. It is folklore that the *backward closure* (*i.e.* suppression of spontaneous transitions by following first the spontaneous transitions and then a transition labeled with a letter) in the Thompson's automaton of E yields the standard automaton of E. Hence the former can be seen as an 'extended version' of the latter and falls in the same category.

The Derived Term Automaton

A second class of algorithms is based on the definition of the *derivation of an expression*. First introduced by Brzozowski [17], the definition of derivation has been slightly, but smartly, modified by Antimirov [18] and yields a non deterministic automaton $\mathcal{A}_E$ which we propose to call the *derived term automaton* of the expression E. This automaton $\mathcal{A}_E$ is smaller than or equal to the standard automaton $\mathcal{S}_E$. The automaton of derived expressions computed in [17] is the determinised automaton of $\mathcal{A}_E$.

An algebraic characterization of regular languages is that every regular language has a finite number of left quotients. The purpose of "Brozozowski" derivatives was to lift that characterization at the level of expressions [17]. Antimirov "partial derivatives" achieve the same lifting in an indirect but more efficient way. To an expression E that denotes a language L is associated a finite set $\mathcal{T}$ of expressions — which we call *derived terms* of E — such that any left quotient of L is a *union* of some of the languages denoted by the expressions in $\mathcal{T}$ [18].

The notion of derived terms is indeed better understood when expressed in the larger framework of power series — languages being series with coefficients in the Boolean semiring — and of expressions *with multiplicity* (*cf.* [15]). A series s is rational — *i.e.* denoted by a regular expression E — iff it is contained in a *finitely generated* module (of series) U which is *closed under left quotient*. The derived terms of E are then expressions that denote a *set of generators* of U. The following definitions give a procedure for computing the derived terms of an expression.

Definition 1 (Brozozowski–Antimirov [18]). *Let* E *be a regular expression on* A *and let* a *be a letter in* A. *The* $\mathbb{B}$-*derivative*[3] *of* E *with respect to* a, *denoted* $\frac{\partial}{\partial a}$ E, *is a set of regular expressions on* A, *recursively defined by:*

---

[2] Probably because in those early times, an automaton *had to be* deterministic.

[3] We call it "$\mathbb{B}$-derivative" and not simply "derivative" for two reasons. First in order to avoid confusion with the derivation defined by Brzozowski, and second because the formulae depend on the semiring of multiplicities and can be defined for other semirings (*cf.* [15]).

$$\frac{\partial}{\partial a} 0 = \frac{\partial}{\partial a} 1 = \emptyset \, ,$$

$$\forall a, b \in A \quad \frac{\partial}{\partial a} b = \begin{cases} \{1\} & \text{if} \quad b = a \\ \emptyset & \text{otherwise} \end{cases}$$

$$\frac{\partial}{\partial a}(E+F) = \frac{\partial}{\partial a} E \cup \frac{\partial}{\partial a} F \tag{17}$$

$$\frac{\partial}{\partial a}(E \cdot F) = \left[\frac{\partial}{\partial a} E \right] \cdot F \cup c(E) \frac{\partial}{\partial a} F \tag{18}$$

$$\frac{\partial}{\partial a}(E^*) = \left[\frac{\partial}{\partial a} E \right] \cdot E^* \tag{19}$$

The induction implied by (17 – 19) should be interpreted by distributing derivation and product over union:

$$\frac{\partial}{\partial a} \left[\bigcup_{i \in I} E_i \right] = \bigcup_{i \in I} \frac{\partial}{\partial a} E_i \, , \qquad \left[\bigcup_{i \in I} E_i \right] \cdot F = \bigcup_{i \in I} (E_i \cdot F) \, .$$

Definition 2. Let E be a regular expression on A and g a non empty word of A^*, i.e. $g = f a$ with a in A. The $\mathbb{B}$-derivative of E with respect to g, denoted $\frac{\partial}{\partial g} E$, is the set of regular expressions on A, recursively defined by formulae (17) – (19) and by:

$$\forall f \in A^+ , \ \forall a \in A \quad \frac{\partial}{\partial f a} E = \frac{\partial}{\partial a} \left(\frac{\partial}{\partial f} E \right) . \tag{20}$$

We shall call derived term of E the expression E itself or any of the expressions which belongs to a set $\frac{\partial}{\partial g} E$ for some g in A^+.

Theorem 2 (Antimirov [18]). The number of derived terms of an expression E is finite and smaller than or equal to $\ell(E) + 1$.

Remark 2. Contrary to the derivation defined by Brzozowski [17], the result of the $\mathbb{B}$-derivation of an expression is *not one* expression but a *set of* expressions. As a result, it overcomes another drawback of its predecessor. The number of Brzozowski derivatives of an expression is not finite directly but only modulo the identities (**A**), (**C**) and (**I**) described above. The computation of the derived terms does not involve any identity.

Definition 3. The derived term automaton of an expression E is the finite automaton $\mathcal{A}_E$ whose states are the derived terms of E and whose transitions are defined by:

(i) if K and K' are derived terms of E and if a is a letter of A, (K, a, K') is a transition of $\mathcal{A}_E$ if and only if K' belongs to $\frac{\partial}{\partial a} K$;
(ii) the initial state of $\mathcal{A}_E$ is E;
(iii) a derived term K is a final state of $\mathcal{A}_E$ if and only if $c(K) = 1$;

We write $E_1 = a^* + a^*b\,H_1 + a^*b\,F_1\,G_1\,H_1$
with $H_1 = (b\,a^*b)^*b\,a^*$, $F_1 = (b\,a^*b)^*a$,
and $G_1 = (b + a\,(b\,a^*b)^*a)^*a$.

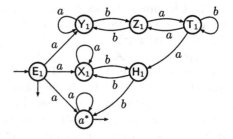

The successive derivations of E_1 with respect to a and b give 7 derived terms:
E_1 itself, a^* , H_1 , $X_1 = a^*b\,H_1$,
$Y_1 = a^*b\,F_1\,G_1\,H_1$, $Z_1 = F_1\,G_1\,H_1$,
and $T_1 = G_1\,H_1$.

Fig. 7. The derived terms of E_1 and its derived term automaton

Figure 7 shows the derived terms of the expression E_1 computed at Figure 4 and the corresponding derived term automaton.

The two classes of algorithms are not without relationships between them. A first one was given by Berry–Sethi who showed that the Brzozowski derivation applied on a " linearized" version of an expression gives the standard automaton of that expression [19, 20]. A more interesting one is established by means of morphisms of automata that we should define first.

Morphisms of Automata

Let $\mathcal{A} = \langle Q, A, E, I, T \rangle$ and $\mathcal{B} = \langle R, A, F, J, U \rangle$ be two $\mathbb{B}$-automata. A (surjective) map $\varphi \colon Q \longrightarrow R$ induces (or *is*) a morphism from $\mathcal{A}$ onto $\mathcal{B}$ if $(p, a, q) \in E$ implies $(\varphi(p), a, \varphi(q)) \in F$ and this morphism is a *($\mathbb{B}$)-quotient* if moreover $(r, a, s) \in F$ and $p \in \varphi^{-1}(r)$ implies that there exists q in $\varphi^{-1}(s)$ such that $(p, a, q) \in E$. *Every automaton has a unique minimal quotient.*

Theorem 3 (Champarnaud–Ziadi [21]). *For any expression* E, *the derived term automaton* $\mathcal{A}_E$ *is a quotient of the standard automaton* $\mathcal{S}_E$.

This result implies in particular the bound of Theorem 2 on the number of derived terms. It is to be noted also that if the derived term automaton is a quotient of the standard automaton, *it is not* its minimal quotient. Theorem 3 has been generalised to expressions with multiplicity but this generalisation requires special care in the definition of the derived terms in the case where the multiplicity semiring is not a positive semiring ([15]).

3.2   An Experimental Point of View

The effective computation of the standard automaton of an expression has been the subject of many works. If the actual efficiency of the computation depends unpon the implementation, it is known that the construction of $\mathcal{S}_E$ is of quadratic complexity (with respect to $\ell(E)$) ([22]).

The determination of the complexity of the computation of the derived term automaton if an expression E is more difficult. The key property, proven in [21], is that every derived term of E is a product of subexpressions of E.

Proposition 4 (Champarnaud–Ziadi [21]). *For every expression* E, *the derived term automaton* $\mathcal{A}_E$ *can be computed with a quadratic complexity (with respect to* $\ell(E)$*).*

The Champarnaud–Ziadi algorithm has been transformed in order to be valid for automata with multiplicity and it has been implemented in VAUCANSON (*cf.* [12] in this volume).

It appears that $\mathcal{A}_E$ is particularly 'economical' — sizewize and by comparison with $\mathcal{S}_E$ — when E is obtained by a Φ algorithm from a finite automaton. We come back to his fact in the conclusion. However, it seems that, *even in this case*, the computation of $\mathcal{S}_E$ followed by a quotient is far more efficient than the direct computation of $\mathcal{A}_E$. Other constructions have been proposed recently that yield automata which are smaller than the standard automaton ([23–25]). Their proper relationships with the derived term automaton, and the efficiency of their computation are still to be worked out by extensive experimentations (*cf.* [26]).

4   Can Expressions and Automata Code for Each Other?

We have seen that a Φ-algorithm is likely to generate, from an automaton $\mathcal{A}$, an expression with a literal length which is exponential in the number of states of $\mathcal{A}$ and that a Ψ-algorithm is likely to build, from an expression E, an automaton whose number of states is (rougly) equal to the literal length of E. These two facts together imply that there is little hope to find algorithms which are inverse of each other in these general families. However, the standard automaton of an expression on one hand, and an expression computed, for instance, by the state elimination method on the other hand, are of such particular form that the problem is certainly to be tackled.

In [27], Caron and Ziadi have described an algorithm, say Θ, which decides whether or not an automaton $\mathcal{A}$ is *the* standard automaton of an expression E; and if the answer is positive, Θ moreover computes an expression which is *almost* E, namely the *star normal form* of E as defined by Brüggemann-Klein [22]. Even if Θ is not properly a Φ-type algorithm since it does not compute an expression for every automaton, it holds:

For any star normal form regular expression E, $\quad \Theta(\Psi_s(E)) = E$.

The problem of finding an algorithm that is inverse of a Φ-algorithm has been addressed in a recent joint paper of mine and Sylvain Lombardy ([28]). We give there a partial solution to that problem in the following way.

There are two main ingredients in the construction of an algorithm Ω that gives back an automaton $\mathcal{A}$ from an expression that has been computed from $\mathcal{A}$. The first one is a *sligthly modified* derivation which, roughly speaking, 'breaks' the sums at the upper level. As a result, in particular, the corresponding derived term automaton may have *more than one* initial state. The second step is to take the *minimal co-quotient* of this new derived term automaton. [The minimal co-quotient is the transposed of the minimal quotient of the transposed automaton.] This Ω is not an inverse of a Φ-algorithm as described above but of a Φ'-algorithm which consists in performing first a *partial linearisation* Λ of the automaton $\mathcal{A}$ and then a normal Φ-algorithm. We then have (*cf.* [28] for more details):

For any automaton $\mathcal{A}$, $\quad \Omega(\Phi'(\mathcal{A})) = \mathcal{A}$.

Reducing the amount of information that one has to bring in with the linearisation Λ is the subject of ongoing research work.

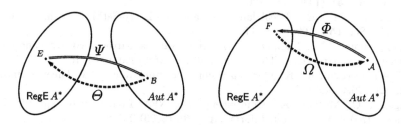

Fig. 8. The Θ and Ω algorithms

References

1. Eilenberg, S.: Automata, Languages, and Machines. Vol. A. Academic Press (1974)
2. Berstel, J.: Transductions and Context-free Languages. B. G. Teubner (1979)
3. McNaughton, R., Yamada, H.: Regular expressions and state graphs for automata. IRE Trans. Electronic Computers **9** (1960) 39–47
4. Wood, D.: Theory of Computation. John Wiley (1987)
5. Yu, S.: Regular languages. In Rozenberg, G., Salomaa, A., eds.: Handbook of Formal Languages. Volume 1., Elsevier (1997) 41–111
6. Conway, J.H.: Regular Algebra and Finite Machines. Chapman and Hall (1971)
7. Krob, D.: Complete systems of B-rational identities. Theoret. Computer Sci. **89** (1991) 207–343
8. Sakarovitch, J.: Eléments de théorie des automates. Vuibert (2003) English translation: Elements of Automata Theory, Cambridge University Press, to appear.
9. Brzozowski, J.A., McCluskey, E.J.: Signal flow graph techniques for sequential circuit state diagrams. IEEE Trans. Electronic Computers **12** (1963) 67–76
10. Lombardy, S., Régis-Gianas, Y., Sakarovitch, J.: Introducing Vaucanson. Theoret. Computer Sci. **328** (2004) 67–76 Journal version of Proc. of CIAA 2003, Lect. Notes in Comp. Sc. 2759, (2003), 96–107 (with R. Poss).
11. Delgado, Morais: Approximation to the smallest regular expression for a given regular language. In Domaratzki, M., Okhotin, A., Salomaa, K., Yu, S., eds.: Proc. of CIAA 04, Lecture Notes in Computer Science 3317, Springer (2004) 312–314
12. Claveirole, T., Lombardy, S., O'Connor, S., Pouchet, L.N., Sakarovitch, J.: Inside Vaucanson. In Farré, J., Litovsky, I., eds.: Proc. of CIAA 05, Springer (2005) this volume.
13. Glushkov, V.M.: The abstract theory of automata. Russian Math. Surveys **16** (1961) 1–53
14. Caron, P., Flouret, M.: Glushkov construction for multiplicities. In Daley, M., Eramian, M., Yu, S., eds.: Pre-Proceedings of CIAA'00. (2000) 52–61
15. Lombardy, S., Sakarovitch, J.: Derivatives of rational expressions with multiplicity. Theor. Comput. Sci. **332** (2005) 141–177
16. Thompson, K.: Regular expression search algorithm. Comm. Assoc. Comput. Mach. **11** (1968) 419–422
17. Brzozowski, J.A.: Derivatives of regular expressions. J. Assoc. Comput. Mach. **11** (1964) 481–494

18. Antimirov, V.: Partial derivatives of regular expressions and finite automaton constructions. Theor. Comput. Sci. **155** (1996) 291–319
19. Berry, G., Sethi, R.: From regular expressions to deterministic automata. Theor. Comput. Sci. **48** (1986) 117–126
20. Berstel, J., Pin, J.E.: Local languages and the Berry-Sethi algorithm. Theor. Comput. Sci. **155** (1996) 439–446
21. Champarnaud, J.M., Ziadi, D.: Canonical derivatives, partial derivatives and finite automaton constructions. Theor. Comput. Sci. **289** (2002) 137–163
22. Brügemann-Klein, A.: Regular expressions into finite automata. Theor. Comput. Sci. **120** (1993) 197–213
23. Hagenah, C., Musholl, A.: Computing ε-free NFAs from regular expressions in $O(n \log^2(n))$ time. Theoret. Inform. Appl. **34** (2000) 257–277
24. Hromkovic, J., Seibert, S., Wilke, T.: Translating regular expressions into small ε-free nondeterministic finite automata. J. Comput. System Sci. **62** (2001) 565–588
25. Ilie, L., Yu, S.: Constructing NFAs by optimal use of positions in regular expressions. In Apolostolico, A., Takeda, M., eds.: Proc. of CPM'02, Lecture Notes in Computer Science 2373, Springer (2002) 279–288
26. Champarnaud, J.M., Nicart, F., Ziadi, D.: Computing the follow automaton of an expression. In Domaratzki, M., Okhotin, A., Salomaa, K., Yu, S., eds.: Proc. of CIAA 04, Lecture Notes in Computer Science 3317, Springer (2004) 90–101
27. Caron, P., Ziadi, D.: Characterization of Glushkov automata. Theor. Comput. Sci. **233** (2000) 75–90
28. Lombardy, S., Sakarovitch, J.: How expressions can code for automata. Theoret. Inform. App. **39** (2005) 217–237

Minimization of Non-deterministic Automata with Large Alphabets*

Parosh Aziz Abdulla, Johann Deneux, Lisa Kaati, and Marcus Nilsson

Dept. of Information Technology, P.O. Box 337, S-751 05 Uppsala, Sweden
{parosh, johannd, kaati, marcusn}@it.uu.se

Abstract. There has been several attempts over the years to solve the bisimulation minimization problem for finite automata. One of the most famous algorithms is the one suggested by Paige and Tarjan. The algorithm has a complexity of $\mathcal{O}(m \log n)$ where m is the number of edges and n is the number of states in the automaton. A bottleneck in the application of the algorithm is often the number of labels which may appear on the edges of the automaton. In this paper we adapt the Paige-Tarjan algorithm to the case where the labels are symbolically represented using Binary Decision Diagrams (BDDs). We show that our algorithm has an overall complexity of $\mathcal{O}(\ell \cdot m \cdot \log n)$ where ℓ is the size of the alphabet. This means that our algorithm will have the same worst case behavior as other algorithms. However, as shown by our prototype implementation, we get a vast improvement in performance due to the compact representation provided by the BDDs.

1   Introduction

Several algorithms have been proposed in the literature for solving the *coarsest refinement problem*: given a finite state automaton and an initial partitioning of the set of states, find the coarsest stable refinement of the given partitioning. The problem is equivalent to the minimization of non-deterministic automata modulo bisimulation, and consequently also gives an algorithm for minimizing deterministic automata modulo language equivalence. Minimization is relevant in many areas of computer science such as concurrency theory, formal verification, set theory, etc. For instance, in formal verification, several existing tools use minimization with respect to bisimulation in order to reduce the size of the state space to be analyzed [1–3]. Also, bisimulation is of particular interest in *regular model checking*. This is a framework which has recently been extensively studied for verification of systems with infinite state spaces (see e.g.[4]).

The idea of regular model checking is to represent the state space of a system using regular languages. Most regular model checking algorithms rely heavily on efficient methods for checking bisimulation [5].

There has been several attempts over the years to solve the coarsest refinement problem. In [6] Hopcroft presents an algorithm for minimization of a deterministic automaton in $\mathcal{O}(n \log n)$ time. The algorithm relies on a "negative strategy":

---

* This work was supported by the the Swedish Research Council (http://www.vr.se/).

J. Farré, I. Litovsky, and S. Schmitz (Eds.): CIAA 2005, LNCS 3845, pp. 31–42, 2006.
© Springer-Verlag Berlin Heidelberg 2006

start from the initial partitioning and perform a number of iterations. During each iteration choose a block (equivalence class) B, and split all the blocks which violate the stability condition with respect to B. The main ingredient is the choice of the blocks which are used in the splitting (the so called "process the smaller half strategy"). The paper [7] solves the problem for the special case of deterministic and unlabeled automata in linear time, using a "positive strategy": start with blocks which are singletons, and perform a number of iterations, where one or more blocks are merged during each iteration. Paige and Tarjan [8] generalized the algorithm of Hopcroft to the case of non-deterministic automata. The key idea is to employ counters which give the number of edges from states to blocks. This makes it possible to avoid partitioning with respect to large blocks. The algorithm runs in $\mathcal{O}(m \log n)$ time where m is the number of edges and n is the number of states in the automaton.

Many applications give rise to automata with large alphabets. For instance, transition systems generated by verification tools such as SPIN [9] usually have very large alphabets [10]. Also, the bottle-neck in applications of regular model checking is often the size of the alphabet in the automata which arise during the analysis [5, 4]. Therefore, this paper adapts the Paige-Tarjan algorithm [8] to consider automata which have large alphabets. To deal with the size of the alphabet, we use a symbolic representation of labels on the edges of the automaton. More precisely, for states q and r, we characterize the set of symbols on which the automaton can move from q to r. This characterization is given through a *Binary Decision Diagram (BDD)* [11]. The main task then is to adapt each step of the Paige-Tarjan algorithm which operates on explicit representation of the transition relation into a symbolic one which operates on BDDs. To achieve that, we use *Algebraic Decision Diagrams (ADDs)* [12] to give a compact representation of the counters. Also, we show that each BDD or ADD operation can be performed in $\mathcal{O}(\ell)$ time where ℓ is the size of the alphabet. We show that this implies an overall complexity of $\mathcal{O}(\ell \cdot m \cdot \log n)$ of our algorithm. In other words, the algorithm will have the same worst case behavior as other algorithms. However, as shown by our prototype implementation, we often get a great improvement in performance due to the compact representation provided by the BDDs and ADDs.

Related Work. The algorithm of [8] operates on an explicit representation of the (unlabeled) automaton. For automata with large alphabets, we report a big improvement compared to [8] using our prototype (see Section 7).

Fernandez [13] presents an algorithm with complexity $\mathcal{O}(m \log n)$ in the case of labeled automata, the algorithm operates on an explicit representation of the automaton, where each edge is labeled with one symbol. In our case, an edge is labeled with a BDD which characterizes a set of symbols. Therefore the worst case complexity of our algorithm is the same as the one reported in [13]. More precisely, we can replace each edge, labeled with a BDD $\mathcal{B}$, by a set of edges each carrying one symbol whose encoding satisfies $\mathcal{B}$.

Bouali and De Simone [14] present a symbolic approach to the problem. The whole automaton and the computed blocks are encoded using BDDs. Such a full symbolic representation is in contrast with our approach where we only encode the alphabet symbolically, while we maintain an explicit representation of the set of states and of the blocks. The authors of [14] do not perform a complexity analysis. However, they mention that they do not gain a drastic improvement compared to the classical algorithm. This indicates that, at least in the case of a large alphabet, it is more efficient to avoid a fully symbolic representation.

The work in [10] combines the negative and positive approaches to bisimulation (described above) in the non-symbolic case. The authors also propose a symbolic algorithm for unlabeled automata, where each block is represented as a BDD. They show that their algorithm performs $\mathcal{O}(n)$ symbolic steps. No experimental results are reported for the symbolic algorithm.

In [15] Klarlund presents an algorithm where the whole automaton (rather than only the alphabet) is represented symbolically. However, this algorithm can only be applied in the case of deterministic automata.

In [16] Fisler and Vardi compare symbolic versions of the Paige-Tarjan algorithm and algorithms described in the two papers [17] and [18]. The latter two papers aim at adapting minimization to the context of the on-the-fly model checking. The paper argues both theoretically and based on experimental data that the Paige-Tarjan algorithm performs better than both.

Outline. In the next two Sections we give preliminaries on automata, equivalence relations, BDDs, and ADDs. In Section 4 we describe our algorithm which consists of performing a number of iterations; and analyze its correctness and complexity. In Section 5 we describe the data structures we use in the implementation of the algorithm. Section 6 describes the steps performed during each iteration. We report on the results we obtain through running our prototype in Section 7. Finally, we give some conclusions and directions for future research in Section 8.

2   Preliminaries

In this section, we give some preliminaries of automata and equivalence relations. Throughout this paper, we will work with a *non-deterministic automaton*, NFA, which is a triple $\langle Q, \Sigma, \Delta \rangle$ where

- Q is a finite set of states, with $|Q| = n$
- Σ is a finite set of symbols, with $|\Sigma| = \ell$.
- Δ is a function $\Delta : Q \times Q \to 2^{\Sigma}$. An *edge* is a pair $\langle q, r \rangle$ such that $\Delta(q, r) \neq \emptyset$. We say that q and r are respectively the *source* and the *target* of the edge $\langle q, r \rangle$. We let m be the number of edges.

In other words, we consider an automaton with n states and m edges. Each edge is labeled with a set of symbols from an alphabet of size ℓ. Without loss of generality, we assume that each state is the source of at least one edge; which implies $m \geq n$. The automaton can change state from q to r on the symbols $\Delta(q, r)$. We write $q \xrightarrow{a} r$ to denote that $a \in \Delta(q, r)$ and $q \longrightarrow r$ to denote that

$\Delta(q, r)$ is not empty. We use $(q \longrightarrow r)$ to denote the set $\{a : a \in \Delta(q, r)\}$, and use $Pre(r)$ to denote the set $\{q : (q \longrightarrow r) \neq \emptyset\}$. An element of $Pre(r)$ is said to be a *predecessor* of r. For a state $q \in Q$ and a set $R \subseteq Q$, we use $(q \longrightarrow R)$ to denote the set $\bigcup_{r \in R}(q \longrightarrow r)$, and $Pre(R)$ to denote the set $\bigcup_{r \in R} Pre(r)$.

We consider equivalence relations on Q. For an equivalence relation $\simeq$, we let $(Q/\simeq)$ be the set of equivalence classes, henceforth called *blocks* of $\simeq$. For $q \in Q$, $a \in \Sigma$, and $B \in (Q/\simeq)$, we define $count(q)(B)(a)$ to be the size of the set $\{r : r \in B$ and $q \xrightarrow{a} r\}$.

For two equivalence relations $\simeq$ and $\simeq'$, we say that $\simeq$ is *coarser* than $\simeq'$ if $\simeq' \subseteq \simeq$. Alternatively, we say that $\simeq'$ is a refinement of $\simeq$. Notice that each block of $\simeq$ is the union of a number of blocks of $\simeq'$.

An equivalence relation $\simeq$ is *stable* with respect to an equivalence relation $\simeq'$, if whenever $q \simeq r$ then $(q \longrightarrow B) = (r \longrightarrow B)$ for each $B \in (Q/\simeq')$. Equivalently, if $q \simeq r$ and $q \xrightarrow{a} q_1$ then there is an r_1 such that $r \xrightarrow{a} r_1$ and $q_1 \simeq' r_1$. In other words, equivalent states in $\simeq$ make moves on the same set of symbols to blocks in $\simeq'$. We say that $\simeq$ is *stable* if it is stable with respect to itself. The *coarsest refinement problem* is defined as follows:

Instance. An equivalence relation $\simeq_{init}$.
Task. Find the coarsest stable refinement of $\simeq_{init}$.

3   BDDs and ADDs

In this section we recall some preliminaries of BDDs and ADDs, and introduce concepts which we will use in our algorithm.

We assume familiarity with *Binary Decision Diagrams (BDDs)* (see e.g. [11, 19, 20]) *Algebraic Decision Diagrams (ADDs)* [12] are extensions of BDDs in the sense that the leaves of an ADD are labeled with natural numbers (rather than only 0 and 1 as is the case with BDDs).

BDDs. We encode each symbol of the alphabet Σ by a finite binary word. Furthermore, we encode sets of symbols of Σ by Boolean expressions which are represented by BDDs. To do that, we use a set V of *BDD variables* where $|V| = \lceil \log_2(|\Sigma|)\rceil$ (recall that $\ell = |\Sigma|$). The variable v_i represents the ith position in the encoding of a word (see the example below). A Boolean expression over V represents the set of symbols whose encodings satisfy the expression. Consequently, each BDD characterizes a set of symbols. In fact, each path from the root to a leaf of a BDD, represents a set of symbols, namely the set of symbols satisfying the path. Sometimes, we identify a BDD with the set of symbols it represents. For instance, given a BDD $\mathcal{B}$ and a symbol $a \in \Sigma$, we use $a \in \mathcal{B}$ to denote that a belongs to the set characterized by $\mathcal{B}$. Also, we use $\mathcal{B}(a)$ to denote the truth value of the formula $a \in \mathcal{B}$. In our algorithm, we use BDDs to represent the function Δ in the definition of an automaton (see Section 2). More precisely, for each $q, r \in Q$, we represent $\Delta(q, r)$ by a BDD $\mathcal{B}$ such that $a \in \mathcal{B}$ iff $a \in \Delta(q, r)$. We write $\Delta(q, r) = \mathcal{B}$ to denote that the set of symbols in $\Delta(q, r)$ is characterized by $\mathcal{B}$.

Operations on BDDs. The classical algorithm for computing a binary operation such as conjunction and disjunction on two BDDs is of time complexity $\mathcal{O}(2^k)$ where k is the number of variables which appear in the two input BDDs (see e.g. [11, 19, 20] for a description of the algorithm). In our case the value of k is bounded by $|V|$. Since $|V| = \lceil \log_2(|\Sigma|) \rceil$ it follows that these operations can performed in $\mathcal{O}(\ell)$ time.

ADDs. In a similar fashion to BDDs, we use an ADD to encode a multiset of symbols in Σ. Also in the case of ADDs, a path from the root to a leaf characterizes a set of symbols. For an ADD $\mathcal{A}$, the paths from the root to the leaf labeled i, characterizes the set of symbols which occur i times in the multiset represented by $\mathcal{A}$. We use $\mathcal{A}(a)$ to denote the number of occurrences a in the multiset represented by $\mathcal{A}$. By the *symbol set* of $\mathcal{A}$ we mean the set $\{a : \mathcal{A}(a) > 0\}$. We perform the following operations on ADDs:

- *Addition*: $\mathcal{A}_1 + \mathcal{A}_2$ is an ADD $\mathcal{A}$ such that $\mathcal{A}(a) = \mathcal{A}_1(a) + \mathcal{A}_2(a)$ for each a. We define the *subtraction* $\mathcal{A}_1 - \mathcal{A}_2$ of two ADDs in a similar manner.
- *Comparison*: $\mathcal{A}_1 \oplus \mathcal{A}_2$ returns a BDD $\mathcal{B}$ such that $\mathcal{B}(a)$ is true iff $\mathcal{A}_1(a) = \mathcal{A}_2(a)$.
- *BDD conversion*: $\overline{\mathcal{A}}$ is a BDD which characterizes the symbol set of $\mathcal{A}$.

Using a similar reasoning to BDDs, all the above operations can be performed in time $\mathcal{O}(\ell)$. Sometimes, we mix BDDs and ADDs in the above operations. In such a case we interpret a BDD $\mathcal{B}$ as an ADD where $\mathcal{B}(a) = 1$ iff $a \in \mathcal{B}$. For instance, given an ADD $\mathcal{A}$ and a BDD $\mathcal{B}$ then $(\mathcal{A} + \mathcal{B})(a)$ is equal to $\mathcal{A}(a)$ in case $a \notin \mathcal{B}$, and is equal to $\mathcal{A}(a) + 1$ otherwise.

Example. We consider the alphabet $\{a, b, c, d, e, f\}$. We use the encoding a: 000, b: 001, c: 010, d: 011, e: 100, f: 101. A dashed line in Figure 1 represents the false branch while the filled line represent the true branch of the BDD (ADD). Figure 1 a) shows a BDD characterizing the set $\{a, b, e\}$, while Figure 1 b) shows an ADD $\mathcal{A}$ with $\mathcal{A}(e) = 3$, $\mathcal{A}(a) = \mathcal{A}(f) = 2$, $\mathcal{A}(d) = 1$, and $\mathcal{A}(b) = \mathcal{A}(c) = 0$.

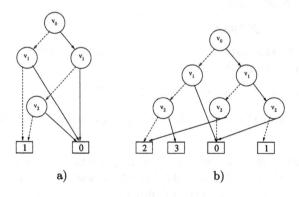

Fig. 1. Example of a BDD and an ADD

4   Algorithm

In this section, we describe our algorithm which consists of performing a number of iterations. Each step of the iteration is described in detail in Section 6. Given an initial equivalence $\simeq_{init}$, the iterations generate two sequences of equivalences of the forms $\simeq_0, \simeq_1, \simeq_2, \ldots, \simeq_t$ and $\cong_0, \cong_1, \cong_2, \ldots, \cong_t$ respectively. We define $\simeq_0$ to be $\simeq_{init}$ and $\cong_0$ to be $Q \times Q$. We derive $\simeq_{i+1}$ and $\cong_{i+1}$ from $\simeq_i$ and $\cong_i$ as follows. Let $B_i \in (Q/\simeq_i)$ and $S_i \in (Q/\cong_i)$ be such that[1] $B_i \subset S_i$ and $|B_i| \leq \frac{|S_i|}{2}$. We define $\simeq_{i+1}$ such that $q \simeq_{i+1} r$ iff the following three conditions are satisfied:

- $q \simeq_i r$.
- $(q \longrightarrow B_i) = (r \longrightarrow B_i)$.
- $\begin{pmatrix} count(q)(B_i)(a) \\ = \\ count(q)(S_i)(a) \end{pmatrix}$ iff $\begin{pmatrix} count(r)(B_i)(a) \\ = \\ count(r)(S_i)(a) \end{pmatrix}$ for each $a \in \Sigma$.

We define $\cong_{i+1}$ such that $q \cong_{i+1} r$ iff the following two conditions are satisfied:

- $q \cong_i r$.
- $q \in B_i$ iff $r \in B_i$.

The iteration continues until we reach the termination point n at which we have $\simeq_t = \cong_t$. In the next Section, we describe the data structures which we use to represent the equivalences $\simeq_i$ and $\cong_i$; and in Section 6 we show how we can implement each step to maintain the above invariants.

Now, we proceed to prove some properties of the generated equivalences. The following lemma shows that $\simeq_i$ is a refinement of $\cong_i$. This implies that, up to the termination point, we will be able to pick $B_i \in (Q/\simeq_i)$ and $S_i \in (Q/\cong_i)$ such that $B_i \subset S_i$ and $|B_i| \leq \frac{|S_i|}{2}$.

Lemma 1. $\simeq_i \subseteq \cong_i$ for all i.

Next, we show partial correctness of the algorithm (Theorem 1). To do that, we show two auxiliary lemmas.

Lemma 2. $\simeq_i$ is stable with respect to $\cong_i$, for all i.

Lemma 3. For any stable refinement $\simeq'$ of $\simeq_{init}$, it is the case that $\simeq' \subseteq \simeq_i$ for each i.

By definition we know that each $\simeq_i$ (and in particular $\simeq_t$) is a refinement of $\simeq_{init}$. From Lemma 2 and the fact that $\simeq_t = \cong_t$ we know that $\simeq_t$ is stable. This, together with Lemma 3 implies the following.

---

[1] As we will show below (Lemma 1), $\simeq_i$ is a refinement of $\cong_i$ and therefore such B_i and S_i exist.

Theorem 1. $\simeq_t$ *is the coarsest stable refinement of* $\simeq_{init}$.

Termination of the algorithm can be shown as follows: We know that, as long as the algorithm has not terminated we have $B_i \subset S_i$ and consequently $\cong_{i+1} \subset \cong_i$. By finiteness of Q it follows that after at most $t = |Q| - 1$ steps we reach a point where there are no $B_t \in (Q/ \simeq_t)$ and $S_t \in (Q/ \cong_t)$ such that $B_t \subset S_t$ and $|B_t| \leq \frac{|S_t|}{2}$. This implies $\simeq_t = \cong_t$.

Theorem 2. *There is a* $t \leq n - 1$ *such that* $\simeq_t = \cong_t$.

Finally, we consider complexity of the algorithm.

Lemma 4. *For each* $q \in Q$ *and* $i < j$ *if* $q \in B_i \cap B_j$ *then* $|B_j| \leq \frac{|B_i|}{2}$.

In Section 6 we will show that each iteration i can be performed in time

$$\mathcal{O}\left(\ell \cdot \left(|B_i| + \sum_{q \in B_i} |Pre(q)| \right) \right)$$

From this and Lemma 4, we get the following.

Theorem 3. *The algorithm has complexity* $\mathcal{O}\left(\ell \cdot m \cdot \log n \right)$.

5 Data Structures

In this section we describe the data structures used in the representation of the equivalences $\simeq_i$ and $\cong_i$ (see Section 4). Also, we use a number of auxiliary data structures which allow efficient implementation of each iteration in the algorithm.

Each state is represented by a record which we identify with the state itself. We maintain three lists of blocks:

- Q which corresponds to blocks in $\simeq_i$. Each state points to the block in Q containing it. Each block in Q is equipped with a natural number which indicates its size.
- X which corresponds to the blocks in $\cong_i$. A block of X is *simple* if contains a single block of Q, and is *compound* otherwise.
- C which is a sublist of X containing only the compound blocks in X.

The elements of the above lists are doubly linked. This allows deletion of elements in constant time. Each block in Q or X is represented by a record which we will identify with the block itself. Each block S in Q contains:

- a natural number which is equal to the size of the block.
- a pointer to a doubly linked list of its elements.
- a pointer to the block of X containing it.

Each block in X contains:

- a pointer to a doubly linked list of the blocks of Q contained in it.
- a pointer to a list of pairs: the first element of the pair is a state q such that q has an edge to a state in S; the second element is an ADD $\mathcal{A}_{(q,S)}$ which encodes $count(q)(S)$, i.e., $\mathcal{A}_{(q,S)}(a) = count(q)(S)(a)$ for each $a \in \Sigma$.

A state r has the following pointers to

- all pairs of the form $\langle q, \mathcal{B} \rangle$ where $\Delta(q,r) = \mathcal{B}$.
- the block in Q which it belongs to.

We shall also use a number of lists which will create and then destroy after each iteration step. These lists are implemented as hash tables, which means that searching for an element in the list can be assumed to take constant time.

6   Refinement Steps

In this section we describe how to implement each iteration of the algorithm of Section 4, so that an iteration takes $\mathcal{O}\left(\ell \cdot \left(|B_i| + \sum_{q \in B_i} |Pre(q)|\right)\right)$ time. An iteration consists of six steps as follows.

Step 1. This step chooses two blocks[2] B and S. Remove a block S from C. Examine the first two blocks in S. Let B be the smaller one. If they are equal in size, then B can be arbitrarily chosen to be anyone of them. This step can be performed in constant time.

Step 2. This step is to maintain the invariant that $q \cong_{i+1} r$ implies that $q \in B$ iff $r \in B$. Remove B from S and create a new block S' in X. The block S' is simple and contains B as its only block. If S is still compound, put it back into C. This step can be performed in constant time.

Step 3. Create a new list L, implemented as a hash table. Each element of L is a record containing a pointer to a state q and an ADD which we call $\mathcal{A}_{L(q)}$. The ADD $\mathcal{A}_{L(q)}$ characterizes $count(q)(B)$, i.e., it gives, for each $a \in \Sigma$, the number of edges from q which go to states in B and whose symbol sets include a. We create L by scanning the elements of B. For each $r \in B$ and each edge $\langle q, r \rangle$ we add q to L with $\mathcal{A}_{L(q)} = \mathcal{B}$ where $\mathcal{B} = \Delta(q,r)$. If q already is in L we modify the value of $\mathcal{A}_{L(q)}$ to be $\mathcal{A}_{L(q)} + \mathcal{B}$, i.e., we update $\mathcal{A}_{L(q)}$ according to the symbols in the set $\Delta(q,r)$.

Since L is a hash table, searching for a state q in L takes constant time. Performing addition on ADDs takes $\mathcal{O}(\ell)$ time (Section 2).

Step 4. We partition each block of Q with respect to B. This will maintain the invariant that $q \simeq_i r$ implies $(q \longrightarrow B) = (r \longrightarrow B)$. We create a new block $D_\mathcal{B}$ for each block D of Q and BDD $\mathcal{B}$ such that there is a state $q \in B$ with

---

[2] These blocks correspond to B_i and S_i chosen during the ith iteration (Section 4).

q in L and $\overline{\mathcal{A}_{L(q)}} = \mathcal{B}$. Intuitively, the block $D_{\mathcal{B}}$ will contain all states which originally belonged to D and which have edges to B on the same set of symbols (namely the set of symbols characterized by $\mathcal{B}$). To perform this operation, each block D in Q will maintain a list L_D, implemented as a hash table. Each element of L_D is a pair, where the first element is a BDD and the second element is a pointer to a block. We traverse the list L created in step 3 above. For each state q in L, we consider the block D in Q to which q currently belongs. We remove q from D. We find the entry in L_D with a BDD equal to $\overline{\mathcal{A}_{L(q)}}$. We insert q in the corresponding block.

In the second phase of step 4, we add the newly created blocks to Q. If a block D has become empty we remove it from Q. If the block in X which contains B or one of the newly created blocks has become compound, we insert it in C.

Computing $\overline{\mathcal{A}_{L(q)}}$ takes time $\mathcal{O}(\ell)$ (see Section 3). Since L_D is a hash table, searching the table takes constant time. Removing q from D and inserting it in the new block takes constant time. Moving and checking emptiness of block takes constant time.

Step 5. We partition each block of Q with respect to $S - B$. This will keep the invariant that $q \simeq_i r$ implies

$$\begin{pmatrix} count(q)(B_i)(a) \\ = \\ count(q)(S_i)(a) \end{pmatrix} \quad \text{iff} \quad \begin{pmatrix} count(r)(B_i)(a) \\ = \\ count(r)(S_i)(a) \end{pmatrix}$$

This step is similar to Step 4 above. The only difference is the manner in which we insert a state in the list L_D. When considering a state q in L, belonging to (say) block D, we compute $\mathcal{B} = \mathcal{A}_{L(q)} \oplus \mathcal{A}_{S(q)}$. The position of q in L_D will be determined by the BDD $\mathcal{B}$ (rather by the BDD $\overline{\mathcal{A}_{L(q)}}$ as was the case in Step 4). Intuitively, the BDD $\mathcal{B}$ characterizes the set of symbols through which the state q moves to $S - B$. This means that, states which will end up in the same block will move to $S - B$ on the same set of symbols, and hence the above mentioned invariant will be maintained.

Step 6. Since B was removed from S, the value of $count(q)(S)(a)$ may have been reduced (in case q has an edge to B labeled with a). This step updates the value of $count(q)(S)(a)$ accordingly. Recall that L contains all states which have edges to B. We scan the list L, and for each state q, we replace the current value $\mathcal{A}$ of $\mathcal{A}_{S(q)}$ by $\mathcal{A} - \mathcal{A}_{L(q)}$ (takes $\mathcal{O}(\ell)$). If $\mathcal{A}$ becomes empty we discard the pair q and its associated ADD $\mathcal{A}_{S(q)}$ from the list pointed to by S. Finally, we make B point to the list L.

Observe that the time spent on an iteration is $\mathcal{O}(\ell)$ per scanned edge and state of B, which gives a total time of $\mathcal{O}\left(\ell \cdot \left(|B_i| + \sum_{q \in B_i} |Pre(q)|\right)\right)$.

7   Experiments

There is no official set of benchmarks for testing algorithms that compute bisimulation equivalence [10]. Therefore, we have implemented a procedure for randomly generating non-deterministic automata. In the procedure, we can change a number of parameters which decide the shape of the generated automata. Such parameters include the number of states, the size of the alphabet, the density of edges between two states, the probability that a certain symbol is included in the symbol set between two states, and the size of such a set.

In Table 1 we compare the execution times of our implementation of the algorithm and a non-symbolic version of the Paige-Tarjan algorithm. To make the comparison meaningful we have implemented both versions of the algorithm in the same code, using the same data structures and the same procedures. As evident from the table, the symbolic version is almost insensitive to the size of the alphabet, while the non-symbolic version exhibits an exponential increase in time until we reach a point where it takes too long time (more than 24 hours). The above experiments are conducted with the number of states being equal to 20. We get a similar behaviour pattern when increasing the number of states. We have tested our prototype on automata with up to 200 states.

We have also compared our implementation with The Concurrency Work-Bench (CWB) [21] and The Concurrency WorkBench of The New Century (CWB-NC) [2]. The results are presented in Table 2. CWB uses minimization techniques based on the Kanellakis and Smolka algorithm [22], while CWB-NC uses the Paige-Tarjan algorithm. Both tools show similar behaviour to the non-symbolic version of our code.

Table 1. Comparing the symbolic and the non-symbolic versions of the algorithm on automata with 20 states. The execution time is measured in seconds. Larger numbers of states give similar behaviours.

Symbols in alphabet	2^2	2^4	2^5	2^7	2^9	2^{10}	2^{11}	2^{12}	2^{40}	2^{80}	2^{100}	2^{120}
Non-symbolic	3.99	4.55	4.81	7.18	32.9	120.7	557.7	1955	–	–	–	–
Symbolic	0.05	0.08	0.09	0.09	0.09	0.09	0.09	0.09	0.09	0.09	0.11	0.12

Table 2. The execution time for our implementation of the algorithm and minimization in CWB and CWB-NC. The automata have 150 states and 250 transitions. Execution time is measured in seconds.

Symbols in alphabet	2^2	2^5	2^{10}	2^{11}	2^{12}	2^{25}	2^{40}	2^{50}	2^{80}	2^{100}	2^{115}
Symbolic	4.69	6.05	6.52	6.60	6.60	6.69	6.84	7.66	8.43	10.15	12.46
CWB	0.13	0.68	10.60	18.50	28.44	–	–	–	–	–	–
CWB-NC	0.31	0.32	–	–	–	–	–	–	–	–	–

In Figure 2 we keep the size of alphabet intact while we increase the probability that a symbol is included in the symbol set of an edge. We observe that while our algorithm copes well with large alphabets, its efficiency decreases with symbol density.

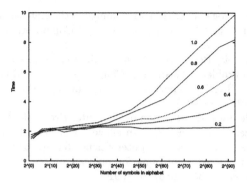

Fig. 2. Increasing the symbol density, while keeping the size of the alphabet fixed. The automata have 150 states and 250 transitions.

8 Conclusions and Future Work

We have presented a version of the Paige-Tarjan algorithm where the edge relation for labeled automata is represented symbolically using BDDs. For automata with large alphabets, our experiments indicate that the algorithm behaves better than algorithms which operate on an explicit representation of the automaton.

One direction for future research, is to consider Boolean encodings of the alphabet which are not canonical (as is the case with BDDs) and then use SAT solvers to perform the necessary operations on the symbolic encoding. It is well-known that SAT solvers outperform BDDs in certain applications, and it could be interesting to find out whether this is the case for minimization of automata. Also, we intend to consider similar algorithms for checking *simulation* relations. This is relevant, for instance, in the context of regular model checking, where several classes of acceleration techniques rely on computing simulations [4].

References

1. Bouali, A.: Xeve, an esterel verification environment. In: Proc. 10th Int. Conf. on Computer Aided Verification. Volume 1427 of Lecture Notes in Computer Science., Springer Verlag (1998) 500–504
2. Cleaveland, R., Sims, S.: The NCSU concurrency workbench. In: Proc. 8th Int. Conf. on Computer Aided Verification. Volume 1102 of Lecture Notes in Computer Science., Springer Verlag (1996) 394–397
3. Fernandez, J.C., Garavel, H., Kerbrat, A., Mateescu, R., Mounier, L., Sighireanu, M.: CADP: A Protocol Validation and Verification Toolbox. In: CAV'96, LNCS 1102 (1996)
4. Abdulla, P., Jonsson, B., Nilsson, M., Saksena, M.: A survey of regular model checking. In: Proc. CONCUR 2004, 15th Int. Conf. on Concurrency Theory. (2004) 348–360
5. Abdulla, P.A., Jonsson, B., Nilsson, M., d'Orso, J.: Algorithmic improvements in regular model checking. In: Proc. 15th Int. Conf. on Computer Aided Verification. Volume 2725 of Lecture Notes in Computer Science. (2003) 236–248

6. Hopcroft, J.E.: An $n \log n$ algorithm for minimizing the states in a finite automaton. In Kohavi, Z., ed.: The Theory of Machines and Computations. Academic Press (1971) 189–196

7. Paige, R., Tarjan, R., Bonic, R.: A linear time solution to the single function coarsest partition problem. Theoretical Computer Science **40** (1985) 67–84

8. Paige, R., Tarjan, R.: Three partition refinement algorithms. SIAM Journal on Computing **16** (1987) 973–989

9. Holzmann, G.: Design and Validation of Computer Protocols. Prentice Hall (1991)

10. Dovier, A., Piazza, C., Policriti, A.: An efficient algorithm for computing bisimulation equivalence. Theoretical Computer Science **311** (2004) 221–256

11. Bryant, R.: Graph-based algorithms for boolean function manipulation. IEEE Trans. on Computers **C-35** (1986) 677–691

12. Bahar, R.I., Frohm, E.A., Gaona, C.M., Hachtel, G.D., Macii, E., Pardo, A., Somenzi, F.: Algebraic decision diagrams and their applications. In: ICCAD '93: Proc. of the 1993 IEEE/ACM international conference on Computer-aided design, IEEE Computer Society Press (1993) 188–191

13. Fernandez, J.C.: An implementation of an efficient algorithm for bisimulation equivalence. Sci. Comput. Program. **13** (1989)

14. Bouali, A., de Simone, R.: Symbolic bisimulation minimisation. In: Proc. Workshop on Computer Aided Verification. Volume 663 of Lecture Notes in Computer Science. (1992) 96–108

15. Klarlund, N.: An $n \log n$ algorithm for online bdd refinement. J. Algorithms **32** (1999) 133–154

16. Fisler, K., Vardi, M.Y.: Bisimulation and model checking. In: Conference on Correct Hardware Design and Verification Methods. (1999) 338–341

17. Bouajjani, A., Fernandez, J., Halbwachs, N.: Minimal model generation (1990) Manuscript.

18. Lee, D., Yannakakis, M.: Online minimization of transition systems. In: Proc. 24th ACM Symp. on Theory of Computing. (1992)

19. Andersen, H.R.: An introduction to binary decision diagrams. Technical Report DK-2800, Department of Information Technology, Technical University of Denmark (1998)

20. Somenzi, F.: Binary decision diagrams (1999)

21. Cleaveland, R., Parrow, J., Steffen, B.: The Concurrency Workbench: A semantics based tool for the verification of concurrent systems. ACM Transactions on Programming Languages and Systems **15** (1993)

22. Kanellakis, P., Smolka, S.: CCS expressions, finite state processes, and three problems of equivalence. Information and Computation **86** (1990) 43–68

Simulating Two-Dimensional Recognizability by Pushdown and Queue Automata[*]

Marcella Anselmo[1] and Maria Madonia[2]

[1] Dipartimento di Informatica ed Applicazioni, Università di Salerno,
I-84081 Baronissi (SA), Italy
anselmo@dia.unisa.it
[2] Dip. Matematica e Informatica, Università di Catania,
Viale Andrea Doria 6/a, 95125 Catania, Italy
madonia@dmi.unict.it

Abstract. The aim of this paper is to investigate sequential models to describe two-dimensional languages. The intent is to add more capabilities to 4NFA in order to encompass a wider class of languages. We show that any (tiling) recognizable language can be simulated by a 4NFA with an extra queue whose size is bounded by the minimum of the two dimensions of a picture; and that 2NFA (i.e. automata moving only in two directions) with an analogous queue are sufficient when the alphabet is unary. A special class of recognizable languages can be simulated also by 4-way pushdown automata with a stack of size bounded by the sum of the two dimensions of the picture. Such a class is also characterized by a recursive definition involving the operations of union, intersection and a new diagonal overlapping operation applied to languages recognized by 2NFA.

1 Introduction

Two-dimensional (2D) languages are the generalization of string languages to two dimensions. Their elements are two-dimensional strings or pictures, i.e. rectangular arrays of symbols taken in a finite alphabet. Many approaches have been presented in the literature in order to generalize formal one-dimensional (1D) language theory to two dimensions. In [6] all the attempts made in this direction till 90's are collected and compared. Furthermore an unifying point of view is presented: the family of picture languages called REC is proposed as the candidate to be "the" generalization of the class of regular one-dimensional languages. Indeed REC family is well characterized from very different points of view and thus inherits several properties from the class of regular 1D languages.

Some recent papers study REC family from the point of view of regular expressions [1, 2, 14], other ones look for recognizability in terms of grammars [4, 14]. In this paper we are more extensively concerned with simulation of REC by some

---

[*] Work partially supported by MIUR Cofin: *Linguaggi Formali e Automi: Metodi, Modelli e Applicazioni.*

J. Farré, I. Litovsky, and S. Schmitz (Eds.): CIAA 2005, LNCS 3845, pp. 43–53, 2006.
© Springer-Verlag Berlin Heidelberg 2006

proper kind of automata. Historically a first attempt to recognize 2D languages by means of automata was done in 1967 by M. Blum and C. Hewitt (cf. [3]) who defined *4-way automata*. A deterministic (non-deterministic) four-way automaton, denoted by 4DFA (4NFA), is defined as an extension of the two-way automaton for strings by allowing it to move in four directions: left, right, up, down. The families of picture languages recognized by some 4DFA and 4NFA are denoted by $\mathcal{L}(4DFA)$ and $\mathcal{L}(4NFA)$ respectively. We will use this notation for any other type of automata: if $\mathcal{M}$ is an automaton of a certain type, then $\mathcal{L}(\mathcal{M})$ is the family of languages accepted by automata as $\mathcal{M}$. Unlike the one-dimensional case, $\mathcal{L}(4DFA)$ is strictly included in $\mathcal{L}(4NFA)$ (cf. [3]). Both families $\mathcal{L}(4DFA)$ and $\mathcal{L}(4NFA)$ are closed under Boolean union and intersection operations and under rotation. The family $\mathcal{L}(4DFA)$ is also closed under complement, while $\mathcal{L}(4NFA)$ is not [11]. On the other hand, $\mathcal{L}(4DFA)$ and $\mathcal{L}(4NFA)$ are not closed under row and column concatenation, and their closure operations [8]. Some restricted versions of 4NFA have been studied, as 3NFA ([12]) and 2NFA ([2]). Even if 4NFA are a direct generalization of classical (one-way or two-way) finite automata for 1D string languages, unfortunately they define only a proper subclass of REC.

Another device to recognize 2D languages was introduced in 1977 by K. Inoue and A. Nakamura [7] and was called *two-way on-line tesselation acceptor* (2OTA). Informally the 2OTA is an infinite array of identical finite-state automata in a two dimensional space. The deterministic version is denoted by 2DOTA and is less powerful than 2OTA. The 2OTA have the worth to recognize exactly REC family. Other devices that generalize their 1D counterpart are alternating finite automata (AFA) defined in [9], alternating pushdown automata (APDA), alternating counter automata (ACA) [15] (see also [13]). Such models, together with 2OTA's one, have a major feature of being somehow *parallel* devices.

In this paper we are interested in recognizability of 2D languages by finite *sequential* automata. We start from 4NFA and add extra capability in order to encompass a wider class of languages, still keeping a sequential structure. In particular we consider 4NFA equipped with bounded stack or queue and compare them with REC family or some other families inside REC. A particular attention is devoted to the case of an unary alphabet. Observe that studying 2D languages on a one-letter alphabet means to study the "shape" of pictures, ignoring their "content". The family of recognizable languages over a unary alphabet is denoted REC(1).

In particular we show that any language in REC can be simulated by a *4NFA equipped with a queue* of size bounded by the minimal dimension of the input picture (denoted 4NQA). Unfortunately the 4NQA are powerful enough to define also some non-recognizable language. The model of 4NQA can be simplified when we restrict to an unary alphabet. A 2NQA (a 4NQA that can move only in two directions) is sufficient to simulate any recognizable unary language. Moreover we show that with some strong restrictions this model exactly characterizes

REC(1). Our simulation follows some basic ideas for analogous simulations of REC family (see [6]).

We then consider 4NFA equipped with a stack. If the size of the stack is bounded by the minimal of the dimensions of the picture (as for 4NQA) it seems that several recognizable languages would be not accepted. Indeed we could not keep in memory a row or a column indifferently. Furthermore, using a stack instead of a queue, when we pop the stack, some necessary information could get lost. Hence we consider 4NFA equipped with a stack of size bounded by the sum of the dimensions of the picture and call them *4-way pushdown automata* (4NPDA). When restricted to one-row pictures, 4NPDA are equivalent to two-way pushdown automata on strings. Since two-way pushdown automata on strings recognize also context-free (string) languages, 4NPDA recognize languages not in REC. Nevertheless we show that 4NPDA are able to recognize a quite large family inside REC, here called $\mathcal{L}(2DOTA\varrho)$. This is the class of languages that are either recognized by 2DOTA or the rotation of a language recognized by 2DOTA. Furthermore, every example provided in the literature of a language in REC but not in $\mathcal{L}(2DOTA)$ is a rotation of a language in $\mathcal{L}(2DOTA)$. We use a characterization of $\mathcal{L}(2DOTA)$ by 2AFA in [10]. The class $\mathcal{L}(2DOTA\varrho)$ is also characterized by a recursive definition: a language in $\mathcal{L}(2DOTA\varrho)$ can be obtained from some languages accepted by 2NFA by iterating their union, intersection and *diagonal overlapping*. The diagonal overlapping is a new operation on pictures and picture languages here defined; in the unary alphabet case it is strictly linked to the diagonal concatenation as defined in [1, 2].

The paper is organized as follows. In Section 2 we briefly recall some preliminary definitions and results later used in the paper. Section 3 contains the main results about 4NQA. Section 4 is devoted to 4NPDA and the class $\mathcal{L}(2DOTA\varrho)$. Section 5 draws some conclusions.

2   Preliminaries

In this section we recall some terminology for two-dimensional languages. For all definitions and classical results refer to [6]. Deterministic and non-deterministic 4-way automata (4DFA and 4NFA, resp.) are a generalization of 2-way (one-dimensional) finite automata where the reading head can move in four directions: Left, Right, Up and Down. When the head can move only in two directions, right and down, we obtain deterministic and non-deterministic 2-way automata (2DFA and 2NFA, resp.). The definition of two-dimensional on-line tessellation acceptor, denoted by 2OTA is in [7]. If $\mathcal{M}$ is an automaton of a certain type, then $\mathcal{L}(\mathcal{M})$ will denote the family of languages accepted by automata as $\mathcal{M}$.

Let Σ be a finite alphabet. A *two-dimensional string* (or a *picture*) over Σ is a two-dimensional rectangular array of elements of Σ. The set of all two-dimensional strings over Σ is denoted by Σ^{**} and a *two-dimensional language* over Σ is a subset of Σ^{**}. Given a picture $p \in \Sigma^{**}$, let $p_{i,j}$ denote the symbol in p with coordinates (i,j), let $\ell_1(p)$ denote the number of rows of p and $\ell_2(p)$ denote the number of columns of p. The pair $(\ell_1(p), \ell_2(p))$ of dimensions of p is called the *size* of the picture p. The set of all two-dimensional strings over Σ of size (n, m) is denoted by $\Sigma^{n \times m}$. For any picture p of size (n, m), we consider picture $\widehat{p}$ of size $(n+2, m+2)$ obtained by surrounding p with a special *boundary symbol* $\# \notin \Sigma$.

A *tiling system* for a language L over Σ with local alphabet Γ is a pair (Θ, π) where Θ is a set of *tiles*, that is pictures of dimension $(2, 2)$ over $\Gamma \cup \{\sharp\}$, and $\pi : \Gamma \cup \{\sharp\} \rightarrow \Sigma$ is an alphabetic mapping. Then, we say that a language $L \subseteq \Sigma^{**}$ is *recognizable by tiling system* (Θ, π) if $L = \pi(L')$ and L' is the set of all pictures p such that the sub-pictures of $\widehat{p}$ are all in Θ. The family of two-dimensional languages recognizable by tiling systems is denoted by $\mathrm{REC}(\Sigma)$, briefly REC when the alphabet can be omitted, and by $\mathrm{REC}(1)$ when a one-letter alphabet is dealt with. Note that one-row languages in REC exactly correspond to regular string languages.

3   Four-Way Queue Automata

In this section we define 4-way queue automata (4NQA) as 4NFA equipped with a queue bounded by the minimum of the input's dimensions and the class $\mathcal{L}(4\mathrm{NQA})$ of languages accepted by 4NQA. We show that REC family is strictly contained in $\mathcal{L}(4\mathrm{NQA})$. In the one-letter alphabet case $\mathrm{REC}(1)$ can be simulated by a weaker model: 2NQA, that is 4NQA that can move only right and down. A restrictive extra condition allows to recognize exactly $\mathrm{REC}(1)$.

Informally, a *4-way non-deterministic queue automaton* $\mathcal{A}$, referred as *4NQA*, is a 4NFA supplied with a queue ("first in, first out" memory) over some alphabet Φ. Its computation depends on the transition function δ: at each step, given the actual state, the symbol read in the actual position and the symbol at the head of the queue, the automaton $\mathcal{A}$, according to δ, non-deterministically, dequeues or not the symbol from the head of the queue, enqueues or not a symbol onto the tail of the queue, changes state and moves by one position in one direction (Left, Right, Up or Down) or stands in the actual position (no_move). As usual, a 4NQA recognizes a picture p if, starting in the top-left corner of p in the initial state, it non-deterministically can reach an accepting state. Moreover during a computation of a 4NQA, the maximal length of the queue is never greater than $min\{\ell_1(p), \ell_2(p)\} + 1$. A *2-way non-deterministic queue automaton*, referred to as *2NQA* is a 4NQA that can move right and down, but not up or left.

Example 1. Let L be the language of pictures that are the column concatenation of two identical squares. More formally $L = \{p \mid \ell_1(p) = n \geq 1, \ell_2(p) = 2n$ and $p(i, j) = p(i, j + n) \; \forall 1 \leq i, j \leq n\}$. The language L is accepted by a 4NQA that compares the i-th column with the $n + i$-th one, for any $i = 1, \cdots, n$, as follows. It enqueues the content of the i-th column in the queue while moving down, then moves to $n + i$-th column following the diagonal, and moving down it dequeues if the symbol at the head of the queue matches the one in the cell. Note that this 4NQA for L acts deterministically.

Proposition 1. *The family REC is strictly contained in $\mathcal{L}(4NQA)$.*

Proof. Let $L \in REC(\Sigma)$, let (Θ, π) be a tiling system over the alphabet Γ for L and let L' be the underlying local language. L is recognized by a 4NQA $\mathcal{A}$, with queue alphabet Θ and states q_x with $x \in \Gamma$, that operates as follows on $p \in \Sigma^{**}$, with $n = \ell_1(p)$ and $m = \ell_2(p)$. $\mathcal{A}$ guesses $l = min\{n, m\}$ and let us suppose, w.l.o.g., $n \leq m$. $\mathcal{A}$ scans p column by column, from top to bottom in the attempt to find, non-deterministically, a picture $p' \in L'$ that corresponds to p in L'. For this, the transition function of $\mathcal{A}$ is designed so that when $\mathcal{A}$ enters in the j-th column ($j > 1$) of p, then the queue contains the guessed sequence of tiles covering the $(j-2)$-th and $(j-1)$-th column of $\widehat{p'}$. So $\mathcal{A}$ using the state, these tiles and the symbols of the j-th column, can guess the tiles covering the $(j-1)$-th and j-th column of $\widehat{p'}$ and can push them in the queue. For example, if $\mathcal{A}$ is reading $p_{i,j}$, then, actually, the symbol at the top of the queue is the guessed

tile $t_1 = \begin{array}{|c|c|} \hline p'_{i-1,j-2} & p'_{i-1,j-1} \\ \hline p'_{i,j-2} & p'_{i,j-1} \\ \hline \end{array}$ for $\widehat{p'}$ and the state is $q_{p'_{i-1,j}}$. Now the automaton $\mathcal{A}$

can guess the tile $t_2 = \begin{array}{|c|c|} \hline p'_{i-1,j-1} & p'_{i-1,j} \\ \hline p'_{i,j-1} & p'_{i,j} \\ \hline \end{array}$ for $\widehat{p'}$ (if at least one such tile exists in

Θ otherwise $\mathcal{A}$ halts without accepting). Then $\mathcal{A}$ dequeues t_1, enqueues t_2, goes down in the state $q_{p'_{i,j}}$ and repeats this procedure. When $\mathcal{A}$ reaches the bottom of the j-th column, it moves right to the $(j+1)$-th column and then up to top position of the column without changing the queue. If the construction of $\widehat{p'}$ can be completed then $\mathcal{A}$ accepts the picture p.

The inclusion is strict since language L in Example 1 is in $\mathcal{L}(4NQA)$, but it is not in REC (see [6]).   □

Remark 1. Bounding the queue of a 4NQA by the minimum of the dimensions of a picture has an important byproduct. When 4NQA are restricted to one-row languages, they are equivalent to 2-way automata on strings with unitary size queue that recognize only regular languages (the queue symbol can be simulated by the states).

In the case of an unary alphabet, Proposition 1 can be specified and gives the following result.

Proposition 2. *Let $|\Sigma| = 1$. The family REC(1) is contained in $\mathcal{L}(2NQA)$.*

Proof. Let $L \in REC(1)$, (Θ, π), Γ, L' and n be as in Proposition 1. The 2NQA, $\mathcal{A}$, that recognizes L is similar to the 4NQA constructed in Proposition 1. The only difference is that, since $|\Sigma| = 1$, it is no more necessary to scan all the positions of the picture p. Therefore, $\mathcal{A}$ works in this way: first it fills up the queue moving downwards in the first column. When it reaches the bottom, it moves to the right, then remaining in the bottom position of the second column, it updates the queue for $n + 1$ times in order to obtain in the queue the sequence of guessed tiles for the first two columns of p. Then $\mathcal{A}$ moves again to the right and repeats the cycle on the next column. If it reaches the bottom-right corner of p then it accepts (see Example 2).   □

Example 2. The language L of squares over an unary alphabet $\Sigma = \{a\}$, that is $L = \{p \in \{a\}^{**} \mid \ell_1(p) = \ell_2(p)\}$, can be easily recognized by a simple 2NFA that follows the diagonal and accepts when it founds the corner. Moreover a tiling system (Θ, π) over the alphabet $\Gamma = \{0, 1, \sharp\}$ for L is the one containing all the $(2,2)$ sub-pictures of a square with 1 on the diagonal and 0 elsewhere, surrounded by $\sharp$. The simulation of such a tiling system following the proof of Proposition 2 provides a 2NQA $\mathcal{A}$ that on a square picture of size $(4, 4)$ acts as follows. The states of $\mathcal{A}$ are q_x where x is the symbol in Γ that has been guessed to be in the considered position. $\mathcal{A}$ moving downwards in the first column, enqueues the following tiles, one at each position: $\begin{smallmatrix} \sharp & \sharp \\ \sharp & 1 \end{smallmatrix}$; $\begin{smallmatrix} \sharp & 1 \\ \sharp & 0 \end{smallmatrix}$; $\begin{smallmatrix} \sharp & 0 \\ \sharp & 0 \end{smallmatrix}$; $\begin{smallmatrix} \sharp & 0 \\ \sharp & 0 \end{smallmatrix}$; $\begin{smallmatrix} \sharp & 0 \\ \sharp & \sharp \end{smallmatrix}$. Then it moves right (at the bottom of the second column) in state $q_\sharp$ and without moving, it dequeues $\begin{smallmatrix} \sharp & \sharp \\ \sharp & 1 \end{smallmatrix}$ and enqueues $\begin{smallmatrix} \sharp & \sharp \\ 1 & 0 \end{smallmatrix}$; (since it is the only tile of the form $\begin{smallmatrix} \sharp & \sharp \\ 1 & \gamma \end{smallmatrix}$ with $\gamma \in \Gamma$) and enters state q_0. Now, it alternates a dequeue and an enqueue of the following tiles, respectively: $\begin{smallmatrix} \sharp & 1 \\ \sharp & 0 \end{smallmatrix}$; $\begin{smallmatrix} 1 & 0 \\ 0 & 1 \end{smallmatrix}$; $\begin{smallmatrix} \sharp & 0 \\ \sharp & 0 \end{smallmatrix}$; $\begin{smallmatrix} 0 & 1 \\ 0 & 0 \end{smallmatrix}$; $\begin{smallmatrix} \sharp & 0 \\ \sharp & 0 \end{smallmatrix}$; $\begin{smallmatrix} 0 & 0 \\ 0 & 0 \end{smallmatrix}$; $\begin{smallmatrix} \sharp & 0 \\ \sharp & \sharp \end{smallmatrix}$; $\begin{smallmatrix} 0 & 0 \\ \sharp & \sharp \end{smallmatrix}$.

At the end of these updates $\mathcal{A}$ moves right in state $q_\sharp$, acting in a similar way for the following columns.

Remark 2. Note that in Proposition 2, the automaton $\mathcal{A}$ that recognizes L is very particular: it scans only the first column and the last row of the input picture p, going downwards in the first column and right in the last row; it enqueues one symbol (without dequeueing) only when it moves down (i.e. only when it scans the first column); it leaves the j-th column (with $j \geq 2$) only after having updated the queue (with one symbol enqueued and one dequeued) exactly $n + 1$ times where n is the number of rows in p.

We will call such a special type of 2NQA a *restricted 2NQA*.

Proposition 3. *Let $|\Sigma| = 1$ and $L \subseteq \Sigma^{**}$. If L is accepted by a restricted 2NQA then $L \in REC(1)$.*

Proof. Let $\mathcal{A}$ be a restricted 2NQA that recognizes L. We construct a tiling system (Θ, π) on a local alphabet Γ. The idea is to construct, given a picture $p = (n, m) \in \Sigma^{**}$, a picture $p' \in \Gamma^{**}$ which can "describe" the computation of the automaton $\mathcal{A}$ on p and such that $p = \pi(p')$. For this, we set $\Gamma = Q \times \Phi \times Q$, where Q is the set of states of $\mathcal{A}$ and Φ is its queue alphabet. Moreover, we define the set of tiles Θ so that the j-th column of p' can depict a sequence of steps of the computation of $\mathcal{A}$ on p, beginning with the step in which $\mathcal{A}$ enters for the first time in that column and ending with the step in which $\mathcal{A}$ leaves that column.

More exactly, define the set Θ so that if, for a fixed column $\bar{\jmath}$ of $\widehat{p'}$, for $i = 1, \ldots, n$ we have $p'_{i,\bar{\jmath}} = (q_{i,\bar{\jmath}}, P_{i,\bar{\jmath}}, q'_{i,\bar{\jmath}})$, then $q_{1,\bar{\jmath}} = q_{2,\bar{\jmath}} = \ldots = q_{n,\bar{\jmath}}$ is the state in which $\mathcal{A}$ reaches the position $(n, \bar{\jmath})$, $q'_{i,\bar{\jmath}}$, for $i = 1 \ldots n$, is the sequence of the states of $\mathcal{A}$ when it remains in the column $\bar{\jmath}$ and $P_{i,\bar{\jmath}}$, for $i = 1, \ldots, n$, is the symbol that $\mathcal{A}$ enqueues when it is in the state $q'_{i-1,\bar{\jmath}}$. In this way, the sequence $P_{1,\bar{\jmath}}, P_{2,\bar{\jmath}}, \ldots, P_{n,\bar{\jmath}}$ represents the queue when $\mathcal{A}$ leaves the column $\bar{\jmath}$.

The symbol $q_{1,\bar{\jmath}} = \ldots = q_{n,\bar{\jmath}}$ is needed to know if two columns can be adjacent: if $\mathcal{A}$ leaves the $\bar{\jmath}$-th column in the state $\bar{q}$, then it must enter in the $(\bar{\jmath}+1)$-th column in the same state (i.e. $q'_{n,\bar{\jmath}} = q_{n,\bar{\jmath}+1} \cdots = q_{1,\bar{\jmath}+1}$).   □

4 Four-Way Pushdown Automata and the Class $\mathcal{L}(2\mathrm{DOTA}\varrho)$

In this section we define 4-way pushdown automata (4NPDA) as 4NFA equipped with a stack bounded by the sum of the dimensions of a picture. This device is able to simulate the class $\mathcal{L}(2\mathrm{DOTA}\varrho)$ of languages either recognized by a 2DOTA or whose rotation is recognized by a 2DOTA. Moreover a language in this class can be recursively defined applying union, intersection and diagonal overlapping to some languages in $\mathcal{L}(2\mathrm{NFA})$. The diagonal overlapping is a new operation on pictures and picture languages here introduced.

Informally, a *4-way non-deterministic pushdown automaton*, referred to as *4NPDA*, works as a classical two-way pushdown automaton on strings, with the only difference that it can now move in four directions: Left, Right, Up, and Down (since it scans 2D pictures). A 4NPDA recognizes a picture p if, starting in the top-left corner of p in the initial state, it non-deterministically can reach an accepting state and, during this computation, the maximal length of the stack is never greater than $\ell_1(p) + \ell_2(p)$. A *2-way non-deterministic pushdown automaton*, referred to as *2NPDA* is a 4NPDA that can move right and down, but not up or left.

Remark 3. When 4NPDA are restricted to one-row languages, that is languages contained in $\Sigma^{1 \times n}$, they are equivalent to 2-way pushdown automata with a stack of length up to the length of the input string. Since two-way pushdown automata on strings recognize also non-regular (string) languages, 4NPDA recognize languages not in REC.

On the other hand, it seems that 4-way automata equipped with a stack of length up to the minimal dimension are not able to recognize several 2D languages in REC.

Let us recall that a two-dimensional alternating automaton (here denoted 4AFA) ([9, 13]) is a generalization of 4NFA where a state can be either existential or universal. A computation that meets an universal (existential, resp.) state accepts if every (at least one, resp.) path from that state is accepting. A two-way two-dimensional alternating automaton (here denoted 2AFA) is a 4AFA that can move rigth and down only.

Example 3. Let $L \subseteq \Sigma^{**}$ be the language of squares whose last row is equal to the last column. More formally $L = \{p \in \Sigma^{**} \mid \ell_1(p) = \ell_2(p) = n$ and for any $i = 1, \cdots, n, \ p(n,i) = p(i,n)\}$. A 2AFA recognizing L is the following. The initial state q_0 is an existential state and the transitions from q_0 for any $\sigma \in \Sigma$ are given by: $\delta(q_0, \sigma) = \{(q_c, no\_move), (q_a, no\_move) \mid a \in \Sigma\}$. The state q_c deterministically accepts if we are in the bottom-right corner. The transitions from an universal state q_a are given by: $\delta(q_a, \sigma) = \{(q_{aR}, R), (q_{aD}, D), (q_D, no\_move)\}$. State q_{aR} deterministically checks whether at the right end of the row there is an a symbol and accepts in this case. In an anologous way, state q_{aD} deterministically checks whether at the bottom of the column there is an a symbol and accepts in this case. State q_D moves one cell in diagonal and enters q_0.

Proposition 4. *The family $\mathcal{L}(2AFA)$ is contained in $\mathcal{L}(4NPDA)$.*

Proof. Let $L \in \mathcal{L}(2AFA)$ and let $\mathcal{A}$ be a 2AFA for L. For the sake of simplicity, suppose that $\mathcal{A}$ at each step moves rigth or down. A 4NPDA $\mathcal{P}$ that simulates $\mathcal{A}$ is the following. When $\mathcal{A}$ reaches an universal state q in position (i, j), then $\mathcal{P}$ has to check if all the possible paths of the computation tree, starting from q in position (i, j), are accepting. So $\mathcal{P}$ fills its stack with some triples (q, d, k), where q is the state, $d \in \{Rigth, Down\}$ is the direction and k is a number indicating which path is actually checked. When $\mathcal{P}$ has completed an accepting path t of $\mathcal{A}$, it can return in position (i, j) by popping his stack, and thus check the next path. Note that, since $\mathcal{A}$ can move only right and down, $\mathcal{P}$'s stack contains at most $\ell_1(p) + \ell_2(p)$ symbols, where p is the input picture.   □

Consider now the family $\mathcal{L}(2DOTA\varrho)$ of all languages in $\mathcal{L}(2DOTA)$ and all their rotations.

Corollary 1. *The family $\mathcal{L}(2DOTA\varrho)$ is contained in $\mathcal{L}(4NPDA)$.*

Proof. If $L \in \mathcal{L}(2DOTA)$ then it is the 180° rotation of a language $L' \in \mathcal{L}(2AFA)$ ([10]) and L' is accepted by a 4NPDA $\mathcal{A}$ (Proposition 4). Hence L is accepted by a 4NPDA that starts by reaching the bottom-right corner and then continues with a reversed copy of $\mathcal{A}$. Moreover $\mathcal{L}(4NPDA)$ is closed under rotation since, in a similar way as before, any rotation of a language accepted by a 4NPDA is also accepted by a 4NPDA that first deterministically reaches some corner. Observe that in any case the sum of the dimensions is the same and so the size of the stack.   □

Let us now introduce the operation of *diagonal overlapping*. Given a picture p, let us denote for any $1 \leq i \leq i' \leq \ell_1(p)$ and $1 \leq j \leq j' \leq \ell_2(p)$, by $p[(i, j), (i', j')]$ the sub-picture of p with top-left corner in position (i, j) and bottom-right corner in position (i', j') (as in [8]).

Definition 1. *Let $p, q \in \Sigma^{**}$ two pictures such that $p_{\ell_1(p), \ell_2(p)} = q_{1,1}$. The diagonal overlapping of p with q, denoted $p(ov)q$, is the language of words $z \in \Sigma^{**}$ with $\ell_1(z) = \ell_1(p) + \ell_1(q) - 1$, $\ell_2(z) = \ell_2(p) + \ell_2(q) - 1$ and such that $z[(1, 1), (\ell_1(p), \ell_2(p))] = p$ and $z[(\ell_1(p), \ell_2(p)), (\ell_1(z), \ell_2(z))] = q$.*

Moreover for $L_1, L_2 \subseteq \Sigma^{**}$, the diagonal overlapping of L_1 with L_2, denoted $L_1(ov)L_2$, is the language $L_1(ov)L_2 = \{p(ov)q \mid p \in L_1, q \in L_2\}$.

Remark 4. Consider an unary alphabet. The diagonal concatenation of $p = (n, m)$ and $q = (n', m')$, as defined in [1, 2], is the picture of size $(n+n', m+m')$. Hence, in the case of an unary alphabet, the descriptional power of the diagonal overlapping is the same as that of the diagonal concatenation. The diagonal overlapping of p with q is the diagonal concatenation of p with a picture obtained from q by erasing one row and one column.

Now we set the recursive definition of *2-way recursive languages*. Observe that in the case of an unary alphabet, the class $\mathcal{L}(\text{2NFA})$ has been characterized in [1, 2] as both the family of rational relations and the family of languages obtained from finite languages using union, diagonal concatenation and its closure.

Definition 2. *Let $L \subseteq \Sigma^{**}$. L is a 2-way recursive language if there exist $X_1, \ldots, X_h, Y_1, \ldots, Y_k \subseteq \Sigma^{**}$, $L = Y_1$, such that, $\forall i = 1, \ldots, h$, $X_i \in \mathcal{L}(\text{2NFA})$ and, $\forall j = 1, \ldots, k$, Y_j can be obtained applying to some languages in the set $\{X_1, \ldots, X_h, Y_1, \ldots, Y_k\}$ a finite number of $\cup$, $\cap$ and (ov) operations where any (ov) operation has a language in $\{X_1, \ldots, X_h\}$ as its first parameter and a language in $\{Y_1, \ldots, Y_k\}$ as its second parameter.*

Example 4. Let L be the language defined in Example 3. L is a 2-way recursive language. Indeed $L = \Sigma^{1,1} \cup \bigcup_{\sigma \in \Sigma} L_\sigma$ where for every $\sigma \in \Sigma$, $L_\sigma = L'_\sigma \cap L''_\sigma \cap (\Sigma^{2,2}(ov)L)$ with $L'_\sigma = \{p \in \Sigma^{**} \mid p_{1,\ell_2(p)} = \sigma\}$, and $L''_\sigma = \{p \in \Sigma^{**} \mid p_{\ell_1(p),1} = \sigma\}$. Remark that $\Sigma^{1,1}$, $\Sigma^{2,2}$, L'_σ and L''_σ are all in $\mathcal{L}(\text{2NFA})$.

Proposition 5. $L \in \mathcal{L}(\text{2AFA})$ *if and only if L is a 2-way recursive language.*

Proof. Let $\mathcal{A}$ be a 2AFA accepting L, δ its transition function and q_0 its starting state. Set $n_\Sigma = \sum_{\sigma \in \Sigma} |\delta(q_0, \sigma)|$. First suppose q_0 is an existential state. If $n_\Sigma > 1$ then L is the union of n_Σ languages in $\mathcal{L}(\text{2AFA})$, following the n_Σ possible choices for the transitions. If $n_\Sigma = 1$ and $\delta(q_0, \sigma) = (q_1, R)$ $(= (q_1, D)$, resp.) then $L = L_{1,2}(ov)L_1$, $(L = L_{2,1}(ov)L_1$, resp.) where $L_{1,2} = \{p \in \Sigma^{1 \times 2} \mid p_{1,1} = \sigma\} \in \mathcal{L}(\text{2NFA})$, $L_{2,1} = \{p \in \Sigma^{2 \times 1} \mid p_{1,1} = \sigma\} \in \mathcal{L}(\text{2NFA})$, and $L_1 \in \mathcal{L}(\text{2AFA})$ is the language recognized by $\mathcal{A}$ with initial state q_1. When q_0 is a universal state an analogous proof holds with intersection instead of union. For the sake of brevity, we omit some details about border conditions and *no_move* transitions.

Vice versa, let L be a 2-way recursive language. The proof is by induction. If $L \in \mathcal{L}(\text{2NFA})$ then $L \in \mathcal{L}(\text{2AFA})$ since a 2AFA is a generalization of a 2NFA. If $L = L_1 \cup L_2$ and L_1, L_2 are 2-way recursive then by inductive hypothesis, for $i = 1, 2$, L_i is accepted by a 2AFA $\mathcal{A}_i$ with initial state q_i. Then we can define a 2AFA $\mathcal{A}$ joining $\mathcal{A}_1$ and $\mathcal{A}_2$ with a new initial existential state q_0 and $\delta(q_0, \sigma) = \{(q_1, no\_move), (q_2, no\_move)\}$. The proof is analogous when $L = L_1 \cap L_2$ and L_1, L_2 are 2-way recursive, with the only difference that q_0 is now a universal state. Finally, suppose $L = L_1(ov)L_2$ where $L_1 \in \mathcal{L}(\text{2NFA})$ and L_2 is a 2-way recursive language. W.l.o.g. suppose that the 2NFA $\mathcal{A}_1$ recognizing L_1 always accepts in the bottom-right corner of a picture. By inductive hypothesis, L_2 is accepted by a 2AFA $\mathcal{A}_2$ with initial state q_2. So we can obtain a 2AFA accepting L by simulating first $\mathcal{A}_1$ (viewed as a 2AFA that can guess the bottom border) and then starting $\mathcal{A}_2$ each time $\mathcal{A}_1$ on some position would enter an accepting state if the position would be a bottom-right corner. Remark that the construction is possible since it works basically connecting initial states of 2AFA unless in the case of (ov) operations. $\square$

Corollary 2. $L \in \mathcal{L}(2DOTA_\varrho)$ *if and only if L is the rotation of a 2-way recursive language.*

Proof. The proof easily follows from Proposition 5 and a result in [10] stating that $L \in \mathcal{L}(2\text{AFA})$ iff it is the 180° rotation of a language in $\mathcal{L}(2DOTA)$.   □

Example 5. Consider again the language L defined in Example 3. The simulation of the 2AFA recognizing L given in Example 3, that follows the proof of Proposition 5, leads to the definition of L as a 2-way recursive language presented in Example 4. Remark that L is in $\mathcal{L}(2\text{AFA})$, but its reverse is not (see [10]).

5   Some Conclusions

In order to represent tiling recognizable two-dimensional languages (REC family) by a sequential device, we have considered 4NFA with some added capabilities. Following the theory of formal (one-dimensional) languages, we considered extra capability consisting of some bounded queue or stack and established some partial results about their relationship with the REC family. The considered models seem not able to describe exactly this family. This is the case also when different limitations on the size of the extra memory are imposed. Moreover, the result cannot be improved also restricting to the deterministic counterparts of the considered models. Indeed, REC family is intrinsically non-deterministic and the deterministic versions of 4NQA and 4NPDA are already able enough to recognize languages not in REC (see Example 1 that can be also adapted to a 4NPDA). Further steps will be to design some model that is conceptually different from the ones for one-dimensional case.

Acknowledgements. We want to greatly thank Dora Giammarresi for helpful discussions and comments.

References

1. Anselmo, M., Giammarresi, D., Madonia, M.: Regular Expressions for Two-Dimensional Languages Over One-Letter Alphabet (Proc. DLT04), Calude C. S., Calude E., Dinneen M. J. (Eds), LNCS **3340** Springer Verlag (2004) 63-75
2. Anselmo, M., Giammarresi, D., Madonia, M.: New operations and regular expressions for two-dimensional languages over one-letter alphabet. Theor. Comp. Sc. (2005) (to appear)
3. Blum, M., Hewitt, C.: Automata on a two-dimensional tape. IEEE Symposium on Switching and Automata Theory. (1967) 155-160
4. Crespi Reghizzi S., Pradella, M.: Tile Rewriting Grammars, (Proc. Developments in Language Theory DLT 2003), LNCS **2710** Springer Verlag (2003) 206-217
5. Giammarresi, D., Restivo, A.: Two-dimensional finite state recognizability. Fundamenta Informaticae **25:3**, 4 (1996) 399-422
6. Giammarresi, D., Restivo, A.: Two-dimensional languages. In: G. Rozenberg *et al* Eds: Handbook of Formal Languages Vol. III. Springer Verlag (1997) 215-268

7. Inoue, K., Nakamura, A.: Some properties of two-dimensional on-line tessellation acceptors. Information Sciences. **13** (1997) 95-121
8. Inoue, K., Takanami, I., Nakamura, A.: A note on two-dimensional finite automata. Information Processing Letters **7:1** (1978) 49-52
9. Inoue, K., Takanami, I., Taniguchi, H.: Two-dimensional alternating Turing machines. Theor. Comp. Sc. **27** (1983) 61-83
10. Ito, A., Inoue, K., Takanami, I.: Deterministic two-dimensional On-line tesselation Acceptors are equivalent to two-way two-dimensional alternating finite automata through 180°-rotation. Theor. Comp. Sc. **66** (1989) 273-287
11. Kari, J., Moore, C.: New results on alternating and non-deterministic two-dimensional finite-state automata (Proc. STACS 2001) LNCS **2010** Springer Verlag (2001)
12. Kinber, E. B.: Three-way Automata on Rectangular Tapes over a One-Letter Alphabet. Information Sciences **35** Elsevier Sc. Publ. (1985) 61-77
13. Lindgren, K., Moore, C., Nordhal, M. G.: Complexity by two-dimensional patterns. J. of Statistical Physics **91** (1998) 909-951
14. Matz, O.: Regular expressions and Context-free Grammars for picture languages. (Proc. STACS'97) LNCS **1200** Springer Verlag (1997) 283-294
15. Okazaki, T., Ito, A., Inoue, K., Wang, Y.: Closure property of space-bounded two-dimensional alternating Turing machines, pushdown automata, and counter automata. Int. J. of Pattern Rec. and Artif. Intelligence **15:7** (2001) 1143-1165

Component Composition Preserving Behavioural Contracts Based on Communication Traces

Arnaud Bailly, Mireille Clerbout, and Isabelle Simplot-Ryl

LIFL, CNRS UMR 8022,
Université de Lille I, Cité Scientifique,
F-59655 Villeneuve d'Ascq Cedex, France
{bailly, clerbout, ryl}@lifl.fr

Abstract. This paper investigates the compositional properties of reusable software components defined with explicit dependencies and behavioural contracts expressing rely-guarantee specifications in the form of communication traces. In this setting, connection of components through their matching ports is indeed compositional and yields a new component or *composite* that respects its constituents' contracts. Thus the behaviour of the composite is computed from the behaviours of its constituents and is known to conform to the contracts without any new proof.

1 Introduction

Components and composition are the embodiment of a very old problem solving strategy: *Divide et Impera*. In the broad field of engineering, this decomposition strategy aims at identifying, given a large problem, how known solutions can be composed to solve the problem. This practice alleviates the burden of complex engineering as known solutions are reused and domain-specific only parts need adhoc solutions. Component software [1] emerged from object-oriented programming as a way to apply compositional engineering to the construction of complex software. The main achievement of the field has been the production of *distributed component frameworks* such as CORBA Component Model (CCM) [2], J2EE and .NET. These frameworks provide technical solutions to software engineers at the implementation and detailed design levels but they are not adequate for reasoning and verifying systems and components interactions.

What is needed is then *component models* and methods that lend themselves to formal compositional reasoning. Architectural Description Languages (ADL [3]) have pioneered the field while trying to give precise meanings to the notion of software architecture and providing tools to reason about it. One achieved work is SOFA [4], an ADL and framework that allows decomposition of *frames* or systems' interfaces into components, interfaces and connectors specified with regular languages over messages, down to primitive components. System behaviour can then be inferred using languages' composition rules. As this work is mostly aimed towards providing adaptable softwares, it gives a formal definition of substitutability that is based on language inclusion. One problem with this

J. Farré, I. Litovsky, and S. Schmitz (Eds.): CIAA 2005, LNCS 3845, pp. 54–65, 2006.

approach is that correct behaviour should be re-proved at each (de)composition step as it is changed by connectors' specifications. Similar works based on *process algebras* (*e.g.* [5–7]) are quite successful at modelling complex behaviours, including reflective behaviours and encoding of structural evolutions of systems. This complexity is of course at the price of the complexity of proofs and the undecidability of most properties.

Some questions that should be addressed by such models are: Given a certain assembly of components, what properties can be inferred from their composition as a system? Is it possible to find a system that has defined expected properties? Is a particular component substitutable with another component without breaking the whole system? Is it possible to preserve properties through composition? In terms of formal languages theory, all these questions can be reduced to the use of synchronization products of languages and the well-known problem of reconstructing a language from its projections onto sub-alphabets. An overview of the problem of composition in the setting of finite state automata is studied in [8], where compositionality of automata depends on the composition rules used. In this paper, we consider some classical form of trace-based specification given in terms of regular languages. And we show that we obtain "good composition properties" using an encoding of the topology of a set of connected components in the alphabet. More precisely, we are stating and proving some desirable properties of a *composite* (set of components seen as a component) that are preserved by composition: The behaviour of the composite respects the contract of the services it provides and uses, and any client using its services will not be blocked by misbehaving clients using other services. A full version of this work including proofs is available as technical report [9].

Composition and decomposition of systems are widely studied in the literature in several settings. Composition of formal specification gives rise in [10] to two different notions of *invariants*: *Existential invariants* guarantee preservation of a property through composition with any other component, while *universal properties* require composition with components holding the same property to be kept through composition. In [11], specifications are given in terms of TLA formulas and the specification of a complete system is a conjunction of component specifications. Then, Composition and Decomposition theorems allow to prove large systems by reasoning about their components. In more "practical" models, like ArchJava for example [12], there exists some kind of "consistency by construction" but often reduced to some syntactical or typing properties. What we obtain here is some kind of "compositional behavioural typing relation" similar to the compositional typing relations in the Pi-calculus, which from our knowledge does not exist in other formalisms.

Paper Overview. Section 2 introduces the model, notations, and specification we use, Section 3 describes the composition itself, deals with the consistency of a set of composed components called a system, and defines a notion of composite extracted from a system, Section 4 concludes the paper and gives some perspectives of this work.

2   Component Model and Specifications

2.1   Component Model

The component model we use is an abstraction of the CORBA Component Model, simple enough to fit a large number of used models. A *component* is an opaque object communicating through *ports*. A port may be *synchronous*, then communication is by method calls, or asynchronous, then messages are structured *events*. Furthermore, a port may represent a service *provided* by the component or *required* by the component from its environment. Synchronous ports are typed by *interfaces*: A provided synchronous port is called a *facet*; a required one is called a *receptacle*. Provided and required asynchronous ports are called respectively *sinks* and *sources*. Components do not operate in isolation; they must be connected through their ports to operate, that is to exchange messages. Throughout this article, we focus on the simpler case where the connections of components are established at deployment time and do not change until the system stops.

We consider behavioural specifications of services, and we emphasize the fact that all the components that offer a specific service should be similar from a client's viewpoint (especially in open systems). Services usage is observable through messages exchanged between various components, so the specifications are given in terms of communication traces, which are sequences of messages. An asynchronous event is modelled by a message sent between two objects, whereas a method call is modelled by two events: a message from the caller to the callee representing the call of the method, and a message from the callee to the caller representing the return of the method call. As we consider distributed systems, each element of the system, a component for example, only knows about its own communications, so its specification is a language (set of traces) whose words (traces) are sequences of messages sent or received by this element. So the language defines a *contract* between the specified element and its potential user(s). In the case of interfaces, this contract relates calls made by the client to returns produced by a component providing this interface. In the case of components, this contract allows relating messages received/produced on provided ports to messages on required ports. This is a very low level form of rely-guarantee specification that can be derived from a lot of known models based on state machines, predicates on traces, ...

Observable events are messages exchanged by elements of the system (*e.g.* a call to a method m). A distinctive feature of our model is the form of the alphabet: A letter representing an event includes sender's and receiver's identity and the names of the ports through which the communication occurs. It is an essential aspect of our formalism that allows us to take into account the configuration resulting from a system configuration. While the specification is abstract and deals with *models of components*, the semantics of composition deals with identified *instances* of components and ports through proper renaming (alphabetic morphisms). These requirements lead to the following definition of the event alphabet:

Definition 1 (Event alphabet). *An event alphabet is composed of letters of the form $(c_1, p_1, c_2, p_2, k, n)$ where:*

- c_1 *is a component and p_1 is the name of a required port of this component,*
- c_2 *is a component and p_2 is the name of a provided port of this component,*
- k *is the "kind": method call (*call*), return from method call (*return*), or asynchronous event (*event*),*
- n *is the name of the method or the event.*

2.2   Definitions – Notations

A *projection* $\Pi_Y : X^* \to Y^*$ is an alphabetical morphism such that $Y \subseteq X$ and $\Pi_Y(x) = x$ if $x \in Y$ and ε otherwise. The prefix-closure of a language L denoted by $pf(L)$ is $pf(L) = \{u \mid \exists v \text{ such that } uv \in L\}$, L is said to be prefix-closed if $L = pf(L)$.

We use in the following two particular products on languages. The *shuffle product* of L_1 and L_2 denoted $L_1 \sqcup\!\sqcup L_2$ is defined as:

$$L_1 \sqcup\!\sqcup L_2 = \bigcup_{u \in L_1, v \in L_2} \{u_1 v_1 u_2 v_2 \dots u_n v_n \mid u = u_1 u_2 \dots u_n, v = v_1 v_2 \dots v_n\}.$$

For languages $L_1 \subseteq \Sigma_1^*$, $L_2 \subseteq \Sigma_2^*$, the *synchronization product* of L_1 and L_2 on Σ_1 and Σ_2 denoted $L_1 \sqcap_{\Sigma_1, \Sigma_2} L_2$ is defined as:

$$L_1 \underset{\Sigma_1, \Sigma_2}{\sqcap} L_2 = \{u \in (\Sigma_1 \cup \Sigma_2)^* \mid \Pi_{\Sigma_1}(u) \in L_1, \Pi_{\Sigma_2}(u) \in L_2\}.$$

We use this definition given by Duboc in [13] instead of De Simone's one [14] since it gives an associative operation:

$$L_1 \sqcap_{\Sigma_1, \Sigma_2} L_2 \sqcap_{\Sigma_2, \Sigma_3} L_3 = (L_1 \sqcap_{\Sigma_1, \Sigma_2} L_2) \sqcap_{\Sigma_1 \cup \Sigma_2, \Sigma_3} L_3$$
$$= L_1 \sqcap_{\Sigma_1, \Sigma_2 \cup \Sigma_3} (L_2 \sqcap_{\Sigma_2, \Sigma_3} L_3).$$

We also use some notations to simplify the writing. Let $\mathcal{E}$ be an event alphabet. For short, we denote

$$\Pi_{(c,p)} = \Pi_{\{(c_1, p_1, c_2, p_2, k, n) \in \mathcal{E} \mid (c_1, p_1) = (c, p) \vee (c_2, p_2) = (c, p)\}}.$$

Let $\mathcal{E}$ and $\mathcal{E}'$ be event alphabets. We denote by $h^{\beta_1, \dots, \beta_n}_{\alpha_1, \dots, \alpha_n}$ the strictly alphabetical morphism:

$$h^{\beta_1, \dots, \beta_n}_{\alpha_1, \dots, \alpha_n} : \mathcal{E} \longrightarrow \mathcal{E}'$$
$$(c_1, p_1, c_2, p_2, k, n) \longmapsto (c_1', p_1', c_2', p_2', k, n) \text{ with}$$
$$c_1' = \beta_i \text{ if } c_1 = \alpha_i \text{ and } c_1' = c_1 \text{ otherwise,}$$
$$p_1' = \beta_i \text{ if } p_1 = \alpha_i \text{ and } p_1' = p_1 \text{ otherwise,}$$
$$c_2' = \beta_i \text{ if } c_2 = \alpha_i \text{ and } c_2' = c_2 \text{ otherwise,}$$
$$p_2' = \beta_i \text{ if } p_2 = \alpha_i \text{ and } p_2' = p_2 \text{ otherwise.}$$

2.3   Specifications

The specifications are given in terms of communication traces. More precisely, each element of the system is specified by a regular language whose elements are valid communication traces of this element (traces where the context and the element both respect the specification). Each trace corresponds to an observation of the system, thus, specifications are prefix-closed languages to take into account observations at any time. In execution traces, it is clear that method calls must preceede the corresponding returns, even if we allow some concurrency inside components. Thus we consider for specification purposes *well-formed* languages. A language $\mathcal{L}$ over an event alphabet $\mathcal{E}$ is said to be well-formed if L is prefix-closed and

$$\mathcal{L} \subseteq pf((\bigsqcup_{(x,y,z,t,\mathtt{call},n) \in \mathcal{E}} ((x,y,z,t,\mathtt{call},n)(x,y,z,t,\mathtt{return},n))^*) $$
$$\bigsqcup_{(x,y,z,t,\mathtt{event},n) \in \mathcal{E}} (x,y,z,t,\mathtt{event},n)^*).$$

An interface specification is a contract offered by an interface to its clients, more precisely, this is a contract on the interface as a *type*: Each port typed by the interface should offer this contract to its clients. Components are also defined as types: each instance of a component must respect the component specification. Thus, to write specifications we use variables as components identities, these variables will be instantiated with the identities of component instances for a particular system configuration.

Definition 2 (Connection variables). *In an event, the variables γ_1 and ϱ_1 (resp. γ_2 and ϱ_2) denote the identity of a component and the name of one of its required (resp. provided) port.*

Definition 3 (Interface). *An interface specification I is a pair $[[meth, \mathcal{L}_I]]$ where meth is a set of method names, $\mathcal{L}_I$ a regular prefix-closed language of $\alpha(I)^*$ with $\alpha(I) = \{(\gamma_1, \varrho_1, \gamma_2, \varrho_2, k, n) \mid n \in meth \wedge k \in \{\mathtt{call}, \mathtt{return}\}\}$ and $\mathcal{L}_I$ is included in*

$$pf((\bigcup_{(\gamma_1,\varrho_1,\gamma_2,\varrho_2,\mathtt{call},n) \in \alpha(I)} ((\gamma_1, \varrho_1, \gamma_2, \varrho_2, \mathtt{call}, n)(\gamma_1, \varrho_1, \gamma_2, \varrho_2, \mathtt{return}, n)))^*).$$

A component specification describes the behaviour of its instances (*i.e.* pieces of software that offer ports), thus, we first have to define ports.

Definition 4 (Port). *A port is a tuple (n, t, g) where n is the port name, t its type (an interface or an asynchronous event type) and g its kind (receptacle, facet, source or sink).*

The event alphabet of a component is the set of events it can send or receive through its ports. So, it is built from the alphabets of the types of its ports. But when we specify a particular component we use a variable γ to denote an instance of this component. In the event of the alphabets of required (resp.

provided) ports, γ replaces γ_1 (resp. γ_2) and the effective name of the port in this component replace ϱ_1 (resp. ϱ_2). Note that this allows us to deal with components having several ports of the same type.

Definition 5 (Component specification). *A component specification C is defined by $C = [[P, \mathcal{L}]]$ with:*

- *P a set of ports whose names are pairwise distinct,*
- *$\mathcal{L}$ a regular well-formed language over $\alpha(C)$ which is the union of:*
  - *$h_{\gamma_2, \varrho_2}^{\gamma, f}(\alpha(I))$ for each $(f, I, \mathbf{facet}) \in P$,*
  - *$h_{\gamma_1, \varrho_1}^{\gamma, r}(\alpha(I))$ for each $(r, I, \mathbf{receptacle}) \in P$,*
  - *$\{(\gamma, s, \gamma_2, \varrho_2, \mathbf{event}, n)\}$ for each $(s, n, \mathbf{source})$ of P,*
  - *$\{(\gamma_1, \varrho_1, \gamma, s, \mathbf{event}, n)\}$ for each $(s, n, \mathbf{sink})$ of P,*

where γ is the variable that represents any instance of this component.

The specification of a particular component instance is then obtained by instantiation of the variable γ with the actual identity of the component instance.

Definition 6 (Component instance). *A component instance of $C = [[P, \mathcal{L}]]$ whose name is c is $c = \langle P, h_\gamma^c(\mathcal{L}) \rangle$, its alphabet is $\alpha(c) = h_\gamma^c(\alpha(C))$.*

A component provides and uses ports. We expect such a piece of code to abide by the specification of its ports, so we first describe three basic properties that a component must respect to be consistent.

For a receptacle, we want messages emitted by an element (most of the time a component) through a receptacle to be accepted by the specification of its type (interface).

Definition 7. *A language $\mathcal{L}$ over an event alphabet $\mathcal{E}$ is consistent for the receptacle $(r, I, \mathbf{receptacle})$ of γ (denoted by $\mathcal{L} \vdash_\gamma (r, I, \mathbf{receptacle})$) if:*

$$\Pi_{(\gamma, r)}(\mathcal{L}) \subseteq h_{\gamma_1, \varrho_1}^{\gamma, r}(\mathcal{L}_I).$$

A component that offers a sink must be able to receive events at any time, which is expressed by the following definition (remember that we are interested in prefix-closed languages):

Definition 8. *A language $\mathcal{L}$ over an event alphabet $\mathcal{E}$ is consistent for the sink $(s, S, \mathbf{sink})$ of γ (denoted by $\mathcal{L} \vdash_\gamma (s, S, \mathbf{sink})$) if:*

$$(u \in \mathcal{L}) \Rightarrow (u(\gamma_1, \varrho_1, \gamma, s, \mathbf{event}, S) \in \mathcal{L}).$$

A component that offers a facet has to respect its specification. We require another property which is of great importance in the setting of open distributed systems: At each time, a facet must be available independently of the external events not controlled by the component (as calls received on the other facets) in order all the components offering the same service to be equivalent from the viewpoint of a client.

Definition 9. *A language $\mathcal{L}$ over an event alphabet $\mathcal{E}$ is consistent for the facet $(f, I, \textbf{facet})$ of γ (denoted by $\mathcal{L} \vdash_\gamma (f, I, \textbf{facet})$) if:*

$$h_{\gamma_2, \varrho_2}^{\gamma, f}(\mathcal{L}_I) \subseteq \Pi_{(\gamma, f)}(\mathcal{L}) \tag{1}$$
and
$$\forall u \in \mathcal{L}, \forall x \in \mathcal{E} \text{ such that } \Pi_{(\gamma, f)}(u)x \in h_{\gamma_2, \varrho_2}^{\gamma, f}(\mathcal{L}_I), \tag{2}$$
$$\exists v \text{ such that } uvx \in \mathcal{L} \text{ and } \forall(\varphi, T, g) \text{ with } g \in \{\textbf{facet}, \textbf{sink}\}, \Pi_{(\gamma, \varphi)}(v) = \varepsilon$$

Part (1) says that the behaviour of an element must conform to the specification of a facet it "offers": An element must accept all specified calls and returns are completely specified by calls. Part (2) indicates that at each time, each event valid for the facet specification should be accessible independently of events not controlled by the component, that is events on other facets or sinks.

The three previous definitions lead us to define a consistent component.

Definition 10 (Consistent component). *A component $C = [[P, \mathcal{L}]]$ is consistent if for each (n, t, g) of P such that g belongs to $\{\textbf{receptacle}, \textbf{facet}, \textbf{sink}\}$:*

$$\mathcal{L} \vdash_\gamma (n, t, g).$$

An instance of a consistent component is said to be consistent.

3   Component Composition

3.1   Connecting Components

In this subsection, we describe how to compose components to obtain systems, that is to say sets of inter-connected components.

Definition 11 (Connection). *A connection is a tuple (c_1, p_1, c_2, p_2) where c_1 and c_2 are component instances, p_1 is the name of a required port of c_1 and p_2 is the name of a provided port of c_2 such that p_1 and p_2 are of the same type. For X a set of connections, we denote the set of elements of X by:*

$$elem(X) = \{(c, p) \mid \exists(c, p, c', p') \in X \text{ or } \exists(c', p', c, p) \in X\}.$$

The event alphabet has been designed to embed the structure of the system in languages. Thus, when connecting components, we instantiate the connection variables to register the connections in the language. This allows us to deal with several instances of the same component as the names of the ports allow us to deal with components having several ports of the same type.

Definition 12 (Connection morphism). *Let $\mathcal{E}$ be an event alphabet and X a set of connections. Then the connection morphism h_X is defined by:*

$$
\begin{aligned}
h_X : \mathcal{E} &\longrightarrow \mathcal{E} \\
(c, p, \gamma_2, \varrho_2, k, n) &\longmapsto (c, p, c', p', k, n) \text{ if } (c, p, c', p') \in X \\
(\gamma_1, \varrho_1, c, p, k, n) &\longmapsto (c', p', c, p, k, n) \text{ if } (c', p', c, p) \in X \\
x &\longmapsto x \text{ otherwise.}
\end{aligned}
$$

Definition 13 (System). *A system* $S = \langle B, X \rangle$ *is built from a set of consistent component instances* $B = \{c_1, \ldots, c_n\}$ *and a set of connections* X *over* B. *The alphabet of* S, *denoted by* $\alpha(S)$ *is:*

$$\alpha(S) = \bigcup_{1 \leq i \leq n} h_X(\alpha(c_i)).$$

The behaviour of S *is deduced from the behaviour of its components and from the connections, it is:* $\mathcal{L}_{B,X} = \mathcal{L}_S = h_X(\mathcal{L}_{c_1}) \sqcap^X_{\alpha(c_1),\alpha(c_2)} \cdots \sqcap^X_{\alpha(c_{n-1}),\alpha(c_n)} h_X(\mathcal{L}_{c_n})$, *with* $\sqcap^X_{\Sigma,\Xi}$ *the synchronization product on the alphabets* $h_X(\Sigma)$ *and* $h_X(\Xi)$.

Notice that as the synchronization product of well-formed languages is well-formed, the language of a system is well-formed. The creation of systems from components allows us to build sub-systems. Then, it is interesting to be able to compose systems in a "compositional" way.

Definition 14 (External connections). *Let* $S_1 = \langle B_1, X_1 \rangle$, $S_2 = \langle B_2, X_2 \rangle$ *be two systems such that* $B_1 \cap B_2 = \emptyset$. *Then, a connection set* X *is said external for these systems if and only if:*

$$elem(X) \cap elem(X_1) = \emptyset$$
and $\quad elem(X) \cap elem(X_2) = \emptyset$
and $\forall (c_1, p_1, c_2, p_2) \in X, \{c_1, c_2\} \cap B_1 \neq \emptyset \wedge \{c_1, c_2\} \cap B_2 \neq \emptyset.$

Definition 15 (Composition of two systems). *Let* $S_1 = \langle B_1, X_1 \rangle$ *and* $S_2 = \langle B_2, X_2 \rangle$ *be two systems such that* $B_1 \cap B_2 = \emptyset$ *and* X *be an external connection set for these systems. Then the composition of the systems by* X, *denoted by* $S = S_1 \circ_X S_2$, *is the system* $S = \langle B_1 \cup B_2, X_1 \cup X_2 \cup X \rangle$ *(with* $\mathcal{L}_S = \mathcal{L}_{B_1 \cup B_2, X_1 \cup X_2 \cup X}$).

The next proposition states that it is possible to hierarchically compute the system languages, which is a basic required property of component systems.

Proposition 1. *Let* $S_1 = \langle B_1, X_1 \rangle$ *and* $S_2 = \langle B_2, X_2 \rangle$ *be two systems with* $B_1 \cap B_2 = \emptyset$. *Then, the system* $S = S_1 \circ_X S_2$ *with* X *an external connection set for* S_1 *and* S_2 *is such that*

$$\mathcal{L}_S = h_X(\mathcal{L}_{S_1}) \sqcap^X_{\alpha(S_1),\alpha(S_2)} h_X(\mathcal{L}_{S_2}).$$

We can now notice two interesting properties of the composition operation.

Proposition 2. *The composition* $(\circ)$ *of systems is commutative.*

Proposition 3. *Let* $S_1 = \langle B_1, X_1 \rangle$, $S_2 = \langle B_2, X_2 \rangle$ *and* $S_3 = \langle B_3, X_3 \rangle$ *be systems such that* B_1, B_2 *and* B_3 *are pairwise disjoint. Let* Y_1 *be external for* S_1 *and* S_2, Y_2 *be external for* S_2 *and* S_3, *and* Y_3 *be external for* S_1 *and* S_3 *such that* $elem(Y_1) \cap elem(Y_2) = elem(Y_1) \cap elem(Y_3) = elem(Y_2) \cap elem(Y_3) = \emptyset$, *then:*

$$(S_1 \circ_{Y_1} S_2) \circ_{Y_2 \cup Y_3} S_3 = S_1 \circ_{Y_1 \cup Y_3} (S_2 \circ_{Y_2} S_3).$$

The problem is now to show that the connections preserve consistency of components. As the components we connect are consistent, the connections are proved to work: any message sent by a component on a connection respect the specification of its partner on this connection. But as we use synchronization products to compute the language of a system, it is not obvious that all the components are still consistent for the non-connected ports: for example it could happen that the trace language of the system does not contain any call to a method m which is supposed to be provided by a component.

3.2   System Consistency

Now, we show that a system is consistent with regard to the behavioural typing: all its components are still consistent after connection. Using the properties of component languages, it is straigthforward to show that for receptacles and sinks.

Notation 1. *Let P be a set of ports and X a set of connections. We denote by $P \setminus X$ the set of ports of P whose name does not belong to $elem(X)$ and $P \cap X$ the set of ports of P whose name belongs to $elem(X)$.*

Proposition 4. *Let $S = \langle B, X \rangle$ be a system. Then, we have:*

$$\forall c = \langle P, \mathcal{L}_c \rangle \in B, \forall (r, I, \textbf{receptacle}) \in P \setminus X, \mathcal{L}_S \vdash_c (r, I, \textbf{receptacle})$$
$$\forall c = \langle P, \mathcal{L}_c \rangle \in B, \forall (si, Si, \textbf{sink}) \in P \setminus X, \mathcal{L}_S \vdash_c (si, Si, \textbf{sink})$$
.

To show a similar property in the case of facet, we have to require another property from the systems we consider. We will consider "loop-free" systems that we call DAG (Directed Acyclic Graph). One of the consistency properties imposes that a component is always able to provide a service it offers independently from actions depending on other clients. This can only be ensured if we forbid cyclic connections: a simple example of this problem is a component c that provides two facets f_1 and f_2, and requires a receptacle r. If we connect r to f_1 and if f_1 and f_2 use services of r to provide their own services then a call on f_2 can lead to a deadlock. This restriction on the system expresses the idea that "ones does not require a service one provides".

Definition 16. *A system $S = \langle B, X \rangle$ is said to be a DAG if and only if the graph $G = \langle B, E \rangle$ is a DAG where $E \subseteq B \times B$ is defined by: $\forall (c_i, c_j) \in B \times B$, $((c_i, c_j) \in E) \Leftrightarrow (\exists (c_i, p_i, c_j, p_j) \in X)$.*

Proposition 5. *Let $S = \langle B, X \rangle$ be a system with $B = \{c_1, \dots, c_n\}$. Then, we have*

$$\forall c = \langle P, \mathcal{L}_c \rangle \in B, \forall (f, I, \textbf{facet}) \in P \setminus X, \mathcal{L}_S \vdash_c (f, I, \textbf{facet}).$$

Sketch of Proof. We add to Definition 16 the definition of the *height* of a component instance c of B: it is the length of the longest path in G whose origin is c and is denoted by $height(c)$. Then we show the proposition by induction on the height of components of the system using the fact that in a DAG system, if there exists a connection (c, p, c', p'), then $height(c) > height(c')$.

As conclusion of this section, a DAG system has been shown to be consistent for its non connected ports.

3.3 Composites

We are now able to define a *composite* as an abstraction of a component system. The abstraction operation hides the internal structure of a system, shows it as a unique component, and renames the external ports in order port names to be unique for a given composite. Let us remark that the composite is here seen as an instance of component. This allows hierarchical reasoning about systems.

Definition 17 (Composite). *A composite is the abstraction of a* DAG *component system. Let $S = \langle B, X \rangle$ be a* DAG *with $B = \{c_1, \ldots, c_n\}$, we can extract from S a composite c*

$$c = abstract(S) = \langle P, \mathcal{L}_c \rangle$$

such that $P = \{(c_i\_p, T, G) \mid \exists c_i = \langle P_i, \mathcal{L}_i \rangle \in B \text{ with } (p, T, G) \in P_i \setminus X\}$
and $\mathcal{L}_c = h_c(\mathcal{L}_S),$

with h_c the abstraction morphism

$$h_c : \alpha(S) \quad\quad\quad \longrightarrow h_c(\alpha(S)) = \alpha(c)$$
$$(\gamma_1, \varrho_1, c_i, p, k, n) \longmapsto (\gamma_1, \varrho_1, c, c_i\_p, k, n) \text{ for each } c_i \text{ and each } p,$$
$$(c_i, p, \gamma_2, \varrho_2, k, n) \longmapsto (c, c_i\_p, \gamma_2, \varrho_2, k, n) \text{ for each } c_i \text{ and each } p,$$
$$x \quad\quad\quad\quad \longmapsto \varepsilon \text{ otherwise.}$$

Proposition 6. *A composite is an instance of a consistent component.*

Sketch of Proof. Once again, it is straigthforward to show that a composite is consistent for its sinks. To show that a composite is consistent for its facets and for its receptacles, we need to introduce a property of the operations we use on languages: For $S = \langle B, X \rangle$, a component c of B, a non-connected port p of c, an identity γ of a composite, and an interface I, we have:

$$h_\gamma(h_{\gamma_i, \varrho_i}^{c, p}(\mathcal{L}_I)) = h_{\gamma_i, \varrho_i}^{\gamma, c\_p}(\mathcal{L}_I) \text{ with } i \in \{1, 2\} \tag{1}$$
$$h_\gamma \circ \Pi_{(c, p)} = \Pi_{(\gamma, c\_p)} \circ h_\gamma. \tag{2}$$

Thus, we get the proposition using:

- (1) and (2),
- the fact that the system abstracted to get the composite is consistent,
- the fact that the synchronization product of well-formed languages is well-formed.

This proposition allows us to directly use composite as components without any proof of their consistency: The model ensures the consistency.

4 Conclusion

The main result of this paper is that our formal model for component-oriented systems is fully compositional: A composite built from components is itself a component that can be used in further composition. The obvious advantage of this property is that when designing systems from components, nothing needs to be re-proved on the system: It is guaranteed to behave according to the specification of its facets and its receptacles. Of course, this property needs to be proved for *atomic* components, which is the subject of other work on formal testing [15].

From this starting point, there are numerous tracks that can be followed. A first extension would be to consider systems that are not DAGs: a lot of "real" systems are DAGs, in particular the ones without asynchronous events, anyway some of them may not be. Thus, we should consider systems that are not DAGs. The compositional property we have shown in this paper is not true in general. So, we will have to determine the class of systems for which the property remains true or to add proof obligations in the other cases. One other important issue that is not addressed in this paper is *substitutability* of components. This issue is tied to the notion of behavioural subtyping introduced in the context of object-oriented programming [16]: a notion of behavioural subtyping of components could be inferred from a classical one for facets. The closely related topic of components' adaptations has been studied in [17, 18] but mostly from the point-of-view of object-oriented programming languages and design. Another important aspect that is not dealt with in this paper is the possible dynamic evolution of connections. We have currently a specification tool that may be used to analyze and design softwares but not yet to control component systems. There are approaches [19, 20] that explicitly model lifecycle of components (mostly objects) thus providing a way to reason on changes in the structure of the system. Such considerations will introduce new reasoning problems in our model.

References

1. Szyperski, C.: Component Software – Beyong Object Oriented Programming. 2nd edn. Addison-Wesley / ACM Press (2002)
2. OMG: CORBA Components, Version 3.0, formal/02-06-65. (2003)
3. Medvidovic, N., Taylor, R.N.: A classification and comparison framework for software architecture description languages. IEEE Transactions On Software Engineering **26** (2000) 70–93
4. Plasil, F., Visnovsky, S.: Behavior protocols for software components. IEEE Transations on Software Engineering **28** (2002) 1056–1076
5. Acherman, F., Nierstrasz, O.: Applications = Components + Scripts – A tour of *Piccola*. In: Software Architectures and Component Technology. Kluwer (2001)
6. Allen, R., Garlan, D.: A formal basis for architectural connection. ACM Transactions on Software Engineering and Methodology **6** (1997) 213–249
7. Magee, J., Dulay, N., Eisenbach, S., Kramer, J.: Specifying distributed software architectures. In Schäfer, W., Botella, P., eds.: 5th European Software Engineering Conference (ESEC). Volume 989 of Lecture Notes in Computer Science., Springer (1995) 137–153

8. ter Beek, M.H., Kleijn, J.: Team automata satisfying compositionality. In Araki, K., Gnesi, S., Mandrioli, D., eds.: International Symposium of Formal Methods Europe (FME). Volume 2805 of Lecture Notes in Computer Science., Pisa, Italy, Springer (2003) 381–400

9. Simplot-Ryl, I., Bailly, A., Clerbout, M.: Component composition preserving behavioral contracts. Technical Report TR-05-01, Université des Sciences et Technologies de Lille, France (2005) http://www.lifl.fr/~ryl/publi/RR-2005-01.pdf.

10. Charpentier, M.: Composing invariants. In Araki, K., Gnesi, S., Mandrioli, D., eds.: International Symposium of Formal Methods Europe (FME). Volume 2805 of Lecture Notes in Computer Science., Pisa, Italy, Springer (2003) 401–421

11. Abadi, M., Lamport, L.: Conjoining specifications. ACM Transactions on Programming Languages and Systems 17 (1995) 507–534

12. Aldrich, J., Chambers, C., Notkin, D.: Architectural reasoning in archjava. In Magnusson, B., ed.: Proc. of the 16th European Conference - Object-Oriented Programming (ECOOP 2002). Volume 2374 of Lecture Notes in Computer Science., Malaga, Spain, Springer (2002) 334–367

13. Duboc, C.: Commutations dans les Monoides libres : un Cadre Théorique pour l'Étude du Parallélisme. PhD thesis, Université de Rouen, France (1986)

14. de Simone, R.: Langages infinitaires et produit de mixage. Theoretical Computer Science 31 (1984) 83–100

15. Simplot-Ryl, I., Clerbout, M., Bailly, A.: Stac: Communication traces based specifictions and tests of software components. In: Proc. of the 15th Nordic Workshop on Programming Theory (NWPT'03), Turku, Finland (2003)

16. Liskov, B., Wing, J.M.: A behavioral notion of subtyping. ACM Transactions on Programming Languages and Systems 16 (1994) 1811–1841

17. Bracciali, A., Brogi, A., Canal, C.: A formal approach to component adaptation. Journal of Systems and Software 74 (2005) 45–54

18. Moisan, S., Ressouche, A., Rigault, J.P.: Behavioral substitutability in component frameworks: A formal approach. In: ESEC/FSE 2003 Specification and Verification of Component-Based Systems Workshop. Volume TR #03-11 of Iowa State University., Helsinki, Finland (2003)

19. Canal, C., Fuentes, L., Troya, J., Vallecillo, A.: Extending CORBA interfaces with pi-calculus for protocol compatibility. In: Proc. TOOLS Europe'2000, Mont Saint-Michel, France, IEEE Computer Society Press (2000) 208–225

20. Harel, D., Kupferman, O.: On object systems and behavioral inheritance. IEEE Transations on Software Engineering 28 (2002) 889–903

Strong Retiming Equivalence of Synchronous Schemes

Miklós Bartha

Memorial University of Newfoundland,
St. John's, NL, Canada
bartha@cs.mun.ca

Abstract. Strong retiming equivalence is the join of two basic equivalence relations of synchronous schemes: strong equivalence and retiming equivalence, which play an important role in the optimization of synchronous systems. Each of these equivalences is characterized separately in an algebraic/category theoretic framework, and the characterization is carried over to the join of them. Tree-reducible schemes are introduced to facilitate the proof that strong retiming equivalence is decidable.

1 Introduction

The concept of a synchronous system arises naturally from that of a systolic system, which has turned out to be one of the most attractive tools in massive parallel computing. During the past few decades, a large number of systolic systems have been designed, many of them manufactured. Transformation methodologies for the design and optimization of systolic systems have been developed, but a rigorous mathematical foundation has not been provided until recently [1, 2, 3].

The present paper aims at providing an algebraic/category theoretic characterization of retiming equivalence and strong equivalence of synchronous systems, by which a decision algorithm can be obtained for the join of these two basic equivalences. The reader is referred to [4] for the category theoretic, and to [5] for the universal algebraic terminology used.

As introduced in [6], a synchronous system is partitioned into functional elements (combinational logic) and registers (clocked memory). Such a system can be described by an edge-weighted directed graph G, called a communication graph, in which the vertices represent functional elements and the edges correspond to interconnections between the functional elements. The weight of each edge in G is a non-negative integer, which indicates the length of a queue of registers placed along the interconnection between the two functional elements corresponding to the endpoints of the edge. The external interface is represented in G by a distinguished vertex, called the host.

In a synchronous system, every functional element has a fixed primitive operation associated with it. These operations are designed to manipulate some simple data (e.g. signals) in the usual algebraic sense. The registers and functional elements are organized by a common clock, which renders the following step-by-step behavior to the system. A configuration of the system is an

J. Farré, I. Litovsky, and S. Schmitz (Eds.): CIAA 2005, LNCS 3845, pp. 66–77, 2006.

assignment of data to each register. With each clock tick, the current configuration is mapped into a new one in such a way that every functional element performs the primitive operation associated with it. The operands (result) of the operation performed by each functional element are taken from (is forwarded to) the nearest registers lying on the interconnections arriving at (leading out of) the functional element. At the same time, data are advanced one register in the queue of registers along each interconnection. If there is no register along an interconnection, then data are always propagated through that interconnection during a single clock cycle. This phenomenon is called rippling. To avoid circular rippling of data within the system, it is assumed that every oriented cycle in the graph of the system contains at least one edge having strictly positive weight.

Synchronous systems are analogous to sequential circuits, and can naturally be viewed as structural Mealy automata [7]. The states of the automaton represented by a system S are the configurations of S, which are structured in as many components as the number of registers in S. The transition function of the automaton is also structured with regard to the state, input, and output components, and it is specified as the combinational logic determined by the interconnected functional elements in S. See [2, 8] for an analysis of the algebraic properties of such automata as morphisms in an appropriate strict monoidal category.

2   Synchronous Schemes

The simple communication graph model of synchronous systems, as presented in the introduction, has two major shortcomings.

1. The operations performed by the functional elements are not necessarily commutative, therefore the edges arriving at each functional element must be ordered.
2. Representing the external interface by one vertex (the host) gives the false impression that the input to the system depends on the output in the same clock cycle. Also, cycles of the communication graph going through the host vertex need not contain edges with a strictly positive weight.

Addressing these two shortcomings, synchronous systems have been redefined in [9] as follows. A *synchronous scheme* over a ranked alphabet $\Sigma = \{\Sigma_n | n \geq 0\}$ is a finite directed graph F having the following additional structure.

1. Each vertex v is labeled by either a symbol in Σ, or one of the symbols in

$$\{ic_j \mid j \in [q]\} \cup \{oc_i \mid i \in [p]\},$$

where p and q are fixed non-negative integers, and $[n] = \{1, \ldots, n\}$. If the label of v is in Σ, then v is called a *box*. Boxes represent functional elements in synchronous systems, and their label indicates the operation associated with them already at the syntactical level. Vertices labeled by the symbols $\{ic_j \mid 1 \leq j \leq q\}$ and $\{oc_i \mid 1 \leq i \leq p\}$ are unique, and they are called *input and output channels*, respectively. We shall assume that each label, not only those in Σ, has a fixed rank associated with it, so that $rank(\text{oc}_i) = 1$ and $rank(\text{ic}_j) = 0$. Then, for each vertex v, the in-degree of v (that is, the number of edges arriving at v) must equal the rank of the symbol labeling v. Furthermore, the outdegree of each output channel is zero.

2. The edges arriving at each vertex v labeled by a symbol of rank n are ordered, which order is captured by saying that these edges enter v at the 1st, ..., n-th *input port*. The notation $u \rightarrow_i v$ indicates that the edge arriving at the ith input port of v originates from vertex u.

3. Each edge e is assigned a non-negative integer weight $w(e)$. This weight specifies the number of registers placed along the interconnection represented by e. It is required that in each oriented cycle of F there exists at least one edge e with $w(e) > 0$. This requirement will be referred to as the exclusion of circular rippling.

Notice that the edges leading out of a vertex u are not ordered. The suggested meaning is that the same value originating from the (single) output port of u is fanned out into several directions in each clock cycle.

A *synchronous system* is a triple $S = (\Sigma, F, \mathcal{I})$, where F is a synchronous Σ-scheme (SΣ-scheme, for short), and $(\Sigma, \mathcal{I})$ is a Σ-algebra. If F is an SΣ-scheme having p output and q input channels, then we shall write $F : p \rightarrow q$. Isomorphism of SΣ-schemes is defined in a straightforward manner as graph isomorphism preserving all labels and weights. In the sequel, we shall not distinguish between isomorphic schemes. Let F^R denote the directed graph obtained from F by reversing the direction of each edge in it. When forgetting the weight of the edges, F^R becomes a flowchart scheme (also known as Elgot scheme [10, 11]). This flowchart will be denoted by $fl(F)$.

3   Retiming Synchronous Schemes

Let F be an SΣ-scheme and u be a box in F labeled by $\sigma \in \Sigma_n$ such that all the edges $e_1, \ldots, e_n$ arriving at the input ports of u have positive weights. *Retiming* u then means subtracting 1 from $w(e_i)$ for each $i \in [n]$, and adding 1 to the weight of each edge leading out of u. *Elementary retiming* is the binary relation ρ on the set of SΣ-schemes by which $F \rho F'$ if F' results from F by retiming a single box in it. *Retiming equivalence* is the smallest equivalence relation containing ρ.

A *retiming count vector* for scheme F is an assignment R of integers to all of its boxes. Extend R to all vertices of F by fixing $R(v) = 0$ for each i/o channel. We say that R is *legal* if for every edge $e : u \rightarrow v$ in F, $w(e) + R(u) - R(v) \geq 0$. If R is legal, then it takes F into a scheme F' that has the same underlying graph structure as F, but the weight $w'(e)$ of each edge $e : u \rightarrow v$ is $w(e) + R(u) - R(v)$. It is clear by this definition that if R is legal for F, then $-R$ is legal for F', and $-R$ takes F' back to F.

Proposition 1. *Synchronous schemes F and F' are retiming equivalent iff there exists a legal retiming count vector R taking F into F'.*

Retiming is a fundamental tool in the optimization of synchronous systems. It allows the registers of a system to be rearranged in order to achieve a more favorable pattern of them inside the scheme of the system. For example, it might be possible to shift the registers around in such a way that the resulting scheme becomes *systolic* in the sense that each edge has a strictly positive weight. The obvious advantage of dealing with a systolic system rather than an ordinary synchronous one is that the clock period (i.e. the length of a clock cycle) can be chosen as small as the maximum amount of time required to perform a single operation in Σ. Even when the total number of registers in the scheme is too small to allow such a transformation, it is possible to first slow the system down by multiplying each weight with the same suitably large positive integer k, and then apply retiming on the resulting scheme to obtain a systolic arrangement. The cost of slowdown is a factor of k regarding the clock period, which might be well worth considering if rippling occurs in the system on very long paths. See [6] for the details.

As to the impact of retiming on the behavior of synchronous systems, it turns out that the damage caused by rearranging the registers is relatively minor. The systems before and after the retiming can simulate each other in the following sense.

Definition 1. *System S_1 can simulate system S_2 if, for every sufficiently old configuration c_2 of S_2, there exists a configuration c_1 of S_1 such that S_1 and S_2 exhibit the same behavior when started from configurations c_1 and c_2, respectively. Systems S_1 and S_2 are simulation equivalent if they can simulate each other. $S\Sigma$-schemes F_1 and F_2 are simulation equivalent if the systems $S_1 = (\Sigma, F_1, \mathcal{I})$ and $S_2 = (\Sigma, F_2, \mathcal{I})$ are such under all interpretations $\mathcal{I}$.*

The fact that retiming equivalence of synchronous schemes implies simulation equivalence is commonly known as the "Retiming Lemma", and it was first proved in [6].

Retiming, as a phenomenon, has been considered earlier in a different graph theoretic context. It has been extensively studied in a model called marked graph [12]. Marked graphs are essentially Petri nets in which all places have in- and out-degree 1. In that context, retiming count vectors are called firing count vectors, and the framework for their study is linear algebra relying on the incidence matrix of the underlying graph. The only conceptual difference between firing marked graphs and retiming synchronous schemes is that in the latter model we do not allow a fixed set of vertices, namely the i/o channels, to be retimed. The reason is that the retiming of these vertices would not be consistent with simulation equivalence. This restriction is minor, however, so that all important results on marked graphs can easily be adopted for synchronous schemes with appropriate modifications.

4   Basic Constructions on Schemes

As we have noted earlier, synchronous schemes have an underlying flowchart structure, which will be in the focus of the constructions that follow. To avoid confusing terminological changes, we shall consider flowchart schemes simply as unweighted synchronous schemes, in which the exclusion of circular rippling does not apply. On the other hand, for the sake of a uniform treatment, all edges will be reversed in synchronous schemes.

The term $F\Sigma$-scheme will be used as a shorthand for Σ-flowchart scheme. An $F\Sigma$-scheme F is called *accessible* if every box of F can be reached from at least one output channel by a directed path. Every $F\Sigma$-scheme can be made accessible simply by deleting its inaccessible boxes, therefore we shall assume from now on that our schemes are all accessible.

The following constructions are concerned with the so called vertical structure of $F\Sigma$-schemes, which is the category $\mathbf{Fl}_\Sigma$ constructed as the coproduct (disjoint union) of the categories $\mathbf{Fl}_\Sigma(n,p)$, $n,p \in N$.

- For each $(n,p) \in N \times N$, $\mathbf{Fl}_\Sigma(n,p)$ has as objects all accessible $F\Sigma$-schemes $n \to p$.
- A morphism $F \to F'$ between $F\Sigma$-schemes $F, F' : n \to p$ is a mapping α from the set of vertices of F into that of F' which preserves:
  a) the labeling of the vertices;
  b) the edges, so that if $u \to_i v$ holds in F, then $\alpha(u) \to_i \alpha(v)$ holds in F'.
- Composition of morphisms is defined in $\mathbf{Fl}_\Sigma(n,p)$ as that of mappings, and the identity morphisms are the identity maps.

It is straightforward to check that the above data indeed determine a category, which is a preorder [4]. In other words, given two objects F and F', there exists at most one morphism $F \to F'$ in $\mathbf{Fl}_\Sigma$. Morphisms in $\mathbf{Fl}_\Sigma$ represent *reductions* of $F\Sigma$-schemes, and inverse morphisms are called *unfoldings*. Unfolding a scheme F thus means blowing it up into a scheme F' such that $F' \to F$ holds.

There is also a horizontal structure of schemes over the set N as objects, in which schemes themselves are the morphisms $n \to p$. In that category, composition is defined as serial composition of schemes. The interested reader is referred to [2, 13] for the description of the 2-category of schemes and their behaviors. Another interesting and more general approach is outlined in [8]. In the present discussion, however, we do not need the horizontal part of this 2-category, and therefore this part will be omitted.

Sometimes it is useful to consider an $F\Sigma$-scheme $F : n \to p$ as a separate partial algebraic structure over the set of vertices of F different from the output channels. In this structure there are n constants, namely the vertices adjacent to the output channels. Furthermore, for each $\sigma \in \Sigma_q$, there are q unary operations $\langle \sigma, i \rangle$, $i \in [q]$ if $q \geq 1$, and one unary operation $\langle \sigma, 0 \rangle$ if $q = 0$. If $i \geq 1$, then the operation $\langle \sigma, i \rangle$ is defined on vertex u of F iff u is labeled by σ, and in that case $\langle \sigma, i \rangle(u)$ is the unique vertex v for which $u \to_i v$. The operation $\langle \sigma, 0 \rangle$ is interpreted as if there was a loop around each vertex labeled by the constant symbol σ, that is, $\langle \sigma, 0 \rangle$ is an appropriate restriction of the identity function. No operation is defined on the input channels. In this algebraic setting, F being accessible means that, with the possible exception of the input channels, F is generated by its constants.

By the above algebraic formalism, a morphism $\alpha : F \to F'$ becomes a strong homomorphism of partial algebras [5], which preserves the given sequence of input channels. A strong congruence relation of F by which the input channels form singleton groups is called a *scheme congruence* of F. Clearly, every scheme morphism $\alpha : F \to F'$ induces a scheme congruence on F, which will be denoted by θ_α. By the homomorphism theorem, if α is onto, then $F/\theta_\alpha \cong F'$, where the isomorphism and the quotient scheme F/θ_α are meant in the usual algebraic sense.

Let F be a synchronous scheme. The relation of *having the same strong behavior* is defined on the vertices of F as the largest scheme congruence μ_F in F. The congruence μ_F gives rise to a minimal scheme F/μ_F in the usual way (cf. [10]), and schemes F_1, F_2 are said to be *strong equivalent* if $F_1/\mu_{F_1} = F_2/\mu_{F_2}$. Clearly, two F$\Sigma$-schemes belong to the same connected component of **Fl**$_\Sigma$ iff they reduce to the same minimal scheme, which is a terminal object in the given component.

By the standard definition in graph theory, a *directed walk* in graph G is an alternating sequence of vertices and edges, which starts and ends with a vertex, and in which each edge points from the vertex immediately preceding it to the vertex immediately following it. Let F be an FΣ-scheme, and $\alpha = v_0 e_1 \ldots e_n v_n$ be a directed walk in F. By the *pattern* of α we mean the sequence $p(\alpha) = \sigma_0 i_1 \ldots i_n \sigma_n$, where σ_j, $0 \leq j \leq n$, is the label of vertex v_j and i_j identifies the output of v_{j-1} where e_j originates from. In general, a pattern of walks is a sequence $p = \sigma_0 i_1 \ldots i_n \sigma_n$ such that $\sigma_j \in \Sigma \cup \{ic_k | k \geq 1\} \cup \{oc_l | l \geq 1\}$ and $1 \leq i_j \leq rank(\sigma_{j-1})$. We say that pattern p is *viable* for vertex u if there exists a directed walk α in F starting from u such that $p = p(\alpha)$. In this case, $end(u, p)$ denotes the last vertex of α. It is easy to see that, for every two vertices u and v of F, $u\mu_F v$ is equivalent to saying that an arbitrary pattern p is viable for u iff p is viable for v.

The category **Fl**$_\Sigma$ is known to have all pushouts [4]. The pushout object of a pair of morphisms $\alpha : F \to G$ and $\beta : F \to H$ is the scheme $F/(\theta_\alpha \sqcup \theta_\beta)$, where $\theta_\alpha \sqcup \theta_\beta$ is the join (least upper bound) of θ_α and θ_β. Constructing the coproduct of two schemes belonging to the same connected component of **Fl**$_\Sigma$ is a similar simple exercise. It is also easy to see that the category **Fl**$_\Sigma$ has all pullbacks and finite products of schemes belonging to the same connected component. The construction of pullbacks and products is analogous to that of their counterparts in the category **Set** of all sets and mappings.

5   Tree-Reducible Schemes

Let $G = (V(G), E(G))$ be an arbitrary directed graph. Recall that a subset $S \subseteq V(G)$ is *strongly connected* if for every $u, v \in S$ there exists a directed path in G from u to v going through vertices of S only. A *strong component* is an (inclusionwise) maximal strongly connected subset. For two vertices $u, v \in V(G)$, we say that v is *reachable* from u, notation $reach(u, v)$, if there exists a directed path from u to v in G. The *closure* of a set $S \subseteq V(G)$ is then the set $\bar{S} = \{v \in V(G) \mid reach(u, v) \text{ and } u \in S\}$. With a slight ambiguity, the notation $\bar{S}$ will also be used for the subgraph of G spanned by $\bar{S}$.

Definition 2. *An* $F\Sigma$-*scheme* $F : n \rightarrow p$ *is* tree-reducible *if the graph obtained from* F *by deleting its input channels (together with all adjacent edges) and shrinking every strong component to one vertex consists of* n *disjoint trees.*

Let F_b denote the subgraph of F determined by its boxes. By Definition 2, if F is tree-reducible, then every strong component S of F_b has a *unique entry edge* by which it can be reached starting from some output channel.

There is an apparent similarity between reducible and tree-reducible flowchart schemes. Recall from [14] that an $F\Sigma$-scheme F is reducible if every strongly connected subset of vertices in F has a unique entry vertex. Definition 2 above requires the existence of a unique entry edge, although for strong components of F only. Eventually, the classes of reducible and tree-reducible schemes are incomparable.

Every $F\Sigma$-scheme F can be unfolded into a tree-reducible scheme in the following way. Recursively, in a top-down manner, whenever a strong component S of F is found that has $k \geq 2$ entry edges, take k identical copies of $\bar{S}$ and redirect each entry edge of S into its "own" copy of $\bar{S}$. The straightforward details of this procedure are left to the reader. The resulting tree-reducible $F\Sigma$-scheme will be denoted by $tr(F)$. The unfolding determines a morphism $\iota_F : tr(F) \rightarrow F$ in the category $\mathbf{Fl}_\Sigma$. The function tr itself is called *tree unfolding*.

Lemma 1. *Let* $\alpha : F \rightarrow G$ *be a morphism in* $\mathbf{Fl}_\Sigma$. *If* F *is tree-reducible, then* α *factors through* ι_G *and an appropriate morphism* $tr(\alpha) : F \rightarrow tr(G)$.

Lemma 1 has a number of important consequences regarding the full subcategory $\mathbf{TFl}_\Sigma$ of $\mathbf{Fl}_\Sigma$ determined by tree-reducible schemes.

Corollary 1. *Tree unfolding defines a right adjoint for the inclusion functor* $\mathbf{TFl}_\Sigma \rightarrow \mathbf{Fl}_\Sigma$.

Proof. Indeed, by Lemma 1, there is a one-to-one correspondence between morphisms $F \rightarrow G$ in $\mathbf{Fl}_\Sigma$ and morphisms $F \rightarrow tr(G)$ in $\mathbf{TFl}_\Sigma$, provided that F is tree-reducible. Thus, $\mathbf{TFl}_\Sigma$ is a coreflexive subcategory of $\mathbf{Fl}_\Sigma$.

The adjunction established in this way implies the following statement by a general category theoretical argument.

Corollary 2. *The category* $\mathbf{TFl}_\Sigma$ *has all pullbacks and pushouts. Every connected component of* $\mathbf{TFl}_\Sigma$ *has finite products, coproducts, and a terminal object. The pushouts and coproducts are the same as they are in* $\mathbf{Fl}_\Sigma$, *whereas the pullbacks, products, and terminal objects are obtained by tree-unfolding the corresponding objects in* $\mathbf{Fl}_\Sigma$.

Recall from [5] that in any algebra A, the *principal* congruence relation of A induced by a pair (a, b) of its elements is the smallest congruence $\theta(a, b)$ joining a with b. If u and v are two boxes of some $F\Sigma$-scheme F such that $reach(u, v)$ and $u\mu_F v$, then the principal scheme congruence $\theta(u, v)$ of F is called an *elementary contraction*.

Definition 3. *A scheme congruence θ of a tree-reducible $F\Sigma$-scheme F is tree-preserving if the scheme F/θ is also tree-reducible.*

As the main result of this section, we now present a theorem characterizing tree-preserving scheme congruences.

Theorem 1. *A scheme congruence of a tree-reducible $F\Sigma$-scheme F is tree-preserving iff it is the join of elementary contractions.*

Now we turn to defining the category $\mathbf{Syn}_\Sigma$ of synchronous Σ-schemes. The objects of this category are all accessible $S\Sigma$-schemes (synchronous Σ-schemes, that is). A morphism $F \to F'$ in $\mathbf{Syn}_\Sigma$ is a morphism $\mathit{fl}(F) \to \mathit{fl}(F')$ in $\mathbf{Fl}_\Sigma$ that preserves the weight of the edges. (Recall that $\mathit{fl}(F)$ is the the flowchart scheme determined by F). Accordingly, a scheme congruence of F is one of $\mathit{fl}(F)$ that is compatible with the weight function. An $S\Sigma$-scheme S is tree-reducible if $\mathit{fl}(F)$ is such. The full subcategory of tree-reducible $S\Sigma$-schemes is denoted by $\mathbf{TSyn}_\Sigma$.

There is a simple way to characterize synchronous schemes as ordinary flowchart schemes, so that the constructions of Sections 4 and 5 can be lifted into the categories $\mathbf{Syn}_\Sigma$ and $\mathbf{TSyn}_\Sigma$. Introducing a new symbol ∇, let Σ_∇ denote the extension of Σ by ∇ as a unary operation symbol. For obvious reasons, vertices labeled by ∇ will be called registers in schemes. With each $S\Sigma$-scheme F, we then associate the $F\Sigma_\nabla$-scheme $\mathit{fl}_\nabla(F)$, which is obtained from $\mathit{fl}(F)$ by subdividing every edge e in it by n registers, where n is the weight of e. In this manner, $\mathbf{Syn}_\Sigma$ can be identified with an appropriate subcategory of $\mathbf{Fl}_{\Sigma_\nabla}$. Any scheme congruence of an $S\Sigma$-scheme F, too, can be specified as the restriction of an appropriate scheme congruence of $\mathit{fl}_\nabla(F)$ to its non-register vertices.

Let $\mathbf{Fl}^0_{\Sigma_\nabla}$ denote the disjoint union of those connected components of $\mathbf{Fl}_{\Sigma_\nabla}$ the schemes in which obey the exclusion of circular rippling, and do not contain cycles consisting of registers only. If F is a scheme in $\mathbf{Fl}^0_{\Sigma_\nabla}$ such that some registers in F have an in-degree greater than one, then unfold F into a scheme $reg(F)$ that does not have such registers, has the same (Σ)-boxes as F, and satisfies the condition that, along every path connecting two boxes, the total number of registers is the same as it is in F. It is easy to see that the unfolding reg defines a right adjoint for the inclusion functor $\mathbf{Syn}_\Sigma \to \mathbf{Fl}^0_{\Sigma_\nabla}$. Thus, $\mathbf{Syn}_\Sigma$ is a coreflexive subcategory of $\mathbf{Fl}^0_{\Sigma_\nabla}$. By this observation, the lifting of all results in Sections 4 and 5 from $\mathbf{Fl}_\Sigma$ and $\mathbf{TFl}_\Sigma$ to $\mathbf{Syn}_\Sigma$ and $\mathbf{TSyn}_\Sigma$ follows the general category theoretical argument already applied under Corollaries 1 and 2.

6 Deciding Strong Retiming Equivalence

In this section we study the relation of strong retiming equivalence on the set of $S\Sigma$-schemes. We shall use the preorders $\mathbf{Fl}_\Sigma$ and $\mathbf{Syn}_\Sigma$ simply as binary relations over the sets Fl_Σ and Syn_Σ of all accessible $F\Sigma$-schemes and $S\Sigma$-schemes, respectively. In both cases, this preorder will be denoted by $\to_s$. Concerning retiming, $\to_r$ will stand for the partial order induced on Syn_Σ by non-negative legal retiming count vectors. Note that if $F \to_r F'$, then $\mathit{fl}(F) = \mathit{fl}(F')$.

Definition 4. *The relation of strong retiming equivalence on the set Syn_Σ is the smallest equivalence relation containing $\rightarrow_s$ and $\rightarrow_r$.*

Strong retiming equivalence will be denoted by $\sim$. The relations of retiming equivalence and strong equivalence, as introduced already in Sections 3 and 4, will be denoted $\sim_r$ and $\sim_s$, respectively.

The practical importance of retiming equivalence has been pointed out in Section 3. The role of strong equivalence in the optimization of synchronous systems is self-explanatory: reduction of schemes means reduction in the size of systems. As to the behavior of schemes, if we assume that the initial configuration in all systems is a standard one by which each register is assigned the same distinguished datum $\perp$, then strong equivalent schemes have the exact same input-output behavior under all interpretations. See [1] for the details. Simulation equivalence, however, in the sense of Definition 1, is guaranteed only for a subset of strongly equivalent schemes. This subset of $\sim_s$ was identified in [3] as finitary strong equivalence, and it was proved that simulation equivalence is the smallest equivalence relation containing $\sim_r$ and finitary strong equivalence. With only a slight generalization of the concept "behavior", however, it can be achieved that simulation equivalence coincide with strong retiming equivalence. This issue will be dealt with in a forthcoming paper.

It is well-known from the literature that strong equivalence of schemes is decidable. In order to decide if $F \sim_s F'$, one must construct the minimal schemes for F and F', and see if they are isomorphic. Regarding retiming equivalence, Murata's [12] similar result on marked graphs can be adopted to prove that $\sim_r$, too, is decidable. Our aim is to prove that the join of these two relations remains decidable. As a first step, we are going to prove the equation

$$\sim = \leftarrow_s \circ \sim_r \circ \rightarrow_s, \tag{1}$$

which will help us to decide the relation $\sim$. Equation (1) says that if two accessible $S\Sigma$-schemes F_1 and F_2 are strong retiming equivalent, then they can be unfolded into appropriate schemes F_1' and F_2' that are already retiming equivalent. We could use (1) to decide $F_1 \sim F_2$ only if we knew the extent to which F_1 and F_2 must be unfolded in order to obtain a suitable pair F_1', F_2'. Our goal is to provide an upper bound for the extent of this unfolding, and we shall indeed find one when the scope of (1) is restricted to tree-reducible $S\Sigma$-schemes.

Lemma 2. $\sim_r \circ \leftarrow_s \subseteq \leftarrow_s \circ \sim_r$.

Proof. Let F, F' and U be $S\Sigma$-schemes such that $F \sim_r U$ and $F' \rightarrow_s U$. Then there exists a legal retiming count vector $R : F \rightarrow U$ and a scheme morphism $\alpha : F' \rightarrow U$. Since $fl(U) = fl(F)$, F can be unfolded into a scheme U' for which $fl(U') = fl(F')$ and $\alpha : U' \rightarrow F$. For every vertex v of U', define $R'(v) = R(\alpha(v))$. It is now easy to check that the retiming R' takes U' to F'.

Corollary 3. $\sim = \leftarrow_s \circ \sim_r \circ \rightarrow_s$.

Proof. It is sufficient to prove that the relation $\rho = \leftarrow_s \circ \sim_r \circ \rightarrow_s$ is transitive. To this end observe that $\rightarrow_s \circ \leftarrow_s \subseteq \leftarrow_s \circ \rightarrow_s$, because the category $\mathbf{Syn}_\Sigma$ has all pullbacks. Thus, we have

$$\leftarrow_s \circ \sim_r \circ \rightarrow_s \circ \leftarrow_s \circ \sim_r \circ \rightarrow_s \subseteq \leftarrow_s \circ \sim_r \circ \leftarrow_s \circ \rightarrow_s \circ \sim_r \circ \rightarrow_s.$$

Hence by Lemma 2,

$$\rho \circ \rho \subseteq \leftarrow_s \circ \leftarrow_s \circ \sim_r \circ \sim_r \circ \rightarrow_s \circ \rightarrow_s = \rho.$$

Repeating the proofs of Lemma 2 and Corollary 3 in the subset $TSyn_\Sigma$ of tree-reducible $S\Sigma$-schemes, we obtain the following result.

Corollary 4. $\sim = tr \circ \leftarrow_s \circ \sim_r \circ \rightarrow_s \circ tr^{-1}$,
where the relation $\rightarrow_s$ is restricted to the subset of tree-reducible schemes.

Theorem 2. Let F and F' be tree-reducible $S\Sigma$-schemes such that $F \sim_r F'$, and assume that θ is a tree-preserving scheme congruence of F. Then $F/\theta \sim_r F'/\theta$, provided that θ is a scheme congruence of F', too.

Proof. We have seen under Theorem 1 that θ is tree-preserving iff it is the join of elementary contractions. Hence, by the second isomorphism theorem, we can assume that $\theta = \theta(u, v)$, where u and v are two distinct internal vertices of F having the same strong behavior and satisfying the condition $reach(u, v)$.

In our argument we shall make use of the following characterization of the congruence $\theta(u, v)$. Define the relation ξ on the set of boxes of F by: $a \xi b$ if there exists a pattern p of walks in $fl(F)$ such that $a = end(z_1, p)$ and $b = end(z_2, p)$, where $\{z_1, z_2\} \subseteq \{u, v\}$. Then $\theta(u, v) = \xi^+$, i.e., the transitive closure of ξ.

Let $R : F \to F'$ be a legal retiming count vector that preserves the congruence θ. We shall prove that if $a \xi b$ holds for any two vertices a, b of F, then $R(a) = R(b)$. Since $\theta = \xi^+$, this immediately implies $R(a) = R(b)$ whenever $a \equiv b \ (\theta)$. Thus, an appropriate retiming count vector $R/\theta : F/\theta \to F'/\theta$ is readily obtained by defining $R/\theta\,(a\theta) = R(a)$ for each group $a\theta$ of the congruence θ.

Let us assume that $a \xi b$. Then there exists a pattern p of walks for which $a = end(z_1, p)$ and $b = end(z_2, p)$, where $z_1, z_2 \in \{u, v\}$. Without loss of generality we can assume that $z_1 = u$ and $z_2 = v$. Since u and v have the same strong behavior in both F and F', we have

$$R(a) - R(u) = R(b) - R(v). \tag{2}$$

Let p_0 be the pattern of an arbitrary path leading from u to v, and consider the patterns $p_0, p_0^2 (= p_0 p_0), \dots, p_0^k$ for all $k \geq 1$. The number of boxes being finite in F, there must be two non-negative integers $k < l$ and an internal vertex z such that

$$z = end(u, p_0^k) = end(u, p_0^l).$$

While keeping the pattern $p = p_0$ fixed, apply (2) iteratively by choosing for u and v the vertices $end(u, p_0^i)$ and $end(u, p_0^{i+1})$, $0 \leq i < l$. Adding up the last $(l - k)$ of the corresponding equations, we obtain that

$$R(z) - R(z) = (l - k) \cdot (R(u) - R(v)),$$

from which $R(u) = R(v)$ follows immediately. The required equation $R(a) = R(b)$ can then be derived again from (2).

Theorem 3. *The relation of strong retiming equivalence is decidable.*

Proof. Let G and G' be $S\Sigma$-schemes. By Corollary 4, $G \sim G'$ iff there exist some tree-reducible schemes F and F' such that $F \rightarrow_s tr(G)$, $F' \rightarrow_s tr(G')$ and $F \sim_r F'$. See Fig. 1a. Then, in the category $\mathbf{TSyn}_\Sigma$, there are morphisms $F \rightarrow tr(G)$ and $F' \rightarrow tr(G')$, which determine two morphisms $fl(F) \rightarrow fl(tr(G))$ and $fl(F') (= fl(F)) \rightarrow fl(tr(G'))$ in $\mathbf{TFl}_\Sigma$. Let ϕ and ϕ' denote the scheme congruences of $fl(F)$ induced by these two morphisms.

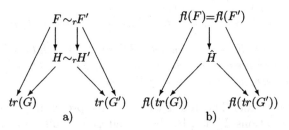

Fig. 1. The proof of Theorem 3 in a diagram

Now construct the product of $fl(tr(G))$ and $fl(tr(G'))$ as a tree-reducible FΣ-scheme $\hat{H}$. Since $\hat{H}$ is a product, there exists a morphism $fl(F) \rightarrow \hat{H}$ that makes the diagram of Fig. 1b commute. For the scheme congruence θ induced by this morphism, we thus have $\theta \subseteq \phi$ and $\theta \subseteq \phi'$. On the other hand, ϕ and ϕ' are also $S\Sigma$-scheme congruences of F and F', for which $F/\phi = tr(G)$ and $F'/\phi' = tr(G')$. It follows that θ, too, is an $S\Sigma$-scheme congruence of both F and F'. Theorem 2 then implies that

$$H = F/\theta \sim_r F'/\theta = H'.$$

See again the diagram of Fig. 1a.

According to the argument above, one can decide strong retiming equivalence of G and G' by the following algorithm.

Step 1. See if $fl(G) \sim_s fl(G')$. If not, then G and G' are not strong retiming equivalent. Otherwise goto Step 2.

Step 2. Construct the schemes H and H', which are the unfoldings of G and G' to the extent determined by the product of $fl(tr(G))$ and $fl(tr(G'))$ in $\mathbf{TFl}_\Sigma$, and test whether H and H' are retiming equivalent.

The schemes G and G' are strong retiming equivalent iff the result of the test performed in Step 2 is positive.

7   Conclusion

We have worked out an algebraic/category theoretic framework to characterize two basic equivalence relations of synchronous schemes: strong equivalence and retiming equivalence. On the basis of this characterization we have proved that strong retiming equivalence, the join of these two equivalences, is decidable. As part of this proof, we have given a characterization of tree-reducible flowchart schemes and tree-preserving scheme congruences, which is an interesting result by itself.

In order to prove that strong retiming equivalence ($\sim$) is decidable, we first showed that $G \sim G'$ iff G and G' can be unfolded into some schemes F and F' that are already retiming equivalent. Our second observation was that if G and G' are tree-reducible, then the schemes F and F' can be chosen "minimal" in the sense that their common underlying flowchart scheme is the product of $fl(G)$ and $fl(G')$ in the category $\mathbf{TFl}_\Sigma$ of tree-reducible Σ-flowchart schemes. The decidability of $\sim$ then followed from some known results on flowchart schemes and marked graphs.

References

1. Bartha, M.: Foundations of a theory of synchronous systems. Theoret. Comput. Sci. **100** (1992) 325–346
2. Bartha, M.: An algebraic model of synchronous systems. Information and Computation **97** (1992) 97–131
3. Bartha, M., Cirovic, B.: On some equivalence notions of synchronous systems. In: Ésik, Z., Fülöp, Z., ed., Proceedings, 11th International Conference on Automata and Formal Languages, Dogogókő, Hungary (2005)
4. Mac Lane, S.: Categories for the Working Mathematician. Springer Verlag, Berlin (1971)
5. Grätzer, G.: Universal Algebra. Springer-Verlag, Berlin (1968) (1979)
6. Leiserson, C.E., Saxe, J.B.: Optimizing synchronous systems. J. VLSI Comput. Systems **1** (1983) 41–67
7. Gécseg, F., Peák, I.: Algebraic Theory of Automata. Akadémiai Kiadó, Budapest (1972)
8. Katis, P., Sabadini, N., Walters, R.F.C.: Feedback, trace, and fixed-point semantics. Theoret. Informatics Appl. **36** (2002) 181–194
9. Bartha, M.: An equational axiomatization of systolic systems. Theoret. Comput. Sci. **55** (1987) 265–289
10. Elgot, C.C.: Monadic computations and iterative algebraic theories. In: Rose, H.E., ed., Logic Colloquium 73, North-Holland, Amsterdam, (1975) 175–230.
11. Elgot, C.C.: Selected Papers. Bloom, S.L., ed., Springer Verlag, New York (1982)
12. Murata, T.: Circuit theoretic analysis and synthesis of marked graphs. IEEE Transactions on Circuits and Systems vol. CAS-24 **7** (1977) 400–405
13. Bloom, S.L., Ésik, Z.: Iteration Theories. Springer Verlag, Berlin (1993)
14. Bloom, S.L., Tindell, R.: Algebraic and graph theoretic characterizations of structured flowchart schemes. Theoret. Comput. Sci. **9** (1979) 265–286

Prime Normal Form and Equivalence of Simple Grammars*

Cédric Bastien[1], Jurek Czyzowicz[1], Wojciech Fraczak[1,2], and Wojciech Rytter[3,4]

[1] Dépt d'informatique, Université du Québec en Outaouais, Gatineau PQ, Canada
{basc01, Jurek.Czyzowicz}@uqo.ca
[2] IDT Canada Inc., Ottawa ON, Canada
wojtek.fraczak@idt.com
[3] Inst. of Informatics, Warsaw University, Warsaw, Poland
rytter@mimuw.edu.pl
[4] New Jersey Institute of Technology, USA

Abstract. A prefix-free language is a prime if it cannot be decomposed into a concatenation of two prefix-free languages. We show that we can check in polynomial time if a language generated by a simple context-free grammar is a prime. Our algorithm computes a canonical representation of a simple language, converting its arbitrary simple grammar into Prime Normal Form (PNF); a simple grammar is in PNF if all its nonterminals define primes. We also improve the complexity of testing the equivalence of simple grammars. The best previously known algorithm for this problem worked in $O(n^{13})$ time. We improve it to $O(n^7 \log^2 n)$ and $O(n^5 \operatorname{polylog} v)$ deterministic time, and $O(n^4 \operatorname{polylog} n)$ randomized time, where n is the total size of the grammars involved, and v is the length of a shortest string derivable from a nonterminal, maximized over all nonterminals. Our improvement is based on a version of Caucal's algorithm from [1].

1 Introduction

An important question in language theory is, given a class of languages, find a canonical representation of any language of this class. Such a representation often permits to solve various decidability problems related to a given class of languages, such as equivalence of languages, non-emptiness, etc. Most often the canonical representation of the language is given by a special form of its grammar, called a normal form. In this paper, we give an algorithm converting a simple grammar into its equivalent, unique representation in a form of so-called Prime Normal Form (PNF). The canonical form of simple grammar was studied by Courcelle, c.f. [2]. The crucial question that our algorithm is confronted with,

---

* The research of the first three authors was supported by NSERC and the research of the fourth author was supported by the grants KBN 4T11C04425 and ITR-CCR-0313219.

J. Farré, I. Litovsky, and S. Schmitz (Eds.): CIAA 2005, LNCS 3845, pp. 78–89, 2006.

is whether a simple language is prime, i.e., not decomposable into a concatenation of two non-trivial prefix-free languages.

In general, the canonical representation of any type of language may be substantially larger than its original grammar. This is also the case for simple languages. Hence verifying the equivalence of simple languages by means of canonical representations may be inefficient. The equivalence problem for simple context-free grammars is a classical question in formal language theory. It is a nontrivial problem, since the inclusion problem for simple languages is undecidable. A. Korenjak and J. Hopcroft, see [3, 4], proved that the equivalence problem is decidable and they gave the first, doubly exponential time algorithm solving it. Their result was improved by D. Caucal to $O(n^3 v(G))$ time, see [1]. The parameter n is the size of the simple grammar and $v(G)$ is the length of a shortest string derived from a nonterminal, maximized over all nonterminals. Caucal's algorithm is exponential since $v(G)$ can be exponential with respect to n. Y. Hirshfeld, M. Jerrum, and F. Moller gave the first polynomial $O(n^{13})$ time algorithm for this problem in [5]. We call it the HJM algorithm.

In the second part of the paper we design an algorithm based on a version of Caucal's algorithm, that has a better complexity than HJM. More precisely, our algorithm works in time $O(n^7 \log^2 n)$. On the other hand a variation of our algorithm works in time $O(n^5 \text{polylog}(v(G)))$, thus beating the complexity of Caucal's algorithm, e.g., for $v(G) \in \Omega(n^3)$. Similarly as the HJM algorithm, we apply the techniques used in the algorithmic theory of compressed strings, based on Lempel-Ziv string encoding. The idea of such an encoding is that, instead of representing a string explicitly, we design a context-free grammar generating the string as a one-word language. As the combinatorial complexity of such a grammar can be significantly smaller than the length of the word, it may be considered as a succinct representation of the word. Such encodings were recently considered by researchers, mainly in the context of efficient pattern matching. There is one problem in this field which is of particular interest to us — the *compressed first mismatch problem* (*First-MP*). Given two strings encoded by a grammar, *First-MP* looks for the position of the first symbol at which the strings differ. Polynomial time algorithms for computing *First-MP* were given independently in [5] and [6], in very disjoint settings. More powerful algorithms were given in [7], where a more complicated problem of fully compressed string-matching was solved. For the purpose of this paper, we will use the result from [8], which we adopted to obtain a faster algorithm.

Simple languages are applied by IDT Canada to perform packet classification at wire speed. Classes of packets are described with the aid of simple languages, and their recognition is made by a so-called Concatenation State Machine, an efficient version of a stateless pushdown automaton. As shown in [9], there is a one-to-one correspondence between Concatenation State Machines and simple grammars. In order to store large sets of classification policies in memory, it is necessary to reuse their common parts. A natural way to do this consists in decomposing simple languages into primes, each of which is stored in memory only once. When a new classification policy is added to memory, we verify if its prime factors are already stored in the data base. The algorithms described in this paper are used to decompose classification policies into primes and to identify primes for reuse.

2   Simple Languages

A context-free grammar $G = (\Sigma, N, P)$ is composed of a finite set Σ of *terminals*, a finite set N of *nonterminals* disjoint from Σ, and a finite set $P \subset N \times (N \cup \Sigma)^*$ of *production rules*. For every $\beta, \gamma \in (N \cup \Sigma)^*$, if $(A, \alpha) \in P$, then $\beta A \gamma \to \beta \alpha \gamma$. A *derivation* $\beta \xrightarrow{*} \gamma$ is a finite sequence $(\alpha_0, \alpha_1, \ldots, \alpha_n)$ such that $\beta = \alpha_0$, $\gamma = \alpha_n$, and $\alpha_{i-1} \to \alpha_i$ for $i \in [1, n]$.

For every sequence of nonterminals $\alpha \in N^*$ of a grammar $G = (\Sigma, N, P)$, we denote by $L_G(\alpha)$ the set of terminal strings derivable from α, i.e., $L_G(\alpha) \stackrel{\text{def}}{=} \{w \in \Sigma^* \mid \alpha \xrightarrow{*} w\}$. Often, if G is known from the context, we will write $L(\alpha)$ instead of $L_G(\alpha)$.

A grammar $G = (\Sigma, N, P)$ is in *Greibach normal form* if for every production rule $(A \to \alpha) \in P$, we have $\alpha \in \Sigma N^*$. A grammar $G = (\Sigma, N, P)$ is a *simple context-free grammar* (simple grammar) if G is a Greibach normal form grammar and such that whenever $A \to a\,\alpha_1$ and $A \to a\,\alpha_2$, for a same $a \in \Sigma$, then $\alpha_1 = \alpha_2$.

A language $L \subseteq \Sigma^*$ is a *simple language* (also called *s-language*) if $L = \{\varepsilon\}$ (where ε denotes the empty word) or if there exists a simple grammar $G = (\Sigma, N, P)$ such that $L_G(A) = L$, for some $A \in N$. The definition implies that every nonterminal of a simple grammar defines a simple language. Since simple languages are prefix codes and are closed by concatenation, the family of simple languages under concatenation constitutes a free monoid with $\{\varepsilon\}$ as unit. Thus, every non-trivial simple language L (i.e. $L \neq \{\varepsilon\}$ and $L \neq \emptyset$) admits a unique decomposition into *prime* (i.e. undecomposable, non-trivial) simple languages, $L = P_1 P_2 \ldots P_n$.

3   Prime Normal Form for Simple Grammars

In this section we give an algorithm converting any simple grammar to its canonical representation called *Prime Normal Form*. A simple grammar is in Prime Normal Form (PNF) if each of its nonterminals represents a prime. We will use the following algebraic notation for left and right division in the free monoid of prefix codes. If $L = L_1 L_2$ for some prefix codes L, L_1, L_2, then by $L_1^{-1} L$ we denote L_2 and by $L L_2^{-1}$ we denote L_1. We call L_1 a left divider and L_2 a right divider of L.

Let L be a prefix code and $L = P_1 P_2 \ldots P_n$ be its decomposition into primes. Prime P_n will be called *final prime* of L, and it will be denoted by $f(L)$. In particular, if L is a prime, then $f(L) = L$.

Lemma 1. *Let* $G = (\Sigma, N, P)$ *be a simple grammar. For every* $X \in N$, *there exists* $Y \in N$, *such that* $f(L(X)) = L(Y)$.

Proof. Let $w \in L(X)f(L(X))^{-1}$, and $X \xrightarrow{*} w\alpha$ be the leftmost derivation in G, with $\alpha \in N^+$. Since $L(\alpha) = f(L(X))$ and $L(\alpha)$ is a prime, α consists of a single nonterminal, i.e., $\alpha \in N$. □

Let $w_0 \alpha_0 \to \ldots \to w_i \alpha_i \to \ldots \to w_n \alpha_n$ be the leftmost derivation $X \xrightarrow{*} w$, with $w_0 = \varepsilon$, $\alpha_0 = X$, $w_n = w$, $\alpha_n = \varepsilon$, $w_i \in \Sigma^*$, and $\alpha_i \in N^*$, for $i \in [0, n]$. We are interested in the subsequence $\pi(X, w) = Y_0, Y_1, \ldots, Y_j$ of $\alpha_0, \alpha_1, \ldots, \alpha_n$, which consists of those elements of $\alpha_0, \ldots, \alpha_n$ that are single nonterminals. E.g., for the leftmost derivation of $abcdef \in L(X)$:

$$\underline{X} \to a Y\underline{Y} \to ab\underline{Y} \to abc\underline{Y} \to abcd Y\underline{Z} \to abcde\,\underline{Z} \to abcdef$$

we have $\pi(X, abcdef) = X, Y, Y, Z$.

Definition 1. *Let $G = (\Sigma, N, P)$ be a simple grammar. We define relation $\mathcal{D}$ over $N \cup \{\varepsilon\}$ as follows. $(X, Y) \in \mathcal{D}$ if and only if:*

- *there exists a rule $(X \to a\alpha Y)$ in P for some $a \in \Sigma$ and $\alpha \in N^*$, or*
- *$Y = \varepsilon$ and there exists a rule $(X \to a)$ in P for some $a \in \Sigma$.*

Relation $\mathcal{D}$ can be seen as a digraph $(N \cup \{\varepsilon\}, \mathcal{D}, \varepsilon)$ with sink ε. In a digraph with a sink, vertex v is called a *d-articulation point* of vertex u if and only if v is present on every path from u to the sink. It was shown in [10] that the order of first (or last) occurrences of the d-articulation points of a vertex v is the same in all paths from v to the sink. Thus, it is natural to represent the set of all d-articulation points for a given vertex v as an ordered list of vertices, $(u_0, u_1, \ldots, u_n)$, where $u_0 = v$ and u_n is the sink.

In [10], it was shown that a prefix code L is prime if and only if the initial state v_1 of the minimal deterministic automaton for L does not have any d-articulation point except sink and v_1 itself. Moreover, the list of d-articulation points $(v_1, v_2, \ldots, v_n)$ corresponds to the prime decomposition of L, the factors being the languages defined by automata having v_i as the initial state and v_{i+1} as the final state (with all outgoing transitions of the final state removed), for $i \in [1, n)$, respectively.

Lemma 2. *For every path π from X to ε in $\mathcal{D}$ there exists a word $w \in L(X)$, such that $\pi = \pi(X, w)$. Conversely, for every $w \in L(X)$, $\pi(X, w)$ defines a path from X to ε in $\mathcal{D}$.*

We say that a grammar $G = (\Sigma, N, P)$ is *reduced* if there is no two different nonterminals defining the same language, i.e., for all $X, Y \in N$, if $L(X) = L(Y)$ then $X = Y$. By Lemma 1, the set of nonterminals $F(X) \overset{\text{def}}{=} \{Y \in N \mid L(Y) = f(L(X))\}$ is nonempty. If the underlying grammar is reduced then $F(X)$ consists of a single nonterminal which, by convenient abuse of notation, will be denoted by $f(X)$.

Theorem 1. *Let $G = (\Sigma, N, P)$ be a reduced simple grammar. For every $X \in N$, $L(X)$ is prime if and only if X does not have d-articulation points in $\mathcal{D}$ except sink and X itself. Moreover, if $Y \in N$ is a d-articulation point of X then $L(Y)$ is a right divider of $L(X)$.*

Proof. By Lemma 1, since G is reduced, every derivation starting in X is of form $X \xrightarrow{*} w' f(X) \xrightarrow{*} w$. Thus, for every $w \in L(X)$, $\pi(X, w)$ contains $f(X)$, i.e., $f(X)$ is a d-articulation point of X in $\mathcal{D}$.

Let Y be a d-articulation point of X in $\mathcal{D}$. By Lemma 2, every derivation starting in X passes by Y, thus Y is a d-articulation point for X in the (infinite) deterministic automaton for X, which implies that $L(Y)$ is a right divider of $L(X)$, cf. [11]. □

Theorem 2. *Given a reduced simple grammar $G = (\Sigma, N, P)$, we can find $f(X)$ for all $X \in N$ in linear time.*

Proof. By Theorem 1, the non-terminal $f(X)$ is exactly the second last d-articulation point for X in $\mathcal{D}$. Calculating $f(X)$ for all $X \in N$ can be done in linear time, by using an algorithm for finding dominators in flow graphs, cf. [12]. □

The algorithm for transforming a simple grammar $G = (\Sigma, N, P)$ into PNF, called $PNF(G, S)$, is presented in Figure 1.

Input: Simple grammar $G = (\Sigma, N, P)$ and $S \in N^+$.
Output: Simple grammar G' in PNF and $S' \in N^+$, such that $L_G(S) = L_{G'}(S')$.

1. Reduce G.
   Find redundant nonterminals by checking if $L(X) = L(Y)$, for all $X, Y \in N$.
   Each redundant nonterminal is substituted in P and in S, and removed from N.
2. For every $X \in N$, find $f(X) \in N$.
   Construct the digraph $\mathcal{D}$ and find the second-last d-articulation point for X.
   If for every $X \in N$, $X = f(X)$, then **return** (G, S).
3. Construct a new grammar $G' = (\Sigma, N, P')$ and new S':
   Define morphism $h : N \mapsto N^*$ as: $h(X) \overset{\text{def}}{=} \begin{cases} X & \text{if } X = f(X) \\ X f(X) & \text{otherwise.} \end{cases}$
   Set S' to $h(S)$, and P' as follows, for $a \in \Sigma$, $X, Y \in N$, $\alpha \in N^*$:
   (a) If $(X \to a\alpha) \in P$ and $X = f(X)$, then $(X \to ah(\alpha))$ is in P'.
   (b) If $(X \to a\alpha f(X)) \in P$ and $X \neq f(X)$, then $(X \to ah(\alpha))$ is in P'.
   (c) If $(X \to a\alpha Y) \in P$, $X \neq f(X)$ and $Y \neq f(X)$, then $(X \to ah(\alpha)Y)$ is in P'.
4. Set G to G', S to S' and go to 1.

Fig. 1. Algorithm $PNF(G, S)$

We present an example of the execution of the algorithm. The input consists of a simple grammar $G = \{(X \to aAA), (X \to bYY), (Y \to aY), (Y \to bBA), (A \to a), (B \to aXA), (B \to b)\}$, and a simple language represented as a word $S = XA$ over nonterminals of G. We obtain the grammar in PNF while keeping track of the decomposition of S. For each iteration, we give the value of S, the grammar G, the digraph $\mathcal{D}$ (solid lines), the d-articulation tree (dotted lines), and the values $f(x)$ for $x \in \{X, Y, A, B\}$ and $h(x)$ for $x \in \{X, Y, A, B, S\}$.

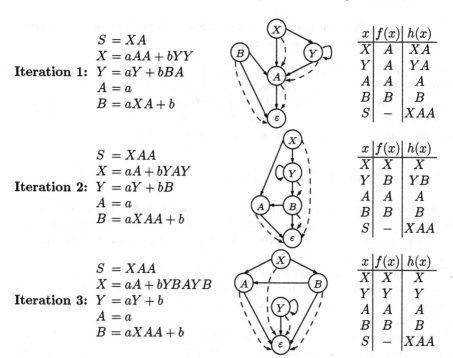

$$
\begin{aligned}
&\phantom{\text{Iteration 1:}}\ S = XA \\
&\phantom{\text{Iteration 1:}}\ X = aAA + bYY \\
&\textbf{Iteration 1:}\ Y = aY + bBA \\
&\phantom{\text{Iteration 1:}}\ A = a \\
&\phantom{\text{Iteration 1:}}\ B = aXA + b
\end{aligned}
$$

x	$f(x)$	$h(x)$
X	A	XA
Y	A	YA
A	A	A
B	B	B
S	$-$	XAA

$$
\begin{aligned}
&\phantom{\text{Iteration 2:}}\ S = XAA \\
&\phantom{\text{Iteration 2:}}\ X = aA + bYAY \\
&\textbf{Iteration 2:}\ Y = aY + bB \\
&\phantom{\text{Iteration 2:}}\ A = a \\
&\phantom{\text{Iteration 2:}}\ B = aXAA + b
\end{aligned}
$$

x	$f(x)$	$h(x)$
X	X	X
Y	B	YB
A	A	A
B	B	B
S	$-$	XAA

$$
\begin{aligned}
&\phantom{\text{Iteration 3:}}\ S = XAA \\
&\phantom{\text{Iteration 3:}}\ X = aA + bYBAYB \\
&\textbf{Iteration 3:}\ Y = aY + b \\
&\phantom{\text{Iteration 3:}}\ A = a \\
&\phantom{\text{Iteration 3:}}\ B = aXAA + b
\end{aligned}
$$

x	$f(x)$	$h(x)$
X	X	X
Y	Y	Y
A	A	A
B	B	B
S	$-$	XAA

Theorem 3. *The algorithm PNF(G, S) correctly computes a PNF simple grammar G′ and S′ such that $L_G(S) = L_{G'}(S')$.*

Proof. Step 1 does not change the semantics of any nonterminal, so it reduces G to an equivalent simple grammar. Step 2 effectively finds final primes for all nonterminals. Step 3 transforms the grammar G into G' by right-factorizing every non-prime nonterminal X by $f(X)$: If X is prime then $L_G(X) = L_{G'}(X)$, otherwise $L_G(X) = L_{G'}(Xf(X))$. Every production $(X \to \alpha) \in P$ is rewritten accordingly into a corresponding production $(X \to \beta) \in P'$. Hence, for all $X \in N$, $L_G(X) = L_{G'}(h(X))$. Thus morphism h converts grammar G together with S to a grammar G' with $S' = h(S)$ such that $L_G(S) = L_{G'}(S')$. Every iteration of the program cuts the length of non-prime nonterminals, in terms of their prime decomposition, by one. Thus, the total number of iterations equals the maximum length of the prime decompositions of nonterminals of the initial grammar. Hence the algorithm terminates. By the exit condition from Step 2, each nonterminal is prime, hence G is in PNF. □

Both steps, 2 and 3, of the algorithm may be computed in linear time, hence the complexity of each iteration of the main loop is dominated by grammar reduction from step 1.

The polynomial time algorithm from Section 6, repeated $O(n^2)$ times may be used to perform the grammar reduction. However, for grammar $G = \{(A_1 \to aA_2A_2), (A_2 \to aA_3A_3), \ldots, (A_{n-1} \to aA_nA_n), (A_n \to a)\}$, language $L_G(A_1)$ has an exponential number of primes with respect to the size of G. Hence the number of iterations of the main loop of PNF(G, S) may be exponential and so may be the size of the resulting PNF grammar. Since simple languages constitute a free monoid, the PNF form is unique.

Corollary 1. *Every simple language L can be represented by a PNF simple grammar $G = (\Sigma, N, P)$ and a starting word $S \in N^*$, such that $L_G(S) = L$. Such a representation is unique. The problem of constructing the PNF representation of L given by a simple grammar is decidable. The PNF representation may be of exponential size with respect to the size of the original grammar.*

4   First Mismatch-Pair Problem

Our approach to transform Caucal's algorithm for the equivalence problem of simple grammar, cf. [1], into a polynomial time one (with respect to the size of the input grammar) is to use compressed representations of sequences of nonterminals, instead of using explicit representations.

We will use the terminology of *acyclic morphisms* because it is more convenient in presenting our algorithms. It is basically equivalent to the representation of a single word by a context-free grammar generating exactly one word, or to a "straight line program".

A *morphism* over a monoid M is an application $H : M \mapsto M$ such that $H(1_M) = 1_M$ and $H(x \cdot y) = H(x) \cdot H(y)$, for all $x, y \in M$. A morphism $H : M \mapsto M$ is fully defined by providing the values for the generators of M. Thus, a morphism H over a finitely generated free monoid N^* is usually defined by providing $H : N \mapsto N^*$. A morphism $H : N \to N^+$ is said to be *acyclic* if we can order elements of N in such a way that for each $A \in N$, we have: $H(A) = A$ or $A > B$ for each symbol B occurring in the string $H(A)$. For an acyclic morphism H over N^* we denote $H^{|N|}$ by H^*, since $H^{|N|+1} = H^{|N|}$. If $H^*(\alpha) = w$ then we say that (H, α) is a compressed representation of w. The size of w can be exponential with respect to the size of its compressed representation.

Let $G = (\Sigma, N, P)$ be a simple grammar. We say that an acyclic morphism $H : N \mapsto N^+$ is *self-proving* in G if for each $A \in N$ we have:

- If $A \to a\,\alpha$ then $H(A) \to a\,\beta$ and $H^*(\alpha) = H^*(\beta)$; and
- If $H(A) \to a\,\beta$ then $A \to a\,\alpha$ and $H^*(\alpha) = H^*(\beta)$.

The concept of self-proving relations was introduced by Courcelle, c.f [13]. The idea of Courcelle and the following Lemma are reformulated in the terms of acyclic morphisms and given here for completeness.

Lemma 3. *If H is an acyclic morphism self-proving in $G = (\Sigma, N, P)$, then $L_G(x) = L_G(H(x))$, for every $x \in N^*$.*

The crucial tool in the polynomial-time algorithms is the compressed *first mismatch-pair* problem, *First-MP*:

Input: an acyclic morphism $H : N \mapsto N^+$ and two strings $x, y \in N^*$;
Output:

- $First\text{-}MP(x, y, H) = nil$, if $H^*(x) = H^*(y)$;
- $First\text{-}MP(x, y, H) = failure$, if one of $H^*(x)$, $H^*(y)$ is a proper prefix of the other;
- $First\text{-}MP(x, y, H) = (A, B) \in N \times N$, where (A, B) is the *first mismatch pair*, i.e., the first symbols occurring at the same position in $H^*(x)$ and in $H^*(y)$, respectively, which are different.

We say that a morphism H is binary if $|H(A)| \leq 2$ for each $A \in N$. The following fact can be shown using the algorithm from [8].

Lemma 4. *Assume that given acyclic morphism $H : N \mapsto N^+$ is binary and that the length of x and y is at most $O(|N|)$, then we can solve $First\text{-}MP(x, y, H)$ in time $O(k^2 \cdot h^2)$, where $k = |N|$ and $h \overset{\text{def}}{=} \min\{k \geq 0 \mid H^k = H^{k+1}\}$ is the depth of the morphism.*

5   The Equivalence Algorithm

Conceptually it is easier to deal with grammars in binary Greibach Normal Form (denoted GNF2). This means that each side of the production is of the form $(A \rightarrow a\alpha)$, where $a \in \Sigma$ and $\alpha \in \{\epsilon\} \cup N \cup N^2$.

Lemma 5. *For each simple grammar G of total size n (the total number of symbols describing G) there is an equivalent simple grammar G' in GNF2 with only $O(n)$ nonterminal symbols. G' can be constructed from G in $O(n)$ time.*

The total size of a grammar in GNF2 is of a same order as the size of N. Hence by the size of a grammar $G = (\Sigma, N, P)$, we mean $n = |N|$.

All known algorithms for the equivalence problem for simple grammars are based on the possibility of computing the quotient of one prefix language by another, assuming that the quotient exists and the languages are given as two nonterminals of a simple grammar.

More precisely, let A and B be two nonterminals of a simple grammar $G = (\Sigma, N, P)$, such that $L(A) = L(B) \cdot L$, for some language $L \subseteq \Sigma^*$. The language L can be derived from A by a leftmost derivation following any word w from $L(B)$, i.e., $A \overset{*}{\to} w\gamma$, for $\gamma \in N^*$, and $L(\gamma) = L$.

Let $\|A\|$ denote the length of the shortest word derivable from A.

Lemma 6. *Let G be a simple grammar of size n. We can compute the lengths of shortest words derivable from all nonterminals of G in time $O(n \log n)$.*

Proof. Finding $\|A\|$ for all $A \in N$ corresponds to the single-source shortest paths problem in an *and/or* graph, which, using Dijkstra algorithm, can be solved in time $O(n \log n)$. □

Lemma 7. *Let A and B be two nonterminals of a simple grammar $G = (\Sigma, N, P)$ such that $L(A) = L(B) \cdot L$, for some $L \subseteq \Sigma^*$. We can compute $\gamma \in N^*$ such that $L(\gamma) = L$ in time $O(n)$. It is guaranteed that $|\gamma| \leq n$.*

Proof. Consider the parse tree for the derivation of a shortest word w from A. The idea is to find a path down the tree which cuts off left of this path subtrees γ generating prefix of w of length $||B||$. Since w is a shortest word, no path of the parse tree contains two occurrences of the same nonterminal hence the depth of the tree is at most n. Therefore $|\gamma| \leq n$ and computing the value takes $O(n)$ time.   □

The result of the algorithm for finding the quotient of A by B as described in the proof of Lemma 7 will be denoted by $quot(A, B)$. The algorithm will give a result for any pair of nonterminals A and B, as long as $||A|| \geq ||B||$. Notice that $L(A) = L(B\ quot(A, B))$ only if $L(B)$ is a left divider of $L(A)$.

Lemma 3 is the starting point for the design of the algorithm *EQUIVA-LENCE*. Assume that we fix a linear order $A_1 < A_2 \ldots < A_n$ of nonterminals, such that whenever $i < j$, we have $||A_i|| \leq ||A_j||$. The idea of the algorithm is to construct a self-proving morphism H or, in the process of its construction, to discover a failure which contradicts $L(A) = L(B)$. The main point of the algorithm is to keep pairs of long strings in compressed form. We keep only strings of linear length, their explicit representations are determined by the morphism H. Each time a new rule is generated by setting $H(A) = B\gamma$, where $\gamma = quot(A, B)$, we create pairs (α, β) such that $A \to a\,\alpha$ and $B\gamma \to a\,\beta$, for every letter a of the terminal alphabet. We keep the generated pairs in set Q. To each pair we apply operation *First-MP*, which "eliminates" the next nonterminal, or finds that we have a pair of identical strings, such pairs are removed from Q. By doing that, the algorithm is checking locally for the proof of the nonequivalence of A and B. If the nonequivalence is not discovered and there is nothing to process, i.e., Q is empty, the algorithm returns the value TRUE, meaning $L(A) = L(B)$.

The algorithm *EQUIVALENCE* is presented in Fig. 2. For technical reasons (to simplify the description of the algorithm) we assume that *First-MP*(x, y, H) gives ordered pairs in the sense that if *First-MP*$(x, y, H) = (A, B)$ then $A > B$. For $\alpha \in N^+$ and $a \in \Sigma$, by $\alpha \xrightarrow{a}$ we denote that there is a $\beta \in N^*$ such that $\alpha \to a\,\beta$, and by $\alpha \xrightarrow{a}\!\!\!\!\!/\,\,$ that there is not. We write $(\alpha, \beta) \xrightarrow{a} (\alpha', \beta')$ to say that $\alpha \to a\,\alpha'$ and $\beta \to a\,\beta'$.

Lemma 8. *The algorithm is correct. The algorithm makes $O(n)$ iterations.*

Proof. In each iteration, either a pair of strings is removed from Q, or a nonterminal is "eliminated" and no more than $|\Sigma|$ pairs of strings are inserted into Q. The crucial property is that whenever $H(A) = B\gamma$, then the nonterminals in $B\gamma$ are of smaller rank than A, ensuring that H is acyclic. Note also that *First-MP* returns a pair (A, B) such that $H(A) = A$, therefore a nonterminal can only be "eliminated" once. After at most $n - 1$ eliminations, *First-MP* will either find that $H^*(\beta_1) = H^*(\beta_2)$ and remove the pair from Q or return $failure$. Thus, the maximum number of iterations is $O(n)$.

Correctness follows from Lemma 3.   □

Corollary 2. *The algorithm EQUIVALENCE(X, Y, G) works in time $O(n\,F(n))$, where n is the size of G, and $F(n)$ is the complexity of the First Mismatch-Pair Problem.*

Input: Simple grammar $G = (\Sigma, N, P)$ and nonterminals $X, Y \in N$;
Output: TRUE if $L_G(X) = L_G(Y)$, FALSE otherwise.
   Initialization:
      $Q := \{(X,Y)\}$;
      for each $A \in N$ **do** $H[A] := A$;
   while Q is not empty **do**
      $(\beta_1, \beta_2) :=$ an element of Q;
      switch $(First\text{-}MP(\beta_1, \beta_2, H))$ **do**
         case *nil* : remove (β_1, β_2) from Q;
         case *failure* : return FALSE;
         case (A, B) :
            $\gamma := quot(A, B)$;
            $H[A] := B\gamma$;   /* *The nonterminal A is "eliminated"* */
            for each $a \in \Sigma$ **do**
               if $(A, B\gamma) \xrightarrow{a} (\beta_1, \beta_2)$ **then** insert (β_1, β_2) into Q;
               if $(A \xrightarrow{a}$ and $B \not\xrightarrow{a})$ or $(A \not\xrightarrow{a}$ and $B \xrightarrow{a})$ **then** return FALSE;
   return TRUE;

Fig. 2. Algorithm $EQUIVALENCE(X, Y, G)$

Lemma 9. *Every instance of First-MP(α, β, H) in EQUIVALENCE(X, Y, G) can be solved in time:*

1. $O(n^6 \log^2 n)$ and
2. $O(n^4 \operatorname{polylog} v(G))$.

where n is the size of G, and $v(G)$ is the length of a shortest string derivable from a nonterminal, maximized over all nonterminals.

Proof. In the proof we use twice Lemma 4.

1. Assume H is an acyclic morphism over N, where $n = |N|$ such that $|H(A)| \leq n$ for each A. Then we can construct a morphism H_b such that $H_b^* = H^*$, over a set of $k \leq n^2$ nonterminals and with depth $h = O(n \log n)$.
   The transformation of the morphism can be done similarly to a balanced transformation into a Chomsky normal form. If $H(A) = B_1 B_2 \ldots B_n$ then we introduce $n - 2$ new auxiliary nonterminals to change it into a balanced binary tree generating $B_1 B_2 \ldots B_n$ from A. We need $O(n)$ new nonterminals per each original one, altogether the number of nonterminals increases to $O(n^2)$, i.e., k is in $O(n^2)$. However the depth is changed only logarithmically. Observe that on each top down path in generation we have at most n original nonterminals, all of them should be different, and at most $O(n \log n)$ auxiliary nonterminals, i.e., h is in $O(n \log n)$. Now, point 1 follows from Lemma 4.
2. We can use the technique from [14] which transforms each grammar generating a single word u into a grammar of depth $O(\log |u|)$ by introducing $O(n \operatorname{polylog} n)$ new nonterminals. Then Lemma 4 can be applied. □

The series of lemmas gives directly the following theorem, due to the fact that after binarization of the morphism the number of variables grows quadratically and the depth only grows by a logarithmic factor.

Theorem 4. *The algorithm EQUIVALENCE(X, Y, G) deciding on the equivalence of two nonterminals X and Y in a simple grammar G, works in time $O(n^7 \log^2 n)$ and $O(n^5 \operatorname{polylog} v(G))$, where n is the size of G, and $v(G)$ is the length of a shortest string derivable from a nonterminal, maximized over all nonterminals.*

6   Randomized Algorithm for *First-MP*

We reduce equality of two compressed texts $H^*(A)$ and $H^*(B)$, to equality of two polynomials of degree at most $\max(|H^*(A)|, |H^*(B)|)$. It is essential that the uncompressed lengths of strings $H^*(A)$ and $H^*(B)$ is only singly exponential. It follows from the construction of the operation *quot* which involves only shortest strings derivable from nonterminals of the grammar G.

Lemma 10 (Randomized Equality Testing). *We can check if $H^*(A) = H^*(B)$ in $O(n \operatorname{polylog} n)$ randomized time.*

Lemma 11. *The first mismatch-pair problem can be solved by a randomized algorithm in time $O(n^2 \operatorname{polylog} n)$.*

Proof. We can check the equality of two prefixes of $H^*(A)$ and $H^*(B)$ at the same time as the equality of $H^*(A)$ and $H^*(B)$. This can be done by changing H into H' which generates only corresponding segments. We omit the details. Then Lemma 10 can be applied. If we can compute the equality of prefixes then we can do a binary search to compute the first mismatch. We have to add as a coefficient the number of iterations in the binary search. This number is logarithmic with respect to the lengths of uncompressed strings, hence it is $O(n)$, since the lengths are only singly exponential. This completes the proof.   □

Theorem 5. *We can solve the equivalence problem for simple grammars by a randomized algorithm in $O(n^4 \operatorname{polylog} n)$ time.*

7   Conclusion

We have given an algorithm converting any simple grammar to its canonical representation called Prime Normal Form. We also improved the complexity of the best existing algorithm verifying equivalence of simple languages. This result may be used to reduce simple grammars, which is the most expensive step of the PNF algorithm. Despite this improvement, this algorithm still works in exponential time in the worst case, since its output may be of exponential size. However, this theoretical limitation does not seem to occur in practice in the context of network packet filtering and classification.

One interesting open problem is to propose a canonical representation of a simple grammar, and an algorithm computing it, such that the size of this representation is polynomial in the size of the original grammar.

References

1. Caucal, D.: A fast algorithm to decide on simple grammars equivalence. In: Optimal Algorithms. Volume 401 of LNCS. Springer (1989) 66–85
2. Courcelle, B.: Une forme canonique pour les grammaires simples deterministes. RAIRO informatique (1974) 19–36
3. Korenjak, A.J., Hopcroft, J.E.: Simple deterministic languages. In: Proc. IEEE 7th Annual Symposium on Switching and Automata Theory. IEEE Symposium on Foundations of Computer Science (1966) 36–46
4. Harrison, M.: Introduction to formal language theory. Addison Wesley (1978)
5. Hirshfeld, Y., Jerrum, M., Moller, F.: A polynomial algorithm for deciding bisimilarity of normed context-free processes. Theoretical Computer Science **158** (1996) 143–159
6. Plandowski, W.: Testing equivalence of morphisms on context-free languages. In: ESA. Volume 855 of LNCS. Springer (1994) 460–470
7. Karpinski, M., Rytter, W., Shinohara, A.: Pattern-matching for strings with short descriptions. In Galil, Z., Ukkonen, E., eds.: Proceedings of the 6th Annual Symposium on Combinatorial Pattern Matching. Number 937, Espoo, Finland, Springer-Verlag, Berlin (1995) 205–214
8. Miyazaki, M., Shinohara, A., Takeda, M.: An improved pattern matching for strings in terms of straight-line programs. Journal of Discrete Algorithms **1** (2000) 187–204
9. Debski, W., Fraczak, W.: Concatenation state machines and simple functions. In: Implementation and Application of Automata, CIAA'04. Volume 3317 of LNCS. Springer (2004) 113–124
10. Czyzowicz, J., Fraczak, W., Pelc, A., Rytter, W.: Prime decompositions of regular prefix codes. In: Implementation and Application of Automata, CIAA 2002. Volume 2608 of LNCS. Springer, Tours, France (2003) 85–94
11. Fraczak, W., Podolak, A.: A characterization of s-languages. Information Processing Letters **89** (2004) 65–70
12. Georgiadis, L., Tarjan, R.E.: Finding dominators revisited: extended abstract. In: Proceedings of the Fifteenth Annual ACM-SIAM Symposium on Discrete Algorithms, SODA 2004, SIAM (2004) 869–878
13. Courcelle, B.: An axiomatic approach to the Korenjak-Hopcroft algorithms. Mathematical Systems Theory **16** (1983) 191–231
14. Rytter, W.: Application of Lempel–Ziv factorization to the approximation of grammar-based compression. Theoretical Computer Science **302** (2003) 211–222

An Incremental Algorithm for Constructing Minimal Deterministic Finite Cover Automata

Cezar Câmpeanu[1], Andrei Păun[2,*], and Jason R. Smith[2]

[1] Department of Computer Science and Information Technology,
University of Prince Edward Island, Charlottetown, P.E.I., Canada C1A 4P3
ccampeanu@upei.ca
[2] Department of Computer Science/Institute for Micromanufacturing,
College of Engineering and Science, Louisiana Tech University,
Ruston, P.O. Box 10348, Louisiana, LA-71272, USA
{apaun, jrs026}@latech.edu

Abstract. We present a fast incremental algorithm for constructing minimal DFCA for a given language. Since it was shown that the DFCA for a language L can have less states than the DFA for L, this technique seems to be the best choice for incrementally building the automaton for a large language, especially when the number of states in the DFCA is significantly less than the number of states in the corresponding minimal DFA. We have implemented the proposed algorithm and have tested it against the best known DFCA minimization technique.

1 Introduction

We have witnessed in recent years a growing interest in the design of incremental algorithms for finite automata [1–10]. The reason behind the (renewed) interest for such incremental algorithms used for building a minimal *Deterministic Finite Automata* (DFA) for a given dictionary (finite language) comes from the observation that such an incremental algorithm could have much smaller memory requirements than a "global" minimization algorithm with little or no increase in the time complexity of the overall minimization process.

The small memory requirements for incremental algorithms (as opposed to "classical" minimization techniques) come from the fact that the DFA for a finite language is built word-by-word and minimized as words are inserted into the DFA. In this way the state complexity (and thus the memory requirements) of the incrementally built DFA could remain small as compared to the state complexity of a *trie* built for the whole dictionary as a first step and then minimizing the *trie* into a small DFA using a fast algorithm such as Hopcroft's which requires $O(n \ log(n))$ time and $O(n)$ space.

In the current paper we continue the research work in the incremental algorithms area, with the observation that for finite languages there is the recently defined concept of *Deterministic Finite Cover Automata* (DFCA) [11]. To conserve even more memory during the intermediate steps of the construction of the

---

* Corresponding author.

J. Farré, I. Litovsky, and S. Schmitz (Eds.): CIAA 2005, LNCS 3845, pp. 90–103, 2006.

automaton we will devise an incremental algorithm for DFCA. We have proved in [12] that when transforming an NFA into a DFA and also into a DFCA the DFA can have exponentially more states than the DFCA; thus, there is a large class of languages for which the DFCA is the desirable representation as opposed to the DFA. For the recent results and properties of DFCA we refer the reader to [11, 13, 14, 12, 15, 16, 17]. We note that a Hopcroft-type algorithm (with $O(n \, log(n))$ time and $O(n)$ space complexities) for the minimization of DFCA was described in [15], but no incremental algorithms for DFCA are known. Another advantage of incremental solutions, beside efficiency, is maintenance, since the technique for increasing the number of words in the dictionary is already built-in. We fill this gap by describing an incremental algorithm for DFCA in the current paper. We have implemented in the *Grail+* package [18] both the algorithm from [15] and the incremental algorithm proposed in the current paper; the preliminary tests suggest that the incremental algorithm is far superior with respect to the memory requirements as opposed to the Hopcroft-like algorithm, while no noticeable slow-down was observed for the languages tested.

The presented algorithm has complexity $O(kn)$ in time and $O(n^2)$ in space for adding a word of size k into a DFCA with n states. The time complexity is considered linear in literature in such a case (see [5]) due to the fact that the size of a word from the language is usually much smaller than the size of the automaton accepting the language. Thus, we provide a fast incremental algorithm (having the same time complexity as the known incremental algorithms for DFA described in [10]), but with a small increase in the memory requirements. This increase is small since, in practice, the complexity n is usually of logarithmical order of the complexity (trie size) of non-incremental algorithms. We will give an example of a language containing 2^n words for which the Hopcroft-like algorithm for DFCA requires $O(2^n)$ space, whereas our algorithm requires $O(n^2)$ space.

For more information on incremental algorithms for DFA we refer the reader to [1, 2, 3, 4, 5, 7, 8, 9, 10]. It is worth noting that the paper [3] could be very interesting as it provides a comparison between the major algorithms (incremental/non-incremental) for the DFA, the comparison being performed using various dictionaries.

2   Preliminaries

We assume the reader is familiar with the basic notations of formal languages and finite automata, cf. e.g. [19, 20, 21]. The cardinality of a finite set A is denoted with $\#A$, the set of words over a finite alphabet Σ is denoted Σ^*, and the empty word is λ. The length of a word $w \in \Sigma^*$ is denoted $|w|$. The set of words over Σ of length at most (respectively, at least) n is denoted $\Sigma^{\leq n}$ (respectively, $\Sigma^{\geq n}$).

For a DFA $D = (\Sigma, Q, q_0, \delta, F)$, we can always assume, without loss of generality, that $Q = \{0, 1, \ldots, n-1\}$ and $q_0 = 0$; we will use this every time is convenient for simplifying our notations. If L is a finite language, we denote by l the maximum among the length of words in L.

Definition 1. *A language L' over Σ is called a cover language for the finite language L if $L' \cap \Sigma^{\leq l} = L$. A deterministic finite cover automaton (DFCA) for L is a deterministic finite automaton (DFA) A, such that the language accepted by A is a cover language of L.*

Definition 2. *Let $x, y \in \Sigma^*$. We define the following similarity relation by: $x \sim_L y$ if for all $z \in \Sigma^*$ such that $xz, yz \in \Sigma^{\leq l}$, $xz \in L$ iff $yz \in L$, and we write $x \not\sim_L y$ if $x \sim_L y$ does not hold.*

Definition 3. *Let $A = (Q, \Sigma, \delta, 0, F)$ be a DFA (or a DFCA). We define, for each state $q \in Q$, $level(q) = \min\{|w| \mid \delta(0, w) = q\}$.*

Definition 4. *Let $A = (Q, \Sigma, \delta, 0, F)$ be a DFCA for L. We consider two states $p, q \in Q$ and $m = \max\{level(p), level(q)\}$. We say that p is similar with q in A, denoted by $p \sim_A q$, if for every $w \in \Sigma^{\leq l-m}$, $\delta(p, w) \in F$ iff $\delta(q, w) \in F$. We say that two states are dissimilar if they are not similar.*

The following theorem gives the procedure to "merge" two similar states.

Theorem 1. *Let $A = (Q, \Sigma, \delta, s, F)$ be a DFCA of L. Suppose that for $p, q \in Q$, $p \sim_A q$, $p \neq q$ and $level(p) \leq level(q)$. Then we can construct a DFCA, $A' = (Q', \Sigma, \delta', s, F')$, for L such that $Q' = Q - \{q\}$, $F' = F - \{q\}$, and for each $t \in Q'$ and $a \in \Sigma$ we have*

$$\delta'(t, a) = \begin{cases} \delta(t, a) & \text{if } \delta(t, a) \neq q, \\ p & \text{if } \delta(t, a) = q \end{cases}.$$

We say that q is merged into p if we can apply the above theorem for p and q.

Definition 5. *A DFCA A for a finite language is a minimal DFCA if and only if any two different states of A are dissimilar.*

Theorem 2. *Any minimal DFCA of L has the same number of states.*

We refer the reader to [11] for the proofs of the above results.

3   Adding a Word to the Language of a DFCA

In this section we will give the algorithm for adding a word to the language accepted by a minimal DFCA while keeping the new DFCA minimal. For better readability, we will set the notations for the subsequent results: $L \subset \Sigma^*$ is a finite language over an alphabet Σ and l is the length of the longest word(s) in L. We also consider $C = (\Sigma, Q_C, \delta_C, 0, F_C)$ a minimal DFCA for L ($L = L(C) \cap \Sigma^{\leq l}$), where $Q_C = \{0, 1, \ldots, n-1\}$. Let $w \in \Sigma^*$, $w = w_1 \ldots w_k$, $w_i \in \Sigma$, $1 \leq i \leq k$ be the new word to be added to the language L; thus, we want to construct the minimal DFCA A recognizing the language $L \cup \{w\}$.

The minimal DFA accepting $\{w\}$ is denoted $W = (\Sigma, Q_W, 0, \delta_w, F_W)$, where

$$Q_W = \{0, 1, \ldots, k+1\},$$
$$\delta_w(i, w_{i+1}) = i + 1, \text{ for all } 0 \leq i < k,$$
$$\delta_w(i, a) = k + 1, \text{ for all } 0 \leq i \leq k \text{ and } a \neq w_i, \text{ or } i = k + 1,$$
$$F_W = \{k\}.$$

Let us denote by $s_i = \delta_C(0, w_1 \ldots w_i)$, and $s_0 = 0$. We will consider and construct different algorithms for two cases: $k \leq l$ or $k > l$.

3.1 Adding a Word Shorter Than the Longest Word in the DFCA, i.e., Case $k \leq l$

We consider now the case where the newly added word w has length less than or equal to l. We will first modify the cover automaton C such that the new automaton A will accept a cover language for $L \cup \{w\}$. The construction is the standard Cartesian product between two automata [19]. We observe that the automaton W has a particular shape (a "line"), making many of the states in the Cartesian product unreachable.

Before giving the actual construction we note that the states of the form $(p, k+1)$ with $p \in Q_C$ from the Cartesian product will have the same transitions as in the automaton C. Moreover, such a state is final in A if and only if $p \in F_C$. Another crucial observation is that for each (p, i) of the new automaton where i is not the sink state of W (i.e. $i \neq k + 1$), $p = s_i$. Due to the particular shape of the automaton W and the fact that C is deterministic, we have that the number of such states (p, i) is equal to the number of different prefixes for w. We now know that the number of states that can be reachable from the start state $(0, 0)$ can be at most $\#Q_C + k + 1$: $\#Q_C$ states of the form $(p, k+1)$ and at most $k+1$ states of the form (p, i) with $i \neq k + 1$. Thus, the original automaton C can be "embedded" in the new automaton with its states becoming the states $(p, k+1)$ in the Cartesian product. It should be clear that the following construction is equivalent to the standard Cartesian product between C and W.

We now construct the DFA $A = (\Sigma, Q_A, \delta_A, 0_A, F_A)$, with $Q_A = Q_C \cup Q_W$; each state $q \in Q_C$ is denoted in Q_A by $(q, k + 1)$ and each state $i \in Q_W$ is denoted by (s_i, i). The initial state is $(s_0, 0) = (0, 0)$, the set of final states is $F_A = \{(q, s) \mid q \in F_C \text{ or } s = k\}$, and the transition function δ_A is given by the the following formula:

$$\delta_A((p, i), a) = \begin{cases} (s_{i+1}, i + 1) & \text{if } i \leq k, \ p = s_i, \text{ and } w_{i+1} = a \\ (\delta_C(p, a), k + 1) & \text{otherwise.} \end{cases}$$

We can now use a standard breadth first search (BFS) algorithm to compute/update the levels of the states in Q_A, as well as detecting any unreachable states of the form $(p, k + 1)$.

The next step is to minimize this DFCA; we are now interested in detecting all the similarities in the automaton A. To do this we will use the notions *level* and *gap* of the states; *level* was defined in Section 2, while the *gap* between each pair of states will be a matrix called the "gap" table [16]. We define the gap between two states p and q (in the automaton C) as the length of the shortest word $z \in \Sigma^*$ that distinguishes p from q:

$$gap_C(p, q) = \min(\{|z| \mid \delta_C(p, z) \in F_C \text{ and } \delta_C(q, z) \notin F_C\}$$
$$\cup \{|z| \mid \delta_C(p, z) \notin F_C \text{ and } \delta_C(q, z) \in F_C\}).$$

The gap in the automaton A is defined similarly.

Remark 1. The level for reachable states (p, i) is at least the level of the state p, for all values of i, since we do not introduce any "shortcuts". For a state $(p, i) \in Q_A$, if $i < k$, then $level_A((p, i)) = i$ and if $i = k + 1$, we have $level_A((p, i)) \geq level_C(p)$.

We shall call from now on the states $(p, k+1)$, "original states" and the states (s_i, i), "cloned" states (see also [2, 10]).

If $x \in \Sigma^*$ is not a prefix of w, we have $\delta_A((0, 0), x) = (\delta_C(0, x), k+1)$. On the other hand, if x is a prefix of w, i.e., $x = w_1 \ldots w_i$, we have $\delta_A((0, 0), x) = (s_i, i)$.

Lemma 1. *If $level_A(s_i, k + 1) = level_C(s_i)$, we have $level_A(s_{i+1}, k + 1) = level_C(s_{i+1})$.*

Proof. Let us assume that $level_A((s_i, k + 1)) = level_C(s_i)$. We distinguish two cases: either $level_C(s_{i+1}) = level_C(s_i) + 1$ or $level_C(s_{i+1}) < level_C(s_i) + 1$.

In the first case $level_C(s_{i+1}) \leq level_A(s_{i+1}, k + 1) \leq level_A(s_i, k + 1) + 1 = level_C(s_i) + 1 = level_C(s_{i+1})$, thus we have that $level_C(s_{i+1}) = level_A((s_{i+1}, k + 1))$.

The second case means that there is $u \in \Sigma^*$ such that $\delta_C(0, u) = s_{i+1}$, $|u| < level_C(s_i) + 1$, $u \neq w_1 \ldots w_i w_{i+1}$, and without the loss of generality we can choose u the shortest with these properties. Therefore, $\delta_A((0, 0), u) = (s_{i+1}, k+1)$ and we have $level_C(s_{i+1}) \leq level_A(s_{i+1}, k + 1) \leq |u| = level_C(s_{i+1})$. □

The following lemma shows that for each cloned state the level will increase only for the cloned state or only for the original state, but not for both.

Lemma 2. *For every $0 \leq i \leq k$ we have the following properties:*

$$\text{if } level_A(s_i, k + 1) > level_C(s_i), \text{ then } level_A(s_i, i) = level_C(s_i);$$
$$\text{if } level_A(s_i, i) > level_C(s_i), \text{ then } level_A(s_i, k + 1) = level_C(s_i).$$

Proof. For $i = 0$, the lemma is true, since $level(s_0, 0) = 0$. Let us now consider $i > 0$, then $level_A(s_i, i) \geq level_C(s_i)$ and $level_A(s_i, k + 1) \geq level_C(s_i)$.
If both inequalities are strict, from the first inequality it immediately follows that $\delta_C(0, w_1 \ldots w_i) = s_i$ and $\delta_C(0, u) = s_i$, for some $u \in \Sigma^{<i}$.
If all these u are prefixes of w, then $(s_i, k + 1)$ is unreachable. Therefore, there is one that is not a prefix of w. We can consider without loss of generality that u is the shortest prefix with these properties.
Since $\delta_A((0, 0), u) = (\delta_C(0, u), k + 1) = (s_i, k + 1)$, it follows that $level_A(s_i, k + 1) \leq level_C(s_i)$, a contradiction. □

Corollary 1. *There are at most $k + 1$ states (s_i, i), $(s_i, k + 1)$, $1 \le i \le k$ for which we have that $level_A((s_i, i)) > level_C(s_i)$ or $level_A((s_i, k+1)) > level_C(s_i)$.*

Remark 2. The gap between two "original" states is the same in A as it is in C, i.e., $gap_A((p, k + 1), q(k + 1)) = gap_C(p, q)$.

Remark 3. Using the definition of similarity, we have that two states (p, i) and (q, j) are similar in A if $gap_A((p, i), (q, j)) + \max\{level_A((p, i)), level((q, j))\} > l$.

The following result drastically reduces the number of possible similarities in the automaton A; we will see that we need to check for similarities only between states considered in Lemma 2 and the other states in A.

Lemma 3. *The states $(p, k+1)$ and $(q, k+1)$ are dissimilar if $level_A(p, k+1) = level_C(p)$ and $level_A(q, k + 1) = level_C(q)$.*

Proof. Assume they are similar. Therefore, using the definitions of similarity and *gap*, we have that $gap_A((p, k+1), (q, k+1)) + \max(level_A(p, k+1), level_A(q, k+1)) > l$. Since the states did not change their levels ($level_A(p, k + 1) = level_C(p)$ and $level_A(q, k + 1) = level_C(q)$) and the function *gap* does not change for pairs of states with $k + 1$ on the second component, we have that $gap_C(p, q) + \max(level_C(p), level_C(q)) > l$, which means $p \sim_C q$, contradicting our assumption of minimality for C. □

Following the result in Lemma 3, our algorithm needs to identify only the similarities between the states of the type (s_i, i) or $(s_i, k + 1)$ and all the other states in the automaton (including similarities between these states).

To achieve this goal we will store in memory all the computed values of *gap* between any two states (from the previous step) and after adding the new word to the language, use this information at the current step to compute/update the similarities between any states.

Let us count how many similarities between "old states" may occur. Any two states q and p are dissimilar in C, but the states $(p, k + 1)$ and $(q, k + 1)$, may become similar. This can happen only if at least one of them changes its level and $gap_A((p, k + 1), (q, k + 1)) + \max\{level_A((p, k + 1)), level_A((q, k + 1))\} > l$, i.e., only when one of them, say p, is equal to s_i, for some $0 \le i \le k$, according to Corollary 1.

Looking only at the $gap_A((s_i, k + 1), (q, k + 1))$ and at the new level(s) for $(s_i, k + 1)$ and $(q, k + 1)$, one can decide immediately whether $(p, k + 1) \sim_A (q, k + 1)$ or not. To compute the (new) levels in A we need to do this just for states $(s_i, k + 1)$, which takes at most $O(n)$ steps. To decide all the similarities between states of the type $(s_i, k + 1)$ and $(q, k + 1)$, one needs exactly n checks for each state $(s_i, k + 1)$, thus in total $O(kn)$ such comparisons.

We now proceed to detect similarities between the states of the form (s_i, i) with $i \le k$ and the rest of the states. We start with the last final state newly introduced, the state (s_k, k). It is obvious that (s_k, k) is of level k and that using a transition labelled with a letter $a \in \Sigma$, the state (s_k, k) will go into a state of the form $(p, k + 1)$: $\delta_A((s_k, k), a) = (p, k + 1)$. To compute the *gap* between

(s_k, k) and any "old state", assuming that we have the gap table for all pairs of old states (see Remark 2), we use the following lemma.

Lemma 4. *For all $q \in F_C$, we have that*

$$gap_A((s_k, k), (q, k+1)) = 1 + \min_{a \in \Sigma}\{gap_C(\delta_C(s_k, a), \delta_C(q, a))\}.$$

For all $q \in Q_C - F_C$, we have then that $gap_A((s_k, k), (q, k+1)) = 0$.

Proof. Since the gap between states with $k+1$ on the second component is not changed as observed in Remark 2, and $(\delta_C(s_k, a), \delta_C(q, a)) \in Q_C \times \{k+1\}$, by the definition of gap we obtain:

$$\begin{aligned} gap_A((s_k, k), (q, k+1)) &= 1 + \min_{a \in \Sigma}\{gap_A(\delta_A((s_k, k), a), \delta_A((q, k+1), a))\} \\ &= 1 + \min_{a \in \Sigma}\{gap_C(\delta_C(s_k, a), \delta_C(p, a))\}. \end{aligned}$$

The second part of the lemma is obvious. $\qquad\qquad\square$

Once the gap between (s_k, k) and all the original states is computed, then the gap between the state $(s_{k-1}, k-1)$ and all the old states plus (s_k, k) can be computed using a similar observation to Lemma 4. Denote by $S_m = \{(s_i, i) \mid i \geq m\} \cup \{(p, k+1) \mid p \in Q_C\}$, where $1 \leq m \leq k$.

Lemma 5. *Assume that the gap_A was computed between all pairs of states in S_m. Then one can compute the gap_A for all pairs of states from S_{m-1}.*

Proof. Since $S_m \subset S_{m-1}$, we already have most of the values of gap_A computed; we only need to determine gap_A for $(s_{m-1}, m-1)$ and all the states from S_m. We notice that in one step the states $(s_{m-1}, m-1)$ and $(p, j) \in S_m$ will go in states from S_m, i.e., $\delta_A((s_{m-1}, m-1), a), \delta_A((p, j), a) \in S_m$, for all $a \in \Sigma$, thus the gap_A for S_{m-1} can be computed. $\qquad\qquad\square$

The exact formula to "extend" the gap_A from S_m to S_{m-1} is given by the following lemma.

Lemma 6. *For any state $q \in Q_C$ and for any $0 \leq i < k$ we have:*

if $(s_i, i) \in F_A$ and $(q, k+1) \in Q_A - F_A$ or vice versa, then $gap_A((s_i, i), (q, k+1)) = 0$;

if $(s_i, i) \in F_A$ and $(q, k+1) \in F_A$, then the gap can be computed as follows:

$$gap_A((s_i, i), (q, k+1)) = 1 + \min_{a \in \Sigma}\{gap_A(\delta_A((s_i, i), a), \delta_A((q, k+1), a))\} =$$

$$\min(\{gap_A((s_{i+1}, i+1), (\delta_C(q, w_i), k+1))\} \cup \{gap_C(\delta_C(s_i, a), \delta_C(q, a)) \mid a \in \Sigma - \{w_i\}\}).$$

We can have a small speedup for the gap computation in the implementation of the algorithm by noticing that $gap_A((s_i, i), (p, k+1)) = gap_C(s_i, p)$ if $gap_C(s_i, p) < k - i$ for all $0 \leq i \leq k - 1$.

Lemma 4 and Lemma 6 suggest the work of the algorithm. We first compute the gap between (s_k, k) and the old states; we now have the gap computed between all the states in S_k. At the second step we can compute the gap between $(s_{k-1}, k-1)$ and the states from S_k obtaining gap for S_{k-1}. At the next step we can compute the gap between $(s_{k-2}, k-2)$ and states from S_{k-1} using values of gap computed for S_{k-1} obtaining gap for S_{k-2}. The process can be iterated up until we have computed all the gap function for S_0, which is actually the gap for all pairs of states in Q_A.

Once the gap matrix is fully computed, the similarities between any two states $p, q \in Q_A$ can be determined easily by checking the levels of p, q and the $gap_A(p, q)$ using Remark 3. We do this just for the "cloned" states and "original" states that change their levels, since all the other pairs of states are dissimilar by Lemma 3.

The Incremental Algorithm: We give now a sketch for the incremental algorithm proposed; a more detailed pseudocode can be found in the appendix along with the C++ source code (implementation in the Grail+ package).

```
Input C, gapC, w, k, l
Output A, gapA
Build A as, described in subsection 3.1
Do a breath first search to compute levelA(p,i) for all (p,i) ∈ QA.
For all q ∈ QC
    Compute gapA((sk,k),(q,k+1)) (cf. Lemma 4)
For i=k-1 down to 0
    For all q ∈ QC
        Compute gapA((si,i),(q,k+1)) (cf. Lemma 6)
For all q ∈ FC
    Compute similarity for the pairs (sk,k), (q,k+1).
For i=k-1 down to 0
    For j=k+1 down to i+1
        Compute similarity for the pairs (si,k+1),(sj,k+1),
For i=k-1 down to 0
    For all q ∈ QC
        Compute similarity for the pairs (si,i),(q,k+1).
Reduce the automaton by merging similar states.
```

The algorithm has been implemented in Grail+ and was tested against the algorithm presented in [15]. The source code of the implementation as well as the Grail+ updated version will be made available by e-mail request and also at the address http://www.latech.edu/~apaun/cover.html. The test language chosen was $L_k = \{w \mid |w| = k\}$ since it was expected that this language will provide good compression results for the DFCA. We obtained the following results[1] that show an excellent performance of our method for the chosen test language. He have been running both algorithms on the same computer (CPU: Pentium

---

[1] It is worth mentioning that the words were inserted incrementally in the standard lexicographical order to the cover automaton. We do not believe that this fact had a significant influence on the time/space efficiency of the proposed algorithm.

4 3.4 GHz; Memory: 1GB DDR400; OS: Linux 2.6.8.1 kernel (Slackware 10.0)).
In the table we give the name of the algorithm, the maximum number of states
in the memory during the execution of the algorithm, the maximum memory
space needed, and the time required for the algorithm to finish (for the Körner
algorithm we give the time required without and then with the trie building).

Algorithm	States	Memory req.	Time/time with trie	l	Alphabet size
Körner	3905	70k	1.512s/1.961s	5	5
Incremnt.	18	1.8k	0.461s	5	5
Körner	19530	1.4M	40.52s/52.706s	6	5
Incremnt.	21	2.2k	3.196s	6	5
Körner	97655	7.0M	24min 49.26s/34min 6.944s	7	5
Incremnt.	24	2.7k	22.420s	7	5

3.2   Adding a Word of Length $|w| = k > l$

We start the discussion in this case by noting that if there exists $x \in L$, such
that $l < |xu| \le k$ and $\delta_C(0, x) = \delta_C(0, xu) = p$ (where $p \in Q_C$), then we need to
"split" the state p, otherwise the word xu of length less than or equal to k will
be also considered in the new cover language. In other words, to make sure that
no other words are in the language accepted by the new DFCA A, all loops in
C must be expanded to chains of length at least l. However, any chain of length
greater than l should go in a "sink" state with the last transition of that chain
because we accept only one word of length greater than l. We will construct the
new automaton as having the level encoded in the state; thus, the states will be
of the form (p, i), where $p \in Q_C$ and $level_A((p, i)) = i$ (the level information will
be attached to each state by construction).

We construct the following DFCA: $A = (\Sigma, Q_A, \delta_A, (n, 0), F_A)$, where:

$$\delta_A((p, i), a) = \begin{cases} (\delta_C(p, a), i+1) & \text{if } i \le l, \\ (\delta_C(s_i, a), i+1) & \text{if } i \le l, \ p = n \text{ and } w_{i+1} \ne a, \\ (n, i+1) & \text{if } p = n \text{ and } w_{i+1} = a, \\ (n, k+1) & \text{in all other cases.} \end{cases}$$

$F_A = \{(q, s) \mid q \in F_C, s \le l\} \cup \{(n, k)\} \cup \{(n, i) \mid s_i \in F_C\}$.
Of course, $Q_A \subset Q_C \times \{0, 1, \ldots, k+1\}$.

Lemma 7. *The DFA A constructed above is accepting $L(A) = L \cup \{w\}$.*

Proof. Let $x \in L$: if x is not a prefix of w, then $\delta_A((n, 0), x) = (\delta_C(0, x), |x|)$.
Since $x \in L$, we have that $\delta_C(0, x) \in F_C$, thus by the definition of F_A and
because $|x| \le l$, we also have that $(\delta_C(0, x), |x|) \in F_A$. This means that if x is
not a prefix of w then $x \in L(A)$.

If x is a prefix of w, i.e., $x = w_1 \ldots w_i$ we also have that $\delta_A((n, 0), x) =
(n, |x|) = (n, i)$. But $(n, i) \in F_A$ if and only if $s_i \in F_C$, which is true if
$x = w_1 \ldots w_i$. Therefore, $L \subseteq L(A)$. We also have that $w \in L(A)$, since
$\delta_A((n, 0), w) = (n, k) \in F_A$.

We will now prove that $L(A) \subseteq L \cup \{w\}$: in other words, for the automaton A, if $x \in L(A)$ then $x \in L \cup \{w\}$. Let $x \in L(A)$, i.e., $\delta_A((n,0),x) \in F_A$. We distinguish two cases: when x is not a prefix of w and when x is a prefix of w.

In the first case, $\delta_A((n,0),x) = (\delta_C(0,x),|x|)$, which implies by the definition of F_A that $|x| \leq l$. But since $\delta_C(0,x) \in F_C$ and $|x| \leq l$, it follows that $x \in L$.

In the second case, x is a prefix of w, so $\delta_A((n,0),x) = (n,|x|)$. Since $x \in L(A)$, $(n,|x|)$ needs to be final in A, thus either $|x| = i$ where $s_i \in F_C$ or $|x| = k$. In other words, x is a prefix of w that is in L or $x = w$, i.e., $x \in L \cup \{w\}$. □

We now describe the properties of the automaton A: we can easily see that $level_A(p,i)) \geq level_C(p)$ for all possible values of p and i. Also, one can note that the state $(n,k+1)$ is a sink state and $level_A((n,k+1)) = l+1$.

Since this automaton has a particular form, we can speed up the process of completing the gap table for the new automaton by giving some formulas for particular pairs of states.

Remark 4. 1. All states (p,l), with $p \in F_C$ are final and they are equivalent to (n,k). Therefore, they can be merged together; the gap between these states is $k+1$.

2. The sink state $(n,k+1)$, is similar with all non-final states which cannot reach a final state with a word of length at most $k-l-1$.

3. The gap between the sink state and (n,k) (final state) is 0.

Using the above remarks and a technique similar to the one in [22] we can now compute the gap function for all states of A. For our algorithm we only need to compute the gap function for the sink state $(n,k+1)$ and all other states. This is done using a BFS traversal for each final state of the graph associated with the new DFA while considering the arrows reversed.

Once we have the gap computed for the sink state and all other states we can proceed to the next step.

Let us compute $gap_A((p,i),(q,j))$ for states $p,q \in Q_C$, and $i,j \leq l$.

Remark 5. If $gap_C(p,q) + \max(i,j) \leq l$, $gap_A((p,i),(q,j)) = gap_C(p,q)$.

For the states with higher levels, i.e., $gap(p,q) + \max(i,j) > l$, one can compute the gap_A table using the technique for computing gap for a (not necessarily minimal) DFA as in [16].

For computing the gap function between the states (n,i) and all other states we use the same technique used in Lemma 6. Due to the space limitations, we leave the details of updating the gap function to the reader.

The minimization algorithm for this case is basically the same as for the case $|w| < l$, with the following differences:

1. the initial construction has to embed the level in the name of the state, and we do this up to level l;
2. we first compute the gap between the sink state $(n,k+1)$ and all other states;
3. the "old" states having several levels will inherit the gap table from C as described in Remark 5;

4. the next steps are the same as in [16], computing the gap function for the "newly introduced" states, using a formula as given below:

$$gap_A((n,i),(p,j)) = \begin{cases} 0, \text{ if } s_i \in F_C \text{ and } p \notin F_C \text{ or } s_i \notin F_C \text{ and } p \in F_C \\ 1 + \min\{gap_A(\delta_A((n,i),a),\delta_A((p,j),a)) \mid a \in \Sigma\}, \\ \qquad\qquad\qquad\qquad\qquad\qquad\qquad\qquad\text{otherwise.} \end{cases}$$

Due to the space limitations, we leave the details of updating the gap function and the details (e.g., pseudocode) of the algorithm to the reader.

Remark 6. The time complexity for adding a word of length k greater than l increases significantly, since each time we "expand" the DFCA for l to a DFA for $L \cup \{w\}$ we can have an explosion in the number of states. This behavior is expected mostly in the case when n is much smaller than k.

To avoid such explosions, the best choice is to start the incremental algorithm with the longest word in the language. When this cannot be done due to specific restrictions imposed by the problem/language considered, one should try to add it as soon as possible.

4   Final Remarks

Our incremental algorithm described in section 3.1 is fast, but it was observed (see e.g.[10]) that such an incremental algorithm could be modified to run even faster if one can perform a preprocessing (which is in fact sorting) of the input set of strings. We already have good results in this direction and submission of another paper describing an incremental algorithm for sorted input data is expected. The string subtraction has a similar algorithm to the string addition. We also devised a string subtraction algorithm, but due to the space limitation of the contribution we have not included it. We also plan to conduct more experiments using real dictionaries and compare the difference in the memory requirements between our incremental algorithms and other DFCA minimization algorithms. It is also worth noting that the string addition algorithm for the case when $|w| > l$ can produce a high number of states, thus it is now efficient to first scan the words in the language and find the longest word (requires $O(n)$ time), and then to start the algorithm with the longest word in L. The discussion for the case $|w| > l$ is valuable if one needs the ability to update (maybe later) the language; for example, adding a new word to a spellchecker should permit also the addition of longer words. It is open whether a faster algorithm for the case $|w| > l$ can be devised, or whether one can design an incremental algorithm of linear space for the string addition into the language of a DFCA.

Acknowledgments

We would like to mention the DFCA fruitful discussions with S. Yu and the insightful suggestions received from the anonymous referees. C. Câmpeanu gratefully acknowledges the support received from NSERC DGP-I249600; A. Păun gratefully acknowledges the support in part by a LA BoR RSC grant and NSF IMR-0414903.

References

1. Carrasco, R.C., Forcada, M.L.: Incremental construction and maintenence of minimal finite-state automata. Computational Linguistics **28** 2 (2002) 207–216
2. Daciuk, J., Mihov, S., Watson, B., Watson, R.E.: Incremental construction of minimal acyclic finite state automata. Computational Linguistics **26** 1 (2000) 3–16
3. Daciuk, J.: Comparison of construction algorithms for minimal, acyclic, deterministic, finite-state automata from sets of strings. Lecture Notes in Computer Science **2608** (2003) 255–261
4. Mihov, S.: Direct construction of minimal acyclic finite states automata. Ann. de l'Université de Sofia "St. Kl. Ohridski", Faculté de Mathematique et Informatique, Sofia, Bulgaria **92** 2 (1998)
5. Sgarbas, K.N., Fakotakis, N.D., Kokkinakis, G.K.: Optimal insertion in deterministic DAWGs. Theoretical Computer Science **301** 1(3) (2003) 103–117
6. Sgarbas, K.N., Fakotakis, N.D., Kokkinakis, G.K.: Two algorithms for incremental construction of directed acyclic word graphs. International Journal on Artificial Intelligence Tools, World Scientific **4** 3 (1995) 369–381
7. Watson, B.W.: A taxonomy of finite automata minimization algorithms. Eindhoven University of Technology, The Netherlands, Computing Science Note **93/44** (1993)
8. Watson, B.W.: Taxonomies and Toolkits of Regular Language Algorithms. Ph.D. thesis, Eindhoven University of Technology, the Netherlands (1995)
9. Watson, B.W.: An incremental DFA minimization algorithm. Finite State Methods in Natural Language Processing; ESSLLI Workshop, Helsinki, Finland, August (2001) 20–24
10. Watson, B.W., Daciuk, J.: An efficient incremental DFA minimization algorithm. Natural Language Engineering **9** 1 (2003) 49–64
11. Câmpeanu, C., Sântean, N., Yu, S.: Minimal cover-automata for finite languages. Theoretical Computer Science **267** 1-2 (2001) 3–16
12. Câmpeanu, C., Păun, A., Kari, L.: Results on transforming NFA into DFCA. Fundamenta Informaticae **64** 1-4 (2005) 53–63
13. Câmpeanu, C., Păun, A.: Counting the number of minimal DFCA obtained by merging states. International Journal of Foundations of Computer Science **14** 6 (2003) 995–1006
14. Câmpeanu, C., Păun, A.: Lower bounds for NFA to DFCA transformations. Proceedings of DFCS 2004, London Ontario, Canada, (2004) 121–130
15. Körner, H.: A time and space efficient algorithm for minimizing cover automata for finite languages. International Journal of Foundations of Computer Science **14** 6 (2003) 1071–1086
16. Păun, A., Sântean, N., Yu, S.: An $O(n^2)$ algorithm for minimal cover-automata for finite languages. Proceedings of the 5th International Conference on Implementation and Application of Automata Implementing Automata CIAA'00 (2000) 243–251
17. Sântean, N.: Towards a Minimal Representation for Finite Languages: Theory and Practice. MSc thesis, Department of Computer Science, The University of Western Ontario, Canada (2000)

102   C. Câmpeanu, A. Păun, and J.R. Smith

18. World Wide Web: The Grail+ project. A symbolic computation environ-
    ment for finite-state machines, regular expressions, and finite languages (2002)
    http://www.csd.uwo.ca/Research/grail.
19. Hopcroft, J.E., Ullman, J.D.: Introduction to Automata Theory, Languages and
    Computation. Addison-Wesley (1979)
20. Salomaa, A.: Formal Languages. Academic Press (1973)
21. Yu, S.: Regular languages. Handbook of Formal Languages, Vol I, eds. G. Rozen-
    berg and A. Salomaa, Springer-Verlag (1997) 41–110
22. Câmpeanu, C., Păun, A., Yu, S.: An efficient algorithm for constructing mini-
    mal cover automata for finite languages. International Journal of Foundations of
    Computer Science **13** 1 (2002) 83–98

A   The Pseudocode for the Algorithm

Input: A DFCA $C = (\Sigma, Q, 0, \delta, F)$ for the language L with the length of the largest word l. We also have as input the new word to be introduced w with $|w| \leq l$, and the precomputed arrays $level$ and gap which store the levels of the states and the gaps between states, respectively.

Output: A DFCA $A = (\Sigma, Q', 0', \delta', F')$ for the language $L \cup \{w\}$ with the arrays $level$ and gap updated.

if $w \in L$ or if $|w| > l$ return   /* do nothing in these cases*/
let $k = |w|$
create $k + 1$ new states with the labels $n, n + 1, \ldots, n + k - 1, n + k$
create the arrays old of size $k + 1$ and $merged$ of size $n + k + 1$ initialized with
0. $old[0] = 0$
for i=1 to k do $old[i] = \delta(old[i - 1], w[i])$
$new = n$
for i=0 to $k - 1$ do
        for all $a \in \Sigma$ do $\delta(new, a) = \delta(old[i], a)$
        $\delta(new, w[i]) = new + 1$; $new = new + 1$
for all $a \in \Sigma$ do $\delta(n + k, a) = \delta(old[k], a)$
Apply the Breadth First algorithm starting in n and compute/update the levels
of all states $old[i]$ with $0 \leq i \leq k$. If such a state p becomes unreachable, then
$merged[p] = 1$
for j=0 to $n - 1$ do /*we compute the gaps between old states and $n + k$*/
        if $j \notin F$ then $gap[n + k, j] = 0$; $gap[j, n + k] = 0$
            else $min = l + 1$
                for all $a \in \Sigma$ do
                    $currentgap = gap[\delta(j, a), \delta(old[k], a)]$
                    if $min > currentgap$ then $min = currentgap$
                $gap[n + k, j] = min + 1$; $gap[j, n + k] = min + 1$
for $i = n + k - 1$ down to n do
        for $j = 0$ to $n - 1$ do /*find the gaps between i and the old states*/
            min=l+1
            for all $a \in \Sigma$ do

$$currentgap = gap[\delta(j,a), \delta(i,a)]$$
$$\text{if } min > currentgap \text{ then } min = currentgap$$
$$gap[i,j] = min + 1; \ gap[j,i] = min + 1$$

for $j = i + 1$ to $n + k$ do /*find the gaps between the new states*/
$$gap[i,j] = min(gap[old[i-n],j], gap[\delta(i,w[i-n]), \delta(j,w[i-n])]+1)$$

/* We have the *gap* matrix completely computed, thus the similarities between the new states and the old states can now be detected */

for $j=0$ to k do
    if $old[j] \neq i$ and $merged[i] + merged[j] == 0$ then
        $lev = max(level[old[j]], level[i])$
        if $gap[old[j],i] + lev > l$ then merge(i, old[j])

for $i = n + k$ dow to n do
    for $j = i - 1$ down to 0 do
        if $merged[j] == 0$ then $lev = max(level[i], level[j])$
            if $gap[i,j] + lev > l$ then merge(i,j)

/* We now delete the rows and columns from the matrix *gap* for the states that were deleted (either merged or unreachable)*/

swap(0,n) /* the new start state n is swapped with the old start state*/
$i = 1; j = n + k$
while $i < j$ do
    while $merged[j] == 1$ do $j = j - 1$ /*j points to the last state that does not disappear*/
    while $merged[i] == 0$ do $i = i + 1$ /* i points to the first state that disappears */
    swap(i,j) /* we update the *gap level* and *merged* arrays*/
    i=i+1; j=j-1

Finite Automata and Unions of Regular Patterns with Bounded Constant Segments

Antonio Cano and Pedro García

Departamento de Sistemas Informáticos y Computación,
Universidad Politécnica de Valencia, Valencia, Spain
{acano, pgarcia}@dsic.upv.es

Abstract. The class of unbounded unions of regular pattern languages with bounded constant segments is identifiable from positive data in the limit [1]. Otherwise, no efficient algorithm that performs the inference of this class of languages is known. We propose a solution to this problem using the existing connexion between the positive variety of languages of dot depth 1/2, $\mathcal{LJ}^+$ [2] and the class of unbounded union of pattern languages $\mathcal{RP}^+\mathcal{L}$.

1 Introduction

Pattern languages have been introduced by Angluin in [3], where she has shown that they are identifiable from positive data. They have been used for machine discovery of protein motifs from amino acid sequences in [4].

A pattern is a word on the alphabet $\Sigma \cup X$, where Σ is a finite alphabet (of constant symbols) and X is a disjoint countable alphabet (of variables). Given a pattern p, the language $L(p)$ is defined as the set of words on Σ obtained by replacing the variables in p by constant words.

The class of pattern languages is efficiently identifiable from positive data in the limit [3]. From the point of view of applications, the use of only one pattern is not enough flexible and it would be more interesting to use several patterns. The problem for doing so is that the class of pattern languages is not closed under union. If we consider the closure under union of the class of pattern languages $\mathcal{P}^+\mathcal{L}$ we obtain a class (unbounded unions of pattern languages) that is not identifiable from positive samples, as any word $w \in \Sigma^*$ is also a pattern such that $L(w) = \{w\}$ and, consequently, the class of unions of pattern languages contains every finite language and also some infinite languages. The same problem still remains when we consider the union of regular pattern languages $\mathcal{RP}^+\mathcal{L}$, that is, patterns in which any variable occurs at most once in the pattern. Shinohara and Arimura [1] have considered an interesting restriction of the class of unbounded unions of regular pattern languages, for any $k > 0$ they consider the class of unions of pattern in which the length of the constant segments is bounded by k (unbounded union of regular pattern languages with bounded constant segments $(\mathcal{RP}_k^+\mathcal{L})$). In other words, a language belongs to $\mathcal{RP}^+\mathcal{L}$ if and only if it belongs to $\mathcal{RP}_k^+\mathcal{L}$ for some $k > 0$. For any k, $\mathcal{RP}_k^+$ is identifiable from positive data in the

J. Farré, I. Litovsky, and S. Schmitz (Eds.): CIAA 2005, LNCS 3845, pp. 104–115, 2006.
© Springer-Verlag Berlin Heidelberg 2006

limit [1]. The proof given by Shinohara and Arimura uses a theorem of Higman on well-quasi ordering. Nevertheless, they do not give an efficient algorithm to identify any class $\mathcal{RP}_k^+\mathcal{L}$.

In this work we propose an efficient algorithm for the inference of $\mathcal{RP}_k^+\mathcal{L}$ using a relation between $\mathcal{RP}^+\mathcal{L}$ and the positive variety of languages $\mathcal{LJ}^+$ [2], also known as languages of dot-depth 1/2.

We show here that, for any $k > 0$, $\mathcal{RP}_k^+\mathcal{L} \subseteq \mathcal{LJ}_{k+1}^+$. From this fact and from the relation $\mathbf{LJ}_k^+ = \mathbf{J}^+ * \mathbf{LI}_k$ [5] the problem of the inference of $\mathcal{RP}_k^+\mathcal{L}$ from positive data can be solved in an easy way through the scheme of inference of languages in varieties of the form $\mathbf{V} * \mathbf{LI}$ proposed in [6] and [7]. So, we give an efficient algorithm to learn languages from $\mathcal{RP}_k^+\mathcal{L}$.

2   Preliminaries

In this section we will describe some facts about formal languages in order to make the notation understandable to the reader. For further details about the definitions, the reader is referred to [8].

Let Σ be a finite alphabet and let Σ^* be the free monoid generated by Σ with concatenation as the binary operation and ϵ as neutral element, and let Σ^+ be the free semigroup generated by Σ with concatenation as the binary operation. Any subset $L \subseteq \Sigma^*$ is called *language*, we will refer to its elements as *words* and the length of a word will be denoted as $|x|$. Let Σ^k (resp. $\Sigma^{\leq k}$) be the set of word of length k (resp. less than or equal to k) on Σ^*.

Given $x \in \Sigma^*$, if $x = uvw$ with $u, v, w \in \Sigma^*$, then u (resp. w) is called *prefix* (resp. *suffix*) of x, whereas v is called a *segment* of x. The set of prefixes (resp. suffixes) of a word x will be denoted as $Pr(x)$ (resp. $Suf(x)$). We will also denote by $Pr_k(x)$ the prefix of length k of x (resp. by $Suf_k(x)$ the suffix of length k of x). Given $x, y \in \Sigma^*$, we say that $x = a_1 a_2 \cdots a_n$, with $a_i \in \Sigma$, $i = 1, 2, \ldots, n$ is a *subword* of y, and we denote this relationship by $x \mid y$ if $y = z_0 a_1 z_1 a_2 \cdots a_n z_n$, with $z_i \in \Sigma^*$ for $i = 0, 1, \ldots, n$.

A Nondeterministic Finite Automaton (*NFA*) is defined as a quintuple $\mathcal{A} = (Q, \Sigma, \delta, Q_0, F)$ where Q is a finite set of states, Σ is a finite alphabet, $Q_0 \subseteq Q$ is the set of initial states, $F \subseteq Q$ is the set of final states and δ is a partial function from $Q \times \Sigma$ into $\mathcal{P}(Q)$, which can be extended to a function from $\mathcal{P}(Q) \times \Sigma$ into $\mathcal{P}(Q)$ by establishing $\delta(Q', a) = \bigcup_{q \in Q'} \delta(q, a)$ for any $Q' \subseteq Q$ and $a \in \Sigma$. It can also be extended to a function from $\mathcal{P}(Q) \times \Sigma^*$ into $\mathcal{P}(Q)$ by establishing $\delta(Q', \epsilon) = Q'$ and $\delta(Q', xa) = \delta(\delta(Q', x), a)$, for every $Q' \subseteq Q$, $x \in \Sigma^*$ and $a \in \Sigma$. If in the previous definition we take $Q_0 = \{q_0\}$ with $q_0 \in Q$ and δ as a function from $Q \times \Sigma^*$ into Q, we obtain the definition of Deterministic Finite Automaton (*DFA*).

A word x is accepted by an automaton $\mathcal{A}$ if $\delta((Q_0), x) \cap F \neq \emptyset$. The set of words accepted by $\mathcal{A}$ is denoted by $L(\mathcal{A})$.

A sequential machine is a sextuple $\mathcal{A} = (Q, \Sigma, \Delta, \delta, \lambda, F)$ where Q, Σ and δ are defined in the same way as in a DFA, Δ is the output alphabet and the output function λ is a function that maps $Q \times \Sigma$ into Δ^*, which can be extended to $Q \times \Sigma^*$ by establishing $\lambda(q, \epsilon) = \epsilon$, and $\lambda(q, xa) = \lambda(q, x)\lambda(\delta(q, x), a)$, for every $q \in Q$, $x \in \Sigma^*$ and $a \in \Sigma$.

We use the model of learning called identification in the limit [9]. An algorithm A identifies a class of languages H *in the limit* if and only if for any $L \in H$, on input of any presentation of L, the infinite sequence of output languages obtained by A converges to L.

2.1   Formal Languages

A language is of level $1/2$ in the Straubing-Thérien hierarchy if it is a finite union of languages of the form $\Sigma^* a_1 \Sigma^* a_2 \Sigma^* \cdots \Sigma^* a_n \Sigma^*$, where $a_1, \ldots, a_n \in \Sigma$. The family of languages of level $1/2$ in the Straubing-Thérien's hierarchy forms the positive variety $\mathcal{J}^+$ corresponding to the variety of ordered monoids $\mathbf{J}^+$ [5].

The languages of dot-depth $1/2$ are finite unions of languages of the form $u_0 \Sigma^* u_1 \Sigma^* \cdots u_{k-1} \Sigma^* u_k$, where $k \geq 0$ and $u_0, \ldots, u_k \in \Sigma^*$. The family of languages of dot-depth $1/2$ forms the positive variety $\mathcal{LJ}^+$ corresponding to the variety of ordered semigroups $\mathbf{LJ}^+$ [5].

The next theoretical result comes from [5] and characterizes some subclasses of $\mathcal{LJ}^+$.

Given some words $u_1, u_2, \ldots, u_n$ of the same length, we define

$$L(u_1, \ldots, u_n) = \{u \in \Sigma^+ \mid u_1, \ldots, u_n \text{ occur in this order as segments of } u\}$$

If we set $u = u_1 u_2 \cdots u_n \in (\Sigma^k)^*$ with $u_i \in \Sigma^k$ for $i \in \{1, \ldots, n\}$, we also denote $L(u_1, \ldots, u_n)$ by $L(u)$.

Theorem 1. *[5] Let L be a language of Σ^+. The following conditions are equivalent.*

(1) *L is of dot-depth $1/2$,*

(2) *L is a finite union of languages of the form $\{u\}$, with $|u| < k - 1$ or $p\Sigma^* \cap L(u_1, \ldots, u_n) \cap \Sigma^* s$, where, for some $k > 1$, $p, s \in \Sigma^{k-1}$ and $u_1, \ldots, u_n$ is a sequence of words of Σ^k.*

For a given $k > 0$, we will denote by $\mathcal{LJ}_k^+$ the languages defined in (2).

It is known that $\mathbf{LJ}^+ = \mathbf{J}^+ * \mathbf{LI}$ and that $\mathbf{LJ}_k^+ = \mathbf{J}^+ * \mathbf{LI}_k$ [5].

$\mathbf{LI}$ is the variety of locally trivial finite semigroups. For any $k > 0$ the variety of languages corresponding to $\mathbf{LI}_k$ consists of languages of the form $X \Sigma^* Y \cup Z$ with $X, Y \subseteq \Sigma^k$ and $Z \subseteq \Sigma^{<k}$, some other definition can be found in [10].

2.2   Pattern Languages

Let Σ be a set of constant symbols containing at least two symbols, and X be a countable set of variable symbols. We assume that $\Sigma \cap X = \emptyset$. A pattern p is a word on $(\Sigma \cup X)^*$. Note that we consider the empty word ϵ. We denote by $\mathcal{P}$ the set of all patterns. The length of a pattern $p \in \mathcal{P}$, will be denoted by $|p|$. A substitution ρ is a homomorphism from patterns to patterns that maps every constant to itself. For a pattern p and a substitution ρ. We say that a pattern

q is a *generalization* of p, or p is an instance of q, and we denote that fact by $p \preceq q$, if there is a substitution ρ such that $\rho(q) = p$.

The language defined by a pattern $p \in \mathcal{P}$ is the set $L(p) = \{w \in \Sigma^* \mid w \preceq p\}$. We denote by $\mathcal{PL}$ the class of all pattern languages.

In this paper, we are specially concerned about a subclass of $\mathcal{P}$. A pattern $p \in \mathcal{P}$ is regular, if each variable appears at most once in p, i. e. for any $x \in X$, the number of occurrences of x in p $|p|_x \leq 1$. A *regular pattern language* is a pattern language defined by a regular pattern. We denote by $\mathcal{RP}$ the set of all regular patters, and by $\mathcal{RPL}$ the set of all regular patterns languages.

We are also concerned with unions of languages defined by patterns. By $\mathcal{P}^+$ we denote the class of all nonempty finite subsets of $\mathcal{P}$. Analogously, by $\mathcal{RP}^+$ we denote the class of all nonempty finite subsets of $\mathcal{RP}$, and by $\mathcal{RP}^+\mathcal{L}$ the corresponding class of languages.

The next proposition shows that the class of unions of pattern languages is exactly the positive variety $\mathcal{LJ}^+$.

Proposition 1. *The class of unions of regular pattern languages $\mathcal{RP}^+\mathcal{L}$ is the positive variety of languages $\mathcal{LJ}^+$.*

Proof. By the definition of $\mathcal{LJ}^+$, it suffices to see that for any pattern p, $L(p) = u_0 \Sigma^* u_1 \Sigma^* \cdots u_{k-1} \Sigma^* u_k$, for some $k \geq 0$ and $u_0, \ldots, u_k \in \Sigma^*$, and that for any language L in this form, there exists a pattern p, such that $L(p) = L$. □

Finally we are interested in unions of bounded pattern languages. Given an integer $k \geq 0$ a k-bounded pattern is a pattern that has at most k constant consecutive symbols. We will denote the set of all these patterns as $\mathcal{P}_k$, and as in the previous cases we will denote by $\mathcal{RP}_k$ and $\mathcal{RP}_k\mathcal{L}$, the sets of k-bounded regular patterns and k-bounded regular pattern languages. From the definition of bounded pattern we obtain the definition of union of k-bounded regular pattern and k-bounded regular pattern languages, that will be denoted by $\mathcal{RP}_k^+$ and $\mathcal{RP}_k^+\mathcal{L}$ respectively.

3   Inferring $\mathcal{J}^+$

In this section we describe an algorithm for the inference of languages that belongs to $\mathcal{J}^+$.

Given a sample $S = \{x_1, x_2, \ldots, x_n\}$ we can associate a language $L_{\mathcal{J}+S} \in \mathcal{J}^+$ as follows

$$L_{\mathcal{J}+S} = \{x \in \Sigma^* \mid \text{ there exists } i \in \{1, \ldots, n\} \text{ such that } x_i \mid x\}.$$

Proposition 2. *$L_{\mathcal{J}+S}$ is the smallest language in $\mathcal{J}^+$ that contains S.*

Proof. If $K \in \mathcal{J}^+$ and $w \in K$, any word x such that $w \mid x$ belongs to K. If furthermore $S \subseteq K$, K contains all words x such that $x_i \mid x$ for some $x_i \in S$. And then, $L_{\mathcal{J}+S} \subseteq K$. □

Algorithm 1 yields a NFA by constructing for every word x_i an automaton that accepts all words which have x_i as subwords, we order S and check the acceptance of any word before constructing the automaton in order to save automaton size.

For the study of the convergence of Algorithm 1 we have that for any alphabet Σ and any language $L \in \mathcal{J}^+(\Sigma^*)$, L can be written as $\bigcup_{1 \le i \le m} \Sigma^* a_{i,1} \Sigma^* \cdots \Sigma^* a_{i,n_i} \Sigma^*$. Then, if we use as input of the algorithm the set $S = \{a_{1,1} \cdots a_{1,n_1}, \ldots, a_{m,1} \cdots a_{m,n_m}\}$, we have that $L_{\mathcal{J}+S} = L$, and the result follows from Proposition 2.

The time complexity of Algorithm 1 is $N \cdot \Sigma$. Let $S = \{x_1, x_2, \ldots, x_n\}$ and let $N = |x_1| + |x_2| + \cdots + |x_n|$. As for any $i \in \{1, \ldots, n\}$ The $\mathcal{J}^+$ Inference Algorithm constructs an automaton whose number of states is $|x_i| + 1$, having every state at most $|\Sigma|$ transitions, the complexity of the algorithm is $N \cdot \Sigma$. Nevertheless, if we consider an implementation where the construction of transitions is linear, the overall algorithm complexity would be linear with the size of the input data.

Algorithm 1. $\mathcal{J}^+$ Inference
Input: S set of words over Σ^*
Output: NFA $\mathcal{A} = (Q, \Sigma, \delta, Q_0, F)$, such that $L(\mathcal{A}) = L_{\mathcal{J}+S}$
Method:
$Q = \emptyset$; $\delta = \emptyset$; $F = \emptyset$; $Q_0 = \emptyset$
Order S by decreasing length as: $S = \{x_1, x_2, \ldots, x_m\}$
For $x_i = a_1 a_2 \ldots a_n \in S$ **Do**
   If $\delta(Q_0, x) \cap F = \emptyset$ **Then**
      $Q = Q \cup \{(i, 0), (i, 1), \ldots, (i, n)\}$
      For $j = 0$ **To** $n - 1$ **Do**
         $\delta = \delta \cup ((i, j), a_j, (i, j + 1))$
         For $c \in \Sigma \backslash \{a_j\}$
            $\delta = \delta \cup ((i, j), c, (i, j))$
      For $c \in \Sigma$
         $\delta = \delta \cup ((i, n), c, (i, n))$
      $Q_0 = Q_0 \cup \{(i, 0)\}$
      $F = F \cup \{(i, n)\}$
   Return $(\mathcal{A})$

---

4   Inferring $\mathcal{LJ}^+$

We recall the following definitions and theorems that will lead us in the inference process. We follow a similar scheme to the scheme used in [6, 7].

Theorem 2 (Ginzburg and Rose, see [11]). *Let $\tau : \Sigma^* \to \Gamma^*$ be the sequential function realized by the transducer $\tau = (P, \Sigma, \Gamma, \delta_1, \lambda, p_0, F)$ and let $\mathcal{A} = (Q, \Gamma, \delta_2, q_0. F')$ be an automaton such that $L = L(\mathcal{A})$. The language $\tau^{-1}(L) \subseteq \Sigma^*$ is recognized by the cascade product $\mathcal{A} \circ \tau = (Q \times P, A, \delta, [q_0, p_0], F' \times F)$, with the transition function defined as $\delta([q, p], a) = (\delta_2(q, \lambda(p, a)), \delta_1(p, a))$.*

We define now the transduction $\tau_{k,F}$, for k and $F \subseteq \Sigma^{k-1}$, that will be used in the sequel.

Definition 1. *For $k > 0$ and a finite set of word $F \subseteq \Sigma^{k-1}$. Let $\tau_{k,F} = (Q, \Sigma, B, \delta, \lambda, q_0, F \cup \Sigma^{<k-1})$ be a sequential machine defined as $Q = \cup_{i=0}^{k-1} \Sigma^i$, $p_0 = \varepsilon$, $B = \bigcup_{i=1}^{k-1} \natural^{k-i} \Sigma^i \cup \Sigma^k$ and for every $p \in Q$ and $a \in A$, the transition and output functions are respectively defined as:*

$$\delta(p, a) = \begin{cases} pa & \text{if } |p| < k - 1 \\ f_{k-1}(pa) & \text{if } |p| = k - 1 \end{cases} \text{ and}$$

$$\lambda(p, a) = \begin{cases} \natural^{k-|pa|}pa & \text{if } |p| < k - 1 \\ pa & \text{if } |p| = k - 1 \end{cases} .$$

The sequential machine $\tau_{k,F}$, for a given $k > 0$ and a word $x \in \Sigma^*$, outputs a word $\tau_{k.F}(x)$ whose symbols are the segments of length k (considering as initial segments $\natural^{k-1}a_1 \mid \natural^{k-2}a_1a_2 \mid \cdots \mid \natural a_1 \cdots a_{k-2}$ being $w = a_1 \cdots a_n \in Prefix(x)$) of x, in order, and the last segment of length $k-1$ belong to F. Examples of $\tau_{k,F}$ for the values $k = 2$ with $F = \{a\}$ and $k = 3$ with $F = \{aa, bb\}$ for $\Sigma = \{a, b\}$ can be seen in Figure 1.

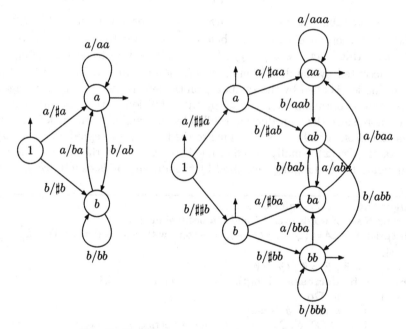

Fig. 1. Transducers $\tau_{2,\{a\}}$ and $\tau_{3,\{aa,bb\}}$

In order to use $\tau_{k,F}$ in some algebraic proofs, we define the morphism h from B^* into $(\Sigma^k)^*$ for any word $b \in B^*$ by setting

$$h(b) = \begin{cases} b & \text{if} \quad b \in \Sigma^k \\ 1 & \text{otherwise} \end{cases}$$

Now, we describe the algorithm 2 in order to infer languages from $\mathcal{LJ}_k^+$. This algorithm will use some of the above elements.

Given a word x, we can associate to this word a language $L_{\mathcal{LJ}_k^+\{x\}}$ in $\mathcal{LJ}_k^+$ as follows,

$$L_{\mathcal{LJ}_k^+\{x\}} = \begin{cases} x & \text{if } |x| < k \\ Pr_{k-1}(x)\Sigma^* \cap L(h(\tau_k(x))) \cap \Sigma^* Suf_{k-1}(x) & \text{if } |x| \geq k. \end{cases}$$

Given a sample $S = \{x_1, x_2, \ldots, x_n\}$, we can extend the previous definition by associating the language $L_{\mathcal{LJ}_k^+ S} \in \mathcal{LJ}^+$ as follows

$$x \in L_{\mathcal{J}_k^+ S} \Leftrightarrow \text{there exists } i, \text{ such that } x \in L_{\mathcal{LJ}_k^+\{x_i\}}.$$

Proposition 3. $L_{\mathcal{LJ}_k^+ S}$ *is the smallest language in* $\mathcal{LJ}_k^+$ *that contains* S.

Proof. It suffices to show that the result holds for $S = \{x\}$ for some $x \in \Sigma^*$. The result is trivial if $|x| < k$.

If $S \in L$ and $L \in \mathcal{LJ}_k^+$ then for any $i \in \{1, \ldots, n\}$ there exists y_i with $\tau_{k,\Sigma^{k-1}}(y_i) \mid \tau_{k,\Sigma^{k-1}}(x_i)$ and $Pr_{k-1}(x_i)\Sigma^* \cap L(h(\tau_{k,\Sigma^{k-1}}(y_i))) \cap \Sigma^* Suf_{k-1}(x_i) \subseteq L$. So, for any $i \in \{1, \ldots, n\}$, $L_{\mathcal{LJ}_k^+\{x_i\}} \subseteq L$. And then, $L_{\mathcal{LJ}_k^+ S} \subseteq L$.   □

The algorithm 2 tries to calculate $L_{\mathcal{LJ}_k^+\{x_i\}}$ for any x_i in S. We order S and check the acceptance of any word before constructing the automaton. To see that the algorithm calculates $L_{\mathcal{LJ}_k^+\{x_i\}}$ for any x_i, it suffices to see that if $|x_i| < k-1$, x_i is accepted by the definition of the cascade product and by the fact that the transduction is filled by the symbols $\sharp$ on the left. If $|x_i| \geq k$, the language of the automaton contains $L(u_1, \ldots, u_n)$ by the definition of the transducer $\tau_{k,F}$, further more since the transduction is filled by the symbols $\sharp$ on the left this implies that the prefix of all words belonging to the language accepted by the automaton is exactly $Pr_k(x)$. Finally, by choosing $F = Suf_{k-1}(x)$, the suffix of all all word belonging to the language accepted by the automaton is exactly $Suf_{k-1}(x)$.

Algorithm 2. $\mathcal{LJ}_k^+$ **Inference**
Input: S set of words over Σ^* and k a positive integer
Output: NFA $\mathcal{A} = (Q, \Sigma, \delta, Q_0, F)$, consistent with S such that $L(\mathcal{A}) = L_{\mathcal{LJ}_k^+ S}$
Method:
$Q = \emptyset$; $\delta = \emptyset$; $F = \emptyset$; $Q_0 = \emptyset$
Order S by decreasing length as: $S = \{x_1, x_2, \ldots, x_m\}$
For $1 \leq i \leq m$ **Do**
   If $\delta(Q_0, x) \cap F = \emptyset$ **Then**
      $\mathcal{A}' = (Q', \Sigma', \delta', Q_0', F') = \mathcal{J}^+$ Inference$(\tau_{k,Suf_{k-1}(x)}(x_i))$
      $\mathcal{A} = \mathcal{A} \cup \mathcal{A}' \circ \tau_{k,Suf_{k-1}(x)}$
   Return $(\mathcal{A}')$

The convergence of Algorithm 2 is a direct consequence of Proposition 3.

The time complexity of Algorithm 2 is $N * |\Sigma|^{k+1}$. Let $S = \{x_1, x_2, \ldots, x_n\}$ and let $N = |x_1| + |x_2| + \cdots + |x_n|$. The size of the transducer $\tau_{k,F}$ is of order $|\Sigma^k|$ but computing $\tau_{k,F}(x_i)$ for $i \in \{1, \ldots, n\}$, is of order $|x_i|$. Since the only remaining steps to be done by the algorithm are: to apply the Algorithm 2 and to calculate the cascade product, the complexity of the Algorithm 2 is $N * |\Sigma|^{k+1}$.

5   Inferring Finite Unions of Pattern Languages with Constant Segments

In this section we show that we can infer k-bounded pattern languages by using the inference algorithm used to learn $\mathcal{LJ}^+$ languages.

In order to do so, we define a new product of automata and transducers. This product is in some sense the inverse of the cascade product.

Definition 2. Let $\mathcal{A} = (Q_1, \Sigma, \delta, q_0, F)$ be a finite deterministic automaton, and let $\tau = (Q_2, \Sigma, \Gamma, \delta', \lambda, p_0, F')$ be a sequential transducer. We define the product $\mathcal{A}\bar{o}\tau = (Q_1 \times Q_2, \Gamma, \delta'', (q_0, p_0), F \times F')$ with $\delta''((q, p), b) = (q', p')$ if $\delta'(p, a) = p'$, $\lambda(p, a) = b$ and $\delta(q, a) = q'$.

The next proposition gives us the meaning of this operation.

Proposition 4. Given a DFA $\mathcal{A} = (Q_1, \Sigma, \delta, q_0, F)$ and a finite transducer $\tau = (Q_2, \Sigma, \Gamma, \delta', \lambda, p_0, F')$, $L(\mathcal{A}\bar{o}\tau) = \tau(L(\mathcal{A}))$.

Proof. Let $w \in \tau(L(\mathcal{A}))$, then there exists $x \in L(\mathcal{A})$ such that $\tau(x) = w$. Then, we have $\delta'(p_0, a) = f'$, $\lambda(p_0, x) = w$ and $\delta(q, x) = f$, for some $f \in F$ and $f' \in F$. And so, $\delta''((q_0, p_0), w) = (f, f') \in F \times F'$, that is $w \in L(\mathcal{A}\bar{o}\tau)$.

Conversely, Let $w \in L(\mathcal{A}\bar{o}\tau)$, this implies that $\delta''((q_0, p_0), w) = (f, f')$ for some $f \in F$ and $f' \in F'$, and there exists $x \in \Sigma^*$ such that $\delta'(p_0, a) = f'$, $\lambda(p_0, x) = w$ and $\delta(q, x) = f$. And so, $\tau(x) = w$ and $x \in L(\mathcal{A})$. And so, $x \in \tau(L(\mathcal{A}))$. $\square$

Note that if there does not exist $p \in P$ and $a, b \in A$ such that $\lambda(p, a) = \lambda(p, b)$ we have that $\mathcal{A}\bar{o}\tau$ is a deterministic automaton.

Theorem 3. $\mathcal{RPL}_k^+$ is included in $\mathcal{LJ}_{k+1}^+$. Furthermore, any language belonging to $\mathcal{RPL}_k^+$ can be obtained as a finite union of languages belonging to $\mathcal{LJ}_{k+1}^+$.

Proof. It suffices to prove the theorem for patterns of the form $u_0 x_1 u_1 \cdots u_{n-1} x_n u_n$, since the class of languages $\mathcal{LJ}^+$ is closed under finite union. Since $p \in \mathcal{RP}_k$ we have that $|u_i| \leq k$ for $1 \leq i \leq n$.

We now give a process to obtain the pattern language $L(p)$ of the form $u_0 \Sigma^* u_1 \cdots u_{n-1} \Sigma^* u_n$ from languages belonging to $\mathcal{LJ}^+$.

Since p is a regular pattern we know that there exists an automaton $\mathcal{A}_p$ such that $L(p) = L(\mathcal{A}_p)$.

Now let $\tau_{k+1, \Sigma^{k-1}}$ be the transducer defined in Definition 1, then by Proposition 4 we know that $L(\mathcal{A}\bar{o}\tau_{k+1, \Sigma^k}) = \tau_{k+1, \Sigma^k}(L(\mathcal{A}))$.

Let $B = \bigcup_{i=1}^{k-1} \#^{k-i} \Sigma^i \cup \Sigma^k$, and let as denote by h the morphism from B^* into $(\Sigma^k)^*$ introduced in Definition 1.

We denote by P the set of acyclic paths of $\mathcal{A}\bar{o}\tau_{k+1, \Sigma^k}$ going from the initial state to some final state. Note that this set is finite. We claim that

$$L(p) = \bigcup_{\substack{X \in P \\ |x|=k, u_0 \in Pre(x) \\ |y|=k, u_n \in Suf(y)}} x\Sigma^* \cap L(h(X)) \cap \Sigma^* y$$

$$\bigcup \{x \in L(p) \mid |x| < k\}.$$

The result is clearly true for any $w \in \Sigma^*$ with $|w| < k$. So, let us suppose $|w| \geq k$.

Let $w \in L(p)$, we know that $\tau_{k+1,\Sigma^k}(w) \in L(\mathcal{A}\bar{o}\tau_{k+1}, \Sigma^k)$, which means that there exists $X \in P$ such that $X \mid \tau_{k+1,\Sigma^k}(w)$, and then, if we take $x = Pr_k(w)$ and $y = Suf_k(w)$, we have that $w \in x\Sigma^* \cap L(h(X)) \cap \Sigma^* y$.

In the other direction let $w \in x\Sigma^* \cap L(h(X)) \cap \Sigma^* y$ for some $x, y \in \Sigma^k$ and $X \in P$. By Proposition 4 and the definition of P, there exists a word $z \in \Sigma^*$ such that $\tau_{k+1,\Sigma^k}(z) = X$ and $z \in L(p)$. Since $z \in L(p)$ and p is k bounded we have that $v_0 v_1 \cdots v_n \mid h(X)$ with $|v_i| = k$ and $v_i = x_i u_i y_i$ for some $x_i, y_i \in \Sigma^*$ with $0 \leq i \leq n$. Then $\tau_{k+1,\Sigma^k}(z) \mid \tau_{k+1,\Sigma^k}(w)$ and $v_0 v_1 \cdots v_n \mid h(\tau_{k+1,\Sigma^k}(z))$, and so, necessarily $w \in L(p)$.   □

This theorem implies that k-bounded regular pattern languages can be identified by the $\mathcal{LJ}_{k+1}^+$ Inference Algorithm in the limit.

The following example shows the behavior of the previous algorithm.

Example 1. Let $p_1 = axayb$ and $p_2 = bxb$ be 1-bounded patterns. Figure 2 shows the automaton that accepts $L(p_1) \cup L(p_2)$.

The automaton constructed in Theorem 3 in order to obtain the words on Σ^2 required to learn the pattern is shown in Figure 3.

This shows that the sequences (aa, ab), (ab, ba, ab), (bb) and (ba, ab) are enough to describe $L(p_1) \cup L(p_2)$. By (aa, ab) we obtain $a\Sigma^* \cap L(aa, ab) \cap \Sigma^* b$, by (ab, ba, ab) we obtain $a\Sigma^* \cap L(ab, ba, ab) \cap \Sigma^* b$, by (bb) we obtain $b\Sigma^* \cap L(bb) \cap \Sigma^* b$ and (ba, ab) we obtain $b\Sigma^* \cap L(ba, ab) \cap \Sigma^* b$. Note that they are the only paths without cycles from the initial to the final states.

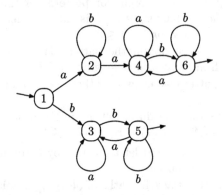

Fig. 2. Automaton accepting $L(p_1 \cup p_2)$ for the patterns $p_1 = axayb$ and $p_2 = bxb$

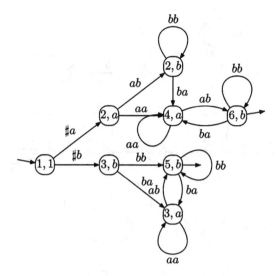

Fig. 3. Automaton accepting $\mathcal{A}(L(p_1 \cup p_2))\overline{\sigma}\tau_2$ for the patterns $p_2 = axayb$ and $p_2 = bxb$

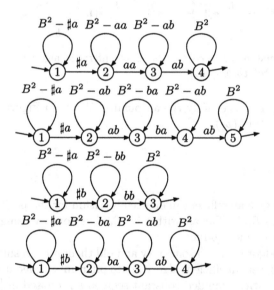

Fig. 4. The automaton obtained for the $\mathcal{J}^+$ inference algorithm for the samples $\{(\sharp a, aa, ab), (\sharp a, ab, ba, ab), (\sharp a, ab, ba, ab, ba, ab), (\sharp b, bb), (\sharp b, bb, bb), (\sharp b, ba, ab)\}$

Otherwise, (aa, ab), (ab, ba, ab), (bb) and (ba, ab) also gives a characteristic set for the inference of $L(p_1) \cup L(p_2)$. Let us consider the set $S = \{aab, abab, ababab, bb, bab, bbb\}$, note that this set contains the characteristic set $\{aab, abab, bb, bab\}$. By appliying the $\mathcal{J}^+$ Inference Algorithm to the set $\tau_{2,\Sigma}(S)$ we obtain the automaton shown in Figure 4.

Finally, Figure 5 shows the automaton obtained from the algorithm used to learn $\mathcal{LJ}_2^+$. We can verify that the minimal automaton obtained for the automa-

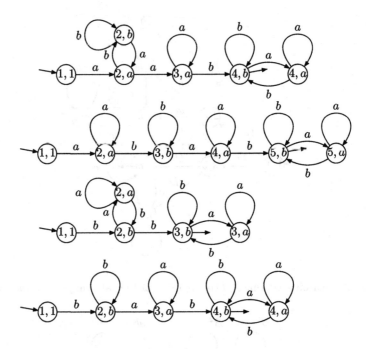

Fig. 5. The automaton obtained for the $\mathcal{LJ}_2^+$ inference algorithm for the samples $S = \{aab, abab, ababab, bb, bbb, bab\}$

ton shown in Figure 5 is exactly the automaton shown in Figure 2 that accepts the language $L(p_1) \cup L(p_2)$.

6   Conclusions

In this article we give an efficient inference algorithm for the positive varieties of languages $\mathcal{J}^+$ and $\mathcal{LJ}^+$. The algorithm for $\mathcal{LJ}^+$ is done by using the algorithm for $\mathcal{J}^+$ and the cascade product.

By using this algorithm and some new and old theoretical results, we solve the open problem of given an efficient algorithm to infer unbounded unions of regular pattern languages with bounded constant segments proposed in [1]. This shows the that study of the algebraic theory of automata can give us some knowledge in order to perform new algorithms to be applied in practice.

References

1. Shinohara, T., Arimura, H.: Inductive inference of unbounded unions of pattern languages from positive data. Theoretical Computer Science **241** (2000) 191–209
2. Pin, J.E., Weil, P.: Polynomial closure and unambiguous product. Theory Comput. Systems **30** (1997) 1–38

3. Angluin, D.: Finding common patterns to a set of strings. in Proc. 11th Ann. Symp. Theoryof Computing (1979) 130–141
4. Arikawa, S., Kuhara, S., Miyano, S., Shinohara, A., Shinohara, T.: A learning algorithm for elementary formal systems and its experiments on identification of trandmembrane domains. in Proc. 25th Hawaii Int. Conf. on System Science **1** (1992) 675–684
5. Pin, J.E., Weil, P.: The wreath product principle for ordered semigroups. Communications in Algebra **30** (2002) 5677–5713
6. Garcia, P., Ruiz, J.: Learning in varieties of the form **V*LI** from positive data. To appear (-)
7. Garcia, P., Ruiz, J.: Learning k-testable and k-piecewise testable languages from positive data. Grammars. Special Issue on Grammar Induction (2004) 125–140
8. Hopcroft, J., Ullman, J.: Introduction to automata theory, languages and computation. Addison-Wesley (1980)
9. Gold, E.M.: Language identification in thelimit. Information and Control (1967) 447–474
10. Pin, J.E.: Varieties of formal languages. North Oxford, London and Plenum, New-York (1986) (Traduction of Variétés de langages formels).
11. Berstel, J.: Transductions and Context Free Languages. Teubner (1979)

Inside Vaucanson

Thomas Claveirole[1], Sylvain Lombardy[2], Sarah O'Connor[1],
Louis-Noël Pouchet[1], and Jacques Sakarovitch[3]

[1] LRDE, EPITA
{claveirole, o-connor, pouchet}@lrde.epita.fr
[2] LIAFA, Université Paris 7
lombardy@liafa.jussieu.fr
[3] LTCI, CNRS/ENST
sakarovitch@enst.fr

Abstract. This paper presents some features of the VAUCANSON platform. We describe some original algorithms on weighted automata and transducers (computation of the quotient, conversion of a regular expression into a weighted automaton, and composition). We explain how complex declarations due to the generic programming are masked from the user and finally we present a proposal for an XML format that allows implicit descriptions for simple types of automata.

1   Introduction

At CIAA'03, we had announced our project VAUCANSON, a software platform for computing with automata and transducers (see [1]). We have made some demonstration of the possibilities of VAUCANSON at CIAA'04. We would like to report now on how some features of VAUCANSON have been implemented at the light of the first years of experiments. This applies to the algorithms as well as to the programming facilities that had to be incorporated within VAUCANSON.

We first describe three of the algorithms implemented in VAUCANSON: those which generalize to automata with multiplicity the Hopcroft algorithm of minimization, the construction of the derived term automaton of a regular expression and the composition of (sub-)normalized transducers.

We then explain how we have overcome the intrinsic difficulty of generic static programming. And we finally introduce the last version of an XML format to describe automata, implemented as input-output in VAUCANSON. In particular, VAUCANSON is complemented with a model of a graphical interface, which relies on the XML format to interact with the VAUCANSON library.

The description of the algorithms is complemented with the results of some benchmarks of the last version of VAUCANSON [1]. All the tests have been run on a server installed at ENST, a bi-Xeon 3.2 GHz with 4 Go of RAM.

2   On the Algorithms

The VAUCANSON platform provides the most usual algorithms on automata: determinization, minimization, product, Thompson automaton of an expression,

---

[1] Downloadable at http://vaucanson.lrde.epita.fr.

J. Farré, I. Litovsky, and S. Schmitz (Eds.): CIAA 2005, LNCS 3845, pp. 116–128, 2006.

standard automaton, ε-transitions removal, *etc.* Each of these algorithms has been written such that it can be applied to the largest range of automata. For instance, product or ε-transitions removal are generic and can be applied to automata with any multiplicity.

As an example, let us mention the automaton $\mathcal{A}_n$, drawn below, that had been used in [1] for benchmarking the determinization and that will serve as the basis of other tests in this paper.

On the latest version of VAUCANSON the determinization test gives the following result for $\mathcal{A}_{20}$ (the minimal deterministic automaton equivalent to $\mathcal{A}_n$ has 2^n states).

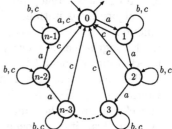

Platform	time (seconds)	space (MB)
FSM	60	447
VAUCANSON	105	1709

We focus now on three algorithms that are extensions for automata with multiplicities of more or less well-known algorithms: a minimization algorithm adapted from Hopcroft algorithm, a rather sophisticated algorithm for building an expression, adapted from a method due to Champarnaud and Ziadi [2], and finally an algorithm for the composition of transducers with multiplicity.

2.1 Minimal Quotient

Definition of the Minimal Quotient. The notion of minimal quotient (or $\mathbb{K}$-covering) is the generalization to weighted automata of the minimal automaton for DFA's. It consists in computing a (smaller) automaton by merging states which have the "same" outgoing transitions. (*cf.* [3, 4]).

More formally, this definition is equivalent to the following one (straightforward from [5]). Let $\mathcal{A} = (I, E, T)$ be an automaton characterized by its initial vector I, its transition matrix E and its final vector T. The minimal quotient of $\mathcal{B}$ is the (unique) smallest automaton $\mathcal{B} = (J, F, U)$ such that:

$$J = IK, \qquad KF = EK, \qquad \text{and} \qquad KU = T,$$

where K is an amalgamation matrix (*i.e.* with one and only one non-zero coefficient, equal to 1, on every row). It is quite obvious that the minimal quotient of $\mathcal{A}$ is equivalent to $\mathcal{A}$.

Algorithm for the Minimal Quotient. The minimal quotient of a DFA can be computed either by the Moore algorithm or by the Hopcroft algorithm [6].[2] These both algorithms consist in refining a partition over states (initialized w.r.t. the terminal states) but they are different: given a class P and a letter a, the Moore algorithm consists in considering the classes of successors of P by a and

---

[2] The Brzozowski algorithm is not a computation of quotient, even if it gives the same result on DFAs.

splitting P, whereas the Hopcroft algorithm consists in considering the classes of predecessors of P by a and splitting them. Therefore, the Hopcroft algorithm can more directly be extended to NFAs or weighted automata:

1. Computation of a backward transition table: for every state q and every letter a, the list of pairs (p, w) is stored, for all transitions from p to q labelled by a with multiplicity w. The current implementation of automata in VAUCANSON already provides this table.
2. The algorithm is initialized by sorting states with respect to their terminal function. This provides the initial partition that has to be refined to be a right congruence. For every part P and every letter a, the pair (P, a) is inserted into a queue l.
3. While l is not empty, the front of l, a pair (P, a) is poped up; for every part Q which has successors by a in P, the part Q is splitted such that two states q and q' remain in the same part if and only if the sum of weights of their outgoing transitions labelled by a that arrive in P are equal. If new parts are created, they are inserted into l (paired with every letter).
4. An automaton whose states are the parts is then created. The terminal function of the part is the (common) terminal function of each of its states, the initial function is the sum, and the multiplicity of (P, a, Q) is the sum, for any state p of P of the multiplicities of transitions (p, a, q) for every q in Q.

Comparison with the Classical Hopcroft Algorithm. The principle of the algorithm is the same as the principle of the minimization algorithm: a backward transition table is computed and a partition is refined by considering predecessors of each part. Nevertheless, the existence of multiplicities has a number of outcomes in every step of the algorithm.

First, the transition table does not contain lists of states, but lists of states paired with weights.

In step 2, the initial partition has as many parts as the terminal function has values. In step 3, it is not sufficient to know wether a state q has a successor in P but which is the multiplicity from q to P. Moreover, one add to l every subpart obtained from Q whereas in the Hopcroft algorithm the smallest among both subparts is inserted, which is crucial to reach the $n \log n$ complexity in the classical case. The complexity of that generalized Hopcroft algorithm is therefore more likely to be quadratic.

Minimizing Deterministic Automata. Minimization of DFAs is a special case of computing the quotient and we have first tested implementations in this case to allow comparison with other platforms. It has been shown in [7] that the de Brujin graph, $\mathcal{B}_n$ is the worst case for Hopcroft minimization algorithm, since it can lead to $n2^n$ steps in the main loop of the algorithm: let $A = \{a, b\}$ be the alphabet; the states of $\mathcal{B}_n$ are labelled by words of length n over A, that gives 2^n states. The state a^n is initial, for every x, y in A, every word w in A^{n-1} there is a transition from xw to wy labelled by y and xw is final if and only if $x = a$. We also test minimization on the the determinized automaton of $\mathcal{A}_n$.

Four procedures are tested; the one proposed by FSM (unknown algorithm), and two algorithms proposed by VAUCANSON: Moore and Hopcroft.[3]

Input	$\mathcal{B}_{12}$	$\mathcal{B}_{17}$	$det(\mathcal{A}_{12})$	$det(\mathcal{A}_{17})$
FSM	0.048	1.791	0.065	2.829
Moore	0.271	37.11	0.470	146.77
Hop.	0.074	45.599	0.338	1752.33

Test of the Generalized Quotient. Let C_1 be the $\mathbb{Z}$-automaton of Figure 1 that maps every word w on $\{a, b\}^2$, seen as a binary number, on its value $\bar{w}$. For every positive integer n, let C_{n+1} be the automaton recursively defined as the product of C_1 by C_n. C_n maps every words w on $\bar{w}^n$. In the following tests, we compute C_n, which has 2^n states and then the minimal quotient V_n of C_n which has $n+1$ states.

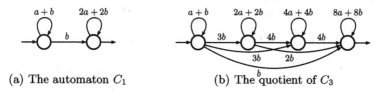

(a) The automaton C_1 (b) The quotient of C_3

Fig. 1. The automata C_n

n	8	9	10	11	12
C_n edges	6817	20195	60073	179195	535537
V_n edges	45	55	66	78	91
Time	0.036	0.112	0.340	0.999	3.161

2.2 Automaton of Derived Terms

The VAUCANSON platform provides several algorithms to convert any regular expression (with multiplicity) into a (weighted) finite automaton. We present here the algorithm that constructs the derived term automaton $\mathcal{A}_E$ of an expression E [8,5]. This automaton is rather small: it has been proven that $\mathcal{A}_E$ is a quotient of the standard (or position, or Glushkov) automaton of E [2,5].

We have implemented the algorithm and the data structure proposed by Champarnaud and Ziadi [2] for the computation of derived terms, together with the necessary improvement in order to deal with multiplicity in expressions. The main point proven in [2] is that every derived term of a regular expression E is a product of subexpressions of E. Therefore, each derived term is represented by a list of nodes in the tree of the regular expression E. Moreover, this tree is equipped with some "links" that help to perform the derivation: for every *-node n, there is a link from the child of n to n itself, and for every ·-node, there is a link from the left child of n to its right child.

---

[3] The Brzozowski algorithm that consists in applying a co-determinization followed by a determinization does not succeed in reasonable time on these inputs.

Two basic functions are $c(E)$ and $first(E, a)$. The function $c(E)$ gives the weight of the empty word in the series described by E and $first(E, a)$ returns a set of pairs weight/position recursively defined by:

$$first(0, a) = \emptyset, \quad first(1, a) = \emptyset,$$

$$\forall b \in A \quad first(b, a) = \begin{cases} (1_{\mathbb{K}}, y) & \text{with } y \text{ position of } a \text{ in } E, \text{ if } a = b, \\ \emptyset & \text{otherwise} \end{cases}$$

$$first(k\,E, a) = \bigcup \{(kx, y) \mid (x, y) \in first(E, a)\}, \quad first(E\,k, a) = first(E, a),$$

$$first(E + F, a) = first(E, a) \cup first(F, a), \quad first(E \cdot F, a) = first(E, a) \cup first(c(E)F, a),$$

$$first(E^*, a) = first(c(E)^* E, a), \text{ if } c(E)^* \text{ is defined in } \mathbb{K}.$$

These functions are easily computed on the tree of the regular expression. The computation of the derivatives of E with respect to a consists, for every position x in $first(E, a)$, to go up to the root of the tree of E and collect the destinations of the links starting from the nodes on that path.

Example 1. Let $E_1 = (5\,F_1)$ with $F_1 = ((2ab) + ((3b) \cdot (4(ab)^*)))^*$.

The derived terms of E_1 are:

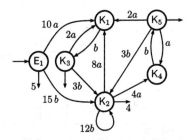

$$K_1 = b \cdot F_1,$$
$$K_2 = (4\,(ab)^*) \cdot F_1,$$
$$K_3 = F_1,$$
$$K_4 = (b \cdot (ab)^*) \cdot F_1, \text{ and}$$
$$K_5 = (ab)^* \cdot F_1.$$

For instance, $\frac{\partial}{\partial a} K_2 = 8K_1 \oplus 4K_4.$ The automaton $\mathcal{A}_{E_1}$.

The tree of E_1 is equipped with links. The coding for E_1 itself is I.

One computes $first(I, a) = \{(10, VI)\}$ and going up from VI, one get:

$$\frac{\partial}{\partial a} E_1 = 10[VII, II].$$

Finally, we get the same automaton with the following coding for derived terms:

$K_0 = [I]$ $K_1 = [VII, II]$ $K_2 = [XI, II]$
$K_3 = [II]$ $K_4 = [XV, XII, II]$ $K_5 = [XII, II]$

For instance,

$$first([XI, II], a) = \{(4, XIV), (8, VI)\}$$
and $\frac{\partial}{\partial a}[XI, II] = 4[XV, XII, II] \oplus 8[VII, II].$

Test on the Derived Terms. A set of expressions is provided by the elimination algorithm applied on $\mathcal{A}_{15}$ with random orderings on states. The automaton of derived terms $\mathcal{A}_E$ of every expression E is computed, and also the quotient $\mathcal{V}_E$ of the standard (Glushkov) automaton of the expression E. One thousand expressions are generated this way and classified w.r.t. their litteral length l_E– which is the size of $\mathcal{S}_E$. We present here means for four significant classes.

Class	l_E	Derived term $\mathcal{A}_E$		Standard $\mathcal{S}_E$	
		$\mathcal{A}_E$ states	time	$\mathcal{V}_E$ states	time
1	110	24	0.123	24	0.012
7	410	53	0.470	51	0.050
14	1035	66	1.169	60	0.138
20	7821	90	13.412	78	1.418

2.3 Composition of Transducers with Multiplicity

A most fundamental result in the theory of transducers is Elgot and Mezei's Composition Theorem ([9]): *The composition of two finite transducers is realized by a finite transducer.* The same result holds true for weighted transducers — up to some definition problems which will not be considered here. The proof is, or can be translated into, an algorithm for the construction of the transducer that realizes the composition. And there are two main proofs for the Composition Theorem.

The first proof follows from Kleene-Schützenberger characterization of rational relations from A^* into B^* as *recognizable series* on A^* with multiplicity in $\mathrm{Rat}\, B^*$. Transducers are thus *representations* of A^* by matrices with entries in $\mathrm{Rat}\, B^*$ and representations can be *composed* in a natural way: this yields a representation for the composition of transducers [10]. This proof has the advantage that it generalizes directly to weighted transducers: they are representations by matrices with entries in $\mathbb{K}\mathrm{Rat}\, B^*$ if $\mathbb{K}$ is the multiplicity semiring. It is thus perfectly "generic" *i.e.* independent from the type of considered transducers and hence fits well with the architecture of VAUCANSON. It is the one we have first implemented. Besides its genericity, this algorithm has a serious drawback: as it deals with *real-time* transducers, the transition "outputs" may be regular expressions and the composition requires the computation of the image (by the second transducer) of all these expressions, a computation that may prove to be costly.

The other proof, certainly better known, relies on the realization of rational relations by projections and intersection with rational (regular) languages (see [11, 12]). We have also implemented *another composition algorithm* which follows more closely this classical proof and which works directly on transducers seen as labeled graphs.

Let us first sketch quickly an algorithm that corresponds to that proof in the unweighted case. In spite of its simplicity, it has not been described so often; it can be seen as a simplified version of the algorithm for the weighted case of [13, 14] which we shall mention again later. It can be also found in [15].

We consider two *normalized* transducers $\mathcal{T} = \langle Q, A^* \times B^*, E, I, T \rangle$ and $\mathcal{U} = \langle R, B^* \times C^*, F, J, U \rangle$, that is transitions of $\mathcal{T}$ are labeled in $A \times 1$ or in $1 \times B$

and those of $\mathcal{U}$ are labeled in $B \times 1$ or in $1 \times C$. The proof of the Composition Theorem as presented in [12] is equivalent to the construction of the transducer

$$T \bowtie \mathcal{U} = \langle Q \times R, A^* \times C^*, G, I \times J, T \times U \rangle$$

by the following rules.

(i) If $(p, (a, 1), q) \in E$ then for all $r \in R$ $((p, r), (a, 1), (q, r)) \in G$.
(ii) If $(r, (1, c), s) \in F$ then for all $q \in Q$ $((q, r), (1, c), (q, s)) \in G$.
(iii) If $(p, (1, b), q) \in E$ and $(r, (b, 1), s) \in F$ then $((p, r), (1, 1), (q, s)) \in G$.

A next possible step is to eliminate the transitions with label $(1, 1)$ by means of a classical closure algorithm.

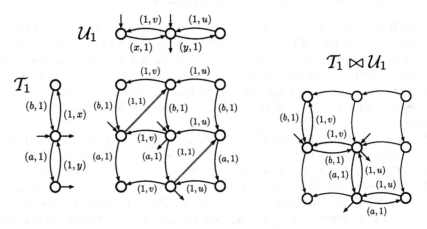

Fig. 2. Composition Theorem on Boolean transducers

This construction can easily be extended to transducers which we shall call *sub-normalized* and which are such that transitions are labeled in $\widehat{A} \times \widehat{B} \setminus (1, 1)$ where $\widehat{A} = A \cup \{1\}$. It amounts to replace (iii) by (iii') If $(p, (x, b), q) \in E$ with $x \in \widehat{A}$ and $(r, (b, y), s) \in F$ with $y \in \widehat{C}$ then $((p, r), (x, y), (q, s)) \in G$.

In this form, it contains as a particular case the composition of letter-to-letter transducers.

It is known that this construction is not correct if multiplicities are to be taken into account. Let us say that two paths in $T \bowtie \mathcal{U}$ are *equivalent* if they correspond to the same pair of paths in T and $\mathcal{U}$. For instance, there is one path labeled (aa, y) in T_1 and one path labeled (y, u) in $\mathcal{U}_1$; and there are *two* equivalent paths labeled (aa, u) in $T_1 \bowtie \mathcal{U}_1$. Hence, $T \bowtie \mathcal{U}$ does not realize the composition of the weighted relations realized by T and $\mathcal{U}$.

In [11], the Composition Theorem is proved for weighted transductions (at least for those with weights taken in a *complete positive and commutative semiring*, which allows to dispose of the question of definition). In this proof, the multiplicity, that is the selection among the equivalent paths, is taken care of, so to speak, by the intersection with a certain local language T.

As we already mentioned, a construction of a weighted transducer that realizes the composition of two weighted transductions is given in [13, 14]. It amounts first to *mark* the transitions which, in the above construction, have a label one component of which is the empty word, and then to choose a *filter*, that is a language on the alphabet of marks which retains *one* path in every set of equivalent paths. Besides implementing a proof of the Composition Theorem, this construction has the advantage of being well-suited to the lazy evaluation of the composition, that is the implementation of an algorithm that does not compute the composed transducer but the output of it on any input word (with the same number of steps as if the composed transducer had been computed). On the other hand, it is easy to verify that the language T in Eilenberg's proof plays the role of a filter.

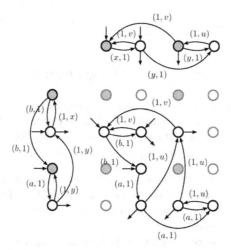

Fig. 3. A composition that preserves multiplicity

We have implemented a construction on transducers that corresponds to this filter T and as it is chosen beforehand we avoid the introduction of marked transductions. We replace them by a preliminary operation on the transducers and the intersection with T is then realized by the deletion of certain states in the product. The construction on T and U can be described as follows:

(a) Split the states of T and their *outgoing* transitions in such a way they are labeled either in $(A \times 1)$ — black states — or in $\widehat{A} \times B$ (or the state is final) — white states; the incoming transitions are duplicated on split states. This is transducer T'.

(b) Split the states of U and their *incoming* transitions in such a way they are labeled either in $(1 \times C)$ — black states — or in $B \times \widehat{C}$ (or the state is initial) — white states; the outgoing transitions are duplicated on split states. This is transducer U'.

(c) Apply the preceeding algorithm [steps (i), (ii) and (iii')] to T' and U' in order to build $T' \bowtie U'$.

(d) Delete the black-black states (every state in $T' \bowtie U'$ is a pair of states).

(e) Trim and eliminate the transitions with label $(1,1)$ by classical closure.

Figure 3 shows the construction applied to T_1 and U_1.

Composition Algorithm. We consider the rewriting rule $ab^n \to ba^n$. This transformation is achieved by the composition of a left sequential transducer by a right sequential transducer, respectively performing rewriting from right to left and left to right. The composition has been implemented using both the composition of representations and the composition of sub-normalized transducers.

Algorithm	n	Nb. states	Nb. transitions	Time
Sub-normalized transducer	20	30084	40356	0.551
	40	232564	305506	4.849
Representation	20	441	882	2.042
	40	1681	3362	36.195

3   Coping with Generic Static Programming

Genericity in Vaucanson. In order to ensure maximal genericity of the functions and algorithms written in the VAUCANSON library, most of the objects that come into the definiton of automata are parameterizable. For instance and to quote a few, one can, but also one has to, define the type of the following entities:

- the alphabet, *i.e.* the type of "letters": characters, pairs of characters, etc.
- the multiplicity, which involves both the *domain* ($\mathbb{B}, \mathbb{Z}, \mathbb{Q}, \mathbb{R}$ for instance) and also the semiring operations considered on these domains: usual $+$ and $\times$, or min and $+$, or max and $+$, etc.
- the transition label type such as letter, polynomial, (rational) series, etc.

As already advocated in [1], the use of C++ static genericity is one of the characteristic features of VAUCANSON. Algorithms are written once, and the assurance is given that they will work for all kinds of automata (concerning the above parameters). In order to achieve efficiency, the use of "classical" virtual methods and abstract classes is avoided. Instead, static mechanisms similar to those described by [16] and [17] are used. The combination of genericity for such a wide range of types and the use of such methods for static mechanism have a heavy counterpart: programming becomes pretty tough, even for most advanced users. The solution to this drawback which threatened the usability of VAUCANSON came through the writing of "context headers".

Context Headers. The VAUCANSON platform now provides a set of context headers, each of them contains all the needed declarations for a classical type of automata such as Boolean automata, automata with multiplicity in $\mathbb{Z}$, max-plus or min-plus automata, or transducers.

The objective is achieved to some extend. The wide range of functions imple-mented in the VAUCANSON library may be used with a minimal amount of decla-rations when applied to classical types of automata. On the other hand, advanced users may also use their own definitions to take the most of the genericity in VAU-CANSON. On the developer's side, genericity is kept and algorithms are written once and specializable in various ways (regarding the automaton type, a partic-ular implementation, etc). By offering predefined types to the user, VAUCANSON provides services which are in fact context-sensitive, as the `new_rat_exp()` or `thompson_of()` functions for instance.

The Future of Context Headers. As explained in [1], the "type" of an entity in VAUCANSON does not refer only to the type of a variable but also to how this variable is implemented. The present headers refer to the general implementation of automata and do not thus insure the best possible efficiency.

Moreover, the writing of a context header is a tedious process, and every user's wish or need cannot be fulfilled by a library of headers: the possible combinations of types are potentially infinite.

A more elegant solution that we plan to implement in a near future will be to provide a kind of *parameterized context*, for which only the most usual parameters are fixed. As an example, an automaton with "numerical" multiplicity would be defined by a header `weighted_automaton` which will have as parameters the type of the letters of the alphabet and the type of the weight: `int`, `float`, etc.

4   The XML Exchange Format for Automata

At CIAA'04, the VAUCANSON group presented an XML description format for automata. This format was elaborated both as a proposal for an exchange format within the community of automata users and as an input-output standard in order to allow communications between VAUCANSON and other softwares dealing with automata[4]. We shall present a new proposal at CIAA'05, and the XML format proposed will be described there. We describe here only the main features of this new format, their motivation, and the way VAUCANSON handles it.

4.1   The XML Proposal

Quick Review of the Format. The description of automata is structured in two parts. The `<type>` tag provides automaton type definition, like Boolean automaton, or weighted ones with the ability to specify weight type, alphabet specification, etc. The `<content>` tag provides the definition of the automaton "structure". The visual representation of automata involves a very large amount of informations. The `<geometry>` data corresponds to the embedding of the automaton in a plane (with informations such as state coordinates or edge type for a transition). The `<drawing>` data contains the definition of attributes that

---

[4] VAUCANSON supports as well the FSM format for loading and saving automata.

characterize the actual drawing of the graph (such as label position or state color for instance). Most of them are indeed implicit and provided by drawing programs; the format only provides the possibility to make them explicit at every level of the description.

From DTD to XSD. The most important difference with our previous proposal is the change from a DTD (Document Type Definition) describing the tags for automata representation to an XSD Schema.

This change is indeed a consequence of the same simplification policy which lead us to the definition of context headers: it is desirable to keep the description of automata simple when describing widely used structures, while giving the possibility to describe the most complex ones.

For XML, this simplification amounts to have default types, in order to omit <type> tag when describing common Boolean automata or transducers.

The problem then arises when describing an automaton or a transducer, the default values for the <type> tag must of course be different. This is not possible with a DTD description. The use of a XSD overcomes this difficulty, since it is possible to define different properties for a same element, according to the embracing context. Is is so possible to locally alter the behavior of a tag, and make it context-sensitive. With this feature, default values for the <type> tag are achieved, whether it is a child of <transducer> or of <automaton>.

It is of course possible to redefine only the tag where default values are inappropriate, inside the <type> tag. For instance, in order to define a weighted automaton on $\mathbb{Z}$, it is sufficient to write a <semiring> tag as a child of <type>, with set attribute set to Z.

4.2   Implementation in Vaucanson

In order to implement support of proposed XML format in VAUCANSON, two main objectives need to be achieved: maintenance easiness in case of format modification or extension and routines availability to access state geometric coordinates specified in the XML document.

Parsing the XML Document. To parse the XML document and create the associated tree, we use the Apache Xerces C++ parser [18]. Xerces is a validating XML parser, and handles well DTD document validation or XSD validation.

Building the Automaton. When reading and interpreting data, the program faces a totally dynamic content. It doesn't know, *a priori*, tag properties it will read. We face the problem of knowledge of the treatment type, not data type. In order to solve this problem, we use the Factory Method design pattern [19].

Factory Method is a creational pattern. It encourages the user to create a common interface for handled objects (in this case tags), while the exact type of the object is chosen by a subclass according to the context. The main routine deals with abstraction since it knows how to manipulate tags, but doesn't know about data it is dealing with.

Acknowledgments

The help and support of all members of the VAUCANSON Group is gratefully acknowledged: A. Demaille for the management of the group at LRDE, R. Poss and Y. Régis-Gianas for keeping an eye on the evolution of the platform, R. Bigaignon, M. Cadilhac, F. Terrones at LRDE and R. Souza at ENST for their participation to the writing of the platform and especially for the benchmarking.

The help of H. Assaoui and Ph. Martins for the installation of the vaucanson server at ENST is also gratefully acknowledged.

References

1. Lombardy, S., Régis-Gianas, Y., Sakarovitch, J.: Introducing VAUCANSON. Theoretical Computer Science **328** (2004) 77–96
2. Champarnaud, J.M., Ziadi, D.: Canonical derivatives, partial derivatives and finite automaton constructions. Theor. Comput. Sci. **289** (2002) 137–163
3. Kuich, W., Walk, K.: Block-stochastic matrices and associated finite-state languages. Computing (Arch. Elektron. Rechnen) **1** (1966) 50–61
4. Sakarovitch, J.: Eléments de théorie des automates. Vuibert (2003) Translation: *Elements of Automata Theory*, Cambridge Universiy Press, to appear.
5. Lombardy, S., Sakarovitch, J.: Derivatives of rational expressions with multiplicity. Theoretical Computer Science **332** (2005) 141–177
6. Hopcroft, J.: An $n \log n$ algorithm for minimizing states in a finite automaton. In: Theory of machines and computations (Proc. Internat. Sympos., Technion, Haifa, 1971). Academic Press, New York (1971) 189–196
7. Berstel, J., Carton, O.: On the complexity of hopcroft's state minimization algorithm. In Domaratzki, M., Okhotin, A., Salomaa, K., Yu, S., eds.: CIAA. Volume 3317 of Lecture Notes in Computer Science., Springer (2004) 35–44
8. Antimirov, V.M.: Partial derivatives of regular expressions and finite automaton constructions. Theor. Comput. Sci. **155** (1996) 291–319
9. Elgot, C.C., Mezei, J.E.: On relations defined by generalized finite automata. IBM J. Res. Develop **9** (1965) 47–68
10. Schützenberger, M.P.: On the definition of a family of automata. Information and Control **4** (1961) 245–270
11. Eilenberg, S.: Automata, languages, and machines. Vol. A. Academic Press [A subsidiary of Harcourt Brace Jovanovich, Publishers], New York (1974) Pure and Applied Mathematics, Vol. 58.
12. Berstel, J.: Transductions and context-free languages. Volume 38 of Leitfäden der Angewandten Mathematik und Mechanik [Guides to Applied Mathematics and Mechanics]. B. G. Teubner, Stuttgart (1979)
13. Pereira, F., Riley, M.: Speech Recognition by Composition of Weighted Finite Automata. In: Finite State Devices for Natural Language. Proc. MIT Press (1997)
14. Mohri, M., Pereira, F.C.N., Riley, M.: The design principles of a weighted finite-state transducer library. Theor. Comput. Sci. **231** (2000) 17–32
15. Lothaire, M.: Algebraic combinatorics on words. Volume 90 of Encyclopedia of Mathematics and its Applications. Cambridge University Press, Cambridge (2002)

16. Burrus, N., Duret-Lutz, A., Géraud, T., Lesage, D., Poss, R.: A static c++ object-oriented programming (scoop) paradigm mixing benefits of traditional oop and generic programming. In: Proc. of MPOOL'03, 18th SIGPLAN Conf. (2003)
17. Régis-Gianas, Y., Poss, R.: On orthogonal specialization in c++: Dealing with efficiency and algebraic abstraction in vaucanson. In: Proc. of POOSC'2003. (2003)
18. Xerces: (http://xml.apache.org/xerces-c/)
19. Gamma, E., Helm, R., Johnson, R., Vlissides, J.: Design Patterns: Elements of Reusable Object-Oriented Software. Addison-Wesley (1995)

Deterministic Recognition of Trees Accepted by a Linear Pushdown Tree Automaton[*]

Akio Fujiyoshi[1] and Ikuo Kawaharada[2]

[1] Department of Computer and Information Sciences, Ibaraki University,
4-12-1 Nakanarusawa, Hitachi, Ibaraki, 316-8511, Japan
fujiyosi@mx.ibaraki.ac.jp
[2] Graduate School of Electro-Communications,
University of Electro-Communications,
1-5-1 Chofugaoka, Chofu, Tokyo, 182-8585, Japan
ikuo@calvyn.cs.uec.ac.jp

Abstract. In this paper, a deterministic recognition algorithm for the class of tree languages accepted by (nondeterministic) linear pushdown tree automata (L-PDTAs) is proposed. L-PDTAs accept an important class of tree languages since the class of their yield languages coincides with the class of yield languages generated by tree adjoining grammars (TAGs). The proposed algorithm is obtained by combining a bottom-up parsing procedure on trees with the CKY (Cocke-Kasami-Younger) algorithm. The running time of the algorithm is $O(n^4)$, where n is the number of nodes of an input tree.

1 Introduction

Nondeterminism plays a very important role in the design of automata, with which we can reduce the number of states and rules of automata. Of course, nondeterminism is not realistic, so we need to consider a systematic way of constructing efficient deterministic recognition algorithms which simulate nondeterminism. It is easy for finite automata because it is a well-known fact that any (nondeterministic) finite automaton can be converted into an equivalent deterministic finite automaton, and we can obtain a deterministic linear time recognition algorithm from it. The same condition holds for finite tree automata because it is known that (nondeterministic) top-down tree automata, (nondeterministic) bottom-up tree automata, and deterministic bottom-up tree automata are convertible between each other [1, 2]. However, when we take automata with a pushdown stack, the condition will be complicated. Fortunately, for pushdown finite automata, we have the CKY (Cocke-Kasami-Younger) algorithm, whose running time is the cube of the length of an input string. On the other hand, the construction of an efficient deterministic recognition algorithm for trees accepted

---

[*] This study is supported in part by a Grant-in-Aid for Young Scientists ((B) 17700004) from the Japanese Ministry of Education, Culture, Sports, Science and Technology.

J. Farré, I. Litovsky, and S. Schmitz (Eds.): CIAA 2005, LNCS 3845, pp. 129–140, 2006.

by a pushdown tree automaton (PDTA) [3] seems difficult because PDTAs have the capability of duplicating their pushdown stack. The fact that the class of yield languages of PDTAs coincides with the class of indexed languages is indirect evidence that the construction of the algorithm might be difficult since the emptiness problem and the uniform membership problem of indexed languages are exponential time complete [4]. However, there exists a restricted version of PDTAs which accepts an interesting class of tree languages.

In this paper, linear PDTAs (L-PDTAs) are considered, and a deterministic recognition algorithm for trees accepted by an L-PDTA is proposed. L-PDTAs are top-down tree automata with a pushdown stack that are disallowed to duplicate their pushdown stack. It is known that the class of tree languages accepted by L-PDTAs coincides with that generated by linear, monadic context-free tree grammars (LM-CFTGs) [5,6], and the class of their yield languages coincides with the class of yield languages generated by tree adjoining grammars (TAGs) [5]. TAGs [7,8,9,10,11,12,13] are a formalism for tree structures which have been widely studied and related to natural languages. The deterministic recognition algorithm presented in this paper is the combination of the CKY algorithm and a bottom-up parsing procedure on trees. It is shown that the algorithm determines whether an input tree can be accepted by a given L-PDTA in $O(n^4)$ time, where n is the number of nodes of an input tree.

2   Preliminaries

In this section, terms, definitions, and former results which will be used in the rest of this paper are introduced.

Let $\mathcal{N}$ be the set of all natural numbers, and let $\mathcal{N}_+$ be the set of all positive integers. The concatenation operator is denoted by '$\cdot$'. For an alphabet Σ, the set of strings over Σ is denoted by Σ^*, and the empty string is denoted by λ.

2.1   Ranked Alphabets and Trees

A *ranked alphabet* is a finite set of symbols in which each symbol is associated with a natural number, called the *rank* of a symbol. Let Σ be a ranked alphabet. For $a \in \Sigma$, the rank of a is denoted by $rank(a)$. For $n \geq 0$, let $\Sigma_n = \{a \in \Sigma \mid rank(a) = n\}$.

A set D is a tree *domain* if D is a nonempty finite subset of $(\mathcal{N}_+)^*$ satisfying the following conditions:

- For any $d \in D$, if $d', d'' \in (\mathcal{N}_+)^*$ and $d = d' \cdot d''$, then $d' \in D$.
- For any $d \in D$ and $i, j \in \mathcal{N}_+$, if $i \leq j$ and $d \cdot j \in D$, then $d \cdot i \in D$.

Let D be a tree domain, and let $d \in D$. Elements in D are called *nodes*. A node d' is a *child* of d if there exists $i \in \mathcal{N}_+$ such that $d' = d \cdot i$. A node is called a *leaf* if it has no child. The node λ is called the *root*. A node that is neither a leaf nor the root is called an *internal node*.

Let Σ be a ranked alphabet. A *tree* over Σ is a function $\alpha : D \to \Sigma$ where D is a tree domain. The set of trees over Σ is denoted by T_Σ. The domain of a tree α is denoted by D_α. For $d \in D_\alpha$, $\alpha(d)$ is called the *label* of d. The *subtree* of α at d is $\alpha/d = \{(d', a) \in (\mathcal{N}_+)^* \times \Sigma \mid (d \cdot d', a) \in \alpha\}$.

A *path* is a sequence of nodes $d_0 d_1 \cdots d_n$ such that $n \geq 0$, $d_0, d_1, \ldots, d_n \in D$ and for $0 \leq i \leq n - 1$, d_{i+1} is a child of d_i.

The expression of a tree over Σ is defined to be a string over elements of Σ, parentheses and commas. For $\alpha \in T_\Sigma$, if $\alpha(\lambda) = b$, $\max\{i \in \mathcal{N}_+ \mid i \in D_\alpha\} = n$ and for each $1 \leq i \leq n$, the expression of α/i is α_i, then the expression of α is $b(\alpha_1, \alpha_2, \ldots, \alpha_n)$. Note that n is the number of the children of the root. For $b \in \Sigma_0$, trees are written as b instead of $b()$. When the expression of α is $b(\alpha_1, \alpha_2, \ldots, \alpha_n)$, it is written that $\alpha = b(\alpha_1, \alpha_2, \ldots, \alpha_n)$, i.e., each tree is identified with its expression.

Let Σ be a ranked alphabet, and let I be a set that is disjoint from Σ. $T_\Sigma(I)$ is defined to be $T_{\Sigma \cup I}$ where $\Sigma \cup I$ is the ranked alphabet obtained from Σ by adding all elements in I as symbols of rank 0.

Let $X = \{x_1, x_2, \ldots\}$ be the fixed countable set of variables. Let $X_0 = \emptyset$ and for $n \geq 1$, let $X_n = \{x_1, x_2, \ldots, x_n\}$. x_1 is situationally denoted by x.

Let $\alpha, \beta \in T_\Sigma$, and let $d \in D_\alpha$. We define $\alpha \langle d \leftarrow \beta \rangle = \{(d', a) \mid (d', a) \in \alpha$ and d is not a prefix of $d'\} \cup \{(d \cdot d'', b) \mid (d'', b) \in \beta\}$, i.e., the tree $\alpha \langle d \leftarrow \beta \rangle$ is the result of replacing α/d by β.

Let ε be the special symbol that can be contained in Σ_0. The *yield* of a tree is a function from T_Σ into Σ^* defined as follows. For $\alpha \in T_\Sigma$, (1) if $\alpha = a \in (\Sigma_0 - \{\varepsilon\})$, then yield$(\alpha) = a$, (1') if $\alpha = \varepsilon$, then yield$(\alpha) = \lambda$ and (2) if $\alpha = a(\alpha_1, \alpha_2, \ldots, \alpha_n)$ for some $a \in \Sigma_n$ and $\alpha_1, \alpha_2, \ldots, \alpha_n \in T_\Sigma$, then yield$(\alpha) = $ yield$(\alpha_1) \cdot $ yield$(\alpha_2) \cdot \cdots \cdot $ yield(α_n). For $L \subseteq T_\Sigma$, the *yield language of* L is the set yield$(L) = \{$yield$(\alpha) \mid \alpha \in L\}$.

2.2   Pushdown Tree Automata

Pushdown tree automata (PDTAs) [3] were introduced by I. Guessarian in order to formalize the class of tree languages generated by context-free tree grammars (CFTGs) [14]. A PDTA can be seen as the combination of an ordinary pushdown finite automaton [15] and a top-down tree automaton [2]. In [3], a variety of PDTAs were introduced, and it was shown that all of them accept the same class of tree languages. The definition of a PDTA in this paper can be described as "a restricted PDTA accepting by empty store" in terms of [3].

Definition 1. A *pushdown tree automaton* (PDTA) is a six-tuple $M = (Q, \Sigma, \Gamma, q_0, Z_0, R)$, where Q is a finite set of *states*, Σ is a ranked alphabet, called the *input alphabet*, Γ is a ranked alphabet such that $\Gamma = \Gamma_0 \cup \Gamma_1$, called the *pushdown alphabet*, $q_0 \in Q$ is the *initial state*, $Z_0 \in \Gamma_0$ is the *start symbol*, and R is a finite set of *rules* of one of the following forms:

Read rule :
  (i) $q(a, A) \rightarrow a$ with $a \in \Sigma_0$, $q \in Q$ and $A \in \Gamma_0$
  (ii) $q(b(x_1, x_2, \ldots, x_n), B) \rightarrow b(q_1(x_1, \pi_1), q_2(x_2, \pi_2), \ldots, q_n(x_n, \pi_n))$ with $n \geq 1$, $b \in \Sigma_n$, $q, q_1, q_2, \ldots, q_n \in Q$, $B \in \Gamma_1$ and $\pi_1, \pi_2, \ldots, \pi_n \in \Gamma_1^* \Gamma_0 \cup \Gamma_1^*$

ε-rule :

(iii) $q(x, A) \to q'(x, \pi)$ with $q, q' \in Q$, $A \in \Gamma_0$ and $\pi \in \Gamma_1^* \Gamma_0$

(iv) $q(x, B) \to q'(x, \pi)$ with $q, q' \in Q$, $B \in \Gamma_1$ and $\pi \in \Gamma_1^* \Gamma_0 \cup \Gamma_1^*$

An *instantaneous description* of M is a triple $q(\alpha, \pi) \in Q \times T_\Sigma \times \Gamma_1^* \Gamma_0$. Let ID be the set of all instantaneous descriptions of M. A *configuration* of M is an element of $T_\Sigma(ID)$. The *move relation* $\vdash_M$ of M is the relation defined as follows. For any configurations $c, c' \in T_\Sigma(ID)$, $c \vdash_M c'$ if there exists a node $d \in D_c$ that satisfies one of the following conditions:

- A type (i) rule $q(a, A) \to a$ is in R, $c/d = q(a, A)$, and $c' = c\langle d \leftarrow a \rangle$.
- A type (ii) rule $q(b(x_1, x_2, \ldots, x_n), B) \to b(q_1(x_1, \pi_1), q_2(x_2, \pi_2), \ldots, q_n(x_n, \pi_n))$ is in R, $c/d = q(b(\alpha_1, \alpha_2, \ldots, \alpha_n), B\rho)$ for some $\alpha_1, \alpha_2, \ldots, \alpha_n \in T_\Sigma$ and $\rho \in \Gamma_1^* \Gamma_0$, and $c' = c\langle d \leftarrow b(q_1(\alpha_1, \pi_1'), q_2(\alpha_2, \pi_2'), \ldots, q_n(\alpha_n, \pi_n'))\rangle$ where for each $1 \le i \le n$, if $\pi_i \in \Gamma_1^* \Gamma_0$, then $\pi_i' = \pi_i$, and if $\pi_i \in \Gamma_1^*$, then $\pi_i' = \pi_i \rho$.
- A type (iii) rule $q(x, A) \to q'(x, \pi)$ is in R, $c/d = q(\alpha, A)$ and $\alpha \in T_\Sigma$, and $c' = c\langle d \leftarrow q'(\alpha, \pi)\rangle$.
- A type (iv) rule $q(x, B) \to q'(x, \pi)$ is in R, $c/d = q(\alpha, B\rho)$ for some $\alpha \in T_\Sigma$ and $\rho \in \Gamma_1^* \Gamma_0$, and $c' = c\langle d \leftarrow q'(\alpha, \pi')\rangle$ where if $\pi \in \Gamma_1^* \Gamma_0$, then $\pi' = \pi$, and if $\pi \in \Gamma_1^*$, then $\pi' = \pi\rho$.

A *computation* is a finite sequence of configurations $c_1 c_2 \cdots c_n$ such that $n \ge 1$, $c_1, c_2, \ldots, c_n \in T_\Sigma(ID)$ and $c_1 \vdash_M c_2 \vdash_M \cdots \vdash_M c_n$. When there exists a computation $c_1 c_2 \cdots c_n$, we write $c_1 \vdash_M^* c_n$. The *tree language accepted by* M is the set $T(M) = \{\alpha \in T_\Sigma \mid q_0(\alpha, Z_0) \vdash_M^* \alpha\}$.

Linear PDTAs (L-PDTAs) [5] are PDTAs that don't have the capability of duplicating their pushdown stack. The class of tree languages accepted by L-PDTAs coincides with that generated by linear, monadic context-free tree grammars (LM-CFTGs) [5,6], and the class of their yield languages coincides with the class of yield languages generated by tree adjoining grammars (TAGs) [5].

Definition 2. Let $M = (Q, \Sigma, \Gamma, q_0, Z_0, R)$ be a PDTA. M is *linear* if it satisfies the following conditions:

- For each type (ii) rule $q(b(x_1, x_2, \ldots, x_n), B) \to b(q_1(x_1, \pi_1), q_2(x_2, \pi_2), \ldots, q_n(x_n, \pi_n))$ in R, $|\{i \mid 1 \le i \le n \text{ and } \pi_i \in \Gamma_1^*\}| = 1$.
- For each type (iv) rule $q(x, B) \to q'(x, \pi)$ in R, $\pi \in \Gamma_1^*$.

Example 1. The following M is an L-PDTA that accepts a tree language whose yield language is $L_{ww} = \{ww \mid w \in \{a, b\}^+\}$. $M = (Q, \Sigma, \Gamma, q_0, Z_0, R)$, where $Q = \{q_0, q_1, q_2, q_A, q_B\}$, $\Sigma = \Sigma_0 \cup \Sigma_2$, $\Sigma_0 = \{a, b\}$, $\Sigma_2 = \{d\}$, $\Gamma_0 = \{Z_0\}$, $\Gamma_1 = \{N, A, B\}$, and R consists of the following rules:

$$q_0(x, Z_0) \to q_1(x, NZ_0), \quad q_1(d(x_1, x_2), N) \to d(q_A(x_1, Z_0), q_1(x_2, NA)),$$
$$q_1(d(x_1, x_2), N) \to d(q_B(x_1, Z_0), q_1(x_2, NB)), \quad q_1(x, N) \to q_2(x, \lambda),$$
$$q_2(d(x_1, x_2), A) \to d(q_2(x_1, \lambda), q_A(x_2, Z_0)), \quad q_A(a, Z_0) \to a,$$

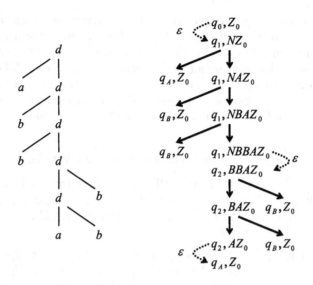

Fig. 1. An example of a tree accepted by M

$$q_2(d(x_1, x_2), B) \to d(q_2(x_1, \lambda), q_B(x_2, Z_0)), \quad q_B(b, Z_0) \to b,$$
$$q_2(x, A) \to q_A(x, \lambda), \text{ and } q_2(x, B) \to q_B(x, \lambda).$$

In Fig. 1, a tree in $T(M)$ and the movement of M for the tree are illustrated.

The recognition algorithm introduced in this paper is based on the CKY algorithm. Thus we need to be able to convert the rules of an L-PDTA into simple ones, which are analogous to productions of a context-free grammar (CFG) in Chomsky normal form [15].

Lemma 1. For any L-PDTA M, we can construct an L-PDTA $M' = (Q, \Sigma, \Gamma, q, Z_0, R)$ such that $T(M) = T(M')$, $Q = \{q\}$, and R consists of rules of one of the following forms:

(i) $q(a, A) \to a$ with $a \in \Sigma_0$, $q \in Q$ and $A \in \Gamma_0$
(ii) $q(b(x_1, x_2, \ldots, x_n), A) \to b(q(x_1, C_1), q(x_2, C_2), \ldots, q(x_n, C_n))$ with $n \geq 1$, $b \in \Sigma_n$, $q \in Q$, $A \in \Gamma_1$ and $C_1, C_2, \ldots, C_n \in \Gamma_0 \cup \{\lambda\}$ such that $|\{i \mid 1 \leq i \leq n \text{ and } C_i = \lambda\}| = 1$
(iii) $q(x, A) \to q(x, BC)$ with $q \in Q$, $A, C \in \Gamma_0$ and $B \in \Gamma_1$
(iv) $q(x, A) \to q(x, BC)$ with $q \in Q$, $A, B, C \in \Gamma_1$

Proof. From the L-PDTA M, we can construct an LM-CFTG that generates $T(M)$ (by Lemma 6.4 in [5]). It is known that any LM-CFTG can be converted into an equivalent LM-CFTG whose productions are one of the following forms:

1. $A \to a$
2. $A(x) \to b(C_1, \ldots, C_{i-1}, x, C_{i+1}, \ldots, C_n)$
3. $A \to B(C)$
4. $A(x) \to B(C(x))$

Here, uppercase characters are nonterminals, and lowercase characters are terminals. The above-mentioned fact is slightly different from the content of the normal form theorem introduced in [5], but it is easy to obtain this normal form in the same way as the construction of Chomsky normal form of CFGs. Thus an LM-CFTG with simple productions that generates $T(M)$ can be obtained. According to the construction method presented in the proof of Lemma 6.3 in [5], we can construct an L-PDTA M' that satisfies the above condition and accepts $T(M)$.   □

An L-PDTA satisfying the condition of Lemma 1 is said to be in *simple form*.

Example 2. The following M' is an L-PDTA in simple form that is equivalent to M in Example 1. $M' = (\{q\}, \Sigma, \Gamma, q, S, R)$, where $\Sigma = \Sigma_0 \cup \Sigma_2$, $\Sigma_0 = \{a, b\}$, $\Sigma_2 = \{d\}$, $\Gamma_0 = \{S, A, B\}$, $\Gamma_1 = \{C, D_1, D_2, D_3, D_4, E_1, E_2, E_3, E_4\}$, and R consists of the following rules:

$$q(x, S) \to q(x, D_1 A), \quad q(x, S) \to q(x, E_1 A), \quad q(x, E_1) \to q(x, D_1 C),$$
$$q(x, S) \to q(x, D_2 B), \quad q(x, S) \to q(x, E_2 B), \quad q(x, E_2) \to q(x, D_2 C),$$
$$q(x, C) \to q(x, D_1 D_3), \quad q(x, C) \to q(x, E_3 D_3), \quad q(x, E_3) \to q(x, D_1 C),$$
$$q(x, C) \to q(x, D_2 D_4), \quad q(x, C) \to q(x, E_4 D_4), \quad q(x, E_4) \to q(x, D_2 C),$$
$$q(d(x_1, x_2), D_1) \to d(q(x_1, A), q(x_2, \lambda)), \quad q(a, A) \to a,$$
$$q(d(x_1, x_2), D_2) \to d(q(x_1, B), q(x_2, \lambda)), \quad q(a, B) \to b,$$
$$q(d(x_1, x_2), D_3) \to d(q(x_1, \lambda), q(x_2, A)), \quad \text{and}$$
$$q(d(x_1, x_2), D_4) \to d(q(x_1, \lambda), q(x_2, B)).$$

In Fig. 2, a tree in $T(M')$ and the movement of M' for the tree are illustrated.

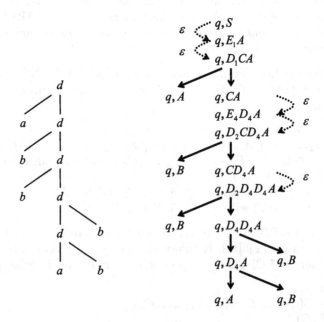

Fig. 2. An example of a tree accepted by M'

3   Recognition Algorithms

Our goal is to present a recognition algorithm which determines whether an input tree is accepted by a given L-PDTA. For the purpose of easier understanding, however, an algorithm in a special case will be presented first. Then the algorithm will be extended for general L-PDTAs.

3.1   A Recognition Algorithm for L-PDTAs with a Monadic Input Alphabet

To explain the utilization of the CKY algorithm for the recognition of trees, we consider the special case where the input alphabet of an L-PDTA, Σ is monadic. In this case, the movement of the recognition algorithm is clear because the shape of any tree in T_Σ is like a string.

Let $\Sigma = \Sigma_0 \cup \Sigma_1$, and let $M = (\{q\}, \Sigma, \Gamma, q, Z_0, R)$ be a PDTA in simple form. By the following function, $CKY(\alpha, Z_0)$ returns $true$ if and only if an input tree $\alpha \in T_\Sigma$ is accepted by M.

CKY:
      input: a tree $\alpha \in T_\Sigma$ and a pushdown symbol $A \in \Gamma$
      output: $true$ or $false$
begin
1   Let m be the number of nodes in α.
2   Let V be an $m \times m$ matrix.
3   Suppose that $\alpha = a_1(a_2(\cdots(a_m)\cdots))$ with $a_1, a_2, \ldots, a_m \in \Sigma$.
4   **for** $i := 1$ **to** m **do begin**
5        $V_{i,1} := \{A \in \Gamma \,|\, q(a_i, A) \to a_i$ or $q(a_i(x), A) \to a_i(q(x, \lambda))$ is in $R\}$
6   **for** $j := 2$ **to** i **do begin**
7            $V_{i-j+1,j} := \emptyset$
8   **for** $k := 1$ **to** $j - 1$ **do**
9               $V_{i-j+1,j} := V_{i-j+1,j} \cup \{A \in \Gamma \mid B \in V_{i-j+1,k},$
                       $C \in V_{i-j+1+k,j-k}$, and $q(x, A) \to q(x, BC)$ is in $R\}$
      end
    end
10 **if** $A \in V_{1,m}$ **then return** $true$ **else return** $false$
end

On line 5, $V_{i,1}$ is set to be all pushdown symbols that can be poped out when the automaton reads a_i. If Σ is not monadic, the construction of the set $V_{i,1}$ is not so easy. Thus we need a bottom-up parsing procedure on an input tree in the general case.

3.2   A Recognition Algorithm for General L-PDTAs

We present a recognition algorithm for trees accepted by a general L-PDTA. Let $M = (\{q\}, \Sigma, \Gamma, q, Z_0, R)$ be a L-PDTA in simple form. This algorithm consists of three parts: $Parse\text{-}Tree$, $Parse$ and CKY. The function $Parse\text{-}Tree$ takes an input and initializes global variables. Then the main procedure $Parse$ is invoked.

Parse is defined recursively and checks the input tree in a bottom-up way. In *Parse*, the function CKY is invoked.

The function *Parse-Tree* takes a tree α as input and returns *accept* if and only if $\alpha \in L(\mathcal{G})$. This function prepares a set $U_{d \cdot i}$ as a global variable for each node d of α and each i-th child of d.

Parse-Tree:
    input: a tree $\alpha \in T_{\Sigma}$
    output: *accept* or *reject*
begin
1   **for** each node $d \in D_{\alpha}$ **do begin**
2   Let n be the number of children of d.
3   **for** $i := 1$ **to** n **do** $U_{d \cdot i} := \emptyset$
    end
4    $Parse(\alpha, \lambda)$
5   **if** $CKY(\alpha, \lambda, Z_0) = true$ **then return** *accept* **else return** *reject*
end

The procedure *Parse* takes a tree and a node as input. The node shows the location in the tree being processed. The purpose of this procedure is to complete the set $U_{d \cdot i}$ for each node d of α and each i-th child of d. Intuitively speaking, the set $U_{d \cdot i}$ will store pushdown symbols that can be poped out when the automaton reads the label of the node d and passes the content of its pushdown stack to the i-th child of d. As this procedure works in a bottom-up way, the set $U_{d \cdot i}$ will be completed from the leaves to the root.

Parse:
    input: a tree $\alpha \in T_{\Sigma}$ and a node $d \in D_{\alpha}$
begin
1   Let $b \in \Sigma$ be the symbol such that $\alpha(d) = b$.
2   Let n be the number of children of d.
3   **if** $n \neq 0$ **then begin**
4   **for** $i := 1$ **to** n **do** $Parse(\alpha, d \cdot i)$
5   **for** each type (ii) rule $q(b(x_1, x_2, \ldots, x_n), A) \rightarrow b(q(x_1, C_1), \ldots,$
        $q(x_{i-1}, C_{i-1}), q(x_i, \lambda), q(x_{i+1}, C_{i+1}), \ldots, q(x_n, C_n))$ in R
        with $C_1, \ldots, C_{i-1}, C_{i+1}, \ldots, C_n \in \Gamma_0$ **do**
6   **if** $\forall j \in \{1, \ldots, i-1, i+1, \ldots, n\}$, $CKY(\alpha, d \cdot j, C_j) = true$
            then $U_{d \cdot i} := U_{d \cdot i} \cup \{A\}$
    end
end

The function CKY takes a tree α, a node $d \in D_{\alpha}$ and a pushdown symbol A as input. In CKY, the algorithm traverses every node in the subtree α/d in the order of depth-first search. Intuitive speaking, when the algorithm reaches a leaf node, it checks whether the path from the root to the leaf can be accepted by M with A as the start symbol. Note that some elements of the matrix V are reused. See Fig. 3.

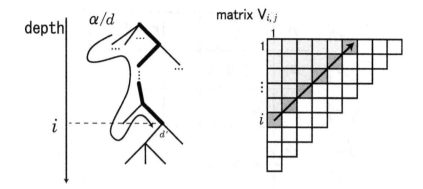

Fig. 3. Traversal of every node in the subtree α/d

CKY:

    input: a tree $\alpha \in T_\Sigma$, a node $d \in D_\alpha$, and a pushdown symbol $A \in \Gamma$

    output: *true* or *false*

begin

1   Let m be the number of nodes in the subtree α/d.

2   Let V be an $m \times m$ matrix.

3    $W := \emptyset$

4   **for** each node $d' \in D_{\alpha/d}$ in the order of depth-first search **do begin**

5   **if** d' is not the root of α/d **then begin**

6            $i := |d'|$

7            $V_{i,1} := U_{d \cdot d'}$

8   **for** $j := 2$ to i **do begin**

9                $V_{i-j+1,j} := \emptyset$

10   **for** $k := 1$ to $j - 1$ **do**

11                  $V_{i-j+1,j} := V_{i-j+1,j} \cup \{A \in \Gamma \mid B \in V_{i-j+1,k},$
                    $C \in V_{i-j+1+k,j-k}$, and $q(x, A) \to q(x, BC)$ is in $R\}$

            end

        end

12   **if** d' is a leaf **then begin**

13            $i := |d'| + 1$

14            $V_{i,1} := \{A \in \Gamma \mid q(a, A) \to a$ is in R and $\alpha(d \cdot d') = a\}$

15   **for** $j := 2$ to i **do begin**

16                $V_{i-j+1,j} := \emptyset$

17   **for** $k := 1$ to $j - 1$ **do**

18                  $V_{i-j+1,j} := V_{i-j+1,j} \cup \{A \in \Gamma \mid B \in V_{i-j+1,k},$
                    $C \in V_{i-j+1+k,j-k}$, and $q(x, A) \to q(x, BC)$ is in $R\}$

            end

19            $W := W \cup V_{1,i}$

        end

    end

20   **if** $A \in W$ **then return** *true* **else return** *false*

end

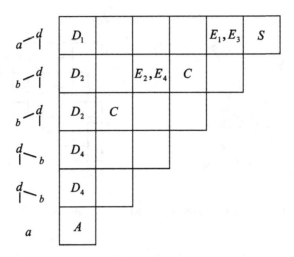

Fig. 4. The content of the matrix V when $d' = 2 \cdot 2 \cdot 2 \cdot 1 \cdot 1$

Example 3. Suppose that we take the automaton M' in Example 2 and input to the algorithmthe the tree illustrated in Fig. 2 (call it α). Imagine that during the process of *Parse-Tree*(α), *Parse*(α, λ) has been completed and $CKY(\alpha, \lambda, S)$ is being processed. In Fig. 4, the content of the matrix V when $d' = 2 \cdot 2 \cdot 2 \cdot 1 \cdot 1$ is illustrated. Because $S \in V_{1,6}$, $CKY(\alpha, \lambda, S)$ returns *true*. Thus *Parse-Tree*(α) returns *accept*.

For the recognition algorithm for general L-PDTAs, we have the following results:

Theorem 1. *For any $\alpha \in T_\Sigma$, $\alpha \in T(M)$ if and only if Parse-Tree(α) returns accept.*

Proof. To show the correctness of the theorem, we prove that the following statement holds for any $A \in N_0$, $\alpha \in T_\Sigma$ and $d \in D_\alpha$.

$$q(\alpha/d, A) \overset{*}{\vdash_M} \alpha/d \text{ iff } CKY(\alpha, d, A) = true \text{ after invoking } Parse(\alpha, d).$$

We prove the "only if" part by induction on the length of computation. **Basis.** If $q(\alpha/d, A) \vdash_M \alpha/d$, then $\alpha/d = a$ for some $a \in \Sigma_0$. *Parse*(α, d) does nothing. Because $q(a, A) \to a$ is in R, A will be in $V_{1,1}$. Therefore $CKY(\alpha, d, A)$ returns *true*. **I.S.** For $k \geq 2$, assume that the statement holds if the length of the computation is less than k. Suppose that $q(\alpha/d, A) \overset{*}{\vdash_M} \alpha/d$ is a computation of length k. Then there exists a path $d_1 d_2 \cdots d_m$ such that $d_1 = d$, d_m is a leaf, and for $1 \leq i \leq m - 1$, the read rule applied to d_i is of the form $q(b_i(x_1, x_2, \ldots, x_{n_i}), A_i) \to b_i(q(x_1, C_{i,1}), \ldots, q(x_{h_i}, \lambda), \ldots, q(x_{n_i}, C_{i,n_i})$ with $b_i = \alpha(d_i) \in \Sigma_{n_i}$, $A_i \in \Gamma_1$, $d_i \cdot h_i = d_{i+1}$, and $C_{i,1}, \ldots, C_{i,h_i-1}, C_{i,h_i+1}, \ldots, C_{i,n_i} \in \Gamma_0$ and the read rule applied to d_m is of the form $q(b_m, A_m) \to b_m$ with $b_m = \alpha(d_m) \in \Sigma_0$ and $A_m \in \Gamma_1$. Intuitively speaking, this path consists of nodes which received the content of pushdown stack from its parent. And the following computation is possible. $q(\alpha/d, A) \overset{*}{\vdash_M} q(\alpha/d, A_1 A_2 \cdots A_m) \overset{*}{\vdash_M} \alpha/d$. Because $q(\alpha/d_i \cdot j, C_{i,j}) \overset{*}{\vdash_M} \alpha/d_i \cdot j$ for $1 \le i \le m-1$ and $1 \le j \le n_i$, the induction hypothesis can be used. We know that for $1 \le i \le m-1$ and $1 \le j \le n_i$, $CKY(\alpha, d_i \cdot j, C_{i,j}) = true$ after invoking $Parse(\alpha, d_i \cdot j)$. Thus after invoking $Parse(\alpha, d)$, $A_i \in U_{d_{i+1}}$ for $1 \le i \le m-1$. Because R contains ε-rules which generate the string of stack symbols $A_1 A_2 \cdots A_m$ from A, A will be in $V_{1,m}$. Therefore $CKY(\alpha, d, A)$ returns $true$.

The "if" part is proved by induction on the number of nodes in the subtree α/d as follows. **Basis.** When $\alpha/d = a$ for some $a \in \Sigma_0$, the statement clearly holds. **I.S.** For $k \ge 2$, assume that the statement holds if the number of nodes in the subtree α/d is less than k. Suppose that the number of nodes in the subtree α/d is k and $CKY(\alpha, d, A) = true$ after invoking $Parse(\alpha, d)$. Then these exist a path $d_1 d_2 \cdots d_m$ and a string of stack symbols $A_1 A_2 \cdots A_m \in \Gamma_1^* \Gamma_0$ such that $d_1 = d$, d_m is a leaf, $A_i \in U_{d_{i+1}}$ for $1 \le i \le m-1$ and $q(\alpha/d, A) \overset{*}{\vdash_M} q(\alpha/d, A_1 A_2 \cdots A_m)$. For $1 \le i \le m-1$, since $A_i \in U_{d_{i+1}}$, a read rule $q(b_i(x_1, x_2, \ldots, x_{n_i}), A_i) \to b_i(q(x_1, C_{i,1}), \ldots, q(x_{h_i}, \lambda), \ldots, q(x_{n_i}, C_{i,n_i})$ with $b_i = \alpha(d_i) \in \Sigma_{n_i}$, $1 \le h_i \le n_i$, and $C_{i,1}, \ldots, C_{i,h_i-1}, C_{i,h_i+1}, \ldots, C_{i,n_i} \in \Gamma_0$ such that $CKY(\alpha, d_i \cdot j, C_{i,j}) = true$ after invoking $Parse(\alpha, d_i \cdot j)$, is in R. By the induction hypothesis, $q(\alpha/d_i \cdot j, C_{i,j}) \overset{*}{\vdash_M} \alpha/d_i \cdot j$ for $1 \le i \le m-1$ and $1 \le j \le n_i$. Therefore $q(\alpha/d, A_1 A_2 \cdots A_m) \overset{*}{\vdash_M} \alpha/d$.

By the statement, for any $\alpha \in T_\Sigma$, $q(\alpha, Z_0) \overset{*}{\vdash_M} \alpha$ if and only if $CKY(\alpha, \lambda, Z_0)$ returns $true$ after invoking $Parse(\alpha, \lambda)$. Therefore the theorem holds.   □

Theorem 2. *The recognition algorithm for general L-PDTAs runs in $O(n^4)$ time, where n is the number of nodes of an input tree.*

Proof. Let $\alpha \in T_\Sigma$ be a tree with n nodes. When α is inputted to the algorithm, the funtion CKY will be invoked $O(n)$ times. The time needed to compute the function CKY is $O(n^3)$. Therefore the total time needed to finish the algorithm is $O(n^4)$.   □

4   Conclusion

In this paper, an $O(n^4)$ time recognition algorithm for trees accepted by an L-PDTA was presented. We expect that the time complexity of the algorithm can be improved to $O(n^3)$. Algorithms with $O(n^4)$ or $O(n^3)$ time complexity might be a little slow in actual applications. However, we expect that there exist faster recognition algorithms for deterministic L-PDTAs. For future work, the development of a recognition algorithm for general PDTAs should be pursued because it might be used for many applications such as the recognition of RNA secondary structures.

References

1. Comon, H., Dauchet, M., Gilleron, R., Jacquemard, F., Lugiez, D., Tison, S., Tommasi, M.: Tree automata techniques and applications. Available on: http://www.grappa.univ-lille3.fr/tata (1997) release October, 1rst 2002.

2. Gécseg, F., Steinby, M.: Tree Languages. In: Handbook of Formal Languages. Volume 3. Springer-Verlag, Berlin (1997) 1–68
3. Guessarian, I.: Pushdown tree automata. Mathematical Systems Theory **16** (1983) 237–263
4. Tanaka, S., Kasai, T.: The emptiness problem for indexed languages is exponential time complete. IEICE Trans. (published in Japanese) **J68-D** (1985) 1727–1734
5. Fujiyoshi, A., Kasai, T.: Spinal-formed context-free tree grammars. Theory of Computing Systems **33** (2000) 59–83
6. Fujiyoshi, A.: Linearity and nondeletion on monadic context-free tree grammars. Information Processing Letters **93** (2005) 103–107
7. Abeillé, A., Rambow, O., eds.: Tree adjoining grammars: formalisms, linguistic analysis and processing. CSLI Publications, Stanford, California (2000)
8. Fujiyoshi, A.: Epsilon-free grammars and lexicalized grammars that generate the class of the mildly context-sensitive languages. In: Proceedings of 7th International Workshop on Tree Adjoining Grammar and Related Formalisms (TAG+7). Vancouver (2004) 16–23
9. Joshi, A.K., Levy, L.S., Takahashi, M.: Tree adjunct grammars. J. Computer & System Sciences **10** (1975) 136–163
10. Joshi, A.K., Schabes, Y.: Tree-adjoining grammars. In: Handbook of Formal Languages. Volume 3. Springer-Verlag, Berlin (1997) 69–124
11. Rajasekaran, S.: Tree-adjoining language parsing in $O(n^6)$ time. SIAM J. Comput. **25** (1996) 862–873
12. Rajasekaran, S., Yooseph, S.: TAL recognition in $O(M(n^2))$ time. J. Computer & System Sciences **56** (1998) 83–89
13. Vijay-Shanker, K., Weir, D.J.: The equivalence of four extensions of context-free grammars. Mathematical Systems Theory **27** (1994) 511–546
14. Rounds, W.C.: Mapping and grammars on trees. Mathematical Systems Theory **4** (1970) 257–287
15. Hopcroft, J.E., Ullman, J.D.: Introduction to Automata Theory, Languages and Computation. Addison Wesley, Reading, Massachusetts (1979)

Shorter Regular Expressions from Finite-State Automata*

Yo-Sub Han and Derick Wood

Department of Computer Science,
The Hong Kong University of Science and Technology
{emmous, dwood}@cs.ust.hk

Abstract. We consider the use of state elimination to construct shorter regular expressions from finite-state automata. Although state elimination is an intuitive method for computing regular expressions from finite-state automata, the resulting regular expressions are often very long and complicated. We examine the minimization of finite-state automata to obtain shorter expressions first. Then, we introduce vertical chopping based on bridge states and horizontal chopping based on the structural properties of given finite-state automata. We prove that we should not eliminate bridge states until we eliminate all non-bridge states to obtain shorter regular expressions. In addition, we suggest heuristics for state elimination that lead to shorter regular expressions based on vertical chopping and horizontal chopping.

Note that we have omitted almost all proofs in this preliminary version.

1 Introduction

It is well known that the family of languages defined by finite-state automata (FAs) is the same as the family of languages described by regular expressions [1]. This result is proved by showing that we can construct FAs from regular expressions and that we can compute regular expressions from FAs.

There are a number of FA constructions; for example, the Thompson construction [2], the position construction [3, 4] and the follow construction [5]. These constructions are inductive and, therefore, preserve the structural properties of regular expressions. For instance, the size of a Thompson automaton is bounded by the size of a given regular expression [6] and the number of states in a position automaton is the number of character appearances in the corresponding regular expression plus one [7].

When converting FAs into regular expressions, we can use either linear equations [8] or state elimination [9]. We consider state elimination. State elimination was already in use in the 1960's, in particular by Brzozowski and McCluskey, Jr. [9] and was carefully formulated by Wood [10]. The idea behind state elimination is simple. We keep removing states, except the start and the final states for

---

* The authors were supported under the Research Grants Council of Hong Kong Competitive Earmarked Research Grant HKUST6197/01E.

J. Farré, I. Litovsky, and S. Schmitz (Eds.): CIAA 2005, LNCS 3845, pp. 141–152, 2006.
© Springer-Verlag Berlin Heidelberg 2006

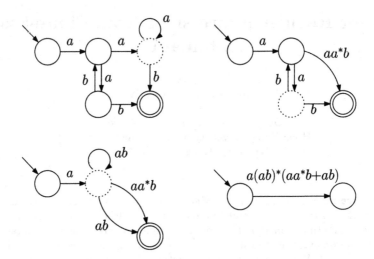

Fig. 1. An example of state elimination. The dotted states are being removed.

a given FA, while maintaining the transition information of the automaton until there are no more states to eliminate. We illustrate state elimination in Fig. 1.

In Section 2, we define some basic notions. In Section 3, we describe state elimination and suggest two ways to obtain smaller finite-state automata. Then, we introduce vertical chopping and horizontal chopping of a given FA in Sections 4 and 5. Furthermore, we show that we should not eliminate bridge states, which are defined in Section 4, until we eliminate all non-bridge states to obtain a shorter regular expression. Finally, we suggest some heuristics for state elimination that lead to shorter regular expressions.

2   Preliminaries

Let Σ denote a finite alphabet of characters and Σ^* denote the set of all strings over Σ. A language over Σ is any subset of Σ^*. The character $\emptyset$ denotes the empty language and the character λ denotes the null string.

A finite-state automaton A is specified by a tuple $(Q, \Sigma, \delta, s, F)$, where Q is a finite set of states, Σ is an input alphabet, $\delta \subseteq Q \times \Sigma \times Q$ is a (finite) set of transitions, $s \in Q$ is the start state and $F \subseteq Q$ is a set of final states. Let $|Q|$ be the number of states in Q and $|\delta|$ be the number of transitions in δ. Then, the size of A is $|A| = |Q| + |\delta|$. Given a transition (p, a, q) in δ, where $p, q \in Q$ and $a \in \Sigma$, we say p has an *out-transition* and q has an *in-transition*. Furthermore, p is a *source state* of q and q is a *target state* of p. A string x in Σ^* is accepted by A if there is a labeled path from s to a final state in F that spells out x. Thus, the language $L(A)$ of a finite-state automaton A is the set of all strings spelled out by paths from s to a final state in F. We define A to be *non-returning* if the start state of A does not have any in-transitions and A to be *non-exiting* if a final state of A does not have any out-transitions. We assume that A has only *useful* states: that is, each state appears on some path from the start state to some final state.

3   State Elimination

We define the *state elimination* of $q \in Q \setminus \{s, f\}$ in A to be the bypassing of state q, q's in-transitions, q's out-transitions and q's self-looping transition with equivalent expression transition sequences. For each in-transition (p_i, α_i, q), $1 \le i \le m$, for some $m \ge 1$, for each out-transition (q, γ, r_j), $1 \le j \le n$, for some $n \ge 1$, and for the self-looping transition (q, β, q) in δ, construct a new transition $(p_i, \alpha_i \cdot \beta^* \cdot \gamma_j, r_j)$. If there exists transition (p, ν, r) in δ for some expression ν, then we merge two transitions to give the bypass transition $(p, (\alpha_i \cdot \beta^* \cdot \gamma_j) + \nu, r)$. We then remove q and all transitions into and out of q in δ. We denote the resulting automaton by $A_q = (Q \setminus \{q\}, \Sigma, \delta_q, s, F)$. State elimination maintains the language accepted by a given automaton while removing states. Note that we have regular expressions instead of single characters on a transition of A_q. We say that a finite-state automaton with regular expressions on transitions is an *expression automaton* (EA) [9, 11].

Given an FA $A = (Q, \Sigma, \delta, s, F)$ that is not non-returning and not non-exiting, we transform A into a new FA A' such that $L(A') = L(A)$ and A' is non-returning and non-exiting by introducing a new start state s' and a new final state f' as follows: $A' = (Q \cup \{s', f'\}, \Sigma, \delta \cup \{(s', \lambda, s)\} \cup \{(f_i, \lambda, f') \mid f_i \in F\}, s', f')$.

Lemma 1. *Let $A = (Q, \Sigma, \delta, s, f)$ be a non-returning and non-exiting expression automaton with at least three states and q be a state in $Q \setminus \{s, f\}$. Then, $L(A_q) = L(A)$ and A_q is non-returning and non-exiting.*

Once we eliminate all states in $Q \setminus \{s, f\}$ for A that is non-returning and non-exiting, we obtain an expression automaton $A_{Q \setminus \{s, f\}} = (\{s, f\}, \Sigma, (s, E, f), s, f)$, where E is the corresponding regular expression for A.

One problem with state elimination is that it may increase the size of labels on transitions exponentially while removing states for a given automaton. For example in Fig. 2, if we remove q from the automaton A, then we have to introduce $O(mn)$ duplicate strings as new transition labels.

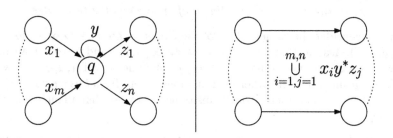

Fig. 2. An example of state elimination that produce many duplicate strings

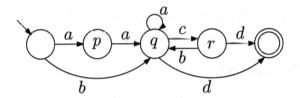

Fig. 3. An example of different regular expressions by different removal sequences for a given finite-state automaton. $E_1 = (aa + b)(a + cb)^*(cd + d)$ is the output of state elimination in $p \rightarrow r \rightarrow q$ order and $E_2 = (aa + b)a^*c(ba^*c)^*(ba^*d + d) + (aa + b)a^*d$ is the output of state elimination in $p \rightarrow q \rightarrow r$ order, where $L(E_1) = L(E_2)$.

Another problem with state elimination is that different removal sequences result in different regular expressions. Although we cannot always avoid exponential blow-up, we can still obtain shorter regular expressions by choosing a better removal sequence. Fig. 3 illustrates this idea.

Recently, Delgado and Morais [12] investigated heuristics for computing a shorter regular expression from a given finite-state automaton A. They define the *weight* of a state q in A. Given a transition $t = (p, \alpha, q)$, the weight of t is the total number of character appearances in α. Then, the weight of a state q in A, which we call *state weight*, is defined as *the sum of in-transition weights + the sum of out-transition weights + the loop weight*. Then, they remove a state that has the lightest weight based on state weight. Although this heuristic is better than random selection, it is straightforward to give examples in which the greedy choice does not lead to shorter regular expressions.

Assume that we have an algorithm to compute an optimal removal sequence for a given automaton A. Then, if we have a smaller automaton A' such that $L(A) = L(A')$, then we can compute the optimal removal sequence more rapidly and the removal sequence will lead to a shorter regular expression.

We define two states p and q in an FA $A = (Q, \Sigma, \delta, s, F)$ to be *equivalent* if the following conditions hold: 1) $p \in F$ if and only if $q \in F$ and 2) $(p, a, t) \in \delta$ if and only if $(q, a, t) \in \delta$, where $t \in Q$ and $a \in \Sigma$. If we have two equivalent states, then we remove one of them, say p, and redirect all in-transitions of p into q. This does not change the language of A but it does reduce the size of A.

Lemma 2. *If two source states of a current state q are equivalent, then we need fewer new transitions when eliminating q after merging the two states.*

Now we consider the target states of the current state $t \in Q$ of an FA $A = (Q, \Sigma, \delta, s, F)$. Assume that t has two target states p and q and two out-transitions of t have the same character; namely, $(t, a, p) \in \delta$ if and only if $(t, a, q) \in \delta$, where $a \in \Sigma$, and p and q have no other in-transitions except from t as shown in Fig. 4. Then, we delete p and attach all out-transitions of p to q so that all out-transitions are from q.

Lemma 3. *If the current state t, in an FA $A = (Q, \Sigma, \delta, s, F)$, has two target states that are reachable only from t via the same transition label, then we need fewer new transitions when removing q after merging the two states.*

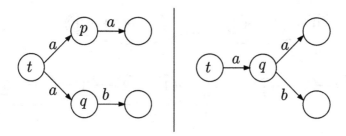

Fig. 4. Note that state t has the same out-transitions to two target states p and q. We make all out-transitions of p leave from q and remove p.

Ilie et al. [13] adopted these ideas to minimize NFAs and designed an $O(m \log n)$ time algorithm using $O(m + n)$ space that discovers equivalent states for a given FA A, where n is the number of states and m is the number of transitions of A. Note that the nondeterministic finite-state automaton (NFA) minimization problem in general is known to be PSPACE-complete [14].

4   Vertical Chopping

Assume that we have a finite-state automaton A that cannot be minimized any further by using equivalent states. Then, we have to compute a removal sequence for A. One question arising from Fig. 3 is why does removing the middle state at the last step lead to a shorter regular expression than when removing it at the second to last step. We observe that the middle state in Fig. 3 has some helpful properties.

Definition 1. *We define a state b in a DFA A to be a* bridge state *if it satisfies the following three conditions:*

1. *State b is neither a start nor a final state.*
2. *For each string $w \in L(A)$, its path in A must pass through b at least once.*
3. *Once w's path passes through state b for the first time, the path can never pass through any states that have been visited before apart from state b.*

Note that we can decompose A into two subautomata A_1 and A_2 such that $L(A) = L(A_1) \cdot L(A_2)$ from the first and the second requirements. However, we may have several duplicate states and transitions in both A_1 and A_2 without the third requirement. Then, it does not give a smaller subautomaton in the worst-case. Fig. 5 illustrates this phenomenon.

The third requirement guarantees that if we partition A at a bridge state b into A_1 and A_2, then all out-transitions of b appear only in A_2. Therefore, A_1 and A_2 have only b as a common state between them. Fig. 6 gives an example of bridge states.

Assume that there is only one final state in A. If there is more than one final state, then we introduce a new final state f' and connect all final states to f'

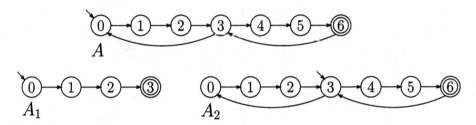

Fig. 5. State 3 satisfies both the first and second conditions in Definition 1 and, therefore, we can partition A into two subautomata A_1 and A_2, where $L(A) = L(A_1) \cdot L(A_2)$. However, A_2 has the same size as A, where state 3 is now the start state of A_2.

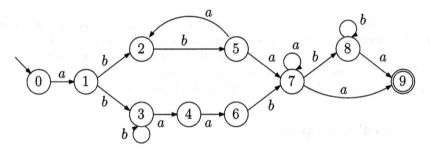

Fig. 6. States 1 and 7 are bridge states

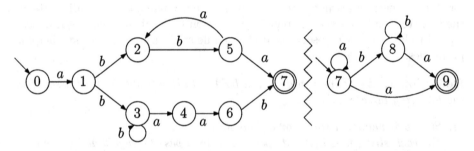

Fig. 7. An example of vertical chopping of the automaton in Fig. 6 at state 7

by null transitions. Given an FA $A = (Q, \Sigma, \delta, s, f)$ and a bridge state $b \in Q$, we partition A into two subautomata A_1 and A_2 as follows: $A_1 = (Q_1, \Sigma, \delta_1, s, b)$ and $A_2 = (Q_2, \Sigma, \delta_2, b, f)$, where Q_1 is a subset of states of A that appear on some path from s and b without visiting b twice in A, $Q_2 = Q \setminus Q_1 \cup \{b\}$, δ_2 is a subset of transitions of A that appear on some path from b to f in A and $\delta_1 = \delta \setminus \delta_2$. Fig. 7 illustrates partitioning at a bridge state.

Lemma 4. *Given an FA A, let A_1 and A_2 be subautomata of A that are partitioned at a bridge state of A. Then, $L(A) = L(A_1) \cdot L(A_2)$.*

Note that if states p and q are bridge states in A, then q is still a bridge state in one of the resulting subautomata after the partitioning of A at p. For example, as shown in Fig. 6, state 1 is a bridge state of A and is a bridge state of A_1, shown in Fig. 7, after chopping at state 7. Let $B = \{b_1, b_2, \ldots, b_k\}$ be a set of bridge states in A, where k is the total number of bridge states in A. Then, $B \setminus \{b_i\}$ is the set of bridge states of A_1 and A_2 after chopping A at state b_i.

We say a path in A is *simple* if it does not have any cycles. Then, from the second requirement of bridge states in Definition 1, we establish the following statement.

Lemma 5. *Let P be a simple path from s to f in A. Then, only the states in P can be bridge states of A.*

Since A is essentially a directed graph, we can compute all bridge states for A using Depth-First Search (DFS) based on Lemma 5.

Theorem 1. *We can compute a set of bridge states for a given automaton $A = (Q, \Sigma, \delta, s, f)$ in $O(|Q| + |\delta|)$ time using DFS.*

Now we demonstrate how bridge states can help to compute a shorter regular expression from a given automaton A. Note that we use state elimination for computing regular expressions. As we have mentioned previously, the removal sequence for state elimination is crucial when we wish to compute a shorter regular expression.

Lemma 6. *If all states in a given automaton $A = (Q, \Sigma, \delta, s, f)$ are bridge states, then state elimination results in the same regular expression whatever the removal sequence of states of A we use.*

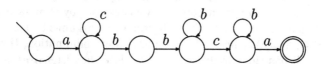

Fig. 8. An example of an FA whose states are all bridge states. Note that state elimination always gives $ac^*bbb^*cb^*a$ no matter which removal sequence we use.

Now we answer the question arising in Fig. 3. We assume that there are no three consecutive bridge states in A. If there are, then we delete the middle bridge state by state elimination. Given an expression automaton $A = (Q, \Sigma, \delta, s, f)$, let $\mathbb{C}(A)$ be the total number of character appearances in transitions of A; that is,

$$\mathbb{C}(A) = \sum_{i,j} |e_{ij}|, \text{ for each } (q_i, e_{ij}, q_j) \in \delta, \text{ where } q_i, q_j \in Q.$$

For example, if A is $(\{s, f\}, \Sigma, (s, E, f), s, f)$, which is the final expression automaton of state elimination for computing a corresponding regular expression, then $\mathbb{C}(A) = |E|$.

Theorem 2. *Given an expression automaton $A = (Q, \Sigma, \delta, s, f)$ and a set B of bridge states of A, the optimal removal sequence must eliminate all states in $Q \setminus B$ before eliminating any bridge states.*

Proof (sketch of proof). Without loss of generality, we assume that we have an optimal removal sequence OPT of state eliminations for A that eliminates a bridge state b first. We prove that there is a shorter regular expression using a different removal sequence and, therefore, OPT is not an optimal sequence.

Since we assume that there are no three consecutive bridge states in A, either a target state or a source state of b must not be a bridge state. Let us assume that a target state is not a bridge state. Let A_b be the resulting expression automaton after the state elimination of b. Then, $\mathbb{C}(A) < \mathbb{C}(A_b)$ by Fig. 2. Let q be the next state to be eliminated after b by OPT. We consider two cases: Case 1 is when q is a target or a source state of b and Case 2 is when q is neither a target state nor a source state of b.

1. If q is a target or a source state of b. Assume that q is a target state of b. In A_b, q has at least the same number of in-transitions compared to q in A and each in-transition of q in A_b has a longer expression than the regular expression of the corresponding in-transitions of q in A. Therefore, $\mathbb{C}(A_p) < \mathbb{C}(A_{bp})$. Moreover, a target state of p in A_{bp} has longer expressions of in-transitions than the corresponding expression of in-transitions in A_p.
2. If q is neither a target nor a source state of b. The state elimination of q produces the same new expressions in both A and A_b. Then, since $\mathbb{C}(A) < \mathbb{C}(A_b)$, we conclude that $\mathbb{C}(A_p) < \mathbb{C}(A_{bp})$.

Let A_{OPT} be the expression automaton computed by OPT and A' be the corresponding expression automaton that we construct by eliminating the same state as OPT does except for b. Then, by the same argument, it is always true that $\mathbb{C}(A') < \mathbb{C}(A_{OPT})$. Once OPT completes state elimination, then $\mathbb{C}(A') < \mathbb{C}(A_{OPT})$ and A' has three states s, f and b. Note that $\mathbb{C}(A_{OPT})$ is the size of the regular expression computed by OPT.

Now we eliminate b from A' and denote the resulting expression automaton by A'_b. Note that $\mathbb{C}(A'_b) = \mathbb{C}(A')$ is the size of the corresponding regular expression that we have computed. Since $\mathbb{C}(A'_b) = \mathbb{C}(A') < \mathbb{C}(A_{OPT})$, we have computed a regular expression that is shorter than the regular expression computed by OPT — a contradiction. Therefore, the optimal removal sequence must eliminate all non-bridge states before eliminating any bridge states. □

Theorem 2 suggests that given an automaton A, we identify all bridge states of A, chop A into several subautomata using bridge states, compute corresponding regular expressions for each subautomaton and catenate the resulting regular expressions to give a regular expression for A. Note that each subautomaton is disjoint from every other subautomaton except for bridge states. Thus, vertical chopping is a divide-and-conquer approach based on the structural properties of A.

5   Horizontal Chopping

Now we have an automaton A without any bridge states and, therefore, we can assume that there is only one start state and one final state in A. Although we cannot avoid computing a removal sequence for A, we can sometimes avoid examining all removal sequences of A to compute such a sequence. For example, we can partition A, shown in Fig. 9, into two subautomata A_u and A_l and compute corresponding regular expressions e_u and e_l for A_u and A_l, respectively. Then, a regular expression for A is $e_u + e_l$, which does not increase the number of character appearances.

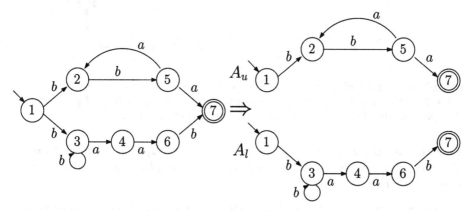

Fig. 9. An example of horizontal chopping for a given automaton without bridge states

Another interesting observation is as follows. Assume that an optimal removal sequence is $5 \rightarrow 3 \rightarrow 4 \rightarrow 6 \rightarrow 2$ for the given FA in Fig. 9. Then, a removal sequence, $3 \rightarrow 4 \rightarrow 6 \rightarrow 5 \rightarrow 2$ gives the same regular expression as before since state elimination of a state in the upper subautomaton does not affect expressions in the lower subautomaton. It implies that sometimes when we compute an optimal removal sequence for a given FA A, we can compute optimal removal sequences for subautomata and combine them. This approach is also a divide-and-conquer approach. Since we partition A horizontally, we call it *horizontal chopping*.

For horizontal chopping of a given FA $A = (Q, \Sigma, \delta, s, f)$, we have to identify subautomata of A such that all subautomata are disjoint from each other except s and f. Our algorithm is based on DFS. When exploring A, we maintain a group index for each state of A. First, we assign a different group index for each child of s in A. Assume p is the current state with group index i and q is the next state to visit in DFS. If q does not have a group index, (then it must have been visited for the first time) q inherits the group index i from p. Otherwise, q already has a group index j and we combine two group indices i and j and regard them as the same group. We continue to explore until we have visited all states in A.

Fig. 10 illustrates how DFS identifies groups from a given automaton. Note that when we visit state q from state p, we merge group 1 and group 2 into a single group.

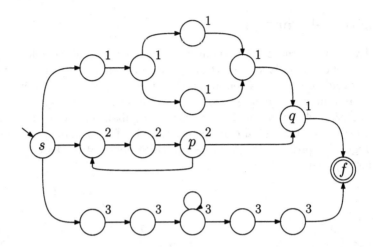

Fig. 10. An example of DFS that identify groups. The label outside a state is its group index. Note that group 1 and group 2 belong to the same group because of q. Therefore, there are two disjoint subautomata that we can use horizontal chopping.

Theorem 3. *Given a finite-state automaton $A = (Q, \Sigma, \delta, s, f)$, we can discover all subautomata that are disjoint from each other except s and f in $O(|Q| + |\delta|)$ time using DFS.*

Moreover, once we partition A horizontally, some states become bridge states of subautomata. For example, state 2 is a bridge state of A_u and states 3, 4 and 6 are bridge states of A_l in Fig. 9. Note that these states are not bridge states of A. Therefore, we can compute bridge states for each subautomaton and perform vertical chopping if there are bridge states; then, again we can repeat horizontal chopping. We continue chopping until no further chopping is possible, and, then compute a removal sequence. Note that state elimination using horizontal chopping and vertical chopping works well for FAs that preserve the structural properties of corresponding regular expressions. For example, for each catenation operation of a given regular expression that is not enclosed by a Kleene star, there is a bridge state in the corresponding Thompson automaton and position automaton. Similarly, for each union operation that is not enclosed by a Kleene star, we can find a horizontal chopping in the corresponding Thompson automaton. On the other hand, we might not be able to perform any vertical chopping or horizontal chopping in the worst-case. However, then it implies that such an FA is already complex and barely preserves any structural properties of the possible regular expressions. In this case, we can only choose brute force.

6   Conclusions

There are several FA constructions from regular expressions and each construction has different properties [7, 6, 3, 5, 4, 2]. On the other hand, there are only two main methods to compute a regular expression from a given FA; namely, linear equations [8] and state elimination [9]. State elimination is an intuitive construction: we compute a regular expression by removing states in a given automaton while maintaining expressions in transitions. The resulting regular expression obtained by state elimination depends on the removal sequence of states. If we choose a good removal sequence, then we obtain a shorter regular expression. On the other hand, we have to try all possible sequences to find the optimal sequence, which is undesirable since there are $O(m!)$ sequences, where m is the number of states. Moreover, state elimination blows up the sizes of regular expressions in transitions. These observations attract us to investigate state elimination for reducing the size of regular expressions and computing a better removal sequence that ensures to have a shorter regular expression.

We have examined NFA minimization to reduce the number of character appearances based on state equivalence. Furthermore, we have investigated the properties of bridge states of an FA and showed that bridge states must be eliminated after eliminating all non-bridge states in A in order to have a shorter regular expression. We can perform vertical chopping of A using bridge states. We have also discovered that we can use horizontal chopping that ensures to compute a state removal sequence of A quickly: once we partition A horizontally, then we can repeat vertical chopping for each subautomaton. We have designed two algorithms for identifying vertical chopping and horizontal chopping of A based on DFS. Both algorithms have a linear running time in the size of A. The combination of vertical chopping and horizontal chopping suggests a divide-and-conquer heuristic for computing a better removal sequence of states of A.

References

1. Kleene, S.: Representation of events in nerve nets and finite automata. In Shannon, C., McCarthy, J., eds.: Automata Studies, Princeton, NJ, Princeton University Press (1956) 3–42
2. Thompson, K.: Regular expression search algorithm. Communications of the ACM **11** (1968) 419–422
3. Glushkov, V.: The abstract theory of automata. Russian Mathematical Surveys **16** (1961) 1–53
4. McNaughton, R., Yamada, H.: Regular expressions and state graphs for automata. IEEE Transactions on Electronic Computers **9** (1960) 39–47
5. Ilie, L., Yu, S.: Follow automata. Information and Computation **186** (2003) 140–162
6. Giammarresi, D., Ponty, J.L., Wood, D., Ziadi, D.: A characterization of Thompson digraphs. Discrete Applied Mathematics **134** (2004) 317–337
7. Caron, P., Ziadi, D.: Characterization of Glushkov automata. Theoretical Computer Science **233** (2000) 75–90
8. Eilenberg, S.: Automata, Languages, and Machines. Volume A. Academic Press, New York, NY (1974)
9. Brzozowski, J., McCluskey, Jr., E.: Signal flow graph techniques for sequential circuit state diagrams. IEEE Transactions on Electronic Computers **EC-12** (1963) 67–76

10. Wood, D.: Theory of Computation. John Wiley & Sons, Inc., New York, NY (1987)
11. Han, Y.S., Wood, D.: The generalization of generalized automata: Expression automata. In: Proceedings of CIAA'04, Springer-Verlag (2004) 156–166 Lecture Notes in Computer Science 3317.
12. Delgado, M., Morais, J.: Approximation to the smallest regular expression for a given regular language. In: Proceedings of CIAA'04, Springer-Verlag (2004) 312–314 Lecture Notes in Computer Science 3317.
13. Ilie, L., Navarro, G., Yu, S.: On NFA reductions. In Karhumaki, J., Maurer, H., Paun, G., Rozenberg, G., eds.: Theory is Forever (Salomaa Festschrift). Lecture Notes in Computer Science 3113, Springer-Verlag, Heidelberg (2004) 112–124
14. Jiang, T., Ravikumar, B.: Minimal NFA problems are hard. SIAM Journal on Computing 22 (1993) 1117–1141

Wind in the Willows – Generating Music by Means of Tree Transducers

Johanna Högberg

Department of Computing Science, Umeå University,
S–901 87 Umeå, Sweden
johanna@cs.umu.se

Abstract. We implement a rule-based system for algorithmic composition. This system, that we call Willow, resides in the TREEBAG environment and consists of a sequence of formal devices, familiar from the
field of tree grammars and tree transducers. Since these devices are well
studied, we can apply known results to derive the descriptive complexity
of the system as a whole.

1 Introduction

In music theory, it is widely believed that music is syntax – to a large extent or
even in its entirety (see [1] for quotations and references supporting this claim). If
this is true, it should be possible to describe some of the basic aspects of musical
composition by means of grammars and automata. Here, we describe a first
attempt in this direction, a system named Willow, and draw some conclusions
regarding the descriptional complexity of the generated tunes.

It is conventional to represent syntax by means of a tree structure (e.g. as a
parse or derivation tree). For the first two bars of the sonata in C-major KV545
by Mozart, the representation could look as shown in Figure 1. The generation
and transformation of trees such as the one in the figure is studied within the
theory of tree grammars and tree transducers, the latter being formal automata
that transform input trees into output trees. Parts of this theory have been implemented in TREEBAG [2], a system that we use in order to implement Willow.

In Figure 2, we see the set-up. The components of Willow, mainly a regular
tree grammar and a number of top-down tree transducers (an *ignorant* transducer is a special kind of top-down tree transducer), are arranged in the fashion
of an assembly line. At the very beginning of the line, the regular tree grammar
generates an initial tree representing a metre, i.e. a rhythmic pattern. The tree is
then transformed step by step by some twelve tree transducers, each of them be-
stowing a specific musical property on the generated piece. For example, the last
top-down tree transducer along the assembly line, namely ACCOMPANIMENT,
adds an accompaniment to an otherwise already finished tune. Because of limited space, the components cannot be described in detail here, but their names
indicate their purpose. The algebra visible in Figure 2 was added for technical
reasons and does not partake in the generation process.

J. Farré, I. Litovsky, and S. Schmitz (Eds.): CIAA 2005, LNCS 3845, pp. 153–162, 2006.
© Springer-Verlag Berlin Heidelberg 2006

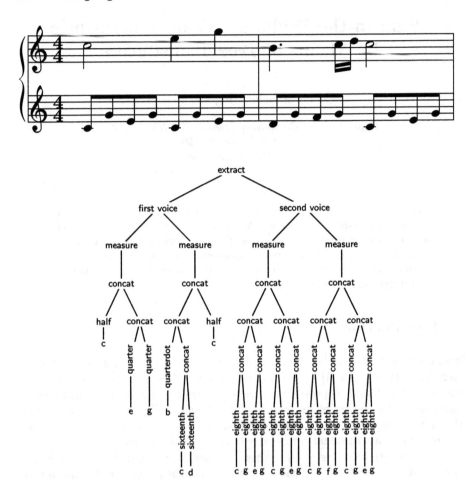

Fig. 1. Above, the first two bars of the sonata in C-major KV545 by Mozart, and below, the same piece represented by a tree

One benefit of Willow is that, since the workers are separate entities, they can be replaced one at a time. Say for example that one worker, perhaps Mr Jazz-transducer, assigns chords mimicking Lillian Hardin, but that the user prefers pop. Then the user could simply substitute Mr Justin-transducer for Mr Jazz-transducer and have things her way. Similarly Mr Walz could substitute Mr March, Ms Guitar Mrs Piano, and Lady Choir old Sir Solo. Another benefit is that the generated music could take the rôle of raw material for a human composer. A computer executing the system could generate an endless supply of themes and tunes, without hesitation or embarrassment. It would then be up to the composer to pick and choose among the material as she pleases, and hopefully there will be some parts that appeal to her. These parts could then be fed into the next step in the construction line; the computer could for example

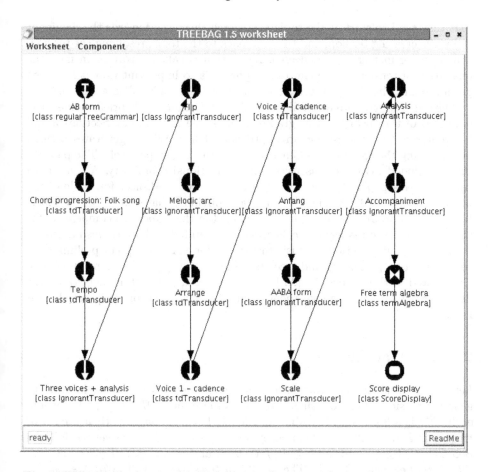

Fig. 2. Willow is implemented in TREEBAG and consists of a regular tree grammar, a number of top-down tree transducers, a free-term algebra, and a score display

suggest an accompaniment or a decoration. Again the human composer would be able to provide the computer with guidance and feedback.

One of the principles that have guided the design of Willow is that every component should be firmly rooted in music theory. Although we shall not discuss music theory in detail here, it is useful to know the following basic facts. Most tunes are based on a set of chords; tuples of tones that are sounded together (or nearly so). For tunes written in a *major scale*, there is an associated set of seven chords called the *triads of the major scale*. In analytic notation, these chords are referred to as I, ii, III, IV, V, vi, and $vii°$.

A *chord progression* is a sequence of chords. Though the chords in a chord progression can be any triads in the scale, depending on the genre, some progressions are more likely than others. E.g. pop music often contains the chord progression shown as (a) in Figure 4, while the progression ii, V, I is associated with jazz, and I, IV, I, V with blues. A common feature of these progressions is that they tend to start at the tonic (I), search their way towards the dominant (V) while creating tension, and then fall back to the tonic, resolving the tension. This cycle of increasing and decreasing tension is called a *phrase*. In fact, the relaxation of tension at the end of the phrase is so important that it has been given a name; the chord progression that ends a phrase is called a *cadence*.

The paper is structured as follows. The next section recalls briefly some basic notations of the theory of tree grammars and tree transducers. Sections 3 and 4 attempt to give the reader an impression of how Willow generates a tune, by discussing the components CHORD and CADENCE, respectively. The paper is then concluded by a brief discussion of descriptional complexity. A full length version of this paper [1], together with a TREEBAG worksheet for Willow, can be downloaded at [3]. It is unfortunate (and obvious) that samples of the music that Willows produces cannot not be included in this paper. To compensate for this, we direct the reader to a collection of generated audio files, also available at [3]. For an introduction to music theory, see for example [4]. For preliminaries concerning tree grammars and tree transducers, see [5], [6] or Appendix A of [2]. Related work includes [7], [8], [9], [10], and [11], although none of these use devices from formal language theory, with the exception of [10], which uses L-systems.

2   Tree Transducers

Let us now recall the notations of tree language theory we shall use in order to generate music. Let Σ be a signature, i.e., a finite union $\Sigma = \bigcup_{k=1}^{n} \Sigma^{(k)}$, where each $\Sigma^{(k)}$ is a finite set of symbols of rank k. Let S be any set, then the set of trees over Σ *indexed by* S, denoted by $\mathrm{T}_\Sigma(S)$, is defined inductively as follows; $S \cup \Sigma^{(0)} \subseteq \mathrm{T}_\Sigma(S)$ and for $k \geq 1$, $f \in \Sigma^{(k)}$, and $t_1, \ldots, t_k \in \mathrm{T}_\Sigma(S)$, the tree $f[t_1 \ldots t_k]$ belongs to $\mathrm{T}_\Sigma(S)$. The set T_Σ of *trees* over Σ is $\mathrm{T}_\Sigma(\emptyset)$. A subset of T_Σ is called a *tree language*.

Let $X = \{x_1, x_2, \ldots\}$ be a set of special symbols, so-called variables, all of rank zero, that is disjoint with every signature in this paper. When we only wish to talk about a subset $\{x_1, \ldots, x_k\}$ of X, we refer to the subset as X_k. If $t \in \mathrm{T}_\Sigma(X)$ for some arbitrary signature Σ, then we denote by $t[\![t_1, \ldots, t_k]\!]$ the tree that results when each occurrence of x_i in t is replaced by t_i, $i \in [k]$.

A top-down tree transducer (or simply, td transducer) is a quintuple $td = (\Sigma, \Sigma', Q, R, q_0)$, where Σ is an input signature, Σ' is an output signature, Q is a signature of states of rank 1, such that $Q \cap (\Sigma \cup \Sigma') = \emptyset$, R is a finite set of rules, and $q_0 \in Q$ is the initial state. Every rule in R has the form $q[f[x_1, \ldots, x_k]] \to t$, where $k \in \mathbb{N}$, $q \in Q$, $f \in \Sigma^{(k)}$, and $t \in \mathrm{T}_{\Sigma'}(Q(X_k))$. To improve legibility, we henceforth write $q f[t_q, \ldots, t_k]$, rather than $q[f[t_q, \ldots, t_k]]$, when $q \in Q$.

For trees $s, s' \in \mathrm{T}_{\Sigma'}(Q(\mathrm{T}_\Sigma))$, there is a *transduction step* $s \mapsto_{td} s'$ by a rule $q f[x_1, \ldots, x_k] \to t \in R$ if $s = s_0[\![q f[t_1, \ldots, t_k]]\!]$ for some tree s_0 containing x_1 exactly once, and $s' = s_0[\![t[\![t_1, \ldots, t_k]\!]]\!]$. We denote the transitive closure of $\mapsto_{td}$ by $\overset{*}{\mapsto}_{td}$ and say that there is a transduction from s to s' if $s \overset{*}{\mapsto}_{td} s'$. Finally, $td(s) = \{s' \in \mathrm{T}_{\Sigma'} \mid q_0[s] \overset{*}{\mapsto}_{td} s'\}$.

Let $td = (\Sigma, \Sigma', Q, R, q_0)$ be a td transducer. We call td a *linear* td transducer if, in every rule, each variable occurs at most once in its right-hand side. A td transducer that is not linear is *copying*. If there is at least one rule r in R whose left-hand side contains a variable that does not occur in the right-hand side, we say that td is *deleting*. Furthermore, if, for all $q \in Q$ and $f \in \Sigma^{(k)}$, there is a rule $q\, f[x_1, \ldots, x_k] \to t \in R$, td is *total*. If there is at most one such rule for all $q \in Q$ and $f \in \Sigma^{(k)}$, then it is *deterministic*. A td transducer is *partial* if it is not total.

3   Chord Progressions

Recall that Willow's assembly line consists of a regular tree grammar that generates an initial tree, and a sequence of twelve td transducers that add an attribute each, thereby contributing to the final representation of a tune. We shall not discuss regular tree grammars in this paper, but the reader may consult [5] to learn more about this device. Out of the twelve td transducers, only CHORD and CADENCE will be described in detail.

The td transducer CHORD assigns chords to the lower nodes of the tree, using states to represent chord transitions. The assignment is done in such a way that when the assigned chords are read from left to right, they appear in accordance

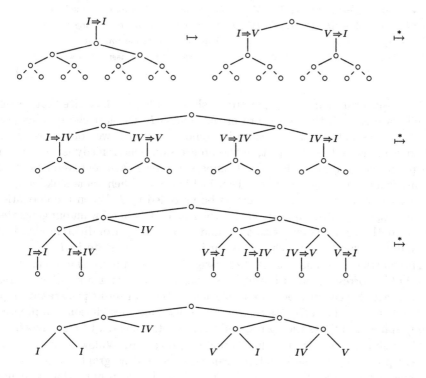

Fig. 3. The td transducer CHORD assigns a chord progression common to pop music

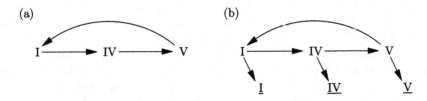

Fig. 4. A chord progression common to pop (a), augmented with sinks (b)

with the chord progression (a) of Figure 4. It is not desirable that all chords are assigned to nodes at the same level, as this would correspond to a tune where the chord changes every n-th note, giving a dull and monotonic impression. In an attempt to attack this problem, we have made CHORD nondeterministic; as soon as a state represents an allowed transition (i.e. an edge between two nodes in the graph of Figure 4), there is one applicable rule which terminates, and one or more applicable rules which continue to elaborate the progression. If a state does not represent an allowed transition (i.e. $I \Rightarrow V$), then no applicable terminating rule exists. A selection of CHORD's rules follows:

$\{ \quad I \Rightarrow I \quad \text{o}[x_1, x_2] \rightarrow \text{o}[I \Rightarrow V \, x_1, V \Rightarrow I \, x_2] \qquad$ *Move from I to I, passing through V.*

$\quad I \Rightarrow V \quad \text{o}[x_1, x_2] \rightarrow \text{o}[I \Rightarrow IV \, x_1, IV \Rightarrow V \, x_2] \qquad$ *Move from I to V, passing through IV.*

$\quad I \Rightarrow IV \quad \text{o}[x_1, x_2] \rightarrow \text{o}[I \Rightarrow IV \, x_1, IV \Rightarrow IV \, x_2] \qquad$ *When moving from I to IV, linger on IV...*

$\quad I \Rightarrow IV \quad \text{o}[x_1, x_2] \rightarrow I \qquad\qquad\qquad\qquad$ *or assign I to the current node.*

$\quad V \Rightarrow V \quad \text{o}[x_1, x_2] \rightarrow \text{o}[V \Rightarrow I \, x_1, I \Rightarrow V \, x_2] \qquad$ *Move from V to V, passing through I.*

$\quad \cdots \qquad\qquad\qquad\qquad\qquad\qquad\qquad\qquad\qquad\qquad\qquad \}$

The transformation of an input tree is shown in Figure 3. Notice that, as our initial state is $I \Rightarrow I$, the first chord of the tune is I. The last chord is however *not* I. This is unfortunate, because it would be useful if we could specify the destination, as well as the start, of the progression. One remedy is to augment the progression graph with sinks. Compare the original progression (a) with the augmented version (b), both given in Figure 4. When some sink, suppose $\underline{I}$, occurs in a derivation, it will always be preceded by I. When the derivation terminates, the $\underline{I}$ will disappear, leaving the I behind. So if we want our generated tune to both begin and end with an I, and have a number of different chords in the middle, it suffices if we choose as our initial state the state $I \Rightarrow \underline{I}$.

This particular version of CHORD assigns a chord progression common to pop, but a corresponding td transducer can be built for many other genres. To facilitate this construction, we implemented the perl script `progression.pl` (available at [3]). The script takes as input a plain text description of a progression graph and outputs the corresponding, nondeterministic, td transducer.

The technique described in this section is also used by Willow to assign other musical properties whose variations can be expressed as graphs. Examples of this kind are the melodic arc, which is not allowed to leap more than four half tones, and the tempo, which is also to be changed incrementally.

4 Adding a Cadence Using Non-determinism

As mentioned in the introduction, the chord progression that ends a phrase is called a cadence. The td transducer CADENCE takes the last two tones of a piece and turns them into a cadence. For this, it is, of course, necessary to find the last two tones in the given tree representation of the piece. This cannot be accomplished by a deterministic td transducer in the general case; there are decisions that must be made early in the transduction, but in accordance with information that can only be obtained towards the end. A nondeterministic partial td transducer, on the other hand, can guess by making a nondeterministic choice. If the guess is erroneous, then the transduction will fail to terminate and no output tree will be produced; but if the guess is correct, the objective is accomplished and the last two notes of the output tree turned into a cadence. For this purpose, we construct a nondeterministic partial td transducer $td = (\Sigma, \Sigma', Q, R, q_s)$, the components of which are as follows.

$$\Sigma = \{\ \circ^{(2)}, \downarrow^{(0)}\ \} \qquad \Sigma' = \Sigma \cup \{\ d^{(1)}, t^{(1)}\ \} \qquad Q = \{\ q_s, q_d, q_t, q_p\ \}$$

$R = \{$

$q_s \circ [x_1, x_2] \to \circ[q_p\, x_1, q_s\, x_2]$	*Search for the parent of the last note,*
$q_s \circ [x_1, x_2] \to \circ[q_d\, x_1, q_t\, x_2]$	*or guess that we have found it.*
$q_d \circ [x_1, x_2] \to \circ[q_p\, x_1, q_d\, x_2]$	*Stay to the right while looking for the second to last note.*
$q_d \downarrow \to d[\downarrow]$	*Place the d marker for 'dominant'.*
$q_t \downarrow \to t[\downarrow]$	*If state q_t encounters anything but a leaf, the transduction fails.*
$q_p \circ [x_1, x_2] \to \circ[q_p\, x_1, q_p\, x_2]$	*Copy the rest of the tree to the output.*
$q_p \downarrow \to \downarrow$	$\}$

One possible transduction is shown in Figure 5. At the very first step, td guesses nondeterministically that it has found the parent of the last note. Clearly, this is not the case. After a number of transduction steps the rightmost tree of the figure has been reached. At this point the transduction must abort, because there are no rules with left-hand side $q_t \circ [x_1, x_2]$. However, this type of dead-end transductions is automatically detected and avoided in TREEBAG. An alternative transduction is shown in Figure 6. Here, the td transducer waits a number of steps before guessing that it has found the sought parent. This time it is correct, so the transduction succeeds in turning the last two notes into a cadence and terminating.

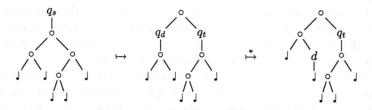

Fig. 5. The transduction fails because of an incorrect earlier guess

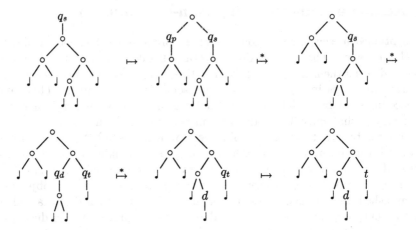

Fig. 6. After a series of correct guesses the nondeterministic td transducer terminates

5   Descriptional Complexity

It was stated in the introduction that an ignorant transducer is a special kind of td transducer, and before we consider the major topic of this section, we should elaborate on what we mean, in this particular case, by "special". The transducers that form Willow are each responsible for one distinct attribute of the finished piece. In other words, rather than completely rebuilding its input tree, a particular transducer contributes by affixing a few labels to the input tree, which is then passed on to the next transducer in the assembly line. The implication is that if the transducers were to be defined using traditional notation, most of their rules would take the following form:

$$q\,f[t_1,\ldots,t_1] \to f[q\,t_1,\ldots,q\,t_1]$$

That is, but for a few exceptions, the rules would dictate that the current node of the input tree should be left untouched, and that the transducer shall continue to work on the subtrees with no change of internal state. E.g. the definition file for SCALE would require more than 3000 rules, out of which less than 300 would cause any change in the input tree whatsoever. To be able to describe the td transducers more concisely, we use the idea of an ignorant transducer. As with a partial td transducer, the definition of an ignorant transducer need not be total, but when an ignorant transducer encounters a state and symbol combination for which it has no appropriate rule, rather than aborting the computation, it keeps the irksome node (i.e. copies it to the output) and continues to work on its subtrees. Hence, an ignorant transducer is a weaker version of the td transducer, as we no longer can express transductions that are partial.

Let us now discuss the descriptive complexity of Willow. The simplicity of its components is probably one of the most appealing properties of Willow. We will now apply results concerning composition of transductions, to show that much of this simplicity is retained when it is the system as a whole that is under consideration. Denote the composition of td transducers td_2 and td_2 by $td_2 \circ td_1$, i.e., $td_2 \circ td_1 = \bigcup_{t' \in td_1(t)} td_2(t')$. We make use of the following result by Baker.

Theorem 1. *[12] The composition $td_2 \circ td_1$ of td transductions td_1 and td_2 is a td transduction if*

1) td_1 is deterministic or td_2 is linear, and
2) td_1 is total or td_2 is nondeleting.

If, in addition, both td_1 and td_2 are linear, deterministic, total, or nondeleting, then $td_2 \circ td_1$ has the respective property as well.

The td transducers that constitute Willow are all nondeleting, which means that the second requirement of Theorem 1 is always met. Recall that regular tree languages are closed under linear td transductions. As a consequence, we can combine the apparatus of AB FORM, CHORD PROGRESSION, and TEMPO in a single regular tree grammar. Applying Theorem 1, we can collapse the sequence consisting of the remaining twelve td transducers by iteratively replacing pairs of them with a single td transducer. Moreover, it is well known that the class of all regular tree languages is closed under linear td transductions. Hence, we can collapse the first three components into a regular tree grammar. We reach a point when the system has been reduced to a regular tree grammar and two td transducers (see Table 1), and cannot be simplified further using Theorem 1. In [13], a type of tree grammar called *tree grammar with branching synchronisation and nested tables of depth n* (branching grammar of depth n, for short) has been introduced, and it has been shown that the class BST_n of tree languages generated is equal to the closure of the regular tree languages under n tree transducers. Hence, we conclude with the following theorem.

Theorem 2. *Willow generates a tree language in BST_2.*

Table 1. The constituents of Willow, ordered as they occur in the generation process. The abbreviations lin., and det. stand for linear and deterministic, respectively.

Component	Device	Lin.	Det.	Collapses to
AB FORM	rtg	n/a	no	reg. tree grammar
CHORD PROGRESSION	td	yes	no	
TEMPO	td	yes	no	
VOICES	td	no	yes	
FLIP	td	yes	yes	
MELODIC ARC	td	yes	no	copy. nondet. td
ARRANGE	td	yes	no	
CADENCE	td	yes	no	
ANFANG	td	yes	no	
AABA FORM	td	no	yes	
SCALE	td	yes	yes	copy. nondet. td
ANALYSIS	td	yes	yes	
ACCOMPANIMENT	td	yes	yes	

6   Limitations and Future Work

The tunes produced by Willow are all in major scales, on the ABAA form, and there are no extrinsic tones or decorations. The accompaniment follows a repetitive pattern governed by chord progression and tempo, and cadences are exceedingly simple. The actual implementation provided works fairly well, but needs further testing to become completely reliable.

A user can regulate the generation process to some degree by selecting, or designing, the td transducers, and setting the order in which they are to be applied. We would like to extend this interaction in order to make it possible to input a theme, e.g. by means of a digital keyboard, and have the system weave a cannon or a fugue around it.

At present, the generated trees are interpreted by the component SCOREDIS-PLAY in a deterministic, but rather ad hoc, manner. This disagrees with the general design of TREEBAG – algebras interpret trees, while displays visualise (or in this case, perform) the results. This makes an algebra for evaluating trees as musical pieces an important future aim.

Acknowledgements. The author wishes to thank the anonymous referees for encouragement and constructive comments.

References

1. Högberg, J.: Wind in the Willows. Technical Report UMINF-05.13, Computing Science, Univ. Umeå (2005)
2. Drewes, F.: Grammatical Picture Generation. Springer (2005)
3. Högberg, J.: Willow – Algorithmic Composition using Tree Automata. Internet resource (2005) Available at http://www.cs.umu.se/~johanna/willow/.
4. Kerman, J., Tomlinson, G.: Listen. Fourth edn. Bedford, Freeman, & Worth (2000)
5. Gécseg, F., Steinby, M.: Tree Automata. Akadémiai Kiadó, Budapest (1984)
6. Fülöp, Z., Vogler, H.: Syntax-Directed Semantics: Formal Models Based on Tree Transducers. Springer-Verlag New York, Inc. (1998)
7. Roads, C.: Grammars as Representations for Music. Computer Music Journal (1979) 48–55
8. Baroni, M.: The concept of musical grammar. Music Analysis **2** (1983) 175–208
9. Lerdahl, F., Jackendoff, R.: Toward a formal theory of tonal music. Journal of Music Theory **21** (1977) 111–171
10. Prusinkiewicz, P.: Score generation with L-systems. In Berg, P., ed.: Proceedings of the International Computer Music Conference 1986. Number 1, Royal Conservatory, The Hague, Netherlands (1986) 455–457
11. Lindblom, B., Sundberg, J.: Towards a Generative Theory of Melody. Swedish Journal of Musicology (1970) 77–88
12. Baker, B.S.: Composition of Top–down and Bottom–up Tree Transductions. Information and Control (1979) 186–213
13. Drewes, F., Engelfriet, J.: Branching Synchronisation Grammars with Nested Tables. Journal of Computer and System Sciences (2004) 611–656

On Deterministic Catalytic Systems*

Oscar H. Ibarra[1,**] and Hsu-Chun Yen[2]

[1] Department of Computer Science,
University of California, Santa Barbara, CA 93106, USA
ibarra@cs.ucsb.edu
[2] Department of Electrical Engineering,
National Taiwan University, Taipei, Taiwan 106, R.O.C.
yen@cc.ee.ntu.edu.tw

Abstract. We look at a 1-membrane catalytic P system with evolution rules of the form $Ca \to Cv$ or $a \to v$, where C is a catalyst, a is a noncatalyst symbol, and v is a (possibly null) string representing a multiset of noncatalyst symbols. (Note that we are only interested in the multiplicities of the symbols.) A catalytic system can be regarded as a *language acceptor* in the following sense. Given an input alphabet Σ consisting of noncatalyst symbols, the system starts with an initial configuration wz, where w is a fixed string of catalysts and noncatalysts not containing any symbol in z, and $z = a_1^{n_1}...a_k^{n_k}$ for some nonnegative integers $n_1, ..., n_k$, with $\{a_1, ..., a_k\} \subseteq \Sigma$. At each step, a maximal multiset of rules is nondeterministically selected and applied in parallel to the current configuration to derive the next configuration (note that the next configuration is not unique, in general). The string z is accepted if the system eventually halts.

It is known that a 1-membrane catalytic system is universal in the sense that any unary recursively enumerable language can be accepted by a 1-membrane catalytic system (even by purely catalytic systems, i.e., when all rules are of the form $Ca \to Cv$). A catalytic system is said to be *deterministic* if at each step, there is a **unique** maximally parallel multiset of rules applicable. It has been an open problem whether deterministic systems of this kind are universal. We answer this question negatively: We show that the membership problem for deterministic catalytic systems is decidable. In fact, we show that the Parikh map of the language ($\subseteq a_1^*...a_k^*$) accepted by any deterministic catalytic system is a simple semilinear set which can be effectively constructed. Since nondeterministic 1-membrane catalytic system acceptors (with 2 catalysts) are universal, our result gives the first example of a variant of P systems for which the nondeterministic version is universal, but the deterministic version is not.

We also show that for a deterministic 1-membrane catalytic system using only rules of type $Ca \to Cv$, the set of reachable configurations from

---

* The research of Oscar H. Ibarra was supported in part by NSF Grants CCR-0208595, CCF-0430945, IIS-0451097 and CCF-0524136. The research of Hsu-Chun Yen was supported in part by NSC Grant 93-2213-E-002-003, Taiwan.
** Corresponding author.

J. Farré, I. Litovsky, and S. Schmitz (Eds.): CIAA 2005, LNCS 3845, pp. 163–175, 2006.
© Springer-Verlag Berlin Heidelberg 2006

a given initial configuration is an effective semilinear set. The application of rules of type $a \to v$, however, is sufficient to render the reachability set non-semilinear. Our results generalize to multi-membrane deterministic catalytic systems. We also consider deterministic catalytic systems which allow rules to be prioritized and investigate three classes of such systems, depending on how priority in the application of the rules is interpreted. For these three prioritized systems, we obtain contrasting results: two are universal and one only accepts semilinear sets.

Keywords: Membrane computing, deterministic catalytic system, deterministic versus nondeterministic, symport/antiport system, counter machine, semilinear set, priority.

1   Introduction

There has been a great deal of research activities in the area of membrane computing (a branch of natural computing) initiated by Gheorghe Păun in a seminal paper [1] over six years ago (see also [2]). Membrane computing identifies an unconventional computing model, namely a P system, from natural phenomena of cell evolutions and chemical reactions. Due to the built-in nature of maximal parallelism inherent in the model, P systems have a great potential for implementing massively parallel systems in an efficient way that would allow us to solve currently intractable problems once future bio-technology (or silicon-technology) gives way to a practical bio-realization (or chip-realization).

A P system is a computing model, which abstracts from the way the living cells process chemical compounds in their compartmental structure. Thus, regions defined by a membrane structure contain objects that evolve according to given rules. The objects can be described by symbols or by strings of symbols, in such a way that multisets of objects are placed in regions of the membrane structure. The membranes themselves are organized as a tree structure (this can be represented by a Venn diagram) where one membrane may contain other membranes. By using the rules in a nondeterministic, maximally parallel manner, transitions between the system configurations can be obtained. A sequence of transitions shows how the system is evolving. Various ways of controlling the transfer of objects from a region to another and applying the rules, as well as possibilities to dissolve, divide or create membranes have been studied. P systems were introduced with the goal to abstract a new computing model from the structure and the functioning of the living cell (as a branch of the general effort of Natural Computing – to explore new models, ideas, paradigms from the way nature computes). Membrane computing has been quite successful: many models have been introduced, most of them Turing complete and/or able to solve computationally intractable problems (NP-complete, PSPACE-complete) in a feasible time (polynomial), by trading space for time. (See the P system website at http://psystems.disco.unimib/it for a large collection of papers in the area, and in particular the monograph [3].)

In the standard semantics of P systems [2, 3, 4], each evolution step of a system $\mathcal{P}$ is a result of applying all the rules in $\mathcal{P}$ in a maximally parallel manner. More precisely, starting from the initial configuration, w, the system goes through a sequence of configurations, where each configuration is derived from the directly preceding configuration in one step by the application of a multiset of rules, which are chosen nondeterministically. For example, a catalytic rule $Ca \rightarrow Cv$ in membrane m is applicable if there is a catalyst C and an object (symbol) a in the preceding configuration in membrane m. The result of applying this rule is the evolution of v from a. If there is another occurrence of C and another occurrence of a, then the same rule or another rule with Ca on the left hand side can be applied. Thus, in general, the number of times a particular rule is applied at anyone step can be unbounded. We require that the application of the rules is maximal: all objects, from all membranes, which *can be* the subject of local evolution rules *have to* evolve simultaneously. Configuration z is reachable (from the starting configuration) if it appears in some execution sequence; z is halting if no rule is applicable on z.

Two popular models of P systems are the catalytic system [2] and the symport/antiport system [5]. An interesting subclass of the latter was studied in [6] – each system is *deterministic* in the sense that the computation path of the system is unique, i.e., at each step of the computation, the maximal multiset of rules that is applicable is unique. It was shown in [6] that any recursively enumerable unary language $L \subseteq o^*$ can be accepted by a deterministic 1-membrane symport/antiport system. Thus, for symport/antiport systems, the deterministic and nondeterministic versions are equivalent and they are universal. It also follows from the construction in [7] that for another model of P systems, called communicating P systems, the deterministic and nondeterministic versions are equivalent as both can accept any unary recursively enumerable language. However, the deterministic-versus-nondeterministic question was left open in [6] for the class of catalytic systems (these systems have rules of the form $Ca \rightarrow Cv$ or $a \rightarrow v$), where the proofs of universality involve a high degree of parallelism [7, 8]. For a discussion of this open question and its importance, see [9, 10]. We answer this question negatively in this paper. Since nondeterministic catalytic systems are universal, our result also gives the first example of a variant of P systems for which the nondeterministic version is universal, but the deterministic version is not.

For a catalytic system serving as a *language acceptor*, the system starts with an initial configuration wz, where w is a fixed string of catalysts and noncatalysts not containing any symbol in z, and $z = a_1^{n_1}...a_k^{n_k}$ for some nonnegative integers $n_1, ..., n_k$, with $\{a_1, ..., a_k\}$ a distinguished subset of noncatalyst symbols (the input alphabet). At each step, a maximal multiset of rules are nondeterministically selected and applied in parallel to the current configuration to derive the next configuration (note that the next configuration is not unique, in general). The string z is accepted if the system eventually halts. Unlike nondeterministic 1-membrane catalytic system acceptors (with 2 catalysts) which are universal, we are able to show using a graph-theoretic approach that the Parikh map of the language ($\subseteq a_1^* ... a_k^*$) accepted by any deterministic catalytic system is a simple semilinear set which can also be effectively constructed. Our result gives the first example of a variant of P systems for which the nondeterministic version is universal, but the deterministic version is not. For deterministic 1-membrane catalytic systems using only rules of type $Ca \rightarrow Cv$, we show the set of reachable configurations from a given initial configuration to be effective semilinear. In contrast, the reachability set is no longer semilinear in general if rules of type $a \rightarrow v$ are also used. Our result generalizes to multi-membrane catalytic systems.

We also consider deterministic catalytic systems which allow rules to be prioritized. Three such systems, namely, *statically prioritized*, *strongly prioritized* and *weakly prioritized* catalytic systems, are investigated. For statically prioritized systems, rules are divided into different priority groups, and if a rule in a higher priority group is applicable, then no rules from a lower priority group can be used. For both strongly prioritized and weakly prioritized systems, the underlying priority relation is a *strict partial order* (i.e., irreflexive, asymmetric, and transitive). Under the semantics of strong priority, if a rule with higher priority is used, then no rule of a lower priority can be used even if the two rules do not compete for objects. This notion of strong priority coincides with the semantics of the priority relation used in [2]. For weakly prioritized systems, a rule is applicable if it cannot be replaced by a higher priority one. For these three prioritized systems, we obtain contrasting results by showing that deterministic strongly and weakly prioritized catalytic systems are universal, whereas statically prioritized systems only accept semilinear sets.

Due to page limitation, some proofs are omitted. Complete proofs will appear later in an expanded (journal) version of this paper.

2   Nonuniversality of Deterministic Catalytic Systems

Consider a catalytic system (CS, for short) in which all rules are of the form: $Ca \rightarrow Cv$ or $a \rightarrow v$, where C is a catalyst, a is a noncatalyst symbol, and v is a (possibly null) string of noncatalyst symbols. (Note that we are only interested in the multiplicities of the symbols.) Unless stated otherwise, we assume that catalytic systems operate under the maximally parallel mode, i.e., at each step the maximal multiset of rules is applied. A CS is said to be *deterministic* if at each step, there is a **unique** maximally parallel multiset of rules applicable. A CS is referred to as a *purely* CS if only rules of the form $Ca \rightarrow Cv$ are used.

Given two configurations c and c', we write $c \xrightarrow{S} c'$ to denote that applying the multiset S at c yields c', and S is a maximally applicable multiset of rules at c. We also write $c \xrightarrow{S_1 \cdots S_k} c'$ to denote the reachability of c' from c through applying sequence $S_1 \cdots S_k$ of multisets of rules (or $c \xrightarrow{*} c'$ if the actual sequence is irrelevant). Given a configuration c, we write $\#_c$ to denote the Parikh map of c, and $\#_c(x)$ the number of occurrences of symbol x in c, where x is either a catalytic or a noncatalytic symbol.

Next we recall the definition of a semilinear set [11]. Let N be the set of nonnegative integers and k be a positive integer. A subset R of N^k is a *linear* set if there exist vectors $v_0, v_1, \ldots, v_t$ in N^k such that $R = \{v \mid v = v_0 + m_1 v_1 + \cdots + m_t v_t,\ m_i \in N\}$. The vectors v_0 (referred to as the *constant vector*) and $v_1, v_2, \ldots, v_t$ (referred to as the *periods*) are called the *generators* of the linear set R. The set $R \subseteq N^k$ is *semilinear* if it is a finite union of linear sets. The empty set is a trivial semilinear set. Every finite subset of N^k is semilinear – it is a finite union of linear sets whose generators are constant vectors. It is also clear that the semilinear sets are closed under (finite) union. It is also known that they are closed under complementation and intersection.

2.1 Deterministic Purely Catalytic Systems

We first consider deterministic purely CSs, i.e., all rules are of the form $Ca \to Cv$. Due to the nature of determinism as well as the number of catalysts being bounded, an infinite computation of a deterministic purely CS is 'periodic' in the sense stated in the following theorem.

Theorem 1. *Given a deterministic purely CS $\mathcal{P}$ and an initial configuration c_0, the following three statements are equivalent:*

1. *$\mathcal{P}$ does not halt;*
2. *there exist c and c' with $\#_{c'} \geq \#_c$ such that $c_0 \overset{*}{\to} c \overset{*}{\to} c'$;*
3. *the computation of $\mathcal{P}$ is of the form $c_0 \overset{T_1 \cdots T_r (S_1 \cdots S_k)^\omega}{\to}$, where $T_1, \ldots, T_r, S_1, \ldots, S_k$ are multisets of rules. (That is, following a finite prefix the computation is 'periodic' with $S_1 \cdots S_k$ repeating forever.)*

Proof. To proceed, we require the following claims whose proofs are omitted due to space limitation:

(**Claim 1**) Suppose $c \overset{H}{\to} d$ and $c' \overset{H'}{\to} d'$, where c, c', d, d' are configurations and H and H' are two multisets of rules. If rule $Ca \to Cv$ is in $H' - H$, then $\#_c(a) < \#_{c'}(a)$.

(**Claim 2**) Given a computation $c_1 \overset{H_1}{\to} c_2 \overset{H_2}{\to} \cdots c_{i-1} \overset{H_{i-1}}{\to} c_i$ and a configuration c_1' with $\#_{c_1'} \geq \#_{c_1}$, then there exist multisets $H_1', \ldots, H_{i-1}'$ and configurations $c_2', \ldots, c_i'$ such that (i) $c_1' \overset{H_1'}{\to} c_2' \overset{H_2'}{\to} \cdots c_{i-1}' \overset{H_{i-1}'}{\to} c_i'$, (ii) $H_j \subseteq H_j', \forall j, 1 \leq j \leq i - 1$, and (iii) $\#_{c_j} \leq \#_{c_j'}, \forall j, 1 \leq j \leq i$.

(**Claim 3**) If $c_1 \overset{H_1 \cdots H_k}{\to} c_2$, $\#_{c_2} \geq \#_{c_1}$ and $c_2 \overset{H_1 \cdots H_k}{\to} c_3$, then it must be the case that $c_1 \overset{H_1 \cdots H_k}{\to} c_2 \overset{H_1 \cdots H_k}{\to} c_3 \cdots \overset{H_1 \cdots H_k}{\to} c_i \cdots$, i.e., $H_1 \cdots H_k$ repeats forever.

We are now in a position to prove our theorem. We first show (1) $\implies$ (2). Assume that $\mathcal{P}$ does not terminate. Let $c_0 \to c_1 \to \cdots \to c_l \to \cdots (l \in N)$ be an infinite computation. According to Higman's and König's lemmas (see [12]), there exist $i < j$ such that $\#_{c_i} \leq \#_{c_j}$; hence, (2) holds. Now we establish (2) $\implies$ (3). Let $H_1 \cdots H_k$ be the sequence of rule sets such that $c_i \overset{H_1 \cdots H_k}{\to} c_j$ and $\#_{c_i} \leq \#_{c_j}$. According to Claim 2, there are rule sets $H_1^t, H_2^t \cdots H_k^t$ and configurations c_{j_t}, $t \geq 1$, such that $c_i \overset{H_1 \cdots H_k}{\rightarrow} c_j \overset{H_1^1 \cdots H_k^1}{\rightarrow} c_{j_1} \overset{H_1^2 \cdots H_k^2}{\rightarrow} c_{j_2} \cdots \overset{H_1^t \cdots H_k^t}{\rightarrow}$ $c_{j_t} \cdots$. Furthermore, for all $1 \leq l \leq k$ and $1 \leq t$, $H_l^t \subseteq H_l^{t+1}$, and $\#_{c_{j_t}} \leq \#_{c_{j_{t+1}}}$. Since the number of catalytic symbols (which bounds the degree of maximal parallelism) is a constant, for all $1 \leq l \leq k$ there must be an t_l such that $H_l^{t_l} = H_l^{t_l+1} = H_l^{t_l+2} = \cdots$. Choose t' to be the maximum among all t_l, such that $H_l^{t'} = H_l^{t'+1}$ for all $1 \leq l \leq k$. Now we have $c_{j_{t'}} \overset{H_1^{t'} \cdots H_k^{t'}}{\rightarrow} c_{j_{t'+1}} \cdots \overset{H_1^{t'} \cdots H_k^{t'}}{\rightarrow} c_{j_{t'+2}}$. By letting $S_l = H_l^{t'}, 1 \leq l \leq k$, Claim 3 guarantees that $S_1 \cdots S_k$ repeat forever at $c_{j_{t'}}$. Therefore. (3) holds. (3) $\Longrightarrow$ (1) is trivial. This completes the proof of the theorem. $\qquad \square$

From (3) of Theorem 1, we immediately have:

Corollary 1. *Given a deterministic purely CS $\mathcal{P}$ and an initial configuration c_0, the reachability set $\{\#_c \mid c_0 \overset{*}{\rightarrow} c\}$ is semilinear.*

Corollary 2. *Given a deterministic purely CS $\mathcal{P}$ and an initial configuration c_0, the problem of determining whether $\mathcal{P}$ halts is decidable.*

Now consider the case when CSs serve as *language acceptors*. Consider a CS $\mathcal{P}$ with initial configuration $wo_1^{n_1} \ldots o_k^{n_k}$, where noncatalytic symbols $o_1, \ldots, o_k$ are distinguished input symbols not in w, and w is a fixed string (independent of $n_1, \ldots, n_k$) not containing symbol $o_1, \ldots, o_k$. The word $o_1^{n_1} \ldots o_k^{n_k}$ is accepted if $\mathcal{P}$ halts. It is known [7] that even for $k = 1$, any unary RE language can be accepted by the a purely CS operating in a nondeterministic manner. Hence, nondeterministic purely CSs are universal. Surprisingly, however, deterministic purely CSs are not universal as the following result indicates.

Theorem 2. *Deterministic purely catalytic systems are not universal.*

2.2 Deterministic Catalytic Systems

Now we consider the full class of deterministic CSs, where the rules are of the form $Ca \rightarrow Cv$ or $a \rightarrow v$. Intuitively, what makes the reachability set of a deterministic purely CS 'simpler' is that any infinite computation of such a system is *periodic* in the sense described in (3) of Theorem 1. Such a periodic behavior is partly due to the fact that the maximum degree of parallelism during the course of the computation of a deterministic purely CS is bounded by the number of catalytic symbols in the initial configuration. Note, however, that the degree of parallelism becomes unbounded if the CS uses rules of type $a \rightarrow v$. In fact, the semilinearity result no longer holds for the full class of deterministic CSs as the following example indicates. It is interesting to note that the degree of parallelism in this example is unbounded.

Example 1: Consider a CS with only one rule $a_1 \rightarrow a_1 a_1$ and initial configuration a_1. Then the Parikh map of the set of all reachable configurations is $\{2^n \mid n \geq 1\}$, which is clearly not semilinear. $\qquad \square$

Although the reachability set of a deterministic (not necessarily purely) CS is not semilinear in general, being deterministic does make the computational power of the model weaker than its nondeterministic counterpart. In what follows, we propose a graph-theoretic approach for reasoning about the behaviors of deterministic CSs.

Consider a deterministic CS $\mathcal{P}$, in which $\{C_1, ..., C_k\}$ is the set of catalytic symbols, and $\Sigma = \{a_1, ..., a_m\}$ is the set of noncatalytic symbols. Let c_0 be the initial configuration which contains (possibly multiple copies of) C_i, $\forall 1 \leq i \leq k$. Two rules r_1 and r_2 are said to be *in conflict* if one of the following holds:

- $r_1 : C_i a_t \rightarrow C_i w_1$, $r_2 : C_j a_t \rightarrow C_j w_2$, and either $w_1 \neq w_2$ or $i \neq j$
- $r_1 : C_i a_t \rightarrow C_i w_1$, $r_2 : a_t \rightarrow w_2$,
- $r_1 : a_t \rightarrow w_1$, $r_2 : a_t \rightarrow w_2$, and $w_1 \neq w_2$

In each of the above, rules r_1 and r_2 compete for the same noncatalyst a_t. (In this case, a_t is said to be *involved* in two conflicting rules.) At any point in time, a deterministic CS can never enable a rule that is in conflict with another rule. Under the unprioritized mode, conflicting rules can be removed without affecting the computation of the CS, regardless of the initial configuration. Note that rules $C_1 a_1 \rightarrow C_1 w_1$ and $C_1 a_2 \rightarrow C_1 w_2$ are not conflicting rules, and in fact, the absence of a_1 (resp. a_2) makes $C_1 a_2 \rightarrow C_1 w_2$ (resp., $C_1 a_1 \rightarrow C_1 w_1$) applicable.

In what follows, we employ a graph-theoretic approach to reasoning about the behaviors of deterministic CSs. We construct a directed labelled graph $G_{\mathcal{P}, c_0} = (V, E)$, called the *execution graph*, such that $V = \Sigma$ and $E = \{(a_i, a_j)_r \mid \exists$ a rule r of the form $C_t a_i \rightarrow C_t w$ or $a_i \rightarrow w$, such that a_j in w, and a_i is not involved in any conflicting rules$\}$. (The subscript r is the label of edge (a_i, a_j). We also write $a_i \xrightarrow{r} a_j$.) A careful examination of $G_{\mathcal{P}, c_0}$ reveals an important property: for each node a_i, the outgoing edges of a_i (if they exist) are of the same label.

To set the stage for the non-universality result of deterministic CSs, we require the following lemma:

Lemma 1. *Consider a deterministic CS $\mathcal{P}$ with $\{C_1, ..., C_k\}$ and $\{a_1, ..., a_m\}$ as the sets of catalysts and noncatalysts, respectively. Let c_0 be the initial configuration. Then:*

1. *$\mathcal{P}$ does not halt on c_0 iff there is a reachable loop from some node a_{i_0} with $\#_{c_0}(a_{i_0}) > 0$ in $G_{\mathcal{P}, c_0}$.*
2. *Let c_0' be a configuration such that $(\forall\ 1 \leq i \leq k,\ \#_{c_0'}(C_i) = \#_{c_0}(C_i))$ and $(\forall\ 1 \leq j \leq m,\ (\#_{c_0}(a_j) > 0 \implies \#_{c_0'}(a_j) = 1) \wedge (\#_{c_0}(a_j) = 0 \implies \#_{c_0'}(a_j) = 0))$. Then $\mathcal{P}$ halts on c_0 iff $\mathcal{P}$ halts on c_0'.*
3. *The problem of determining whether $\mathcal{P}$ halts on c_0 is decidable in polynomial time.*

Deterministic CSs also have the following *monotonic property* regarding non-terminating computations.

Lemma 2. *Given a deterministic CS $\mathcal{P}$, if $\mathcal{P}$ does not halt from configuration c, then $\mathcal{P}$ does not halt from any configuration c' such that $\#_{c'} \geq \#_c$.*

Hence, we have the following result.

Theorem 3. *For a deterministic CS P and a fixed string w, the set $L = \{o_1^{n_1}...o_k^{n_k}$ | P halts on $wo_1^{n_1}...o_k^{n_k}\}$ is effective semilinear. In fact, L is either empty, or of the form $o_1^{n_1}...o_k^{n_k}$, where $n_i = *$ or 0, $1 \leq i \leq k$.*

We immediately have the following, which strengthens Theorem 2:

Corollary 3. *Deterministic catalytic systems are not universal.*

In contrast, it is known that *nondeterministic* 1-membrane CSs are universal [8] (see also [13]) even operating under the 3-**Max-Parallel** mode. The universality result holds for either purely CSs with three catalysts, or CSs with two catalysts. In fact, to simulate a Turing machine M the 1-membrane CS need no more than k noncatalysts for some *fixed k*, independent of M, as [13] shows.

Consider the following extension of CS:

- *multi-membrane* CSs, where each rule in a membrane looks like: $Ca \rightarrow Cv$ or $a \rightarrow v$, where the symbols in v have designated target membranes specifying where they are to be moved. The catalyst C remains in the membrane containing the rule. In this case w represents the configurations $w_1, ...w_m$ in the m membranes.

It turns out that our results obtained thus far can be extended to multi-membrane CSs. Hence, deterministic multi-membrane CSs are not universal. Theorem 1 and Corollary 1 (characterizing semilinear reachability sets) also hold for deterministic purely catalytic multi-membrane CSs (i.e., without $a \rightarrow v$ type of rules). The proofs are similar to that for the 1-membrane case.

3   Prioritized Deterministic Catalytic Systems

Now let us look at catalytic systems which allow rules to be prioritized according to the following two types of priority relations. Let R be the set of rules of a CS. For a priority relation ρ over R, we write $\rho(r_1) < \rho(r_2)$ (or simply $r_1 < r_2$, if ρ is understood) to denote that $(r_1, r_2) \in \rho$, meaning that r_2 takes precedence over r_1. ρ is said to be of

- *Type A*:   if ρ is irreflexive, asymmetric, transitive, and the complement of ρ, i.e., $\bar{\rho} = \{(r, r') \mid \neg((r, r') \in \rho) \wedge \neg((r', r) \in \rho)\}$, is an equivalence relation. Clearly, $\bar{\rho}$ induces equivalence classes $\Omega_1, \Omega_2, ..., \Omega_k$, for some k, such that $\forall 1 \leq i < j \leq k$, $\forall r \in \Omega_i, r' \in \Omega_j, \rho(r) < \rho(r')$. The subscript i of Ω_i can be thought of as the priority level of rules in Ω_i. For $r \in \Omega_i$, we also write $\bar{\rho}(r) = i$. (The interested reader is referred to [14] for an example of applying this notion of a priority relation to reasoning about concurrent systems.)
- *Type B*:   if ρ is an irreflexive, asymmetric, and transitive relation. That is, ρ is a *strict partial order*.

Example 2: Consider a strict partial order ρ over $R = \{r_1, ..., r_6\}$: $(r_5 > r_3 > r_2 > r_1)$; $(r_6 > r_4 > r_2 > r_1)$; $(r_5 > r_4)$;   and $(r_6 > r_3)$. Then $\bar{\rho} = \{(r_5, r_6), (r_6, r_5), (r_3, r_4), (r_4, r_3)\} \cup \{(r_i, r_i) \mid 1 \leq i \leq 6\}$, which is an equivalence relation. Hence, ρ is of type A. Furthermore, $\bar{\rho}$ partitions R into the following equivalence classes $\Omega_1 = \{r_1\}, \Omega_2 = \{r_2\}, \Omega_3 = \{r_3, r_4\}, \Omega_4 = \{r_5, r_6\}$, such that for $1 \leq i < j \leq 4$, rules in Ω_i have a lower priority than those in Ω_j.   □

3.1   Systems w.r.t. Type A Priority Relation

Let $\mathcal{P}$ be a deterministic CS, c and c' be two configurations, and H be a multiset of rules. With respect to a priority relation ρ of type A (with $\bar{\rho}$ inducing equivalence classes $\Omega_1, \Omega_2, ..., \Omega_k$),

1. (*static priority*): c' is said to follow c through the application of H under the *statically prioritized mode*, written as $c \xrightarrow{H}_t c'$, if H is the maximal multiset satisfying the following:
    (i) $\forall\ r_i, r_j \in H, \bar{\rho}(r_i) = \bar{\rho}(r_j)$ (i.e., r_i and r_j are in the same Ω_l, for some l),
    (ii) $\neg\ \exists\ r, r \notin H, r$ is applicable in c and $\bar{\rho}(r) > \bar{\rho}(r')$ for some rule $r' \in H$.
    In words, H is the maximal multiset of rules such that if a rule in a higher priority group is applicable, then no rules from a lower priority group can be used.

We first show the following result which characterizes the computations of non-halting CSs.

Lemma 3. *Given a deterministic purely CS $\mathcal{P}$ operating under the statically prioritized mode, and an initial configuration c_0, $\mathcal{P}$ does not halt iff there exist c and c' with $\#_{c'} \geq \#_c$ such that $c_0 \xrightarrow{*}_t c \xrightarrow{*}_t c'$.*

At this point, we do not know whether the reachability set of a deterministic statically prioritized purely CS is semilinear or not. Lemma 3, in conjunction with Higman's and König's lemmas, is sufficient to yield the decidability of the halting problem for such prioritized CSs. Hence, we have the following, whose proof parallels that of Theorem 2.

Theorem 4. *Deterministic purely catalytic systems under the statically prioritized mode are not universal.*

We now consider the full class of deterministic statically prioritized CSs with both catalytic and noncatalytic rules. It turns out that the graph-theoretic approach employed in Section 2.2 remains valid for this new class of CSs.

Let ρ be the underlying priority relation of type A. Given a deterministic statically prioritized CS $\mathcal{P}$ and an initial configuration c_0, we construct a directed labelled graph $G^t_{\mathcal{P}, c_0} = (V, E)$, where V is the set of noncatalytic symbols, and $E = \{(a_i, a_j)_r \mid \exists$ a rule r of the form $C_t a_i \rightarrow C_t w$ or $a_i \rightarrow w$, such that a_j in w, and no rule r' of equal or higher priority level (i.e., $\bar{\rho}(r') \geq \bar{\rho}(r)$) is in conflict with $r\}$. It is important to explain why E constructed above does not leave out edges corresponding to applicable rules. Suppose r is a rule in conflict with another rule of equal priority level in ρ. $\mathcal{P}$ being deterministic prohibits r from being enabled; hence, r can be dropped without affecting the computation of $\mathcal{P}$. Similarly, if r is in conflict with a rule r' of higher priority level, then r can never be applied since r and r' become enabled simultaneously, and only the one of the higher priority level prevails. Again, r plays no role in $\mathcal{P}$'s computation in this case. It is therefore clear that like the execution graph in the unprioritized case, $G^t_{\mathcal{P}, c_0}$ also enjoys the property that for each node in V, the outgoing edges of the node are uniquely labelled. What makes this property critical is that if a noncatalyst a_i is in the current configuration of $\mathcal{P}$, the only way to prevent the unique rule associated with a_i (in the execution graph) from being applied indefinitely is for $\mathcal{P}$ to apply rules of higher priority level forever, implying $\mathcal{P}$ to be non-halting. Therefore, it becomes fairly easy to see that $\mathcal{P}$ is non-halting iff $G^t_{\mathcal{P},c_0}$ has a reachable loop from some node whose corresponding symbol appears in c_0. In view of this key observation, Lemmas 1, 2 and Theorem 3 also hold for deterministic statically prioritized CSs. Hence, we have:

Theorem 5. *For a deterministic statically prioritized CS $\mathcal{P}$ and a fixed string w, the set $L = \{o_1^{n_1}...o_k^{n_k} \mid \mathcal{P}$ halts on $wo_1^{n_1}...o_k^{n_k}\}$ is effective semilinear. In fact, L is either empty, or of the form $o_1^{n_1}...o_k^{n_k}$, where $n_i = *$ or 0, $1 \leq i \leq k$.*

3.2   Systems w.r.t. Type B Priority Relation

Again, let $\mathcal{P}$ be a deterministic CS, c and c' be two configurations, and H be a multiset of rules. With respect to a priority relation ρ of type B, the following two notions of priority are considered.

1. (*Strong priority*): c' is said to follow c through the application of H under the strongly prioritized mode, written as $c \xrightarrow{H}_s c'$, if H is the maximal multiset satisfying the following:
   (a) $\forall$ rule $r_1 \in H$, $\neg \exists r_2 \notin H$ such that $\rho(r_1) < \rho(r_2)$ and $(H - \{r_1\}) \cup \{r_2\}$ is still applicable,
   (b) $\forall r_1, r_2 \in H$, $\neg(\rho(r_1) < \rho(r_2))$
   In words, if a rule with higher priority is used, then no rule of a lower priority can be used, even if the two rules do not compete for objects. Note that this priority notion coincides with the one used in [2].
2. (*Weak priority*): c' is said to follow c through the application of H under the weakly prioritized mode, written as $c \xrightarrow{H}_w c'$, if H is the maximal multiset satisfying the following:
   $\forall$ rule $r_1 \in H$, $\neg \exists r_2 \notin H$ such that $\rho(r_1) < \rho(r_2)$ and $(H - \{r_1\}) \cup \{r_2\}$ is still applicable.
   In words, none of the rules in H can be replaced by a higher priority one.

We use the following simple example to illustrate the difference between the above two notions of priority.

Example 3: Consider a deterministic CS $\mathcal{P}$ with the following rules:

Rule $r_1 : Cb_1 \rightarrow Cb_2$;   Rule $r_2 : Ca_1 \rightarrow Ca_2$;   Rule $r_3 : Da_1 \rightarrow Da_3$;
Rule $r_4 : Ec_1 \rightarrow Ec_2$;   Rule $r_5 : Fc_1 \rightarrow Fc_3$;   Rule $r_6 : Gd_1 \rightarrow Dd_2$;
(Priority relation): $\rho(r_1) > \rho(r_2) > \rho(r_3)$; $\rho(r_4) > \rho(r_5)$

Then

$$CDEFGa_1b_1c_1d_1 \xrightarrow{\{r_1,r_4,r_6\}}_s CDEFGa_1b_2c_2d_2$$
$$CDEFGa_1b_1c_1d_1 \xrightarrow{\{r_1,r_3,r_4,r_6\}}_w CDEFGa_3b_2c_2d_2$$

Note that under the weak priority semantics, the application of r_1 makes r_3 applicable, since r_2 (competing for the catalyst C with r_1) is 'disabled' by r_1. Under the strong priority semantics, however, the application of r_1 disables r_3 (since $\rho(r_3) < \rho(r_1)$) even though these two rules do not compete for objects.   □

In contrast to Theorem 2 (also Theorem 3) that deterministic unprioritized CSs are not universal, allowing strongly or weakly prioritized rules boosts the computational power as the following result shows.

Theorem 6. *Deterministic purely CSs under the weakly prioritized (or strongly prioritized) mode are universal.*

Proof. (Sketch) The proof involves the construction of a purely CS that simulates a given deterministic k-counter machine which starts with one counter having value n and the other counters empty. We only consider the case $k = 2$, the generalization for any k being straightforward.

Let M be a deterministic two-counter machine. Each of M's transitions is of one of the following forms:

- (Increment) $s : c + +, \text{goto } s'$ (on state s, increment counter c by one and move to state s');
- (Test-for-zero/Decrement) $s : \text{if } c = 0, \text{ goto } s_1 \text{ else } c - -, \text{goto } s_2$ (on state s, if counter c is zero, go to state s_1; otherwise, decrement counter c by one and move to state s_2).

We show how to construct a deterministic purely CS $\mathcal{P}$ under the either the strongly or the weakly prioritized mode such that starting with one counter empty and the other counter having value n, M halts iff $\mathcal{P}$ halts on the initial configuration $w(o_1)^n$, where w is a string of catalytic and noncatalytic symbols not including the symbol o_1. Let the two counters of M be c_1 and c_2.

At any instant, the configuration of $\mathcal{P}$ is of the form $C_1 C_2 D_1 D_2 s(o_1)^{n_1}(o_2)^{n_2} t$, where C_1, D_1 (resp., C_2, D_2) are catalysts associated with the simulation of M's transitions operating on counter c_1 (resp., c_2), s represents the current state of M, n_1 and n_2 keep track of the values of counters c_1 and c_2, respectively, and t is a noncatalyst whose purpose will be explained later.

We are now in a position to see how the two types of M's transitions are simulated. Without loss of generality, we assume the operations to be simulated operate on counter c_1; the cases on counter c_2 are similar. Let $C_1 C_2 D_1 D_2 s(o_1)^{n_1}(o_2)^{n_2} t_2$ be the current configuration.

- Transition $s : c_1 + +, \text{goto } s'$ (assuming that from s', the next transition operates on counter c_1.)
  $\mathcal{P}$ utilizes the following rules:
  $$r_1 : C_1 s \to C_1 q_s o_1; \quad r_2 : C_1 q_s \to C_1 q_s'; \quad r_3 : C_1 q_s' \to C_1 s' t_2;$$
  $$h_1' : C_2 t_2 \to C_2 t_2'; \quad h_2' : C_2 t_2' \to C_2 t_2''; \quad h_3' : C_2 t_2'' \to C_2.$$
  Note that symmetrically we also have rules $h_1 : C_1 t_1 \to C_1 t_1'$; $h_2 : C_1 t_1' \to C_1 t_1''$ $h_3 : C_1 t_1'' \to C_1$. If the next transition to be executed on state s' operates on counter c_2, then rule r_3 becomes $C_1 q_s' \to C_1 s' t_1$.
  Using the above rules, incrementing counter c_1 is simulated through the following sequence:

$$C_1C_2D_1D_2s(o_1)^{n_1}(o_2)^{n_2}t_2$$
$$\overset{\{r_1,h_1'\}}{\to}_w C_1C_2D_1D_2q_s(o_1)^{n_1+1}(o_2)^{n_2}t_2'$$
$$\overset{\{r_2,h_2'\}}{\to}_w C_1C_2D_1D_2q_s'(o_1)^{n_1+1}(o_2)^{n_2}t_2'',$$
$$\overset{\{r_3,h_3'\}}{\to}_w C_1C_2D_1D_2s'(o_1)^{n_1+1}(o_2)^{n_2}t_2,$$

It will be seen later that the length of the above sequence (i.e., three steps) is exactly the same as that of simulating a test-for-zero/decrement.

- Transition s : if $c_1 = 0$, goto s_1 else $c_1 - -$, goto s_2

$\mathcal{P}$ has the following rules, in addition to the h_1', h_2' and h_3' defined above. Assume that from s_1 and s_2, M's transitions operate on counter c_1; the other cases are similar.

$f_1 : C_1s \to C_1q_{s_2}b;$ $f_2 : C_1o_1 \to C_1;$ $f_3 : C_1q_{s_2} \to C_1q_{s_1};$ $f_4 : D_1q_{s_1} \to D_1s_1 t_2;$ $f_5 : D_1q_{s_2} \to D_1s_2 t_2;$ $f_6 : D_1b \to D_1d;$ $f_7 :$
$C_1d \to C_1;$

The priority relation has

$f_1 > f_2 > f_3;$ $\{h_1,h_2,h_3\} > f_2;$ $f_7 > f_2 > f_3;$ $f_6 > \{f_4,f_5\};$
$\{r_1,r_2,r_3\} > f_2.$

Care has to be taken regarding f_2, which decrements counter c_1. Priority relation $\{r_1,r_2,r_3\} > f_2$ is to prevent f_2 from being falsely applied when simulating an 'increment'. Note that f_3 and f_5 are conflicting rules. The simulation involves the following sequence:

$$C_1C_2D_1D_2s(o_1)^{n_1}(o_2)^{n_2} t_2 \overset{\{f_1,h_1'\}}{\to}_w C_1C_2D_1D_2q_{s_2}b(o_1)^{n_1}(o_2)^{n_2}t_2'$$
$$\overset{\{f_2,f_6,h_2'\}}{\to}_w C_1C_2D_1D_2q_{s_2}d(o_1)^{n_1-1}(o_2)^{n_2}t_2'',$$
$$\overset{\{f_5,f_7,h_3'\}}{\to}_w C_1C_2D_1D_2s_2(o_1)^{n_1-1}(o_2)^{n_2}t_2, \quad \text{provided } n_1 > 0;$$

or

$$\overset{\{f_3,f_6,h_2'\}}{\to}_w C_1C_2D_1D_2q_{s_1}d(o_2)^{n_2}t_2'',$$
$$\overset{\{f_4,f_7,h_3'\}}{\to}_w C_1C_2D_1D_2s_1(o_2)^{n_2}t_2, \qquad \text{provided } n_1 = 0;$$

In the second step of the above sequence, the application of f_6 disables f_5, allowing f_3 to be applied if counter c_1 is zero. In the third step, the use of f_7 disables both f_2 and f_3, while allowing either f_4 or f_5 to be applied.

Clearly, M halts iff $\mathcal{P}$ terminates. It is also obvious that $\mathcal{P}$ is deterministic. It is easy to observe that the above argument works for deterministic purely CSs under both the strongly prioritized and the weakly prioritized modes.   □

References

1. Păun, G.: Computing with membranes. Turku University Computer Science Research Report No. 208 (1998)
2. Păun, G.: Computing with membranes. Journal of Computer and System Sciences 61 (2000) 108–143
3. Păun, G.: Membrane Computing: An Introduction. Springer-Verlag (2002)
4. Păun, G., Rozenberg, G.: A guide to membrane computing. Theoretical Computer Science 287 (2002) 73–100

5. Păun, A., Păun, G.:   The power of communication: P systems with symport/antiport. New Generation Computers **20** (2002) 295–306
6. Freund, R., Păun, G.: On deterministic P systems. See P Systems Web Page at http://psystems.disco.unimib.it (2003)
7. Sosik, P.: P systems versus register machines: two universality proofs. In: Pre-Proceedings of Workshop on Membrane Computing (WMC-CdeA2002), Curtea de Argeş, Romania (2002) 371–382
8. Freund, R., Kari, L., Oswald, M., Sosik, P.: Computationally universal P systems without priorities: two catalysts are sufficient. Theoretical Computer Science **330** (2005) 251–266
9. Calude, C., Păun, G.: *Computing with Cells and Atoms: After Five Years* (new text added to Russian edition of the book with the same title first published by Taylor and Francis Publishers, London, 2001). To be published by Pushchino Publishing House. (2004)
10. Păun, G.: Further twenty six open problems in membrane computing., Written for the Third Brainstorming Week on Membrane Computing, Sevilla, Spain (see P Systems Web Page at http://psystems.disco.unimib.it) (2005)
11. Ginsburg, S.: The Mathematical Theory of Context-Free Languages. New York: McGraw-Hill (1966)
12. Higman, G.: Ordering by divisibility in abstract algebras. Proc. London Math. Soc. **3** (1952) 326–336
13. Ibarra, O., Yen, H., Dang, Z.: The power of maximal parallelism in P systems. In: Eighth International Conference on Developments in Language Theory (DLT'04). LNCS 3340, Springer (2004) 212–224
14. Bause, F.: On the analysis of Petri nets with static priorities. Acta Informatica **33** (1996) 669–685

Restricting the Use of Auxiliary Symbols
for Restarting Automata*

Tomasz Jurdziński[1] and Friedrich Otto[2]

[1] Institute of Computer Science, University of Wrocław,
51-151 Wrocław, Poland
tju@ii.uni.wroc.pl
[2] Fachbereich Mathematik/Informatik, Universität Kassel,
34109 Kassel, Germany
otto@theory.informatik.uni-kassel.de

Abstract. The most general models of restarting automata make use of auxiliary symbols in their rewrite operations. Here we put restrictions on the way in which restarting automata use auxiliary symbols, and we investigate the influence of these restrictions on their expressive power. In fact, we consider two types of restrictions. First, we consider the *number of auxiliary symbols* in the tape alphabet of a restarting automaton as a measure of its descriptional complexity. Secondly, we consider the *number of occurrences of auxiliary symbols* on the tape as a dynamic complexity measure. We establish some lower and upper bounds with respect to these complexity measures concerning the ability of restarting automata to recognize the (deterministic) context-free languages and some of their subclasses.

1 Introduction

The restarting automaton was introduced by Jančar et al. as a formal tool to model the *analysis by reduction*, which is a technique used in linguistics to analyze sentences of natural languages [1]. It consists of a stepwise simplification of a given sentence so that the syntactical correctness or incorrectness of the sentence is not affected. It is applied primarily in languages that have a free word-order. Already several programs used in Czech and German (corpus) linguistics are based on the idea of restarting automata [2, 3].

A (two-way) restarting automaton, RLWW-automaton for short, is a device M that consists of a finite-state control, a flexible tape containing a word delimited by sentinels, and a read/write window of a fixed size. This window is moved along the tape by move-right and move-left operations until the control decides (nondeterministically) that the content of the window should be rewritten by some *shorter* string. In fact, the new string may contain auxiliary symbols that do not belong to the input alphabet. After the rewrite operation, M can continue

---

* This work was supported by a grant from the Deutsche Forschungsgemeinschaft. It was performed while Tomasz Jurdziński was visiting the University of Kassel.

J. Farré, I. Litovsky, and S. Schmitz (Eds.): CIAA 2005, LNCS 3845, pp. 176–187, 2006.

to move its window until it either halts and accepts, or halts and rejects, or restarts, that is, it places its window over the left end of the tape, reenters the initial state, and continues with the computation. Thus, each computation of M can be described through a sequence of cycles.

Also various restricted versions of the restarting automaton have been considered. A *one-way restarting automaton*, RRWW-automaton for short, does not use any move-left operations. If, in addition, it is required to perform a restart step immediately after executing a rewrite operation, then it is an RWW-automaton.

Many well-known classes of formal languages have been characterized in terms of restricted variants of the restarting automaton. For example, the deterministic R(R)WW-automaton characterizes the class of Church-Rosser languages [4, 5] of McNaughton et al. [6], the monotone R(R)WW-automaton characterizes the class CFL of context-free languages [7], and various types of deterministic monotone R(R)WW-automata characterize the class DCFL of deterministic context-free languages [7].

Here we place some restrictions on the way in which restarting automata make use of auxiliary symbols. This direction of research is motivated by the fact that originally the analysis by reduction does not involve the use of auxiliary symbols. On the other hand, the expressive power of restarting automata without auxiliary symbols is relatively weak, as not even all context-free languages can be recognized by them [7]. Thus, we introduce an intermediate level, at which auxiliary symbols can be used only in a restricted way. Actually, we consider two types of restrictions. First we consider the number of auxiliary symbols in the tape alphabet as a measure of the *descriptional complexity* of the restarting automaton, and secondly we interpret the number of occurrences of auxiliary symbols on the tape as a *dynamic* complexity measure. We analyze the influence of these restrictions on the ability of various types of restarting automata to recognize certain well-studied classes of formal languages.

In Section 2 we give the necessary definitions in short. In Section 3 we investigate the expressive power of deterministic restarting automata that use auxiliary symbols in a restricted way only. Then, in Section 4, we study how many auxiliary symbols (in the alphabet or on the tape) are needed by nondeterministic RWW-automata to accept any context-free language, and we show that all k-linear languages ($k \geq 2$) are accepted by RLWW-automata with only two occurrences of a single auxiliary symbol. In addition, for $k = 2$ we improve upon this result by showing that a single occurrence of a single auxiliary symbol suffices. Because of the page limit not all proofs are given in the paper. For a complete and detailed presentation we refer to the technical report [8].

Notation. Throughout the paper ε will denote the empty word, and for $i, j \in \mathbb{N}$, $[i, j] := \{ l \in \mathbb{N} \mid i \leq l \leq j \}$.

2   Definitions

Here we describe in short the type of restarting automaton we will be dealing with. More details can be found in [9].

A *two-way restarting automaton*, RLWW-automaton for short, is a nondeterministic machine that is described by an 8-tuple $M = (Q, \Sigma, \Gamma, \mathcal{c}, \$, q_0, k, \delta)$, where Q is a finite set of states, Σ is a finite input alphabet, and Γ is a finite tape alphabet containing Σ. The symbols $\mathcal{c}, \$ \notin \Gamma$ serve as markers for the left and right border of the work space, respectively, which cannot be removed from the tape. Further, $q_0 \in Q$ is the initial state, $k \geq 1$ is the size of the *read-write window*, and δ is the transition relation that associates to a pair (q, u) consisting of a state q and a possible content u of the read/write window a finite set of possible transition steps. There are five types of transition steps:

1. A *move-right step* (MVR) causes M to shift the read/write window one position to the right and to change the state. However, the read/write window cannot move across the right sentinel $\$$.
2. A *move-left step* (MVL) causes M to shift the read/write window one position to the left and to change the state. However, the read/write window cannot move across the left sentinel $\mathcal{c}$.
3. A *rewrite step* causes M to replace the content u of the read/write window by a shorter string v, thereby shortening the tape, and to change the state. Further, the read/write window is placed immediately to the right of the string v.
4. A *restart step* causes M to place its read/write window over the left end of the tape, so that the first symbol it sees is the left sentinel $\mathcal{c}$, and to reenter the initial state q_0.
5. An *accept step* causes M to halt and accept.

If $\delta(q, u) = \emptyset$ for some pair (q, u), then M necessarily halts, and we say that M *rejects* in this situation. Further, the transition relation must satisfy the additional requirement that within each computation of M, rewrite steps and restart steps occur alternatingly with a rewrite step coming first.

A *configuration* of M is a string $\alpha q \beta$ where q is a state, and either $\alpha = \varepsilon$ and $\beta \in \{\mathcal{c}\} \cdot \Gamma^* \cdot \{\$\}$ or $\alpha \in \{\mathcal{c}\} \cdot \Gamma^*$ and $\beta \in \Gamma^* \cdot \{\$\}$; here q represents the current state, $\alpha\beta$ is the current content of the tape, and it is understood that the window contains the first k symbols of β or all of β when $|\beta| \leq k$. A *restarting configuration* is of the form $q_0 \mathcal{c} w \$$, where q_0 is the initial state and $w \in \Gamma^*$; if $w \in \Sigma^*$, then $q_0 \mathcal{c} w \$$ is an *initial configuration*. Thus, initial configurations are a particular type of restarting configurations.

In general, the automaton M is *nondeterministic*, that is, there can be two or more instructions with the same left-hand side (q, u). If that is not the case, the automaton is *deterministic*.

Each computation of a two-way restarting automaton M consists of certain phases. A phase, called a *cycle*, starts in a restarting configuration, the window moves along the tape performing MVR and MVL operations and a single rewrite operation until a restart operation is performed and thus a new restarting configuration is reached. If no further restart operation is performed, any finite computation necessarily finishes in a halting configuration – such a phase is called a *tail*. During a tail at most one rewrite operation may be executed.

An input $w \in \Sigma^*$ is *accepted by* M, if there is a computation which, starting with the initial configuration $q_0 \cent w\$$, finishes by executing an accept instruction. By $L(M)$ we denote the language consisting of all words accepted by M; we say that M *recognizes* (*accepts*) the language $L(M)$.

Various subclasses of RLWW-automata have been studied. They are obtained by combining two types of restrictions:

(a) Restrictions on the movement of the read/write window (expressed by the first part of the class name): RL- denotes no restriction, RR- means that no MVL operations are available, R- means that no MVL operations are available and that each rewrite step is immediately followed by a restart.

(b) Restrictions on the rewrite-instructions (expressed by the second part of the class name): -WW denotes no restriction, -W means that no auxiliary symbols are available (that is, $\Gamma = \Sigma$), -ε means that no auxiliary symbols are available and that each rewrite step is simply a deletion (that is, if $(q', v) \in \delta(q, u)$ is a rewrite instruction of M, then v is obtained from u by deleting some symbols).

By det-RLWW we denote the class of *deterministic* RLWW-automata, and analogously for the other types of restarting automata. Further, for each type X of automata, we denote the class of languages that are accepted by automata from that class by $\mathcal{L}(\mathsf{X})$.

Finally, we define some new complexity measures for restarting automata with auxiliary symbols. For each type X of restarting automata with auxiliary symbols, and integers $i, j \in \mathbb{N}$, aux(j, i)-X, a-aux(j, i)-X, and g-aux(j, i)-X denote the class of restarting automata M of type X for which the number of auxiliary symbols in the tape alphabet does not exceed the number i and,

− for aux: the number of occurrences of auxiliary symbols in any configuration during *any* computation of M starting from an initial configuration is not larger than j;

− for a-aux: the number of occurrences of auxiliary symbols in any configuration during *any accepting* computation of M starting from an initial configuration is not larger than j;

− for g-aux: for each $x \in L(M)$, there exists an accepting computation of M such that the number of occurrences of auxiliary symbols in any configuration during that computation is not larger than j.

In some cases we may replace the constant j by a non-constant function, which is used to measure the number of occurrences of auxiliary symbols on the tape as a function of the length of the input.

As our main interest concerns those classes with only a single auxiliary symbol in the alphabet, we introduce the notation aux(j)-X as a shorthand for aux$(j, 1)$-X.

Observe that, for each type $\mathsf{X} \in \{\mathsf{RL}, \mathsf{RR}, \mathsf{R}, \mathsf{det\text{-}RL}, \mathsf{det\text{-}RR}, \mathsf{det\text{-}R}\}$, XW and aux$(0)$-XWW denote essentially the same class of automata.

Proposition 1. *The following relationships hold for each $i \in \mathbb{N}$ and each function $j : \mathbb{N} \to \mathbb{N}$:*

1. $\mathcal{L}(\text{Y-aux}(j, i)\text{-RLWW}) = \mathcal{L}(\text{Y-aux}(j, i)\text{-RRWW})$ *for each type* $\text{Y} \in \{\text{a-, g-}\}$.
2. $\mathcal{L}(\text{aux}(j, i)\text{-RLWW}) \subseteq \mathcal{L}(\text{aux}(2j, i)\text{-RRWW})$.

Proof. (1) For each RLWW-automaton M, there exists an RRWW-automaton M' such that M and M' use the same tape alphabet, they recognize the same language, and in each accepting computation M' executes exactly the same rewrite steps as M does in the corresponding computation [10]. More precisely, in each cycle of a computation M' guesses crossing tables for M and simultaneously verifies that its guesses are correct. In the affirmative M' has successfully simulated the corresponding cycle of M; otherwise M' has made a mistake, and therefore it terminates the simulation and halts without accepting. Thus, as long as M' simulates the computation of M correctly, both automata will always have the same number of occurrences of auxiliary symbols on their tapes.

(2) When M' makes an incorrect guess, then this can result in the introduction of at most j additional occurrences of auxiliary symbols, as M' only applies rewrite operations of M. Hence, in this case M' may have up to $2j$ occurrences of auxiliary symbols on its tape. $\qquad\square$

3 Deterministic Restarting Automata

In [11] a non-context-free language L_{lr} is presented such that $L_{lr} \in \mathcal{L}(\text{det-RW})$. On the other hand, there exist context-free languages which are not even recognized by RRW-automata [7]. Thus, we have the following results.

Corollary 1.

(a) $\text{DCFL} \subsetneq \mathcal{L}(\text{aux}(0)\text{-det-RWW})$.
(b) *The classes* CFL *and* $\mathcal{L}(\text{aux}(0)\text{-det-RWW})$ *are incomparable under inclusion.*

It is known that auxiliary symbols increase the expressive power of deterministic RWW-automata [7]. Here, we show that already a single occurrence of a single auxiliary symbol has that effect.

Proposition 2. *The language* $L_{pow} := \{ a^{2^n} \mid n \in \mathbb{N} \}$ *belongs to the class* $\mathcal{L}(\text{aux}(1)\text{-det-RWW})$.

Proof. A det-RWW-automaton M for the language L_{pow} works as follows, where A is the only auxiliary symbol :

1. It accepts an input of the form a, aa or $aaaa$ immediately.
2. If the tape content does not contain an occurrence of the symbol A, then a rewrite step of the form $aaaa\$ \to Aaa\$$ is applied.
3. If the tape content does contain an occurrence of A, then
    - M rejects, if the tape content has a prefix of the form $\text{¢}a^i A$ for some integer $i < 4$;

- M applies a rewrite step of the form $\math022a^4A \to \math022a^2$, if the tape content has a prefix of the form $\math022a^4A$;
- M applies a rewrite step of the form $a^4A \to Aa^2$, if the tape content has a prefix of the form $\math022a^iA$ for some integer $i > 4$.

It follows easily that $L(M) = L_{pow}$, and that no configuration of M that is reachable from an initial configuration ever contains more than a single occurrence of the auxiliary symbol A.   □

Using the pumping lemma for restarting automata [10], it can be shown easily that L_{pow} is not accepted by any RLW-automaton. Thus, we obtain the following proper inclusions.

Corollary 2. *For each type* $X \in \{\text{det-R(R)WW}, \text{det-RLWW}, \text{R(R)WW}, \text{RLWW}\}$,

$$\mathcal{L}(\text{aux}(0)\text{-X}) \subsetneq \mathcal{L}(\text{aux}(1)\text{-X}).$$

As shown in [9] (Section 5), det-RL-automata even accept some languages that are not growing context-sensitive. Hence, we see that the language class $\mathcal{L}(\text{aux}(0)\text{-det-RLWW})$ is not included in the class GCSL of growing context-sensitive languages. As GCSL includes the class of Church-Rosser languages, which coincides with the class $\mathcal{L}(\text{det-RRWW})$, we obtain the following consequences.

Corollary 3. *For each* $i \in \mathbb{N}_+$ *and each function* $j : \mathbb{N} \to \mathbb{N}$,

$$\mathcal{L}(\text{aux}(0)\text{-det-RLWW}) \not\subset \mathcal{L}(\text{aux}(j,i)\text{-det-RRWW}) \subsetneq \mathcal{L}(\text{aux}(j,i)\text{-det-RLWW}).$$

Currently we do not know whether all context-free languages can be accepted by det-RLWW-automata. However, we can at least show that this is impossible when the number of occurrences of auxiliary symbols is restricted too much.

Proposition 3. *The language* $L_{pal2} := \{\, ww^R vv^R \mid w, v \in \{0,1\}^* \,\}$ *is not accepted by any deterministic* RLWW-*automaton that uses only* $o(n/\log^5 n)$ *occurrences of auxiliary symbols.*

The proof of this proposition, which is based on Kolmogorov complexity, is quite involved. It can be found in [8]. This result yields the following lower bound result.

Corollary 4. *If* CFL *is contained in the language class* $\mathcal{L}(\text{aux}(j,i)\text{-det-RLWW})$ *for some function* j *and some integer* i, *then* $j(n) \notin o(n/\log^5 n)$.

It is currently not even known whether the deterministic RLWW-automaton is at all less expressive than the nondeterministic RLWW-automaton. However, as the language L_{pal2} is 2-linear, and as the class of 2-linear languages is included in aux(1)-RLWW (see Theorem 4), we have at least the following separation result.

Corollary 5. *For each function* $j(n) \in o(n/\log^5 n)$ *and each integer* $i > 0$,

$$\mathcal{L}(\text{aux}(j,i)\text{-det-RLWW}) \subsetneq \mathcal{L}(\text{aux}(j,i)\text{-RLWW}).$$

4 Nondeterministic Restarting Automata

Here we investigate the complexity of context-free languages with respect to the number of auxiliary symbols used. As already R-automata can accept some languages that are not even growing context-sensitive [12], while some context-free languages cannot be accepted by RRW-automata [7], we have the following basic fact.

Corollary 6. *The language classes* $\mathcal{L}(\text{aux}(0)\text{-}X)$ *and* CFL *are incomparable under set inclusion for each type* $X \in \{$RLWW, RRWW, RWW$\}$.

However, each context-free language can be accepted by an RWW-automaton that has only a single auxiliary letter.

Theorem 1. CFL *is included in* $\mathcal{L}(\text{aux}(n, 1)\text{-RWW})$.

Proof. Let G be a context-free grammar in Chomsky normal form with the set N of nonterminals, let $m := |N|$, and let $\hat{L}$ be the set of all sentential forms that can be derived in G.

For each $\alpha \in \hat{L}$, we consider a derivation tree for α. If α is sufficiently long, then there exists a subtree with at least $4m$ (and at most $8m$) leaves. The RWW-automaton guesses a subword of α which corresponds to such a subtree and replaces it by the encoding of the nonterminal appearing at the root of that subtree.

In order to use this technique when there is only one auxiliary symbol in the alphabet, we encode the i-th nonterminal of G by $Aa^i A$, where A is the only auxiliary symbol of the RWW-automaton considered and a is a fixed terminal symbol. As each rewrite step shortens the sentential form by at least $4m - 1$ symbols, the rewrite steps remain length-reducing even when the above encoding for nonterminals of G is being used. $\square$

If only the accepting computations with the smallest number of occurrences of auxiliary symbols are taken into account, then a technique of Hemaspaandra et al. for space efficient computations [13, 14] can be used to derive the following result.

Theorem 2. CFL *is included in* $\mathcal{L}(\text{g-aux}(\log n, 1)\text{-RWW})$.

For the rest of the paper we restrict our attention to a particular class of context-free languages. A language L is called k-*linear* [15] if there is a context-free grammar $G = (N, \Sigma, P, S)$ for L that contains a starting rule of the form $S \to S_1 \ldots S_k$ such that S does not occur in any other rule of G, and S_i is the starting symbol of a linear subgrammar $G_i = (N_i, \Sigma, P_i, S_i)$ for each $i \in \{1, \ldots, k\}$. Further, $N_i \cap N_j = \emptyset$ for each $i \neq j$, and S_i does not occur on the righthand side of any rule of G_i ($1 \leq i \leq k$). Thus, L is the concatenation $L_1 \cdot L_2 \cdot \ldots \cdot L_k$ of the linear languages $L_i := L(G_i)$ ($1 \leq i \leq k$). By k-LIN we denote the class of k-linear languages.

Theorem 3. $\bigcup_{k \in \mathbb{N}} k\text{-LIN} \subsetneq \mathcal{L}(\text{aux}(2)\text{-RLWW})$.

Proof. The computation of an RLWW-automaton M can be described transparently by a finite set of *meta-instructions* of the form $(E_1, u \to v, E_2)$ and (E, Accept), where E_1, E_2, and E are regular languages, which are called the *regular constraints* of the meta-instruction. In a restarting configuration of the form $q_0 \textcent w\$$, M nondeterministically chooses a meta-instruction. If $(E_1, u \to v, E_2)$ is chosen, then M halts and rejects, if w does not admit a factorization of the form $w = w_1 u w_2$ such that $\textcent w_1 \in E_1$ and $w_2\$ \in E_2$. Otherwise, one such factorization is chosen nondeterministically and the restarting configuration $q_0 \textcent w_1 v w_2 \$$ is reached. If (E, Accept) is chosen, then M halts and accepts, if $\textcent w\$ \in E$, otherwise, it halts and rejects.

Let L be a k-linear language, and let G be a k-linear grammar that generates L. First, we describe the idea of accepting L using only two occurrences of auxiliary symbols on the tape, but without restricting the number of auxiliary symbols in the alphabet.

For an input word x we first guess a G_1-derivation $S_1 \Rightarrow^* x_1$ for a prefix x_1 of x such that $x = x_1 \ldots x_k$, $x_i \in L(G_i)$ for $i \in [1, k]$, in a bottom-up fashion. We start by choosing a production $X \to \alpha$ for $X \in N_1$ and $\alpha \in \Sigma^*$. That is, we perform a rewrite step $\alpha \to X$. Then we simulate consecutive steps of the derivation in reverse order by applying meta-instructions

$$(\textcent \Sigma^*, \alpha X \beta \to Y, \Sigma^* \$)$$

for $X, Y \in N_1$, $\alpha, \beta \in \Sigma^*$, corresponding to productions $Y \to \alpha X \beta$ of G_1.

When a tape content of the form $S_1 y$ is reached, where $y \in \Sigma^*$, we begin to simulate a G_2-derivation for $L_2 = L(G_2)$ by first executing the last step in a derivation of $x_2 \in L_2$. Thereafter, the tape contains two auxiliary symbols: $S_1 \in N_1$ and $X \in N_2$. This means that we have already found a prefix $x_1 \in L_1$ and started to simulate a G_2-derivation for $x_2 \in L_2$. So we can remove S_1. Further, we process consecutive factors analogously. In general, we can describe this behaviour by the following meta-instructions, where $u, y, v \in \Sigma^*$, $i \in [1, k]$:

$$
\begin{aligned}
&(\textcent \Sigma^*, u \to X, \Sigma^* \$) && \text{for } (X \to u) \in P_1, \\
&(\textcent \Sigma^*, uXy \to Y, \Sigma^* \$) && \text{for } X, Y \in N_i, (Y \to uXy) \in P_i, \\
&(\textcent S_i \Sigma^*, u \to X, \Sigma^* \$) && \text{for } X \in N_{i+1}, (X \to u) \in P_{i+1}, \\
&(\textcent, S_i \to \varepsilon, \Sigma^* X \Sigma^* \$) && \text{for } X \in N_{i+1}, \\
&(\textcent S_k \$, \text{Accept}).
\end{aligned}
$$

However, this schema does not guarantee that the automaton is length-reducing, for example, a production $X \to y$ where $|y| \leq 1$ can be applied. Further, our aim is to use only one auxiliary symbol in the alphabet.

Without loss of generality we can assume that the grammar does neither contain any productions of the form $X \to Y$ for $|Y| \leq 1$ and $X \notin \{S_1, \ldots, S_k\}$ nor of the form $S_i \to X$ for $i \in [1, k]$ and $X \in N$. Further, we can assume that Σ contains at least two symbols, say 0 and 1 (as context-free languages over a one-letter alphabet are regular). In order to apply the above strategy using only one auxiliary symbol, an occurrence of this auxiliary symbol will be followed by a binary encoding (of a fixed length) of the actual nonterminal of G. In order to make the resulting rewrite operations length-reducing, 'short' factors x_i will not be processed separately and for the remaining 'long' factors, we simulate several derivation steps by a single rewrite operation. In this way we will have sufficient space for the encodings.

Let $p := 2 \cdot \max(\lceil \log |N| \rceil, \lceil \log k \rceil)$, and let $X_1, \ldots, X_{|N|}$ be the nonterminals of G. For each occurrence of the only auxiliary symbol A of M on the tape, the p symbols following A will be interpreted as follows: the first $p/2$ symbols encode the number i of the nonterminal X_i, and the next $p/2$ symbols encode j, the index of the last factor x_j processed previously. For $X_i \in N$, we use $\text{bin}(X_i)$ to denote the $(p/2)$-bit encoding of i, and for $i \in [1, k]$, $\text{bin}(i)$ denotes the $(p/2)$-bit encoding of i.

Finally, let $r := \max\{ |\alpha| \mid (X \to \alpha) \in P \} + p$. The automaton M will proceed according to the following strategy:

1. If the tape does not contain any occurrences of the auxiliary symbol, and if the length of the tape content is not longer than $k \cdot r$, then M decides whether the input belongs to L in a tail computation.

2. If the tape does not contain any occurrences of the auxiliary symbol, but the length of the tape content exceeds the number $k \cdot r$, then M guesses a minimal index j such that $|x_j| > r$. Next M guesses a derivation $X \Rightarrow_G^* u$ such that $p + 1 < |u| \le r$, $u \in \Sigma^*$, and $X \in N$, M finds an occurrence of the factor u within the tape content, and executes the rewrite step $u \to A\text{bin}(X)\text{bin}(0)$.

3. To simulate a derivation step in a single factor, M has a meta-instruction of the form

$$(\mathbb{c}\Sigma^*, uA\text{bin}(Y)\text{bin}(j)v \to A\text{bin}(X)\text{bin}(j), \Sigma^*\$)$$

   for each production $X \to uYv$, where $X, Y \in N_i$ and $i > j \ge 0$.

4. To finish the derivation of a factor x_i, M has a meta-instruction of the form

$$(\mathbb{c}, yuA\text{bin}(Y)\text{bin}(j-1)v \to A\text{bin}(S_i)\text{bin}(i), \Sigma^*\$)$$

   for each $y = x_j x_{j+1} \ldots x_{i-1}$ such that $x_l \in L_l$ and $|x_l| \le r$ for $l \in [j, i-1]$, and for each production $S_i \to uYv$.

5. To start the processing of a new factor, M guesses the next value $j > i$ such that $|x_j| > r$, where i is the index of the previously processed factor. Next M chooses a derivation $X \Rightarrow_G^* u$ such that $p + 1 < |u| \le r$, $X \in N_j$, finds the factor u on the tape, and executes the meta-instruction

$$(\mathbb{c}A\text{bin}(S_i)\text{bin}(i)\Sigma^*, u \to A\text{bin}(X)\text{bin}(i), \Sigma^*\$).$$

6. In order to remove an occurrence of the auxiliary symbol which is not needed anymore from the tape (together with the encoding of the nonterminal which follows this symbol), M uses the meta-instructions

$$(\mathbb{c}, A\text{bin}(S_i)\text{bin}(i) \to \varepsilon, \Sigma^* A\text{bin}(X)\text{bin}(i)\Sigma^*\$)$$

for $X \in N_j$, $j > i$.

7. Finally, for each $y = x_j x_{j+1} \ldots x_{i-1}$ and $y' = x_{i+1} \ldots x_k$ such that $x_l \in L_l$ and $|x_l| \leq r$ for $l \in [j, k] - \{i\}$, $i \in [1, k]$, M has the meta-instruction

$$(\mathtt{\mathcal{C}}yA\mathrm{bin}(S_i)\mathrm{bin}(j-1)y'\$, \mathsf{Accept}).$$

The above meta-instructions define a length-reducing RLWW-automaton which recognizes $L(G)$ and which uses at most two occurrences of the single auxiliary symbol A.   □

From the proof above we obtain the following consequence.

Corollary 7. LIN $\subsetneq \mathcal{L}(\mathsf{aux}(1)\text{-RLWW})$.

Actually, this result can be extended as follows, improving on Theorem 3 at least for the case $k = 2$.

Theorem 4. 2-LIN $\subsetneq \mathcal{L}(\mathsf{aux}(1)\text{-RLWW})$.

Proof. Let $G = (N, \Sigma, P, S)$ be a 2-linear grammar with starting production $S \to S_1 S_2$ and linear subgrammars $G_i = (N_i, \Sigma, P_i, S_i)$ for $i = 1, 2$. We describe a restarting automaton M for $L := L(G)$ that never has more than a single occurrence of an auxiliary symbol on its tape, but that uses many different auxiliary symbols. Then we will point out how to get rid of all but one auxiliary symbol by employing an appropriate encoding.

In the following description we will make use of a constant $c \in \mathbb{N}_+$ that we will specify later. Given an input word of length below $2c + 2$, M accepts or rejects immediately in a tail computation. For an input x satisfying $|x| \geq 2c+2$, M must determine whether x has a factorization $x = x_1 x_2$ such that $x_1 \in L(G_1)$ and $x_2 \in L(G_2)$. As a first step towards this aim, M chooses nondeterministically one of the cases (i) $|x_1|, |x_2| > c$, (ii) $|x_1| \leq c$ (and so $|x_2| > c$), or (iii) $|x_2| \leq c$ (and so $|x_1| > c$).

In cases (ii) and (iii) M guesses a G_i-derivation of x_i from S_i in reverse order for the factor x_i satisfying $|x_i| > c$ using only a single occurrence of an auxiliary symbol on the tape, verifying that the remaining factor x_j, $j \neq i$, belongs to $L(G_j)$ in the final step.

Finally, in case (i) M works as follows. First, it guesses a G_1-derivation for x_1 in reverse order. Thereafter, M simulates a G_2-derivation

$$\begin{aligned} S_2 &\Rightarrow s_0 X_1 r_0 \Rightarrow s_0 s_1 X_2 r_1 r_0 \\ &\Rightarrow^* s_0 s_1 \ldots s_{m-1} X_m r_{m-1} \ldots r_1 r_0 \\ &\Rightarrow s_0 s_1 \ldots s_{m-1} s_m r_{m-1} \ldots r_1 r_0 \end{aligned}$$

of $x_2 = s_0 s_1 \ldots s_{m-1} s_m r_{m-1} \ldots r_1 r_0$ from S_2, where $X_{i-1} \to s_{i-1} X_i r_{i-1}$ is the i-th step of this derivation for $1 \leq i \leq m$, $X_0 := S_2$, and $X_m \to s_m$ is the last step. As M must remember the position of the nonterminal X_i within the current content of the tape, it uses a finite number of symbols at the suffix of the tape content to indicate where the encoding of this nonterminal is located. Unfortunately, M cannot apply any rewrite step to the suffix as long as $i \leq j$, where j is the minimal value for which $r_j \neq \varepsilon$. Therefore, the initial part of length j of the G_2-derivation is treated separately. Eventually, the restarting configuration $q_0 \mathtt{¢} X_j s_j \ldots s_{m-1} s_m r_{m-1} \ldots r_j \mathtt{\$}$ is reached.

If $s_j \neq \varepsilon$ and $r_j \neq \varepsilon$, then the simulation of the derivation step $X_j \to s_j X_{j+1} r_j$ will require more than one rewrite step of M. Therefore, we use a fixed number of input symbols that follow directly after the auxiliary symbol and a fixed number of input symbols that are adjacent to the right sentinel $\mathtt{\$}$ to encode information about the derivation step to be simulated and to coordinate the rewrite steps.

As this requires some extra space for the encodings, M will simulate at least c steps of the G_2-derivation at once, using several cycles. The matter is complicated by the fact that we have to distinguish between those parts of the G_2-derivation where the factors r_i are empty and those parts, where these factors are non-empty.

The automaton M accepts the language L, but it is not length-reducing, and furthermore, it uses many different auxiliary symbols. Fortunately, we can transform it into a length-reducing automaton with only a single auxiliary symbol in its alphabet by using an appropriate encoding. The size of the constant c is determined as part of this encoding. The details can be found in [8].   □

5   Conclusions and Open Problems

We have seen that two occurrences of a single auxiliary symbol suffice to accept every k-linear language, and that for $k = 2$, already a single occurrence suffices. On the other hand, we have seen that a bounded number of occurrences of auxiliary symbols does not suffice to accept all context-free languages by deterministic RLWW-automata. However, many problems concerning the new measures remain open. For example, is there an infinite hierarchy with respect to the number of auxiliary symbols in the tape alphabet? Or is it possible to show that a single auxiliary symbol is always sufficient by using appropriate encodings? What can be said in general on the number of occurrences of auxiliary symbols on the tape? Is there an infinite hierarchy with respect to the number of occurrences of auxiliary symbols? Other interesting questions concern the context-free languages. For example, is there a constant d such that each context-free language is accepted by a nondeterministic RLWW-automaton that uses at most d occurrences of auxiliary symbols? Recall that each *deterministic* context-free language is accepted by a monotone det-R-automaton [7], that is, for these languages no auxiliary symbols are required at all.

Acknowledgement. The authors thank František Mráz and Martin Plátek from Charles University, Prague, for many fruitful discussions on restarting automata in general and on the topic of this paper in particular.

References

1. Jančar, P., Mráz, F., Plátek, M., Vogel, J.: Restarting automata. In Reichel, H., ed.: FCT 1995, LNCS 965, Springer, Berlin (1995) 283–292
2. Oliva, K., Květoň, P., Ondruška, R.: The computational complexity of rule-based part-of-speech tagging. In Matoušek, V., Mautner, P., eds.: TSD 2003, LNCS 2807, Springer, Berlin (2003) 82–89

3. Plátek, M., Lopatková, M., Oliva, K.: Restarting automata: motivations and applications. In Holzer, M., ed.: Workshop 'Petrinetze' and 13. Theorietag 'Formale Sprachen und Automaten', Institut für Informatik, Technische Universität München (2003) 90–96

4. Niemann, G., Otto, F.: Restarting automata, Church-Rosser languages, and representations of r.e. languages. In Rozenberg, G., Thomas, W., eds.: Developments in Language Theory - Foundations, Applications, and Perspectives, DLT 1999, World Scientific, Singapore (2000) 103–114

5. Niemann, G., Otto, F.: Further results on restarting automata. In Ito, M., Imaoka, T., eds.: Words, Languages and Combinatorics III, World Scientific, Singapore (2003) 352–369

6. McNaughton, R., Narendran, P., Otto, F.: Church-Rosser Thue systems and formal languages. J. Assoc. Comput. Mach. **35** (1988) 324–344

7. Jančar, P., Mráz, F., Plátek, M., Vogel, J.: On monotonic automata with a restart operation. J. Autom. Lang. Comb. **4** (1999) 283–292

8. Jurdziński, T., Otto, F.: Restarting automata with restricted utilization of auxiliary symbols. Mathematische Schriften Kassel 2/05, Universität Kassel (2005)

9. Otto, F.: Restarting Automata - Notes for a Course at the 3rd International PhD School in Formal Languages and Applications. Mathematische Schriften Kassel 6/04, Universität Kassel (2004)

10. Plátek, M.: Two-way restarting automata and j-monotonicity. In Pacholski, L., Ružička, P., eds.: SOFSEM 2001, LNCS 2234, Springer, Berlin (2001) 316–325

11. Plátek, M., Otto, F., Mráz, F., Jurdziński, T.: Restarting automata and variants of j-monotonicity. Mathematische Schriften Kassel 9/03, Universität Kassel (2003)

12. Jurdziński, T., Otto, F., Mráz, F., Plátek, M.: On the complexity of 2-monotone restarting automata. In Calude, C., Calude, E., Dinneen, M., eds.: DLT 2004, LNCS 3340, Springer, Berlin (2004) 237–248

13. Hemaspaandra, L., Mukherji, P., Tantau, T.: Computation with absolutely no space overhead. In Ésik, Z., Fülöp, Z., eds.: DLT 2003, LNCS 2710, Springer, Berlin (2003) 325–336

14. Hemaspaandra, L., Mukherji, P., Tantau, T.: Overhead-free computation, dcfls, and cfls. In: The Computing Research Repository cs. CC/0410035. (2004)

15. Salomaa, A.: Formal Languages. Academic Press (1973)

A Class of Rational n-WFSM Auto-intersections

André Kempe[1], Jean-Marc Champarnaud[2], Jason Eisner[3], Franck Guingne[1,4], and Florent Nicart[1,4]

[1] Xerox Research Centre Europe, Grenoble Laboratory,
6 chemin de Maupertuis, 38240 Meylan, France
Andre.Kempe@xrce.xerox.com
http://www.xrce.xerox.com
[2] PSI Laboratory, Université de Rouen, CNRS, 76821 Mont-Saint-Aignan, France
Jean-Marc.Champarnaud@univ-rouen.fr
http://www.univ-rouen.fr/psi/
[3] Johns Hopkins University, Computer Science Department,
3400 N. Charles St., Baltimore, MD 21218, United States
jason@cs.jhu.edu
http://www.cs.jhu.edu/~jason/
[4] LIFAR Laboratory, Université de Rouen, 76821 Mont-Saint-Aignan, France
{Franck.Guingne, Florent.Nicart}@univ-rouen.fr
http://www.univ-rouen.fr/LIFAR/

Abstract. Weighted finite-state machines with n tapes describe n-ary rational string relations. The join n-ary relation is very important in applications. It is shown how to compute it via a more simple operation, the auto-intersection. Join and auto-intersection generally do not preserve rationality. We define a class of triples $\langle A, i, j \rangle$ such that the auto-intersection of the machine A on tapes i and j can be computed by a delay-based algorithm. We point out how to extend this class and hope that it is sufficient for many practical applications.

1 Introduction

Multi-tape finite-state machines (FSMs) [1, 5] are a natural generalization of the familiar finite-state acceptors (one tape) and transducers (two tapes). Multi-tape machines have been used in the morphology of Semitic languages, to synchronize the vowels, consonants, and templatic pattern into a surface form [3, 6].

The n-ary relation defined by a (weighted) n-tape FSM is a (weighted) *rational* relation. *Finite* relations are defined by *acyclic* FSMs, and are well-studied since they can be viewed as relational databases whose fields are strings [7]. E.g., a two-column database can be represented by an acyclic finite-state transducer.

Unfortunately, one pays a price for generalizing to multi-column databases with *infinitely* many rows, as defined by *cyclic* FSMs. Cyclic FSMs are closed under the rational operations, but not under all relational operations, as finite databases are. For example, transducers are not closed under intersection [1].

In this paper we consider a practically useful generalization of transducer intersection, *multi-tape join*, which is analogous to *natural join* of databases. More precisely, we study an equivalent but simpler problem, *auto-intersection*.

J. Farré, I. Litovsky, and S. Schmitz (Eds.): CIAA 2005, LNCS 3845, pp. 188–198, 2006.

The emptiness or rationality of the result is generally undecidable [7]. Therefore we define a simple class Θ of triples $\langle A, i, j \rangle$ such that the auto-intersection of the machine A w.r.t. tapes i and j is rational. Our auto-intersection algorithm for this class is based on the notion of delay [8, 9]. We focus on the case of an auto-intersection w.r.t. two tapes, which is sufficient to explain the basic ideas and problems, and we briefly discuss the general case. We conclude by pointing out possible extensions of the class Θ.

Weighted n-ary relations and their machines are introduced in Section 2. Join and auto-intersection operations are presented in Section 3. A class of compilable auto-intersections and the associated algorithm are defined in Section 4.

2   Definitions

We recall some definitions about n-ary weighted relations and their machines, following the usual definitions for multi-tape automata [2, 10], with semiring weights added just as for acceptors and transducers [11, 12]. See [7] for details.

Weighted n-Ary Relations: A weighted n-ary relation is a function from $(\Sigma^*)^n$ to $\mathbb{K}$, for a given finite alphabet Σ and a given weight semiring $\mathcal{K} = \langle \mathbb{K}, \oplus, \otimes, \bar{0}, \bar{1} \rangle$. A relation assigns a weight to any n-tuple of strings. A weight of $\bar{0}$ can be interpreted as meaning that the tuple is not in the relation.[1] We are especially interested in *rational* (or *regular*) n-ary relations, i.e. relations that can be encoded by n-tape weighted finite-state machines, which we now define.

We adopt the convention that variable names referring to n-tuples of strings include a superscript (n). Thus we write $s^{(n)}$ rather than $\vec{s}$ for a tuple of strings $\langle s_1, \ldots s_n \rangle$. We also use this convention for the names of objects that contain n-tuples of strings, such as n-tape machines and their transitions and paths.

Multi-tape Weighted Finite-State Machines: An *n-tape weighted finite-state machine* (WFSM or n-WFSM) $A^{(n)}$ is defined by a six-tuple $A^{(n)} = \langle \Sigma, Q, \mathcal{K}, E^{(n)}, \lambda, \varrho \rangle$, with Σ being a finite alphabet, Q a finite set of states, $\mathcal{K} = \langle \mathbb{K}, \oplus, \otimes, \bar{0}, \bar{1} \rangle$ the semiring of weights, $E^{(n)} \subseteq (Q \times (\Sigma^*)^n \times \mathbb{K} \times Q)$ a finite set of weighted n-tape transitions, $\lambda : Q \to \mathbb{K}$ a function that assigns initial weights to states, and $\varrho : Q \to \mathbb{K}$ a function that assigns final weights to states. We say that $q \in Q$ is an initial state if $\lambda(q) \neq \bar{0}$, and a final state if $\varrho(q) \neq \bar{0}$.

Any transition $e^{(n)} \in E^{(n)}$ has the form $e^{(n)} = \langle p, \ell^{(n)}, w, n \rangle$. We refer to these four components as the transition's source state $p(e^{(n)}) \in Q$, its label $\ell(e^{(n)}) \in (\Sigma^*)^n$, its weight $w(e^{(n)}) \in \mathbb{K}$, and its target state $n(e^{(n)}) \in Q$. We refer by $E(q)$ to the set of out-going transitions of a state $q \in Q$ (with $E(q) \subseteq E^{(n)}$).

A *path* $\gamma^{(n)}$ of length $k \geq 0$ is a sequence of transitions $e_1^{(n)} e_2^{(n)} \cdots e_k^{(n)}$ where $n(e_i^{(n)}) = p(e_{i+1}^{(n)})$ for all $i \in [\![1, k-1]\!]$. The path's label $\ell(\gamma^{(n)})$ is the element-wise concatenation of the labels of its transitions. The path's weight $w(\gamma^{(n)})$ is

---

[1] It is convenient to define the *support* of an arbitrary weighted relation $\mathcal{R}^{(n)}$, as being the set of tuples to which the relation gives non-$\bar{0}$ weight.

$$w(\gamma^{(n)}) \stackrel{\text{def}}{=} \lambda(p(e_1^{(n)})) \otimes \left(\bigotimes_{j \in [\![1,k]\!]} w\left(e_j^{(n)}\right) \right) \otimes \varrho(n(e_k^{(n)})) \qquad (1)$$

The path is said to be *successful*, and to *accept* its label, if $w(\gamma^{(n)}) \neq \bar{0}$. We denote by $\Gamma_{A^{(n)}}$ the set of all successful paths of $A^{(n)}$, and by $\Gamma_{A^{(n)}}(s^{(n)})$ the set of successful paths (if any) that accept the n-tuple of strings $s^{(n)}$. Now, the machine $A^{(n)}$ defines a weighted n-ary relation $\mathcal{R}(A^{(n)}) : (\Sigma^*)^n \to \mathbb{K}$ that assigns to each n-tuple, $s^{(n)}$, the total weight of all paths accepting it:

$$\mathcal{R}_{A^{(n)}}(s^{(n)}) \stackrel{\text{def}}{=} \bigoplus_{\gamma^{(n)} \in \Gamma_{A^{(n)}}(s^{(n)})} w(\gamma^{(n)}) \qquad (2)$$

3   Operations

We now describe some central operations on n-ary weighted relations and their n-WFSMs [13]. The auto-intersection operation is introduced, with the aim of simplifying the computation of the join operation. Our notation is inspired by relational databases. For mathematical details of simple operations see [7].

Simple Operations: The set of n-ary weighted rational relations can be constructed as the closure of the elementary n-ary weighted relations (those whose support consists of at most one tuple) under the basic rational operations of *union*, *concatenation* and *Kleene closure*. These rational operations can be implemented by simple constructions on the corresponding nondeterministic n-tape WFSMs [14]. These n-tape constructions and their semiring-weighted versions are exactly the same as for acceptors and transducers, since they are indifferent to the n-tuple transition labels.

The *projection* operator $\pi_{\langle j_1, \dots j_m \rangle}$, with $j_1, \dots j_m \in [\![1, n]\!]$, maps an n-ary relation to an m-ary one by retaining in each tuple components specified by the indices $j_1, \dots j_m$ and placing them in the specified order. Indices may occur in any order, possibly with repeats. Thus the tapes can be permuted or duplicated: $\pi_{\langle 2,1 \rangle}$ inverts a 2-ary relation. The *complementary projection* operator $\overline{\pi}_{\{j_1, \dots j_m\}}$ removes the tapes $j_1, \dots j_m$ and preserves the order of other tapes.

Join Operation: Our *join* operator differs from database join in that database columns are named, whereas our tapes are numbered. Since tapes must explicitly be selected by number, join is neither associative nor commutative.

For any distinct $i_1, \dots i_r \in [\![1, n]\!]$ and any distinct $j_1, \dots j_r \in [\![1, m]\!]$, we define a *join* operator $\bowtie_{\{i_1=j_1, \dots i_r=j_r\}}$. It combines an n-ary and an m-ary relation into an $(n + m - r)$-ary relation defined as follows:[2]

---

[2] For example the tuples $\langle abc, def, \epsilon \rangle$ and $\langle def, ghi, \epsilon, jkl \rangle$ combine in the join $\bowtie_{\{2=1,3=3\}}$ and yield the tuple $\langle abc, def, \epsilon, ghi, jkl \rangle$, with a weight equal to the product of their weights.

$$\left(\mathcal{R}_1^{(n)} \bowtie_{\{i_1=j_1,\dots i_r=j_r\}} \mathcal{R}_2^{(m)}\right) (\langle u_1, \dots u_n, s_1, \dots s_{m-r}\rangle) \stackrel{\text{def}}{=} \mathcal{R}_1^{(n)}(u^{(n)}) \otimes \mathcal{R}_2^{(m)}(v^{(m)}) \qquad (3)$$

$v^{(m)}$ being the unique tuple s. t. $\overline{\pi}_{\{j_1,\dots j_r\}}(v^{(m)}) = s^{(m-r)}$ and $(\forall k \in [\![1,r]\!])\, v_{j_k} = u_{i_k}$.

The *intersection* of two n-ary relations is the n-ary relation defined by the join operator $\bowtie_{\{1=1,2=2,\dots n=n\}}$. Examples of *single-tape join* (where $r = 1$) are the join $\bowtie_{\{1=1\}}$ (the intersection of two acceptors) and the join $\bowtie_{\{2=1\}}$ that can be used to express transducer composition. The cross product $\times$, as in $\mathcal{R}_1^{(n)} \times \mathcal{R}_2^{(m)}$, can be expressed as $\bowtie_{\emptyset}$, the join of no tapes ($r = 0$). Our main concern in this paper is multi-tape join ($r > 1$).

Some practical applications require the multi-tape join operation, for example: probabilistic normalization of n-WFSMs conditioned on r tapes,[3] or searching for cognates [16]. Unfortunately, rational relations are *not* closed under arbitrary joins [7]. The join operation is so useful that it is helpful to have a partial algorithm: hence our motivation for studying auto-intersection.

Auto-intersection: For any distinct $i_1, j_1, \dots i_r, j_r \in [\![1, n]\!]$, we define an *auto-intersection* operator $\sigma_{\{i_1=j_1,i_2=j_2,\dots i_r=j_r\}}$. It maps a relation $\mathcal{R}^{(n)}$ to a subset of that relation, preserving tuples $s^{(n)}$ whose elements are equal in pairs as specified, but removing other tuples from the support of the relation.[4] The formal definition is:

$$\left(\sigma_{\{i_1=j_1,\dots i_r=j_r\}}(\mathcal{R}^{(n)})\right)(\langle s_1, \dots s_n\rangle) \stackrel{\text{def}}{=} \begin{cases} \mathcal{R}^{(n)}(\langle s_1, \dots s_n\rangle) & \text{if } (\forall k \in [\![1,r]\!])s_{i_k} = s_{j_k} \\ \overline{0} & \text{otherwise} \end{cases} \qquad (4)$$

It is easy to check that auto-intersecting a relation is different from joining the relation with its own projections. Actually, join and auto-intersection are related by the following equalities:

$$\mathcal{R}_1^{(n)} \bowtie_{\{i_1=j_1,\dots i_r=j_r\}} \mathcal{R}_2^{(m)} = \overline{\pi}_{\{n+j_1,\dots n+j_r\}}\left(\sigma_{\{i_1=n+j_1,\dots i_r=n+j_r\}}(\mathcal{R}_1^{(n)} \times \mathcal{R}_2^{(m)})\right) \qquad (5)$$

$$\sigma_{\{i_1=j_1,\dots i_r=j_r\}}(\mathcal{R}^{(n)}) = \mathcal{R}^{(n)} \bowtie_{\{i_1=1,j_1=2,\dots i_r=2r-1,j_r=2r\}} \underbrace{\left(\pi_{\langle 1,1\rangle}(\Sigma^*) \times \cdots \times \pi_{\langle 1,1\rangle}(\Sigma^*)\right)}_{r \text{ times}} \qquad (6)$$

Thus, for any class of difficult join instances whose results are non-rational or have undecidable properties [7], there is a corresponding class of difficult auto-intersection instances, and vice-versa. Conversely, a partial solution to one problem would yield a partial solution to the other.

The case $r = 1$ is *single-pair* auto-intersection. An auto-intersection on multiple pairs of tapes ($r > 1$) can be defined in terms of multiple single-pair auto-intersections:

$$\sigma_{\{i_1=j_1,\dots i_r=j_r\}}(\mathcal{R}^{(n)}) \stackrel{\text{def}}{=} \sigma_{\{i_r=j_r\}}(\cdots \sigma_{\{i_1=j_1\}}(\mathcal{R}^{(n)})\cdots) \qquad (7)$$

---

[3] This is a straightforward generalization of J. Eisner's construction for probabilistic normalization of transducers ($n = 2$) conditioned on one tape ($r = 1$) [15].

[4] The requirement that the $2r$ indices be distinct mirrors the similar requirement on join and is needed for (6) to hold. But it can be evaded by duplicating tapes: the illegal operation $\sigma_{\{1=2,2=3\}}(\mathcal{R})$ can be computed as $\overline{\pi}_{\{3\}}(\sigma_{\{1=2,3=4\}}(\pi_{\langle 1,2,2,3\rangle}(\mathcal{R})))$.

Nonetheless, it may be wise to compute $\sigma_{\{i_1=j_1,\ldots i_r=j_r\}}$ all at once rather than one tape pair at a time. The reason is that even when $\sigma_{\{i_1=j_1,\ldots i_r=j_r\}}$ is rational, a finite-state strategy for computing it via (7) could fail by encountering non-rational intermediate results. For example, consider applying $\sigma_{\{2=3,4=5\}}$ to the rational 5-ary relation $\{\langle a^i b^j, c^i, c^j, x, y\rangle \mid i, j \in \mathbb{N}\}$. The final result is rational (the empty relation), but the intermediate result after applying just $\sigma_{\{2=3\}}$ would be the non-rational relation $\{\langle a^i b^i, c^i, c^i, x, y\rangle \mid i \in \mathbb{N}\}$.

4   Single-Pair Auto-intersection

As indicated by (5), a join can be computed via an auto-intersection, which can be decomposed as a sequence of single-pair auto-intersections as in (7). We therefore focus on the single-pair case, which is sufficient to explain the basic ideas and problems. As a consequence of Post's Correspondence Problem, there exists no fully general algorithm for auto-intersection [7]. We show that it is however possible to compile the auto-intersection $\sigma_{\{i=j\}}(A)$ for a limited class of triples $\langle A, i, j\rangle$ whose definition is based on the notion of delay.

By *delay* we mean the difference of length of two strings of an n-tuple:[5] $\delta_{\langle i,j\rangle}(s^{(n)}) = |s_i| - |s_j|$ (with $i, j \in [\![1, n]\!]$). The delay of a path γ is determined from its respective labels on tapes i and j: $\delta_{\langle i,j\rangle}(\gamma) = |\ell_i(\gamma)| - |\ell_j(\gamma)|$.

For any $\mathcal{R}_1^{(n)}$, its autointersection $\mathcal{R}^{(n)} = \sigma_{\{i=j\}}(\mathcal{R}_1^{(n)})$ assigns a weight $\bar{0}$ to each string tuple $s^{(n)}$ such that $s_i \neq s_j$. For simplicity, our auto-intersection construction will ensure this by never creating any successful paths γ for which $\ell_i(\gamma) \neq \ell_j(\gamma)$. One consequence is that all successful paths of our constructed $A^{(n)} = \sigma_{\{i=j\}}(A_1^{(n)})$, where $A_1^{(n)}$ expresses $\mathcal{R}_1^{(n)}$, will have a delay equal to 0: $\forall \gamma \in \Gamma_{A^{(n)}}, \; \ell_i(\gamma) = \ell_j(\gamma) \Rightarrow |\ell_i(\gamma)| = |\ell_j(\gamma)| \Rightarrow \delta_{\langle i,j\rangle}(\gamma) = 0$.

To be more specific, let $\Gamma^0 \subseteq \Gamma_{A_1^{(n)}}$ be the set of successful paths of $A_1^{(n)}$ with a delay of 0. Then our construction will "copy" an appropriate subset of Γ^0 into the constructed $A^{(n)}$. Note that $\forall \gamma = \gamma_1 \gamma_2 \cdots \gamma_r \in \Gamma^0$, $\sum_{h=1}^r \delta_{\langle i,j\rangle}(\gamma_h) = \delta_{\langle i,j\rangle}(\gamma) = 0$.

4.1   Bounded Delay Auto-intersection

We now focus temporarily on n-WFSMs such as $A_1^{(n)}$ in Figure 1, whose cycles all have a positive delay with respect to the tapes i, j of the single-pair auto-intersection.

Such an n-WFSM might contain paths with arbitrarily large delay. However, if we consider only its paths $\gamma \in \Gamma^0$, it turns out that they must have *bounded delay*. That is, that there is a bound $\delta_{\langle i,j\rangle}^{\max}(A_1^{(n)})$ for the WFSM such that $|\delta_{\langle i,j\rangle}(\gamma_1)| \leq \delta_{\langle i,j\rangle}^{\max}(A_1^{(n)})$ for any prefix γ_1 of any $\gamma \in \Gamma^0$.

In this section, we outline how to compute the bound $\delta_{\langle i,j\rangle}^{\max}(A_1^{(n)})$. Then, while the algorithm of the next section (4.2) is copying paths from $A_1^{(n)}$, it can avoid

---

[5] We use the notion of delay similarly as in the synchronization of transducers [8, 9].

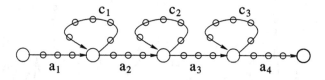

Fig. 1. An example n-WFSM $A_1^{(n)}$, having four acyclic factors a_h and three cycles c_h with positive delay

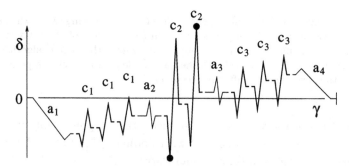

Fig. 2. Hypothetical monitoring of the delay of successively longer prefixes γ_1 of one path γ through $A_1^{(n)}$ whose total delay $\delta_{\langle i,j\rangle}(\gamma) = 0$. Global extrema are marked. By assumption, each of the cycles c_1, c_2, c_3 has positive delay.

extending any prefix whose delay's absolute value exceeds $\delta_{\langle i,j\rangle}^{\max}(A_1^{(n)})$. (Such a prefix is useless because it will not extend into a path in Γ^0, let alone a path with $\ell_i(\gamma) = \ell_j(\gamma)$.)

If we plotted the delay for successively longer prefixes γ_1 of a given path $\gamma \in \Gamma^0$, as γ_1 ranges from ϵ to γ, we would obtain a curve that begins and ends with delay $\delta_{\langle i,j\rangle}(\gamma_1) = 0$, as shown in Figure 2. How can we bound the maximum $\hat{\delta}_{\langle i,j\rangle}(\gamma_1)$ and minimum $\check{\delta}_{\langle i,j\rangle}(\gamma_1)$ along this curve?

A lower bound is given by $\check{\delta}_{\langle i,j\rangle}^{LR}(A_1^{(n)}) \le 0$, defined as the minimum delay of any *acyclic* path that begins at an initial state of $A_1^{(n)}$. Why? Since $\gamma \in \Gamma^0$ is a successful path, any prefix γ_1 of γ can be regarded as an acyclic path of this sort with zero or more cycles inserted. But these cycles can only increase the total delay (by the assumption that their delay is positive), so $\delta_{\langle i,j\rangle}(\gamma_1) \ge \check{\delta}_{\langle i,j\rangle}^{LR}(A_1^{(n)})$.

An upper bound is given by $\hat{\delta}_{\langle i,j\rangle}^{RL}(A_1^{(n)}) \ge 0$, defined as the *negation* of the minimum delay of any acyclic path that ends at a final state of $A_1^{(n)}$. By symmetry, that minimum delay is a lower bound on the delay of any *suffix* γ_2 of γ. But if we factor $\gamma = \gamma_1\gamma_2$, we have $\delta_{\langle i,j\rangle}(\gamma_1) + \delta_{\langle i,j\rangle}(\gamma_2) = \delta_{\langle i,j\rangle}(\gamma) = 0$, since $\gamma \in \Gamma^0$. It follows that $\hat{\delta}_{\langle i,j\rangle}^{RL}(A_1^{(n)})$ is an upper bound on the delay of γ_1.

The minimum $\check{\delta}_{\langle i,j\rangle}^{LR}(A_1^{(n)})$ is finite because there are only finitely many acyclic paths from initial states to consider. $\hat{\delta}_{\langle i,j\rangle}^{RL}(A_1^{(n)})$ is similar. Exhaustively considering all these acyclic paths by backtracking, as illustrated in Figure 3, takes

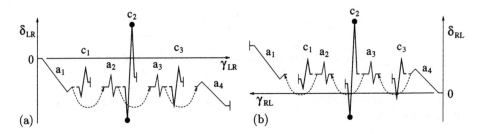

Fig. 3. Monitoring the delay on all acyclic paths of $A_1^{(n)}$, exploring (a) forward from initial states and (b) backward from final states. In (b), the sign of the delay is negated. Global extrema are marked. Gaps denote points where the search algorithm backtracked to avoid completing a cycle. Dashed arrows lead from a choice point to alternative paths that are explored after backtracking.

exponential time in the worst case.[6] However, that is presumably unavoidable since the decision problem associated with finding $\check{\delta}_{\langle i,j\rangle}^{LR}(A_1^{(n)})$ is NP-complete (by a trivial reduction from Hamiltonian Path).

Visually, *all* acyclic prefix paths are represented in Figure 3a, so a given acyclic prefix path must fall entirely above the minimum of Figure 3a. A possibly cyclic prefix path as in Figure 2 can only be higher still, since all cycles have positive delay. A visual argument can also be made from Figure 3b.

These prefix-delay bounds, $\delta_{\langle i,j\rangle}(\gamma_1) \in [\![\check{\delta}_{\langle i,j\rangle}^{LR}(A_1^{(n)}), \hat{\delta}_{\langle i,j\rangle}^{RL}(A_1^{(n)})]\!]$, in fact apply whenever γ_1 is a prefix of a $\gamma \in \Gamma^0$ that traverses no cycle of negative delay. If on the other hand γ traverses no cycle of *positive* delay, we have similarly $\delta_{\langle i,j\rangle}(\gamma_1) \in [\![\check{\delta}_{\langle i,j\rangle}^{RL}(A_1^{(n)}), \hat{\delta}_{\langle i,j\rangle}^{LR}(A_1^{(n)})]\!]$, where these bounds are found by considering maximum rather than minimum delays. In either case, we see that

$$|\delta_{\langle i,j\rangle}(\gamma_1)| \le \delta_{\langle i,j\rangle}^{\max}(A_1^{(n)}) \tag{8}$$

$$\overset{\text{def}}{=} \max\left(|\hat{\delta}_{\langle i,j\rangle}^{LR}(A_1^{(n)})|, \ |\hat{\delta}_{\langle i,j\rangle}^{RL}(A_1^{(n)})|, \ |\check{\delta}_{\langle i,j\rangle}^{LR}(A_1^{(n)})|, \ |\check{\delta}_{\langle i,j\rangle}^{RL}(A_1^{(n)})|\right) \tag{9}$$

Definition of the Class: Let Θ be the class of all the triples $\langle A_1^{(n)}, i, j\rangle$ such that $A_1^{(n)}$ does not contain a path traversing both a cycle with positive delay and a cycle with negative delay (with respect to tapes i and j). The Algorithm AUTOINTERSECTSINGLEPAIR (see Section 4.2) computes the auto-intersection $A^{(n)} = \sigma_{\{i=j\}}(A_1^{(n)})$ for any triple in Θ, thanks to the property that it has a delay not exceeding the limit $\delta_{\langle i,j\rangle}^{\max}(A_1^{(n)})$ defined in (9).

---

[6] In practice, one would first trim $A_1^{(n)}$ to remove edges and states that do not appear on any successful path. This may reduce the problem size, without affecting the defined relation or its auto-intersection.

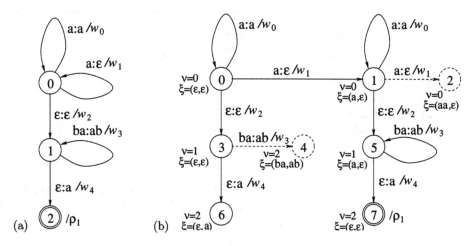

(a) An n-WFSM $A_1^{(2)}$ and (b) its auto-intersection $A^{(2)} = \sigma_{\{1=2\}}(A_1^{(2)})$ (dashed parts are not constructed)

Fig. 4. (a) An n-WFSM $A_1^{(2)}$ and (b) its auto-intersection $A^{(2)} = \sigma_{\{1=2\}}(A_1^{(2)})$ (dashed parts are not constructed)

4.2 Algorithm for Bounded Delay Auto-intersection

We take first the example of the n-WFSM $A_1^{(2)}$ of Figure 4a. The triple $\langle A_1^{(2)}, 1, 2 \rangle$ is obviously in the class Θ. The delay of the auto-intersection $A^{(2)} = \sigma_{\{1=2\}}(A_1^{(2)})$ is bounded by $\delta_{(1,2)}^{\max}(A_1^{(2)}) = 1$. The support $((a{:}a \cup a{:}\varepsilon)^* (ba{:}ab)^* \varepsilon{:}a)$ of $A_1^{(2)}$ is equal to $\{ \langle a^{i+j}(ba)^h, a^i(ab)^h a \rangle \mid i, j, h \in \mathbb{N} \}$.

To construct the auto-intersection,[7] we copy states and transitions one by one from $A_1^{(2)}$ (Figure 4a) to $A^{(2)}$ (Figure 4b), starting with the initial states. We assign to each state q of $A^{(2)}$ two variables: $\nu[q] = q_1$ is the associated state of $A_1^{(2)}$, and $\xi[q] = (s, u)$ gives the "leftover strings" of the path read while reaching q: s has been read on tape i but not yet on tape j, and vice-versa for u. (Thus the delay accumulated so far is $|s| - |u|$. In practice either s or u will be ε.)

In our example, we start at the initial state $q_1 = 0$, with $\nu[0] = 0$ and $\xi[0] = (\varepsilon, \varepsilon)$. Then, we copy the three outgoing transitions of $q_1 = 0$, with their original labels and weights, as well as creating their respective target states with appropriate ν and ξ. If a target state has already been created with this ν and ξ, we reuse it. If not, we create it and proceed to copy *its* outgoing transitions.

The target state of a transition e has an $\xi[n(e)]$ that is obtained from the $\xi[p(e)]$ of its source state, concatenated with the relevant components of its label

---

[7] Our construction bears resemblance to known transducer synchronization procedures. The algorithm of Frougny and Sakarovitch [8] and Mohri's algorithm [9] can, however, not cope with n-FSMs having unbounded delay, such as the one in Figure 4a. Furthermore, they generate synchronized n-FSMs, which is not necessarily what one is aiming for. The algorithm [8] is based on a $\mathbb{K}$-covering of the transducer. Our algorithm is based on a general reachability-driven construction, as [9], but the labeling of the transitions is quite different since our algorithm performs a copy of the original labeling, and we also construct only such paths whose delay does not exceed some limit that we are able to determine.

AUTOINTERSECTSINGLEPAIR$(A_1^{(n)}, i, j, \delta_{\langle i,j \rangle}^{\max}) \rightarrow A^{(n)}$:

1     $A^{(n)} \leftarrow \langle \Sigma \leftarrow \Sigma_1, \ Q \leftarrow \emptyset, \ \mathcal{K} \leftarrow \mathcal{K}_1, \ E^{(n)} \leftarrow \emptyset, \ \lambda, \ \rho \rangle$

2     $Stack \leftarrow \emptyset$

3   for $\forall q_1 \in \{ Q_1 : \lambda(q_1) \neq \bar{0} \}$ do

4   GETPUSHSTATE$(q_1, (\varepsilon, \varepsilon))$

5   while $Stack \neq \emptyset$ do

6             $q \leftarrow pop(Stack)$

7             $q_1 \leftarrow \nu[q]$

8             $(s, u) \leftarrow \xi[q]$

9   for $\forall e_1 \in E(q_1)$ do

10                   $(s', u') \leftarrow$ CREATELEFTOVERSTRINGS$(\ s \cdot \pi_{(i)}(\ell(e_1)),\ u \cdot \pi_{(j)}(\ell(e_1)))$

11   if $\ (s' = \varepsilon \vee u' = \varepsilon) \wedge (\ |(|s'| - |u'|)| \leq \delta_{\langle i,j \rangle}^{\max}(A_1^{(n)})\ )$

12   then $q' \leftarrow$ GETPUSHSTATE$(\ n(e_1), (s', u'))$

13                                 $E \leftarrow E \cup \{\ \langle q, \ell(e_1), w(e_1), q' \rangle\ \}$

14   return $A^{(n)}$

CREATELEFTOVERSTRINGS$(\dot{s}, \dot{u}) \rightarrow (s', u')$:

15     $x \leftarrow longestCommonPrefix(\dot{s}, \dot{u})$

16   return $(x^{-1} \cdot \dot{s}, x^{-1} \cdot \dot{u})$

GETPUSHSTATE$(q_1, (s', u')) \rightarrow q'$:

17   if $\ \exists q \in Q : \nu[q] = q_1 \wedge \xi[q] = (s', u')$

18   then $q' \leftarrow q$

19   else $q' \leftarrow createNewState(\ )$

20                   $\nu[q'] \leftarrow q_1$

21                   $\xi[q'] \leftarrow (s', u')$

22   if $\ s' = \varepsilon \wedge u' = \varepsilon$

23   then $\lambda(q') \leftarrow \lambda(q_1)$

24                                 $\rho(q') \leftarrow \rho(q_1)$

25   else $\lambda(q') \leftarrow \bar{0}$

26                                 $\rho(q') \leftarrow \bar{0}$

27                   $Q \leftarrow Q \cup \{q'\}$

28                   $push(Stack, q')$

29   return q'

Fig. 5. The main algorithm AUTOINTERSECTSINGLEPAIR. It relies on a prior computation of $\delta_{\langle i,j \rangle}^{\max}(A_1^{(n)})$.

$\ell(e)$. The longest common prefix of s and u in $\xi[n(e)] = (s, u)$ is then removed. For example, for the cyclic transition e on $q = 5$ (a copy of that on $q_1 = 1$), the leftover strings of the target are $\xi[n(e)] = \langle ab, ab \rangle^{-1}(\langle a, \varepsilon \rangle \langle ba, ab \rangle) = \langle a, \varepsilon \rangle$. Also, $\nu[n(e)] = 1$. This implies that $n(e) = p(e)$ because they have the same ξ and ν.

    In Figure 4b, new state $q = 2$ and its incoming transition are not created because here the delay of 2 (determined from $\xi[q]$) has an absolute value that exceeds $\delta_{\langle 1,2 \rangle}^{\max}(A_1^{(2)}) = 1$, which means that any path to new state $q = 2$ cannot be in $A^{(2)}$. State $q = 4$ and its incoming transitions are not created either, because both leftover strings in $\xi[4]$ are non-empty, which means that any path traversing $q = 4$ has different strings on tape 1 and 2 and can therefore not be in $A^{(2)}$. State $q = 6$ is non-final, although $q_1 = 2 = \nu[6]$ is final, because $\xi[6]$ is not $(\varepsilon, \varepsilon)$, which means that any path ending in $q = 6$ has different strings on tape 1 and 2. As expected, the support $((a{:}a)^*\ a{:}\varepsilon\ (a{:}a)^*\ (ba{:}ab)^*\ \varepsilon{:}a)$ of the constructed auto-intersection $A^{(2)}$ is equal to $\{\ \langle a^{i+j+1}(ba)^h, a^{i+j+1}(ba)^h \rangle \mid i, j, h \in \mathbb{N}\ \}$.

Algorithm: The formal algorithm AUTOINTERSECTSINGLEPAIR in Figure 5 finds the auto-intersection, provided only that $\delta_{\langle i,j \rangle}^{\max}(A_1^{(n)})$ is indeed an upper bound on the absolute value of the delay of any prefix γ_1 of any successful path γ in $A_1^{(n)}$ such that $\ell_i(\gamma) = \ell_j(\gamma)$.

We have seen how to find such a bound when $\langle A_1^{(n)}, i, j \rangle$ is in the class Θ. Such a bound may also exist in other cases. Even when such a bound is not known or does not exist, one could impose one arbitrarily, in order to obtain an approximate auto-intersection.

The loop at line 5 must terminate, since a finite state set Q will be constructed for $A^{(n)}$ and each state is pushed only once. Q is finite because distinct states $q \in Q$ must have distinct values for $\nu[q]$ and/or $\xi[q]$. The number of values of $\nu[q] = q_1$ is limited by $|Q_1|$ (the number of states of A_1), and the number of values of $\xi[q] = (s, u)$ both by $|\Sigma_1|$ and $\delta_{\langle i,j \rangle}^{\max}$ because either s or u is empty and the other string is not longer than $\delta_{\langle i,j \rangle}^{\max}$. As a result, $|Q| < 2\,|Q_1|\,\dfrac{|\Sigma_1|^{\delta_{\langle i,j \rangle}^{\max}+1}-1}{|\Sigma_1|-1}$.

5   Conclusion

We conclude with two enhancements of the auto-intersection construction. Both attempt to remove cycles of A that prevent $\langle A, i, j \rangle$ from falling in Θ.

First, one can eliminate paths γ such that $\ell_i(\gamma)$ not only differs from $\ell_j(\gamma)$, but differs from $\ell_j(\gamma')$ for all γ' such that $A(\gamma') \neq \bar{0}$, or vice-versa. Given $\langle A^{(n)}, i, j \rangle$, define $A_i^{(1)}$ to be the projection $\pi_{\langle i \rangle}(A^{(n)})$.[8] Define $A_j^{(1)}$ similarly, and put $A'^{(n)} = (A^{(n)} \bowtie_{\{i=1\}} A_j^{(1)}) \bowtie_{\{j=1\}} A_i^{(1)}$.[9] Now $\sigma_{\{i=j\}}(A)$ can be found as $\sigma_{\{i=j\}}(A')$, which helps if $\langle A', i, j \rangle$ falls in Θ.

The second point is related to the generalization (7) for auto-intersection on multiple pairs of tapes. Given a problem $\sigma_{\{i_1=j_1, \ldots i_r=j_r\}}(A)$, we nondeterministically select a pair (i_h, j_h) (if any) such that $\langle A, i_h, j_h \rangle \in \Theta$, and use our method to compute $A' = \sigma_{\{i_h=j_h\}}(A)$. We now attempt to continue in the same way by

---

[8] More precisely, $A_i^{(1)}$ should define a "neutrally weighted" version of the projected language, in which non-$\bar{0}$ string weights have been changed to $\bar{1}$. To obtain this, replace all $\bar{0}$ and non-$\bar{0}$ weights in the weighted acceptor $\pi_{\langle i \rangle}(A^{(n)})$ with FALSE and TRUE respectively to get an ordinary unweighted acceptor over the Boolean semiring; determinize this by standard methods; and then replace all FALSE and TRUE weights with $\bar{0}$ and $\bar{1}$ respectively.

[9] These single-tape joins are guaranteed to succeed (for commutative semirings): they can be computed similarly to transducer composition.

auto-intersecting A' on the remaining $r - 1$ tapes. Note that A' may have fewer cycles than A, so we may have $\langle A', i_{h'}, j_{h'} \rangle \in \Theta$ even if $\langle A, i_{h'}, j_{h'} \rangle \notin \Theta$.

Acknowledgments

We wish to thank Mark-Jan Nederhof for pointing out the relationship between auto-intersection and Post's Correspondence Problem (personal communication), and the anonymous reviewers of our paper for their advice.

References

1. Rabin, M.O., Scott, D.: Finite automata and their decision problems. IBM Journal of Research and Development **3** (1959) 114–125
2. Elgot, C.C., Mezei, J.E.: On relations defined by generalized finite automata. IBM Journal of Research and Development **9** (1965) 47–68
3. Kay, M.: Nonconcatenative finite-state morphology. In: Proc. 3rd Int. Conf. EACL, Copenhagen, Denmark (1987) 2–10
4. Harju, T., Karhumäki, J.: The equivalence problem of multitape finite automata. Theoretical Computer Science **78** (1991) 347–355
5. Kaplan, R.M., Kay, M.: Regular models of phonological rule systems. Computational Linguistics **20** (1994) 331–378
6. Kiraz, G.A.: Multitiered nonlinear morphology using multitape finite automata: a case study on Syriac and Arabic. Computational Lingistics **26** (2000) 77–105
7. Kempe, A., Champarnaud, J.M., Eisner, J.: A note on join and auto-intersection of n-ary rational relations. In Watson, B., Cleophas, L., eds.: Proc. Eindhoven FASTAR Days. Number 04–40 in TU/e CS TR, Eindhoven, Netherlands (2004) 64–78
8. Frougny, C., Sakarovitch, J.: Synchronized rational relations of finite and infinite words. Theoretical Computer Science **108** (1993) 45–82
9. Mohri, M.: Edit-distance of weighted automata. In: Proc. 7th Int. Conf. CIAA (2002). Volume 2608 of Lecture Notes in Computer Science., Tours, France, Springer Verlag, Berlin, Germany (2003) 1–23
10. Eilenberg, S.: Automata, Languages, and Machines. Volume A. Academic Press, San Diego (1974)
11. Kuich, W., Salomaa, A.: Semirings, Automata, Languages. Number 5 in EATCS Monographs on Theoretical Computer Science. Springer Verlag, Berlin, Germany (1986)
12. Mohri, M., Pereira, F.C.N., Riley, M.: A rational design for a weighted finite-state transducer library. Lecture Notes in Computer Science **1436** (1998) 144–158
13. Kempe, A., Guingne, F., Nicart, F.: Algorithms for weighted multi-tape automata. Research report 2004/031, Xerox Research Centre Europe, Meylan, France (2004)
14. Rosenberg, A.L.: On n-tape finite state acceptors. In: IEEE Symposium on Foundations of Computer Science (FOCS). (1964) 76–81
15. Eisner, J.: Parameter estimation for probabilistic finite-state transducers. In: Proc. of the 40th Annual Meeting of the Association for Computational Linguistics, Philadelphia (2002)
16. Kempe, A.: NLP applications based on weighted multi-tape automata. In: Proc. 11th Conf. TALN, Fes, Morocco (2004) 253–258

Experiments with Deterministic ω-Automata for Formulas of Linear Temporal Logic

Joachim Klein and Christel Baier

Universität Bonn, Institut für Informatik I, Römerstrasse 164, 53117 Bonn, Germany
jklein@ltl2dstar.de, baier@cs.uni-bonn.de

Abstract. This paper addresses the problem of generating deterministic ω-automata for formulas of linear temporal logic, which can be solved by applying well-known algorithms to construct a nondeterministic Büchi automaton for the given formula on which we then apply a determinization algorithm. We study here in detail Safra's determinization algorithm, present several heuristics that attempt to decrease the size of the resulting automata and report on experimental results.

1 Introduction

Automata on infinite words, in particular ω-automata and the related ω-regular languages, play a crucial role in logic, for verification purposes and in other areas, see e.g. [1, 2]. In the context of model checking, to check if a system satisfies a given specification, both the system and specification can be regarded as ω-automata, allowing to perform operations like union and intersection or checking for language emptiness with graph algorithms on the automata. As it is often easier for the users of a model checker to specify the properties that they want to verify using a formula in a suitable logic, e.g. linear time logic (LTL), an algorithm for translating formulas to corresponding ω-automata is needed. For LTL formulas, traditionally a conversion to nondeterministic Büchi automata (NBA) is used. Despite a worst case exponential blowup in the size of the formula, in practice the formulas tend to be small and due to good optimizing tools the resulting NBA are of a manageable size for many interesting formulas. For standard model checking, the nondeterminism of the Büchi automaton does not pose a problem. However, for some applications, such as the verification of Markov decision processes [3, 4, 5], the quantitative analysis relies on the representation of the formula by deterministic ω-automata. As deterministic Büchi automata are not as expressive as NBA, it is necessary to use deterministic automata with more complex acceptance types, such as Rabin and Streett automata. Safra [6, 7] proposed an algorithm for the determinization of NBA. In the worst case, Safra's construction yields an exponential blowup, which was shown to be optimal up to a constant factor in the exponent [8, 9]. The transformation from LTL formulas to deterministic Rabin automata (DRA) via NBA and Safra's algorithm leads to a worst case double exponential blowup, which roughly meets the lower bound established by Kupferman and Vardi [10].

J. Farré, I. Litovsky, and S. Schmitz (Eds.): CIAA 2005, LNCS 3845, pp. 199–212, 2006.
© Springer-Verlag Berlin Heidelberg 2006

The purpose of this paper is to study the question whether using Safra's construction to generate deterministic ω-automata for LTL formulas is feasible in practice. We present a series of heuristic optimization methods. Some of them can be understood as refinements of Safra's algorithm, while others operate on the resulting automata or on the formula level. Although an exponential blowup is unavoidable in the worst-case, our empirical studies using our tool *ltl2dstar* show that for many LTL formulas (benchmark formulas from [11, 12, 13] and randomly chosen formulas), the resulting deterministic ω-automata have reasonable size, in many cases of the same magnitude as NBA.

Organization of the Paper. Section 2 recalls the definitions of the relevant automata types. Section 3 summarizes the main steps of Safra's determinization algorithm and presents several heuristics to improve the Safra algorithm. In Section 4, we present techniques to reduce the automaton size that are independent of the chosen determinization algorithm. Section 5 explains the main features of our tool *ltl2dstar* and reports on experimental studies with a series of benchmark examples. Section 6 concludes the paper.

2 ω-Automata

Throughout the paper, we assume some familiarity with formal languages, finite automata and ω-automata. We briefly recall the basic concepts and explain our notations concerning ω-automata with Büchi, Rabin and Streett acceptance. For further details see e.g. [1, 2]. At a few places, we will also need LTL formulas. Due to the length restrictions we skip an explanation of LTL and refer to [14, 15].

A nondeterministic ω-automaton over a nonempty, finite alphabet Σ is a tuple $\mathcal{A} = (Q, \Sigma, \delta, q_0, Acc)$ where Q is a finite state space, $\delta : Q \times \Sigma \to 2^Q$ the transition function and $q_0 \in Q$ the initial state. The last component Acc denotes the acceptance condition of $\mathcal{A}$. For Büchi automata, Acc is a set of accepting states, $Acc = F$ for some $F \subseteq Q$. For Rabin or Streett automata, Acc is a set $\{(L_1, U_1), \dots, (L_r, U_r)\}$ of pairs[1] (L_n, U_n) consisting of sets $L_n, U_n \subseteq Q$. $\mathcal{A}$ is called deterministic if $|\delta(q, a)| = 1$ for all $q \in Q$ and $a \in \Sigma$. We write NBA, NRA, NSA, DBA, DRA and DSA to denote the nondeterministic or deterministic version of Büchi, Rabin or Streett automata, respectively. $|\mathcal{A}|$ denotes the number of states in $\mathcal{A}$ (i.e., $|\mathcal{A}| = |Q|$). The extended transition relation $\delta : Q \times \Sigma^* \to 2^Q$ is defined by $\delta(q, \varepsilon) = \{q\}$ and $\delta(q, ax) = \bigcup_{p \in \delta(q,a)} \delta(p, x)$ for $a \in \Sigma$ and $x \in \Sigma^*$.

Given an infinite word $\rho = a_1 a_2 \dots$ over Σ, a run for ρ in $\mathcal{A}$ denotes any finite or infinite state-sequence $\pi = q_0, q_1, \dots$ where $q_0 \in Q_0$ and $q_i \in \delta(q_{i-1}, a_i)$, $i = 1, 2, \dots$ and such that π is either infinite or $\pi = q_0, \dots, q_j$ where $\delta(q_j, a_{j+1}) = \emptyset$. We write $\inf(\pi)$ to denote the set of states that occur infinitely often in π. An infinite run π is called accepting with respect to the Büchi acceptance condition F if F is visited infinitely often in π, i.e., if $\inf(\pi) \cap F \neq \emptyset$. For the Rabin acceptance condition $\{(L_1, U_1), \dots, (L_r, U_r)\}$, π is called accepting if there exists

---

[1] Another common notation uses pairs (E_n, F_n) in reversed order, i.e. $E_n = U_n$ and $F_n = L_n$.

an index $n \in \{1, \ldots, r\}$ such that $\inf(\pi) \cap U_n = \emptyset$ and $\inf(\pi) \cap L_n \neq \emptyset$. For the Streett acceptance condition $\{(L_1, U_1), \ldots, (L_r, U_r)\}$, π is called accepting if, for all indices $n \in \{1, \ldots, r\}$, $\inf(\pi) \cap L_n = \emptyset$ or $\inf(\pi) \cap U_n \neq \emptyset$. Any finite run is non-accepting. The accepted language $\mathcal{L}(\mathcal{A})$ of an NBA (DBA, NRA, DRA, NSA, DSA) $\mathcal{A}$ is the set of all infinite words $\sigma \in \Sigma^\omega$ that have an accepting run in $\mathcal{A}$. As Streett acceptance is dual to Rabin acceptance, a DRA $\mathcal{A}$ regarded as a DSA recognizes exactly the complement language of $\mathcal{A}$. It is well known that the classes of languages accepted by an NBA, NRA, DRA, NSA and DSA agree exactly with the class of ω-regular languages, while DBA are strictly less expressive.

3   Heuristics to Improve Safra's Construction

We will first recall the main steps of Safra's algorithm to convert an NBA $\mathcal{A}$ into an equivalent DRA $\mathcal{A}'$ and then present several techniques that can decrease the size of the resulting DRA, and thus can also lead to a speedup of the construction. In the sequel, let $\mathcal{A} = (Q, \Sigma, \delta, q_0, F)$ be the NBA to be determinized.

Safra's Algorithm. Safra's idea [6, 7] was to use multiple powerset constructions in parallel to track the runs originating in accepting states in addition to the classical powerset construction, which allows to detect which runs are finite and need to be rejected. These different powersets are organized in a tree-structure called *Safra trees*, which become the states in the DRA. A Safra tree consist of nodes that have a *name*, which allows us to refer to them and keep track of their existence over multiple trees, and a *label*, a set of states from the original NBA associated with this node. In addition, each node has a boolean flag. The transition function of the DRA will transform a Safra tree to its successor by separately applying the powerset construction to the labels of every node of the tree. The initial tree (i.e., initial state in the DRA) will have only a root node with $\{q_0\}$ as its powerset, therefore the label of the root node in all trees will correspond to the standard powerset construction. As we want to keep track of runs originating from accepting states, we create a new child for every node that contains an accepting state in its label. The label of the newly branched child consists of all the accepting states from the parent's label. If at a future point this node has an empty label (the runs it tracked were finite), we can remove the node and record in the acceptance condition that these runs should be rejected. As there is no limit on the branching of new nodes, the trees can grow infinitely large. To get finite trees, both height and width of the trees have to be bounded. The width can be limited by the observation that it is not necessary that a state appears in the labels of multiple siblings. To have a well defined rule which sibling is chosen to keep such a state, Safra proposes ordering the siblings by "age", with the state only kept in the oldest sibling. After this simplification, the labels of sibling nodes are disjoint. To bound the height, we notice that the union of the labels of the children of a node in a Safra tree is always a subset of the label of the parent node, as they track a subset of runs that the parent tracks. When a parent and one of its child have exactly the same labels, they both redundantly track the same runs and we can remove the child node. We set a flag in the parent node to note this event, as it guarantees that all runs tracked by the parent have visited at least one accepting state since the last time the node was flagged. This will be used by the acceptance condition to detect accepting cycles. The same reduction is used when the states of the parent's label are distributed over multiple children. After this step, the parent's label is a proper superset of the union of the child labels, limiting the height. In fact, any proper Safra tree has at most $|Q|$ nodes (up to $|2Q|$ temporarily during construction).

Formally, a Safra tree is an ordered tree T with node-set $N \subseteq \{0, 1, \ldots, 2|Q| - 1\}$ augmented with a marking function $marked : N \to \{\texttt{true}, \texttt{false}\}$, and a labeling function $label : N \to 2^Q \setminus \{\emptyset\}$ such that the label of a parent node is a proper superset of the union of the labels of the children and the labels of sibling nodes are disjoint. A DRA $\mathcal{A}' = (Q', \Sigma, \delta', q_0', Acc)$, equivalent to the original NBA $\mathcal{A}$, is obtained as follows. Q' is the set of all Safra trees. The initial state q_0' is the unique Safra tree with only one node, named 0, labeled with $\{q_0\}$ and unmarked. The transition function δ' transforms a Safra tree T into its successor $\delta'(T, a)$ by the following procedure:[2]

1. **Unmark.** Set $marked(n) = \texttt{false}$ for all nodes n in T.
2. **Branch accepting.** For every node n in T with $label(n) \cap F \neq \emptyset$, create a new, unmarked node as the youngest child of n labeled with $label(n) \cap F$. The new node is named with an unused name from $\{0, 1, \ldots, 2|Q| - 1\}$.
3. **Powerset.** For every node n, replace $label(n)$ with $\bigcup_{q \in label(n)} \delta(q, a)$.
4. **Normalize siblings.** For every two sibling nodes such that they share a state $q \in Q$ in their labels, remove q from the label of the youngest node and all its children.
5. **Remove empty.** Remove all nodes with empty labels.
6. **Mark.** For every node whose label equals the union of the labels of its children, remove all descendants of this node and mark it.

The acceptance condition is $Acc = \{(L_n, U_n) : 0 \leq n < 2|Q|\}$ where L_n is the set of all Safra trees with node n marked and U_n the set of all Safra trees without node n. This construction ensures that $\mathcal{L}(\mathcal{A}) = \mathcal{L}(\mathcal{A}')$ and $|\mathcal{A}'| = 2^{\mathcal{O}(|Q| \cdot \log |Q|)}$. To decrease the size of the resulting DRA, we present four methods that can be integrated in the algorithm.

I. True-Loops on Accepting States. An NBA state q is said to have a true-self-loop if $q \in \delta(q, a)$ for all symbols $a \in \Sigma$. Let $AccTrueLoop$ be the set of accepting states of the NBA $\mathcal{A}$ with a true-self-loop. That is, $AccTrueLoop = \{q \in F : q \in \delta(q, a) \text{ for all } a \in \Sigma\}$. Clearly, any run that eventually enters $AccTrueLoop$ can be modified to an accepting run. Thus, we may abort Safra's construction any time the label of the root node of a Safra tree T contains a state $q \in AccTrueLoop$. In this case, we put $\delta'(T, a) = T$ for all $a \in \Sigma$ and make T accepting in the sense that we insert the acceptance pair $(\{T\}, \emptyset)$.

---

[2] Clearly, in practice it suffices to just generate the Safra trees as states of the DRA that are actually reachable from the initial Safra tree q_0' and the acceptance condition can be easily simplified by removing never accepting or redundant pairs.

This simple heuristic is very useful, as without it, Safra's construction tends to generate many different Safra trees unnecessarily tracking alternative runs, even though an accepting run (an NBA state in *AccTrueLoop*) has already been found.

II. All Successors Are Accepting. If all NBA states q in the label of a node n (of a Safra tree) have only successors that are accepting in NBA $\mathcal{A}$ then a single powerset construction is sufficient as we only have to track if all runs from q are finite; the infinite runs from q are all accepting as no non-accepting state in the NBA can be reached. Safra's construction handles this special case well by default. If $label(n) \subseteq F$ then node n will be marked and has no children (a child with $label(n)$ is branched in step 2 and deleted in step 6, marking n). If all successors of $label(n)$ are also in F then node n will stay marked and have no children in subsequent trees or it will be deleted when the runs it tracks are finite. A possibility for optimization remains, as it takes an additional step in the beginning for Safra's construction to fall into the pattern described above. Let q be a state in $\mathcal{A}$ and $succ^*(q) = \bigcup_{x \in \Sigma^*} \delta(q, x)$ the set of all states reachable from q. We define $succAcc = \{q \in F : succ^*(q) \subseteq F\}$. If after the construction of a new tree with Safra's algorithm, the label of a node n of the Safra tree has only states that are members of $succAcc$ and is not marked, it can be marked (and the tree will thus be placed into L_n of the acceptance condition). This can be done in an additional step:

7. **Additional marking.** For any unmarked node n with $label(n) \subseteq succAcc$ remove all children of n and mark n.

Calculating $succAcc$ can be done in linear time in the size of $\mathcal{A}$:

1. Calculate the strongly connected components (SCCs) of $\mathcal{A}$.
2. In backward topological ordering, visit the SCCs and check:
   (i) If all states in the current SCC are accepting and all SCCs that are successors of the current SCC are marked, then mark the current SCC.
   (ii) If the current SCC contains only a single non-accepting state q that has no edge leading back to itself and all SCCs reachable from q are marked, then mark the current SCC $\{q\}$.

Then, $succAcc$ consists of all states in marked SCCs. Step 2(ii) treats non-accepting NBA states $q \in Q \setminus F$ with $\delta(q, a) \subseteq succAcc$ as if they were accepting.

III. Naming the Nodes in Safra Trees. New nodes in Safra trees are only created in step 2 (Branch accepting) of Safra's construction. As we can choose any unused name, we have significant freedom in choosing the name for the new node. As the set of Safra trees that are created during Safra's construction becomes the set of states in the DRA, we are interested in having the smallest number of different Safra trees. One way to keep the number of different Safra trees low is to try to name new nodes in a way that the resulting tree matches an already existing tree, thus adding no additional state to the DRA. To do this, we mark the new nodes and then search for a matching tree among the already existing trees. If no matching tree is found, the new nodes are named as normal and a new state in the DRA is created for the tree. This can be implemented by calculating the Safra trees the normal way, naming new nodes temporary with a special symbol, e.g. '*'. We simultaneously have to keep track of the names of nodes deleted during steps 4, 5 and 6 of Safra's construction, as they are still in use in step 2 where the new nodes are named and can therefore not be reused. It is clear that nodes that are created and then directly deleted again do not have to be tracked, as we can pretend to have named them with a convenient name that is unused.

Let T_* be a Safra tree after the steps of Safra's construction, with new nodes marked with '*' and $deleted \subseteq \{0, 1, \ldots, 2|Q| - 1\}$ the set of names of the deleted nodes. Possible candidates for a match must have the same structure as T_*. Formally, we define *structural equality* as an equivalence on Safra trees with $T_1 \equiv_{\text{struct}} T_2$ iff T_1 and T_2 agree up to the names of the nodes. That is, there is a isomorphism $f : T_1 \to T_2$, which means a bijection from the node set of T_1 to the node set of T_2 that preserves the labels, markings and topological structure. An already constructed Safra tree T and a newly constructed tree T_* *match* if the following three conditions are met: (i) $T \equiv_{\text{struct}} T_*$, (ii) for all nodes n named '*' in T_*, the corresponding node $f(n)$ in T is not named with a name from *deleted* and (iii) for all nodes n not named '*' in T_*, the corresponding node $f(n)$ in T has the same name as the node in T_*. One way to keep track of the trees that are possible candidates for matching is to partition the already existing trees by structural equality. This can be implemented, for example, by a hash map that allows for efficient access to all trees that are structural equal to T_*.

IV. Reordering. Safra's construction assumes a strict ordering of the sibling nodes in Safra trees, used in step 4 to reestablish the requirement on Safra trees that siblings have disjoint labels. The strict ordering is not necessary in all cases and can sometimes be relaxed. In our tool *ltl2dstar* we used a technique that attempts to collapse Safra trees that differ only in the ordering of "independent" nodes. We skip further explanations here as this approach could only yield a minor reduction in our experiments.

4   Other Techniques

The following techniques attempt to decrease the size of a deterministic ω-automaton (DRA or DSA) for a given LTL-formula φ. These methods are independent from the chosen algorithm to generate a deterministic automaton from φ as they operate on a given DRA/DSA or on the formula level.

Rabin or Streett Automata. Some applications need a translation from LTL formulas to deterministic ω-automata, but do not particularly care if the automaton is a Rabin or a Streett automaton. It is well known that for some languages Streett automata can be exponentially more compact than Rabin automata, and vice versa, so this flexibility can have huge benefits. The switch from an DSA to an equivalent DRA (or vice versa) is computationally hard. If we start with an LTL formula φ then we may exploit the duality of Rabin and Streett acceptance and construct a DRA for $\neg\varphi$, yielding a DSA for φ. Already for small formulas this simple trick can be very useful as illustrated in the following table. The first two columns contain the number of states using the standard Safra's construction, the last two columns the number of states when the optimization techniques suggested here were used.

Formula	DRA	DSA	DRA (opt.)	DSA (opt.)
$(\Box\Diamond a) \to (\Box\Diamond b)$	61	7	12	7
$((\Box\Diamond a) \to (\Box\Diamond b)) \wedge ((\Box\Diamond c) \to (\Box\Diamond d))$	67051	298	18526	49

In the sequel, we concentrate on techniques that attempt to decrease the size of a DRA for a given LTL formula φ. By duality, analogue techniques are also applicable to DSA.

Bisimulation Quotient. One of the standard algorithms for minimization of deterministic finite automata is to calculate the quotient automaton that arises by identifying all states accepting the same language. We now adapt this idea to DRA by taking into account the acceptance signature of the runs. Let $\mathcal{A} = (Q, \Sigma, \delta, q_0, Acc)$ be an DRA where $Acc = \{(L_n, U_n) : n = 1, \ldots, r\}$. Let $acc(q)$ denote the acceptance signature of state q, that is, the pair (I_L, I_U) where $I_L = \{n : q \in L_n\}$ and $I_U = \{n : q \in U_n\}$. Bisimulation equivalence $\equiv$ on Q is defined by $q \equiv p$ iff $acc(\delta(q, z)) = acc(\delta(p, z))$ for all $z \in \Sigma^*$. Clearly, $q \equiv p$ implies that the set of infinite words that have an accepting run starting in q agrees with the set of infinite words that have an accepting run starting in p. In the classification of [16], the above equivalence on the states of a DRA can be viewed as a notion of *direct bisimulation* for Rabin automata. In fact, an alternative, but equivalent coinductive definition of $\equiv$ could be given in the typical bisimulation-style.

Let $[q] = \{p \in Q : p \equiv q\}$ be the bisimulation equivalence class of state q. For $S \subseteq Q$, let $S/_{\equiv} = \{[q] : q \in S\}$. The quotient automaton $\mathcal{A}/_{\equiv} = (Q', \Sigma, \delta', q_0', \Omega')$, also a DRA, has the state space $Q = Q/_{\equiv}$, initial state $q_0' = [q_0]$ and the acceptance condition $Acc' = \{(L_1/_{\equiv}, U_1/_{\equiv}), \ldots, (L_r/_{\equiv}, U_r/_{\equiv})\}$. The transition relation is given by $\delta'([q], a) = [\delta(q, a)]$. It is easy to see that δ is well-defined and that the accepted languages of $\mathcal{A}$ and $\mathcal{A}/_{\equiv}$ coincide (see [17]). To calculate the quotient automaton, we may apply the standard partitioning-splitter technique [18].

Union of DRA. If the starting point of the construction of a DRA is an LTL formula, rather than an NBA, then for formulas $\varphi = \varphi_1 \vee \varphi_2$ whose outermost operator is disjunction, we may avoid the construction of an NBA for φ by first constructing two DRA $\mathcal{A}_1$ and $\mathcal{A}_2$ for the subformulas φ_1 and φ_2 and finally composing these two DRA into a DRA via a union-operator (implemented as a simple product construction on the two DRAs). The generated union DRA might be smaller than a DRA generated for the whole formula, as the subformulas are shorter and probably simpler, which can lead to smaller NBA and DRA for the subformulas.

(Co-)Safety Formulas and Deterministic Automata. Safety properties are languages $L \subseteq \Sigma^\omega$ that can be characterized via their bad prefixes. That is, L is a safety property iff any word $z \in \Sigma^\omega \setminus L$ has a finite prefix x such that none of the words xz' belongs to L. Co-safety properties are the duals of safety properties. Any safety and co-safety ω-regular languages can be represented by a DBA. For a certain type of LTL formulas that represent safety and co-safety languages, a corresponding DBA can be generated directly, i.e., without using Safra's construction [19, 20]. As any DBA can be viewed as DRA or DSA, these algorithms (which are implemented in the scheck-tool [20]) yield an alternative to our construction for certain (co-)safety formulas.

5   Experimental Results

Safra's construction and the optimizations described in the previous sections were implemented in the tool *ltl2dstar* (**LTL** to deterministic **S**treett and **R**abin automata) which is available via http://www.ltl2dstar.de/. Another implementation of Safra's algorithm [21] represented Safra trees with BDDs and used a partly implicit calculation of successors. In our tool, we use explicit data structures for the Safra trees and calculate each successor tree separately, using hash maps to efficiently find similar trees and match them to their respective state in the deterministic automaton.

The basic building blocks available for the construction of DRA/DSA are:

- Safra: the generation of a DRA for an LTL formula φ by creating an NBA with an external LTL-to-NBA translator and then applying Safra's construction on the NBA. Additionally, the procedure can be started with the negated formula $\neg\varphi$ to obtain a DSA for φ. If both a DRA and a DSA are generated then the smaller one is returned.
- scheck: If the formula is syntactically (co-)safe then an DBA (which can be viewed as a DRA or DSA) is constructed with the external tool scheck [20].
- union: If the formula has the form $\varphi_1 \vee \varphi_2$ then we may construct DRA for φ_1 and φ_2 and return the union of the two automata.[3]

These blocks can be combined such that the smallest of the generated automata (DRA or DSA obtained with Safra and scheck or union, if applicable) is returned. As long as we do not use optimizations which operate on the automaton after it is fully generated, we can abort an alternative construction as soon as the size of the generated automaton is superior to the already existing automaton. If, however, we use the bisimulation quotienting technique, we cannot abort directly, as the quotient might ultimately be smaller than the smallest automaton obtained so far. For efficiency reasons, we suggest an heuristic approach with a

---

[3] The dual opportunity to apply an intersection-operator for DSA if $\varphi = \varphi_1 \wedge \varphi_2$ is covered by considering $\neg\varphi \equiv \neg\varphi_1 \vee \neg\varphi_2$.

maxgrowth factor α. If the smallest automaton computed so far has N states then the size limit of alternative computations is αN which allows the possibility of a subsequent reduction of the current automaton via quotienting to $\frac{1}{\alpha}$ of its original size. Limiting the construction of the automata like this is obviously sensitive to the order in which the different constructions are carried out. As a heuristic for a good ordering, we used the sizes of the NBA for the relevant formulas (the original formula φ and its negation) and start the construction with the smallest NBA.

In the context of his diploma thesis, the first author performed a series of experiments to investigate the gain of the proposed heuristics. Here, we summarize the main results and refer to [17] for further details. Our experiments were performed with the 39 benchmark formulas of [11, 12], 55 formulas[4] based on patterns from [13] and sets of 100 and 1000 random LTL formulas generated with the test bench *lbtt* [22]. The chosen LTL-to-NBA translator[5] was *ltl2ba* [27]. All experiments were conducted on a Pentium-M 1.5 GHz with 512 MB RAM, running Linux.

Table 1 compares our suggested heuristics (including generating either a DRA or DSA, depending on which one is smaller) to the standard Safra construction (generating only DRA). $\Sigma(|\mathcal{A}|)$ denotes the total number of states of the generated automata, while $\Sigma(t)$ is the total running time. Despite the additional computations required for the generation of multiple automata and the bisimulation technique (with maxgrowth factor $\alpha = 10$), the overall running time of our approach is roughly the same (or faster) as for simply using the unoptimized Safra's algorithm.

Table 1. Overall effect of the proposed heuristics as implemented in *ltl2dstar*

	[11, 12]		Patterns		100 random		1000 random	
	$\Sigma(|\mathcal{A}|)$	$\Sigma(t)$	$\Sigma(|\mathcal{A}|)$	$\Sigma(t)$	$\Sigma(|\mathcal{A}|)$	$\Sigma(t)$	$\Sigma(|\mathcal{A}|)$	$\Sigma(t)$
Standard Safra (DRA)	1320	1.02 s	341121	358.98 s	1625	0.66 s	43375	12.58 s
ltl2dstar (DRA/DSA)	268	1.04 s	6399	73.83 s	474	1.49 s	4480	14.91 s
Size reduction	-79.7 %		-98.1 %		-70.8 %		-89.7 %	

We will now consider the performance of the proposed heuristics separately.

Experiments with the On-the-Fly Techniques. Table 2 illustrates the practical performance of the effect of the heuristics explained in Section 3 for Safra's construction. The first row shows the total sizes of the generated DRA where all on-the-fly optimizations were used. The second row shows the absolute difference to the standard Safra's construction without the on-the-fly techniques. To

---

[4] http://patterns.projects.cis.ksu.edu/documentation/patterns/ltl.shtml
[5] For a comparison with other LTL-to-NBA translators, such as Modella [23], SPIN [24, 25] and LTL→NBA [26] in the context of subsequent determinization, we refer to [17].

Table 2. Results for the on-the-fly heuristics

	[11, 12]	Patterns	100 random	1000 random
$\Sigma(|\mathcal{A}|)$ with all opt.	926	246455	642	6743
No optimization	+394	+94666	+983	+36632
No 'Trueloop detection'	+195	+1467	+651	+26254
No 'All successors accepting'	+113	+95	+38	+400
No 'Node renaming'	+40	+92687	+8	+90
No 'Reordering'	+16	+0	+8	+31
$\Sigma(t)$ (no opt.)	0.48 s	358.50 s	0.70 s	12.89 s
$\Sigma(t)$ (all opt.)	0.39 s	270.14 s	0.56 s	5.57 s

assess the individual impact of each heuristic I-IV, a run was carried out with just this heuristic disabled. (In all cases, the methods that are not on-the-fly, like quotienting and the union construction, were disabled.)

The effectiveness of all the on-the-fly heuristics combined was highest for the random formulas, where they resulted in a reduction by around 60% for the 100 and 84% for the 1000 random formulas. This is mostly due to the "true-loop detection", followed by "all successors accepting". For the formulas from [11] and [12], the overall reduction is lower (around 30%) and "all successors accepting" plays a bigger role than for the random formulas. The pattern formulas, while also having an overall reduction of around 30%, exhibit a completely different behavior. Here, the "node renaming" is almost exclusively responsible for the overall reduction. It seems that "node renaming" works better for bigger automata, which can be explained by the fact that a single tree that can be matched early in the construction can result in a huge reduction of states, as an incompatible naming generated by our default "first free name"-strategy would result in the duplication (also with different names) of many of the successor states. The bigger the automaton gets, the more states would be duplicated, so "node renaming" has a bigger effect. In all cases, the reordering heuristic does not have a big effect. Another interesting point is the computation time (shown in the last two rows). With all on-the-fly optimizations enabled, the running time was shorter (around 20-50%) than with the on-the-fly heuristics disabled. Thus, the benefit of handling fewer states far outweighs the additional effort needed to carry out the optimizations.

Experiments with the Heuristics Suggested in Section 4. We already mentioned that the difference between DRA- and DSA-sizes can be enormous which motivates the flexibility in using Rabin or Streett automata. In fact, it turned out that the minimum sizes of the deterministic automaton obtained by constructing both an DRA and an DSA are often rather close to NBA. Table 3 shows a comparison between the automata sizes of DRA, DSA and NBA for the pattern formulas.

Table 3. Automata sizes for the pattern formulas (number of states, for DRA and DSA additionally the number of acceptance pairs, NBA generated with *ltl2ba*)

	Global			Before R			After Q			Between Q and R			After Q until R		
	NBA	DRA	DSA	NBA	DRA	DSA	NBA	DRA	DSA	NBA	DRA	DSA	NBA	DRA	DSA
Absence	1	2/1	2/1	4	4/1	4/1	2	3/1	3/1	4	7/2	4/1	3	6/2	3/1
Universality	1	2/1	2/1	4	4/1	4/1	2	3/1	3/1	4	7/2	4/1	3	6/2	3/1
Existence	2	2/1	3/1	3	5/2	3/1	5	3/1	4/1	3	6/2	3/1	2	5/1	4/2
Bounded Existence (2)	6	11/2	6/1	8	8/1	8/1	9	11/3	7/1	16	62/3	8/1	12	52/3	7/1
Precedence	3	5/2	3/1	4	4/1	4/1	6	5/2	8/1	4	9/2	4/1	3	6/2	3/1
Response	2	4/1	3/1	5	8/1	8/1	3	6/1	4/1	6	22/3	4/1	6	32/3	5/2
Precedence Chain (1-2)	5	4/1	4/1	6	7/2	5/1	7	6/3	5/1	8	29/2	5/1	12	32/2	389/4
Precedence Chain (2-1)	5	4/1	4/1	5	5/1	5/1	7	7/2	5/1	10	111/4	5/1	10	79/4	4/1
Response Chain (2-1)	11	45/3	6/1	20	16/2	7/1	12	82/4	7/1	35	3563/7	9/1	30	56050/11	157/4
Response Chain (1-2)	5	20/2	14/3	10	5/1	5/1	4	24/2	5/2	15	18/1	19/3	24	11395/8	1976/11
Constr. Response (1-2)	5	21/2	15/3	10	5/1	5/1	4	25/2	5/2	15	18/1	19/3	24	31742/8	3952/11

Table 4. Results for the bisimulation quotient technique

	[11, 12]		Patterns		100 random		1000 random	
	$\Sigma(|\mathcal{A}|)$	$\Sigma(t)$	$\Sigma(|\mathcal{A}|)$	$\Sigma(t)$	$\Sigma(|\mathcal{A}|)$	$\Sigma(t)$	$\Sigma(|\mathcal{A}|)$	$\Sigma(t)$
No opt., no bisim.	1320	0.5 s	341121	362.5 s	1625	0.7 s	43375	12.9 s
No opt., with bisim.	-636	0.5 s	-217780	373.1 s	-631	0.7 s	-29990	12.9 s
No bisimulation	860	0.4 s	246435	272.8 s	638	0.7 s	6701	7.1 s
With bisimulation	-474	0.4 s	-142792	281.1 s	-132	0.7 s	-1383	7.2 s

To evaluate the performance of the bisimulation technique, we compare the difference in the size of the original DRA and their bisimulation quotients (See Table 4). It turns out that our simple equivalence provides a surprisingly big reduction in the size of the automata at a very moderate cost (less than 3% increase in running time). For the pattern formulas, the effect is highest, with reductions by around 60%. For the formulas from [11] and [12] the reductions are around 50%. For these two formula sets, building the quotient automaton works roughly as well when the other heuristics are enabled, leading to a combined reduction of around 70%! For the random formulas, the quotient-technique decreases the already reduced automata by an additional 20%, which improves the (already high) reduction from the on-the-fly optimizations for the 1000 formulas to an impressive 90%.

For the 20%-30% of the non-random benchmark formulas that have the required form, the union construction yields a reduction of ca. 10%-25%. For the 30%-60% of the formulas that are syntactically (co-)safe and thus valid input for scheck, a reduction of around 20%, for the pattern formulas of around 50%, is achieved. For a small number of formulas, the automata generated directly using Safra's construction are slightly smaller than those generated using one of the special constructions.

6   Conclusion

We have considered Safra's construction in the context of translating LTL formulas to deterministic Rabin or Streett automata and suggested several heuristics to decrease the automaton-size. With various tests, we evaluated the performance of its implementation in the tool *ltl2dstar* and the effect of our heuristics. In summary, for many formulas, Safra's construction (with the presented heuristics) is usable in practice and results in deterministic ω-automata with acceptable sizes The proposed heuristics turned out to have a big impact in practice (overall reductions of 70% and more) and contribute a great deal to the practical feasibility of using Safra's construction for LTL formulas. Perhaps surprisingly, the simple quotient technique (via a variant of direct bisimulation) performed extremely well in practice on the DRA and DSA: we observed an overall reduction of more than 50% with a negligible increase of running time.

We concentrated on Safra's construction; for a comparison with an alternative construction by Muller/Schupp [28] see [29] in this volume. A comparison with the construction by Emerson and Sistla [30] would be interesting as well. The observation that the bisimulation technique leads to significant reductions indicates that Safra's construction produces many bisimulation equivalent states. It might be possible to avoid the creation of these redundant states in the first place. Although our rather strong notion of (direct) bisimulation for DRA (or DSA) turned out to be very useful, weaker notions of bisimulation equivalence might yield a better reduction. In fact, for Büchi automata, several other, more advanced notions like *fair* or *delayed* (bi)simulation have been proposed (e.g. [16]). If similar approaches can work for deterministic Rabin or Streett automata remains to be seen. Further improvements might be possible by using the techniques of [31] and [32] for the subset of DRA that are Büchi-type.

References

1. Thomas, W.: Languages, automata, and logic. Handbook of formal languages **3** (1997) 389–455
2. Grädel, E., Thomas, W., Wilke, T., eds.: Automata Logics, and Infinite Games: A Guide to Current Research. Volume 2500 of LNCS. Springer (2002)
3. de Alfaro, L.: Formal Verification of Probabilistic Systems. PhD thesis, Stanford University, Department of Computer Science (1997)
4. Baier, C., Kwiatkowska, M.: Model checking for a probabilistic branching time logic with fairness. Distributed Computing **11** (1998) 125–155
5. Vardi, M.: Probabilistic linear-time model checking: An overview of the automata-theoretic approach. In: Proc. Formal Methods for Real-Time and Probabilistic Systems (ARTS). Volume 1601. (1999) 265–276
6. Safra, S.: On the complexity of ω-automata. In: Proc. 29th Annual Symposium on Foundations of Computer Science (FOCS), IEEE Computer Society Press (1988) 319–327
7. Safra, S.: Complexity of Automata on Infinite Objects. PhD thesis, The Weizmann Institue of Science, Rehovot, Israel (1989)
8. Michel, M.: Complementation is more difficult with automata on infinite words. Technical report, CNET Paris (1988)
9. Löding, C.: Optimal bounds for the transformation of omega-automata. In: FSTTCS'99. Volume 1738 of Lecture Notes in Computer Science., Springer (1999) 97–109
10. Kupferman, O., Vardi, M.Y.: Freedom, weakness, and determinism: From linear-time to branching-time. In: Proc. 13th IEEE Symposium on Logic in Computer Science. (1998) 81–92
11. Etessami, K., Holzmann, G.J.: Optimizing Büchi automata. In: CONCUR. Volume 1877 of Lecture Notes in Computer Science., Springer (2000) 153–167
12. Somenzi, F., Bloem, R.: Efficient Büchi automata from LTL formulae. In: Computer Aided Verification (CAV'2000), Proc. Volume 1855 of Lecture Notes in Computer Science., Springer (2000) 248–263
13. Dwyer, M.B., Avrunin, G.S., Corbett, J.C.: Patterns in property specifications for finite-state verification. In: ICSE. (1999) 411–420
14. Emerson, E.A.: Temporal and modal logic. In van Leeuwen, J., ed.: Handbook of Theoretical Computer Science, Volume B: Formal Models and Semantics. Elsevier Science Publishers (1990) 995–1072

15. Clarke, E., Grumberg, O., Peled, D.: Model Checking. MIT Press (2000)
16. Etessami, K., Wilke, T., Schuller, R.A.: Fair simulation relations, parity games, and state space reduction for Büchi automata. In: ICALP'2001. Volume 2076 of Lecture Notes in Computer Science., Springer (2001) 694–707
17. Klein, J.: Linear time logic and deterministic omega-automata. Diploma thesis, Universität Bonn, Institut für Informatik (2005)
18. Paige, R., Tarjan, R.E.: Three partition refinement algorithms. SIAM Journal on Computing **16** (1987) 973–989
19. Kupferman, O., Vardi, M.Y.: Model checking of safety properties. In: Computer Aided Verification (CAV'99), Proceedings. Volume 1633 of Lecture Notes in Computer Science., Springer (1999)
20. Latvala, T.: On model checking safety properties. Research Report A76, Helsinki University of Technology, Laboratory for Theoretical Computer Science, Espoo, Finland (2002)
21. Tasiran, S., Hojati, R., Brayton, R.K.: Language containment of non-deterministic ω-automata. In: CHARME'95. Volume 987 of Lecture Notes in Computer Science., Springer (1995) 261–277
22. Tauriainen, H.: Automated testing of Büchi automata translators for linear temporal logic. Research report, Helsinki University of Technology, Laboratory for Theoretical Computer Science (2000)
23. Sebastiani, R., Tonetta, S.: "More Deterministic" vs. "Smaller" Büchi Automata for Efficient LTL Model Checking. In: CHARME 2003, Proc. Volume 2860 of Lecture Notes in Computer Science., Springer (2003) 126–140
24. Holzmann, G.J.: The Model Checker Spin. IEEE Trans. on Software Engineering **23** (1997) 279–295 Special issue on Formal Methods in Software Practice.
25. Gerth, R., Peled, D., Vardi, M.Y., Wolper, P.: Simple on-the-fly automatic verification of linear temporal logic. In: PSTV'95, Proc. Volume 38 of IFIP Conference Proceedings., Chapman & Hall (1995) 3–18
26. Fritz, C.: Constructing Büchi automata from linear temporal logic using simulation relations for alternating Büchi automata. In: CIAA 2003. Volume 2759 of Lecture Notes in Computer Science., Springer (2003) 35–48
27. Gastin, P., Oddoux, D.: Fast LTL to Büchi automata translation. In: Computer Aided Verification (CAV'2001), Proceedings. Volume 2102 of Lecture Notes in Computer Science., Springer (2001) 53–65
28. Muller, D.E., Schupp, P.E.: Simulating alternating tree automata by nondeterministic automata: New results and new proofs of the theorems of Rabin, McNaughton and Safra. Theoretical Computer Science **141** (1995) 69–107
29. Althoff, C.S., Thomas, W., Wallmeier, N.: Observations on determinization of Büchi automata. In: CIAA'05, Proceedings. Lecture Notes in Computer Science, Springer (2005) , this volume.
30. Emerson, E.A., Sistla, A.P.: Deciding branching time logic. In: STOC'84, ACM Press (1984) 14–24
31. Krishnan, S.C., Puri, A., Brayton, R.K.: Deterministic ω Automata vis-a-vis Deterministic Buchi Automata. In: Algorithms and Computation, 5th International Symposium (ISAAC'94). Volume 834 of Lecture Notes in Computer Science., Springer (1994) 378–386
32. Löding, C.: Efficient minimization of deterministic weak omega-automata. Information Processing Letters **79** (2001) 105–109

Computing Affine Hulls over $\mathbb{Q}$ and $\mathbb{Z}$ from Sets Represented by Number Decision Diagrams

Louis Latour

Université de Liège,
Institut Montefiore, B28,
4000 Liège, Belgium
latour@montefiore.ulg.ac.be

Abstract. Number Decision Diagrams (NDD) are finite automata representing sets of integer vectors and have recently been proposed as an efficient data structure for representing sets definable in Presburger arithmetic. In this context, some work has been done in order to generate formulas or sets of generators from the NDDs. Taking another step in this direction, this paper present algorithms that takes as input an NDD and computes the affine hull over $\mathbb{Q}$ or over $\mathbb{Z}$ of the set represented by the NDD, i.e., the smallest set defined by a conjunction of equations or by a conjunction of equations and congruence relations that includes the set represented by the NDD. Our algorithms run in time $\mathcal{O}(|Q| \cdot |\Sigma_r^n| \cdot n)$ and $\mathcal{O}(|Q|^3 \cdot |\Sigma_r^n| \cdot n^3)$ respectively, where n is the number of components of the vectors represented by the NDD, and $|Q|$ and Σ_r^n are the number of states and the alphabet of the NDD. On a prototype implementation, the computations of affine hulls of NDDs with more than 100000 states are done in seconds.

1 Introduction

It has been known for a long time that finite automata can be used for representing sets of integer vectors (see [1]). In particular, sets definable in Presburger arithmetic, i.e., first-order logic over the integers with addition and the order relation, can be represented by finite automata. Many applications rely on Presburger arithmetic, including integer programming problems, compiler optimization techniques, program analysis tools and model-checking.

There exist different equivalent representations of Presburger definable sets (see [1]), including formulas, semi-linear sets and finite automata, and different approaches have been developed for handling Presburger definable sets. Finite automata have recently been investigated as an efficient data structure for representing Presburger definable sets in practical applications [2, 3]. Finite automata present two main advantages, there is a canonical representation and efficient procedures exist for set operations and inclusion tests. However, simple arithmetic operations, such as affine transformation, can be costly if performed on automata. Therefore, it may appear efficient to handle both automaton and formula representations of the set and perform the operations on the most appropriate representation. Also, having access to a simple formula representation of

J. Farré, I. Litovsky, and S. Schmitz (Eds.): CIAA 2005, LNCS 3845, pp. 213–224, 2006.
© Springer-Verlag Berlin Heidelberg 2006

the sets can shed light on the sometimes hidden relationships between variables, or give a useful broad view of the set. It also provides a link to theorem provers.

Working with both automata and formulas implies being able to move from one representation to the other. While generating automata from formulas is now well understood [4], the issue of generating formulas from automata has only been dealt with more recently. Algorithm for restricted classes of sets appeared in [5], [6] and [7], and a solution for the general case has been presented in [8]. In this paper, we approach the problem of extracting information from automata differently, and instead of generating a formula matching exactly the set represented, we compute the affine hull over $\mathbb{Q}$ and over $\mathbb{Z}$, i.e., the smallest affine space over $\mathbb{Q}$ or affine module over $\mathbb{Z}$ that includes the set represented by the automaton. The main interests are that the computations are fast (linear if arithmetic operations are performed in constant time), and affine spaces and affine modules are easily dealt with since they can be represented by n equations and congruence relations or by n generators together with an element of the set, where n is the number of vector components. Furthermore, for a number of applications, affine hulls already provide useful information. For example, in the context of verification, one could simplify a model by removing some variables via the equations and congruence relations. Finally, the algorithms presented in this paper could be integrated in a more general algorithm computating exact formulas for sets represented by automata, as it is done in [6] where affine hulls are computed in order to identify the left-hand sides (i.e. the vector of coefficients) of the inequations occurring in the formula.

An algorithm computing the affine hull over $\mathbb{Q}$ of sets of positive vectors represented by finite automata (with a least significant digit first encoding) has been already presented in [9]. The time complexity of this algorithm is $\mathcal{O}(|Q| \cdot |\Sigma_r^n| \cdot n^3)$, where $|Q|$ is the number of states, n is the number of components in the vectors of the represented set and Σ_r^n is the alphabet of the automaton. Also, a finite automaton representing sets of integer vectors can be viewed as a program, the states being the control locations and the transitions being affine assignments based on the fact that adding a digit d as suffix to an encoding of a number z is equivalent to multiply z by the encoding basis and adding d (when using a most significant digit first encoding scheme). Therefore, some results in the field of static analysis of program can be applied, and in particular, the method proposed in [10] for computing affine relations among variables in a program can be used with minor adaptations for computing the affine hull over $\mathbb{Q}$ of sets represented by finite automata. The time complexity is then $\mathcal{O}(|Q| \cdot |\Sigma_r^n| \cdot n^3)$. In this paper, we present a more efficient algorithm whose time complexity is $\mathcal{O}(|Q| \cdot |\Sigma_r^n| \cdot n)$, and $\mathcal{O}(|Q| \cdot |\Sigma_r^n| \cdot n^2)$ if a minimal set of generators is required.

Regarding the affine hull over $\mathbb{Z}$, nothing has been done directly on sets represented by finite automata. In the context of static analysis, an algorithm for computing the affine and congruence relations satisfied in a control point of an affine programs has been presented in [11]. Although the computation is proved to be finite, there is no bound on the number of operations required. More recently, [12] describes a polynomial time algorithm for computing affine relations over $\mathbb{Z}_m$, i.e. integer arithmetic modulo m, satisfied by the variables at a given control location. In this paper, we give the first polynomial time algorithm for computing the affine hull over $\mathbb{Z}$ of sets represented by finite automata. The exact time complexity of our algorithm is $\mathcal{O}(|Q|^3 \cdot |\Sigma_r^n| \cdot n^3)$. Note that our algorithm for computing affine hulls over $\mathbb{Q}$ is part of our algorithm for computing the affine hulls over $\mathbb{Z}$.

This paper is organized as follows. In Section 2, we recall basic properties regarding automata theory as well as linear algebra. In Section 3, we show how finite automata can represent sets of integer vectors. In Section 4, we present an efficient representation for generators of vector spaces, $\mathbb{Z}$-modules and $\mathbb{Z}_m$-modules. In Sections 5 and 6, we present our algorithms for computing affine hulls over $\mathbb{Q}$ and over $\mathbb{Z}$ respectively. Some experimental results are provided in Section 7, and we conclude in Section 8. The proofs of the results presented in this paper are given in [13].

2   Preliminaries

We start with some preliminaries from linear algebra and automata theory. In what follows, for any finite set S, the number of elements in S will be denoted by $|S|$.

2.1   Finite Automata

An *alphabet* is a finite nonempty set of symbols. A *word* over an alphabet Σ is a finite sequence of symbols taken from Σ. The symbol ε denotes the empty word, i.e., the word containing no symbol. The *length* of a word w, denoted by $|w|$, is the number of symbols in w. A *language* over Σ is a set of words over Σ, and Σ^* denotes the set of all words over Σ.

A *deterministic finite automaton (DFA)* $\mathcal{A}$ is a quintuple $(Q, \Sigma, \delta, s_{init}, Q_F)$, where Q is a finite set of states, Σ is the input alphabet, $\delta : Q \times \Sigma \to Q$ is the transition function, s_{init} is the initial state and $Q_F \subseteq Q$ is the set of final states.

Function δ is extended to words: $\hat{\delta}(s, \varepsilon) = \{s\}$ and $\hat{\delta}(s, uw) = \bigcup_{s' \in \delta(s,u)} \hat{\delta}(s', w)$. If $s' = \delta(s, u)$ for $s, s' \in Q$ and $u \in \Sigma$, then we say that there is a *transition* from s to s' *labeled* by u. By extension, there is a *path* from s to s' *labeled* by w if $s' = \hat{\delta}(s, w)$. The *language* of $\mathcal{A}$, denoted by $L(\mathcal{A})$ is the set of words labeling paths from the initial state to a final state. The set of words labeling paths from a state s_1 to a state s_2 in $\mathcal{A}$ is denoted as $L_{\mathcal{A}}(s_1 \to s_2)$.

The DFA $\mathcal{A} = (Q, \Sigma, \delta, s_{init}, Q_F)$ is *reduced* if for all words $w \neq \varepsilon$ labeling a path rooted at s_{init}, there exists a word $v \in \Sigma^*$ such that $wv \in L(\mathcal{A})$.

2.2   Basics on Linear Algebra

The following definitions and results can be found in elementary linear algebra textbooks.

As usual, $\mathbb{Q}$, $\mathbb{Z}$ and $\mathbb{N}$ denote the sets of rational numbers, integers and naturals, and $\mathbb{Z}_m = \mathbb{Z}/(m\mathbb{Z})$, i.e., the equivalence classes of $\mathbb{Z}$ modulo m. In the following, $\mathbb{D}$ will denote any set among $\mathbb{Q}$, $\mathbb{N}$, $\mathbb{Z}$ and $\mathbb{Z}_m$. In the case of $\mathbb{Z}_m$, any addition or multiplication of elements in $\mathbb{Z}_m$ correspond to addition or multiplication in $\mathbb{Z}$ modulo m so that the result is in $\{0, \ldots, m-1\}$. The set of vectors with n components in $\mathbb{D}$ is denoted $\mathbb{D}^n$. The i-component of a vector x is written $x[i]$. The superscript $\cdot^T$ denotes transposition. For any set $S \subseteq \mathbb{D}^n$, vector $a \in \mathbb{D}^n$ and scalar $\gamma \in \mathbb{D}$, we denote by $a + S$ and γS the sets $\{a + x \mid x \in S\}$ and $\{\gamma x \mid x \in S\}$ respectively.

For $m, n \in \mathbb{N}$, $m, n \geq 1$, $\mathbb{D}^{m \times n}$ is the set of $m \times n$-matrices with entry in $\mathbb{D}$. For a matrix $A \in \mathbb{D}^{m \times n}$, the row index set of A is $\{1, \ldots, m\}$ and the column index set is $\{1, \ldots, n\}$, and the entry located in the ith row and jth column is written $A[i, j]$. The ith row of A is denoted $A[i, *]$ and similarly, the jth column is denoted $A[*, j]$. Let $S \subseteq \mathbb{D}^n$. The $\mathbb{D}$-linear hull of S, denoted $\text{lin}_{\mathbb{D}}(S)$, and the $\mathbb{D}$-affine hull of S, denoted $\text{aff}_{\mathbb{D}}(S)$, are defined as follows.

$$\text{lin}_{\mathbb{D}}(S) = \{\sum_{i=1}^{n} \lambda_i x_i \mid \lambda_i \in \mathbb{D}, x_i \in S\}, \tag{1}$$

$$\text{aff}_{\mathbb{D}}(S) = \{\sum_{i=1}^{n} \lambda_i x_i \mid \lambda_i \in \mathbb{D}, x_i \in S, \sum_{i=1}^{n} \lambda_i = 1\}. \tag{2}$$

Example 1. Let $S = \{(1, 0), (1, 2), (1, 4)\}$. $\text{aff}_{\mathbb{Q}}(S) = \{(1, k) \mid k \in \mathbb{Q}\}$ and $\text{aff}_{\mathbb{Z}}(S) = \{(1, 2 * k) \mid k \in \mathbb{Z}\}$.

The vectors $x_1, \ldots, x_n \in \mathbb{D}^n$ are *linearly independent over* $\mathbb{D}$ iff $\sum_{j=1}^{n} \alpha_j x_j = 0$ with $\alpha_j \in \mathbb{D}$ implies that $\alpha_j = 0$ for $j = 1, \ldots, n$. If the vectors are not linearly independent, they are *linearly dependent over* $\mathbb{D}$. A set of vectors G is *free over* $\mathbb{D}$ iff the vectors in G are linearly independent over $\mathbb{D}$. A set $G \subseteq \mathbb{D}^n$ $\mathbb{D}$-*generates* a set $S \subseteq \mathbb{D}^n$ iff $\text{lin}_{\mathbb{D}}(G) = S$. If in addition, G is free over $\mathbb{D}$, then G is a $\mathbb{D}$-basis of S.

A subset $M \subseteq \mathbb{D}^n$ of vectors with entries in $\mathbb{D}$ is a $\mathbb{D}$-*module* iff $M \neq \emptyset$ and $M = \text{lin}_{\mathbb{D}}(M)$. A subset $S \subseteq \mathbb{D}^n$ is a $\mathbb{D}$-*affine module* iff $S = a + M$, where $a \in \mathbb{D}^n$ and M is a $\mathbb{D}$-module.

Proposition 1. *Let* $S \subseteq \mathbb{D}^n$. *The set* $\text{lin}_{\mathbb{D}}(S)$ *(resp.* $\text{aff}_{\mathbb{D}}(S)$*) is the smallest* $\mathbb{D}$-*module (resp.* $\mathbb{D}$-*affine module) containing* S. *The* $\mathbb{D}$-*module* M *such that* $\text{aff}_{\mathbb{D}}(S) = a + M$ *for some* $a \in \mathbb{D}^n$ *is unique.*

Proposition 2. *Any* $\mathbb{D}$-*module* $S \subseteq \mathbb{D}^n$ *has a* $\mathbb{D}$-*basis, and all* $\mathbb{D}$-*basis of* S *have the same number of elements* $d \leq n$ *called the* dimension *of* S.

Since $\mathbb{Q}$ is a field, $\mathbb{Q}$-modules and $\mathbb{Q}$-affine modules have more properties than their counterparts over the rings $\mathbb{Z}$ and $\mathbb{Z}_m$ (except if m is prime, in which case $\mathbb{Z}_m$ is also a field). Consequently, $\mathbb{Q}$-modules and $\mathbb{Q}$-affine modules have specific names and are called *vector space* and *affine space* respectively. For example, one property displayed by vector spaces but not by $\mathbb{Z}$-modules is the fact that for any vector space V, any set S of linearly independent vectors in V can be extended to form a basis of V.

2.3   Size and Complexity

We define the size of numbers as follows. The size of an integer number $a \in \mathbb{Z}$ is 1 if $a = 0$, and $1 + \lfloor \log |a| \rfloor$ otherwise. The size of a rational a/b where $a \in \mathbb{Z}$, $b \in \mathbb{N} \setminus \{0\}$ and $\gcd(a, b) = 1$ is 1 if $a = 0$ and $\lfloor 1 + \log |a| + \log |b| \rfloor$ otherwise.

In order to reason about the complexity of the algorithms presented in this paper, we assume that direct memory accesses are performed in constant time and that arithmetic operations are perform in unit time.

3   Automata-Based Representation of Integer Vector Sets

In this section, we explain how automata can represent sets of integer vectors. The main idea consists in establishing a mapping between vectors and words. Our encoding scheme of vectors is based on the positional expression of numbers (most significant digit first) with a signed-complement system for negative integers.

Given an *encoding basis* $r \in \mathbb{N}$, with $r > 1$, an *r-encoding of an integer* $a \in \mathbb{Z}$ is a word w over Σ_r, such that if $w = u_p u_{p-1} \ldots u_0$ where each $u_i \in \Sigma_r = \{0, \ldots, r - 1\}$, $u_p = 0$ if $a \geq 0$ and $u_p = r - 1$ if $a < 0$, and $a = -r^p \cdot \frac{u_p}{r-1} + \sum_{i=0}^{p-1} u_i r^i$.

In order to encode a vector $z \in \mathbb{Z}^n$, one simply reads synchronously one digit from the encodings of all its components, provided that these encodings share the same length. This requirement can always be met by prefixing the encoding by a sequence of copies of the leading digit of the initial encoding. So, an *r-encoding of an integer vector* $z \in \mathbb{Z}^n$ is a word w over Σ_r^n, such that if $w = u_p u_{p-1}, \ldots u_0$ where each $u_i \in (\Sigma_r^n, u_p \in (0, r-1)^n$, and for each $j \in \{1, \ldots, n\}$, we have $z[j] = -r^p \cdot \frac{u_p[j]}{r-1} + \sum_{i=0}^{p-1} u_i[j] r^i$.

The fact that w is an r-encoding of z is denoted by $\langle w \rangle_r = z$. Also, we simply write 0 for the symbol $(0, \ldots, 0) \in \Sigma_r^n$.

Based on the definition of the encoding scheme, for all encodings $u \in (\Sigma_r^n)^+$ and words $v \in (\Sigma_r^n)^*$, we have $\langle uv \rangle_r = r^{|v|} \langle u \rangle_r + \langle 0v \rangle_r$.

Let $S \subseteq \mathbb{Z}^n$. If the language $L(S)$ containing all the encodings of all the vectors in S is regular, then any DFA $\mathcal{A}$ accepting $L(S)$, i.e. such that $L(\mathcal{A}) = L(S)$, is a *Number Decision Diagram (NDD)*, and we say that $\mathcal{A}$ *represents* S. In this paper, we use the following notations. We denote by $S_{\mathcal{A}(s_{init} \to s)}$ the set of vectors whose encoding labels paths from s_{init} to s in the NDD $\mathcal{A}$, and by $S_{\mathcal{A}}$ the set represented by the NDD $\mathcal{A}$. The encoding scheme that we use here is the same as the one proposed in [1] and extended to $\mathbb{Z}$ in [2].

It is known (see [1]) that the sets definable in the first order theory $\langle \mathbb{Z}, +, <, V_r \rangle$ correspond exactly to the sets that can be represented by finite-state automata using the r-encoding scheme that has just been discussed. Note that $\langle \mathbb{Z}, +, <, V_r \rangle$ is the first-order logic over the integers with addition and the ordering relation, with an additional predicate $V_r(x, y)$ returning true if y is the greatest power of r dividing x and false otherwise.

In the remaining of this paper, r-encodings are simply called encodings since we will always use the same encoding basis r.

4   Triangular Sets

The algorithms presented in this paper manipulate intensively vector spaces, $\mathbb{Z}$-modules and $\mathbb{Z}_m$-modules. In order to have more efficient procedures, we maintain sets of generators in a particular form: the *triangular form* [12]. For a non-zero vector x, we call i the *leading index* of x and $x[i]$ the *leading entry* of x if $x[i] \neq 0$ and $x[j] = 0$ for $j \in \{1, \ldots, i - 1\}$. A set of non-zero vectors T is *triangular* iff the leading entries of all vectors in T are positive and for all distinct vectors $x, x' \in T$, the leading indices of x and x' are distinct. Intuitively, a set is triangular if the vectors are the rows of a echelon matrix A with no zero-row, i.e. each row of A has a non-zero element and if $A[i, k]$ and $A[j, k']$ are the first non-zero element of the ith and jth rows respectively with $j > i$, then $k' > k$. Note that a triangular set of integer vectors is a set of linearly independent vectors over $\mathbb{Q}$ and $\mathbb{Z}$.

There exist efficient procedures for generating an integer basis in triangular form of a vector space or of a $\mathbb{Z}$-module given a set of integer generators.

Proposition 3. *There exists an algorithm* GetTriangQBasis *which, given a finite set $G \subseteq \mathbb{Z}^n$ as input, generates a triangular set $\overline{G} \subseteq \mathbb{Z}^n$ such that*

- *$\mathrm{lin}_\mathbb{Q}(G) = \mathrm{lin}_\mathbb{Q}(\overline{G})$,*
- *the sizes of the components of vectors in $\overline{G}$ are bounded by $n \cdot (k + \log n)$ where k is the bound on the component size of vectors in G, and*
- *the time complexity of* GetTriangQBasis *is $\mathcal{O}(|G| \cdot n^2)$.*

Proposition 4. *There exists an algorithm* GetTriangZBasis *which, given a finite set $G \subseteq \mathbb{Z}^n$ as input, generates a triangular set $\overline{G} \subseteq \mathbb{Z}^n$ such that*

- *$\mathrm{lin}_\mathbb{Z}(G) = \mathrm{lin}_\mathbb{Z}(\overline{G})$,*
- *the sizes of the components of vectors in $\overline{G}$ are bounded by $k \cdot n \cdot \log(\sqrt{n})$, where k is the bound on the component size of vectors in G, and*
- *the time complexity of* GetTriangZBasis *is $\mathcal{O}(|G| \cdot k \cdot n^3 \cdot \log(\sqrt{n}))$.*

Note that computing a basis is more difficult over $\mathbb{Z}$ than over $\mathbb{Q}$ since a set of linearly independent vectors over $\mathbb{Z}$ cannot be extended to form a basis as it is the case over $\mathbb{Q}$.

Proposition 5. *Given a triangular set $T \subseteq \mathbb{Z}^n$ and a vector $x_0 \in \mathbb{Z}^n$, there exists an algorithm that generates a set of congruences and a set of equations such that*

- *the solutions of the system of equations (resp. equations and congruences) are exactly the elements in $x_0 + \mathrm{lin}_\mathbb{Q}(T)$ (resp. $x_0 + \mathrm{lin}_\mathbb{Z}(T)$).*
- *the coefficient sizes appearing in the congruences and in the equations are bounded by $\mathcal{O}(n \log n + nk)$, k being a bound on the size of the numbers in the vectors in T and x_0.*

Proposition 6. *There exists an algorithm* UpdateTriangZm, *which, given a strictly positive integer m, a triangular set $T \subseteq \mathbb{Z}_m^n$ and a vector $x \in \mathbb{Z}_m^n$, generates a triangular set $T' \subseteq \mathbb{Z}_m^n$ such that*

- $\mathrm{lin}_{\mathbb{Z}_m}(T') = \mathrm{lin}_{\mathbb{Z}_m}(T \cup \{x\})$.
- *The time complexity of* UpdateTriangZm *is* $\mathcal{O}(n^2 \cdot q)$.

Proposition 7. *The length of any sequence of triangular sets* $T_1, \ldots, T_k \subseteq \mathbb{Z}_m^n$ *such that for all* $i \in \{1, \ldots, k-1\}$ $T_{i+1} = $ UpdateTriangZm(m, T_i, x_i) *for some* $x_i \in \mathbb{Z}_m^n$ *is bounded by* $n \log m$.

5 Affine Hulls over $\mathbb{Q}$

In this section, we present an algorithm which takes as input a reduced NDD $\mathcal{A} = (Q, \Sigma_r^n, \delta, s_{init}, Q_F)$ and generates the affine hull over $\mathbb{Q}$ of the set represented by $\mathcal{A}$.

We briefly present the algorithm based on [10], and then present a more efficient algorithm which takes advantage of the special affine transformation corresponding to transitions in NDDs. In addition, this more efficient version is also part of the more sophisticated algorithm for computing the affine hull over $\mathbb{Z}$.

The idea of the algorithm based on [10] is to explore the paths of $\mathcal{A}$ rooted at the initial state s_{init} and to compute for each state s a vector x_s and a triangular set of vectors G_s such that $x_s \in S_{\mathcal{A}(s_{init} \to s)}$ and $x_s + \mathrm{lin}_{\mathbb{Q}}(G_s) \subseteq \mathrm{aff}_{\mathbb{Q}}(S_{\mathcal{A}(s_{init} \to s)})$. When handling a path labeled by w from s_{init} to s, the algorithm applies the following recursive procedure.

- If x_s has not yet been set, one sets x_s equal to $\langle w \rangle_r$ and we propagate w from s, that is, we apply the procedure to all paths from s_{init} to s' labeled by wu with $u \in \Sigma_r^n$ such that $\delta(s, u) = s'$.
- Otherwise, if $\langle w \rangle_r \in x_s + \mathrm{lin}_{\mathbb{Q}}(G_s)$, then we do not propagate w. If on the other hand, $\langle w \rangle_r \notin x_s + \mathrm{lin}_{\mathbb{Q}}(G_s)$, one has to add $\langle w \rangle_r - x_s$ to G_s and to propagate w from s.

Since for each s, one sets at most once x_s and one adds at most n vectors to G_s, the number of iterations is bounded, and at some point, no more path needs to be explored. It can be proved that at this point, $x_s + \mathrm{lin}_{\mathbb{Q}}(G_s) = \mathrm{aff}_{\mathbb{Q}}(S_{\mathcal{A}(s_{init} \to s)})$ for all states s. Finally, one has to take the union of the affine hulls corresponding to final states and again, take the affine hull over $\mathbb{Q}$ of this set.

We can improve the algorithm presented above. The main property is expressed in the following lemma.

Lemma 8. *Let* $s, s' \in Q$ *with* $\hat{\delta}(s, v) = s'$ *for some* v, *and let* $V, V_{s'} \subseteq \mathbb{Q}^n$ *be vector spaces such that* $\mathrm{aff}_{\mathbb{Q}}(S_{\mathcal{A}}) = x_F + V$ *and* $\mathrm{aff}_{\mathbb{Q}}(S_{\mathcal{A}(s_{init} \to s')}) = x' + V_{s'}$ *for some* $x_F, x' \in \mathbb{Z}^n$. *For all* $x_1, x_2 \in S_{\mathcal{A}(s_{init} \to s)}$, *we have* $x_1 - x_2 \in V_{s'} \subseteq V$.

Thanks to the previous property, we note that in the algorithm sketched above, if $\langle w \rangle_r - x_s$ is added to G_s, then $\langle w \rangle_r - x_s$ can be added to all $G_{s'}$ where s' is reachable from s. We deduce that it is not necessary to compute at each individual state s one basis G_s and one element x_s such that $x_s + \mathrm{lin}_{\mathbb{Q}}(G_s) = \mathrm{lin}_{\mathbb{Q}}(S_{\mathcal{A}(s_{init} \to s)})$. One only needs to consider one element x_s per state and one basis G for the whole NDD. Also, from each state, one has to propagate only one path. Indeed, if $w_1, w_2 \in L_{\mathcal{A}}(s_{init} \rightarrow s)$ and $\langle w_1 \rangle_r - \langle w_2 \rangle_r$ is added to G, then for $v \in \Sigma_r^n$, $\langle w_1 v \rangle_r - \langle w_2 v \rangle_r \in \mathrm{lin}_{\mathbb{Q}}(G)$. Finally, in the above description, we did not specify the order with which one consider the propagated paths. Adopting a breadth first search approach allows us to manipulate smaller numbers.

Our algorithm QAffineHull takes a reduced NDD as input and works as follows.

1. Initially, the set G is empty. Also, for each state, one stores a vector $x_s \in \mathbb{Z}^n$ which is initially set to $\bot$.
2. It considers paths of increasing length originating from s_{init}, starting with all paths of length 1, and at the kth iteration, it handles paths of length k that have been propagated so far. When handling a path labeled by w from s_{init} to s, there are two possibilities.
   - If $x_s = \bot$, x_s is set to $\langle w \rangle_r$, and one will consider at the next iteration the paths labeled by wu for all $u \in \Sigma_r^n$ with $\delta(s, u) = s'$ for some s'.
   - If $x_s \neq \bot$, then we add $\langle w \rangle_r - x_s$ to G.
3. When all states have been visited once, we pick one final state $s_F \in Q_F$ and we add to G all vectors $x_s - x_{s_F}$ where $s \in Q_F$. Then, the algorithm terminates and it returns G as well as the vector x_{s_F}.

Theorem 9. *Let $l_{\min} \leq |Q|$ be the smallest positive integer such that for all states $s \in Q$, there exists an encoding w_s such that $\hat{\delta}(s_{init}, w_s) = s$ with $|w_s| \leq l_{\min}$. Let $x_F \in \mathbb{Z}^n$ and $G \subseteq \mathbb{Z}^n$ such that $(G, x_F) = \mathsf{QAffineHull}(\mathcal{A})$. We have*

- *$x_F + \mathrm{lin}_{\mathbb{Q}}(G) = \mathrm{aff}_{\mathbb{Q}}(S_{\mathcal{A}})$,*
- *$|G| \leq |Q| \cdot \Sigma_r^n$,*
- *The time complexity of QAffineHull is $\mathcal{O}(|Q| \cdot |\Sigma_r^n| \cdot n)$,*
- *The size of the numbers in G are bounded by $\mathcal{O}(l_{\min})$.*

Finally, according to Proposition 3, we can compute a triangular set $\overline{G}$ of at most n generators from the set G computed via the algorithm QAffineHull. The sizes of the numbers in $\overline{G}$ are then bounded by $\mathcal{O}(n \cdot (|Q| + \log n))$ and the time complexity for the call GetTriangQBasis(G) is $\mathcal{O}(|Q| \cdot |\Sigma_r^n| \cdot n^2)$. In addition, thanks to Proposition 5, we can compute a system of linear equations $a_i x = 0$, $i = |\overline{G}| + 1, \ldots, n$ such that $x \in x_F + \mathrm{lin}_{\mathbb{Q}}(G) \Leftrightarrow \bigwedge_{i=|\overline{G}|+1,\ldots,n} a_i(x - x_F) = 0$.

6   Affine Hulls over $\mathbb{Z}$

In this section, we give an algorithm for computing the affine hull in $\mathbb{Z}^n$ of the set represented by a reduced NDD $\mathcal{A} = (Q, \Sigma_r^n, \delta, s_{init}, Q_F)$.

Note first that in general, if $(G, x_F) = \mathsf{QAffineHull}(\mathcal{A})$, the set $x_F + \mathrm{lin}_{\mathbb{Z}}(G)$ is not equal to $\mathrm{aff}_{\mathbb{Z}}(S_{\mathcal{A}})$. This stems from the fact that Lemma 8 does not hold in the integer case because it does not consider the factor $r^{|v|}$ of the affine transformations corresponding to the path from s_1 to s_2. Taking this factor into consideration leads to the following lemma.

Lemma 10. *Let $s \in Q$ with $\hat{\delta}(s, v) \in Q_F$ for some v, and let $M \subseteq \mathbb{Z}^n$ be the $\mathbb{Z}$-module such that $\mathrm{aff}_{\mathbb{Z}}(S_A) = x_F + M$ for some $x_F \in \mathbb{Z}^n$. For all $x_1, x_2 \in S_{A(s_{init} \to s)}$, we have $r^{|v|} \cdot (x_1 - x_2) \in M$.*

Based on the above lemma, we can extend Theorem 9 and prove the following property regarding the output of algorithm QAffineHull.

Lemma 11. *Let $d_{\min}$ be the smallest positive integer such that for all states $s \in Q$, there exists an encoding w_s such that $\hat{\delta}(s, w_s) \in Q_F$ with $|w_s| \leq d_{\min}$. Let $M, G \subseteq \mathbb{Z}^n$ and $x_F \in \mathbb{Z}^n$ such that $\mathrm{aff}_{\mathbb{Z}}(S_A) = x_F + M$ and $(G, x_F) = $ QAffineHull(A).*

- *for all $s \in Q$, for all $x_1, x_2 \in S_{A(s_{init} \to s)}$, $x_1 - x_2 \in \mathrm{lin}_{\mathbb{Z}}(G)$, and,*
- *for all $g \in G$, $r^{d_{\min}} g \in M$.*

We now turn on the actual computation of $\mathrm{aff}_{\mathbb{Z}}(S_A)$. A first approach, similar to what is done in [10] for the affine hull over $\mathbb{Q}$, is to compute a finite G_s for each state s such that if $x_s \in S_{A(s_{init} \to s)}$, then $x_s + \mathrm{lin}_{\mathbb{Z}}(G_s) \subseteq \mathrm{aff}_{\mathbb{Z}}(S_{A(s_{init} \to s)})$. This can be done by keeping a basis of G_s and considering paths of increasing length until reaching a fixpoint at which for all states s, for all $w \in L_A(s_{init} \to s)$, $\langle w \rangle_r \in x_s + \mathrm{lin}_{\mathbb{Z}}(G_s)$. The problems with this approach are that numbers in the basis of G_s can grow exponentially, and secondly, there is no bound on the length of the paths before reaching the fixpoint. Based on Lemma 11, those two problems can be solved in the following way. Let $G_{pre}, M \subseteq \mathbb{Z}^n$ and $x_F \in \mathbb{Z}^n$ such that $(G_{pre}, x_F) = $ QAffineHull(A), and $\mathrm{aff}_{\mathbb{Q}}(S_A) = x_F + M$. Since for all states s and $x_s \in S_{A(s_{init} \to s)}$, $\langle w \rangle_r - x_s \in \mathrm{lin}_{\mathbb{Z}}(G_{pre})$, $\langle w \rangle_r - x_s$ is a linear combination over $\mathbb{Z}$ of vectors in G_{pre}, for any $\mathbb{Z}$-basis $\overline{G_{pre}}$ of $\mathrm{lin}_{\mathbb{Z}}(G_{pre})$, the decomposition of $\langle w \rangle_r - x_s$ with respect to $\overline{G_{pre}}$ is unique. Also, since for all $g \in G_{pre}$, $r^{d_{\min}} g \in M$, this also holds for vectors $\overline{g} \in \overline{G_{pre}}$, and adding any combination of $r^{d_{\min}} \overline{g}$ to any $\langle w \rangle_r - x_s$ does not change the affine hull over $\mathbb{Z}$. So, once the decomposition of $\langle w \rangle_r - x_s$ with respect to $\overline{G_{pre}}$ has been performed, we can work in $\mathbb{Z}_{r^{d_{\min}}}$, i.e. work in integer arithmetic modulo $r^{d_{\min}}$.

Based on the above considerations, our algorithm ZAffineHull takes a reduced NDD as input and works as follows.

1. Via the algorithm QAffineHull, one computes a set G_{pre} and a vector x_F. Then, one computes a basis $\overline{G_{pre}}$ of $\mathrm{lin}_{\mathbb{Z}}(G_{pre})$ and set $p = |\overline{G_{pre}}|$. Then for each state s, one associates a triangular set $\Gamma_s \subseteq \mathbb{Z}_{r^{d_{\min}}}^p$ initially empty.
2. One considers paths of increasing length originating from s_{init}, starting with all paths of length 1. Given the label w of a path from s_{init} to s, the procedure works as follows.
   - If $x_s = \bot$, then x_s is set to $\langle w \rangle_r$ and one propagates w from s, that is, for all $u \in \Sigma_r^n$ with $\delta(s, u) = s'$ for some $s' \in Q$, one handles the path labeled by wu at the next iteration.
   - If $x_s \neq \bot$, then one decomposes $\langle w \rangle_r - x_s$ into a linear combination $\sum_{g_i \in \overline{G_{pre}}} \gamma_i g_i$, which is always possible with $\gamma_i \in \mathbb{Z}$. Let $c \in \mathbb{Z}^p$ with $c[i] = \gamma_i \bmod r^{d_{\min}}$ and $c[i] \in \{0, \ldots, r^{d_{\min}} - 1\}$, and let $\Gamma_s' = $ UpdateTriangZm$(r, d_{\min}, \Gamma_s, c)$. There are 2 possibilities.

- If $\Gamma'_s \neq \Gamma_s$, then Γ_s is set to Γ'_s and one propagates w from s.
- Otherwise, one does nothing and w is not propagated.

3. One updates a triangular set $\Gamma \subseteq \mathbb{Z}^p_{r^{d_{\min}}}$, initially empty, via UpdateTriangZm with all vectors $c \in \Gamma_s$ for all $s \in Q_F$.

4. Finally one generates the set $G \subseteq \mathbb{Z}^n$ by adding the vectors $g \in \mathbb{Z}^n$ such that $g = \sum_{g_i \in \overline{G_{pre}}} c[i] \cdot g_i$ for some $c \in \Gamma$, $g = r^{d_{\min}} g_i$ for some $g_i \in \overline{G_{pre}}$, or $g = x_s - x_F$ for some final state $s \in Q_F$. Then, one returns G together with x_F.

Theorem 12. *Let $l_{\min}, d_{\min} \leq |Q|$ be the smallest positive integers such that for all states $s \in Q$, there exist encodings w_l, w_d such that $\hat{\delta}(s_{init}, w_l) = s$ with $|w_l| \leq l_{\min}$ and $\hat{\delta}(s, w_d) = s_F$ for some $s_F \in Q_F$ with $|w_d| \leq d_{\min}$. Let $x_F \in \mathbb{Z}^n$, $G \subseteq \mathbb{Z}^n$ such that $(G, x_F) = \mathsf{ZAffineHull}(\mathcal{A})$. We have*

- $x_F + \mathrm{lin}_{\mathbb{Z}}(G) = \mathrm{aff}_{\mathbb{Z}}(S_{\mathcal{A}})$,
- $|G| \leq |Q| + 2n$ *and the size of numbers in G are bounded by $\mathcal{O}(n \cdot \log(\sqrt{n}) \cdot l_{\min} + d_{\min})$,*
- *the time complexity of* $\mathsf{ZAffineHull}$ *is* $\mathcal{O}(|Q| \cdot |\Sigma^n_r| \cdot (\log(\sqrt{n}) \cdot l_{\min} + d^2_{\min}) \cdot n^3)$.

Note that if $(G, x_F) = \mathsf{ZAffineHull}(\mathcal{A})$, then by applying the function GetTriangZBasis to G, we can generate a basis $\overline{G}$ of $\mathrm{lin}_{\mathbb{Z}}(G)$ in time $\mathcal{O}(|Q| \cdot (l_{\min} + d_{\min}) \cdot n^5)$ and the size of the numbers in $\overline{G}$ are bounded by $\mathcal{O}((l_{\min} + d_{\min}) \cdot n^3)$. Also, thanks to Proposition 5, from $\overline{G}$ and x_F, we can generate a set of equations and congruence relations describing $\mathrm{aff}_{\mathbb{Z}}(S_{\mathcal{A}})$.

7   Experimental Results

The algorithms presented in this paper have been implemented within the LASH library[1]. Note that the algorithms have been slightly modified in order to use the serial encoding as presented in [14], which significantly decreases the running time. By using the serial encoding, we simplify the transition relation at the expense of additional states. As a rule of thumb, the number of states is multiplied by the number of components of the represented vectors, and the number of transition can be exponentially decreased. As encoding basis, we have taken $r = 2$.

The time and memory used for the computation of the algorithms QAffineHull and ZAffineHull in a prototype implementation running on a pentium-M at 1,5 GHz are given in the table below. The computations include the generation of a triangular set $\overline{G}$ such that $x_F + \mathrm{lin}_{\mathbb{Q}}(\overline{G}) = \mathrm{aff}_{\mathbb{Q}}(S_{\mathcal{A}})$ or $x_F + \mathrm{lin}_{\mathbb{Z}}(\overline{G}) = \mathrm{aff}_{\mathbb{Z}}(S_{\mathcal{A}})$. The columns indicate successively the set on which the computation is performed, the number of components of the vectors in the set, the number of states in the corresponding NDD (with alphabet Σ_2), the values of $l_{\min}$ and $d_{\min}$ (see Theorems 9 and 12), and finally the time and memory requirement for the computation of QAffineHull and ZAffineHull successively. Note that all sets $S_1, \ldots, S_{12}$ are defined by a boolean combination of several equations, inequations and congruence relations. In addition, $S_1, \ldots, S_6$ are $\mathbb{Z}$-affine modules which is not the case of $S_7, \ldots, S_{12}$.

---

[1] Available at http://www.montefiore.ulg.ac.be/~boigelot/research/lash/

		$\mathcal{A}$			QAffineHull		ZAffineHull	
Set	n	Nb. States	$l_{\min}$	$d_{\min}$	Time (sec.)	Mem (Mb)	Time (sec.)	Mem (Mb)
S_1	7	64874	3	12	1.0	6.1	3.5	46.7
S_2	6	115727	2	15	1.6	10.4	4.6	64.5
S_3	6	287713	6	27	3.3	27.4	22.5	162.1
S_4	6	215685	4	4	3.3	22.5	10.8	123.4
S_5	10	281135	4	5	3.1	31.4	119.9	379.3
S_6	11	112754	2	5	2.3	13.1	10.9	183.4
S_7	7	279598	4	7	4.3	29.2	63.2	203.8
S_8	7	42067	5	10	0.8	4.3	6.4	30.6
S_9	6	54186	5	5	1.2	5.4	6.6	30.8
S_{10}	7	50580	5	6	0.7	5.1	7.2	36.7
S_{11}	6	52177	4	8	0.9	4.9	4.2	29.3
S_{12}	6	44920	6	7	1.0	4.4	4.5	25.4

In the above table, we note that in the sets considered, the values of $l_{\min}$ and $d_{\min}$ are small compared to $|Q|$, even more so if one uses the serialized encoding. There exist sets for which the values of $l_{\min}$ and $d_{\min}$ have the same magnitude as $|Q|$. For example, the NDDs representing the sets $x = 0 \mod 2^k$ in base 2 have k states and $l_{\min} \simeq d_{\min} \simeq k$. Our intuition is that whenever the characteristics numbers of a set (i.e., the maximal value for finite set, the coefficient of the inequation in a quantifier-free Presburger formula, ...) are small then, $l_{\min}$ and $d_{\min}$ are also small and our algorithms perform very well.

8   Conclusion

In this paper, we have presented two algorithms, QAffineHull and ZAffineHull, that take a reduced NDD $\mathcal{A}$ as input and compute the affine hull over $\mathbb{Q}$ and over $\mathbb{Z}$ respectively of the set represented by $\mathcal{A}$. More precisely, they generate a pair (G, x_F) with a finite set $G \subseteq \mathbb{Z}^n$ and $x_F \in \mathbb{Z}^n$ such that $x_F + \lin_{\mathbb{Q}}(G)$ (resp. $x_F + \lin_{\mathbb{Z}}(G)$) is the affine hull over $\mathbb{Q}$ (resp. $\mathbb{Z}$) of the set represented by $\mathcal{A}$. The size of the numbers manipulated in QAfineHull (resp. ZAffineHull) are bounded by $\mathcal{O}(|Q|)$ (resp. $\mathcal{O}(n \log(\sqrt{n}) \cdot |Q|)$) and the time complexity is $\mathcal{O}(|Q| \cdot |\Sigma_r^n| \cdot n)$ (resp. $\mathcal{O}(|Q|^3 \cdot |\Sigma_r^n| \cdot n^3)$). The algorithms perform very well for NDDs such that the distances from the initial state to each state and the distances from each state to an accepting state are small, as we have shown in a prototype implementation.

References

1. Bruyère, V., Hansel, G., Michaux, C., Villemaire, R.: Logic and p-recognizable sets of integers. Bulletin of the Belgian Mathematical Society 1 (1994) 191–238
2. Wolper, P., Boigelot, B.: An automata-theoretic approach to Presburger arithmetic constraints. In: Proceedings of Static Analysis Symposium. Volume 983 of Lecture Notes in Computer Science., Glasgow, Springer-Verlag (1995) 21–32

3. Boudet, A., Comon, H.: Diophantine equations, Presburger arithmetic and finite automata. In: Proceedings of CAAP'96. Number 1059 in Lecture Notes in Computer Science, Springer-Verlag (1996) 30–43

4. Klaedtke, F.: On the automata size for Presburger arithmetic. In: Proceedings of the 19th Annual IEEE Symposium on Logic in Computer Science (LICS 2004), IEEE Computer Society Press (2004) 110–119

5. Leroux, J.: Algorithmique de la vérification des systèmes à compteurs. Approximation et accélération. Implémentation de l'outil FAST. PhD Thesis, Ecole Normale Supérieure de Cachan, Cachan, France (2003)

6. Latour, L.: From automata to formulas: Convex integer polyhedra. In: Proceedings of 19th IEEE Symposium on Logic in Computer Science (LICS 2004), IEEE Computer Society Press (2004) 120–129

7. Lugiez, D.: From automata to semi-linear sets: a solution for polyhedra and even more general sets. Technical Report 21-2004, Lab. d'informatique de Marseilles (2004)

8. Leroux, J.: A polynomial time Presburger criterion and synthesis for number decision diagram. Technical report, Université de Montréal (2004)

9. Leroux, J.: The affine hull of a binary automaton is computable in polynomial time. Electr. Notes Theor. Comput. Sci. **98** (2004) 89–104

10. M. Müller-Olm, H. Seidl: A note on Karr's algorithm. In Josep Diaz, Juhani Karhumki, Arto Lepistö, eds.: Proceedings of the 31st International Colloquium on Automata, Languages and Programming (ICALP 2004). Volume 3142 of Lecture Notes in Computer Science., Springer-Verlag Heidelberg (2004)

11. Granger, P.: Static analysis of linear congruence equalitites among variables of a program. In Abramsky, S., Maibaum, T.S.E., eds.: TAPSOFT'91: Proc. of the International Joint Conference on Theory and Practice of Software Development. Springer, Berlin, Heidelberg (1991) 169–192

12. M. Müller-Olm, H. Seidl: Analysis of modular arithmetic. In: To appear in the European Symposium on Programming (ESOP 2005). Lecture Notes in Computer Science, Springer-Verlag Heidelberg (2005)

13. Latour, L.: Computing affine hulls over $\mathbb{Q}$ and $\mathbb{Z}$ from sets represented by number decision diagrams. Technical Report 2005-49, Centre Fédéré en Vérification (2005)

14. Boigelot, B., Latour, L.: Counting the solutions of presburger equations without enumerating them. Theoretical Computer Science **313** (2004) 17–29

Tree Automata and XPath on Compressed Trees

Markus Lohrey[1] and Sebastian Maneth[2]

[1] FMI, University of Stuttgaert, Germany
lohrey@informatik.uni-stuttgart.de
[2] Faculté I & C, EPFL, Switzerland
sebastian.maneth@epfl.ch

Abstract. The complexity of various membership problems for tree automata on compressed trees is analyzed. Two compressed representations are considered: dags, which allow to share identical subtrees in a tree, and straight-line context-free tree grammars, which moreover allow to share identical intermediate parts of a tree. Several completeness results for the classes NL, P, and PSPACE are obtained. Finally, the complexity of the XPath evaluation problem on trees that are compressed via straight-line context-free tree grammars is investigated.

1 Introduction

During the last decade, the massive increase in the volume of data has motivated the investigation of algorithms on *compressed data*, like for instance compressed strings, trees, or pictures. The general goal is to develop algorithms that directly work on compressed data without prior decompression. Considerable amount of work has been done concerning algorithms on compressed strings, see e.g. [1, 2]. In this paper we investigate the computational complexity of algorithmic problems on *compressed trees*. Trees serve as a fundamental data structure in many fields of computer science, e.g. term rewriting, model checking, XML, etc. In fact, in each of these domains, compressed trees in form of *dags* (directed acyclic graphs), which allow to share identical subtrees in a tree, are used as a key for obtaining more efficient algorithms, see for instance [3] (term graph rewriting), [4] (model checking with BDDs), and [5, 6] (querying compressed XML documents). Recently, *straight-line context-free tree grammars* (SL cf tree grammars) were proposed as another compressed representation of trees in the context of XML [7]. Whereas a dag can be seen as a *regular* tree grammar [8] that generates exactly one tree, an SL cf tree grammar is a *context-free tree grammar* [8] that generates exactly one tree. SL cf tree grammars allow to share identical intermediate parts in a tree. This results in better compression rates in comparison to dags: in the theoretical optimum, SL cf tree grammars lead to doubly exponential compression rates, whereas dags only allow singly exponential compression rates. In [9], a practical algorithm (BPLEX) for generating a small SL cf tree grammar that produces a given input tree is presented. Experiments with existing XML benchmark data show that BPLEX results in significantly better compression rates than dag-based compression algorithms.

J. Farré, I. Litovsky, and S. Schmitz (Eds.): CIAA 2005, LNCS 3845, pp. 225–237, 2006.
© Springer-Verlag Berlin Heidelberg 2006

In Section 3 we study the problem of evaluating compressed trees via *tree automata* [8, 10]. Tree automata play a fundamental role in many applications where trees have to be processed in a systematic way. In the context of XML, for instance, tree automata are used to type check documents against an XML type [11, 12]. These applications motivate the investigation of general decision problems for tree automata like emptiness, equivalence, and intersection non-emptiness. Several complexity results are known for these problems, see e.g. [8]. Membership problems for tree automata were investigated in [13] for ranked trees (see Table 1 for the results of [13]) and [14] for unranked trees from the perspective of computational complexity. Here we extend this line of research by investigating the computational complexity of membership problems for various classes of tree automata on compressed trees (dags and SL cf tree grammars). For deterministic/nondeterministic top-down/bottom-up tree automata we analyze the fixed membership problem (where the tree automaton is not part of the input) as well as the uniform membership problem (where the tree automaton is also part of the input). Moreover, we consider subclasses of SL cf tree grammars that allow more efficient algorithms for evaluating tree automata. In particular, linearity and the restriction that for some constant k, every production of the SL cf tree grammar contains at most k parameters (variables) lead to better complexity bounds. For all cases, we present upper and lower bounds which vary from NL (nondeterministic logspace) to PSPACE (polynomial space). Our results are collected in Table 1. We also briefly consider the parameterized complexity [15] of membership problems for tree automata.

In Section 4 we consider the problem of evaluating core XPath expressions over compressed trees. XPath is a widely used language for selecting nodes in XML documents and is the core of many modern XML technologies. The query problem for XPath asks whether a given node in a given (unranked) tree is selected by a given XPath expression. For uncompressed trees, the complexity of this problem is intensively studied in [16, 17]. For input trees that are represented as dags, XPath evaluation was investigated in [5, 6]. In [6] it was shown that the evaluation problem for core XPath (the navigational part of XPath) over dag-compressed trees is PSPACE-complete. Here, we extend this result to linear SL cf tree grammars (Theorem 9). This is remarkable, since linear SL cf tree grammars lead to (provably) better compression rates than dags, which is also confirmed by our experimental results for the BPLEX-algorithm (which produces linear SL cf tree grammars) from [9].

Proofs that are omitted in the main part of this paper will appear in the full version.

2   Preliminaries

For background in complexity theory see [18]. The set of all finite strings over a (not necessarily finite) alphabet Σ is Σ^*. The empty string is ε. The length of a string u is $|u|$. We write $u \preceq v$ for $u, v \in \Sigma^*$ if u is a prefix of v. The reflexive and transitive closure of a binary relation $\to$ is denoted by $\overset{*}{\to}$.

Trees, Dags, and SL cf Tree Grammars. A *ranked alphabet* is a pair $(\mathcal{F}, \text{arity})$, where $\mathcal{F}$ is a finite set of function symbols and arity : $\mathcal{F} \to \mathbb{N}$ assigns to each $\alpha \in \mathcal{F}$ its arity (or rank). Let $\mathcal{F}_i = \{\alpha \in \mathcal{F} \mid \text{arity}(\alpha) = i\}$. Function symbols in $\mathcal{F}_0$ are called *constants*. In examples we use symbols $a \in \mathcal{F}_0, h \in \mathcal{F}_1$, and $f \in \mathcal{F}_2$. Mostly we omit the function arity in the description of a ranked alphabet. An $\mathcal{F}$-*labeled tree* t (or *ground term* over $\mathcal{F}$) is a pair $t = (\text{dom}_t, \lambda_t)$, where (i) $\text{dom}_t \subseteq \mathbb{N}^*$ is finite, (ii) $\lambda_t : \text{dom}_t \to \mathcal{F}$, (iii) if $v \preceq w \in \text{dom}_t$, then also $v \in \text{dom}_t$, and (iv) if $v \in \text{dom}_t$ and $\lambda_t(v) \in \mathcal{F}_n$, then $vi \in \text{dom}_t$ if and only if $1 \leq i \leq n$. Note that the edge relation of the tree t can be defined as $\{(v, vi) \in \text{dom}_t \times \text{dom}_t \mid v \in \mathbb{N}^*, i \in \mathbb{N}\}$. The size of t is $|t| = |\text{dom}_t|$. With an $\mathcal{F}$-labeled tree t we associate a term in the usual way: If $\lambda_t(\varepsilon) = \alpha \in \mathcal{F}_i$, then this term is $\alpha(t_1, \ldots, t_i)$, where t_j is the term that corresponds to the subtree of t rooted at the node $j \in \mathbb{N}$. The set of all $\mathcal{F}$-labeled trees is $T(\mathcal{F})$. Let us fix a countable set $\mathcal{X}$ of variables. The set of all $\mathcal{F}$-labeled trees with variables from $\mathcal{X}$ is $T(\mathcal{F}, \mathcal{X})$. Formally, we consider variables as new constants and define $T(\mathcal{F}, \mathcal{X}) = T(\mathcal{F} \cup \mathcal{X})$. A tree $t \in T(\mathcal{F}, \mathcal{X})$ is *linear*, if every variable $x \in \mathcal{X}$ occurs at most once in t. A *term rewriting system*, briefly TRS, over a ranked alphabet $\mathcal{F}$ is a finite set $\mathcal{R} \subseteq (T(\mathcal{F}, \mathcal{X}) \setminus \mathcal{X}) \times T(\mathcal{F}, \mathcal{X})$ such that for all $(s, t) \in \mathcal{R}$, every variable that occurs in t also occurs in s. The *one-step rewrite relation* $\to_\mathcal{R}$ over $T(\mathcal{F}, \mathcal{X})$ is defined as usual, see for instance [19].

Dags (directed acyclic graphs) are a popular compressed representation of trees that allows to share identical subtrees. An $\mathcal{F}$-labeled *dag* is a triple $D = (V_D, \lambda_D, E_D)$ where (i) V_D is a finite set of nodes, (ii) $\lambda_D : V_D \to \mathcal{F}$ labels each node with a symbol from $\mathcal{F}$, (iii) $E_D \subseteq V_D \times \mathbb{N} \times V_D$ (i.e. edges are directed and labeled with natural numbers), (iv) every $v \in V_D$ contains precisely one i-labeled outgoing edge for every $1 \leq i \leq \text{arity}(\lambda_D(v))$, and (v) (V_D, E_D) is acyclic and contains precisely one node $\text{root}_D \in V_D$ without incoming edges. The size of D is $|D| = |V_D|$. A *root-path* in D is a path $v_1, i_1, v_2, i_2 \cdots, v_n$ in the graph (V_D, E_D), i.e., $v_k \in V_D$ $(1 \leq k \leq n)$ and $(v_k, i_k, v_{k+1}) \in E_D$ $(1 \leq k < n)$ that moreover starts in the root node, i.e., $v_1 = \text{root}_D$. Such a path can be identified with the label-sequence $i_1 i_2 \cdots i_{n-1} \in \mathbb{N}^*$. An $\mathcal{F}$-labeled dag D over $\mathcal{F}$ can be unfolded into an $\mathcal{F}$-labeled tree $\text{eval}(D)$: $\text{dom}_{\text{eval}(D)}$ is the set of all root-paths in D (viewed as a subset of $\mathbb{N}^*$), and if the root-path $p \in \mathbb{N}^*$ ends in the node $v \in V_D$, then we set $\lambda_{\text{eval}(D)}(p) = \lambda_D(v)$. Clearly the size of $\text{eval}(D)$ is bounded exponentially in $|D|$.

Example 1. For the dag D on the right we have $\text{eval}(D) = g(f(h(a), h(a)), f(h(a), h(a)), h(a))$. Moreover, the size of D is 4. We have $\text{dom}_{\text{eval}(D)} = \{\varepsilon, 1, 2, 3, 11, 12, 21, 22, 31, 111, 121, 211, 221\}$.

Recently, a compressed representation of trees, which generalizes dags, was introduced: *straight-line context-free tree grammars* (*SL cf tree grammars*) [7]. An SL cf tree grammar is a tuple $G = (\mathcal{F}, N, S, P)$, where (i) $N \cup \mathcal{F}$ is a ranked alphabet, (ii) N is the set of nonterminals, (iii) $\mathcal{F}$ is the set of terminals, (iv) $S \in N$ is the start nonterminal and has rank 0, (v) P (the set of productions) is a TRS over $N \cup \mathcal{F}$ that contains for every $A \in N$ exactly one rule of the form $A(x_1, \ldots, x_n) \to t_A$, where $n = \text{arity}(A)$ and $x_1, \ldots, x_n$ are pairwise different variables, and (vi) the relation $\{(A, B) \in N \times N \mid B \text{ occurs in } t_A\}$ is acyclic. These conditions ensure that for every $A \in N$ of rank n there is a unique tree $\text{eval}_G(A)(x_1, \ldots, x_n) \in T(\mathcal{F}, \{x_1, \ldots, x_n\})$ with $A(x_1, \ldots, x_n) \xrightarrow{*}_P \text{eval}_G(A)(x_1, \ldots, x_n)$. Let $\text{eval}(G) = \text{eval}_G(S) \in T(\mathcal{F})$. Thus, an SL cf tree grammar is a context free tree grammar [8] that generates exactly one tree. Alternatively, an SL cf tree grammar is a *recursive program scheme* [20] that generates a finite tree. The size of G is $|G| = \sum_{A \in N} |t_A|$. We say that G is an SL cf tree grammar *with k parameters* ($k \geq 0$) if $\text{arity}(A) \leq k$ for every $A \in N$. The SL cf tree grammar G is *linear* if for every production $A(x_1, \ldots, x_n) \to t_A$ in P the tree t_A is linear.

SL cf tree grammars generalize string generating straight-line programs [2] in a natural way from strings to trees. The following example shows that SL cf tree grammars may lead to doubly exponential compression rates; thus, they can be exponentially more succinct than dags: Let the (non-linear) SL cf tree grammar G_n consist of the following productions: $S \to A_0(a)$, $A_i(x) \to A_{i+1}(A_{i+1}(x))$ for $0 \leq i < n$, and $A_n(x) \to f(x, x)$. Then $\text{eval}(G_n)$ is a complete binary tree of height 2^n. Thus, $|\text{eval}(G_n)| \in O(2^{2^n})$. Note that G_n has only one parameter. On the other hand, it is easy to prove by induction over the number of productions that *linear* SL cf tree grammars can only achieve exponential compression rates. But linear SL cf tree grammars are still more succinct than dags: The tree $h(h(\cdots h(a) \cdots))$ with 2^n many occurrences of h can be generated by a linear SL cf tree grammar of size $\mathcal{O}(n)$, which is not possible with dags.

An SL cf tree grammar $G = (\mathcal{F}, N, S, P)$ with 0 parameters (i.e., $\text{arity}(A) = 0$ for every nonterminal $A \in N$) can be easily transformed in logspace into an $\mathcal{F}$-labeled dag that generates the same tree: we take the disjoint union of all right-hand sides of productions from P, where the root of the right-hand side for the nonterminal A gets the additional label A. Then we merge for every nonterminal A all nodes with label A. Note that since $\text{arity}(A) = 0$ for every $A \in N$, nonterminals can only occur as leafs in right-hand sides of G. Thus, this merging process results in a dag. For instance, the SL cf tree grammar with the productions $S \to g(A, A, B)$, $A \to f(B, B)$, $B \to h(a)$ corresponds to the dag from Example 1. Vice versa, from an $\mathcal{F}$-labeled dag we can construct in logspace an equivalent SL cf tree grammar with 0 parameters by taking the nodes of the dag as nonterminals. Thus, dags can be seen as special SL cf tree grammars. This justifies our choice to denote with eval both the evaluation function for dags and unrestricted SL cf tree grammars.

Tree Automata. A (nondeterministic) *top-down tree automaton*, briefly TDTA, is a tuple $\mathcal{A} = (Q, \mathcal{F}, q_0, \mathcal{R})$, where Q is a finite set of states, $Q \cup \mathcal{F}$ is a ranked alphabet with $\text{arity}(q) = 1$ for all $q \in Q$, $q_0 \in Q$ is the initial state, and $\mathcal{R}$ is a TRS such that all rules have the form $q(\alpha(x_1, \ldots, x_n)) \to \alpha(q_1(x_1), \ldots, q_n(x_n))$, where $q, q_1, \ldots, q_n \in Q$, $x_1, \ldots, x_n$ are pairwise different variables, and $\alpha \in \mathcal{F}$ has rank n. $\mathcal{A}$ is a *deterministic TDTA* if no two rules in $\mathcal{R}$ have the same left-hand side. The tree language that is accepted by a TDTA $\mathcal{A}$ is $T(\mathcal{A}) = \{t \in T(\mathcal{F}) \mid q_0(t) \xrightarrow{*}_{\mathcal{R}} t\}$. A (nondeterministic) *bottom-up tree automaton*, briefly

BUTA, is a tuple $\mathcal{A} = (Q, \mathcal{F}, Q_f, \mathcal{R})$, where Q and $\mathcal{F}$ are as above, $Q_f \subseteq Q$ is the set of final states, and $\mathcal{R}$ is a TRS such that all rules have the form $\alpha(q_1(x_1), \ldots, q_n(x_n)) \rightarrow q(\alpha(x_1, \ldots, x_n))$, where $q, q_1, \ldots, q_n \in Q$, $x_1, \ldots, x_n$ are pairwise different variables, and $\alpha \in \mathcal{F}$ has rank n. $\mathcal{A}$ is a *deterministic BUTA* if no two rules in $\mathcal{R}$ have the same left-hand side. The tree language that is accepted by a BUTA $\mathcal{A}$ is $T(\mathcal{A}) = \{t \in T(\mathcal{F}) \mid \exists q \in Q_f : t \xrightarrow{*}_{\mathcal{R}} q(t)\}$. It is straight-forward to transform a nondeterministic BUTA into an equivalent nondeterministic TDTA and vice versa, and a logspace transducer is able to to do these transformations. Thus, in the following we do not distinguish between nondeterministic BUTA and nondeterministic TDTA, and we call them simply tree automata (TA). A subset of $T(\mathcal{F})$ is *recognizable* if it is accepted by a TA. Using a powerset construction, every recognizable tree language can be also accepted by a deterministic BUTA, but this involves an exponential blowup in the number of states. For deterministic TDTA the situation is different; they only recognize a proper subclass of the recognizable tree languages. The size $|\mathcal{A}|$ of a TA is the sum of the sizes of all left and right hand sides of rules. Let $\mathcal{G}$ be a class of SL cf tree grammars (e.g., the class of all dags). The *membership problem* for the fixed TA $\mathcal{A}$ and the class $\mathcal{G}$ is the following decision problem:

INPUT: $G \in \mathcal{G}$
QUESTION: Does eval$(G) \in T(\mathcal{A})$ hold?

For a class $\mathcal{C}$ of tree automata, the *uniform membership problem* for $\mathcal{C}$ and the class $\mathcal{G}$ is the following decision problem:

INPUT: $G \in \mathcal{G}$ and $\mathcal{A} \in \mathcal{C}$
QUESTION: Does eval$(G) \in T(\mathcal{A})$ hold?

The upper part of Table 1 collects the complexity results that were obtained in [13] for uncompressed trees. The statement that for instance the membership problem for TA is NC^1-complete means that for every fixed TA the membership problem is in NC^1 and that there exists a fixed TA for which the membership problem is NC^1-hard. More details on tree automata can be found in [8, 10].

3   Membership Problems for Dags and SL CF Tree Grammars

The time bounds in the following theorem are based on dynamic programming. Note that only the number k of parameters appears in the exponent. The idea of the proof is to run the tree automaton $\mathcal{A}$ bottom up on the right-hand sides of G's productions. For the parameters we have to assume at most n^k different possibilities of states of $\mathcal{A}$ which (a determinized simulation of) $\mathcal{A}$ maps to a state of $\mathcal{A}$.

Theorem 1. *For a given TA $\mathcal{A}$ with n states and a linear SL cf tree grammar G with k parameters we can check in time $\mathcal{O}(n^{k+1} \cdot |G| \cdot |\mathcal{A}|)$ whether eval$(G) \in T(\mathcal{A})$.*

Table 1. Complexity results for (uniform) membership problems

		det. TDTA	det. BUTA	TA
uncompressed trees [13]	**fixed**	NC^1-complete		
	uniform	L-complete	LOGDCFL, L-hard	LOGCFL-complete
dags	**fixed**	NL-complete	P-complete	
	uniform			
lin. SL + fixed number para.	**fixed**	P-complete		
	uniform			
SL + fixed number para.	**fixed**	P-complete		PSPACE-complete
	uniform			
unrestricted SL	**fixed**	P-complete	PSPACE-complete	
	uniform			

For a given deterministic BUTA $\mathcal{A}$ with n states and a given SL cf tree grammar with k parameters we can check in time $\mathcal{O}(n^k \cdot |G| \cdot |\mathcal{A}|)$ whether $\mathrm{eval}(G) \in T(\mathcal{A})$.

Recall that a dag can be seen as a (linear) SL cf tree grammar without parameters. Thus, Theorem 1 can be also applied to dags in order to obtain a polynomial time algorithm for the uniform membership problem for TA and dags. Using a straightforward reduction from the P-complete monotone circuit-value problem, we obtain:

Theorem 2. *There exists a fixed deterministic BUTA $\mathcal{A}$ such that the membership problem for $\mathcal{A}$ and dags is P-hard.*

Remark 1. By Theorem 1 and 2, the (uniform) membership problem for (deterministic) BUTA on dags is P-complete. This result may appear surprising when compared with a recent result from [21]: the membership problem for so called dag automata is NP-complete. But in contrast to our approach, a dag automaton operates directly on a dag, whereas we consider ordinary tree automata that run on the unfolded dag. This makes a crucial difference for the complexity of the membership problem.

By the next theorem, a deterministic TDTA can be evaluated on a dag in NL (nondeterministic logspace). The crucial fact is that a deterministic TDTA $\mathcal{A}$ accepts a tree t if and only if the path language of t (which is, roughly speaking, the set of all words labeling a maximal path in the tree t) is included in some regular string language L [10], where L is accepted by a finite automaton $\mathcal{B}$ that is logspace constructible from $\mathcal{A}$. Now we just guess a path in the input dag and simulate $\mathcal{B}$ on this path. The NL lower bound is obtained by a reduction from the graph accessibility problem for dags.

Theorem 3. *The uniform membership problem for deterministic TDTA and dags is in NL. Moreover, there exists a fixed deterministic TDTA such that the membership problem for $\mathcal{A}$ and dags is NL-hard.*

By combining the statements in Theorem 1–3 we obtain the results for dags in Table 1.

SL cf tree grammars allow higher compression rates than dags. This makes computational problems harder when input trees are represented via SL cf tree grammars. The following result reflects this phenomenon. The PSPACE lower bound can be shown by a reduction from QSAT (quantified boolean satisfiability), see e.g. [18].

Theorem 4. *The uniform membership problem for TA and SL cf tree grammars is in PSPACE. Moreover, there exists a fixed deterministic BUTA such that the membership problem for $\mathcal{A}$ and SL cf tree grammars is PSPACE-hard.*

Only for deterministic TDTA we obtain more efficient algorithms in the context of unrestricted SL cf tree grammars. The polynomial time upper bound in the next theorem is again based on the concept of the path language of a tree. For an SL cf tree grammar G, the path language of $\mathrm{eval}(G)$ can be generated by a small context-free string grammar. The lower bound follows from a result of [22] about string straight-line programs.

Theorem 5. *The uniform membership problem for deterministic TDTA and SL cf tree grammars is in P. Moreover, there is a fixed deterministic TDTA such that the membership problem for $\mathcal{A}$ and linear SL cf tree grammars with only one parameter is P-hard.*

From Theorem 1 and 5 (resp. Theorem 4 and 5) we obtain the complexity results for linear SL cf tree grammars with a fixed number of parameters (resp. unrestricted SL cf tree grammars) in Table 1, see lin. SL + fixed number para. (resp. unrestricted SL). The following result completes our characterization presented in Table 1.

Theorem 6. *The uniform membership problem for TA and (non-linear) SL cf tree grammars with only one parameter is PSPACE-hard.*

Proof. We prove the theorem by a reduction from QSAT [18]. Let us take a quantified boolean formula $\psi = Q_1 x_1 \cdots Q_n x_n \, \varphi$, where $Q_i \in \{\forall, \exists\}$ and φ is a boolean formula with variables from $\mathcal{X} = \{x_1, \ldots, x_n\}$. W.l.o.g. we may assume that in φ the negation operator $\neg$ only occurs directly in front of variables. Let $\bar{\mathcal{X}} = \{\neg x \mid x \in \mathcal{X}\}$. We define an SL cf tree grammar G as follows: The set of terminals contains the binary function symbol f, a unary function symbol t_i for every $x_i \in \mathcal{X}$, and a constant a. The set of nonterminals contains the start nonterminal S, and for every subformula α of ψ it contains a nonterminal A_α of arity 1. The productions of G are:

$$S \to A_\psi(a) \qquad\qquad A_\alpha(y) \to f(A_\beta(t_i(y)), A_\beta(y)) \text{ if } \alpha \in \{\forall x_i\beta, \exists x_i\beta\}$$
$$A_\alpha(y) \to y \text{ if } \alpha \in \mathcal{X} \cup \bar{\mathcal{X}} \qquad A_\alpha(y) \to f(A_\beta(y), A_\gamma(y)) \qquad \text{if } \alpha \in \{\beta \wedge \gamma, \beta \vee \gamma\}$$

An occurrence of the symbol t_i on a path in the tree $\mathrm{eval}(G)$ indicates that the variable x_i is set to true. Note that from a nonterminal A_α, where α begins with a quantification $\exists x_i$ or $\forall x_i$ we first generate a branching node (labeled with the binary symbol f). Moreover, the left branch gets in addition the unary symbol t_i, which indicates that x_i is set to true. The absence of t_i in the right branch indicates that x_i is set to false.

We define a nondeterministic TDTA $\mathcal{A}$ as follows: The state set of $\mathcal{A}$ contains all subformulas of ψ plus an additional state q. The initial state of $\mathcal{A}$ is the whole formula ψ. The set $\mathcal{R}$ of transition rules of $\mathcal{A}$ consists of the following rules:

$$q(f(y,z)) \to f(q(y), q(z))$$
$$q(t_i(y)) \to t_i(q(y)) \qquad\qquad \text{for all } i$$
$$q(a) \to a$$
$$\alpha(f(y,z)) \to f(\beta(y), q(z)) \text{ if } \alpha = \exists x_i\beta \text{ for some } i$$
$$\alpha(f(y,z)) \to f(q(y), \beta(z)) \text{ if } \alpha = \exists x_i\beta \text{ for some } i$$
$$\alpha(f(y,z)) \to f(\beta(y), \beta(z)) \text{ if } \alpha = \forall x_i\beta \text{ for some } i$$
$$\alpha(f(y,z)) \to f(\beta(y), q(z)) \text{ if } \alpha = \beta \vee \gamma \text{ for some } \gamma$$
$$\alpha(f(y,z)) \to f(q(y), \gamma(z)) \text{ if } \alpha = \beta \vee \gamma \text{ for some } \beta$$
$$\alpha(f(y,z)) \to f(\beta(y), \gamma(z)) \text{ if } \alpha = \beta \wedge \gamma$$
$$\alpha(t_i(y)) \to t_i(\alpha(y)) \qquad \text{if } \alpha \in (\mathcal{X} \cup \bar{\mathcal{X}}) \setminus \{x_i, \neg x_i\}$$
$$\alpha(t_i(y)) \to t_i(q(y)) \qquad \text{if } \alpha = x_i$$
$$\alpha(a) \to a \qquad\qquad \text{if } \alpha \in \bar{\mathcal{X}}$$

Figure 1 shows the tree $\mathrm{eval}(G)$ for the true quantified boolean formula $\forall x_1 \exists x_2$: $(x_1 \wedge \neg x_2) \vee (\neg x_1 \wedge x_2)$, where in addition every node is labeled with a state of the automaton $\mathcal{A}$ such that the overall labeling is an accepting run.

By the first three rules for state q, $q(t) \xrightarrow{*}_{\mathcal{R}} t$ for every ground tree t. Thus, if we reach the state q, then the corresponding subtree is accepted. If the current state α is an existential subformula $\exists x_i\beta$, then we guess nondeterministically one of the two subtrees of the current f-labeled node (i.e., we choose an assignment for x_i) and verify β in that subtree. The other subtree is accepted by sending q to that subtree. Similarly, if the current state α is a universal subformula $\forall x_i\beta$, then we verify β in both subtrees, i.e., for both assignments for x_i. The rules for $\alpha = \beta \vee \gamma$ and $\alpha = \beta \wedge \gamma$ can be interpreted similarly. Note that by construction of G and $\mathcal{A}$, if the current state α is of the form $\exists x_i\beta$, $\forall x_i\beta$, $\beta \vee \gamma$, or $\beta \wedge \gamma$, then the current tree node in $\mathrm{eval}(G)$ is an f-labeled node. On the other hand, if the current state is from $\mathcal{X} \cup \bar{\mathcal{X}}$, then the current tree node in $\mathrm{eval}(G)$ is labeled with a symbol t_j or the constant a. If the current state is a variable x_i, then we

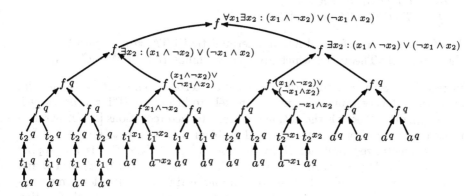

Fig. 1

search for the symbol t_i in the chain of t_j-labeled nodes below the current node. We accept by going into the state q as soon as we find t_i: $x_i(t_i(y)) \rightarrow t_i(q(y))$ If we do not find t_i and end up in the constant a, then we block; note that there is no rule of form $x_i(a) \rightarrow a$. On the other hand, if the current state is a negated variable $\neg x_i$, then we verify that there is no t_i in the chain of t_j-labeled nodes below the current node. Thus, we block as soon as we find t_i; note that there is no rule with left-hand side $\neg x_i(t_i(y))$. On the other hand, if we finally reach the constant a in state $\neg x_i$, then we accept via the rule $\neg x_i(a) \rightarrow a$. From the previous discussion, it is not hard to see that the formula ψ is true if and only if $\mathrm{eval}(G) \in L(\mathcal{A})$. $\qquad\square$

From Theorem 1 and Theorems 4–6 we obtain the results for SL cf tree grammars with a fixed number of parameters in Table 1.

We end this sections with two results concerning the parameterized complexity of membership problems for tree automata. *Parameterized complexity* [15] is a branch of complexity theory with the goal to understand which input parts of a hard (e.g. NP-hard) problem are responsible for the combinatorial explosion. A *parameterized problem* is a decision problem where the input is a pair $(k, x) \in \mathbb{N} \times \Sigma^*$. The first input component k is called the *input parameter* (it may also consist of several natural numbers). A typical example of a parameterized problem is the parameterized version of the clique problem, where the input is a pair (k, G), G is an undirected graph, and it is asked whether G has a clique of size k. A parameterized problem (with input (k, x)) is in the class FPT (fixed parameter tractable), if the problem can be solved in time $f(k) \cdot |x|^c$. Here c is a fixed constant and f is an arbitrary (e.g., exponential) computable function on $\mathbb{N}$. This means that the non-polynomial part of the algorithm is restricted to the parameter k.

Theorem 7. *The following parameterized problem is in FPT:*

INPUT: An SL cf tree grammar G with k parameters and a TA $\mathcal{A}$ with n states.

INPUT PARAMETER: (k, n)
QUESTION: eval$(G) \in T(\mathcal{A})$?

Proof. We first transform $\mathcal{A}$ into a deterministic BUTA with at most 2^n states. Then we apply Theorem 1 which gives us a running time of $2^{kn} \cdot |G| \cdot |\mathcal{A}|$. □

In recent years, a structural theory of parameterized complexity with the aim of showing that certain problems are unlikely to belong to FPT was developed. Underlying this theory is the notion of parameterized reductions [15]: A parameterized reduction from a parameterized problem A (with input $(k, x) \in \mathbb{N} \times \Sigma^*$) to a parameterized problem B (with input $(\ell, y) \in \mathbb{N} \times \Gamma^*$) is a mapping $f : \mathbb{N} \times \Sigma^* \rightarrow \mathbb{N} \times \Gamma^*$ such that: (i) for all $(k, x) \in \mathbb{N} \times \Sigma^*$, $(k, x) \in A$ if and only if $f(k, x) \in B$, (ii) $f(k, x)$ is computable in time $g(k) \cdot |x|^c$ for some computable function g and some constant c, and (iii) for some computable function h, if $f(k, x) = (\ell, y)$, then $\ell \leq h(k)$. A parameterized problem A is fpt-reducible to a parameterized problem B if there exists a parameterized reduction from A to B. One of the classes in the upper part of the parameterized complexity spectrum is the class AW[P]. For the purpose of this paper it is not necessary to present the quite technical definition of AW[P]. Roughly speaking, AW[P] results from taking the closure (w.r.t. fpt-reducibility) of a parameterized version of the PSPACE-complete QSAT problem. Problems that are AW[P]-hard are very unlikely to be in FPT.

Theorem 8. *The following problem is AW[P]-hard w.r.t. fpt-reducibility:*

INPUT: A deterministic BUTA $\mathcal{A}$ and an SL cf tree grammar G with k parameters
   INPUT PARAMETER: k
   QUESTION: eval$(G) \in T(\mathcal{A})$?

The theorem can be shown by a parameterized reduction from the following problem pFOMC (parameterized first-order model-checking), which is AW[P]-hard w.r.t. fpt-reducibility [23]:

   INPUT: A directed graph $H = (V, E)$ and a sentence ϕ of first-order logic (built up from the atomic formulas $x = y$ and $E(x, y)$ (for variables x and y) using boolean connectives and quantification over nodes of H).
   INPUT PARAMETER: The number of different variables that are used in ϕ
   QUESTION: Is ϕ true in the graph H?

4   XPath Evaluation

In this section, we consider XML-trees that are compressed via SL cf tree grammars and study the node selecting language XPath over such trees. For more background on XPath see [16, 17]. We restrict our attention to linear SL cf tree grammars. Skeletons of XML documents are usually modeled as *rooted unranked labeled trees*. Analogously to Section 2, an unranked tree with labels from an (unranked) alphabet Σ can be defined as a pair $t = (\text{dom}_t, \lambda_t)$, where (i)

$\text{dom}_t \subseteq \mathbb{N}^*$ is finite, (ii) $\lambda_t : \text{dom}_t \to \mathcal{F}$, (iii) if $v \preceq w \in \text{dom}_t$, then also $v \in \text{dom}_t$, and (iv) if $vi \in \text{dom}_t$ then also $vj \in \text{dom}_t$ for every $1 \le j \le i$. For the purpose of this section, it is more suitable to view such an unranked tree $t = (\text{dom}_t, \lambda_t)$ as a relational structure $t = (\text{dom}_t, \text{child}, \text{next-sibling}, (Q_a)_{a \in \Sigma})$, where $Q_a = \lambda_t^{-1}(a) \subseteq \text{dom}_t$, child $= \{(v, vi) \in \text{dom}_t \times \text{dom}_t \mid v \in \mathbb{N}^*, i \in \mathbb{N}\}$, and next-sibling $= \{(vi, v(i+1)) \in \text{dom}_t \times \text{dom}_t \mid v \in \mathbb{N}^*, i \in \mathbb{N}\}$. Thus, $\text{child}(u,v)$ is the child-relation in t and $\text{next-sibling}(u,v)$ if and only if v is the right sibling of u. From the basic tree relations child and next-sibling further tree relations that are called *XPath-axes* can be defined. For instance let descendant $:=$ child* (the reflexive and transitive closure of child) and following-sibling $:=$ next-sibling*. For the definition of the other XPath axes see for instance [16]. In the following we consider the four XPath axes child, descendant, next-sibling, and following-sibling; handling of other axes is straightforward and needs no further ideas.

The node selection language *core XPath* [16] can be seen as the tree navigational core of XPath. Its syntax is given by the following EBNF; here, χ is an XPath-axis and $a \in \Sigma \cup \{*\}$ (where $*$ is a new symbol):

corexpath ::= locationpath | / locationpath

locationpath ::= locationstep (/ locationstep)*

locationstep ::= χ :: a | χ :: a [pred]

      pred ::= (pred and pred) | (pred or pred) | not(pred) | locationpath

Let Q_* be the unary predicate that is true for every node of a tree t. We define the semantics of core XPath by translating a given tree $t = (\text{dom}_t, \text{child}, \text{next-sibling}, (Q_a)_{a \in \Sigma})$ and a given expression $\pi \in \mathcal{L}(\text{corexpath})$ (resp. $e \in \mathcal{L}(\text{pred})$) into a binary relation $\mathcal{S}[\pi, t] \subseteq \text{dom}_t \times \text{dom}_t$ (resp. a unary relation $\mathcal{E}[e, t] \subseteq \text{dom}_t$). Let $\pi, \pi_1, \pi_2 \in \mathcal{L}(\text{locationpath})$, $e, e_1, e_2 \in \mathcal{L}(\text{pred})$, and let χ be an XPath axes (recall that ε is the root of a tree).

$$\mathcal{S}[\chi :: a[e], t] := \{(x, y) \in \text{dom}_t \times \text{dom}_t \mid (x, y) \in \chi, y \in Q_a, y \in \mathcal{E}[e, t]\}$$
$$\mathcal{S}[/\pi, t] := \text{dom}_t \times \{x \in \text{dom}_t \mid (\varepsilon, x) \in \mathcal{S}[\pi, t]\}$$
$$\mathcal{S}[\pi_1/\pi_2, t] := \{(x, y) \in \text{dom}_t \times \text{dom}_t \mid \exists z : (x, z) \in \mathcal{S}[\pi_1, t], (z, y) \in \mathcal{S}[\pi_2, t]\}$$
$$\mathcal{E}[e_1 \text{ and } e_2, t] := \mathcal{E}[e_1, t] \cap \mathcal{E}[e_2, t]$$
$$\mathcal{E}[e_1 \text{ or } e_2, t] := \mathcal{E}[e_1, t] \cup \mathcal{E}[e_2, t]$$
$$\mathcal{E}[\text{not}(e), t] := \text{dom}_t \setminus \mathcal{E}[e, t]$$
$$\mathcal{E}[\pi, t] := \{x \in \text{dom}_t \mid \exists y : (x, y) \in \mathcal{S}[\pi, t]\}$$

Recall that by definition SL cf tree grammars generate ranked trees. In order to generate XML skeletons, i.e., unranked trees, with SL cf tree grammars, we encode unranked trees by binary trees (and hence ranked trees) using a standard encoding: For an unranked tree $t = (\text{dom}_t, \text{child}, \text{next-sibling}, (Q_a)_{a \in \Sigma})$ define the binary encoding $\text{bin}(t) = (\text{dom}_t, \text{child1}, \text{child2}, (Q_a)_{a \in \Sigma})$, where (i) $(u, v) \in$ child1 if and only if $(u, v) \in$ child and there does not exist $w \in \text{dom}_t$ with $(w, v) \in$ next-sibling (i.e., v is the left-most child of u), and (ii) child2 $=$ next-sibling. Note that t and $\text{bin}(t)$ have the same set of nodes. The following theorem is our main result in this section. PSPACE-hardness follows from the corresponding result for dags [6].

Theorem 9. *The following problem is PSPACE-complete:*

INPUT: A linear SL cf tree grammar G generating a binary tree with eval$(G)=$ bin(t) *for some (unique) unranked tree t, two nodes u, v of* eval(G), *and a core XPath expression* $\pi \in \mathcal{L}$(corexpath).

QUESTION: $(u, v) \in \mathcal{S}[\pi, t]$?

For the proof of the PSPACE upper bound in Theorem 9 we first translate a given XPath expression into a first-order formula that uses the XPath axes as atomic predicates. We then show that such a first-order formula can be evaluated on eval(G) for a given linear SL cf tree grammar by an alternating Turing machine [18] that works in polynomial time with respect to the size of the formula and the size of the grammar. For this it is crucial that nodes of eval(G) can be represented in polynomial space (with respect to the size of G) and hence can be guessed in polynomial time. This does not hold for non-linear SL cf tree grammars which can generate trees of doubly exponential size. Finally, one can use the fact that PSPACE is precisely the class of all problems that can be solved on an alternating Turing machine in polynomial time, cf. [18].

5   Open Problems and Conclusions

An interesting class of SL cf tree grammars that is missing in our present complexity analysis of tree automata is the class of *linear* SL cf tree grammar (with an unbounded number of parameters in contrast to Theorem 1). The results in this paper leave a gap from P to PSPACE for the uniform membership problem for TA and linear SL cf tree grammars (with an unbounded number of parameters). Our algorithm BPLEX from [9] outputs linear SL cf tree grammars. Note that BPLEX, even when bounding the number of parameters by a small constant (like 2 or 3), clearly outperforms compression by dags. The results presented here show that with respect to tree automata membership problems and XPath evaluation, exactly the same complexity bounds hold for linear SL cf tree grammars with a bounded number of parameter as for dags [5, 6]. This motivates us to believe that linear SL cf tree grammars are better suited than dags as memory efficient representations of XML documents. Precise trade-offs between the representations have to be determined in practice; we are currently implementing our ideas as part of BPLEX. For the XPath evaluation problem, the complexity for non-linear SL cf tree grammars remains open. We conjecture that the PSPACE upper bound from Theorem 9 cannot be generalized to the non-linear case.

References

1. Lohrey, M.: Word problems on compressed word. In Diaz, J., Karhumäki, J., Lepistö, A., Sannella, D., eds.: Proc. ICALP 2004, Turku (Finland). Number 3142 in Lecture Notes in Computer Science, Springer (2004) 906–918

2. Rytter, W.: Grammar compression, LZ-encodings, and string algorithms with implicit input. In Diaz, J., Karhumäki, J., Lepistö, A., Sannella, D., eds.: Proc. ICALP 2004, Turku (Finland). Number 3142 in Lecture Notes in Computer Science, Springer (2004) 15–27

3. Plump, D.: Term graph rewriting. In Ehrig, H., Engels, G., Kreowski, H.J., Rozenberg, G., eds.: Handbook of Graph Grammars and Computing by Graph Transformation. Volume 2. World Scientific (1999) 3–61

4. Bryant, R.E.: Symbolic boolean manipulation with ordered binary-decision diagrams. ACM Computing Surveys **24** (1992) 293–318

5. Buneman, P., Grohe, M., Koch, C.: Path queries on compressed XML. In Freytag, J.C., et al., eds.: Proc. VLDB 2003, Morgan Kaufmann (2003) 141–152

6. Frick, M., Grohe, M., Koch, C.: Query evaluation on compressed trees (extended abstract). In: Proc. LICS'2003, IEEE Computer Society Press (2003) 188–197

7. Maneth, S., Busatto, G.: Tree transducers and tree compressions. In Walukiewicz, I., ed.: Proc. FoSSaCS 2004, Barcelona (Spain). Number 2987 in Lecture Notes in Computer Science, Springer (2004) 363–377

8. Comon, H., Dauchet, M., Gilleron, R., Jacquemard, F., Lugiez, D., Tison, S., Tommasi, M.: Tree automata techniques and applications. Available on: http://www.grappa.univ-lille3.fr/tata (2002)

9. Busatto, G., Lohrey, M., Maneth, S.: Efficient memory representation of XML documents. In: Proc. DBPL 2005, Trondheim (Norway), Springer (2005) to appear.

10. Gécseg, F., Steinby, M.: Tree automata. Akadémiai Kiadó (1984)

11. Murata, M., Lee, D., Mani, M.: Taxonomy of XML Schema Languages using Formal Language Theory. In: Proc. Extreme Markup Languages 2000, Montréal (Canada) (2000)

12. Neven, F.: Automata theory for XML researchers. SIGMOD Record **31** (2002) 39–46

13. Lohrey, M.: On the parallel complexity of tree automata. In Middeldorp, A., ed.: Proc. RTA 2001, Utrecht (The Netherlands). Number 2051 in Lecture Notes in Computer Science, Springer (2001) 201–215

14. Segoufin, L.: Typing and querying XML documents: some complexity bounds. In: Proc. PODS 2003, ACM Press (2003) 167–178

15. Downey, R.G., Fellows, M.R.: Parametrized Complexity. Springer (1999)

16. Gottlob, G., Koch, C., Pichler, R.: Efficient algorithms for processing XPath queries. In: Proc. VLDB 2002, Morgan Kaufmann (2002) 95–106

17. Gottlob, G., Koch, C., Pichler, R.: The complexity of XPath query evaluation. In: Proc. PODS 2003, ACM Press (2003) 179–190

18. Papadimitriou, C.H.: Computational Complexity. Addison Wesley (1994)

19. Baader, F., Nipkow, T.: Term Rewriting and All That. Cambridge University Press (1998)

20. Courcelle, B.: A representation of trees by languages I. Theoretical Computer Science **6** (1978) 255–279

21. Anantharaman, S., Narendran, P., Rusinowitch, M.: Closure properties and decision problems of dag automata. Information Processing Letters **94** (2005) 231–240

22. Markey, N., Schnoebelen, P.: A PTIME-complete matching problem for SLP-compressed words. Information Processing Letters **90** (2004) 3–6

23. Papadimitriou, C.H., Yannakakis, M.: On the complexity of database queries. Journal of Computer and System Sciences **58** (1999) 407–427

Deeper Connections Between LTL and Alternating Automata

Radek Pelánek and Jan Strejček

Faculty of Informatics, Masaryk University in Brno,
Botanická 68a, 602 00 Brno, Czech Republic
{xpelanek, strejcek}@fi.muni.cz

Abstract. It is known that Linear Temporal Logic (LTL) has the same expressive power as alternating 1-weak automata (A1W automata, also called alternating linear automata or very weak alternating automata). A translation of LTL formulae into a language equivalent A1W automata has been introduced in [1]. The inverse translation has been developed independently in [2] and [3]. In the first part of the paper we show that the latter translation wastes temporal operators and we propose some improvements of this translation. The second part of the paper draws a direct connection between fragments of the Until-Release hierarchy [4] and alternation depth of nonaccepting and accepting states in A1W automata. We also indicate some corollaries and applications of these results.

1 Introduction

The study of connections between temporal logics and automata proved to be very fruitful. The best example is the translation of *linear temporal logic (LTL)* formulae into nondeterministic Büchi automata [5, 6], which is one of the cornerstones of the automata-based model checking of LTL properties [7].

It is known for a long time that nondeterministic Büchi automata are more expressive than LTL [8]. Only a few years ago, the *alternating 1-weak Büchi automata* (or *A1W automata* for short, also known as *alternating linear automata* or *very weak alternating automata*) have been identified as the type of automata with the same expressive power as LTL. Muller, Saoudi, and Schupp [1] have introduced a translation of LTL formulae into equivalent A1W automata. The translation of A1W automata into equivalent LTL formulae has been presented independently by Rohde [2], and Löding and Thomas [3].

The LTL→A1W translation has been recently used to build new and more efficient algorithms translating LTL formulae into nondeterministic Büchi automata [9, 10]. Another application of this translation arises in connection with verification algorithms working directly on alternating automata (for pointers see [11]). The growing popularity of A1W automata is hindered by the fact that it is often hard to see what language is recognized by an automaton. Here is the point where the A1W→LTL translation can help as LTL formulae are easy to understand, especially if they contain only few occurrences of temporal operators.

J. Farré, I. Litovsky, and S. Schmitz (Eds.): CIAA 2005, LNCS 3845, pp. 238–249, 2006.
© Springer-Verlag Berlin Heidelberg 2006

Unfortunately, the "standard" A1W→LTL translation does not provide optimal results as it wastes *next* operators. For example, the automaton corresponding to the formula $a \cup (b \wedge (b \cup c))$ is translated into formula $a \cup (b \wedge X(b \cup c))$. In this paper we propose an improved A1W→LTL translation reducing the number of *next* operators in the resulting formula. Our improved translation also prefers the use of less expressive and easy-to-read unary temporal operators *eventually* or *globally* instead of binary operator *until*. We prove that for an A1W automaton produced by the standard translation of an LTL formula φ our translation provides a formula with the same (or even lower) nesting depths of *until*, *next*, and *eventually* operators comparing to these nesting depths in φ.

The improved translation also allows to define classes of A1W automata with the same expressive power as LTL fragments with temporal operators *until*, *next*, and *eventually*, where the nesting depth of each operator can be bounded. Several interesting and previously studied LTL fragments fit into this general pattern, namely fragments of the *until hierarchy* [12, 13], fragments without *eventually* operator and with bounded nesting depth(s) of *next* or *until* or both operators studied in [14, 15], and the fragment without *until* operator known as *restricted LTL* [16].

The second part of this paper presents connections between A1W automata and some LTL fragments that are not covered by the pattern above, namely fragments of the *until-release (alternating) hierarchy* [4] and fragments of the *hierarchy of temporal properties* [17, 18]. In particular, we show that alternation of *until* and *release* operators in a formula corresponds to alternation of nonaccepting and accepting states in an equivalent A1W automaton. Some corollaries of this correspondence are presented as well.

The paper is structured as follows. In Section 2 we recall the definitions of LTL and alternating 1-weak automata together with standard translations between these formalisms. Section 3 provides an improved version of A1W→LTL translation and indicates some applications. Section 4 is devoted to the connection between A1W automata and the until-release hierarchy. Section 5 sums up presented results and mentions some topics for future research. All proofs are omitted due to the space limitations; they can be found in the full version of this paper [19].

2   Preliminaries

2.1   Linear Temporal Logic (LTL)

The syntax of LTL is given by the abstract syntax equation

$$\varphi ::= \top \mid a \mid \neg\varphi \mid \varphi_1 \wedge \varphi_2 \mid X\varphi \mid F\varphi \mid \varphi_1 \cup \varphi_2,$$

where $\top$ stands for *true* and a ranges over a countable set $\Lambda = \{a, b, c, \ldots\}$ of *letters*. We also use $\perp$ to abbreviate $\neg\top$, $G\varphi$ to abbreviate $\neg F\neg\varphi$, and $\varphi R \psi$ to abbreviate $\neg(\neg\varphi \cup \neg\psi)$. The temporal operators X, F, U, G, R are called *next*, *eventually*, *until*, *globally*, and *release*, respectively. Let us note that $F\varphi$ can be equivalently defined as an abbreviation for $\top \cup \varphi$.

We define the semantics of LTL in terms of languages over infinite words. An *alphabet* is a finite set $\Sigma \subseteq \Lambda$. A *word* over alphabet Σ is an infinite sequence $w = w(0)w(1)w(2)\ldots \in \Sigma^\omega$ of letters from Σ. For every $i \in \mathbb{N}_0$, by w_i we denote the suffix of w of the form $w(i)w(i+1)w(i+2)\ldots$.

The *validity* of an LTL formula φ for $w \in \Sigma^\omega$ is defined as follows:

$$
\begin{aligned}
&w \models \top \\
&w \models a && \text{iff} && a = w(0) \\
&w \models \neg\varphi && \text{iff} && w \not\models \varphi \\
&w \models \varphi_1 \wedge \varphi_2 && \text{iff} && w \models \varphi_1 \wedge w \models \varphi_2 \\
&w \models \mathsf{X}\varphi && \text{iff} && w_1 \models \varphi \\
&w \models \mathsf{F}\varphi && \text{iff} && \exists i \in \mathbb{N}_0 : w_i \models \varphi \\
&w \models \varphi_1 \mathsf{U} \varphi_2 && \text{iff} && \exists i \in \mathbb{N}_0 : w_i \models \varphi_2 \wedge \forall 0 \le j < i : w_j \models \varphi_1
\end{aligned}
$$

Given an alphabet Σ, an LTL formula φ defines the language $L^\Sigma(\varphi) = \{w \in \Sigma^\omega \mid w \models \varphi\}$.

Now we define a notation for LTL fragments given by bounds on nesting depths of temporal operators. Let $O \in \{\mathsf{X}, \mathsf{F}, \mathsf{U}\}$ be a temporal operator. The nesting depth of O in a formula φ, written $O\text{-}depth(\varphi)$, is defined in the following way, where Z and Z' range over unary and binary (temporal as well as boolean) operators respectively.

$$
\begin{aligned}
O\text{-}depth(\top) &= 0 \\
O\text{-}depth(a) &= 0 \\
O\text{-}depth(Z\varphi) &= \begin{cases} O\text{-}depth(\varphi) + 1 & \text{if } Z = O \\ O\text{-}depth(\varphi) & \text{otherwise} \end{cases} \\
O\text{-}depth(\varphi_1 Z' \varphi_2) &= \begin{cases} \max\{O\text{-}depth(\varphi_1), O\text{-}depth(\varphi_2)\} + 1 & \text{if } Z' = O \\ \max\{O\text{-}depth(\varphi_1), O\text{-}depth(\varphi_2)\} & \text{otherwise} \end{cases}
\end{aligned}
$$

For all $m, n, k \in \mathbb{N}_0 \cup \{\infty\}$, we set

$$\mathrm{LTL}(\mathsf{U}^m, \mathsf{X}^n, \mathsf{F}^k) = \{\varphi \mid \mathsf{U}\text{-}depth(\varphi) \le m,\ \mathsf{X}\text{-}depth(\varphi) \le n,\ \mathsf{F}\text{-}depth(\varphi) \le k\}.$$

We abuse this fragment notation by omitting the upper indices equal to ∞. Moreover, we usually omit the whole operator if its index is 0. For example, by $\mathrm{LTL}(\mathsf{X}^n, \mathsf{F})$ we mean the fragment $\mathrm{LTL}(\mathsf{U}^0, \mathsf{X}^n, \mathsf{F}^\infty)$.

2.2 Alternating 1-Weak Büchi Automata (A1W)

The transition function of an alternating automaton assigns to each state and letter a positive boolean formula over states. The set of *positive boolean formulae* over set Q (denoted $\mathcal{B}^+(Q)$) consists of formulae $\top$ (true), $\bot$ (false), all elements of Q, and boolean combinations over Q built with $\wedge$ and $\vee$. A subset S of Q is a *model* of $\varphi \in \mathcal{B}^+(Q)$ iff φ is satisfied by the valuation assigning true just to states in S. A set S is a *minimal model* of φ (denoted $S \models \varphi$) iff S is a model of φ and no proper subset of S is a model of φ.

An *alternating Büchi automaton* is a tuple $A = (\Sigma, Q, q_0, \delta, F)$, where Σ is a finite alphabet, Q is a finite set of states, $q_0 \in Q$ is an initial state, $\delta : Q \times \Sigma \to$

$\mathcal{B}^+(Q)$ is a transition function, and $F \subseteq Q$ is a set of accepting states. By $A(p)$ we denote the automaton A with initial state $p \in Q$ instead of q_0.

A run of an alternating automaton is a (potentially infinite) tree. A *tree* is a set $T \subseteq \mathbb{N}_0^*$ such that if $xc \in T$, where $x \in \mathbb{N}_0^*$ and $c \in \mathbb{N}_0$, then also $x \in T$ and $xc' \in T$ for all $0 \leq c' < c$. A *Q-labeled tree* is a pair (T, r) where T is a tree and $r : T \to Q$ is a labeling function. A *run* of an automaton $A = (\Sigma, Q, q_0, \delta, F)$ over word $w \in \Sigma^\omega$ is a Q-labeled tree (T, r) such that $r(\varepsilon) = q_0$ and for each $x \in T$ the set $S = \{r(xc) \mid c \in \mathbb{N}_0, xc \in T\}$ satisfies $S \models \delta(r(x), w(|x|))$. A run (T, r) is *accepting* iff for each infinite path π in T it holds that $Inf(\pi) \cap F \neq \emptyset$, where $Inf(\pi)$ is the set of all labels (i.e. states) appearing infinitely often on π. An automaton A *accepts* a word $w \in \Sigma^\omega$ iff there exists an accepting run of A over w. A language of all words accepted by an automaton A is denoted by $L(A)$.

Let $Succ(p)$ denote the set $Succ(p) = \{q \mid \exists a \in \Sigma, S \subseteq Q : S \cup \{q\} \models \delta(p, a)\}$ of all possible successors of p, and $Succ'(p) = Succ(p) \setminus \{p\}$. An automaton is called *1-weak* if there exists an ordering $<$ on the set of states Q such that $q \in Succ'(p)$ implies $q < p$. In the following we use *A1W automaton* or simply *automaton* meaning 'alternating 1-weak Büchi automaton'. Further, instead of $S \models \delta(a, p)$ we write $p \overset{a}{\to} S$ and say that an automaton has a transition leading from p to S under a. A state p of an automaton has a *loop* whenever $p \in Succ(p)$.

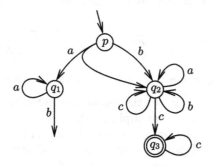

Fig. 1. The automaton accepting the language $a^*b\{a, b, c\}^*c^\omega$

An A1W automaton $A = (\Sigma, Q, q_0, \delta, F)$ can be drawn as a graph; nodes are the states and every transition $p \overset{a}{\to} S$ is depicted as a branching edge labelled with a and leading from node p to the nodes in S. Edges that are not leading to any node correspond to the cases when S is the empty set. Initial and accepting states are indicated in the standard way. For example, Figure 1 depicts an automaton accepting the language $a^*b\{a, b, c\}^*c^\omega$.

2.3 LTL→A1W Translation [1, 11]

In this subsection we treat every (sub)formula of the form $F\varphi$ as an abbreviation for $\top \mathsf{U} \varphi$.

Let φ be an LTL formula and Σ be an alphabet. The formula can be translated into an automaton A satisfying $L(A) = L^\Sigma(\varphi)$, where $A = (\Sigma, Q, q_\varphi, \delta, F)$ and

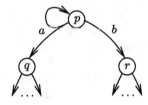

Fig. 2. Part of an automaton translated into the formula $\varphi_p = (a \wedge \mathsf{X}\varphi_q) \,\mathsf{U}\, (b \wedge \mathsf{X}\varphi_r)$

- the states $Q = \{q_\psi, q_{\neg\psi} \mid \psi \text{ is a subformula of } \varphi\}$ correspond to the subformulae of φ and their negations,
- the transition function δ is defined inductively as:

$$\delta(q_\top, a) = \top$$
$$\delta(q_a, b) = \top \text{ if } a = b, \ \delta(q_a, b) = \bot \text{ otherwise}$$
$$\delta(q_{\neg\psi}, a) = \overline{\delta(q_\psi, a)}$$
$$\delta(q_{\psi \wedge \rho}, a) = \delta(q_\psi, a) \wedge \delta(q_\rho, a)$$
$$\delta(q_{\mathsf{X}\psi}, a) = q_\psi$$
$$\delta(q_{\psi\mathsf{U}\rho}, a) = \delta(q_\rho, a) \vee (\delta(q_\psi, a) \wedge q_{\psi\mathsf{U}\rho})$$

where $\overline{\alpha}$ denotes the positive boolean formula dual to α defined by induction on the structure of α as:

$$\overline{\top} = \bot \qquad \overline{q_{\neg\psi}} = q_\psi \qquad \overline{\beta \wedge \gamma} = \overline{\beta} \wedge \overline{\gamma}$$
$$\overline{\bot} = \top \qquad \overline{q_\psi} = q_{\neg\psi} \qquad \overline{\beta \vee \gamma} = \overline{\beta} \vee \overline{\gamma}$$

- the set of accepting states is $F = \{q_{\neg(\psi\mathsf{U}\rho)} \mid \psi \,\mathsf{U}\, \rho \text{ is a subformula of } \varphi\}$.

We use the notation $A^\Sigma(\varphi)$ for the automaton given by the translation of an LTL formula φ with respect to an alphabet Σ.

For example, the translation applied on the formula $\varphi = (a \,\mathsf{U}\, b) \wedge \mathsf{FG}c$ and the alphabet $\Sigma = \{a, b, c\}$ produces the automaton depicted on Figure 1, where p, q_1, q_2, q_3 stand for $q_\varphi, q_{a\mathsf{U}b}, q_{\mathsf{FG}c}, q_{\mathsf{G}c}$, respectively.

2.4 A1W→LTL Translation [2, 3]

Let $A = (\Sigma, Q, q_0, \delta, F)$ be an A1W automaton. For each $p \in Q$ we define an LTL formula φ_p such that $L^\Sigma(\varphi_p) = L(A(p))$ (in particular $L^\Sigma(\varphi_{q_0}) = L(A)$). The definition proceeds by induction respecting the ordering of states; the formula φ_p employs formulae of the form φ_q where $q \in Succ'(p)$. This is the point where the 1-weakness of the automaton is used. To illustrate the inductive step of the translation, let us consider the situation depicted on Figure 2. The formula corresponding to state p is $\varphi_p = (a \wedge \mathsf{X}\varphi_q) \,\mathsf{U}\, (b \wedge \mathsf{X}\varphi_r)$.

Before we give a formal definition of φ_p, we introduce some auxiliary formulae. Let $a \in \Sigma$ be a letter and $S \subseteq Q$ be a set of states.

$$\theta(a, S) = a \wedge \bigwedge_{q \in S} \mathsf{X}\varphi_q \qquad \alpha_p = \bigvee_{\substack{p \xrightarrow{a} S \\ p \in S}} \theta(a, S \setminus \{p\}) \qquad \beta_p = \bigvee_{\substack{p \xrightarrow{a} S \\ p \notin S}} \theta(a, S)$$

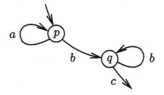

Fig. 3. An automaton for the formula $a \cup (b \wedge (b \cup c))$ and alphabet $\{a, b, c\}$

The formula $\theta(a, S)$ represent a situation where the automaton makes a transition under a into the set of states S. Formulae α_p and β_p correspond to all transitions leading from state p; α_p covers transitions with a loop while β_p covers the others. The definition of φ_p then depends on whether p is an accepting state or not.

$$\varphi_p = \begin{cases} \alpha_p \cup \beta_p & \text{if } p \notin F \\ (\alpha_p \cup \beta_p) \vee G\alpha_p & \text{if } p \in F \end{cases}$$

Given an automaton A with an initial state q_0, we set $\varphi(A) = \varphi_{q_0}$.

3 Improved A1W→LTL Translation

The weak point of the A1W→LTL translation presented above is that for each successor $q \in Succ'(p)$ of a state p the formula φ_p contains a subformula $X\varphi_q$ even if the X operator is not needed. This is illustrated by the automaton A in Figure 3 produced by translating formula $a \cup (b \wedge (b \cup c))$ with respect to alphabet $\{a, b, c\}$. The reverse translation provides an equivalent formula $\varphi(A) = a \cup (b \wedge X(b \cup c))$.

Let $p \overset{a}{\to} S$ be a transition and $X \subseteq S$. We now formulate conditions that are sufficient to omit the X operator in front of φ_q (for every $q \in X$) in the subformula of φ_p corresponding to the transition $p \overset{a}{\to} S$.

Definition 1. *Let $p \overset{a}{\to} S$ be a transition of an automaton A. A set $X \subseteq S \setminus \{p\}$ is said to be X-free for $p \overset{a}{\to} S$ if the following conditions hold.*

1. *For each $q \in X$ there is $S'_q \subseteq S$ such that $q \overset{a}{\to} S'_q$.*
2. *Let $Y \subseteq X$ and for each $q \in Y$ let $S'_q \subseteq Q$ be a set satisfying $q \overset{a}{\to} S'_q$ and $q \notin S'_q$. Then there exists a set $S'' \subseteq (S \setminus Y) \cup \bigcup_{q \in Y} S'_q$ satisfying $p \overset{a}{\to} S''$.*

Figure 4 illustrates the conditions for X-freeness. Please note that it can be the case that $p \in S$. Further, in the first condition it can be the case that $q \in S'_q$.

It is easy to see that the empty set is X-free for every transition. Further, every subset of an X-free set for a transition is X-free for the transition as well. On the other hand, Figure 5 demonstrates that a union of two X-free sets need not be X-free.

Let Xfree be an arbitrary but fixed function assigning to each transition $p \overset{a}{\to} S$ a set that is X-free for $p \overset{a}{\to} S$. We now introduce an improved A1W→LTL translation. Roughly speaking, the translation omits the X operators in front of subformulae which correspond to the states in X-free sets given by the function Xfree.

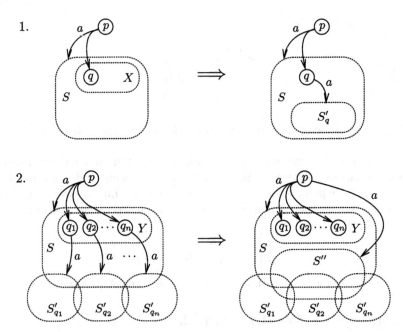

Fig. 4. The conditions for X-freeness

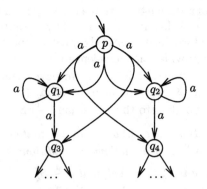

Fig. 5. The sets $\{q_1\}, \{q_2\}$ are X-free for $p \xrightarrow{a} \{q_1, q_2\}$ while the set $\{q_1, q_2\}$ is not

The improved A1W→LTL translation exhibits similar structure as the original one. Instead of formulae of the form $\theta(a, S)$ representing a transition under a leading from an arbitrary state p to S, we define a specialized formula $\theta'_p(a, S)$ for each transition $p \xrightarrow{a} S$.

$$\theta'_p(a, S) = a \wedge \bigwedge_{\substack{q \in S \setminus \text{Xfree}(p \xrightarrow{a} S) \\ q \neq p}} X\varphi'_q \wedge \bigwedge_{q \in \text{Xfree}(p \xrightarrow{a} S)} \varphi'_q$$

$$\alpha'_p = \bigvee_{\substack{p \xrightarrow{a} S \\ p \in S}} \theta'_p(a, S) \qquad\qquad \beta'_p = \bigvee_{\substack{p \xrightarrow{a} S \\ p \notin S}} \theta'_p(a, S)$$

In the following definition of a formula φ'_p we identify some cases when U can be replaced by "weaker" operators F or G. To this end we define two special types of states. A state p is of the F-*type* if there is a transition $p \xrightarrow{a} \{p\}$ for every $a \in \Sigma$. A state p is of the G-*type* if every transition of the form $p \xrightarrow{a} S$ satisfies $p \in S$.

$$\varphi'_p = \begin{cases} \beta'_p & \text{if } p \notin Succ(p) \\ \bot & \text{if } p \in Succ(p),\, p \notin F,\, p \text{ is of G-type} \\ F\beta'_p & \text{if } p \in Succ(p),\, p \notin F,\, p \text{ is of F-type and not of G-type} \\ \alpha'_p \, U\, \beta'_p & \text{if } p \in Succ(p),\, p \notin F,\, p \text{ is neither of F-type nor of G-type} \\ \top & \text{if } p \in Succ(p),\, p \in F,\, p \text{ is of F-type} \\ G\alpha'_p & \text{if } p \in Succ(p),\, p \in F,\, p \text{ is of G-type and not of F-type} \\ (\alpha'_p \, U\, \beta'_p) \vee G\alpha'_p & \text{if } p \in Succ(p),\, p \in F,\, p \text{ is neither of F-type nor of G-type} \end{cases}$$

By $\varphi^{\text{Xfree}}(A)$ we denote the formula φ'_{q_0} given by the improved translation using the function Xfree. The following Theorems 1 and 2 say that the translation is correct and that it does not waste temporal operators.

Theorem 1. *Let A be an A1W automaton over alphabet Σ. Let Xfree be a function assigning an X-free set to each transition of A. Then $L(A) = L^{\Sigma}(\varphi^{\text{Xfree}}(A))$.*

Theorem 1 is proved by induction with respect to ordering of states in the automaton A. The theorem is a direct corollary of the following lemma.

Lemma 1. *Let $p \xrightarrow{a} S$ be a transition of an A1W automaton A such that for each $q \in Succ'(p)$ the equivalence $\varphi_q \iff \varphi'_q$ holds. Then $\theta(a, S \setminus \{p\}) \implies \theta'_p(a, S)$. Further, $\theta'_p(a, S) \implies \beta_p \vee \alpha_p$. Moreover, if $p \notin S$ then $\theta'_p(a, S) \implies \beta_p$.*

Theorem 2. *For each formula $\varphi \in \text{LTL}(U^m, X^n, F^k)$ and each alphabet Σ there exists a function Xfree such that $\varphi^{\text{Xfree}}(A^{\Sigma}(\varphi)) \in \text{LTL}(U^m, X^n, F^k)$.*

The function Xfree can be effectively constructed from the transition relation of the automaton. For further details about the construction and for full proofs see [19].

The improved translation enables us to study relations between fragments of the form $\text{LTL}(U^m, X^n, F^k)$ and classes of A1W automata. In particular, we can provide alternative definitions of language classes corresponding to some previously studied LTL fragments, namely fragments of the form $\text{LTL}(U^k, X, F)$ constituting the so-called *until hierarchy* [12, 13], fragments of the form $\text{LTL}(U, X^n)$, $\text{LTL}(U^m, X)$, or $\text{LTL}(U^m, X^n)$ studied in [14, 15], and the fragments $\text{LTL}(X, F)$ also called *restricted LTL* [16]. Due to the lack of space we mention only the alternative definition of languages definable in LTL(X, F). The other cases are a bit more complicated and can be found in [19].

Lemma 2. *A language is definable by a formula of* LTL(X, F) *if and only if there exists an A1W automaton recognizing the language such that every state with a loop is of* F-*type or* G-*type.*

4   Until-Release Hierarchy and A1W Automata

The *until-release hierarchy* of LTL formulae has been introduced in [4]. It is based on alternation depth of U and R operators. Therefore it is also called *alternating hierarchy.* This hierarchy has a strong connection to the *hierarchy of temporal properties* introduced by Manna and Pnueli [17, 18]. Moreover, there is a relation between classes of until-release hierarchy and complexity of their model checking problem (see [4]).

Definition 2. *The classes* UR_i, RU_i *of the Until-Release hierarchy are defined inductively.*

- *The classes* UR_0 *and* RU_0 *are both identical to* LTL(X).
- *The class* UR_{i+1} *is the least set containing* RU_i *and closed under the application of operators* $\wedge, \vee, X,$ *and* U.
- *The class* RU_{i+1} *is the least set containing* UR_i *and closed under the application of operators* $\wedge, \vee, X,$ *and* R.

Let us note that the hierarchy collapses on the third level with respect to its expressive power. More precisely, each language is definable by LTL if and only if it is definable by a positive boolean combination of UR_2 and RU_2 formulae. These formulae are contained in UR_3 as well as in RU_3. In the following we identify a fragment of the alternating hierarchy with the set of languages defined by formulae of this fragment.

We now define the alternation depth of nonaccepting and accepting states in the graph of an A1W automaton. We also define classes of languages recognized by automata with a given alternation depth.

Definition 3. *Let* $A = (\Sigma, Q, q_0, \delta, F)$ *be an A1W automaton. For each* $i \in \mathbb{N}_0$ *we inductively define sets of states* σ_i *and* π_i *as follows.*

- σ_0 *is the smallest set of states satisfying*
  - $\{p \mid p \notin F \text{ and } Succ(p) = \emptyset\} \subseteq \sigma_0$ *and*
  - *if* $p \notin F$ *and* $Succ(p) \subseteq \sigma_0$ *then* $p \in \sigma_0,$
- π_0 *is the smallest set of states satisfying*
  - $\{p \mid p \in F \text{ and } Succ(p) = \emptyset\} \subseteq \pi_0$ *and*
  - *if* $p \in F$ *and* $Succ(p) \subseteq \pi_0$ *then* $p \in \pi_0,$
- σ_{i+1} *is the smallest set of states satisfying*
  - $\sigma_i \cup \pi_i \subseteq \sigma_{i+1}$ *and*
  - *if* $p \notin F$ *and* $Succ'(p) \subseteq \sigma_{i+1}$ *then* $p \in \sigma_{i+1},$

− π_{i+1} *is the smallest set of states satisfying*
- $\sigma_i \cup \pi_i \subseteq \pi_{i+1}$ *and*
- *if* $p \in F$ *and* $Succ'(p) \subseteq \pi_{i+1}$ *then* $p \in \pi_{i+1}$.

We also define functions $\sigma_A, \pi_A : Q \longrightarrow \mathbb{N}_0$ *as*

$$\sigma_A(p) = min\{i \mid p \in \sigma_i\} \quad and \quad \pi_A(p) = min\{i \mid p \in \pi_i\}.$$

Finally, for each $i \in \mathbb{N}_0$ *we define sets* Σ_i *and* Π_i *as*

$$\Sigma_i = \{L(A) \mid A = (\Sigma, Q, q_0, \delta, F) \text{ is an A1W automaton and } \sigma_A(q_0) \leq i\},$$
$$\Pi_i = \{L(A) \mid A = (\Sigma, Q, q_0, \delta, F) \text{ is an A1W automaton and } \pi_A(q_0) \leq i\}.$$

The following theorem says that a language is definable by a formula of UR_i if and only if it is recognized by an A1W automaton with alternation depth of nonaccepting and accepting states at most i. An analogous statement holds for RU_i and alternation depth of accepting and nonaccepting states. It is worth mentioning that the proof of the following theorem is not as simple as one can think when looking at the definition of a formula φ_p in the standard A1W→LTL translation. See [19] for details.

Theorem 3. *For each* $i \in \mathbb{N}_0$ *it holds that* $\mathsf{UR}_i = \Sigma_i$ *and* $\mathsf{RU}_i = \Pi_i$.

The theorem allows us to transform the results proved for the until-release hierarchy in [4] into statements about our hierarchy of Σ_i and Π_i classes. This is exemplified by the two following corollaries. For definitions of language classes mentioned in the latter corollary (safety, guarantee, obligation,...) we refer to [17, 18].

Corollary 1. *The hierarchy of* Σ_i *and* Π_i *classes collapses on the third level, i.e.* $\Sigma_3 = \Pi_3 = \Sigma_i = \Pi_i$ *for all* $i > 3$.

Corollary 2. *A language definable in LTL is in safety, guarantee, obligation, response, persistence, or reactivity class iff it is in* Π_1, Σ_1, $\Pi_2 \cap \Sigma_2$, Π_2, Σ_2, *or* $\Pi_3 \cap \Sigma_3$, *respectively.*

5   Summary and Future Work

The paper presents two main results. The first is the improved translation of A1W automata into LTL formulae that are language equivalent. The second result is a new automata-based definition of classes in the until-release hierarchy [4]. We also provide some corollaries of these results and indicate further applications.

Besides the presented results our research brought several topics for future work. For example, we would like to know whether there are some more general or/and simpler conditions for a set to be X-free (see Definition 1). Another interesting question is the relation between the sizes of LTL formulae and equivalent A1W automata. Both standard and improved A1W→LTL translations can be modified to produce formulae that can be represented by directed acyclic graphs of linear size with respect to the size of the original automata. However, we conjecture that A1W automata can be exponentially more succinct than LTL if we stick with the standard representation of LTL formulae.

Acknowledgment. Authors have been partially supported as follows: R. Pelánek by Czech Science Foundation (GAČR), grants No. 201/03/0509 and 102/05/H050, and J. Strejček by the research centre "Institute for Theoretical Computer Science (ITI)", project No. 1M0021620808.

References

1. Muller, D.E., Saoudi, A., Schupp, P.E.: Weak alternating automata give a simple explanation of why most temporal and dynamic logics are decidable in exponential time. In: Proceedings of the 3rd IEEE Symposium on Logic in Computer Science (LICS 1988), IEEE Computer Society Press (1988) 422–427
2. Rohde, S.: Alternating automata and the temporal logic of ordinals. PhD thesis, University of Illinois at Urbana-Champaign (1997)
3. Löding, C., Thomas, W.: Alternating automata and logics over infinite words (extended abstract). In van Leeuwen, J., et al., eds.: Theoretical computer science: exploring new frontiers of theoretical informatics: International Conference IFIP TCS 2000. Volume 1872 of Lecture Notes in Computer Science., Springer-Verlag (2000) 521–535
4. Černá, I., Pelánek, R.: Relating hierarchy of temporal properties to model checking. In: Mathematical Foundations of Computer Science (MFCS). Volume 2747 of Lecture Notes in Computer Science., Springer (2003)
5. Wolper, P., Vardi, M.Y., Sistla, A.P.: Reasoning about infinite computation paths (extended abstract). In: 24th Annual Symposium on Foundations of Computer Science, IEEE (1983) 185–194
6. Vardi, M.Y., Wolper, P.: Reasoning about infinite computations. Information and Computation **115** (1994) 1–37
7. Vardi, M.Y., Wolper, P.: An automata-theoretic approach to automatic program verification. In: Proceedings of the First Symposium on Logic in Computer Science, Cambridge (1986) 322–331
8. Wolper, P.: Temporal logic can be more expressive. Information and Control **56** (1983) 72–99
9. Gastin, P., Oddoux, D.: Fast LTL to Büchi automata translation. In Berry, G., Comon, H., Finkel, A., eds.: Proceedings of the 13th Conference on Computer Aided Verification (CAV'01). Volume 2102 of Lecture Notes in Computer Science., Springer (2001) 53–65
10. Tauriainen, H.: On translating linear temporal logic into alternating and nondeterministic automata. Research Report A83, Helsinki University of Technology, Laboratory for Theoretical Computer Science (2003)
11. Vardi, M.Y.: Alternating automata: Unifying truth and validity checking for temporal logics. In McCune, W., ed.: Proceedings of the 14th International Conference on Automated Deduction. Volume 1249 of LNAI., Springer (1997) 191–206
12. Thérien, D., Wilke, T.: Temporal logic and semidirect products: An effective characterization of the until hierarchy. In: 37th Annual Symposium on Foundations of Computer Science (FOCS '96), IEEE (1996) 256–263

13. Etessami, K., Wilke, T.:   An until hierarchy and other applications of an Ehrenfeucht-Fraïssé game for temporal logic. Information and Computation **160** (2000) 88–108
14. Kučera, A., Strejček, J.: The stuttering principle revisited. Acta Informatica (2005) To appear.
15. Kučera, A., Strejček, J.: Characteristic patterns for LTL. In: Proceedings of SOFSEM 2005. Volume 3381 of Lecture Notes in Computer Science., Springer-Verlag (2005) 239–249
16. Perrin, D., Pin, J.E.: Infinite words. Volume 141 of Pure and Applied Mathematics. Elsevier (2004)
17. Manna, Z., Pnueli, A.: A hierarchy of temporal properties. In: Proc. ACM Symposium on Principles of Distributed Computing, ACM Press (1990) 377–410
18. Chang, E., Manna, Z., Pnueli, A.: Characterization of temporal property classes. In Kuich, W., ed.: Automata, Languages and Programming, 19th International Colloquium (ICALP '92). Volume 623 of Lecture Notes in Computer Science., Springer-Verlag (1992) 474–486
19. Pelánek, R., Strejček, J.: Deeper connections between ltl and alternating automata. Technical Report FIMU-RS-2004-08, Faculty of Informatics, Masaryk University in Brno (2004) Available at **http://www.fi.muni.cz/reports/**.

The Structure of Subword Graphs and Suffix Trees of Fibonacci Words⋆

Wojciech Rytter

Instytut Informatyki, Uniwersytet Warszawski,
Banacha 2, 02–097, Warszawa, Poland
Department of Computer Science, New Jersey Institute of Technology
rytter@mimuw.edu.pl

Abstract. We use automata-theoretic approach to analyze properties of
Fibonacci words. The directed acyclic subword graph (dawg) is a useful
deterministic automaton accepting all suffixes of the word. We show that
dawg's of Fibonacci words have particularly simple structure. The simple structure of paths in these graphs gives simplified alternative proofs
and new interpretation of several known properties of Fibonacci words.
The structure of lengths of paths in the compacted subword graph corresponds to a number-theoretic characterization of occurrences of subwords
in terms of Zeckendorff Fibonacci number system. Using the structural
properties of dawg's it can be easily shown that for a string w we can
check if w is a subword of a Fibonacci word in time $O(|w|)$ and $O(1)$
space. Compact dawg's of Fibonacci words show a very regular structure
of their suffix trees and show how the suffix tree for the Fibonacci word
grows (extending the leaves in a very simple way) into the suffix tree for
the next Fibonacci word.

1   Introduction

Fibonacci words form a famous family of words, due to many interesting properties related to text algorithms and combinatorics on words, see [1, 2]. In particular Fibonacci words have $\Theta(n \log n)$ positioned squares and they have linear number of *runs*: maximal periodic subsegments (x is said to be *periodic* iff
$period(x) \le |x|/2$). The structure of runs in general strings is rather mysterious,
and the structure of runs in Fibonacci words helps to understand this structure.
In this sense Fibonacci words are very representative. A very good source for
properties of these words is for example the book [2]. We rediscover/discover
several known/unknown properties of Fibonacci words in a novel way: analyzing
the automaton for the set of subwords. Let F_n be the n-th Fibonacci word, where

$$F_0 = a, \; F_1 = ab, \; F_{n+1} \; = \; F_n \cdot F_{n-1}$$

Denote by Φ_n the n-th Fibonacci number, where $|F_n| = \Phi_n$. Define also the
infinite Fibonacci word $\mathcal{F}_\infty \; = \; \mathcal{F}_\infty(1, 2, 3, 4, \ldots)$, such that each F_n is a prefix
of $\mathcal{F}_\infty$. Hence

⋆ Research supported by the grants 4T11C04425 and CCR-0313219.

J. Farré, I. Litovsky, and S. Schmitz (Eds.): CIAA 2005, LNCS 3845, pp. 250–261, 2006.

$$\mathcal{F}_\infty = abaababaabaababaabaabaabaababaabaababaabaabaabaabaabaabaabaabaabaabaabaabaabaabaab\ldots$$

By an *occurrence* of u in $\mathcal{F}_\infty$ we mean a position i such that $\mathcal{F}_\infty[i+1\ldots i+|u|] = u$. Denote by *first-occ(u)* the first occurrence of u in $\mathcal{F}_\infty$, and by *occ(u)* the set of all occurrences. The structure of lengths of paths in the dawg's of Fibonacci words is closely related to the Fibonacci number system. This system consists in representing a number as a sum of Fibonacci numbers, in such a way that no two consecutive Fibonacci numbers are used. The sum of zero number of integers equals zero. The corresponding representation of the number is called $\mathcal{Z}$-representation.

Theorem 1. [Zeckendorff Theorem, [3]]
Every nonnegative integer is uniquely represented in the Fibonacci number system. Every number $F_n \leq k \leq F_{n+1} - 1$ contains F_n as the largest term in its $\mathcal{Z}$-representation.

Define the *dual Fibonacci system*. In this system each positive integer x is represented as a sum of different Fibonacci numbers, however we require that if Φ_i is not taken then Φ_{i+1} is taken in the sum, whenever any Fibonacci number after Φ_i is taken. It follows directly from Zeckendorff's Theorem that:

Lemma 1. *Every integer $k > 0$ is uniquely represented in the dual Fibonacci number system.*

If X is a set of integers then define:

$$X \oplus j = \{x + j \ : \ x \in X\}.$$

Denote by g_i (the i-th truncated Fibonacci word) the word F_i with the last two letters removed. Using the dawg's we show that for each nonempty subword u of $\mathcal{F}_\infty$ we have:

$$occ(u) = occ(g_i) \oplus \textit{first-occ}(u),$$

where g_i is the shortest truncated Fibonacci word containing u.

Let $\mathcal{Z}_n$ be the set of nonnegative integers which do not use Fibonacci numbers $\Phi_0, \Phi_1, \ldots, \Phi_{n-1}$ in their Fibonacci representation. It follows directly from the structure of the dawg that:

$$occ(g_{n+1}) = occ(F_n) = \mathcal{Z}_n \text{ for } n > 1 \text{ and } occ(F_1) = occ(F_2), occ(F_0) = \mathcal{Z}_1$$

The sorted set $\mathcal{Z}_k[0], \mathcal{Z}_k[1], \mathcal{Z}_k[2], \ldots$ is closely related to Fibonacci words, denote by $\mathcal{D}_k$ the displacement structure of $\mathcal{Z}_k$:

$$\mathcal{D}_k = (\mathcal{Z}_k[1] - \mathcal{Z}_k[0], \ \mathcal{Z}_k[2] - \mathcal{Z}_k[1], \ \mathcal{Z}_k[3] - \mathcal{Z}_k[2], \ \mathcal{Z}_k[4] - \mathcal{Z}_k[3], \ \ldots).$$

The following fact is very useful in the analysis of the structure of runs in $\mathcal{F}_\infty$. It shows that the dsiplacement sequence is isomorphic to $\mathcal{F}_\infty$.

Lemma 2. $\mathcal{D}_k = h_k(\mathcal{F}_\infty)$, where $h_k(a) = \Phi_k$, $h_k(b) = \Phi_{k-1}$.

It follows easily from the structure of the dawg's that every run in $\mathcal{F}_\infty$ (except aa, $(ab)^2$) is of the form $(F_i)^k g_{i-1}$, where $k \in \{2,3\}$. A similar analysis of the structure of runs of squares has been already done by Iliopoulos, Moore, and Smyth in [4]. However their proofs were syntactic, and here we present different graph-theoretic proofs, based on the structure of the dawg of $\mathcal{F}_\infty$ and on a natural number-theoretic interpretation of the sets of lengths of its paths.

2   The Structure of Subword Graphs

We construct the infinite labelled graph $\mathcal{G}_\infty$, The nodes of $\mathcal{G}_\infty$ are all integers $i \geq 0$, the edges are constructed as follows:

$$(i-1) \stackrel{\mathcal{F}_\infty(i)}{\longrightarrow} i, \text{ for } i > 0, \qquad \Phi_i - 2 \stackrel{b}{\rightarrow} \Phi_{i+1} - 1, \text{ for odd } i,$$

$$\text{and } \Phi_i - 2 \stackrel{a}{\rightarrow} \Phi_{i+1} - 1, \text{ for even } i.$$

The graph $\mathcal{G}_\infty$ is, in a certain sense, a subword graph of the infinite Fibonacci word F_∞. The initial segments of this graph are dawg's of finite Fibonacci words. Denote by finite-paths($\mathcal{G}_\infty$) the set of all finite words spelled by the paths of $\mathcal{G}_\infty$ originating at 0, and by finite-subwords($\mathcal{F}_\infty$) the set of all finite sub-words of $\mathcal{F}_\infty$. The following fact follows from Theorem 6, which wil be proved later.

Theorem 2. finite-paths($\mathcal{G}_\infty$) = finite-subwords($\mathcal{F}_\infty$).

We say that a path is an a-path if it is an infinite path in $\mathcal{G}_\infty$ which starts at 0, and chooses the edge labelled a whenever there is a choice. Similarly define b-path. Denote by a-path($\mathcal{G}_\infty$) the infinite word spelled by the a-path, similarly define b-path($\mathcal{G}_\infty$). The b-path($\mathcal{G}_\infty$) can be treated as the infinite lexicographically maximal *pseudo-suffix* of $\mathcal{F}_\infty$ (each prefix of b-path($\mathcal{G}_\infty$) is a prefix of maximal suffix of some finite Fibonacci word).

Theorem 3. a-path($\mathcal{G}_\infty$) $= a \cdot \mathcal{F}_\infty$, b-path($\mathcal{G}_\infty$) $= b \cdot \mathcal{F}_\infty$.

The edges of the form $(i, i+1)$ are called *main edges*. The suffixes of $\mathcal{F}_\infty$ are infinite words resulting by cutting off a finite prefix of $\mathcal{F}_\infty$.

Theorem 4. a-path($\mathcal{G}_\infty$) and b-path($\mathcal{G}_\infty$) are not suffixes of $\mathcal{F}_\infty$.
    The infinite string corresponding to a path π of $\mathcal{G}_\infty$ is a suffix of $\mathcal{F}_\infty$ iff almost all edges of π (all but a finite number) are main edges.

The nodes of outdegree greater than one are called fork nodes. We say that a path starting from 0 is a *fork-path* iff it ends at a fork node in $\mathcal{G}_\infty$. The next theorem follows from the structure of the compacted infinite dawg $\mathcal{G}_\infty$. However we introduce later the compacted dawg's in terms of finite words.

Theorem 5. *For each $k > 1$ there is exactly one fork-path of length k in $\mathcal{G}_\infty$. This fork-path corresponds to the representation of k in the dual Fibonacci number system.*

*For each $\Phi_{n+1} - 2 < k \leq \Phi_{n+2} - 2$ there is a path of length k from the source
to the fork node $\Phi_{n+2} - 2$.*

Proof. It is easy to see that each path of total length k from the source to
a fork node in the compacted version of $\mathcal{G}_\infty$, see Figure 4, corresponds to a
representation of a number k in the dual Fibonacci system, the example of
representing $k = 60$ is shown in Figure 4.

If we have paths of length $k - 1$ then only a path ending at a fork node generates
two paths of length k. The theorem and Lemma 1 implies directly in a novel
way the following well known Sturmian property of $\mathcal{F}_\infty$.

Corollary 1. *There are exactly $k + 1$ different subwords of length k in $\mathcal{F}_\infty$.*

Let $\mathcal{G}_n$ be the subgraph of $\mathcal{G}_\infty$ induced by the nodes $[0 \ldots \Phi_n]$, see Figure 1.
Denote by $dawg(w)$ the acyclic directed subword graph of a word w, see for
example [1, 5, 2] for the definition. We assume that the nodes on the *main branch*
of such a graph are consecutive integers starting with 0.

Theorem 6. *For each $n > 1$ $dawg(F_n) = \mathcal{G}_n$ and $paths(\mathcal{G}_n) = suffixes(F_n)$.*

Proof. The thesis follows from the on-line construction of $dawg(F_n)$, see [1]. It
is enough to show that no extra nodes outside the main branch are created. If
$dawg(F_n) = \mathcal{G}_n$ then the next $|F_{n-1}| - 2$ symbols do not create new nodes or
new edges since g_n is a prefix and suffix of g_{n+1}, which consequently has the
period $|F_{n-1}|$. One extra edge is created from $|F_n| - 2$ to $|F_{n+1} - 1|$ because the
next read symbol terminates the period $|F_{n-1}|$. We omit the details.

We refer the reader to [1] for the definition of the critical factorization point.
The starting position of a lexicographically maximal suffix, maximized over all
possible orders of the alphabet, is the critical factorization point. This implies
the following fact:

Theorem 7. $\Phi_n - \min\{ |a\text{-}path(\mathcal{G}_n)|, |b\text{-}path(\mathcal{G}_n)| \}$ *is the critical factorization
point of the n-th Fibonacci word.*

This gives alternative proof, see [6], of the following fact.

Corollary 2. $\Phi_{n-1} - 1$ *is a critical factorization point of F_n.*

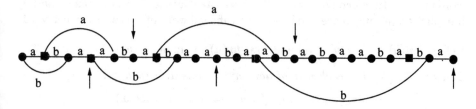

Fig. 1. The subword graph $dawg(F_6)$, the *fork nodes* (of outdegree 2) are drawn as
squares. The arrows show the ends of prefixes which are Fibonacci words.

Each $dawg(F_n)$ can be compactly described in $O(n)$ space, see Figure 2 for the first compaction, in which each chain (a sequence of nodes of indegree and out-degree one) is represented by a single edge. We can further compact $dawg(F_n)$. Let us remove all nodes except fork nodes, the source and the sink. Call remaining nods essential. Then for each edge outgoing from an essential node replace it by an edge going to the next essential node, with label representing the word "spelled" by the compressed path, see Figure 3. The resulting compacted sub-word graph is denoted by $cdawg(F_n)$.

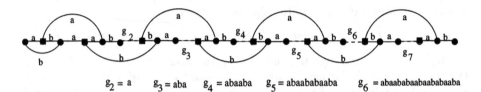

$$g_2 = a \qquad g_3 = aba \qquad g_4 = abaaba \qquad g_5 = abaababaaba \qquad g_6 = abaababaabaababaaba$$

Fig. 2. The *structure* of $dawg(F_9)$, of 12th Fibonacci word (of length 89). The dashed edges correspond to chains.

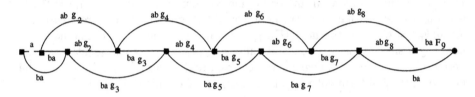

Fig. 3. The power of compaction: $cdawg(F_{11})$ of the Fibonacci word of length 233. Observe that all labels (but one) are reverses of Fibonacci words.

By $O(1)$ space we mean constant number of nonnegative integers not greater than n.

Theorem 8. *We can test if a word w is a subword of a Fibonacci word in time $O(|w|)$ and $O(1)$ space.*

Proof. It is easy to see that we can test if a specified subword of w is a Fibonacci word in linear time and $O(1)$ space. Then we can traverse $\mathcal{G}$ without remembering it explicitly. In some places we have to test if a subword of w is a Fibonacci word.

Define $fin(u) = occ(u) \oplus |u|$ and $first\text{-}fin(u) = \min(fin(u))$.

Lemma 3. (A) *For each pair of nonempty words u, w we have:*

$$first\text{-}fin(u) = first\text{-}fin(w) \Leftrightarrow occ(u) = occ(w).$$

(B) *For each nonempty subword u of $\mathcal{F}_\infty$ we have*
$occ(u) = occ(g_i) \oplus first\text{-}occ(u)$, *where g_i is the shortest truncated Fibonacci word containing u.*

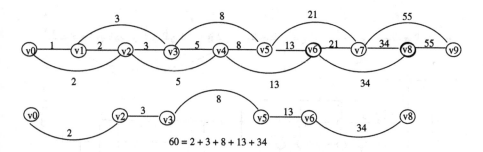

Fig. 4. We consider only fork nodes and put the lengths of the edges as the lengths of compacted paths. The representation of $k = 60$ in the dual Fibonacci system corresponds to a path $(v_0, v_2, v_3, v_5, v_6, v_8)$. It illustrates the fact that for each k exactly one word corresponds to a path from the source to a fork node.

Example. The shortest truncated Fibonacci word containing aa, as well as $F_3 = abaab$ is $g_4 = abaaba$. We have $occ(F_3) = occ(g_4) = \{0, 5, 8, 13, 18, 21, 26, 29, \ldots\}$, and *first-occ*$(aa) = 2$, hence

$$occ(aa) = occ(F_3) \oplus 2 = occ(g_4) \oplus 2 = \{2, 7, 10, 15, 20, 23, 28, 31, \ldots\}.$$

The structure of the graph $\mathcal{G}$ implies easily several number-theoretic properties of the Fibonacci words. It follows from Lemma 3 and the structure of the graph $\mathcal{G}$, see Figure 4, that:

Theorem 9.

1. $occ(g_{n+1}) = occ(F_n) = \mathcal{Z}_n$ for $n > 1$
2. $occ(F_1) = occ(F_2)$, $occ(F_0) = \mathcal{Z}_1$.
3. For each subword $u \notin \{F_0, F_1\}$ of $\mathcal{F}_\infty$ we have $occ(u) = \mathcal{Z}_i \oplus$ *first-occ*(u), where g_i is the smallest truncated Fibonacci word containing u as a subword.

Proof. The subword u "moves" to the right by starting at *first-occ*(u) in $\mathcal{G}$ and making shortcuts. Each shortcut corresponds to taking a Fibonacci number, no two consecutive Fibonacci numbers are taken.

We investigate also the structure of the set

$$FIN(k) = \{\textit{first-fin}(u) : u \text{ is of size } k \}$$

The structure of this set easily follows from the way how paths of length $k - 1$ are extended into paths of length k. Only fork nodes $i \in FIN(k - 1)$ generate two elements of $FIN(k)$, each other node i in $FIN(k - 1)$ generates a single element $i + 1$ in $FIN(k)$, see Figure 5. We have:

$$FIN(k + 1) = FIN(k) \oplus 1 \cup \{\Phi_{i+1} - 1\} \text{ where } \Phi_i - 2 \in FIN(k)$$

This implies directly the following fact.

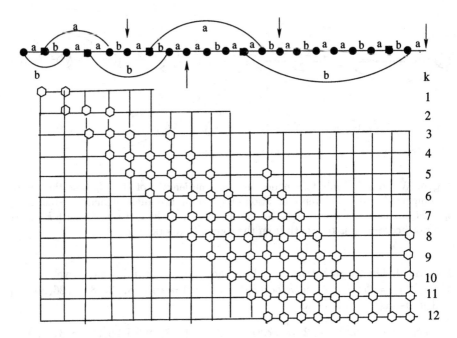

Fig. 5. The structure of nodes of G which are endpoints of all $k + 1$ different strings of length k. The end-positions of Fibonacci prefixes are indicated by vertical arrows.

Lemma 4. *The set $FIN(k)$ consists of a single interval or of two disjoint intervals.*

$$FIN(\Phi_n - 1) = [\Phi_n - 1 \ldots 2 \cdot \Phi_n - 1];$$

We say that a subword w of $\mathcal{F}_\infty$ is a right special subword, iff wa and wb are subwords of $\mathcal{F}_\infty$. Such subwords are responsible for the increase of the number of subwords with respect to their length. These are the words corresponding to paths to fork nodes, they are considered for example in [7]. It is easy to see from the structure of $\mathcal{G}$ that right special subwords are exactly suffixes of g_i's. On the other hand each suffix of g_i is a reverse of a prefix of $\mathcal{F}_\infty$. Let w^R denote the reverse of w. We gave a new proof of another property of $\mathcal{F}_\infty$:

a word w is a right special factor of $\mathcal{F}_\infty$ iff w^R is a prefix of $\mathcal{F}_\infty$.

3   The Structure of Runs in Fibonacci Words

We say that a run w is a p-run iff $period(w) = p$. The run is short if $|w| < 3 \cdot period(w)$. The structure of runs has been already investigated in [8, 4]. Every occurrence of a subword in $\mathcal{F}_\infty$ implies an occurrence of some word g_i starting at the same position. Hence the runs correspond to adjacent occurrences or overlaps of words g_i. Consequently we have the following fact.

Lemma 5. [8] *Every run of $\mathcal{F}_\infty$ is of one of two types:*

(**Short runs**) $w = F_k \cdot F_k \cdot g_{k-1}$, *or* (**Long runs**) $w = F_k \cdot F_k \cdot F_k \cdot g_{k-1}$.

Denote by $rep(x)$ the repetition order of the string (finite or infinite) x as

$$rep(x) = \sup\{|w|/period(w) : w \in \text{finite-subwords}(x)\}.$$

The maximal repetitions correspond to long runs in $\mathcal{F}_\infty$. This implies the following fact (already shown in [8]).

Corollary 3. [8] $rep(\mathcal{F}_\infty) = 2 + \phi$, *where* $\phi = \frac{1+\sqrt{5}}{2}$ *is the golden ratio.*

It follows from the structure of runs that there is no subword aaa in $\mathcal{F}_\infty$. Using the displacement sequence $\mathcal{D}_k$, due to its recursive Fibonacci-like structure, we can easily show the following (already shown using different methods) properties of Fibonacci words.

Corollary 4. *There are no subwords in $\mathcal{F}_\infty$ of type x^4, where x is nonempty. For $n > k$, the number of occurrences of F_k in F_n is $F_{n-k} - odd(n-k)$, where $odd(x) = 1$ if x is an odd integer, and $odd(x) = 0$ otherwise.*

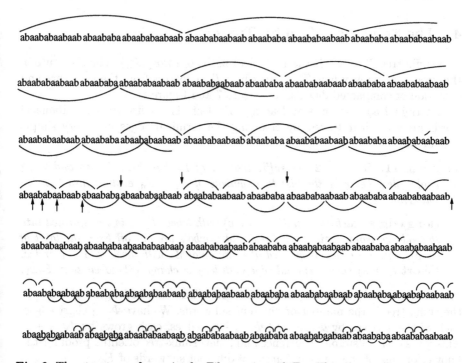

Fig. 6. The structure of *runs* in the Fibonacci word F_{11}. The arrows show endpoints of Fibonacci prefixes. F_{11} has 65 runs. The 21 1-runs of aa are not shown in the figure. The runs are distributed as follows: there are 12 2-runs, 13 3-runs, 8 5-runs, 5 8-runs, 3 13-runs, 2 21-runs and 1 34-run.

All runs correspond to occurrences of g_i's. However $\mathcal{Z}_i$ is the set of all occurrences of g_i. The crucial role in understanding the structure of runs in F_n plays the Displacement Lemma (Lemma 2). We know that the displacement sequence is isomorphic to Fibonacci sequence, hence we can easily compute number of different types of runs by computing numbers of a's and b's in prefix segments of $\mathcal{F}_\infty$. Using Lemma 2 we can describe the structure of runs in F_n, see Figure 6.

Theorem 10. [Structure of Runs] *The Fibonacci word F_n has: F_{n-3} Φ_0-runs; $F_{n-4} - 1$ Φ_1-runs, and F_{n-k-2} Φ_k-runs for $2 \leq k \leq n - 2$.*

This gives alternative (compared with [9]) proof for the number of all runs.

Corollary 5. [9] *F_n has $2 \cdot F_{n-2} - 3$ runs.*

We say that a square xx is primitive iff x is a primitive word, similarly define primitive cubes. The run $F_i F_i g_{i-1}$ contains $|g_{i-1}|$ primitive squares and $F_i F_i F_i g_{i-1}$ contains $\Phi_i + |g_{i-1}|$ primitive squares. The short runs correspond to bab in $\mathcal{F}_\infty$ and long runs correspond to aa in $\mathcal{F}_\infty$. Due to the Fibonacci-like structure of displacement sequences (Lemma 2) and Theorem 10 we can calculate (in a new easier way) the number of all positioned primitive squares and all primitive positioned cubes in finite Fibonacci words.

4   The Structure of Suffix Trees

The suffix tree T_n of F_n is the tree of all paths of $cdawg(F_n)$. The structure of this tree and the way how T_n evolves into T_{n+1} follows from the structure and evolution of compacted dawg's, see Figure 7 and Figure 8.

A terminal edge is an edge leading to a leaf. The suffix trees of Fibonacci words grow at their leaves, by changing the terminal edges in a very simple regular way.

Theorem 11. *For $n > 2$ the suffix tree T_n of F_n has Φ_{n-1} leaves and Φ_{n-2} internal nodes. Let x be the last two symbols of F_{n+1}. T_n evolves into T_{n+1} in the following way:*

- **(long edges)** *each terminal edge (u, v) with label xF_{n-2} is transformed into the subtree isomorphic to S_n, two end symbols are cut off from the label of (u, v), and two edges originated at v are created, with labels $x^R F_{n-1}$ and x,*
- **(short edges)** *each terminal edge with label x changes its labels to $x \cdot F_{n-1}$.*

We know precisely how the suffix trees grow. The sum of lengths of edges of the suffix tree is the number of different subwords. We have Φ_{n-3} short edges, each of them grows by Φ_{n-1}, and Φ_{n-2} long edges, each grows by $\Phi_{n-1} + 2$. This gives easily a simple recurrence and a new suffix-tree oriented proof for the known formula of the number $Sub(n)$ of different subwords of F_n.

Corollary 6. *For $n > 2$ we have:*

$$Sub(n + 1) = Sub(n) + \Phi_{n-3} \cdot \Phi_{n-1} + \Phi_{n-2} \cdot (\Phi_{n-1} + 2)$$
$$Sub(n) = \Phi_{n-1}\Phi_{n-2} + 2 \cdot \Phi_{n-1} - 1$$

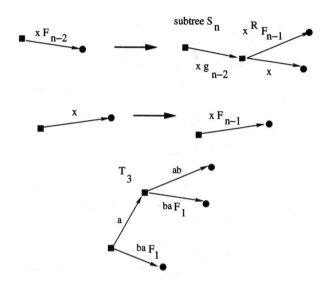

Fig. 7. The suffix tree T_3 and the general rules to generate T_{n+1} from T_n. The word $x \in \{ab, \ ba\}$.

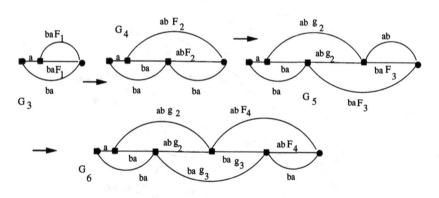

Fig. 8. The evolution of the compacted graph $cdawg(F_6)$

We say that two labelled trees are structurally isomorphic iff they are isomorphic as unordered trees in graph-theoretic sense, disregarding the labels. The following fact also follows from the structure of cdawg's.

Theorem 12. [Fibonacci-like structure of suffix trees of Fibonacci words] *For $n > 4$ the two subtrees rooted at the sons of the root of the suffix tree $T(F_n)$ are structurally isomorphic to the suffix trees $T(F_{n-1})$ and $T(F_{n-2})$, respectively.*

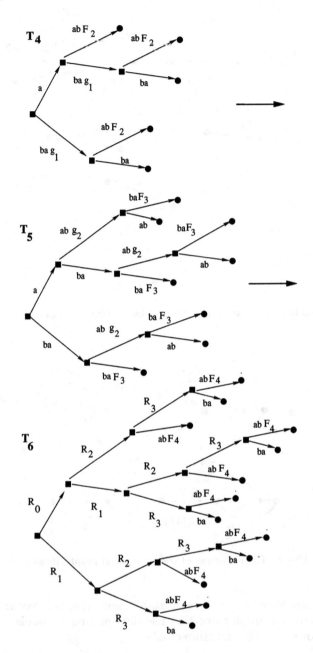

Fig. 9. The evolution of the suffix tree $T_6 = T(F_6)$. Observe that g_1 is the empy string and that the labels $ab\ g_i$ (for even i) and $ba\ g_j$ (for odd j) are reverses of Fibonacci words, denote $R_k = F_k^R$. We can obtain *in the limit* an infinite suffix tree $\mathcal{T}_\infty$ of $\mathcal{F}_\infty$. Each path in $\mathcal{T}_\infty$ will have the sequence of labels $R_{i_1}, R_{i_2}, R_{i_3} \ldots$, where $i_1 \in \{0,1\}$ and for each k we have: $i_{k+1} \in \{i_k + 1, i_k + 2\}$.

Acknowledgment. I thank Łukasz Mikulski [10] for helpful comments related to Lemma 4. He has written an independent and more formal proof of this lemma. The subword graphs for general Sturmian words have been already considered in [11]. There is a huge literature on Sturmian words (each Fibonacci word is a Sturmian one).

References

1. Crochemore, M., Rytter, W.: Jewels of stringology: text algorithms. World Scientific (2003)
2. Smyth, W.: Computing Patterns in Strings. Addison-Wesley (2003)
3. Zeckendorff, E.: Représentation des nombres naturels par une somme des nombres de fibonacci ou de nombres de lucas. Bulletin de la Société Royale des Sciences de Liège **41** (1972) 179–182
4. Costas Iliopoulos, D.M., Smyth, W.: A characterization of the squares in a fibonacci string. Theor. Comput. Sci. **172** (1997) 281–291
5. Charras, C., Lecroq, T.: Handbook of Exact String Matching Algorithms. King's College London Publications (2004)
6. Harju, T., Nowotka, D.: Density of critical factorizations. ITA **36** (2002) 315–327
7. Berstel, J., Karhumaki, J.: Combinatorics on words – a tutorial. Bulletin of the EATCS **79** (2003) 178–228
8. Mignosi, F., Pirillo, G.: Repetitions in the fibonacci infinite word. RAIRO Inform. Theor. Appl. **26** (1992) 199–204
9. Kolpakov, R., Kucherov, G.: Finding maximal repetitions in a word in linear time. In: FOCS '99: Proceedings of the 40th Annual Symposium on Foundations of Computer Science, Washington, DC, USA, IEEE Computer Society (1999) 596
10. Mikulski, Ł.: Personal communication (2005)
11. Epifanio, C., Mignosi, F., Shallit, J., Venturini, I.: Sturmian graphs and a conjecture of moser. In Calude, C., Calude, E., Dinneen, M.J., eds.: Developments in Language Theory. Volume 3340 of Lecture Notes in Comput. Sci., Springer (2004) 175–187

Observations on Determinization of Büchi Automata

Christoph Schulte Althoff, Wolfgang Thomas, and Nico Wallmeier

RWTH Aachen, Lehrstuhl Informatik 7, 52056 Aachen, Germany
{althoff, thomas, wallmeier}@i7.informatik.rwth-aachen.de

Abstract. The two determinization procedures of Safra and Muller-Schupp for Büchi automata are compared, based on an implementation in a program called OmegaDet.

1 Introduction

A central result in the theory of ω-automata is McNaughton's Theorem [1]. In its original formulation it says that a nondeterministic Büchi automaton can be converted into a deterministic Muller automaton. Many constructions have been proposed to show this determinization result (cf. [2], [3] for hints to the literature). In most cases, the target automaton is a deterministic Rabin automaton, which can be considered as a special form of Muller automaton. It is well-known that the blow-up in number of states has to be greater than in the classical subset construction; there is a lower bound of $2^{O(n \log n)}$ for the number of states of a deterministic Rabin automaton, given a Büchi automaton with n states ([4], [5]).

Safra [6] was the first to find a construction which matches this lower bound. It seems now the standard way of showing Büchi automata determinization. But there is a second construction, again matching the lower bound, due to Muller and Schupp [7]. Teaching experience of the second author indicates that the Muller-Schupp proof can be explained more easily (the reader can judge him/herself below). The two constructions are sufficiently different to justify a closer comparison. This is the aim of present paper.

The study is based on an implementation of the two algorithms in a program called OmegaDet. As it turns out, such an implementation is necessary not only for a serious experimental performance comparison of the two procedures but also for a better conceptual understanding of their behaviour. The two algorithms are too involved to be analyzed by hand if one is interested in studying say a dozen examples. We report here on some insights we obtained in this investigation, both regarding a better understanding of the characteristics (and the similarities) of two the algorithms and of their performance. We observe that (apart from some peripheral cases), the Safra algorithm uses stronger abstractions than the one of Muller-Schupp and thus yields smaller automata. (Maybe this is a reason for the difficulties the Safra algorithm poses for exposition in lectures.) Moreover, our experiments led to an improvement of the Muller-Schupp procedure which can reduce the state space of the target automaton.

J. Farré, I. Litovsky, and S. Schmitz (Eds.): CIAA 2005, LNCS 3845, pp. 262–272, 2006.
© Springer-Verlag Berlin Heidelberg 2006

The paper is structured as follows. In the subsequent Section 2 we present the determinization procedures, with an emphasis on singling out those points where they coincide and where they differ. In this exposition, we use the insights from our experiments; we start with an explanation of the Muller-Schupp algorithm and more briefly discuss the Safra construction. We do not give any details about the correctness proofs. In Section 3 we give a brief introduction to (the user's view of) the program OmegaDet, in which also the subset based construction of Hayashi and Miyano [8] for co-Büchi automata determinization is included. We report on observations obtained in case studies and suggest the above mentioned improvement of the Muller-Schupp algorithm. In Section 4 we comment on the context of our work as well as on perspectives for extensions.

2   The Algorithms of Safra and Muller-Schupp

We consider Büchi automata in the format $\mathcal{A} = (Q, \Sigma, q_0, \Delta, F)$ where Q is the finite set of states, Σ the input alphabet, q_0 the initial state, $\Delta \subseteq Q \times \Sigma \times Q$ the transition relation, and $F \subseteq Q$ the set of "final states". The automaton $\mathcal{A}$ accepts the ω-word $\alpha \in \Sigma^\omega$ if a a run $\rho \in Q^\omega$ exists (defined in the standard way) with infinitely many occurrences of states in F. In other words, one may consider the *run tree* t_α of $\mathcal{A}$ on α, which has a root (considered to be at "level 0") labelled q_0, and displays level by level the states reached after the α-prefixes $\alpha(0) \ldots \alpha(i-1)$ for $i = 0, 1, 2, \ldots$. Formally, a vertex on level i labelled p has the successor nodes labelled $q_1, \ldots, q_k$ if for p and the letter $a = \alpha(i)$ the transitions $(p, a, q_1), \ldots, (p, a, q_k)$ are applicable. We assume the tree to be sibling ordered, with reference to an ordering of the set of states. The *run dag* r_α of $\mathcal{A}$ on α is obtained inductively from t_α, level by level, by deleting a vertex v labelled q if on the same level a vertex u labelled q appears to the left; in this case an edge is added from the parent vertex of v to u. Clearly, the input word α is accepted by $\mathcal{A}$ iff in the run dag r_α there is an infinite path from the root on which an F-state occurs infinitely often (henceforth we just speak of a "successful path").

A deterministic Rabin automaton (we say "Rabin automaton" to be short) has the format $\mathcal{A} = (Q, \Sigma, q_0, \delta, \Omega)$ where Q, Σ, q_0 are as for Büchi automata, $\delta : Q \times \Sigma \to Q$ is the transition function, and $\Omega = ((E_1, F_1), \ldots, (E_k, F_k))$ a list of "accepting pairs" with $E_j, F_j \subset Q$. The automaton accepts the input word $\alpha \in \Sigma^\omega$ if for the unique run $\rho \in Q^\omega$ of $\mathcal{A}$ on α an index j exists such that some F_j-state is visited infinitely often in ρ but each E_j-state only finitely often.

The starting point for the transformation of a Büchi automaton $\mathcal{A} = (Q, \Sigma, q_0, \Delta, F)$ into an equivalent Rabin automaton (i.e., recognizing the same ω-language) is to use a finite abstraction of the infinity of the finite prefixes of run trees. If the Büchi automaton has scanned the prefix $\alpha(0) \ldots \alpha(i-1)$ of the input, the run tree up to level i is built up. Taking the run dag instead, one observes that a structure of finite width suffices (since each state can occur at most once on each level). The main point of the transformation of $\mathcal{A}$ into a finite deterministic automaton is to invent a finite number of representations of the infinitely many possible run dag prefixes, in a way that the existence of an infinite path with infinitely many F-states can still be detected. For this, it is necessary to separate the different threads of the run tree (or run dag) for recording of the occurrence of final states. Both algorithms, the procedures by Safra and Muller-Schupp, use tree structures for this purpose. A node in such a tree provides the information which states are presently visited in certain threads of the run tree; in particular, the root records the totality of presently reachable states (as in the classical subset construction). Also both procedures adopt the convention that a state is kept only at its leftmost occurrence on a tree level, thus inheriting the rule mentioned above for constructing run dags.

2.1 Muller-Schupp Trees

Let us first introduce the tree structures used by Muller and Schupp, called Muller-Schupp trees in the present paper. A *Muller-Schupp tree* is a finite sibling-ordered strictly binary tree (i.e., each vertex except the leaves has precisely two sons), whose vertices are named with positive natural numbers and additionally are labelled by two items: a subset of Q and a color from the set $\{\text{red}, \text{yellow}, \text{green}\}$. Since by construction the set of states at a parent node is the disjoint union of the sets at the two sons, it would suffice to keep state-sets as labels only for the leaves; however, for easier readability of the trees we prefer to use the state-set labelling throughout.

The Muller-Schupp trees can be motivated in three stages, starting from the computation tree t_α of the given Büchi automaton on some input word α. The first step consists in partitioning the sons of a vertex v into two classes, those which carry a final state and those which carry a non-final state. The former are collected in a set and declared as the label of the left son of v, the latter (non-final) ones form the label of the right son (of course, one of the two sons can vanish). Call the resulting tree with at most binary branching the "acceptance tree" t_α^1. It is easy to verify that

t_α has a successful path iff t_α^1 has a path branching left infinitely often

If we keep only the occurrences of a state q which occur leftmost on the respective level of the tree t_α^1, obtaining the tree t_α^2, the equivalence above holds also for t_α^2 instead of t_α^1.

The tree t_α^2 grows in a deterministic fashion level by level, given α. Note that each level has at most as many entries as there are states in $\mathcal{A}$, so t_α^2 is of bounded width. The idea is to take as states of the deterministic Rabin automaton compressed versions of the t_α^2-prefixes, level by level: A path segment from a left son, respectively a right son, or from the root, to the next branching point v is contracted into v. Then a strictly binary tree is obtained. The states of such a path segment are forgotten except some information about the presence of final states, given by three different colors which the remaining vertex v can have: red, yellow, and green. It is clear that the number of such trees is finite.

The update step upon processing an input letter a (corresponding to the extension of t_α^2 by one level), is performed by attaching sons to the leaves according to the subset construction, starting from the state set at each leaf. Of course, no son is introduced to a leaf if from none of its states a continuation of the run via

a is possible. This case leads to the deletion of the whole path back to the last branching point. Vertex names which are freed by this can be reused, however not in the same update step. In the remaining case a left son, a right son, or both are introduced, depending on whether there are only final states, only non-final states, or both in the resulting state set. When a final state is encountered, the vertex carrying it is colored green. By the cancellation policy (to keep only the leftmost occurrence of a state) and the path compression procedure it can happen that path segments are merged in a single vertex (again setting free name of the spared vertex). In this case the parent vertex may receive final states from a son with which it is merged; we say then that it "receives a new final state".

A vertex is colored red if the path segment it represents has no final state, yellow if it has a final state but did not receive this state in the last step, and it is colored green if it received a final state in the last step, either at a leaf via the subset construction or by a merge step, for example with a vertex previously colored yellow.

Using this update procedure, it turns out that t_α^2 has a path branching left infinitely often iff in the sequence of corresponding Muller-Schupp trees some vertex v stays forever from some point onwards and has the color green again and again. This is captured by a Rabin acceptance condition of pairs (E_i, F_i) where i ranges over the finite reservoir of vertex names: E_i contains those trees where i is missing, and F_i has those trees where i occurs colored green.

Formally, the update for a tree t and input letter a is carried out as follows:

Update of Muller-Schupp tree

1. Copy the given tree t, changing all colors green to yellow
2. Apply the subset construction (via letter a) to each leaf, add left and right son carrying the reached final, respectively non-final states; color these sons green and red, respectively.
3. Keep only the leftmost occurrence of each state.
4. Delete the vertices which are only on paths leading to leaves whose value is the empty set.
5. As long as there exists a vertex of degree one merge this vertex with its successor, inheriting the color green if this successor was colored green or yellow.
6. Proceeding from the leaves, label each parent by the union of the two state sets from the labelling of the two sons.

2.2   Safra Trees

The Safra trees are more succinct in the sense that they suppress as much as possible the record of non-final states. Starting from the update step of the Muller-Schupp algorithm (which of course was not the way these algorithms were invented), the Safra construction introduces a technical simplification when the subset construction is applied: Here only the left son (containing the final states reached) is kept in the tree, no right son for the non-final states is introduced.

When from these non-final states at later stages final states are reached, new son vertices are created successively in the Safra tree; in this situation more than binary branching may occur. In a Muller-Schupp tree the intermediate vertices with non-final state-sets amount to a binary encoding of the Safra trees. However, due to different coloring policies, the embedding of a Safra tree into the corresponding Muller-Schupp tree cannot in general be lifted to an embedding of the Safra state space into the Muller-Schupp state space. In particular, a Safra automaton can also be larger than the corresponding Muller-Schupp automaton; cf. the remark at the end of Section 3. A didactic advantage of the Muller-Schupp trees is that they convey more directly the structure of the computation tree of the given Büchi automaton.

The difference of colorings reflects different recordings of visits of final states. The Muller-Schupp procedure uses the coloring policy to signal "new visits to final states". The Safra algorithm marks a node by color green according to the so-called breakpoint construction, signalling that all states of the node can be reached via a *past* visit to a final state. Similarly as for Muller-Schupp trees, a run is accepting if some vertex stays indefinitely from some point onwards and is colored green again and again. For the formal definition of Safra trees and their update function we refer the reader to [6] or [9].

Example 1. Let $\mathcal{A}_0$ be the Büchi automaton

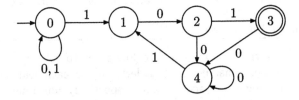

which accepts the 0-1-sequences which have the segment 11 only finitely often but 101 infinitely often. In the figure on the next page we present the run dag for the input word $10101010\ldots$, right to it the run of Safra trees, and aside that the run of Muller-Schupp trees. We skip the intermediate stages in the construction process between two successive trees. A vertex is named by a number; following the stroke we list the states belonging to its label. In a Muller-Schupp tree, a vertex colored red is given as a dashed rectangle, colored yellow as a simple rectangle, and colored green as a double-line rectangle. Similarly, the vertices of a Safra tree receiving the mark green are displayed in double-line rectangles.

3   Implementation, Experiments, Conclusions

OmegaDet is a program written in C++ which offers implementations of four determinization procedures for Büchi automata:

– the Safra construction
– the Muller-Schupp construction

Input	Run dag	Safra	Muller-Schupp

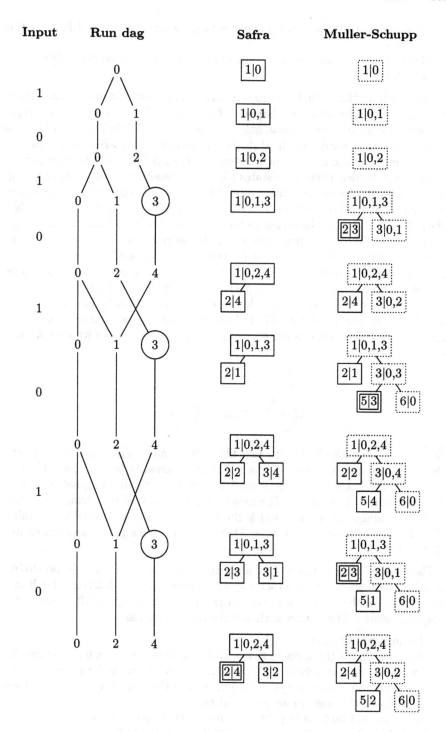

- an optimized Muller-Schupp construction (which is presented later in this section)
- the Hayashi-Miyano construction (which can be applied to co-Büchi automata)

The fourth option is included since many examples we considered turned out to be co-Büchi automata. This happens, for example, in cases where the accepting loops consist of a single state only. In this case the Büchi condition holds iff from some time onwards only final states are encountered (co-Büchi acceptance). Other examples were not co-Büchi automata as such but could be transformed to this shape by declaring more states (than previously) as final, without changing the accepted language. Thus a useful preprocessing consists in successively declaring as final all states from which in one step only final states are reachable, which does not change the language but might lead to a co-Büchi automaton.

The Hayashi-Miyano construction is a simple refinement of the subset construction, needing only $2^{O(n)}$ states (essentially two subsets) and will be preferable if a large automaton can be presented as a co-Büchi automaton. An implementation exists also in the LASH package at Liège (see [8, 10, 11]).

The program OmegaDet asks the user to supply a Büchi automaton as a text file. The format of text file is best explained by an example. Consider the following Büchi automaton $\mathcal{A}_1$ which accepts all ω-words with only finitely many b.

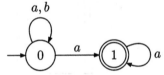

2
ab
1
0 a 0
0 b 0
0 a 1
1 a 1

The first line of the text file is the number n of states of the Büchi automaton, whose state set is then assumed to be $\{0, ..., n-1\}$. The initial state is 0. The second line contains the used alphabet Σ as a string of single ASCII symbols. Each symbol of the string is used as a single letter. Afterwards the final states are numerated in the third line separated by spaces. Then the transitions of the automaton are listed.

The user can choose the desired algorithms in a menu. He has the possibility to either simulate a run interactively or to compute the deterministic Rabin automaton. In the latter case, the program reports progress after every 200 computed states. The output is then delivered in four parts:

- the number of states
- the list of Safra trees, respectively Muller Schupp trees, each introduced by a name si, respectively ki (for $i = 0, 1, ...$) together with the word (the first in the canonical ordering of words) via which the state is reached, and then a display of the tree (to be explained below),
- the transition table, using the state names si, respectively ki,
- the list of accepting pairs and number of accepting pairs

For the display of trees, a textual representation is used which indicates the sons of some node by the subsequent lines, marked as sons by indentation after a pointer symbol +->. So brother nodes are listed with same indentation. The colors red, yellow, green are presented as the symbols -, 0, +, following each vertex in Muller-Schupp trees; in Safra trees a mark ! is attached to a vertex if it has color green.

As an example of the output we list the automaton according to Safra generated by the example above.

```
Deterministic Rabin automaton
according to Safra:                    Transition table:
                                              a    b
4 States:                              s0   s1   s0
s0:                                    s1   s2   s0
     [1|0]                             s2   s3   s0
                                       s3   s3   s0
s1: a
     [1|0,1]                           Acceptance pairs:
                                       for vertex 2 (sizes 2,1):
s2: aa                                 ({s0,s1},{s3})
     [1|0,1]
     +-> [2|1]                         Overall: 1 pair with non-empty
                                       acceptance set
s3: aaa
     [1|0,1]
     +-> [2|1]!
```

We used the program for various Büchi automata, among them also the automata suggested by Michel [4] for showing the $2^{O(n \log n)}$ lower bound for complementation of Büchi automata (see also [3] and [9]). Recall that the Büchi automaton $\mathcal{M}_n$ considered in [4] has states $0, \ldots, n$, the input alphabet $\{1, \ldots, n, \sharp\}$ and the following transition graph:

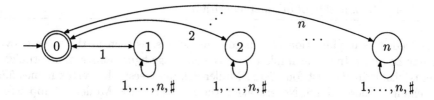

While we could compute the Rabin automaton according to Safra's construction easily up to automaton $\mathcal{M}_5$ (where a million states are reached for the first time), the Rabin automaton following Muller-Schupp has about 5 million states already for $\mathcal{M}_3$, and the system ran out of memory for $\mathcal{M}_4$ (see Table 1). The reader can obtain an impression of the program Omega-

Table 1. Comparison of Safra, Muller-Schupp and optimized Muller-Schupp

	Safra		Muller-Schupp		Opt. Muller-Schupp	
	States	Pairs	States	Pairs	States	Pairs
M_1 (2 states)	7	1	9	5	9	5
M_2 (3 states)	33	2	4,058	8	262	7
M_3 (4 states)	385	5	4,823,543	11	23,225	9
M_4 (5 states)	13,601	7	memory exceeded		3,656,802	11
M_5 (6 states)	1,059,057	9	memory exceeded		memory exceeded	

Det by calling `http://www-i7.informatik.rwth-aachen.de/d/research/omegadet.html`; there the program itself, as well as the text files for the automata $M_1, \ldots, M_5$ and the output files are listed.

It was already mentioned in the previous section that the Muller-Schupp trees tend to be larger due to the inclusion of vertices whose labels are formed from non-final states. A more serious effect, however, is the procedure for introducing new vertices as sons of the leaves and the naming scheme pursued here. Many trees can be generated which have the same structure of vertex labels (and colors), whereas a difference occurs in the vertex naming. An idea to spare vertex names is to add new sons only for leaves which contain final states as well as non-final states. This may result in the freeing of vertex names which may then be reused more quickly.

Formally, we proceed as follows in this modification of the Muller-Schupp algorithm:

Optimized update of Muller-Schupp tree

---

1. Copy the given tree t, changing all colors green to yellow
2. Apply the subset construction (via letter a) to each leaf.
3. Keep only the leftmost occurrence of each state.
4. For all leaves which contain final states as well as non-final states add left and right son carrying the reached final, respectively non-final states; color these sons green and red, respectively.
5. Color all leaves containing only final states green.
6. Items 4., 5. and 6. of original algorithm

Indeed, this modification can spare many states, as seen in the table above (fourth column). In the example run of the one-page figure above, the optimization is visible in the last four listed Muller-Schupp trees: The vertex names 5,6 are changed there to 4,5. Nevertheless, the number of the Muller-Schupp trees grows still much faster than the number of Safra trees.

More case studies are reported in [12]. A simple general statement relating the numbers of states of the two constructions is not obvious, since we observed several cases where the Safra construction gives a slightly larger automaton than the Muller-Schupp procedure. This happens, for example, for the automaton A_1 considered above, where the Safra construction yields four states and the

Muller-Schupp construction (the normal one as well as the optimized one) only two states. The delayed signalization of "success" (by an extended initialization) yields different Safra trees, distinguished by different colorings, for a unique Muller-Schupp tree. A possibility to spare states in the Safra construction, which appears in the exposition of [3], is to exchange the application of the powerset construction and the creation of sons. In the example just mentioned this spares one state, however still leads to a larger Safra automaton than the Muller-Schupp one.

4   Outlook

We have presented the determinization procedures of Safra and Muller-Schupp, working out their similarities and their differences. Remarks on the implementation focussed on the input and output format and the explanation of simple case studies. In Michel's example we found a drastic difference between the two procedures, giving an advantage to Safra's algorithm. We explained this effect and suggested an improvement of the Muller-Schupp algorithm, giving (in some cases) much smaller automata.

As a result of our experimental studies we found a tighter connection between the two algorithms than expected, and we found the superiority of the Safra procedure for building small automata.

Despite much research, the determinization algorithms have so far not reached the stage of application examples of any serious scale, in definite contrast to the many implementations based on Büchi automata and alternating automata, applied mostly in model-checking. On the other hand, determinization is a necessary prerequisite in certain domains, for example in the solution of games with regular winning conditions (where a presentation by nondeterministic automata does not suffice). It seems that before reaching real practice, determinization still needs more investigation, not only with respect to the procedures as such (as done in this paper) but also concerning the phases of "preprocessing" and "postprocessing". The preprocessing phase would involve an analysis of the given Büchi automaton, possibly its reduction e.g. with methods of [13] and the test whether it can as well be represented as a co-Büchi automaton. In the latter case, the simpler determinization procedure of Hayashi and Miyano [8] can be applied (see e.g. [10]). The postprocessing would deal with the reduction or even minimization of deterministic Rabin automata, and it would have to deal with a parameter which we did not consider in the present paper: the complexity of the acceptance condition (number of accepting pairs in a Rabin automaton). So the present paper just addresses a single aspect in the general problem of implementing Büchi automaton determinization.

Acknowledgement

We thank Detlef Kähler for his presentation of [14] in our seminar and remarks on a preliminary version of the paper; we relied on his work at several places.

The second author acknowledges fruitful discussions with Christof Löding while preparing a lecture on the Muller-Schupp algorithm.

References

1. McNaughton, R.: Testing and generating infinite sequences by a finite automaton. Information and Control **9** (1966) 521–530
2. Thomas, W.: Automata on Infinite Objects. In van Leeuwen, J., ed.: Handbook of Theoretical Computer Science. Volume B, Formal models and semantics. Elsevier Science Publishers B. V. (1990) 133–191
3. Perrin, D., Pin, J.E.: Infinite Words: Automata, Semigroups, Logic and Games. Volume 141 of Pure and Applied Mathematics. Elsevier (2004)
4. Michel, M.: Complementation is more difficult with automata on infinite words. CNET, Paris (1988)
5. Löding, C.: Optimal bounds for the transformation of omega-automata. In: Proc. of the 19th Conference on Foundations of Software Technology and Theoretical Computer Science. Volume 1738 of Lecture Notes in Computer Science., Springer-Verlag (1999) 97–109
6. Safra, S.: On the Complexity of ω-Automata. In: Proc. of the 29th Symp. on Foundations of Computer Science, Los Alamitos, CA, IEEE Computer Society Press (1988) 319–327
7. Muller, D., Schupp, P.: Simulating Alternating Tree Automata by Nondeterministic Automata: New Results and New Proofs of the Theorems of Rabin, McNaughton and Safra. Theoretical Computer Science **141** (1995) 69–107
8. Miyano, S., Hayashi, T.: Alternating Finite Automata on ω-Words. Theor. Comput. Sci. **32** (1984) 321–330
9. Thomas, W.: Languages, Automata and Logic. In: Handbook of Formal Language Theory. Volume III. Springer-Verlag (1997) 389–455
10. Boigelot, B., Jodogne, S., Wolper, P.: An Effective Decision Procedure for Linear Arithmetic with Integer and Real Variables. ACM Transaction on Computational Logic (to appear) (2005)
11. : (The Liège Automata-based Symbolic Handler (LASH)) Available at http://www.montefiore.ulg.ac.be/~boigelot/research/lash/.
12. Schulte-Althoff, C.: Construction of deterministic ω-automata: A comparative analysis of the algorithms by safra and muller/schupp. Diplomarbeit, RWTH Aachen (2005)
13. Etessami, K., Wilke, T., Schuller, R.A.: Fair Simulation Relations, Parity Games, and State Space Reduction for Büchi Automata. In: Proc. of ICALP 2001. Volume 2076 of Lecture Notes in Computer Science., Springer-Verlag (2001) 694–707
14. Kähler, D.: Determinisierung von ω-Automaten. Diplomarbeit, Christian-Albrechts-Universität zu Kiel (2001)

The Interval Rank of Monotonic Automata

Tamara Shcherbak*

Ural State University, 620083 Ekaterinburg, Russia
tomsya@mail.ur.ru

Abstract. We solve the 'order preserving' version of the generalized Černý problem (also known as the rank problem). Namely, for all n and k such that $2 \leq k \leq n$, we determine the least number $\ell(n,k)$ such that for each monotonic automaton with n states and interval rank k there exists a word of length $\ell(n,k)$ that compresses the state set of the automaton to an interval of length k.

1 Motivation and Overview

A deterministic finite automaton (DFA) $\mathcal{A} = \langle Q, \Sigma, \delta \rangle$ is called *monotonic* if its state set Q admits a linear order $\leq$ such that for each letter $a \in \Sigma$ the transformation $\delta(\_, a)$ of Q *preserves* $\leq$. This means that $\delta(q,a) \leq \delta(q',a)$ whenever $q \leq q'$. Though monotonic automata form quite a natural subclass of the class of counter-free automata, they not yet well studied and remain mysterious in some respects: for instance, no combinatorial characterization of the class of rational languages recognized by monotonic automata has been found so far.

Recall that the *rank* of a DFA $\mathcal{A} = \langle Q, \Sigma, \delta \rangle$ is the least cardinality of sets of the form $\delta(Q, w)$ where w runs over Σ^*. Automata of rank 1 are also known as *synchronizable* (or *directed*): for a synchronizable automaton $\mathcal{A}$, there exists a word whose action 'resets' $\mathcal{A}$, i.e. brings all its states to a particular one. Any word with this property is said to be a *reset* word for the automaton $\mathcal{A}$. The famous *Černý conjecture* [1] claims that each synchronizable automaton with n states possesses a reset word of length at most $(n-1)^2$. Its generalization known as the *rank conjecture* (cf., e.g., [2]) claims that for every DFA $\mathcal{A} = \langle Q, \Sigma, \delta \rangle$ with n states and rank k there is a word $w \in \Sigma^*$ of length at most $(n-k)^2$ such that $|\delta(Q, w)| = k$. Both conjectures are open in general and reveal many interesting connections with other areas of mathematics and computer science, see the recent survey [3].

Synchronization properties of monotonic automata have been studied in the recent paper [4]. It has turned out that the presence of a stable order on the state set speeds up synchronization: for every monotonic DFA $\mathcal{A} = \langle Q, \Sigma, \delta \rangle$ with n states and rank k there is a word $w \in \Sigma^*$ of length at most $n - k$ such that $|\delta(Q, w)| = k$ [4–Theorem 1]. A related but more complicated problem (also

---

* The work was supported by the Federal Education Agency of Russia, grant no. 49123 and the Russian Foundation for Basic Research, grant 05-01-00540.

J. Farré, I. Litovsky, and S. Schmitz (Eds.): CIAA 2005, LNCS 3845, pp. 273–281, 2006.
© Springer-Verlag Berlin Heidelberg 2006

discussed in [4]) arises when one modifies the above notion of the rank in the following way. For any non-empty subset $P \subset Q$, let $[P]$ denote the least interval of the chain $\langle Q, \leq \rangle$ containing P. Now, given a monotonic DFA $\mathcal{A} = \langle Q, \Sigma, \delta \rangle$, one defines its *interval rank* as the least cardinality of intervals of the form $[\delta(Q, w)]$ where w runs over Σ^*. Clearly, monotonic automata of interval rank k have usual rank at most k but the converse is not true for $k > 1$, and the interval rank of a monotonic automata with n states and rank 2 can be equal even to n.

It is to be expected that compressing to small intervals requires more effort than compressing to just small subsets that can be scattered over the state set in an arbitrary way. Let $\ell(n, k)$ stand for the least number such that for each monotonic automaton with n states and interval rank $k \geq 2$, there exists a word of length $\ell(n, k)$ that compresses the state set of the automaton to an interval of length k. A series of examples [4] shows that no linear function of n can serve as an upper bound for the function $\ell(n, 2)$ [4–Propositions 1 and 2]. On the other hand, Theorem 2 of [4] gives the following quadratic upper bound for the function $\ell(n, k)$ for all $n > k \geq 2$:

$$\ell(n, k) \leq \frac{(n - k)(n - k - 1)}{2} + 1. \tag{1}$$

This bound has been shown to be exact for all 'sufficiently large' k, that is, for all $k \geq \lfloor \frac{n}{2} \rfloor$ [4–Propositions 3 and 4]. However, the problem of determining the function $\ell(n, k)$ for $2 \leq k < \lfloor \frac{n}{2} \rfloor$ was left open in [4]. In the present paper we solve this problem by showing that for all $n \geq k \geq 2$ one has

$$\ell(n, k) \leq \lceil \frac{n(n - 2)}{4} - \frac{(k + 1)(k - 2)}{2} \rceil \tag{2}$$

and exhibiting a series of examples that demonstrate that this bound is precise for $2 \leq k < \lfloor \frac{n}{2} \rfloor$.

The proofs, though elementary in their essence, are far from being easy and require relatively long calculations. Due to size limitations, we include here detailed proofs only for the case $k = 2$ while results and examples related to the case $k > 2$ are presented on a less formal level.

2   An Upper Bound for $\ell(n, 2)$

We may assume that the state set Q of our monotonic automaton $\mathcal{A} = \langle Q, \Sigma, \delta \rangle$ is the set $\{1, 2, 3, \ldots, n\}$ of the first n positive integers with the usual order $1 < 2 < 3 < \cdots < n$. For $x, y \in Q$ such that $x \leq y$, we denote by $[x, y]$ the interval $\{x, x + 1, x + 2, \ldots, y\}$. Given a word $w \in \Sigma^*$ and nonempty subset $X \subseteq Q$, we write $X \cdot w$ for the set $\{\delta(x, w) \mid x \in X\}$.

Now assume that the interval rank of the automaton $\mathcal{A}$ equals 2.

Lemma 1. *If* $Q \cdot w = [m, m + 1]$, *then*

$$\delta(q, w) = \begin{cases} m & \text{whenever } q \leq m, \\ m + 1 & \text{whenever } q \geq m + 1. \end{cases}$$

Proof. As the word w compresses the set Q to the interval $[m, m + 1]$ either $\delta(q, w) = m$ or $\delta(q, w) = m + 1$ for every $q \in Q$. Suppose that $\delta(m, w) = m + 1$ and consider the action of w^2 on Q. We see that

$$Q.w^2 = (Q.w).w = [m, m + 1].w = \{m + 1\}$$

whence rank of $\mathcal{A}$ is equal to 1, a contradiction. Thus, $\delta(m, w) = m$ and hence $\delta(q, w) = m$ for all $q \leq m$ by the monotonicity of the automaton. The second half of the lemma is proved in a symmetric way.

Let W_2 be the set of all words $w \in \Sigma^*$ such that $||Q.w|| = 2$.

Lemma 2. *For every word $v \in \Sigma^*$ and for every word $w \in W_2$, the interval $[Q.v]$ contains the interval $[Q.w]$.*

Proof. Arguing by contradiction, assume there exist $v \in \Sigma^*$ and $w \in W_2$ such that $[Q.w] = [m, m + 1] \not\subseteq [Q.v] = [x, y]$. Then either $m + 1 \leq x$ or $y \leq m$. Suppose for certainty that $m + 1 \leq x$ and consider the action of the word vw on Q:

$$Q.vw = (Q.v).w = [x, y].w = \{m + 1\}.$$

Here the last equality follows from Lemma 1 because $x, y \geq m + 1$. Hence rank of $\mathcal{A}$ is 1, a contradiction.

Corollary 1. *All words in W_2 compress Q to the same interval.*

Theorem 1. *For each monotonic automaton $\mathcal{A} = \langle Q, \Sigma, \delta \rangle$ of interval rank 2, the set W_2 contains a word of length at most $\left\lceil \frac{n(n-2)}{4} \right\rceil$.*

Proof. Denote the set of all non-singleton intervals of the chain $\langle Q, \leq \rangle$ by $\mathrm{int}_2(Q)$ and consider the automaton $\mathcal{I} = \langle \mathrm{int}_2(Q), \Sigma, \delta' \rangle$ where $\delta'(I, a) = [I.a]$ for any interval $I \in \mathrm{int}_2(Q)$ and for any letter $a \in \Sigma$. We call $\mathcal{I}$ the *interval automaton* of the monotonic automaton $\mathcal{A}$. The set $\mathrm{int}_2(Q)$ is naturally ordered by inclusion. We represent this order on the figures below by drawing the states of the automaton $\mathcal{I}$ as a triangular array in which intervals of the same size are aligned in the same horizontal row and the interval $[x, y]$ is placed immediately above $[x, y - 1]$ and $[x + 1, y]$.

Let $[m, m + 1]$ be the unique interval of size 2 to which the state set Q of $\mathcal{A}$ can be compressed. It is easy to see that every word in W_2 labels a path from $Q = [1, n]$ to $[m, m + 1]$ in the automaton $\mathcal{I}$, and conversely, every word labeling such a path belongs to W_2. We partition the set $\mathrm{int}_2(Q)$ into three zones: $\mathcal{Z}_1 = \{[x, y] \mid y \leq m\}$, $\mathcal{Z}_2 = \{[x, y] \mid m < x\}$ and $\mathcal{Z}_3 = \{[x, y] \mid x \leq m < y\}$, see Fig. 1.

From Lemma 2 it follows that every path starting at the state $Q = [1, n]$ in the automaton $\mathcal{I}$ never leaves the zone $\mathcal{Z}_3$. Therefore a minimum length path from Q to $[m, m + 1]$ passes only through intervals in $\mathcal{Z}_3$ and visits each of them at most once.

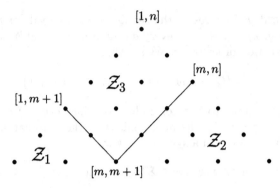

Fig. 1

In fact, we can say more by applying an argument from [4]. An interval $I \in$ int$_2(Q)$ is called *extreme* if it contains one of the two extreme states of the chain $\langle Q, \leq \rangle$. It is shown in the proof of Theorem 2 in [4] that if a minimum length path from Q to some interval I visits a non-extreme interval J then no extreme interval occurs in the subpath between J and I. Therefore the maximum number of intervals visited by a minimum length path from Q to $[m, m+1]$ is less than or equal to

$$pp(m) = (m-1)(n-m-1) + \max\{m, n-m\},$$

where the first summand is the number of non-extreme intervals in the zone $\mathcal{Z}_3$ and the second summand is the number of extreme intervals in the longest outer side of $\mathcal{Z}_3$. Fig. 2 shows one of the paths visiting all $p(m)$ 'allowed' intervals.

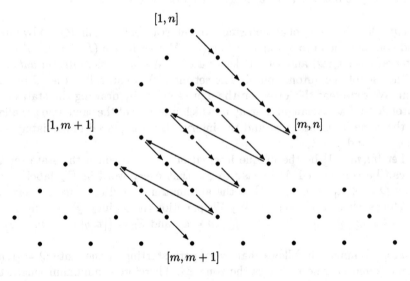

Fig. 2

Thus, the minimum length of a word in W_2 does not exceed

$$p(m) - 1 = \begin{cases} (n - m - 1)m & \text{if } m \leq n - m, \\ (n - m)(m - 1) & \text{if } m \geq n - m. \end{cases}$$

If n is even, this function reaches its maximum $\frac{n(n-2)}{4}$ at $m = \frac{n}{2}$; if n is odd, the maximum is equal to $\frac{(n-1)^2}{4}$ and it is reached at $m = \frac{n-1}{2}$ when $m \leq n - m$ and at $m = \frac{n+1}{2}$ when $m \geq n - m$. Since $\frac{(n-1)^2}{4} = \frac{n(n-2)}{4} + \frac{1}{4}$, we can express the bound as $\left\lceil \frac{n(n-2)}{4} \right\rceil$ independently of the parity of n.

3   Tightness of the Bound of Theorem 1

In order to show that the upper bound $\left\lceil \frac{n(n-2)}{4} \right\rceil$ for $\ell(n, 2)$ is tight, we have to present for each $n > 1$ an n-state monotonic automaton of interval rank 2 such that no word of length less than $\left\lceil \frac{n(n-2)}{4} \right\rceil$ compresses the states of the automaton to an interval of size 2. For each odd $n > 3$ such an automaton is exhibited in [4–Propositions 1 and 2], and the example for $n = 3$ is rather obvious: $\langle \{1, 2, 3\}, \{a\}, \delta \rangle$ with $\delta(1, a) = \delta(2, a) = 2$, $\delta(3, a) = 3$. Therefore in what follows we assume that $n = 2m$ is even. The case $n = 2$ is trivial so we assume that $n \geq 4$.

Thus, for each $m = 2, 3, \ldots$, we define an automaton $\mathcal{A}_m$ with the state set $Q_m = \{1, 2, \ldots, 2m\}$. The input alphabet Σ of $\mathcal{A}_m$ consists of three letters A, B and C whose action on the set Q_m is defined as follows:

$$\delta(q, A) = \begin{cases} 2 & \text{if } q \leq m, \\ 2m & \text{if } q > m; \end{cases} \tag{3}$$

$$\delta(q, B) = \begin{cases} 1 & \text{if } q = 1, \\ q + 1 & \text{if } 1 < q < m, \\ q & \text{if } q \geq m; \end{cases} \tag{4}$$

$$\delta(q, C) = \begin{cases} 1 & \text{if } q < m, \\ 2 & \text{if } q = m, \\ m + 1 & \text{if } q = m + 1, \\ q - 1 & \text{if } q > m + 1. \end{cases} \tag{5}$$

The next figure shows the action of Σ on the set Q_m for $m = 4$.

It is easy to see that the actions (3)–(5) preserve the natural order on the set Q_m. Therefore the automaton $\mathcal{A}_m$ is monotonic.

Recall that a subset $X \subseteq Q$ is said to be *invariant* with respect to a transformation φ of the set Q if $X\varphi \subseteq X$. It is clear that the intervals $[1, m]$ and $[m + 1, 2m]$ are invariant under the actions (3)–(5). Therefore for any word $w \in \Sigma^*$ the set $Q_m . w$ contains at least one state in $[1, m]$ and at least one state in $[m + 1, 2m]$ whence the rank of $\mathcal{A}_m$ is at least 2, and so is the interval rank of the automaton.

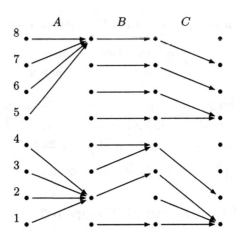

Fig. 3. The automaton $\mathcal{A}_4$

Proposition 1. *There exists a word $w \in \Sigma^*$ such that $Q_m \cdot w = [m, m+1]$.*

Proof. For each $k = 1, \ldots, m$, consider the interval $I_k = [m, m + k]$. From (4) and (5) we obtain $I_k \cdot CB^{m-2} \subseteq [m, m + k - 1] = I_{k-1}$. On the other hand, $Q_m \cdot AB^{m-2} \subseteq [m, 2m] = I_m$, and thus $Q_m \cdot w \subseteq [m, m + 1]$ for $w = AB^{m-2}(CB^{m-2})^{m-1}$. As observed above, the interval rank of $\mathcal{A}_m$ is at least 2 whence $Q_m \cdot w = [m, m + 1]$ as required.

The reader may verify that in the interval automaton corresponding to the automaton $\mathcal{A}_m$ the word $w = AB^{m-2}(CB^{m-2})^{m-1}$ labels a path of the form shown in Fig. 2 above.

As above, let W_2 be the set of all words $v \in \Sigma^*$ such that $\|[Q_m \cdot v]\| = 2$.

Proposition 2. *The length of any word $v \in W_2$ is at least $m(m - 1)$.*

Proof. From Corollary 1 we deduce that $Q_m \cdot v = [m, m+1]$, whence $[1, m] \cdot v = \{m\}$ and $[m + 1, 2m] \cdot v = \{m + 1\}$ as the intervals $[1, m]$ and $[m + 1, 2m]$ are invariant. Another consequence of the invariancy of these intervals is that $[Q \cdot uA] = [2, 2m]$ for any word $u \in \Sigma^*$.

Every word $v \in W_2$ must contain at least one occurrence of A since A is the only letter that changes the state 1. If we write v as $v = uAw$ where the suffix w contains no occurrence of A, then it is clear that the word Aw also belongs to W_2. This means that we may assume that $v = Aw$ where $w \in \{B, C\}^*$.

Calculate the actions of the following words on the state m:

$$\delta(m, AB^k) = \delta(m, CB^k) = \begin{cases} 2 + k & \text{if } k < m - 2, \\ m & \text{if } k \geq m - 2; \end{cases} \tag{6}$$

$$\delta(m, AB^k C) = \delta(m, CB^k C) = \begin{cases} 1 & \text{if } k < m - 2, \\ 2 & \text{if } k \geq m - 2. \end{cases} \tag{7}$$

Since $\delta(m, v) = m$, from (6) and (7) it follows that the word v contains no factors of the forms AB^kC and CB^kC with $0 \leq k < m - 2$. Therefore $v = AB^{k_1}CB^{k_2}\cdots CB^{k_s}$, where $k_1, k_2, \ldots, k_s \geq m - 2$. Further, we notice that the only letter that moves the states from the interval $[m+1, 2m]$ down is C and in order to move the state $2m$ to the state m the word v must have at least $m - 1$ occurrences of the letter C. Thus, $s \geq m$ and the length of v is at least $m(m-1)$.

As $m = \frac{n}{2}$, the automaton $\mathcal{A}_m$ is indeed a witness for the lower bound $\ell(n, 2) \geq \frac{n(n-2)}{4}$ for each even $n \geq 4$.

4   The Value of $\ell(n, k)$ for $2 < k < \lfloor \frac{n}{2} \rfloor$

Now let $\mathcal{A} = \langle Q, \Sigma, \delta \rangle$ be a monotonic automaton with interval rank $k > 2$. Let W_k denote the set of all words $w \in \Sigma^*$ such that $|[Q \cdot w]| = k$.

Theorem 2. *For each automaton $\mathcal{A} = \langle Q, \Sigma, \delta \rangle$ of interval rank k the set W_k contains a word of length at most*

$$\lceil \frac{n(n-2)}{4} - \frac{(k+1)(k-2)}{2} \rceil. \tag{8}$$

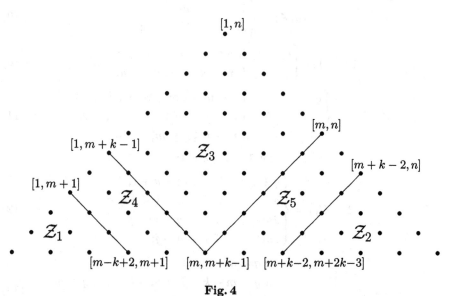

Fig. 4

Some extra complications in the proof of Theorem 2 in comparison with the one of Theorem 1 are caused by the fact that for $k > 2$ there is no uniqueness: different words from W_k may compress the state set Q to different intervals of size k. One can however prove that the number of different intervals of the form $[Q \cdot w]$ with $w \in W_k$ does not exceed $k - 1$ (and this bound is tight). Moreover, if $[m, m + k - 1]$ is one of these intervals then the leftmost and the rightmost intervals of size k that can be reached from Q are $[m - k + 2, m + 1]$ and respectively $[m + k - 2, m + 2k - 3]$.

These observations lead to a partitioning of the set $\text{int}_k(Q)$ of all at least k-element intervals of Q into the five zones shown on Fig. 4. Every path from the interval $[1, n]$ to the interval $[m, m+k-1]$ passes only through intervals from the zones $\mathcal{Z}_3$, $\mathcal{Z}_4$ and $\mathcal{Z}_5$. It can be also shown that no such path can penetrate both the zones $\mathcal{Z}_4$ and $\mathcal{Z}_5$ 'too deeply' (see Lemma 4 of the appendix for a precise formulation of the latter property). This together with the argument from [4] restricting the number of extreme intervals in a minimum length path yields the upper bound of Theorem 2.

In order to show that the upper bound is tight for $2 < k < \lfloor \frac{n}{2} \rfloor$, we have to exhibit for each $n > 2k$ an n-state monotonic automaton of interval rank k such that no word of length less than $\left\lceil \frac{n(n-2)}{4} - \frac{(k+1)(k-2)}{2} \right\rceil$ compresses the states of the automaton to an interval of size k. Here is the construction for even $n = 2m$, the construction for odd n being similar. The input alphabet Σ_k of our automaton $\mathcal{B}_{m,k} = \langle Q_m, \Sigma_k, \delta \rangle$ consists of $2k - 1$ letters $A, B_1, \ldots, B_{k-1}, C_1, \ldots, C_{k-1}$ that act on Q_m as follows:

$$\delta(q, A) = \begin{cases} 1 & \text{if } q \leq m, \\ 2m - 1 & \text{if } q > m; \end{cases} \tag{9}$$

$$\delta(q, B_1) = \begin{cases} q & \text{if } q \leq m + k - 1 \text{ or } q = 2m, \\ q - 1 & \text{if } m + k - 1 < q < 2m; \end{cases} \tag{10}$$

$$\delta(q, B_i) = \begin{cases} q & \text{if } q \leq m - i \text{ or } q > m + k - i + 1, \\ m + k - i & \text{if } m < q \leq m + k - i + 1, \\ m - i & \text{if } m - i \leq q \leq m, \end{cases} \tag{11}$$

$$\text{for } 1 < i \leq k - 1;$$

$$\delta(q, C_1) = \begin{cases} q + 1 & \text{if } q < m - k + 1, \\ q & \text{if } m - k + 1 \leq q \leq m, \\ 2m - 1 & \text{if } m < q \leq m + j, \\ 2m & \text{if } q > m + j; \end{cases} \tag{12}$$

$$\delta(q, C_j) = \begin{cases} q + 1 & \text{if } q = m - k + 1, \\ q & \text{if } q < m - k + j \text{ or } m - k + j < q \leq m, \\ 2m - 1 & \text{if } m < q \leq m + j, \\ 2m & \text{if } q > m + j, \end{cases} \tag{13}$$

$$\text{for } 1 \leq j \leq k - 1.$$

Fig. 5 shows the action of Σ_4 on the state set Q_m for $m = 6$.

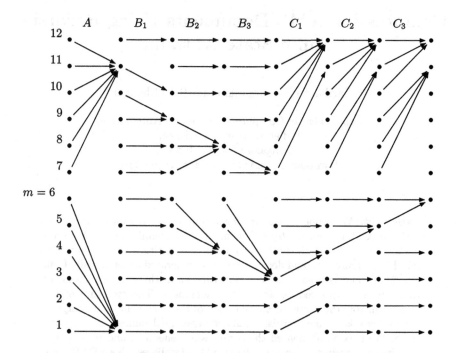

Fig. 5. The automaton $\mathcal{B}_{6,4}$

For each $\ell = 1, \ldots, k - 1$, consider the word $w_\ell = B_1^{m-k} B_2 \cdots B_{k-\ell} C_\ell$. Then it is not hard to verify that the word $A w_1^{m-k+1} w_2 w_3 \cdots w_{k-1} B_1^{m-k}$ compresses the set Q_m to the interval $[m, m + k - 1]$. With somewhat more effort one can prove that the interval rank of the automaton $\mathcal{B}_{m,k}$ is equal to k and that every word in W_k must have the length at least $m(m-1) - \frac{(k+1)(k-2)}{2}$ thus confirming the tightness of the bound (8).

Acknowledgment. The author is grateful to Dr. D. S. Ananichev for suggesting the problem and for his guidance and to Prof. M. V. Volkov and Prof. J. Almeida for several useful remarks.

References

1. Černý, J.: Poznámka k homogénnym eksperimentom s konecnými automatami. Mat.-Fyz. Cas. Slovensk. Akad. Vied. **14** (1964) 208–216 [in Slovak].
2. Rystsov, I.: Rank of a finite automaton. Cybernetics and System Analysis **28** (1992) 323–328
3. Mateescu, A., Salomaa, A.: Many-valued truth functions, Černý's conjecture and road coloring. Bull. EATCS **68** (1999) 134–150
4. Ananichev, D.S., Volkov, M.V.: Synchronizing monotonic automata. Theoret. Comput. Sci. **327** (2004) 225–239

Compressing XML Documents Using Recursive Finite State Automata

Hariharan Subramanian and Priti Shankar*

Department of Computer Science and Automation,
Indian Institute of Science,
Bangalore 560012, India
{hariharan, priti}@csa.iisc.ernet.in

Abstract. We propose a scheme for automatically generating compressors for XML documents from Document Type Definition(DTD) specifications. Our algorithm is a lossless adaptive algorithm where the model used for compression and decompression is generated automatically from the DTD, and is used in conjunction with an arithmetic compressor to produce a compressed version of the document. The structure of the model mirrors the syntactic specification of the document. Our compression scheme is on-line, that is, it can compress the document as it is being read. We have implemented the compressor generator, and provide the results of experiments on some large XML databases whose DTD's are specified. We note that the average compression is better than that of XMLPPM, the only other on-line tool we are aware of. The tool is able to compress massive documents where XMLPPM failed to work as it ran out of memory. We believe the main appeal of this technique is the fact that the underlying model is so simple and yet so effective.

1 Introduction

Extensible Markup Language(XML) [1] is a standard meta language used to describe a class of data objects, called XML documents and to specify how they are to be processed by computer programs. XML is rapidly becoming a standard for the creation and parsing of documents. However, a significant disadvantage is document size, which is a consequence of verbosity arising from markup information. It is commonly observed that non-standardized text formats for describing equivalent data are significantly shorter. Theoretically, therefore, one should be able to compress XML documents down to the same size as the compressed versions of their non-standard counterparts. XML documents have their structure specified by DTD which specify the syntax of the documents. From an information-theoretic standpoint, portions of the document that have to do with its layout should not add to its entropy. It is therefore natural to investigate the use of syntactic models for the compression of such data. Present day XML databases are massive and the need for compression is pressing.

---

* Contact Author.

J. Farré, I. Litovsky, and S. Schmitz (Eds.): CIAA 2005, LNCS 3845, pp. 282–293, 2006.
© Springer-Verlag Berlin Heidelberg 2006

A desirable feature of a compression scheme is the ability to be able to query the compressed document without decompressing the whole document. Whereas we do not address this problem in this paper, the fact that syntax plays a crucial rule in the compression model is an indication that the scheme might be amenable to extensions that can achieve this. At present the scheme *is totally automatic* where the user specifies just the DTD and the compressor and decompressor are generated. DTD syntax, is very similar to that of Extended Context Free Grammars[2]. The left hand side of each rule is an element and the right hand side is a regular expression over elements. One could therefore construct a model that mirrors the DTD in the same way that recursive descent parsers mirror the underlying LL(1) [2] grammar. What is of importance here is that the model tracks the structure of the document, and is able to make accurate predictions of the expected symbols. More importantly, whenever the predicted symbol is unique, there is no need to encode it at all as the decoder generates the same model from the DTD and is thus able to generate the unique expected symbol. Most markup symbols fall into this category of symbols. Character data associated with a single element is automatically directed to the same model for arithmetic compression irrespective of the *instance* of the element in the DTD.

The syntax directed translation scheme converts the DTD into a set of Deterministic Finite Automata (DFA) one for each element in the DTD. Each transition is labeled by an element, and the action associated with a transition is a call to a simulator for the DFA for the element labeling that transition. Every element that has some attributes or character data has an associated container. The scheme we describe automatically groups all data for the same element into a single container which is compressed incrementally using a single model for an arithmetic order-4 compressor[3,4]. We have run experiments on five large databases and compared the performance of our tool with that of two well known XML-aware compression schemes, XMill[5] and XMLPPM[6]. Two of these databases, DBLP[7] and UniProt[8] are well known. The other three (XMark[9], Michigan[10] and XOO7[11]) are XML benchmark projects. The tool XMLPPM could not compress two of the databases as it ran out of memory. The average compression ratio of our scheme is better than that of XMLPPM and significantly better than that of XMill. The time and space overheads are somewhat larger than those of XMill. This is an inherent drawback of a scheme based on arithmetic coding, which has to perform costly table updating operations after seeing every symbol. However XMill cannot perform on-line compression as can XMLPPM and our tool XAUST(*X*ML compression with *AU*tomata and a *STa*ck). Section 2 describes related work. Section 3 is a short background on arithmetic coding. Section 4 is a summary of the structure of XML documents and DTD, and this is followed by a description of our scheme. Section 5 compares our compression results with those of XMill and XMLPPM and that of a general purpose compressor `bzip2`[12]. Section 6 concludes the paper.

2   Related Work

The use of syntax in the compression of program files is not new. Cameron[13] has used Context Free Grammars (CFG) for compressing programs. Given estimates for derivation step probabilities, he has shown how to construct practical encoding systems for compression of programs whose syntax is defined by a CFG. The models are, however, fairly complex in their operation. For the scheme to be effective, these probabilities have to be learned on sample text. Syntax based schemes have also been used for machine code compression [14, 15, 16, 17]. The XML-specific compression schemes that we are aware of are XMLZIP[18], XMill and XMLPPM. The last two have tried to take advantage of the structure in XML data by either transforming the file after parsing, breaking up the tree into components[5] or injecting hierarchical element structure symbols into a model that multiplexes several models based on the syntactic structure of XML [6]. They do not require the DTD to compress the document, and even if it is available it is not used (XMill can use it but only interactively).

XMLZIP parses XML data and creates the underlying tree. It then breaks up the tree into many components, the *root* component at depth d and a component for each of the subtrees at depth d. Each of the subtrees is compressed using Java's ZIP-DEFLATE archive library. The advantage of such a scheme is that it allows limited random access to parts of the document without the need to have the whole tree in main memory.

XMill separates the structure from the content and compresses them separately. Data items are grouped into containers and each container is compressed separately. Different compressors are applied to compress different containers depending on the content. The criterion for grouping data into a container is not just the tagname but also the path from the root to the tagname. XMill does not compress the document on-line.

XMLPPM uses a modeling technique called Multiplexed Hierarchical Modeling (MHM), based on the SAX[19] encoding and on PPM[20] modeling. The technique employs two basic ideas: multiplexing several text compression models based on the syntactic structure of XML (one model for element structure, one for attributes, and so on), and injecting hierarchical element structure symbols into the multiplexed models (these are essentially root to leaf paths to the element). Multiplexing enables more effective hierarchical structure modeling. A common case for these dependencies is for the enclosing element tag to be strongly correlated with enclosed data. MHM exploits this by injecting the enclosing tag symbol into the element, attribute or string model immediately before an element, attribute or string is encoded. Injecting a symbol means telling the model that it has been seen but not explicitly encoding or decoding it.

At the cost of a degraded compression quality tools have been designed that allow certain kinds of queries on the compressed versions. Examples of such schemes are [21, 22, 23].

We first describe the well known arithmetic encoding technique that is embedded into our scheme and is an essential component of it.

3   Arithmetic Coding and Finite Context Modeling

3.1   Arithmetic Coding

Arithmetic coding does not replace every input symbol with a specific code. Instead it processes a stream of input symbols and replaces it with a single floating point output number. The longer (and more complex) the message, the more bits are needed in the output number.

The output from an arithmetic coding process is a single number less than 1 and greater than or equal to 0. This single number can be uniquely decoded to create the exact stream of symbols that went into its construction. In order to construct the output number, the symbols being encoded need to have a set of probabilities assigned to them. Initially the range of the message is the interval [0, 1). As each symbol is processed, the range is narrowed to that portion of it allocated to the symbol.

3.2   Finite Context Modeling

In a finite context scheme, the probabilities of each symbol are calculated based on the *context* the symbol appears in. In its traditional setting, the context is just the symbols that have been previously encountered. The *order* of the model refers to the number of previous symbols that make up the context. In an adaptive order k model, both the compressor and the decompresser start with the same model. The compressor encodes a symbol using the existing model and then updates the model to account for the new symbol. Typically a model is a set of frequency tables one for each context. After seeing a symbol the frequency counts in the tables are updated. The frequency counts are used to approximate the probabilities and the scheme is adaptive because this is being done as the symbols are being scanned. The decompresser similarly decodes a symbol using the existing model and then updates the model. Since there are potentially q^k possibilities for level k contexts where q is the size of the symbol space, update can be a costly process, and the tables consume a large amount of space. This causes arithmetic coding to be somewhat slower than dictionary based schemes like the Ziv-Lempel[24] scheme.

4   Automata Representing XML Documents

XML documents contain *element tags* which include start tags like `<name>` and end tags like `</name>`. Elements can nest other elements and therefore a tree structure can be associated with an XML document. Elements can also contain plain text, comments and special processing instructions for XML processors. In addition, opening element tags can have attributes with values such as **gender** in `<person gender=''female''>`. Detailed specifications are given in [1].

XML documents have to conform to a specified syntax usually in the form of a DTD. Usually XML documents are parsed to ensure that only valid data reaches an application. Most XML parsing libraries use either the SAX interface or the DOM(Document Object Model) interface. SAX is an event based interface suitable for search tools and algorithms that need one pass. The DOM model on the other hand is suitable for algorithms that have to make multiple passes.

Since XML documents are stored as plain text files one possibility is to use standard compression tools like bzip2 or ppm*. Cheney[6] has performed a study of the compression using such general purpose tools and observed that each general purpose compressor performs poorly on at least one document. Since XML documents are governed by a rather restrictive set of rules the obvious way to go, is to try to use the rules to predict what symbols to expect. Further if the rules are already known a-priori then the compressor which is tuned to take advantage of the rules can be generated directly from the rules themselves. This is what we achieve in our scheme XAUST.

The scheme proposed in this paper assumes that the DTD describing the data is known to both the sender and the receiver. Typically, an element of a DTD consists of distinct beginning and ending tags enclosing regular expressions over other elements. Elements can also contain plain text, comments and special instructions for XML processors ("processing instructions"). Opening element tags can have attributes with values.

Example 1. Consider a DTD defined as follows:

```
<!DOCTYPE addressBook[
<!ELEMENT addressBook (card*)>
<!ELEMENT card ((name | (givenName, familyName)), email, note?)>
<!ELEMENT name (#PCDATA)>
<!ELEMENT givenName (#PCDATA)>
<!ELEMENT familyName (#PCDATA)>
<!ELEMENT email (#PCDATA)>
<!ELEMENT note (#PCDATA)>
]>
```

Below is an instance of an XML document conforming to this DTD.

```
<addressBook>
<card>
<givenName>Hariharan</givenName>
<familyName>Iyer</familyName>
<email>hari@gmail.com</email>
</card>
<card>
<name>Priti Shankar</name>
<email>priti@gmail.com</email>
<note>Hariharan's advisor</note>
</card>
</addressBook>
```

The strings following each element declaration are just regular expressions over element names and therefore each of them can be associated with a DFA.

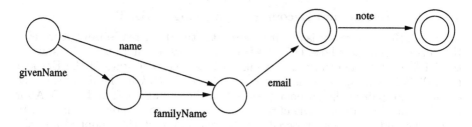

Fig. 1. DFA for the right hand side of the production for n_n in example 1

The DFA for the right hand side of the rule for element `card` is shown in Fig., 1. There are two kinds of states in this automaton, those having a single output transition and those with multiple output transitions. Symbols that label single output transitions need not be encoded as their probability is 1. Thus encoding of symbols by the arithmetic compressor needs to be performed only at states with more than one outgoing transition. An arithmetic encoding procedure is called at each such state for each element. As we observed in Section 3, the arithmetic encoder maintains tables of frequencies which it updates each time it encodes a symbol. Each element which has a `#PCDATA` attribute will result in a call to an arithmetic encoder which uses a common model for all instances of that element attribute and encodes them using the same set of frequency tables. A typical sequence of actions is then as follows: Enter the start state of a DFA representing the right side of a rule; if there is only one edge out of the state then do nothing; if that element has a `#PCDATA` attribute then encode the string of symbols using the frequency tables associated with that element; if there is more than one edge encode the element labeling the edge taken, using an arithmetic encoder for that state, and transit to the the start state of the DFA for that element; the decoder mimics the action of the encoder generating symbols that are certain and using the arithmetic decoder for symbols that are not.

XAUST uses a single container for the character data associated with each element though this has the capability to use the context (i.e. the path along which it reached this element). The reason is best illustrated by the example below:

Example 2. Consider the element below

```
<!ELEMENT Project (date, date, ...)>
<!ELEMENT Employee (date, ...)>
<!ELEMENT date (#PCDATA)>
```

The `date` in `Employee` is the joining date. The first and second `date` in `Project` are the starting and ending dates respectively of the project. XAUST uses a single model for `date` and the reason is clear. Experimentation indicates that having different models for `date` in this case is counter-productive as different models for essentially the same kind of data consume an inordinate amount of memory with little or no gain in compression ratio.

4.1   Compression and Decompression Using XAUST

A state of the compressor is a pair (**element, state**) where **element** represents the current element whose DFA XAUST is traversing, and **state** the state of the DFA where it currently is. Assume that the current state of the Encoder is (i, j). When an open tag is encountered for element k in the document, the current state pair of the encoder is stored on the calling stack and the DFA for the element k is entered. The current state of the encoder now becomes $(k, 0)$. When the end tag is encountered for element k, the stack is popped and the new state of the encoder becomes $(i, j + 1)$. As mentioned earlier, tags are not encoded if the number of output transitions is equal to 1. For example, for the case below we need not encode the tag D but we have to encode B and C.

```
<!ELEMENT A ((B | C), D)>
```

Every state has an arithmetic model which it uses to encode the next state. Note that this is different from the model used to encode character data, which is handled as described below.

Consider the element below.

```
<!ELEMENT A ((#PCDATA | B)*)>
```

There are two transitions from the start state of the DFA for element A. One of them invokes the arithmetic model for PCDATA which is common for all PCDATA associated with any instance of element A in the document. The other transition invokes the DFA for element B after pushing the current state in the stack.

The pseudo-code for Encoder (Compressor) and Decoder (Decompresser) is given below. For the sake of brevity only these two routines are shown. Encoding and decoding attributes are also not shown. We can see the similarity between Encoder and Decoder routines.

```
void Encoder()
{
  ExitLoop = true;
  //StateStruct is a pair of int(ElementIndex, StateIndex)
  //ElementIndex represents the automaton
  //StateIndex is the state in the above automaton
  StateStruct CurrState(0, 0);

  while(ExitLoop == false)
  {
    Type = GetNextType(FilePointer, ElementIndex);

    switch(Type)
    {
    case OPENTAG:
      //Encode ElementIndex in CurrState context
      EncodeOpenTag(CurrState, ElementIndex);
      Stack.push(CurrState);
      CurrState = StateStruct(ElementIndex, 0);
      break;
```

```
      case CLOSETAG:
        //Encode CLOSETAG in CurrState context
        EncodeCloseTag(CurrState);
        if(Stack.empty() == true)
        {
          ExitLoop = true;
        }
        else
        {
          CurrState = Stack.pop();
          //Make state transition in CurrState.ElementIndex
          //automaton and get the next state
          CurrState.StateIndex = MakeStateTransition(CurrState,
                                            ElementIndex);
        }
        break;

      case PCDATA:
        //Encode Pcdata in Currstate context
        EncodePcdata(CurrState);
        CurrState.StateIndex = MakeStateTransition(CurrState, PCDATA);
        break;
    }
  }
}

void Decoder()
{
  ExitLoop = true;
  StateStruct CurrState(0, 0);

  while(ExitLoop == false)
  {
    //Decode the type in CurrState context
    Type = DecodeNextType(FilePointer, CurrState, ElementIndex);

    switch(Type)
    {
    case OPENTAG:
      //Write open tag of the Element of ElementIndex
      WriteOpenTag(ElementIndex);
      Stack.push(CurrState);
      CurrState = StateStruct(ElementIndex, 0);
      break;

    case CLOSETAG:
      //Write close tag of the Element of ElementIndex
      WriteCloseTag(ElementIndex);
      if(Stack.empty() == true)
```

```
     {
       ExitLoop = true;
     }
     else
     {
       CurrState = Stack.pop();
       CurrState.StateIndex = MakeStateTransition(CurrState,
                                                  ElementIndex);
     }
     break;

   case PCDATA:
     DecodePcdata(CurrState);
     CurrState.StateIndex = MakeStateTransition(CurrState, PCDATA);
     break;
   }
 }
}
```

5   Experimental Results

We have examined the comparative performance of three tools XMill, XMLPPM and XAUST on five large XML documents. The sizes of these documents are displayed in Table 1. We define the *Compression Ratio* as the ratio of the size of the compressed document to the size of the original document expressed as a percentage. The compression ratios for all three schemes are shown in Fig., 2 along with that of a general purpose compressor bzip2. The compression ratios of XAUST and XMLPPM are considerably better than that of XMill for all but one of the documents. XMLPPM, however, ran out of memory for two documents. It also takes significantly longer than XAUST whereas XMill is very fast and economical in its use of space. The disadvantage of XMill is that it cannot perform on-line compression. We expect that our scheme will do well wherever the markup content is high as tags whose probability of occurrence is 1 are not included in the compressed stream. Figure 2 also shows the compression ratios for tags alone. XAUST compresses tags more efficiently than in other schemes.

Table 1. Sizes of XML documents that were compressed

Name	Size (in MB)
auction	113
dblp	253
uniprot	1070
michigan	495
x007	128

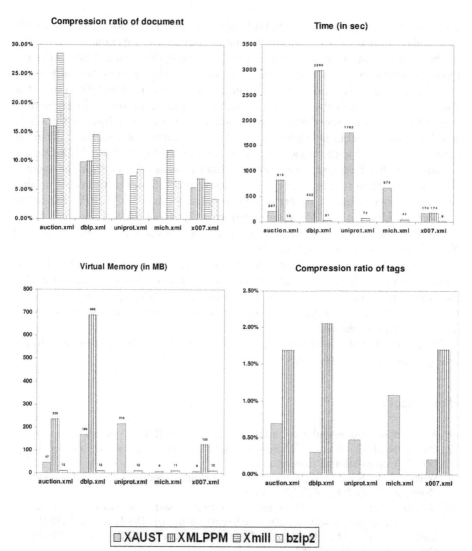

Fig. 2. Statistics for Compression Ratios, Running Times and Memory Usage for XMill, XAUST, XMLPPM and **bzip2**. XMLPPM ran out of memory for uniprot.xml and mich.xml. Running times are shown for only XML-aware schemes.

XAUST does not need a SAX parser as do XMill and XMLPPM as some form of parsing is already embedded in its action.

6   Conclusion and Future Work

We have presented a scheme for the compression of XML documents where the underlying arithmetic model for the compression of tags is a finite state automaton generated directly from the DTD of the document. The model is automatically switched on transiting from one automaton to another storing enough information on the stack so that return to the right state is possible; this ensures that the correct model is always used for compression. (In fact it precisely achieves the *multiplexing of models* mentioned in XMLPPM in a completely natural manner). On return, the stack is used to recover the state from which a transition was made. The scheme is reminiscent of a recursive descent parser except that it is not subject to the LL(1) restrictions. Our technique directly generates the compressor from the DTD in the appropriate format with no user interaction except the input of the DTD. Our experiments on five large databases indicate that the scheme is better on the average than XMLPPM in terms of compression ratio, much faster in terms of running time and more economical in terms of memory usage. In fact XMLPPM ran out of memory for UniProt and Michigan documents. The tool XMill runs much faster and in less space, but its average performance is considerably inferior to that of XAUST as can be observed from Fig. 2.

The dynamic space requirements for the compressor are dominated by the size of the tables for the arithmetic compressor which grow exponentially with the size of the context (order 4 is used here). Also updating these tables after each symbol is processed makes the compression rather slow in comparison with dictionary based schemes.

Future work will concentrate on modifying this scheme to facilitate simple tree queries on the XML text.

References

1. XML: W3C recommendation. http://www.w3.org/TR/REC-xml (2004)
2. Backhouse, R.C.: Syntax of Programming Languages - Theory and Practice. Prentice Hall International, London (1979)
3. Witten, I.H., Neal, R.M., Cleary, J.G.: Arithmetic coding for data compression. Commun. ACM **30** (1987) 520–540
4. Nelson, M.: Arithmetic coding and statistical modeling. http://dogma.net/markn/articles/arith/part1.htm. Dr. Dobbs Journal (1991)
5. Liefke, H., Suciu, D.: XMILL: An efficient compressor for XML data. In: SIGMOD Conference. (2000) 153–164
6. Cheney, J.: Compressing XML with Multiplexed Hierarchical PPM Models. In: Proceedings of the Data Compression Conference, IEEE Computer Society (2001) 163–172
7. DBLP: (http://www.informatik.uni-trier.de/~ley/db)
8. UniProt: (http://www.ebi.uniprot.org)
9. XMark: (http://monetdb.cwi.nl/xml/generator.html)
10. Michigan: (http://www.eecs.umich.edu/db/mbench)
11. XOO7: (http://www.comp.nus.edu.sg/~ebh/xoo7.html)
12. Bzip2: (http://www.bzip.org)
13. Cameron, R.D.: Source encoding using syntactic information source models. IEEE Transactions on Information Theory **34** (1988) 843–850
14. Ernst, J., Evans, W.S., Fraser, C.W., Lucco, S., Proebsting, T.A.: Code compression. In: PLDI. (1997) 358–365

15. Franz, M.: Adaptive compression of syntax trees and iterative dynamic code op-
    timization: Two basic technologies for mobile object systems. In: Mobile Object
    Systems: Towards the Programmable Internet. Springer-Verlag: Heidelberg, Ger-
    many (1997) 263–276
16. Franz, M., Kistler, T.: Slim binaries. Commun. ACM **40** (1997) 87–94
17. Fraser, C.W.: Automatic inference of models for statistical code compression. In:
    PLDI. (1999) 242–246
18. XMLZIP: (http://www.xmls.com)
19. SAX: (http://www.megginson.com/sax)
20. Cleary, J.G., Teahan, W.J.: Unbounded length contexts for PPM. The Computer
    Journal **40** (1997) 67–75
21. Tolani, P.M., Haritsa, J.R.: XGRIND: A query-friendly XML compressor. In:
    ICDE. (2002) 225–234
22. Min, J.K., Park, M.J., Chung, C.W.: XPRESS: A queriable compression for XML
    data. In: SIGMOD Conference. (2003) 122–133
23. Arion, A., Bonifati, A., Costa, G., D'Aguanno, S., Manolescu, I., Pugliese, A.:
    Efficient query evaluation over compressed XML data. In: EDBT. (2004) 200–218
24. Ziv, J., Lempel, A.: A universal algorithm for sequential data compression. IEEE
    Transactions on Information Theory **23** (1977) 337–343

Non-backtracking Top-Down Algorithm for Checking Tree Automata Containment

Tadahiro Suda and Haruo Hosoya

Graduate School of Information Science and Technology,
University of Tokyo, Japan
{tada, hahosoya}@is.s.u-tokyo.ac.jp

Abstract. Checking tree automata containment is a fundamental operation in static verification of XML processing programs. However, tree automata containment problem is known to be EXPTIME-complete and a standard algorithm with determinization of automata easily blows up even in practical cases. Hosoya, Vouillon, and Pierce have proposed a top-down algorithm that efficiently works for a large class of typical instances. However, there still remains a considerable inefficiency because of repeated calculation incurred by backtracking. In this paper, we propose a *non-backtracking* top-down algorithm which improves this inefficiency. In the algorithm, we introduce "dependencies" among performed computations and, by exploiting these, we can recover certain kinds of information lost by backtracking. One difficulty in constructing such algorithm is, however, that, since some dependency information can be useless, we may be misled to needless computation by using such information. To alleviate this problem, we carefully check the usefulness of each dependency whenever we use it. Since these checks introduce a subtlety to our algorithm, we rigorously formalize it with a correctness proof. Our preliminary experiments show that our algorithm works more efficiently compared to the previous algorithm.

1 Introduction

Tree automata are a finite-state machine model for accepting trees. This paper aims at studying an efficient algorithm for the containment problem of tree automata.

The primary motivation of this study is the application to static typechecking for XML processing. XML [1] is a world-wide emerging standard for tree-structured documents that allows user-defined *schemas* for imposing structural constraints on those data. The purpose of static typechecking is to analyze a program for processing such XML documents and guarantee, before the execution, that generated documents conform to the schema given by the user. Though various methods for static typechecking have been proposed [2–7], the containment check between schemas is often used as the most important core (in particular, in XDuce [2], CDuce [3], XQuery [4], and several theoretical frameworks [5, 7]). As tree automata have been proved to be the most natural model

J. Farré, I. Litovsky, and S. Schmitz (Eds.): CIAA 2005, LNCS 3845, pp. 294–306, 2006.

for schemas (e.g., [8]),[1] we focus on the containment problem of tree automata in this paper.

Unfortunately, the containment problem of tree automata is known to have a high complexity: EXPTIME-complete [11]. Since, in XML typechecking, we often consider tree automata with a large number of states (more than 100 states), naive algorithms are often not usable. In particular, a standard algorithm which involves determinization of automata easily blows up since it needs to transform input automata to completely separate automata with the number of states exponential in the size of the input.

Hosoya, Vouillon, and Pierce have proposed a top-down algorithm [12] for checking tree automata containment efficiently in typical cases. Their algorithm checks a given goal of containment by recursively expanding it to subgoals in a top-down way. During this check, the algorithm keeps track of already-encountered containment goals as a set of "assumptions" in order to avoid repetition of checking the same containment. However, in a later computation, the assumptions may turn out to be false. At that moment, the algorithm performs backtracking, which is not only costly by itself but also may incur repetition of the same computation because some valuable information can be lost.

In this paper, we propose a non-backtracking top-down algorithm which improves this inefficiency. In addition to already-encountered containments as in the original top-down algorithm, our algorithm maintains dependency relations among these containments. By exploiting this dependency information, we can recover the above-mentioned information lost by backtracking and thus avoid the wasteful repetition of computation. However, some dependency information proved during the calculation can be useless (i.e., one containment depends on another containment that actually does not hold), a naive introduction of this mechanism would again cause extra computation. In order to overcome this difficulty, we carefully craft our algorithm in a way that eliminates dependency relations as soon as they are proved to be useless. Since the algorithm becomes quite subtle because of this handling of useless dependencies, we rigorously formalize our algorithm and prove its correctness. We have also implemented the algorithm and compared it with the original top-down algorithm using several non-trivial examples. The result indicates that our algorithm runs approximately 3 times to 8 times more efficiently than the previous one in these examples.

The rest of this paper is organized as follows. We first give preliminary notations in Sec. 2. In Sec. 3, we first informally explain the existing top-down algorithm, where we point out the inefficiency caused by backtracking, and then describe the problem arising from naively introducing dependency information. In Sec. 4, we formalize our non-backtracking algorithm that desirably handles dependencies and prove its correctness. We discuss related work in Sec. 5. Finally, we verify the efficiency of our algorithm in practical cases by preliminary experiments in Sec. 6. Due to space constraints, we omit the proofs of theorems from this paper. These can be found in [13].

---

[1] There are numerous schema languages, but most can be expressed more or less by tree automata. (e.g., DTD [1], XML-schema [9], RELAX NG [10]).

2   Preliminaries

Let $\mathcal{L}$ be a finite set of *labels*, ranged over by l. We define a *tree t* as a labeled binary tree by the following grammar:

$$t ::= \# \mid l(t, t)$$

A *tree automaton M* is a triplet $(\mathcal{L}, Q, \delta)$ where $\mathcal{L}$ is a finite set of labels, Q is a finite set of *states*, and δ is a transition function from states to *types*. Types are defined as subsets of $\{\#\} \cup \{l(s, s') \mid l \in \mathcal{L}, s, s' \in Q\}$. We use the meta-variables s, S, and T to range over Q, 2^Q, and types, respectively. Also, we write $\delta(S)$ for $\bigcup_{s \in S} \delta(s)$. For any type T appearing in M, we write $[\![T]\!]_M$ to denote the set of all the trees matched by T, formally, the least solution of the following equations: let us write $[\![a]\!]_M$ for $[\![\{a\}]\!]_M$ and

$$
\begin{aligned}
[\![\phi]\!]_M &= \phi \\
[\![\#]\!]_M &= \{\#\} \\
[\![l(s, s')]\!]_M &= \{l(t, t') \mid t \in [\![\delta(s)]\!]_M, \ t' \in [\![\delta(s')]\!]_M\} \\
[\![\{a_1, \cdots, a_n\}]\!]_M &= \bigcup_{i=1}^{n} [\![a_i]\!]_M
\end{aligned}
$$

For any set S of states, we define the *language* $[\![S]\!]_M$ of S as $[\![\delta(S)]\!]_M$. In the rest of paper, we simply write $[\![\cdot]\!]$ for $[\![\cdot]\!]_M$ when M is clear from the context. Also, we write $[\![s]\!]$ for $[\![\{s\}]\!]$. The tree automata containment problem is formalized as follows: for a tree automaton M and two sets of states S and S', answer "yes" if and only if $[\![S]\!] \subseteq [\![S']\!]$.

3   Problems

Hosoya, Vouillon, and Pierce have proposed a "top-down" algorithm for checking tree automata containment [12]. In their algorithm, containment check of given two sets of states proceeds by recursively unfolding states by the transition function. That is, it starts with checking the given pair of state sets by comparing the types yielded by unfolding the states; this eventually leads to checks of other pairs of state sets, and then we repeat unfoldings and comparisons similarly for these. In order to avoid repetition of checking the same pair, the algorithm keeps an "assumption" set to remember pairs of state sets that have already been seen: later when it encounters a pair that is already in the assumption set, it stops further check of this.

For example, let us consider checking the containment $[\![s_1]\!] \subseteq [\![s_2]\!]$ for the tree automaton in Fig. 1 by their algorithm. In the example, we write an assumption set in the following form:

$$\{\ s_1 \prec s_1', \ \cdots, \ s_n \prec s_n' \ \}$$

Intuitively, each $s_i \prec s_i'$ stands for $[\![s_i]\!] \subseteq [\![s_i']\!]$.

We start with the empty assumption set. To check $[\![s_1]\!] \subseteq [\![s_2]\!]$, we first add $s_1 \prec s_2$ to the assumption set:

$$\{\ s_1 \prec s_2 \ \}$$

$$\mathcal{L} = \{a, b, c, d, e, f\} \quad Q = \{s_1, \cdots, s_8\}$$

$$\delta : s_1 \mapsto \{a(s_1, s_1), b(s_3, s_4)\} \qquad\qquad s_7 \mapsto \{\#, a(s_2, s_2)\}$$
$$s_2 \mapsto \{a(s_2, s_2), b(s_5, s_7), b(s_6, s_8)\} \quad s_8 \mapsto \{\#, a(s_2, s_2), b(s_2, s_2)\}$$
$$s_3 \mapsto \{c(s_4, s_4), d(s_9, s_9), e(s_4, s_4)\} \qquad s_9 \mapsto \{f(s_3, s_3)\}$$
$$s_4 \mapsto \{\#, a(s_1, s_1)\} \qquad\qquad\qquad s_{10} \mapsto \{f(s_5, s_5)\}$$
$$s_5 \mapsto \{c(s_8, s_8), d(s_{10}, s_{10}), e(s_2, s_2)\} \quad s_{11} \mapsto \{f(s_5, s_5), f(s_6, s_6)\}$$
$$s_6 \mapsto \{c(s_2, s_2), d(s_{11}, s_{11}), e(s_8, s_8)\}$$

Fig. 1. An example of tree automaton

We then unfold s_1 and s_2 by the transition function δ and check the following containment of types assuming the validity of containments in the assumption set (i.e., assuming that $[\![s_1]\!] \subseteq [\![s_2]\!]$ holds):

$$[\![\{a(s_1, s_1), b(s_3, s_4)\}]\!] \subseteq [\![\{a(s_2, s_2), b(s_5, s_7), b(s_6, s_8)\}]\!]$$

It is enough to compare the elements on both sides that have the same label. Thus we check both of the following two containments:

(A) $[\![a(s_1, s_1)]\!] \subseteq [\![a(s_2, s_2)]\!]$ **(B)** $[\![b(s_3, s_4)]\!] \subseteq [\![\{b(s_5, s_7), b(s_6, s_8)\}]\!]$

First, for the containment (A), showing $[\![s_1]\!] \subseteq [\![s_2]\!]$ suffices. Since $s_1 \prec s_2$ is already in the assumption set, we stop checking this containment further and we judge right away that it holds.

Next, for the containment (B), it suffices to show:

$$[\![s_3]\!] \times [\![s_4]\!] \subseteq ([\![s_5]\!] \times [\![s_7]\!]) \cup ([\![s_6]\!] \times [\![s_8]\!])$$

The right hand side of this containment can be transformed into the conjunctive normal form as follows: let us write $\mathcal{T}$ for the set of all trees and

$$(([\![s_5]\!] \times \mathcal{T}) \cap (\mathcal{T} \times [\![s_7]\!])) \cup (([\![s_6]\!] \times \mathcal{T}) \cap (\mathcal{T} \times [\![s_8]\!]))$$
$$= (([\![s_5]\!] \times \mathcal{T}) \cup (\mathcal{T} \times [\![s_8]\!])) \cap (([\![s_6]\!] \times \mathcal{T}) \cup (\mathcal{T} \times [\![s_7]\!]))$$
$$\cap ([\![\{s_5, s_6\}]\!] \times \mathcal{T}) \cap (\mathcal{T} \times [\![\{s_7, s_8\}]\!])$$

Since $[\![s_3]\!] \times [\![s_4]\!] \subseteq ([\![s_5]\!] \times \mathcal{T}) \cup (\mathcal{T} \times [\![s_8]\!])$ is equivalent to "$[\![s_3]\!] \subseteq [\![s_5]\!]$ or $[\![s_4]\!] \subseteq [\![s_8]\!]$" and similarly for the other clauses in the last formula, it is enough to check all of the followings.

(C) $[\![s_3]\!] \subseteq [\![s_5]\!]$ or $[\![s_4]\!] \subseteq [\![s_8]\!]$ **(D)** $[\![s_3]\!] \subseteq [\![s_6]\!]$ or $[\![s_4]\!] \subseteq [\![s_7]\!]$
(E) $[\![s_3]\!] \subseteq [\![\{s_5, s_6\}]\!]$ **(F)** $[\![s_4]\!] \subseteq [\![\{s_7, s_8\}]\!]$

Backtracking. Note that the algorithm needs to check disjunctions of containments and this is the cause of backtracking. Let us see this from how the algorithm works for (C).

We begin with checking the first containment $[\![s_3]\!] \subseteq [\![s_5]\!]$, for which we first add $s_3 \prec s_5$ to the assumption set:

$$\{\ s_1 \prec s_2,\ s_3 \prec s_5\ \}$$

We then unfold s_3 and s_5 by δ and check the following containment:

$$[\![\{c(s_4, s_4), d(s_9, s_9), e(s_4, s_4)\}\}]\!] \subseteq [\![\{c(s_8, s_8), d(s_{10}, s_{10}), e(s_2, s_2)\}\}]\!]$$

In order for this containment to hold, we need to show each of the following three checks:

(G) $[\![c(s_4, s_4)]\!] \subseteq [\![c(s_8, s_8)]\!]$ **(H)** $[\![d(s_9, s_9)]\!] \subseteq [\![d(s_{10}, s_{10})]\!]$
(I) $[\![e(s_4, s_4)]\!] \subseteq [\![e(s_2, s_2)]\!]$

For the check of (G), since we only need to check $[\![s_4]\!] \subseteq [\![s_8]\!]$, we add $s_4 \prec s_8$ to the assumption set as

$$\{\ s_1 \prec s_2,\ s_3 \prec s_5,\ s_4 \prec s_8\ \}$$

and check $[\![\{\#, a(s_1, s_1)\}]\!] \subseteq [\![\{\#, a(s_2, s_2)\}]\!]$ as given by the unfolding of the states s_4 and s_8. This succeeds by the trivial relation $[\![\#]\!] \subseteq [\![\#]\!]$ and the fact that the assumption set already contains $s_1 \prec s_2$. In order to show (H), all we need is to check $[\![s_9]\!] \subseteq [\![s_{10}]\!]$. This holds since the unfolding of the states reduces this relation to checking $[\![s_3]\!] \subseteq [\![s_5]\!]$ and $s_3 \prec s_5$ is already in the assumption set. As a result of this check, the assumption set becomes

$$\{\ s_1 \prec s_2,\ s_3 \prec s_5,\ s_4 \prec s_8,\ s_9 \prec s_{10}\ \}.$$

Finally, the containment (I) requires checking $[\![s_4]\!] \subseteq [\![s_2]\!]$, but it does not hold since $\# \in \delta(s_4)$ and $\# \notin \delta(s_2)$. This makes the containment (I) false, leading $[\![s_3]\!] \subseteq [\![s_5]\!]$ to fail.

Here, since we have assumed $[\![s_3]\!] \subseteq [\![s_5]\!]$ but it turns out to be false, we roll back to the point (C). Since this is just before $s_3 \prec s_5$ was added to the assumption set, the set is now reverted to

$$\{\ s_1 \prec s_2\ \}.$$

This backtracking is a source of inefficiency for the following reasons.

1. After the backtracking, we check the second check $[\![s_4]\!] \subseteq [\![s_8]\!]$ of the disjunction in (C). However, the algorithm repeats the same calculation that has already been done in the check of (G).
2. After finishing the check of (C), we continue with (D), which eventually leads to the check of $[\![s_4]\!] \subseteq [\![s_2]\!]$. Even though this relation has already been refuted when checking (I), the algorithm needs the same check once again.

Introducing Dependency Information. We propose a technique to improve the above inefficiency of the previous top-down algorithm. Our algorithm works similarly to the previous one but it additionally maintains more refined information including containment dependencies (expressing that "a containment depends on other containments") and refuted containments and uses these for avoiding the above-mentioned needless calculation. Since our new algorithm never reverts dependency information to a previous point in a blind way, we call it a *non-backtracking* algorithm as oppose to the previous backtracking one. For example, note that, in checking (G) above, when we judged $[[s_4]] \subseteq [[s_8]]$, we assumed the relation $[[s_1]] \subseteq [[s_2]]$. For this, our algorithm maintains the dependency "$[[s_4]] \subseteq [[s_8]]$ depends on $[[s_1]] \subseteq [[s_2]]$." This information is useful since, later when we need to check $[[s_4]] \subseteq [[s_8]]$, we can stop going further but instead immediately say "succeed, provided $[[s_1]] \subseteq [[s_2]]$ holds."

However, in order to obtain an enough efficient algorithm, we need a care in constructing our new algorithm. Among dependencies that have been proved during the course of computation, there are useless ones expressing "a containment A depends on a false containment B". It would make the algorithm slower if we naively return as described in the last paragraph whenever we encounter A for the next time. This is because the "conditional success" will later be canceled by B's falsity any way and the computation from now to then will be wasted. One might think that such a dependency is stupid from the first place, but the issue is that B's falsity cannot be known at the moment where the dependency is generated. As an example, the dependency "$[[s_9]] \subseteq [[s_{10}]]$ depends on $[[s_3]] \subseteq [[s_5]]$" was proved in the check of (H). However, $[[s_3]] \subseteq [[s_5]]$ was refuted later: the dependency turns out to be useless at the refutation point.

Our approach to this issue is to check uselessness of each dependency (i.e., validity of the depended containments) whenever we use it. However, such treatment is not straightforward since blindly performing such a check will make algorithm infinitely loop. Our observation is that the depended containments that are unsafe to check can be characterized as those "still under checking," and a formalization of an algorithm involving a careful classification of containment relations is our main technical contribution in this paper.

4 Algorithm

We first introduce the following notation to express the containments that are handled in our algorithm: a containment *cont* is either of the form $s \prec S$ (standing for "$[[s]] \subseteq [[S]]$"), of the form $T \prec T'$ (standing for "$[[T]] \subseteq [[T']]$"), or of the form $s \prec S \mid s' \prec S'$ (standing for "$[[s]] \subseteq [[S]]$ or $[[s']] \subseteq [[S']]$"). We also use π to range over sets of containments of the form $s \prec S$.

Our algorithm maintains an (extended) dependency set $\mathcal{A} = (U, D, F)$ where U and F are sets of pairs of the form $s \prec S$ and D is a set of triplets of the form $\pi \vdash s \prec S$. We store under-checking containments in U, dependencies ("$s \prec S$ depends on the containments in π") in D, and failed containments in F. For a set D of dependencies, D_{pair} denotes $\{s \prec S \mid \pi \vdash s \prec S \in D\}$. A dependency set (U, D, F) is *well-defined* if it satisfies $U \cap F = \phi$, $U \cap D_{pair} = \phi$, $F \cap D_{pair} = \phi$

and, moreover, for any (s, S), there is at most one triplet of the form $\pi \vdash s \prec S$ in D. In the rest of this paper, we assume that any dependency set is well-defined. A containment set π is *consistent* if $[\![s]\!] \subseteq [\![S]\!]$ holds for all $s \prec S$ in π and a dependency set (U, D, F) is *consistent* if it satisfies the following conditions:

- If $\pi \vdash s \prec S \in D$ and π is consistent, then $[\![s]\!] \subseteq [\![S]\!]$.
- If $s \prec S \in F$, then $[\![s]\!] \not\subseteq [\![S]\!]$.

(Note that the set U does not constrain the consistency of the dependency set.)
    Our algorithm is defined by a set of rules that derive the following relation

$$\mathcal{A}, cont \rightsquigarrow \mathcal{A}', \rho$$

where $\rho ::= \pi \mid \perp$ and π is a subset of the under-checking pairs U of $\mathcal{A}$. This relation reads "the algorithm checks a given containment $cont$ under a given dependency set $\mathcal{A}$ and, as the result, it transforms $\mathcal{A}$ to $\mathcal{A}'$ and returns ρ". The meaning of the last part "returns ρ" depends on the form of ρ.

$\rho = \pi$: "if both $\mathcal{A}$ and π are consistent, then $cont$ holds."
$\rho = \perp$: "if $\mathcal{A}$ is consistent, then $cont$ does not hold."

Since we are actually interested in simply checking $[\![s_0]\!] \subseteq [\![S_0]\!]$ for given s_0 and S_0, we start the algorithm by giving $\mathcal{A} = (\phi, \phi, \phi)$ and $cont = s_0 \prec S_0$. (Note that, when it succeeds, $\rho(= \pi) = \phi$ since we have $U = \phi$ and ensure $\pi \subseteq U$.)

Derivation Rules. First, let us see the derivation rules for the case $cont = s \prec S$ (where $\mathcal{A} = (U, D, F)$, $\mathcal{A}' = (U', D', F')$ and $\mathcal{A}_i = (U_i, D_i, F_i)$).

$$\frac{s \in S}{\mathcal{A}, s \prec S \rightsquigarrow \mathcal{A}, \phi} \text{ (Mem)} \qquad \frac{s \prec S \in U}{\mathcal{A}, s \prec S \rightsquigarrow \mathcal{A}, \{s \prec S\}} \text{ (InU)} \qquad \frac{s \prec S \in F}{\mathcal{A}, s \prec S \rightsquigarrow \mathcal{A}, \perp} \text{ (InF}_t\text{)}$$

$$\frac{s \notin S \quad s \prec S \notin U \cup F \cup D_{pair} \quad (U \cup \{s \prec S\}, D, F), \delta(s) \prec \delta(S) \rightsquigarrow \mathcal{A}', \pi}{\mathcal{A}, s \prec S \rightsquigarrow (U' \backslash \{s \prec S\}, D' \cup \{\pi' \vdash s \prec S\}, F'), \pi' \text{ where } \pi' = \pi \backslash \{s \prec S\}} \text{ (Unfold)}$$

$$\frac{s \notin S \quad s \prec S \notin U \cup F \cup D_{pair} \quad (U \cup \{s \prec S\}, D, F), \delta(s) \prec \delta(S) \rightsquigarrow \mathcal{A}', \perp}{\mathcal{A}, s \prec S \rightsquigarrow (U' \backslash \{s \prec S\}, D', F' \cup \{s \prec S\}), \perp} \text{ (Unfold}_t\text{)}$$

$$\frac{\pi \vdash s \prec S \in D \quad \text{for all } 1 \leq i \leq m, \; \mathcal{A}_{i-1}, s_i \prec S_i \rightsquigarrow \mathcal{A}_i, \pi_i}{\text{where } \pi = \{s_1 \prec S_1, \cdots, s_m \prec S_m\} \text{ and } \mathcal{A}_0 = (U \cup \{s \prec S\}, D \backslash \{\pi \vdash s \prec S\}, F)}{\mathcal{A}, s \prec S \rightsquigarrow (U_m \backslash \{s \prec S\}, D_m \cup \{\pi' \vdash s \prec S\}, F_m), \pi' \text{ where } \pi' = \bigcup_{i=1}^m \pi_i \backslash \{s \prec S\}} \text{ (InD)}$$

$$\frac{\pi \vdash s \prec S \in D \quad \text{for all } 1 \leq i \leq j-1, \; \mathcal{A}_{i-1}, s_i \prec S_i \rightsquigarrow \mathcal{A}_i, \pi_i}{\mathcal{A}_{j-1}, s_j \prec S_j \rightsquigarrow \mathcal{A}_j, \perp \quad \mathcal{A}_j, \delta(s) \prec \delta(S) \rightsquigarrow \mathcal{A}', \pi'}{\text{where } \pi = \{s_1 \prec S_1, \cdots, s_m \prec S_m\} \text{ and } \mathcal{A}_0 = (U \cup \{s \prec S\}, D \backslash \{\pi \vdash s \prec S\}, F)}{\mathcal{A}, s \prec S \rightsquigarrow (U' \backslash \{s \prec S\}, D' \cup \{\pi'' \vdash s \prec S\}, F'), \pi'' \text{ where } \pi'' = \pi' \backslash \{s \prec S\}} \left(\begin{array}{c}\text{InD\&}\\\text{Unf}\end{array}\right)$$

$$\frac{\pi \vdash s \prec S \in D \quad \text{for all } 1 \leq i \leq j-1, \; \mathcal{A}_{i-1}, s_i \prec S_i \rightsquigarrow \mathcal{A}_i, \pi_i}{\mathcal{A}_{j-1}, s_j \prec S_j \rightsquigarrow \mathcal{A}_j, \perp \quad \mathcal{A}_j, \delta(s) \prec \delta(S) \rightsquigarrow \mathcal{A}', \perp}{\text{where } \pi = \{s_1 \prec S_1, \cdots, s_m \prec S_m\} \text{ and } \mathcal{A}_0 = (U \cup \{s \prec S\}, D \backslash \{\pi \vdash s \prec S\}, F)}{\mathcal{A}, s \prec S \rightsquigarrow (U' \backslash \{s \prec S\}, D', F' \cup \{s \prec S\}), \perp} \left(\begin{array}{c}\text{InD\&}\\\text{Unf}_t\end{array}\right)$$

If $s \in S$, we can easily conclude $[\![s]\!] \subseteq [\![S]\!]$ by the definition of languages. We thus return $\rho = \phi$ as the result of this check (Mem). When $s \prec S \in U$ (where (U, D, F) is the original dependency set), we stop the further check of $s \prec S$ and immediately return $\rho = \{s \prec S\}$ as the result (InU). This rule means the trivial statement "if $[\![s]\!] \subseteq [\![S]\!]$ holds, then $[\![s]\!] \subseteq [\![S]\!]$ holds." If $s \prec S \in F$, then this implies that we have already checked $[\![s]\!] \nsubseteq [\![S]\!]$ and therefore we return $\rho = \perp$ immediately (InF$_f$). When $s \prec S$ is neither in U, F, nor D_{pair}, then this means that we encounter $s \prec S$ for the first time and therefore we first add $s \prec S$ to U (this ensures the termination of our algorithm since the number of containments in $U \cup F \cup D_{pair}$ increases monotonously) and then check $\delta(s) \prec \delta(S)$ under the new dependency set $(U \cup \{s \prec S\}, D, F)$. Suppose that the check succeeds with $\mathcal{A}' = (U', D', F')$ and π. Then, its direct meaning is that $[\![s]\!] \subseteq [\![S]\!]$ depends on π. However, this actually implies that $[\![s]\!] \subseteq [\![S]\!]$ depends on $\pi' = \pi \setminus \{s \prec S\}$ (intuitively because we can construct a proof tree such that every application of InU with $s \prec S$ is recursively replaced by the proof tree showing $[\![s]\!] \subseteq [\![S]\!]$ depends on π). Thus we add $\pi' \vdash s \prec S$ to D', remove $s \prec S$ from U', and then return $\rho = \pi'$ (Unfold). On the other hand, suppose that $[\![s]\!] \subseteq [\![S]\!]$ is refuted as a result of checking $\delta(s) \prec \delta(S)$. In this case, we remove $s \prec S$ from U', add $s \prec S$ to F', and return $\rho = \perp$ (Unfold$_f$).

If $\pi \vdash s \prec S \in D$, then this means that we have already proved that $s \prec S$ depends on the consistency of π. However, since the dependency may be useless, that is, π may be inconsistent, we successively check each pair in π. (Before checking these pairs, we add $s \prec S$ to U and remove $\pi \vdash s \prec S$ from D in order to avoid rechecking $s \prec S$.) Suppose that all checks of pairs $s_i \prec S_i$ in π succeed $(1 \leq i \leq m)$, each proving that it depends on π_i for some π_i. From this result and the above dependency $\pi \vdash s \prec S$, we know that $s \prec S$ depends on $\bigcup_{i=1}^{m} \pi_i$. Then, similarly to Unfold, since the obtained dependency implies that $s \prec S$ depends on $\pi' = \bigcup_{i=1}^{m} \pi_i \setminus \{s \prec S\}$, we add $\pi' \vdash s \prec S$ to D', remove $s \prec S$ from U', and return $\rho = \pi'$ (InD). When some pair $s_j \prec S_j$ in π turns out to be false, this makes π inconsistent and hence $\pi \vdash s \prec S$ becomes useless. In this case, we recheck $s \prec S$ by unfolding these states, similarly to Unfold and Unfold$_f$, under the dependency set resulted from checking $s_1 \prec S_1$ through $s_j \prec S_j$ with $s \prec S$ in U (InD&Unf and InD&Unf$_f$).

Next, we show the rules for $cont = T \prec T'$.

$$\frac{T = \phi}{\mathcal{A}, T \prec T' \rightsquigarrow \mathcal{A}, \phi} \text{ (Empty)} \qquad \frac{T = \{\#\} \quad \# \in T'}{\mathcal{A}, T \prec T' \rightsquigarrow \mathcal{A}, \phi} \text{ (Leaf)} \qquad \frac{T = \{\#\} \quad \# \notin T'}{\mathcal{A}, T \prec T' \rightsquigarrow \mathcal{A}, \perp} \text{ (Leaf$_f$)}$$

$$\frac{T = \{a_1, \cdots, a_m\}(m \geq 2) \quad \text{for all } 1 \leq i \leq m, \ \mathcal{A}_{i-1}, \{a_i\} \prec T' \rightsquigarrow \mathcal{A}_i, \pi_i}{\mathcal{A}_0, T \prec T' \rightsquigarrow \mathcal{A}_m, \bigcup_{i=1}^{m} \pi_i} \text{ (Union)}$$

$$\frac{\begin{array}{c} T = \{a_1, \cdots, a_m\}(m \geq 2) \quad \text{for all } 1 \leq i \leq j-1, \ \mathcal{A}_{i-1}, \{a_i\} \prec T' \rightsquigarrow \mathcal{A}_i, \pi_i \\ \mathcal{A}_{j-1}, \{a_j\} \prec T' \rightsquigarrow \mathcal{A}_j, \perp \end{array}}{\mathcal{A}_0, T \prec T' \rightsquigarrow \mathcal{A}_j, \perp} \text{ (Union$_f$)}$$

$$T = \{l(s, s')\} \quad \text{for all } 1 \leq i \leq 2^m, \; \mathcal{A}_{i-1}, s \prec S_i | s' \prec S'_i \rightsquigarrow \mathcal{A}_i, \pi_i$$

$$\text{where} \begin{cases} \{l'(s, s') \in T' \mid l' = l\} = \{l(s_1, s'_1), \cdots, l(s_m, s'_m)\}, \\ I_i \subseteq \{1, \cdots, m\}, \; S_i = \{s_k \mid k \in I_i\} \text{ and } S'_i = \{s'_k \mid k \notin I_i\} \end{cases}$$

$$\frac{}{\mathcal{A}_0, T \prec T' \rightsquigarrow \mathcal{A}_{2^m}, \bigcup_{i=1}^{2^m} \pi_i} \quad \text{(Conj)}$$

$$T = \{l(s, s')\} \quad \text{for all } 1 \leq i \leq j-1, \; \mathcal{A}_{i-1}, s \prec S_i | s' \prec S'_i \rightsquigarrow \mathcal{A}_i, \pi_i$$

$$\mathcal{A}_{j-1}, s \prec S_j | s' \prec S'_j \rightsquigarrow \mathcal{A}_j, \bot$$

$$\text{where} \begin{cases} \{l'(s, s') \in T' \mid l' = l\} = \{l(s_1, s'_1), \cdots, l(s_m, s'_m)\}, \\ I_i \subseteq \{1, \cdots, m\}, \; S_i = \{s_k \mid k \in I_i\} \text{ and } S'_i = \{s'_k \mid k \notin I_i\} \end{cases}$$

$$\frac{}{\mathcal{A}_0, T \prec T' \rightsquigarrow \mathcal{A}_j, \bot} \quad \text{(Conj}_f\text{)}$$

If $T = \phi$, then $\llbracket T \rrbracket (= \phi) \subseteq \llbracket T' \rrbracket$ trivially holds and therefore we return $\rho = \phi$ right away (**Empty**). If $T = \{\#\}$, then $\llbracket T \rrbracket \subseteq \llbracket T' \rrbracket$ is equivalent to $\# \in T'$. Therefore, in this case, we return $\rho = \phi$ immediately when $\# \in T'$ holds (**Leaf**), while we return $\rho = \bot$ when $\# \notin T'$ (**Leaf**$_f$). If $T = \{a_1, \cdots, a_m\}$, then we successively check $a_i \prec T'$ for each $i = 1, \cdots, m$. And if all checks of $a_i \prec T'$ succeed with π_i as a result, this proves that $T \prec T'$ depends on $\rho = \bigcup_{i=1}^m \pi_i$ and therefore we return ρ (**Union**). On the other hand, if some pair $a_j \prec T'$ ($a_j \in T$) is refuted, then this concludes $\llbracket T \rrbracket \nsubseteq \llbracket T' \rrbracket$ and therefore we return $\rho = \bot$ (**Union**$_f$). When $T = \{l(s, s')\}$, it is enough to compare $l(s, s')$ with the elements labeled with l in T'. Suppose that such elements in T' are $l(s_i, s'_i)$ for $1 \leq i \leq m$. Then the relation $\llbracket T \rrbracket \subseteq \llbracket T' \rrbracket$ is equivalent to

$$\llbracket s \rrbracket \times \llbracket s' \rrbracket \subseteq \bigcup_{i=1}^m (\llbracket s_i \rrbracket \times \llbracket s'_i \rrbracket) = \bigcap_{I \subseteq \{1, \cdots, m\}} \left(\bigcup_{i \in I} \llbracket s_i \rrbracket \times T \right) \cup \left(T \times \bigcup_{i \notin I} \llbracket s'_i \rrbracket \right)$$

by transforming the right hand similarly to the process in Sec. 3. We thus check "$\llbracket s \rrbracket \subseteq \llbracket \bigcup_{i \in I} s_i \rrbracket$ or $\llbracket s' \rrbracket \subseteq \llbracket \bigcup_{i \notin I} s'_i \rrbracket$" for each subset I of $\{1, \cdots, m\}$ (**Conj** and **Conj**$_f$).

Finally, the rules for the case $cont = s \prec S \mid s' \prec S'$ are:

$$\frac{\mathcal{A}, s \prec S \rightsquigarrow \mathcal{A}', \pi}{\mathcal{A}, s \prec S | s' \prec S' \rightsquigarrow \mathcal{A}', \pi} \quad \text{(Front)} \qquad \frac{\mathcal{A}, s \prec S \rightsquigarrow \mathcal{A}', \bot \quad \mathcal{A}', s' \prec S' \rightsquigarrow \mathcal{A}'', \pi}{\mathcal{A}, s \prec S | s' \prec S' \rightsquigarrow \mathcal{A}'', \pi} \quad \text{(Post)}$$

$$\frac{\mathcal{A}, s \prec S \rightsquigarrow \mathcal{A}', \bot \quad \mathcal{A}', s' \prec S' \rightsquigarrow \mathcal{A}'', \bot}{\mathcal{A}, s \prec S | s' \prec S' \rightsquigarrow \mathcal{A}'', \bot} \quad \text{(Neither}_f\text{)}$$

Here, we need to check whether or not at least one of $\llbracket s \rrbracket \subseteq \llbracket S \rrbracket$ and $\llbracket s' \rrbracket \subseteq \llbracket S' \rrbracket$ holds. Hence, we first check $\llbracket s \rrbracket \subseteq \llbracket S \rrbracket$ and, if it succeeds with π, then we return $\rho = \pi$ without checking $\llbracket s' \rrbracket \subseteq \llbracket S' \rrbracket$ (**Front**); if $\llbracket s \rrbracket \subseteq \llbracket S \rrbracket$ is refuted, then we check $\llbracket s' \rrbracket \subseteq \llbracket S' \rrbracket$ (**Post** and **Neither**$_f$).

Theorem 1. *The complexity of the algorithm is bounded in $2^{\mathcal{O}(|Q|)}$.*

Theorem 2 (Soundness). *Suppose $\mathcal{A}, s \prec S \rightsquigarrow \mathcal{A}', \pi$. If both $\mathcal{A}$ and π are consistent, then $\llbracket s \rrbracket \subseteq \llbracket S \rrbracket$ holds and $\mathcal{A}'$ is consistent.*

Theorem 3 (Completeness). *Suppose* $A, s \prec S \rightsquigarrow A', \bot$. *If* A *is consistent, then* $[\![s]\!] \not\subseteq [\![S]\!]$ *holds and* A' *is consistent.*

5   Related Work

Since the tree automata containment problem is a key to XML type-checking, several authors have investigated various techniques for practical algorithms. As mentioned in Introduction, Hosoya, Vouillon, and Pierce have proposed a top-down algorithm [12]. Our algorithm in the present paper is constructed on top of theirs and adds an improvement to avoid backtracking by keeping track of dependencies among containments to be checked. Frisch has also pursued for improving the top-down algorithm [14]. He has pointed out that functional data structures used in the original top-down algorithm for performing backtracking can actually be replaced by destructive data structures (a hash table with a stack). Our experiments implement an algorithm incorporating his remark and confirmed that this replacement can indeed contribute to the efficiency (Sec. 6). Frisch has also proposed a different approach [14] that, given a containment to check, generates a set of certain forms of constraints and delegates this to a *local constraint solver* [15]. An empirical comparison with this algorithm is still planed.

Another completely different approach has been investigated by Tozawa and Hagiya [16]. They have used binary decision diagrams (BDDs) for representing sets of sets of states of given tree automata and solving the containment problem by using a series of operations on BDDs. Their algorithm behaves in a bottom-up way and therefore some combinations of states may potentially be examined even when it is not needed. Nevertheless they have given some experimental results that indicate a potential advantage over the top-down approach.

6   Experiments

In our preliminary experiments, we compare the following three algorithms.

NonBack. Our non-backtracking top-down algorithm.

Origin. Hosoya-Vouillon-Pierce's original top-down algorithm [12] using functional data structures, maintaining no dependencies of containments or failed containments.

Stack. Frisch's version of top-down algorithm using destructive data structures (mentioned in the previous section), maintaining only failed containments (no dependencies of containments).

We have experimented on the third algorithm in order to see whether the cheaper optimization suggested by Frisch can compete with our rather involved treatment. We have used seven examples (explained below) as inputs to the algorithms and measured the amortized elapsed time that each algorithm takes for each example. We have also counted the number of times that states were unfolded by

Example	Algorithm	Time(Sec.)	Unfold	Example	Algorithm	Time(Sec.)	Unfold
addrbook	NonBack	0.0028	126	xbel	NonBack	0.0044	313
	Origin	0.0060	975		Origin	0.0137	2701
	Stack	0.0026	126		Stack	0.0044	339
bookmarks	NonBack	0.0564	1050	complex_pat	NonBack	1.1094	189
	Origin	0.2315	40597	($n = 6$)	Origin	6.7649	17253
	Stack	0.0496	1050		Stack	6.6449	724
html2latex	NonBack	0.0837	1146	docbook	NonBack	1.5548	2134
	Origin	0.7094	139735		Origin	>1h.	—
	Stack	0.1668	2444		Stack	0.9097	2134

Fig. 2. Measurement result of experiments

the transition function during the check. The experiment has been done in the following environment: Intel Mobile PentiumIII 700MHz with 256 mega bytes memory under Linux (kernel version 2.4.7). The result is shown in Fig. 2.

In each of the first four examples, we take a small but non-trivial program written in XDuce and measure the time spent for checking all the containments needed in typechecking the program. Although these programs are not "real" applications, these contain typical patterns of XML programming and some of these (bookmarks and html2latex) use a relatively large schema, i.e., XHTML, and hence experimenting on these is a meaningful benchmark. The result shows that our non-backtracking algorithm works about 3 times to 8 times faster than the original algorithm. It also shows that the running time is similar in our algorithm and in Frisch's version except that ours is about twice faster in html2latex. Hence, it indicates that the cheaper optimization can be enough for many cases.

In the next example (complex_pat), we examine the containment between A and $B_1 | \ldots | B_n$ where $A, B_1, \ldots, B_n$ are defined as follows using the notation of regular expression types [12].

$$A = a[T_1*], a[T_2*], \ldots\ldots\ldots\ldots\ldots, a[T_n*]$$
$$B_i = a[T_1*], \ldots, a[S_i], a[T_{i+1}*], \ldots, a[T_n*] \ (i = 1, \ldots, n-1)$$
$$B_n = a[T_1*], \ldots\ldots\ldots\ldots, a[T_{i+1}*], a[S_n*]$$
$$T_i = b_i[X] \quad S_i = b_i[Y]$$

(B_n has an additional $*$ in the last label whereas the other B_i's does not. This is for ensuring the containment to hold.) In the above, X and Y are defined as some types (not shown here) where the containment between X and Y holds, but its check needs a large computation. Although this example itself is not taken from a real application, a similar one could appear in checking a pattern match (in the style of XDuce) that extracts, from a given sequence of a fixed length, the first element whose content matches a particular type. The result in Fig. 2 shows that, for the case $n = 6$, our algorithm runs 6 times more efficiently than Frisch's version, and in fact, the ratio is proportional to n. Hence, this result implies that, only with his simple optimization techniques, the algorithm can still behave in a catastrophic manner in some cases.

In the final example (docbook), we perform a single containment check between version 2 and version 4 of the DocBook schema [17]. This series of schemas is one of the largest popular schemas for XML and hence is a challenging example for the containment algorithms. The result is that the original top-down algorithm could not finish checking in a reasonable amount of time whereas the other algorithms finish in about 1 second. Frisch's algorithm is about 70% faster than ours. However, note that the numbers of unfoldings are exactly the same for these. Since, from the way the algorithm is constructed, the number of unfoldings is always equal or smaller in our algorithm and since the additional overhead is about 70% even in such a large example, we can expect that the relative slowdown can be bounded by 70% in almost any situation. Considering that there are cases where we can save the algorithm from a catastrophic slowdown, we believe that this overhead is acceptable in practice.

Acknowledgment. We would like to express our deepest gratitude to Susumu Nishimura for his advice in improving the presentation of this paper. We also thank Alain Frisch for his precious comments and suggestions. This work was partly supported by The Inamori Foundation and Japan Society for the Promotion of Science.

References

1. Bray, T., Paoli, J., Sperberg-McQueen, C.M., Maler, E.: Extensible markup language (XML™). http://www.w3.org/XML/ (2000)
2. Hosoya, H., Pierce, B.C.: XDuce: A typed XML processing language. ACM Transactions on Internet Technology **3** (2003) 117–148
3. Benzaken, V., Castagna, G., Frisch, A.: CDuce: a white paper. In: PLAN-X: Programming Language Technologies for XML. (2002)
4. Fankhauser, P., Fernández, M., Malhotra, A., Rys, M., Siméon, J., Wadler, P.: XQuery 1.0 Formal Semantics. http://www.w3.org/TR/query-semantics/ (2001)
5. Milo, T., Suciu, D., Vianu, V.: Typechecking for XML transformers. In: Proceedings of the Nineteenth ACM SIGMOD-SIGACT-SIGART Symposium on Principles of Database Systems, ACM (2000) 11–22
6. Murata, M.: Transformation of documents and schemas by patterns and contextual conditions. In: Principles of Document Processing '96. Volume 1293 of Lecture Notes in Computer Science., Springer-Verlag (1997) 153–169
7. Tozawa, A.: Towards static type checking for XSLT. In: Proceedings of ACM Symposium on Document Engineering. (2001)
8. Murata, M., Lee, D., Mani, M.: Taxonomy of XML schema languages using formal language theory. In: Extreme Markup Languages. (2001)
9. Fallside, D.C.: XML Schema Part 0: Primer, W3C Recommendation. http://www.w3.org/TR/xmlschema-0/ (2001)
10. Clark, J., Murata, M.: RELAX NG. http://www.relaxng.org (2001)
11. Seidl, H.: Deciding equivalence of finite tree automata. SIAM Journal of Computing **19** (1990) 424–437
12. Hosoya, H., Vouillon, J., Pierce, B.C.: Regular expression types for XML. In: Proceedings of the International Conference on Functional Programming (ICFP). (2000) 11–22
13. Suda, T., Hosoya, H.: Non-backtracking top-down algorithm for checking tree automata containment. http://arbre.is.s.u-tokyo.ac.jp/ (2005) full version.

14. Frisch, A.: Théorie, conception et réalisation d'un langage de programmation fonctionnel adapté à XML. PhD thesis, Universit Paris 7 (2004)
15. Dowling, W.F., Gallier, J.H.: Linear-time algorithms for testing the satisfiability of propositional horn formulas. Journal of Logic Programming **1** (1984) 267–284
16. Tozawa, A., Hagiya, M.: XML schema containment checking based on semi-implicit techniques. In: 8th International Conference on Implementation and Application of Automata. Volume 2759 of Lecture Notes in Computer Science., Springer-Verlag (2003) 213–225
17. OASIS: DocBook. http://www.docbook.org (2002)

Size Reduction of Multitape Automata

Hellis Tamm*, Matti Nykänen, and Esko Ukkonen

Department of Computer Science,
P.O. Box 68, 00014 University of Helsinki, Finland
{hellis.tamm, matti.nykanen, esko.ukkonen}@cs.helsinki.fi

Abstract. We present a method for size reduction of two-way multi-tape automata. Our algorithm applies local transformations that change the order in which transitions concerning different tapes occur in the automaton graph, and merge suitable states into a single state. Our work is motivated by implementation of a language for string manipulation in database systems where string predicates are compiled into two-way multitape automata. Additionally, we present a (one-tape) NFA reduction algorithm that is based on a method proposed for DFA minimization by Kameda and Weiner, and apply this algorithm, combined with the multitape automata reduction algorithm, on our multitape automata.

1 Introduction

Multitape automata, introduced by Rabin and Scott [1], are a more difficult research area than one-tape automata. Although the equivalence problem of deterministic (one-way) multitape automata is decidable [2], the same problem for nondeterministic multitape automata is not, and we are not aware of any minimization procedure for multitape automata.

In this paper, we present a method to reduce the size of two-way multi-tape automata. Our main motivation for this work is the implementation of the Alignment Declaration Language, a language for expressing string predicates, designed in the purposes of developing a string handling and manipulating database system [3]. While this language provides means to declare string predicates, these declarations must be converted into an executable form to be used in database queries. As an intermediate form in this conversion, we use two-way multitape automata. To make the final executable more concise and efficient to simulate, we are interested in reducing the size of these automata. The automaton model that we consider is a modified version of the Rabin-Scott model. Our algorithm uses certain local factoring transformations that change the order in which transitions concerning different tapes occur in the automaton graph, and merge suitable states into a single state. The algorithm runs in polynomial time with respect to the number of states of the automaton.

---

* Supported by the Academy of Finland grant 201560.

J. Farré, I. Litovsky, and S. Schmitz (Eds.): CIAA 2005, LNCS 3845, pp. 307–318, 2006.

Also, we can view these multitape automata as if they were one-tape nondeterministic automata (NFA) instead, and apply appropriate techniques to reduce their size. More specifically, we consider a method from [4] to reduce the size of NFAs.

We combine this NFA reduction method along with our multitape automata size reduction algorithm into an algorithm that alternatingly applies these procedures on a given automaton until no more size reduction can be achieved. By experiments, this approach is quite successful.

Some details which are omitted in this paper can be found in [5] where we presented the multitape automata size reduction algorithm and applied it along with a minimization procedure for deterministic automata.

2 Alignment Declaration Language

The Alignment Declaration language is designed to describe string comparison and manipulation operations over several strings that are manipulated together. A basic statement of this language is an *on*-statement of the form < *scan part*> on < *condition part*> where both the scan and condition parts are optional. A scan part starts with a word **scan** or **rightscan** followed by a list of string variables, and its effect is to move the positions of currently considered characters of corresponding strings, respectively, to the next or the previous position. A condition part is a Boolean combination of character comparisons, such as x='a', x=y, x=[or x=], which evaluate true if, respectively, the current character of a string denoted by a variable x is 'a', the same as the current character of a string denoted by y, the left endmarker, or the right endmarker. Initially, the current character for any string is the left endmarker. An on-statement holds if and only if, after taking into account possible changes of current characters of the strings pointed out by the scan part, the condition part evaluates true.

An on-statement is an expression in the Alignment Declaration language. Other expressions are defined as follows. If Φ_1 and Φ_2 are expressions then their concatenation $\Phi_1\Phi_2$ is an expression, **repeat** * **times** Φ_1 **end** is an expression, and **choose** $\Phi_1|\Phi_2$ **end** is an expression. The expression $\Phi_1\Phi_2$ holds if and only if Φ_1 holds and Φ_2 holds when evaluated starting from the same currently considered character positions where the evaluation of Φ_1 ends. The expression **repeat** * **times** Φ_1 **end** holds if and only if a k-fold concatenation of Φ_1 with itself holds for some $k \geq 0$. The expression **choose** $\Phi_1|\Phi_2$ **end** holds if and only if Φ_1 or Φ_2 holds.

Some shorthands are defined in the language. For example, **repeat** * **times** scan x on x='a' end can be written as scan* x on x='a'. Different string alphabets can be applied by using the **keep**-statement (see the example below). A more complete description of the language can be found in [3].

Here is an example of an alignment declaration describing a property involving two strings x and y from the alphabet $\{a, b\}$ such that y is the reversal of x:

```
reversal(x, y)
keep x in 'a', 'b'
keep y in 'a', 'b'
  scan* x on
  scan x on x=]
  repeat * times
    rightscan x on
    scan y on x=y
  end
  rightscan x on x=[
  scan y on y=]
end
end
```

3 Alignment Declarations as Multitape Automata

In this section we discuss how the alignment declarations are translated into two-way multitape automata. First, we present the automaton model that is specially designed for our application, and then we show how the automata are obtained.

We describe the n-tape automaton model as follows. There is a window whose width is one symbol and height is n symbols, so that one symbol of each tape shows through that window at any given time. We call the showing symbol of a given tape the *current symbol* for that tape. Initially, the current symbols for all tapes are their left endmarkers. If we want to read the next symbol from a tape, we move that tape *left* with respect to the window. And if we want to read the previous symbol from a tape, we move that tape *right*. These tape movements are indicated in the automaton as transitions with the labels L_i and R_i where L and R are special symbols not belonging to the alphabet of the automaton, and i is the tape involved. For reading an input string, there are transitions with the labels like a_i where a is a symbol read from the tape $i \in \{1, ..., n\}$. In addition, transitions may involve special symbols [and] denoting the endmarkers, and the symbol @ that is used to denote any string character or the right endmarker. Also, the automaton can have transitions on empty string ϵ.

Formally, an n-tape automaton is given by a quintuple $(Q, \Sigma, \delta, q_I, F)$ where Q is a finite set of states, Σ is the input alphabet, $\delta : Q \times (\Sigma'_{\{1,...,n\}} \cup \{\epsilon\}) \rightarrow 2^Q$ is the transition function where $\Sigma' = \Sigma \cup \{[,],@\} \cup \{L, R\}$ and $\Sigma'_{\{1,...,n\}} = \{a_i \mid a \in \Sigma', i \in \{1, ..., n\}\}$, $q_I \in Q$ is the initial state and $F \subseteq Q$ is the set of final states. The number of states $|Q|$ is the *size* of the automaton.

Initially, the automaton is in the initial state. Let u be a string formed by concatenating the labels of all transitions that appear on some path in the automaton graph going from the initial state to a final state. We consider u to be an *accepting computation* if there exists an n-tuple $(w_1, ..., w_n)$ where $w_i \in \Sigma^*$ for $i = 1, ..., n$, such that if we read u from left one symbol at a time then, on seeing any c_i where $c \in \Sigma \cup \{[,]\}$ the symbol currently read from w_i is c, on seeing $@_i$ the current symbol of w_i is not the left endmarker, and on seeing L_i or R_i the current symbol of w_i is taken to be the next or the previous one, respectively. In this case, the n-tuple $(w_1, ..., w_n)$ is *accepted* by the automaton. The set of all n-tuples accepted by an automaton A is the *language* of A.

Now, let Φ be an alignment declaration with string variables $x_1, ..., x_n$. Then Φ can be translated into an n-tape automaton A as follows. First, every Boolean formula in all *on*-statements of Φ is transformed so that it consists of only **and** and **or** operations combining character comparisons in a form x='a', x=[or x=]. To create A, we use a function Compile() described below which takes either an alignment declaration or a part of it as its first input argument and the automaton state as its second input argument, possibly creates new states and transitions into the automaton and calls itself recursively, and finally outputs an automaton state.

In the beginning, let A consist of a single final state q_F. Then, a call to the function Compile(Φ, q_F) builds up A and yields the initial state q_I of A. Let Φ_1 and Φ_2 denote either expressions in the Alignment Declaration language or parts of such Boolean formulas described above. Let q be an automaton state. Then we define the function Compile() by induction over the structure of the alignment declaration as follows:

1) Compile($\Phi_1\Phi_2, q$) = Compile(Φ_1 **and** Φ_2, q) = Compile(Φ_1, Compile(Φ_2, q));
2) Compile(**choose** $\Phi_1|\Phi_2$ **end**, q) = Compile(Φ_1 **or** Φ_2, q) = q_1 where q_1 is a new state with ϵ-transitions to Compile(Φ_1, q) and Compile(Φ_2, q);
3) Compile(**repeat** * **times** Φ_1 **end**, q) = q_1 where q_1 is a new state with ϵ-transitions to q and Compile(Φ_1, q_1);
4) Compile(**on** Φ_1, q) = Compile(Φ_1, q);
5) Compile(**scan** $x_{i_1}, ..., x_{i_k}$ **on** Φ_1, q) = q_1 where $i_j \in \{1, ..., n\}$ and $q_1, ..., q_k$ are new states with transitions $q_j \xrightarrow{L_{i_j}} q_{j+1}$ for $j = 1, ..., k$, with q_{k+1} = Compile(Φ_1, q);
6) Compile(**rightscan** $x_{i_1}, ..., x_{i_k}$ **on** Φ_1, q) = q_1 where $i_j \in \{1, ..., n\}$ and $q_1, ..., q_{2k}$ are new states with transitions $q_{2j-1} \xrightarrow{@_{i_j}} q_{2j}$, $q_{2j} \xrightarrow{R_{i_j}} q_{2j+1}$, and $q_{2j-1} \xrightarrow{L_{i_j}} q_{2j+1}$ for $j = 1, ..., k$, with q_{2k+1} = Compile(Φ_1, q);
7) Compile($x_i = \sigma, q$) = q_1 where $i \in \{1, ..., n\}$, $\sigma \in \Sigma \cup \{[,]\}$, and q_1 is a new state with a transition $q_1 \xrightarrow{\sigma_i} q$;
8) Compile($true, q$) = q_1 where q_1 is a new state with ϵ-transition to q;
9) Compile($false, q$) = q_1 where q_1 is a new state with no transitions.

The ϵ-transitions can be eliminated from A. Next, the automaton is modified to eliminate some redundant checks and tape movements from it. For this reason, the automaton is *expanded* so that it remembers in each state the last transition labels for all tapes which appeared on any path from the initial state to the given state. Those transitions that can be seen as redundant or impossible-to-follow, by this local inspection of labels, are eliminated from the automaton. Also, the states that are not on any path from the initial state to a final state are eliminated.

To continue with the example of Section 2, the 2-tape automaton, obtained by applying the function Compile() on the alignment declaration reversal(x, y) where the ϵ-transitions are eliminated, is shown in Figure 1 (left). Here, the first tape corresponds to variable x and the second one to y. The expanded automaton A_{rev} is shown in Figure 1 (right).

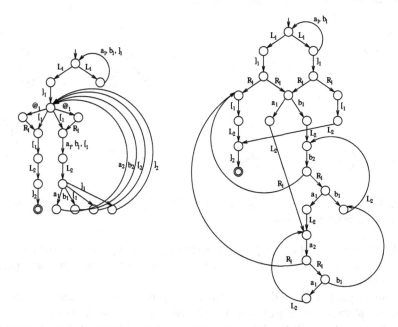

Fig. 1. The automaton corresponding to the alignment declaration reversal(x, y) (left) and the expanded automaton A_{rev} (right)

4   Reduction Algorithm for Multitape Automata

We have designed an algorithm to reduce the size of an n-tape automaton $A = (Q, \Sigma, \delta, q_I, F)$. The algorithm is based on the following four language preserving automaton transformations.

Swap Upwards. Let $q' \in Q$ be a non-initial and non-final state with $k \geq 1$ incoming and one outgoing transition. Let the transitions associated with q' be $q_1 \xrightarrow{(a_1)_{i_1}} q', ..., q_k \xrightarrow{(a_k)_{i_k}} q'$ and $q' \xrightarrow{b_j} q$, such that j refers to a tape that is different from all tapes $i_l, l \in \{1, ..., k\}$. Then q' and its incoming and outgoing transitions can be removed and replaced with new non-initial and non-final states $q'_1, ..., q'_k$ and transitions $q_1 \xrightarrow{b_j} q'_1, ..., q_k \xrightarrow{b_j} q'_k$, and $q'_1 \xrightarrow{(a_1)_{i_1}} q, ..., q'_k \xrightarrow{(a_k)_{i_k}} q$.

Sink Combine. Let $q_1, ..., q_k$ be some non-initial states of A, all having exactly one incoming transition labelled a_i from a state q of A where q is different from all q_i, $i \in \{1, ..., k\}$. Then $q_1, ..., q_k$ can be combined into one state q', meaning that $q_1, ..., q_k$ and their incoming and outgoing transitions are removed and replaced by a new non-initial state q' which is final if and only if any of $q_1, ..., q_k$ is final, with all outgoing transitions of $q_1, ..., q_k$ now leaving q', and the transition $q \xrightarrow{a_i} q'$.

Swap Downwards and *Source Combine* are defined symmetrically. All transformations are schematically presented in Figure 2.

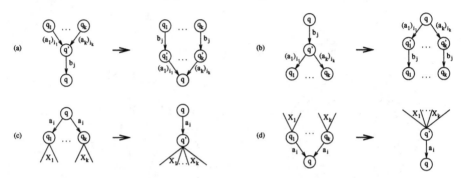

Fig. 2. Automata transformations: (a) Swap Upwards; (b) Swap Downwards; (c) Sink Combine; (d) Source Combine

Let $q \in Q$ and $i \in \{1, ..., n\}$. A transition is called a *future transition* for the state q and tape i if it is the first transition involving this tape on some path in A that starts from q.

A central part of the reduction algorithm (presented in Figure 3) is the procedure `MoveTransitionUp()`. Let $a \in \Sigma'$. We want to find a set of future transitions for q and i, with the label a_i, such that by calling `MoveTransitionUp()` for each of these transitions and the state q, we can reduce the number of states of A by a certain amount. When this procedure is invoked with a transition (q_1, a_i, q_2) and the state q, its goal is to decrease the number of states and transitions of A by "moving" the transition (q_1, a_i, q_2) in the automaton graph "up", applying *Swap Upwards* and *Sink Combine* transformations on the way, until this transition, along with one or more other transitions with the same label, will be replaced by a transition out of q (instead of q_1).

If we denote a set of future transitions for q and i bearing the label a_i, by $ft_{q,i,a}$, then let us denote the set of all paths in A, which start from q and end by any transition in $ft_{q,i,a}$, by $P_{ft_{q,i,a}}$. Consider the following conditions imposed on the path set $P_{ft_{q,i,a}}$. Let p be a path in the set $P_{ft_{q,i,a}}$ and let the two last states on p be q' and q''. Then the conditions are as follows:

(i) there are no loops in p, except that q'' may be equal to q;

(ii) every state on p that appears after q and before q'' is non-initial and non-final, all of its incoming and outgoing transitions are traversed by some path in $P_{ft_{q,i,a}}$, and all of its incoming transitions involve a tape that is different from i;

(iii) if q' has more than one outgoing transition then q'' is non-initial and has only one incoming transition.

procedure MoveTransitionUp$(A, (q_1, a_i, q_2), q)$
1. **if** transition (q_1, a_i, q_2) exists in A **then**
2.   use *Sink Combine* transformation to merge all such states that are reachable
        from q_1 by a transition labelled by a_i and suitable for this transformation;
3.   **if** $q \neq q_1$ and $outdegree(q_1) = 1$ **then**
4.   use *Swap Upwards* transformation on the outgoing transition of q_1
            and let T be a set of transitions with the label a_i
            created by this transformation;
5.   **for all** $(q_1', a_i, q_2') \in T$ where $q_1', q_2' \in Q$ **do**
6.   MoveTransitionUp$((q_1', a_i, q_2'), q)$;

procedure Upwards$(A, tape)$
1. $m := 0$;
2. $reduced := true$;
3.   **while** $reduced = true$ **do**
4. $reduced := false$;
5.   **for all** $q \in Q$ as long as $reduced = false$ **do**
6.   find a set $FT_{q,tape} = \bigcup_{a \in \sigma' \subseteq \Sigma'} FT_{q,tape,a}$ such that for each $a \in \sigma'$,
            $FT_{q,tape,a}$ is as in (P1);
7.   **for all** $a \in \sigma'$ where $|FT_{q,tape,a}| > 1$ **do**
8.   find a state q' such that $FT_{q',tape,a} = FT_{q,tape,a}$, $FT_{q',tape,a}$ is as
                in (P1), and the longest path from q' to the originating state of
                any transition in $FT_{q,tape,a}$ is of minimal length;
9.   **for all** $t \in FT_{q',tape,a}$ **do**
10.   MoveTransitionUp(A, t, q');
11. $m := m + |FT_{q',tape,a}| - 1$;
12. $reduced := true$;
13. **return** m;

Reduce A
1. $m := 0$;
2. $A_1 := \text{CopyOf}(A)$;
3. $reduced := true$;
4.   **while** $reduced = true$ **do**
5. $reduced := false$;
6.   **for** $tape := 1$ **to** n **do**
7. $m_{up} := \text{Upwards}(A, tape)$;
8. $m_{down} := \text{Downwards}(A_1, tape)$;
9.   **if** $m_{up} > 0$ **or** $m_{down} > 0$ **then**
10.   **if** $m_{up} \geq m_{down}$ **then**
11. $A_1 := \text{CopyOf}(A)$;
12. $m := m + m_{up}$;
13.   **else**
14. $A := \text{CopyOf}(A_1)$;
15. $m := m + m_{down}$;
16. $reduced := true$;
17. **return** A, m;

Fig. 3. Procedures MoveTransitionUp(), Upwards(), and the reduction algorithm

Now, the following propositions hold:

(P1) There is a unique maximal set $FT_{q,i,a}$ of future transitions for q and i, with the label a_i, such that the conditions (i) – (iii) hold for the set $P_{FT_{q,i,a}}$;

(P2) The series of calls to MoveTransitionUp() where it is invoked with every transition in $FT_{q,i,a}$ and q, results in size reduction of A by $|FT_{q,i,a}| - 1$ states.

Also, given another $b \in \Sigma'$ with the set $FT_{q,i,b}$ satisfying (P1), the application of transformations of (P2) for the set $FT_{q,i,a}$ does not affect the application of transformations of (P2) for the set $FT_{q,i,b}$. The proofs of these propositions can be found in [5, Propositions 5.1 – 5.3].

Also, symmetric conditions can be specified that allow to eliminate automaton states by applying a procedure that uses the *Source Combine* and *Swap Downwards* transformations.

The reduction algorithm uses a variable m to indicate the number of states eliminated from A. The idea of the algorithm is that for each tape of A, as many states as possible are eliminated from A using the procedure Upwards(), and from its copy A_1 using a symmetric procedure Downwards() (not shown). Given the automaton tape *tape*, Upwards() finds for each state q a set $FT_{q,tape}$ that is the union of all sets $FT_{q,tape,a}$ of future transitions for q and *tape*, with some symbol a, such that $FT_{q,tape,a}$ is as in (P1) above. For all $FT_{q,tape,a}$ that consist of at least two transitions, a state q' is found which has the same set of future transitions $FT_{q',tape,a}$ for this tape and symbol that satisfies (P1), and which is as close to the transitions in $FT_{q,tape,a}$ as possible. Then the procedure MoveTransitionUp() is called for all of the transitions in $FT_{q',tape,a}$ and q', and by (P2) above, the value of m is increased by $|FT_{q',tape,a}| - 1$. After considering every such set $FT_{q,tape,a}$, the loop over all states is started again. This process continues until no further reductions of A can be achieved using this approach for any state of A. The return value of Upwards() indicates the number of states eliminated by it.

In case any states were eliminated from either A or A_1, a smaller one of these automata is retained and the next round with a next tape is performed using two copies of that automaton. Also, the value of m is updated accordingly. This process is continued until no more states are eliminated for any tape.

For a fixed number of tapes and fixed alphabet, the time complexity of the algorithm is $O(|Q|^4)$ [5].

5 Reducing the Size of an NFA

Our multitape automata can also be viewed as (one-tape) NFAs over the alphabet $\Sigma'_{\{1,\ldots,n\}}$. Therefore, it is interesting to apply NFA size reduction methods as well. We propose here one such method.

Let A be an NFA. The *reversal* of A (denoted by A^R) is obtained from A by reversing the direction of all transitions and interchanging the initial and final states. Let p and q be some states of A. If the set of all words that can be formed by concatenating the transition labels on some path from p to a final state of A equals to the similarly created set for q then the states p and q are called *equivalent*. We can make A deterministic by applying *subset construction* [6] on it.

Size reduction of NFAs has been recently considered in several articles, such as [7, 8, 9]. Here we consider a method for NFA reduction based on [4]. Let A be an NFA and let C be an automaton obtained from A^R by subset construction. That is, any state of C is a subset of the state set of A. By Kameda and Weiner [4], two states of A are equivalent if and only if they appear exactly in the same states of C. They mention that this is useful for DFA minimization. Namely, if A is a DFA then by merging the equivalent states one can find a minimal DFA. In the case of A being an NFA, this method can be used for the size reduction of the automaton although the result is not necessarily a minimal NFA.

Similarly, we can find the equivalent states of the reversal automaton. Let B be an automaton obtained by applying the subset construction on A. Then, two states of A^R are equivalent if and only if they appear exactly in the same states of B. By the appropriate merging of the equivalent states of A^R, we can reduce the size of A^R (and use this to reduce A).

Ilie and Yu [7] consider the right-invariant and left-invariant equivalences which are refinements of the above state equivalence relations. Thus, the reductions according to the above equivalences result in automaton size reduction of at least the same amount as obtained by [7]. Also, merging the equivalent states in NFA can produce *useless* states, that is, states which are not on any path from an initial state to a final state. These states can be eliminated, too.

Similarly to [7], we can possibly get a smaller NFA by combining the reductions corresponding to the two equivalences above. We propose the following method for NFA reduction.

First, find and merge the equivalent states of an NFA according to the method above, and eliminate the useless states from the automaton. Second, find and merge the equivalent states of the reversal of the resulting automaton, eliminating the useless states as well. If the automaton size was reduced by the second method, then again, apply the first method, etc. That is, alternatingly apply two reduction methods (with the elimination of useless states), until no more reduction of the automaton occurs.

6   Reducing the Size of a Multitape Automaton

To continue with the example of Sections 2 and 3, if we apply the NFA reduction algorithm presented at the end of Section 5 to the automaton A_{rev}, then its size is reduced from 23 states to 11 states. The resulting automaton denoted by $Red_{NFA}(A_{rev})$ is shown in Figure 4 (left).

Now, applying the multitape automata reduction algorithm of Section 4 after the NFA reduction can lead to a further size reduction of the automaton. If we apply this algorithm to $Red_{NFA}(A_{rev})$ then the result is the automaton $Red_{multi}(Red_{NFA}(A_{rev}))$ having 9 states as shown in Figure 4 (right). Further application of the NFA reduction algorithm on this automaton does not make it any smaller.

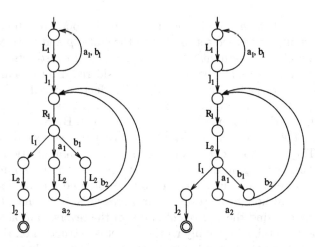

Fig. 4. The automata $Red_{NFA}(A_{rev})$ (left) and $Red_{multi}(Red_{NFA}(A_{rev}))$ (right)

On the other hand, we can also reduce A_{rev} by applying the multitape automata reduction algorithm first. The resulting automaton (not shown) has 16 states. Now, if we apply the NFA reduction procedure on this automaton, the result is the same as the automaton $Red_{NFA}(A_{rev})$. Further reduction of this automaton is as above.

In this example, the end result of applying these two algorithms one after another does not depend on which of them was applied first. However, generally, this is not the case.

Finally, we propose the following algorithm to reduce the size of a multitape automaton A that alternatingly applies two size-reducing algorithms. Apply two sequences of algorithms consisting of the NFA reduction procedure of Section 5 and the multitape automata reduction algorithm of Section 4 by turn on A, at one time starting with the NFA reduction algorithm and the other time starting with the multitape automata reduction algorithm, and stopping when no more size reduction occurs to A. Output the smaller of the resulting two automata.

7   Experimental Results

To test the algorithm presented at the end of Section 6, we have considered a set of alignment declarations expressing different string properties, and made experiments with the corresponding automata. The results of the experiments are presented in the table in Figure 5. For each string predicate, the table shows the number of tapes n and the alphabet size $|\Sigma|$, the size of the original automaton $|A_{orig}|$ (the result of applying the function Compile() on the corresponding alignment declaration) after eliminating ϵ-transitions from it, and the size of the expanded automaton $|A_{exp}|$ after ϵ-transition elimination. The reduction algorithm is applied on the ϵ-transition-free expanded automaton A_{exp} of each string predicate. The table shows the size of the automaton during the reduction

String predicate	n	$|\Sigma|$	$|A_{orig}|$	$|A_{exp}|$	Automaton size during the reduction process			
reversal	2	2	17	23	Red_{NFA} 11	Red_{Multi} 9	Red_{NFA} 9	
					Red_{multi} 16	Red_{NFA} 11	Red_{multi} 9	Red_{NFA} 9
substring	2	2	11	18	Red_{NFA} 9	Red_{multi} 9		
					Red_{multi} 17	Red_{NFA} 9	Red_{multi} 9	
subsequence	2	2	11	17	Red_{NFA} 7	Red_{multi} 7		
					Red_{multi} 16	Red_{NFA} 7	Red_{multi} 7	
prefix	2	2	9	16	Red_{NFA} 7	Red_{multi} 7		
					Red_{multi} 15	Red_{NFA} 7	Red_{multi} 7	
suffix	2	2	18	25	Red_{NFA} 11	Red_{multi} 11		
					Red_{multi} 22	Red_{NFA} 11	Red_{multi} 11	
concatenation	3	2	21	20	Red_{NFA} 13	Red_{multi} 12	Red_{NFA} 12	
					Red_{multi} 19	Red_{NFA} 13	Red_{multi} 12	Red_{NFA} 12
shuffle	3	2	21	51	Red_{NFA} 12	Red_{multi} 10	Red_{NFA} 10	
					Red_{multi} 45	Red_{NFA} 12	Red_{multi} 10	Red_{NFA} 10
overlap	3	2	15	48	Red_{NFA} 21	Red_{multi} 20	Red_{NFA} 20	
					Red_{multi} 44	Red_{NFA} 20	Red_{multi} 19	Red_{NFA} 19
edit distance	3	4	24	168	Red_{NFA} 28	Red_{multi} 27	Red_{NFA} 27	
					Red_{multi} 143	Red_{NFA} 28	Red_{multi} 27	Red_{NFA} 27

Fig. 5. Automata sizes before and during the reduction process

process, given in two rows: the upper row shows the automaton size in the sequence where the NFA reduction algorithm is applied first, and the lower row shows the automaton size in the sequence where the multitape automata reduction algorithm is applied first. The numbers in the columns with Red_{NFA} and Red_{multi} indicate the size of the automaton in the reduction process, after applying the NFA reduction or the multitape automata reduction algorithm, respectively.

Even if both of these reduction sequences end up with the automata of the same size, the automata may be different. For most cases in our experiments, the reduced automaton is smaller than the original one, although this is not always so, as for automata of *overlap* and *edit distance* predicates. However, if one has in mind the efficiency of simulating the computations of automata, then avoiding redundant checks of tape symbols and those paths that are not possible to follow, seem to be important. Fortunately, most of the size growth in the expanded automata seems to disappear as the result of the reduction process.

References

1. Rabin, M.O., Scott, D.: Finite automata and their decision problems. IBM J. Res. Develop. **3** (1959) 114–125
2. Harju, T., Karhumäki, J.: The equivalence problem of multitape finite automata. Theoretical Computer Science **78** (1991) 347–355
3. Grahne, G., Hakli, R., Nykänen, M., Tamm, H., Ukkonen, E.: Design and implementation of a string database query language. Inform. Syst. **28** (2003) 311–337
4. Kameda, T., Weiner, P.: On the state minimization of nondeterministic automata. IEEE Trans. Comput. **C-19** (1970) 617–627
5. Tamm, H.: On minimality and size reduction of one-tape and multitape finite automata. PhD thesis, Department of Computer Science, University of Helsinki, Finland (2004)
6. Hopcroft, J.E., Ullman, J.D.: Introduction to Automata Theory, Languages, and Computation. Addison-Wesley (1979)
7. Ilie, L., Yu, S.: Reducing NFAs by invariant equivalences. Theoretical Computer Science **306** (2003) 373–390
8. Ilie, L., Navarro, G., Yu, S.: On NFA reductions. In: Theory is forever. Volume 3113 of Lecture Notes in Computer Science., Springer (2004) 112–124
9. Champarnaud, J.M., Coulon, F.: NFA reduction algorithms by means of regular inequalities. Theoretical Computer Science **327** (2004) 241–253

Robust Spelling Correction[*]

Manuel Vilares[1], Juan Otero[1], and Jesús Vilares[2]

[1] Department of Computer Science, University of Vigo,
Campus As Lagoas s/n, 32004 Ourense, Spain
{vilares, jop}@uvigo.es
[2] Department of Computer Science, University of A Coruña,
Campus de Elviña s/n, 15071 A Coruña, Spain
jvilares@udc.es

Abstract. The paper introduces a robust spelling correction technique to deal with ill-formed input strings, including unknown parts of unknown length. In contrast to previous works, we derive profit from a finer dynamic programming construction, which takes advantage of the underlying grammatical structure, leading to an improved computational behavior and error repair quality. The formal description applies a deductive approach in order to simplify this task, separating it from the interpretation strategy, and including cut-off facilities.

1 Introduction

Although spelling correction has been a central subject in natural language processing (NLP) for a long time [1], recent years have seen a renewal of interest in it due to the increasing amount of textual information available in electronic format. Here, the state of the art [2] focuses on contextual and non-contextual error correction. In relation to the former, most proposals are based on NLP techniques and/or statistical-language models, integrating linguistic knowledge [3, 4]. For the latter, techniques look for possible editing sequences to reflect the error occurrence phenomenon in spelling. These strategies study correction patterns, most of them taking into account the *edit distance* [5], but also on occasion introducing constraints on the spelling process [6] in order to cut down the computational time needed for the correction.

Even non-contextual strategies can be of interest in a number of practical applications, when no training corpus is available and/or it is not easy to obtain statistics for estimating the linguistic model, these algorithms can be considered as a preliminary phase in a more sophisticated contextual approach such as shallow and partial interpretation. Our proposal extends an original non-contextual regional least-cost spelling correction proposal [7] in order to provide both robustness in noisy conditions and general parameterizable cut-off criteria. In relation to previous works, we provide a formal definition framework and an improved computational behavior.

---

[*] Research supported by the Spanish Government under projects TIN2004-07246-C03-01, TIN2004-07246-C03-02, and the Autonomous Government of Galicia under projects PGIDIT03SIN30501PR and PGIDIT02SIN01E.

J. Farré, I. Litovsky, and S. Schmitz (Eds.): CIAA 2005, LNCS 3845, pp. 319–328, 2006.

2   The Operational Model

Our aim is to parse a word $w_{1..n} = w_1 \ldots w_n$ according to an RG $\mathcal{G} = (N, \Sigma, P, S)$. We denote by w_0 (resp. w_{n+1}) the position in the string, $w_{1..n}$, previous to w_1 (resp. following w_n). We generate from $\mathcal{G}$ a *numbered minimal acyclic finite automaton* for the language $\mathcal{L}(\mathcal{G})$. In practice, we choose a device [8] generated by GALENA [9]. A *finite automaton* (FA) is a 5-tuple $\mathcal{A} = (\mathcal{Q}, \Sigma, \delta, q_0, \mathcal{Q}_f)$ where: $\mathcal{Q}$ is the set of states, Σ the set of input symbols, δ is a function of $\mathcal{Q} \times \Sigma$ into $2^{\mathcal{Q}}$ defining the transitions of the automaton, q_0 the initial state and $\mathcal{Q}_f$ the set of final states. We denote $\delta(q, a)$ by $q.a$, and we say that $\mathcal{A}$ is *deterministic* iff $\mid q.a \mid \leq 1$, $\forall q \in \mathcal{Q}$, $a \in \Sigma$. The notation is transitive, $q.w_{1..n}$ denotes the state $(\overset{n-2}{\ldots}(q.w_1)\overset{n-2}{\ldots}).w_n$. As a consequence, w is *accepted* iff $q_0.w \in \mathcal{Q}_f$, that is, the *language accepted by* $\mathcal{A}$ is defined as $\mathcal{L}(\mathcal{A}) = \{w, \text{ such that } q_0.w \in \mathcal{Q}_f\}$. An FA is *acyclic* when the underlying graph is. We define a *path in the* FA as a sequence of states $\rho = \{q_1, \ldots, q_n\}$, such that $\forall i \in \{1, \ldots, n-1\}$, $\exists a_i \in \Sigma$, $q_i.a_i = q_{i+1}$.

We also apply a minimization process [10]. In this sense, we say that two states, p and q, are *equivalent* iff the FA with p as initial state and the one that starts in q recognize the same language. An FA is *minimal* iff no pair in $\mathcal{Q}$ is equivalent. Although the standard recognition is deterministic, the repair one could introduce non-determinism by exploring alternatives associated to possibly more than one recovery strategy. So, in order to get polynomial complexity, we avoid duplicating intermediate computations in the repair of $w_{1..n} \in \Sigma^+$, storing them in a table $\mathcal{I}$ of *items*, $\mathcal{I} = \{[q, i], q \in \mathcal{Q}, i \in [1, n+1]\}$, where $[q, i]$ looks for the suffix $w_{i..n}$ to be analyzed from $q \in \mathcal{Q}$.

Our description uses *parsing schemata* [11], a triple $\langle \mathcal{I}, \mathcal{H}, \mathcal{D} \rangle$, with $\mathcal{H} = \{[a, i], a = w_i\}$ an initial set of items called *hypothesis* that encodes the word to be recognized[1], and $\mathcal{D}$ a set of *deduction steps* that allow items to be derived from previous ones. These are of the form $\{\eta_1, \ldots, \eta_k \vdash \xi \,/\, conds\}$, meaning that if all antecedents η_i are present and the conditions *conds* are satisfied, then the consequent ξ is generated. In our case, $\mathcal{D} = \mathcal{D}^{\text{Init}} \cup \mathcal{D}^{\text{Shift}}$, where:

$$\mathcal{D}^{\text{Init}} = \{\vdash [q_0, 1]\} \qquad \mathcal{D}^{\text{Shift}} = \{[p, i] \vdash [q, i+1] \,/\, \exists [a, i] \in \mathcal{H}, \; q = p.a\}$$

We associate a set of items S_p^w, called *itemset*, to each $p \in \mathcal{Q}$; and apply these deduction steps until no new item is generated. The word is recognized iff a *final item* $[q_f, n+1]$, $q_f \in \mathcal{Q}_f$ has been generated. We can assume that $\mathcal{Q}_f = \{q_f\}$, and that there is only one transition from (resp. to) q_0 (resp. q_f). To get this, it is sufficient to augment the original FA with two states which become the new initial and final states, and are linked to the original ones through empty transitions, our only concession to the notion of minimal FA.

3   Spelling Correction

We talk about an *error* in a word to mean the difference between what was intended and what actually appears, and we call *point of error* the point at

---

[1] A word $w_{1...n} \in \Sigma^+$, $n \geq 1$ is represented by $\{[w_1, 1], [w_2, 2], \ldots, [w_n, n]\}$.

which that difference occurs. So, a *repair* should be understood as a modification allowing the recognizer both to recover the process and to avoid cascaded errors, that is, errors precipitated by a previous erroneous repair diagnosis. This is the goal of *regional repairs* [7], which we succinctly remember now.

Working on acyclic FAs, we define an order relation $p < q$, with $p, q \in Q$ iff a path exists in the FA from p to q. A pair of states (p, q) is a *region*, $\mathcal{R}_p^q$, in the FA when it defines a sub-automaton with initial (resp. final) state in p (resp. q). So, we say that a state $r \in \mathcal{R}_p^q$ iff there exists a path ρ in $\mathcal{R}_p^q$, such that $r \in \rho$, $r \neq p, q$. Given $r \in Q$, it can be proved that there is only one *minimal region*, $\mathcal{M}(r)$, in the FA containing it.

To begin with, we assume that we are dealing with the first error detected. We extend the structure of items, as a pair $[p, i]$, with an error counter e; resulting in a new structure $[p, i, e]$. Given a *point of error* w_j, the associated *point of detection* is the initial state of the minimal region, $\mathcal{M}(w_j) = \mathcal{R}_p^q$, containing w_j. Associated to the point of error (resp. detection) w_j (resp. w_i), we consider the corresponding *error* (resp. *detection*) item $[q, j, \_]$ (resp. $[p, i, \_]$). To filter out undesirable repairs, we introduce criteria to select those with minimal cost. For each $a, b \in \Sigma$ we assume insert, $I(a)$; delete, $D(a)$, replace, $R(a, b)$, and transpose, $T(a, b)$, costs. We apply, from the detection item, the deduction steps $\mathcal{D}_{error} = \mathcal{D}^{Shift} \cup \mathcal{D}_{error}^{Insert} \cup \mathcal{D}_{error}^{Delete} \cup \mathcal{D}_{error}^{Replace} \cup \mathcal{D}_{error}^{Transpose}$, defined as follows:

$$\mathcal{D}^{Shift} = \{[r, l, e] \vdash [s, l+1, e], \ \exists [a, l] \in \mathcal{H}, \ s = r.a\}$$
$$\mathcal{D}_{error}^{Insert} = \{[r, l, e] \vdash [r, l+1, e+I(a)]\}$$
$$\mathcal{D}_{error}^{Delete} = \{[r, l, e] \vdash [s, l, e+D(w_l)] \Big/ \begin{array}{l} \mathcal{M}(q_0.w_{1..j}) = \mathcal{R}_{q_s}^{q_d} \\ r.w_l = s \in \mathcal{R}_{q_s}^{q_d} \text{ or } s = q_d \end{array} \}$$
$$\mathcal{D}_{error}^{Replace} = \{[r, l, e] \vdash [s, l+1, e+R(w_l, a)], \Big/ \begin{array}{l} \mathcal{M}(q_0.w_{1..j}) = \mathcal{R}_{q_s}^{q_d} \\ r.a = s \in \mathcal{R}_{q_s}^{q_d} \text{ or } s = q_d \end{array} \}$$
$$\mathcal{D}_{error}^{Transpose} = \{[r, l, e] \vdash [s, l+2, e+T(w_l, w_{l+1})] \Big/ \begin{array}{l} \mathcal{M}(q_0.w_{1..j}) = \mathcal{R}_{q_s}^{q_d} \\ r.w_{l+1}.w_l = s \in \mathcal{R}_{q_s}^{q_d} \text{ or } s = q_d \end{array} \}$$

where $w_{1..j}$ looks for the current point of error. We also redefine $\mathcal{D}^{Init}$ as $\{\vdash [q_0, 1, 0]\}$. In any case, the error hypotheses apply on transitions behind the repair region. The process continues until a repair covers that region, accepting a character in the remaining string. When no repair is possible, the process extends to the next region, taking the final state of the previous one as the new point of error. We apply a principle of optimization, saving only those items with minimal counters.

When the current error is not the first one, we can modify a previous repair in order to avoid cascaded errors, by adding the cost of the new error hypotheses to profit from the experience gained from previous ones. This allows us to get a quality close to global methods [7], with a time complexity, in the worst case

$$\mathcal{O}(\frac{n!}{\tau! * (n-\tau)!} * (n+\tau) * 2^\tau * \text{fan-out}_\mu^\tau)$$

where τ and *fan-out*$_\mu$ are, respectively, the maximal error counter computed and the maximal fan-out of the automaton in the scope of the repairs considered. The input string is recognized iff a final item $[q_f, n+1, e]$, $q_f \in Q_f$, is generated.

4   Spelling Incomplete Strings

In order to handle incomplete strings, we extend the input alphabet by introducing two new symbols. So, "?" stands for one unknown character, and "∗" stands for an unknown sequence of input characters. Once the underlying FA detects that the next input symbol to be shifted is one of these two extra symbols, we apply the following set of deduction steps, $\mathcal{D}_{\text{incomplete}}$:

$$\mathcal{D}_{\text{incomplete}}^{\text{Shift}} = \{[p,i,e] \vdash [q,i+1,e+I(a)] \ / \ \exists \ [?,i] \in \mathcal{H}, \ q = p.a\}$$
$$\mathcal{D}_{\text{incomplete}}^{\text{Loop\_shift}} = \{[p,i,e] \vdash [q,i,e+I(a)] \ / \ \exists \ [*,i] \in \mathcal{H}, \ q = p.a, \ \not\exists \ q.w_{i+1}\}$$
$$\mathcal{D}_{\text{incomplete}}^{\text{Loop\_shift\_end}} = \{[p,i,e] \vdash [q,i+1,e+I(a)] \ / \ \exists \ [*,i] \in \mathcal{H}, \ q = p.a, \ \exists \ q.w_{i+1}\}$$

where $I(a)$ is the insertion cost for $a \in \Sigma$. From an intuitive point of view, $\mathcal{D}_{\text{incomplete}}^{\text{Shift}}$ applies any shift transition independently of the current lookahead available, provided that this transition is applicable with respect to the FA configuration and that the next input symbol is an unknown character. In relation to $\mathcal{D}_{\text{incomplete}}^{\text{Loop\_shift}}$, it simulates shift actions on items corresponding to FA configurations for which the next input symbol denotes an unknown sequence of characters, when no standard shift action links up to the right-context. Given that in this latter case new items are created in the same itemset, these transitions may be applied any number of times to the same computation thread, without scanning the input string. These deduction steps are applied until a recognition branch links up to the right-context by using a shift action, resuming the standard recognition mode, as it is described by $\mathcal{D}_{\text{incomplete}}^{\text{Loop\_shift\_end}}$.

In this manner, when we deal with sequences of unknown characters, we can examine different paths in the FA resolving the same "∗" symbol. Although this could be useful for subsequent syntactic or semantic processing, an uncontrolled over-generation is not of practical interest in most cases. We solve this by tabulating the number of characters used to rebuild the word, using the error counter, and applying the principle of optimization. These steps are applied until new items cannot be generated. The time bound is, also, in the worst case,

$$\mathcal{O}(\frac{n!}{\tau! * (n - \tau)!} * (n + \tau) * 2^{\tau} * \text{fan-out}_{\mu}^{\tau})$$

The correction is defined by a final item $[q_f, n+1, e]$, $q_f \in \mathcal{Q}_f$.

5   The Robust Frame

We are now ready to introduce the robust construction. We must now guarantee the capacity to recover the recognizer from any unexpected situation derived either from gaps in the scanner or from errors. To deal with this, it is sufficient to combine the rules previously introduced. More exactly, we have that the new set of deduction steps, $\mathcal{D}_{\text{robust}}$, is given by:

$$\mathcal{D}_{\text{robust}} = \mathcal{D}^{\text{Init}} \cup \mathcal{D}^{\text{Shift}} \cup \mathcal{D}_{\text{error}}^{\text{Insert}} \cup \mathcal{D}_{\text{error}}^{\text{Delete}} \cup \mathcal{D}_{\text{error}}^{\text{Replace}} \cup$$
$$\mathcal{D}_{\text{error}}^{\text{Transpose}} \cup \mathcal{D}_{\text{incomplete}}^{\text{Shift}} \cup \mathcal{D}_{\text{incomplete}}^{\text{Loop\_shift}} \cup \mathcal{D}_{\text{incomplete}}^{\text{Loop\_shift\_end}}$$

where there is no overlapping between the deduction subsets. The final robust recognizer also has a time complexity, in the worst case

$$\mathcal{O}(\frac{n!}{\tau! * (n - \tau)!} * (n + \tau) * 2^\tau * \text{fan-out}_\mu^\tau)$$

with respect to the length n of the ill-formed sentence. The input string is recognized iff a final item $[q_f, n + 1, e]$, $q_f \in \mathcal{Q}_f$, is generated.

6 Pruning Strategies

In dealing with spelling correction, ill-formed expressions can often be resolved in different manners, which forces us to consider a framework involving ambiguities. Although most of these ambiguities will be eliminated in subsequent and more sophisticated analysis tasks, a number of them can already be treated at this stage. Disregarding pure statistical aspects, we focus on the formalization of cut-off schemata in order to limit the repair space and, as a consequence, reduce the computational impact derived from exploring useless repair paths.

Nevertheless, the interpretation of an FA as a sequential transitional formalism imposes an essential guideline on the design of any pruning strategy. If we also take into account that the dynamic frame previously defined updates error counters at each new item generation, it appears that pruning techniques based on threshold error criteria seem to be particularly well adapted. So, we can consider a set of simple cut-off schemata, combining the repair hypotheses in order to allow the user to implement human-like correction strategies.

6.1 Path-Based Pruning

We refer here to a classic technique [5, 12] consisting of pruning repair branches on items with an error below a given threshold. From an operational viewpoint, the consideration of this pruning mechanism does not require any modification in the item structure, and we must only apply a test on the error counter each time a new item is generated. If the counter computed is greater than the defined threshold, ρ, we simply prune the parse process on the corresponding branch by stopping any action on that item. So, we can only take into account what is now in our parse scheme:

$$\forall I \vdash [p, i, e] \in \mathcal{D}_{\text{robust}}, \ e < \rho$$

As an example, considering the discrete metric assigning a unitary cost to each repair deduction step in robust mode, we could cut-off all repair branches with an error counter higher than a fixed proportion on the length of the word.

6.2 Sequence-Based Pruning

Another possible approach is to limit the number of consecutive errors included in a path, pruning them on items in these sequences with a quality below a given threshold, σ. In order to implement this pruning strategy, we must first introduce an additional error counter, e_l, representing the local error count accumulated along a sequence of repair hypotheses in the path we are now exploring. So, items take the new structure $[p, i, e_g, e_l]$, where the error counter e_g is the same as that considered in the original robust algorithm. At this point, we re-define the following deduction steps from the original scheme for the robust mode:

$$\mathcal{D}^{\text{Shift}} = \{[p, i, e_g, e_l] \vdash [q, i + 1, e_g, 0], \; \exists [a, i] \in \mathcal{H}, \; q = p.a\}$$

which implies that each time a shift action is performed, a sequence of possible repair hypotheses is broken and, as a consequence, no sequence-based pruning can be considered in that case. At this point, all that remains is to test that no sequence of deduction steps in $\mathcal{D}_{\text{robust}}$ exceeds the threshold σ. So, we have that the complete previous deduction step

$$[p, i, e_g] \vdash [q, j, e_g + \triangle] \in \mathcal{D}_{\text{robust}}$$

is now replaced by another one of the form

$$[p, i, e_g, e_l] \vdash [q, j, e_g + \triangle, e_l + \triangle] \in \mathcal{D}_{\text{robust}}, \; e_l + \triangle < \sigma$$

So, for example, we could contemplate cutting off any branch including a sequence of repair hypotheses.

6.3   Type-Based Pruning

Sometimes we may be more interested in detecting the presence of some particular hypotheses in a path of the FA or even in a sequence of this path. This translates into applying the previous path and sequence based approaches to a particular kind of deduction hypotheses. Taking, for example, the case of $\mathcal{D}_{\text{robust}}^{\text{Insert}}$ and assuming a threshold τ to locate the pruning action on a path, we have that the new deduction steps are now:

$$\forall I \vdash [p, i, e_g, e_l] \in \mathcal{D}_{\text{robust}}^{\text{Insert}}, \; e_g < \tau$$

and, if we deal with a sequence on a path, we have that:

$$[p, i, e_g, e_l] \vdash [q, j, e_g + \triangle, e_l + \triangle] \in \mathcal{D}_{\text{robust}}^{\text{Insert}}, \; e_l + \triangle < \tau$$

assuming that standard shift actions re-initialize to zero local counters. However, we need a pair of counters associated to each kind of deduction steps in order to consider type-based pruning for insert, delete, replace or transpose hypotheses. As an example, we could cut-off any branch considering more than two delete hypotheses in the same branch.

7   Experimental Results

We consider a lexicon for Spanish built from GALENA [9], which includes 514,781 different words, to illustrate this aspect. The lexicon is recognized by an FA containing 58,170 states connected by 153,599 transitions, of sufficient size to allow us to consider it as a representative starting point for our purposes. In order to take the edit distance [5] as the error metric for measuring the quality of a repair, it is sufficient to consider discrete costs $I(a) = D(a) = 1$, $\forall a \in \Sigma$ and $R(a,b) = T(a,b) = 1$, $\forall a,b \in \Sigma$, $a \neq b$. In particular, this choice will allows us to compare our proposal with the original conditions for Savary's one [12].

Our goal is now to illustrate the robustness in a variety of situations. We look for a set of tests that will show both the effects from the topological distribution of errors and unknown sequences in the input string and, whenever possible, the structural influence of the operational kernel in the recognition process. Three different kinds of patterns are considered for modeling ill-formed input strings.

The former, which we call *unknown*, is given by words which do not include spelling errors, but only unknown symbols. This, for example, is the case of the ill-formed word **agu*teis**. Taking a path-threshold 2, the completion is **aguasteis** (*you watered*). The second kind of pattern, which we call *error-correction*, gathers words including only errors. For the error input **augasteis** with path-threshold 2, the correction is **aguasteis**. The third pattern, which we call *overlapping*, groups words combining both unknown symbols and spelling errors. In the case of **aga*teis** with path-threshold 2, the repair is **aguasteis**,

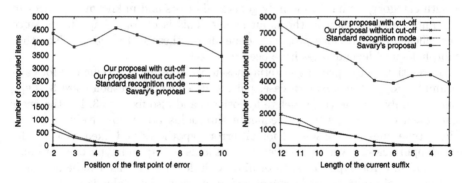

Fig. 1. Items generated for the *unknown* example

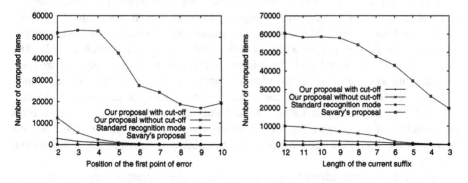

Fig. 2. Items generated for the *error-correction* example

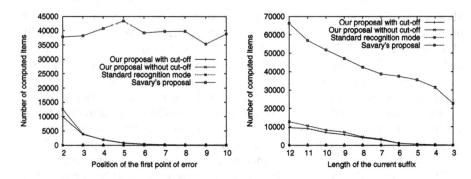

Fig. 3. Items generated for the *overlapping* example

which is generated by rebuilding the unknown sequence "*" with ''s'' and, later, re-taking the error mode to insert ''u'' before the second ''a''.

The results are shown, for the *unknown*, *error-correction* and *overlapping* examples in Figs. 1, 2 and 3; respectively. In all cases, we have started from the same sample of words, which has the same distribution observed in the original lexicon in terms of lengths of the strings dealt with. On these words and for each length category, we have randomly generated errors and unknown sequences in a number and position in the input string. This is of some importance since the efficiency of previous proposals depends on these factors [5, 12]. No other morphological dependencies have been detected.

In relation to the pruning criteria chosen, we consider a specific one for each example. So, in the *unknown* case, path and sequence thresholds are 3. Type ones are only considered for delete hypothesis and also fixed to 3. For the *error correction* example, path and sequence thresholds are, respectively, 3 and 2. Here, type ones are considered for all error hypotheses and fixed to 1. In the overlapping case, path and sequence thresholds are 4; and type ones are also fixed for all error hypotheses. In dealing with deletions it has a value of 3, and in the case of insertion, replacement and transposition its value is 1.

The number of items generated by the system during the robust recognition process has been taken as the reference for appreciating the efficiency of our method, rather than purely temporal criteria, which are more dependent on its implementation. These items are measured in relation to both the position of the first point at which a difference which was attended to by the user occurs in the word and the length of the suffix from it. So, we are sure to take into account the degree of penetration in the FA at that point, which determines the effectiveness of the repair strategy since it influences the number of repair schemata to follow. In particular, in our proposal, it determines the number of regions in the FA including the point of error or the first unknown point and, as a consequence, the possibility of considering a non-global resolution.

In each figure, we compare four different graphs corresponding to our pruning proposal, the results without cut-off, the Savary's approach [12] with the same path-threshold of our pruning schemata and, finally, the number of items that would be generated in standard recognition mode if we had considered the correct input string from which we have obtained the erroneous one analyzed by the previous three graphs corresponding to robust techniques. So, we can estimate the computational behavior of the different robust techniques considered, but we can also to illustrate the computational effort exclusively due to the application of the robust mechanisms in each case. In relation to the Savary's proposal, the original algorithm allows to consider path-based pruning and, in order to introduce unknown symbols, we have simply extended it by simulating insertions.

These results show a noticeable improvement in computational complexity due to the consideration of pruning techniques. Here, it is important to remember that errors and unknown sequences were randomly generated and therefore we have not profited from any linguistic knowledge in order to design efficient pruning criteria. In spite of this apparent lack of performance, the application of these cut-off techniques has augmented the precision [2] by 4'06% for the *unknown* example, 7'76% for the *error correction* one, and 1'95% for the *overlapping* case. In relation to this, although the errors in our tests have been randomly generated, we must remember that we have fixed the original, and correct, corpus. As a consequence, we can easily estimate this parameter.

The graphs corresponding to the standard recognition mode illustrate the complexity of the robust strategy. This is due, essentially, to the number of FA paths to be explored, which also explains the greater amount of items generated when the point of origin for the application of the robust mode is close to the beginning of the word. Finally, comparison with the Savary's method, in the best of our knowledge the most efficient proposal on spelling correction, seems to put into evidence the validity of our approach from the point of view of the efficiency.

8   Conclusions

The gap with human performance in spelling correction, which is mainly due to the mismatch between what was in the text, what actually appears in the input and the set of available dictionary entries, should be covered by a flexible and robust strategy at various levels.

A robust model for non-contextual spelling correction is described, which allows the algorithm to deal with distortions caused by incomplete string acquisition, simulating human performance in non-contextual word recognition. Our goal is to compensate the noise effect resulting from ill-formed word recognition, in order to avoid degradation in the performance of the recognizer. The consideration of cut-off criteria provides the capability to control the correction mechanisms, conducting the process through the nearest neighbors of a given character string in a dictionary.

---

[2] The rate reflecting when the algorithm provides the repair attended by the user.

References

1. Peterson, J.: Computer Programs For Spelling Correction. Springer-Verlag, Inc., Berlin, Germany / Heidelberg, Germany / London, UK / etc. (1980)
2. Kukich, K.: Techniques for automatically correcting words in text. ACM Computing Surveys **24** (1992) 377–439
3. Agirre, E., Gojenola, K., Sarasola, K., Voutilainen, A.: Towards a single proposal in spelling correction. In Boitet, C., Whitelock, P., eds.: Proc. of the 36th Annual Meeting of the ACL, San Francisco, California, Association for Computational Linguistics, Morgan Kaufmann Publishers (1998) 22–28
4. Elmi, M., Evens, M.: Spelling correction using context. In Boitet, C., Whitelock, P., eds.: Proc. of the 36th Annual Meeting of the ACL, San Francisco, California, Association for Computational Linguistics, Morgan Kaufmann Publishers (1998) 360–364
5. Oflazer, K.: Error-tolerant finite-state recognition with applications to morphological analysis and spelling correction. Computational Linguistics **22** (1996) 73–89
6. Du, M., Chang, S.: A model and a fast algorithm for multiple errors spelling correction. Acta Informatica **29** (1992) 281–302
7. Vilares, M., Otero, J., Graña, J.: Regional finite-state error repair. Lecture Notes in Computer Science **3317** (2005) 269–280
8. Lucchesi, C., Kowaltowski, T.: Applications of finite automata representing large vocabularies. Software-Practice and Experience **23** (1993) 15–30
9. Graña, J., Barcala, F., Alonso, M.: Compilation methods of minimal acyclic automata for large dictionaries. Lecture Notes in Computer Science **2494** (2002) 135–148
10. Daciuk, J., Mihov, S., Watson, B., Watson, R.: Incremental construction of minimal acyclic finite-state automata. Computational Linguistics **26** (2000) 3–16
11. Sikkel, K.: Parsing Schemata. PhD thesis, Univ. of Twente, The Netherlands (1993)
12. Savary, A.: Typographical nearest-neighbor search in a finite-state lexicon and its application to spelling correction. Lecture Notes in Computer Science **2494** (2001) 251–260

On Two-Dimensional Pattern Matching by
Finite Automata*

Jan Žďárek and Bořivoj Melichar

Department of Computer Science and Engineering,
Faculty of Electrical Engineering, Czech Technical University in Prague,
Karlovo náměstí 13, 121 35 Praha 2, Czech Republic
{melichar, zdarekj}@fel.cvut.cz

Abstract. This paper presents a general concept of two-dimensional
pattern matching using conventional (one-dimensional) finite automata.
Then two particular models and methods, implementations of the general
principle, are presented. The first of these two models presents an automata based version of the Bird and Baker approach with lower space
complexity than the original algorithm. The second introduces a new
model for two-dimensional approximate pattern matching using the two-
dimensional Hamming distance.

1   Introduction

In recent years there has been unceasing interest in two and more dimensional
pattern matching problems. Such interest is substantiated by the growing computational strength of our computers allowing multidimensional data, e.g. NMR
scans, photographs, etc., to be processed.

In this paper the idea of dimensional (linear) reduction is used to provide a
generic algorithm of 2D pattern matching using finite automata, *FA* for short.
This has been known for a very long time and is widely used (for a nice survey in
the area of 2D matching see [1]). In our approach, by the dimensional reduction
of the problem we obtain a mapping between final states and one-dimensional
strings of the d dimensional pattern and a new preprocessed $d - 1$ dimensional
text array that is over an alphabet of automaton final state labels. Then linear
reduction is used again and after $d-1$ steps we finally obtain the one-dimensional
problem. From now on let us restrict our deliberation to describing the most
practical case, i.e. 2D pattern matching by finite automata.

Based on the generic algorithm, a couple of automata based models and
algorithms for 2D exact and 2D approximate pattern matching using a 2D
Hamming distance are presented. For this purpose some of the wide scale of
classical FA solving one-dimensional exact and approximate pattern matching
problems [2,3,4] are reused. The proposed methods in fact generalize the one-
dimensional pattern matching approach based on finite automata.

---

* This research is partially supported by the MŠMT under research program MSM
6840770014.

J. Farré, I. Litovsky, and S. Schmitz (Eds.): CIAA 2005, LNCS 3845, pp. 329–340, 2006.
© Springer-Verlag Berlin Heidelberg 2006

1.1   Basic Notions

Let A be a finite alphabet and its elements are called symbols. A set of strings over A is denoted by A^* and A^ℓ is a set of strings of length ℓ. The empty string is denoted by ε. Language L is any subset of A^*, $L \subseteq A^*$. Let $P \in A^m$ and $T \in A^n$ be a pattern and a text, respectively, $m \leq n$. An exact occurrence of P in T is index i, such that $P[1, \ldots, m] = T[i, \ldots, i + m - 1]$, $i + m - 1 \leq n$. If some string R is a substring of T and the relevant edit distance is $D(P, R) \leq k$ then R is an approximate occurrence of P in T with at most k errors.

An array (picture, 2D string) is a rectangular arrangement PA of symbols taken from a finite alphabet. The set of all arrays over alphabet A is denoted by A^{**} and a 2D language over A is thus any subset of A^{**}. The set of all arrays of size $(n \times n')$ over A, where $n, n' > 0$, is denoted by $A^{n \times n'}$. ([5] discusses the theory of 2D languages in detail.) The size of an array is the size of its rectangular shape, denoted by $|PA|$ or $(x \times y)$, and its numerical value is the product of its x and y components, $|PA| = xy$. A 2D exact occurrence of $PA \in A^{m \times m'}$ in $TA \in A^{n \times n'}$ is a pair (i, j), such that $PA[1, \ldots, m; 1, \ldots, m'] = TA[i, \ldots, i + m - 1; j, \ldots, j + m' - 1]$. If for some sub-array X of TA and a relevant 2D edit distance $2D\text{-}dist(PA, X) \leq k$ then X is a 2D approximate occurrence of PA in TA with at most k errors.

A finite automaton (FA) is a quintuple (Q, A, δ, I, F). Q is a finite set of states, A is a finite input alphabet, $F \subseteq Q$ is a set of final states. If FA is nondeterministic (NFA), then δ is a mapping $Q \times (A \cup \{\varepsilon\}) \mapsto \mathcal{P}(Q)$ and $I \subseteq Q$ is a set of initial states. A deterministic FA (DFA) is (Q, A, δ, q_0, F), where δ is a (partial) function $Q \times A \mapsto Q$; $q_0 \in Q$ is the only initial state.

By custom the term finite automaton is used where a pattern matching automaton (PMA) would be more appropriate. The PMA is a program based on a run of an FA, e.g. the AC automaton (or machine) uses "forward" δ and "backward" *fail* functions [6]. A PMA may be able to do some additional operations, e.g. it may have some "actions" assigned to some or all of its transitions or states (a generalization of a transducer).

1.2   Types of Pattern Matching Automata

In 1997 Melichar and Holub [4] showed that 1D pattern matching problems are sequential problems and therefore it is possible to solve them using FA. Moreover, they presented a six-dimensional classification of all 192 then known 1D pattern matching problems for an alphabet of finite size.

The classification criteria (see Fig. 1) are: 1. nature of the pattern; 2. integrity of the pattern; 3. number of patterns; 4. way of matching (exact or approximate using various distances); 5. importance of symbols in the pattern; 6. number of instances of the pattern.

The original model has been updated recently [7] in its fourth dimension with distances used in the area of musicology (Δ, Γ) [8]. Those distances were not known at the time of publication of [4] and as a consequence, the number of problems described by this classification has risen from 192 to 336. Together, these criteria allow us to classify conveniently all pattern matching problems.

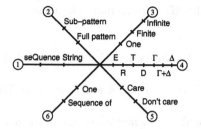

Criterion	1	2	3	4	5	6
	S	F	O	E	C	O
	Q	S	F	R	D	S
			I	T		
Abbrev.				D		
				$G(\Delta)$		
				$L(\Gamma)$		
				$H(\Gamma + \Delta)$		

Fig. 1. Updated classification of one-dimensional pattern matching problems

Example 1. A common problem in text editors is to find a mistyped word. This involves using approximate string matching of one pattern using the Levenshtein distance. This problem can be simply referred to as an *SFODCO* problem.

One can use the notion of a family of pattern matching problems. In this case symbol "?" is used instead of a particular letter. For example *SFF???* describes the family of all problems concerning full pattern matching of multiple strings.

2   Generic Algorithm

Reusing finite automata from 1D pattern matching into 2D pattern matching has several advantages: the same formal method of modelling pattern matching algorithms in both cases and a description of all problems using a unified view. Furthermore, automata process a text in a time proportional to the text's length, for fixed alphabet A in linear time. (Otherwise the time complexity should be multiplied by a $\log|A|$ factor.) There are known simulation methods of NFA [9, 10,11], and for some types of problems there are known algorithms constructing appropriate DFA directly, some of them even in linear time [2].

The idea of solving multidimensional pattern matching problems using PMA is simple: multiple automata should be used passing their results among them, reducing the dimension of the problem by one in each step. In the last step classical pattern matching can be used. (A preliminary version of Alg. 1 along with some of our ideas presented below has appeared in [7].)

3   2D Exact Pattern Matching

Let pattern array PA be viewed as a sequence of strings. Without loss of generality let these strings be its columns. To locate columns of the pattern array within columns of the text array requires searching for several strings. They are contained in set of strings PS and its cardinality may be less than the number of columns of PA, which can be used to reduce the state complexity of the matching automaton. Testing for identical columns in PA can be done in $\mathcal{O}(|PA|)$ time by a trie construction algorithm (the trie construction algorithm is given in [2] or [6]).

Algorithm 1. A generic algorithm of the 2D pattern matching using pattern matching automata
Method:
1: Dictionary matching automaton $M(PS)$ (of type $SFF?CO$, see Tab. 1) is constructed.
2: Automaton $M(PS)$ is applied to each column of TA and new array TA' is generated.
3: For further matching a one-dimensional representation of the pattern array PA should be computed (*representing string R*).
4: String matching automaton M' ($SFO?CO$) searching for R with at most k errors is built; $k = 0$ in case of the exact matching ($SFOECO$).
5: Automaton M' locates string R inside the rows of TA', reporting eventual (1D) occurrences of R in TA' and therefore also 2D occurrences of PA in the original TA.

3.1 A Finite Automata Model of 2D Exact Pattern Matching

Let m be the number of columns and let m' be the number of rows of pattern array PA, and let m_d be the number of distinct columns of PA, $m_d \leq m$. In the following text all steps of Alg. 1 will be implemented describing the idea of 2D exact pattern matching using pattern matching automata.

According to step 1 of Alg. 1, the $M(PS)$ automaton of type $SFF?CO$ should be used. For the purposes of 2D exact pattern matching it is a dictionary matching automaton ($SFFECO$), because the location of the exact occurrences of the individual patterns should be found (Alg. 1, step 2).

$SFFECO$ automaton $M(PS) = (Q, A, \delta, \{q_0\}, F)$, accepts a language $L(M)$, $L(M) = A^*P$, where $P \in PS$. The construction of automaton $M(PS)$ for searching for set PS, $PS = \{P_1, P_2, \ldots, P_{m_d}\}$, consists of a trie construction of m_d patterns and adding a selfloop at its initial state q_0. The construction of NFA $M(PS)$ is given in [3].

A deterministic version of $M(PS)$ and how it works over TA is given in Sec. 3.2.

The Representing String. In step 3 of Alg. 1 construction of the *representing string R* of pattern array PA is required. String R represents the original 2D pattern array in such a way that every column becomes its representing symbol in R. This representing string is a result of linear reduction, and it is a one-dimensional representation of a 2D entity in symbols of a new alphabet. Here these symbols are labels of final states of $M(PS)$.

Example 2. Let $PA \in A^{3\times 3}$, $PA = \begin{array}{|c|c|c|} \hline a & b & a \\ \hline c & a & c \\ \hline c & d & c \\ \hline \end{array}$ and let columns $PA[1] = PA[3] = acc$
and $PA[2] = bad$ be accepted by states f_1 and f_2, respectively, and let $f_1, f_2 \in F$ be final states of automaton $M(PS)$. Then the representing string R of PA in rows of TA' will be 121.

Searching for 2D Exact Occurrences Using the Exact Pattern Matching Automaton. After application of $M(PS)$ on every column of TA the text array TA' is prepared for application of some one-dimensional pattern matching method, e.g. PMA for exact pattern matching.

In this step automaton M' of type $SFO??O$ will be used for matching in the rows of TA'. For the purposes of 2D exact pattern matching this is the simplest automaton, the $SFOECO$ automaton.

$SFOECO$ automaton M' is constructed over the alphabet $F \cup \{0\}$, i.e. over the set of final state labels of automaton $M(PS)$, united with at least one symbol that represents the rest of the states of $M(PS)$ (recall the idea of a reduced alphabet). In detail, $M' = (Q', F \cup \{0\}, \delta', \{q'_0\}, F')$ and accepts language $L(M) = (F \cup \{0\})^* R$, where $R \in F^m$, $F = \{s_1, s_2, \ldots, s_{m_d}\}$, $|F| = m_d = |PS|$, and m is the length of the rows of PA.

NFA M' searches for pattern R of length m in each row of TA' individually (Alg. 1, step 5). M' searches for occurrences of R and therefore it can report also 2D occurrences of PA, because at the moment R is found it has been verified that all columns of PA are found in the appropriate place and order.

3.2   Deterministic Finite Automata for 2D Exact Pattern Matching

The Bird and Baker algorithm uses for the 2D exact pattern matching the well known algorithms of Aho-Corasick and Knuth-Morris-Pratt [12], and their method works in linear time. This fact is a strong motivation for us to achieve linear time with our method, too.

Our model of 2D exact pattern matching requires two finite automata: the $M(PS)$ automaton for preprocessing of TA is the $SFFECO$ automaton; the M' automaton for searching for string R is the $SFOECO$ automaton.

These automata have a neat structure, so they are useful as a model, but they are also nondeterministic. There is no problem with this fact, as these NFA's can be either simulated or determinised before use. However, in order to achieve linear time complexity for 2D exact pattern matching using our method, direct constructions of equivalent deterministic finite automata should be used. Indeed, this is possible in this case (see [2]): DFA $M(PS)$ can be constructed as a *linear dictionary-matching automaton* with time complexity $\mathcal{O}(\log |A| |PA|) = \mathcal{O}(mm')$, supposing alphabet A is fixed. Its space complexity is $\mathcal{O}(\log |A| |PA|) = \mathcal{O}(mm')$,

Elements of TA' are computed as follows: let $M(PS) = (Q, A, \delta, q_0, F)$ be DFA, $q \in Q$, q is the active state after reading a symbol from the element $TA[i,j]$, then $TA'[i,j] = q$; $q \in Q$, $\forall i,j$ $1 \leq i \leq n$, $1 \leq j \leq n'$.

DFA M' can be constructed as a *linear string-matching automaton* with time and space complexity $\mathcal{O}(|R|) = \mathcal{O}(m)$.

Theorem 1. *The presented method of 2D exact pattern matching using the direct construction of DFA's has asymptotic time complexity $\mathcal{O}(|TA|)$.*
(Proof omitted.)

This time complexity is the same as in the Bird and Baker solution, i.e. it is linear with the size of a given text array.

The space complexity is designated as $\mathcal{O}\left(|TA|\right)$, and it depends on the space for temporary data (and on the sizes of the pattern matching automata, which are smaller).

3.3   Optimized 2D Exact Pattern Matching

The new text array TA' has the same size as TA, and because we are dealing with pictures, it is clear that its size can be very large. Hence a significant saving can be achieved if we could avoid using it.

We can use some natural properties of finite automata to reduce the space complexity of 2D exact pattern matching. To be able to restart a run of a deterministic finite automaton only its transition function, active state and current position in the input text are required. Automaton $M(PS)$ matches in all columns of TA individually, so $\mathcal{O}(n)$ extra space is needed to store all active states of $M(PS)$ in each row of TA. Once one row of TA' is computed by $M(PS)$, it is possible to do matching in it using automaton M' to find possible 2D occurrences. Then the space of the row can be reused, efficiently eliminating the need to store the whole array TA'.

Theorem 2. *Two-dimensional exact pattern matching by finite automata has asymptotic space complexity* $\mathcal{O}\left(|PA| + n\right)$.

Proof. The space complexity of automata $M(PS)$ and M', $\mathcal{O}(|PA|)$ and $\mathcal{O}(m)$, respectively, remains unchanged. Since $M(PS)$ treats each column and M' each row individually, to be able to restart the preprocessing phase it is required to store the active states of $M(PS)$ only. The extra space required is $\mathcal{O}(n)$, the number of columns of TA.

Steps 2 and 5 of Alg. 1 are now "interleaved", therefore both automata should be stored in memory at the same time. The asymptotic space complexity of the 2D exact pattern matching is then $\mathcal{O}(|PA|) + \mathcal{O}(m) + \mathcal{O}(n) = \mathcal{O}(|PA| + n)$. $\square$

Note 1. To save some processing time, it is sufficient to start matching for 2D occurrences (Alg. 1, step 5) in row $TA'[x, m']$, $1 \leq x \leq n$, where the topmost occurrences may be located.

4   2D Approximate Pattern Matching

In this section a new automata-based method of 2D approximate pattern matching using a 2D Hamming distance is introduced. The 2D Hamming distance (2D matching with mismatches) D_{2H} is analogous to the Hamming distance D_H in 1D matching [3,13].

$D_H(v, w)$ between two strings $v, w \in A^*$, $|v| = |w|$ is the minimum number of edit operations *replace* (change of symbol), needed to convert string v to w. Distance $D_{2H}(P, R)$ between two arrays P and R is the minimum number of edit operations *replace* needed to convert array P to R, $P, R \in A^{**}$, $|P| = |R|$.

In 2D exact matching a simple dimensional reduction was sufficient to do the task, but here more information about each prefix is needed: not only that some prefix of one or more strings of PS can end at the actual element, but that there can be a certain number of (1D) mismatches in it.

Let us refer again to the generic algorithm. First, an approximate dictionary matching automaton $M(PS)$ for the approximate matching of a set of strings using the Hamming distance should be built ($SFFRCO$). $M(PS)$ accepts a language $L(M) = A^* H_k(PS)$, where

$$H_k(PS) = \{X; \ X \in A^*, D_H(X, P) \leq \min(k, m' - 1) \ \wedge \ P \in PS\}, \qquad (1)$$

k is a given number of allowed 2D mismatches in the 2D occurrence of pattern array PA and m' is the length of the columns of PA (supposing we start the processing vertically).

Since $M(PS)$ searches for a set of strings, it consists of $SFORCO$ sub-automata for approximate pattern matching using the Hamming distance. ($SFORCO$ automata and their usage are discussed for example in [3].)

The reason why the distance $\min(k, m' - 1)$ in formula (1) should be used is that the $SFORCO$ sub-automaton for pattern of length m' can find its occurrences with at most $m' - 1$ mismatches in every column of TA, while $k \leq mm' - 1$.

The final states of $M(PS)$ indicate which one of the (1D) patterns was found, and the amount of mismatches found in a particular occurrence within the columns of TA.

Let $M(PS) = (Q, A, \delta, I, F)$ be the $SFFRCO$ automaton for the approximate matching of a set of patterns using the Hamming distance.

Proposition 1. SFFRCO *automaton $M(PS)$ may have after each reading of the input symbol and executing all subsequent transitions*

1. *at most m_d final states active,*
2. *among these active final states at most one final state indicating the exact occurrence of pattern P_i of PS in the text array,*
3. *at most m_d active final states, indicating occurrences of m_d different patterns with l mismatches, $0 < l \leq k'$, where $k' = \min(k, |P| - 1)$, $P \in PS$. (Proof omitted.)*

As a consequence of Proposition 1, symbols of a secondary alphabet will have $|PS|$ parts, each $\lceil \log_2(k' + 1) \rceil$ bits long, representing the number of mismatches found (k') and one "no match" situation in each string of PS.

Let $M(PS) = (Q, A, \delta, I, F)$, $q \in Q$ be the active state after reading the symbol from element $TA[i, j]$. Let an ordered couple (s, x) be the label of a final state of $M(PS)$, where s is a string identification (number of its matching $SFORCO$), to which a final state belongs, and x is the number of mismatches found in it. Let $\oslash \notin Q$ be a special symbol not among the labels of states.

Then it holds for $\forall i, j, s \ 1 \leq i \leq n, 1 \leq j \leq n', 1 \leq s \leq |PS|$:

$$TA'[i, j, s] = \begin{cases} x \ ; \ q \text{ active}, q \in F, q = (s, x), \\ \oslash \ ; \ s^{th} \text{ sub-automaton has no active final state.} \end{cases} \qquad (2)$$

Let l_s be the number of mismatches for each pattern number s and $k' = \min(k, |P_s| - 1)$, $P_s \in PS$. Every element of TA' provides the following information about the potential occurrence of a column of PA ending at a particular element in the original array TA:

1. exact match, $l_s = 0$,
2. approximate match with l_s mismatches, $0 < l_s \leq k'$,
3. no match, $TA'[i, j, s] = \oslash$ ($l_s > k'$ mismatches found).

String R, representing the original pattern array PA in the rows of TA', should be constructed from "s" parts of (s, x) labels of final states, which are the same in each $SFORCO$ sub-automaton M_s of $M(PS)$.

Searching for 2D Approximate Occurrences Using the 2D Hamming Distance. Here the $SFOLCO$ automaton should be used, which is a PMA able to match pattern R using Γ distance. It will search for the representing string R and also count the numbers of errors found in each column of a possible 2D occurrence. According to [8], let A' be an ordered alphabet and a, b be two symbols of alphabet A', then Γ *distance* $D_\Gamma(v, w)$ between two strings $v, w \in A^*$, $|v| = |w|$, is $\sum_{i=1}^{|v|} |v[i] - w[i]|$.

Let F in this section denote the set of final states of finite automaton $M(PS)$ and let secondary alphabet A' be set F extended with a special symbol "$\oslash$": $A' = F \cup \{\oslash\}$. Symbols of alphabet A' denote the number of errors found at a given element of TA in the particular pattern from PS. Symbol $\oslash$ represents the "no match" situation, where the number of errors in a particular string at the given element is greater than the number of mismatches k' allowed in it.

Let M' be $M' = (Q', A', \delta', \{q'_{0,0}\}, F')$, δ' is a mapping $Q' \times (A')^m \mapsto \mathcal{P}(Q')$, where Q' are states of M' and $m = |PS|$. The active final state of M' indicates that an approximate 2D occurrence of PA in TA has been found. Furthermore, it shows the total number of 2D mismatches found in a particular 2D occurrence, up to the given maximum k.

Symbols of A' are ordered using the second part x of the (s, x) couple, i.e. the number of mismatches found in string $P_s \in PS$. Let the distances between two symbols, final state labels of $M(PS)$, be defined as follows:

$$|(s, x) - (t, y)| = \begin{cases} |x - y| \text{ ; } s = t, \text{ if } (x \vee y) = \oslash, \text{ then } \oslash = m' \\ m' \quad\text{ ; } s \neq t. \end{cases} \tag{3}$$

Example 3. To illustrate formula (3) let us compare symbols: $|(1, 0) - (1, 3)| = 3$, $|(2, 3) - (5, 0)| = m'$, $|(1, 0) - (1, \oslash)| = m'$, $|(3, \oslash) - (3, \oslash)| = 0$.

These comparisons are used in the error counting in TA'. If symbol (i, j) is found in a position where $(i, 0)$ is expected, then

$$l = \begin{cases} j \text{ ; } j \neq \oslash, \\ m' \text{ ; } j = \oslash. \end{cases} \tag{4}$$

l mismatches is added to the current value of err, if $err + l \leq k$. Let err be the current value of mismatches found in a particular occurrence of the representing string. If $j = \varnothing$, $k \geq m'$ errors are allowed and $err + m' \leq k$, m' mismatches are added to the current value, because a column of PA of length m' was not found at its expected position.

Let k be the number of mismatches allowed, $k < |P_i|$, $P_i \in PS$. In this case the number of 2D mismatches in any occurrence is lower than the length of the columns of PA. Then the $SFOLCO$ automaton has a slightly simpler form than in the general case, as it allows at most $|P_i| - 1 = k'$ mismatches while searching for the representing string.

A slightly more complicated case is when $k \geq m'$ is given. This means that the number of 2D errors is greater than the number of mismatches that $M(PS)$ is able to find in one dimension. To be able to count 2D errors by one-dimensional means, $\varnothing$ transitions are introduced in automaton M', representing $m' = |R|$ errors, $R \in PS$. Hence each state may have at most $m' + 1$ outgoing transitions, only initial state $q'_{0,0}$ has more, because of the selfloop.

Construction of the $SFOLCO$ automaton M' is shown in Alg. 2.

Algorithm 2. Construction of NFA for the approximate pattern matching of string R over the set of identifiers of final states of NFA $M(PS)$

Input: Pattern R over the set of final states of $M(PS)$, $|R| = m$, and m' be the length of patterns in set PS. The maximum number of 2D errors allowed k, $k \leq mm'$.

Output: NFA M', $M' = (Q', A', \delta', \{q'_{0,0}\}, F')$, accepting language $L(M') = A'^* \Gamma(R) = \{wx;\ w, x \in A'^*, D_\Gamma(x, R) \leq k\}$.

Sets Q', F' and mapping δ' are constructed in the following way:

Method:

$Q' \leftarrow \{q'_{0,0}\}$ {the initial state}

for $i \leftarrow 0$ **to** k

$\quad first \leftarrow \left\lfloor \dfrac{|i-1|}{m'} \right\rfloor + 1$ { "depth" of the first non-initial state in the ith row }

$\quad$ **for** $j \leftarrow first$ **to** m

$\quad\quad Q' \leftarrow Q' \cup \{q'_{j,i}\}$ { add a new state }

$\quad\quad$ **if** $j = m$ **then**

$\quad\quad\quad F' \leftarrow F' \cup \{q'_{j,i}\}$ { add a new final state }

$\quad\quad\quad$ Assign an alias $q'_{j,i} \leftarrow i$.   { the number of errors found }

$\quad\quad$ **end**

$\quad\quad$ **if** $j = 1$ **then**

$\quad\quad\quad$ **if** $i < m'$ **then** $\delta'\left(q'_{j-1,0}, (R[j], i)\right) \leftarrow q'_{j,i}$

$\quad\quad\quad\quad\quad$ **else** $\delta'\left(q'_{j-1,0}, (R[j], \varnothing)\right) \leftarrow q'_{j,i}$ { if $i = m'$ }

$\quad\quad$ **else**

$\quad\quad\quad x \leftarrow \max(0, i - m')$

$\quad\quad\quad$ **if** $j = first$ **then** $last \leftarrow i \pmod{m'}$

$\quad\quad\quad\quad\quad$ **else** $last \leftarrow \min(i, m')$

$\quad\quad\quad$ **for** $l \leftarrow 0$ **to** $last$

$\quad\quad\quad\quad$ **if** $(i \geq m') \wedge (l = 0)$ **then** $\delta'\left(q'_{j-1,x}, (R[j], \varnothing)\right) \leftarrow q'_{j,i}$

$\quad\quad\quad\quad\quad\quad$ **else** $\delta'\left(q'_{j-1,x+l}, (R[j], i - x - l)\right) \leftarrow q'_{j,i}$

$\quad\quad$ **end**

$\quad$ **end**

end end

$\delta'(q'_{0,0}, a) \leftarrow \delta'(q'_{0,0}, a) \cup \{q'_{0,0}\}$, $\forall a \in A'$ { the selfloop of the initial state }

4.1   Practical 2D Pattern Matching Using the 2D Hamming Distance

Our model of this type of 2D approximate pattern matching requires two PMA: *SFFRCO* and *SFOLCO*. These are nondeterministic and there are no known direct methods for constructing their deterministic versions (in contrast to 2D exact matching).

In such a situation we can either transform NFA to DFA using the standard subset construction [14] or simulate a run of the NFA. The former method may result in quite high space complexity, hence in the rest of this section the latter method is used: a simulation of a run of $M(PS)$ and M'.

For the simulation of the run of $M(PS)$ we use dynamic programming for pattern matching using the Hamming distance [3,9,15]. This method for string matching computes matrix D of size $(m + 1) \times (n + 1)$ for a pattern of length m and a text of length n. Each element of D usually contains the edit distance between the string ending at a current position in text T and the prefix of pattern P. The advantages of this method are that it is very simple and can be implemented memory-efficiently, and for a pattern of length m it requires only $\mathcal{O}(m)$ space. It works in time $\mathcal{O}(mn)$ for a text of length n, and this complexity is independent of the number of errors. Ukkonen [15] improved the expected time of the standard dynamic programming for approximate string matching to $\mathcal{O}(nk')$, by computing only the zone of the dynamic programming matrix consisting of the prefix of each column ending with the last k' in the column, where k' is the maximum number of mismatches in the occurrence. This improvement does not help much in our case, because for 2D approximate matching we usually need more than m errors to be allowed and then we have $k' = m - 1$.

From the construction of $M(PS)$ we see that there is at most m_d sub-automata for the approximate pattern matching of $m_d \leq m$ strings of PA. These sub-automata can be simulated by the dynamic programming in time $\mathcal{O}(mm'nn')$, which is independent of the number of 2D errors.

Automaton M' has a special structure and can be easily simulated in time $\mathcal{O}(mnn' - mm'n)$. Its simulation algorithm has appeared in [7].

Theorem 3. *The described realization of our method of 2D approximate pattern matching with finite automata using the 2D Hamming distance has asymptotic time complexity $\mathcal{O}(|TA||PA|)$. (Proof omitted.)*

Proposition 2. *The space complexity of the basic version of 2D approximate pattern matching using the 2D Hamming distance presented above is $\mathcal{O}(m|TA|)$. (Proof omitted.)*

4.2   Optimized 2D Approximate Pattern Matching Using the 2D Hamming Distance

According to the idea from Sec. 3.3, in order to reduce the space complexity we have to be able to restart a run of finite automaton $M(PS)$ in columns of TA. We use dynamic programming to simulate sub-automata of $M(PS)$, so $\mathcal{O}(mm')$space is needed to store the current state of the dynamic programming (state of $M(PS)$) in each row of TA. Once one row of TA' is computed, it is possible to do the matching in it using the simulation algorithm of automaton M' to find possible 2D occurrences. Then the space of the row can be reused, effectively eliminating the need to store the whole array TA'.

Theorem 4. *The space complexity of the optimized version of 2D approximate pattern matching using the 2D Hamming distance is $\mathcal{O}\left(n|PA|\right)$.*

Proof. Once again following steps of Alg. 1: (1-2) We have n columns of TA, and in each of them there run m_d, $m_d \leq m$, dynamic programming simulations of $M(PS)$ sub-automata in $\mathcal{O}(mm')$ space each, that is $\mathcal{O}(mm'n)$. To store the results of simulation in each column $\mathcal{O}(m)$ space is needed, that is $\mathcal{O}(mn)$. (3) We also have to store an assignment of PA columns to the sub-automata of $M(PS)$ in the representing string with the space complexity $\mathcal{O}(m)$. (4-5) The simulation algorithm of M' has asymptotic space complexity $\mathcal{O}(m)$.

Since steps 2 and 5 of Alg. 1 are interleaved, all space requirements should be summed up and the resulting asymptotic space complexity is $\mathcal{O}\left(mm'n + mn + 2m\right) = \mathcal{O}\left(n|PA|\right)$. □

5   Conclusion

The main contribution of this work is a general finite automata based approach to modelling of two-dimensional pattern matching problems. Based on the generic algorithm, two particular methods have been presented, one for 2D exact pattern matching and one for 2D approximate pattern matching using the 2D Hamming distance. In practice these are the most important kinds of 2D pattern matching, because most of the pictures stored in and by computers are rectangular in shape. However, there are two-dimensional edit distances, like R, C, L, RC [16], and we wish to find suitable automata models for them, too.

Beside automata based models we have dealt with issues in implementing them. In general it is impossible to use a simulation of nondeterministic models and obtain linear time complexity. Yet, there exist direct construction methods of equivalent deterministic pattern matching automata, and with the use of these our method is able to work in linear time, too. Moreover, we have shown a way to reduce the space needed to the size of only one row of the text array.

Then we presented the model of two-dimensional approximate pattern matching using the 2D Hamming distance. It has no known direct deterministic implementation, but it is possible to simulate its pattern matching automata.

The main point of our work is that it reuses a great deal of pattern matching automata in a new area of application. We offer a systematic approach for describing two-dimensional pattern matching.

References

1. Amir, A.: Theoretical issues of searching aerial photographs: a bird's eye view. In Balík, M., Holub, J., Šimánek, M., eds.: Proceedings of the Prague Stringology Conference 2004, Czech Technical University in Prague, Czech Republic (2004) 1–23

2. Crochemore, M., Hancart, C.: Automata for matching patterns. In Rozenberg, G., Salomaa, A., eds.: Handbook of Formal Languages. Springer-Verlag, Berlin (1997) 399–462
3. Melichar, B.: Approximate string matching by finite automata. In Hlaváč, V., Šára, R., eds.: Computer Analysis of Images and Patterns. Number 970 in Lecture Notes in Computer Science, Springer-Verlag, Berlin (1995) 342–349
4. Melichar, B., Holub, J.: 6D classification of pattern matching problems. In Holub, J., ed.: Proceedings of the Prague Stringology Club Workshop '97, Czech Technical University in Prague, Czech Republic (1997) 24–32
5. Giammarresi, D., Restivo, A.: Two-dimensional languages. In: Handbook of Formal Languages. Volume III (Beyond Words). Springer-Verlag, Heidelberg (1997) 216–267
6. Aho, A.V., Corasick, M.J.: Efficient string matching: an aid to bibliographic search. Commun. ACM **18** (1975) 333–340
7. Žďárek, J., Melichar, B.: Finite automata and two-dimensional pattern matching. In Heričko, M., Rozman, I., Jurič, M.B., Rajkovič, V., Urbančič, T., Bernik, M., Bučar, M., Brodnik, A., eds.: Proceedings of the 7th International Multiconference Information Society IS'2004. Volume D., Ljubljana, Slovenia, Institut "Jožef Stefan" (2004) 185–188
8. Cambouropoulos, E., Crochemore, M., Iliopoulos, C.S., Mouchard, L., Pinzon, Y.J.: Algorithms for computing approximate repetitions in musical sequences. In Raman, R., Simpson, J., eds.: Proceedings of the 10th Australasian Workshop On Combinatorial Algorithms, Perth, WA, Australia (1999) 129–144
9. Sellers, P.H.: The theory and computation of evolutionary distances: Pattern recognition. J. Algorithms **1** (1980) 359–373
10. Wu, S., Manber, U.: Fast text searching: allowing errors. Commun. ACM **35** (1992) 83–91
11. Holub, J.: Simulation of nondeterministic finite automata in pattern matching. Dissertation thesis, Czech Technical University in Prague, Czech Republic (2000)
12. Knuth, D.E., Morris, Jr, J.H., Pratt, V.R.: Fast pattern matching in strings. SIAM J. Comput. **6** (1977) 323–350
13. Hamming, R.W.: Error detecting and error correcting codes. The Bell System Technical Journal **29** (1950) 147–160
14. Hopcroft, J.E., Ullman, J.D.: Introduction to automata theory, languages and computations. Addison-Wesley, Reading, MA (1979)
15. Ukkonen, E.: Finding approximate patterns in strings. J. Algorithms **6** (1985) 132–137
16. Baeza-Yates, R.A., Navarro, G.: New models and algorithms for multidimensional approximate pattern matching. J. Discret. Algorithms **1** (2000) 21–49

Incremental and Semi-incremental Construction of Pseudo-Minimal Automata

Jan Daciuk[1,*], Denis Maurel[2], and Agata Savary[2]

[1] Gdańsk University of Technology, Poland
jandac@eti.pg.gda.pl
[2] Université François Rabelais, Tours, France
{denis.maurel, agata.savary}@univ-tours.fr

Pseudo-minimal automata ([1],[2]) are minimal acyclic automata that have a proper element (a transition or a state) for each word belonging to the language of the automaton. That proper element is not shared with any other word, and it can be used for implementing a function on words belonging to the language. For instance, dynamic perfect hashing (e.g. a mapping from n unique words to n consecutive numbers, such that addition of new elements does not change the order of the previous elements) can be implemented using a pseudo-minimal automaton ([3]).

The only existing algorithm for the construction of pseudo-minimal automata ([1]) requires the input data to be sorted in an unusual way (in reverse lexicographic order). We propose three other algorithms that can use lexicographically sorted data, unsorted data, or data sorted on decreasing length. All these algorithms result from slight modifications of known algorithms for the incremental and semi-incremental construction of minimal deterministic acyclic automata ([4], [5]). They are based on the following property: in a pseudo-minimal automaton, there is no path on which a divergent state (i.e. a state with more than one outgoing transition) follows a convergent state (i.e. a state with more than one incoming transition).

In a minimal deterministic acyclic automaton, there may be no two different equivalent states, i.e. states having the same right language (set of words spelled out on all paths from the given state to any final state). That is not the case for a pseudo-minimal automaton, in which each state q such that

$$|\vec{\mathcal{L}}(q)| > 1 \qquad (1)$$

may have an equivalent state somewhere in the automaton (where $\vec{\mathcal{L}}(q)$ is the right language of q). The modifications introduced to the abovementioned algorithms rely on the verification of condition (1).

In the original algorithms for sorted (case 1) and unsorted data (case 2), cf. [4], as well as for data sorted on decreasing length (case 3), cf. [5], each time we add a new word to the automaton, we perform a local minimization of a path corresponding to one or more word suffixes (the suffix of the previously added word in case 1, or the suffix of the current word in case 2, and the suffixes of several previously added words in case 3). This suffix minimization is done by

---

* Invited professor at the University of Tours, October through November 2004.

J. Farré, I. Litovsky, and S. Schmitz (Eds.): CIAA 2005, LNCS 3845, pp. 341–342, 2006.
© Springer-Verlag Berlin Heidelberg 2006

checking, for every suffix' state, if that state has an equivalent state already in the automaton. If an equivalence is discovered both states are merged.

In order for the automaton to be pseudo-minimal instead of minimal, the local minimization has to be modified so that merging of states happens only if states are equivalent and condition (1) is not met. As in cases 1 and 2, the local minimization happens recusively backwards (starting from a final state), and the cardinality of the right language is easy to track on the fly. However, in case 3, the information about condition (1) has to be stored explicitly. After the addition of a new word and before the local minimization, all states from the start state to the newly created divergent state (if any) are marked as not verifying condition (1).

We have performed a correctness proof of the three algorithms we have proposed. The complexity of each of them is linear with regard to the number of symbols in the input data, provided that the operations on the so-called *register* (data structure containing a single representative state of each equivalence class of the automaton under construction) can be carried out in constant time. In incremental algorithms, all through the construction process, the intermediate automaton remains pseudo-minimal, i.e. the computation space usage of the whole algorithm is optimal.

We have perfomed experiments on 3 word lists extracted from English, French and Polish natural language corpora. Lists contained only unique words. For the algorithm for unsorted data, words came in the order they appeared in corpora. For other algorithms, they were sorted appropriately. The comparison of construction speed was done with respect to the first stage of the algorithm by [1] (its first stage produces a pseudo-minimal automaton while the whole algorithm produces a minimal automaton).

The results show that the three new algorithms proposed here are slower (up to 2.4 times for English, up to 3.7 times for French and up to 3 times for Polish) than the original algorithm by [1]. However, that algorithm requires unusual sorting of input data, which can not always be done (e.g. for the sake of disk space, or because of the nature of dynamic perfect hashing).

References

1. Revuz, D.: Dictionnaires et lexiques: méthodes et algorithmes. PhD thesis, Institut Blaise Pascal, Paris, France (1991) LITP 91.44.
2. Maurel, D.: Pseudo-minimal transducer. Theoretical Computer Science (2000) 129–139
3. Daciuk, J., Maurel, D., Savary, A.: Dynamic perfect hashing with finite-state automata. In: Proceedings of Intelligent Information Systems. New Trends in Intelligent Information Processing and Web Mining. Advances in Soft Computing, Springer (2005)
4. Daciuk, J., Mihov, S., Watson, B., Watson, R.: Incremental construction of minimal acyclic finite state automata. Computational Linguistics **26** (2000) 3–16
5. Watson, B.: A fast new (semi-incremental) algorithm for the construction of minimal acyclic DFAs. In: Third Workshop on Implementing Automata, Rouen, France, Lecture Notes in Computer Science, Springer (1998) 91–98

Is Learning RFSAs Better Than Learning DFAs?

Pedro García[1], José Ruiz[1], Antonio Cano[1], and Gloria Alvarez[2]

[1] Universidad Politécnica de Valencia. Valencia, Spain
[2] Pontificia Universidad Javeriana - Seccional Cali. Cali, Colombia
{pgarcia, jruiz, acano, galvarez}@dsic.upv.es

Abstract. Inference of RFSAs has been recently presented [1] as an alternative to inference of DFAs if the target language has been obtained by a random generation of NFAs. We propose in this paper the algorithm RPNI2, which is a variation of the previous RPNI, that also outputs DFAs as hypothesis. The experiments done using the same data as in [1] show that RPNI2 has an error rate very similar to the rate obtained in the inference of RFSAs, but the size of the hypothesis is substantially smaller.

1 Description of the Algorithms RPNI and RPNI2

The RPNI (Regular Positive and Negative Inference) algorithm can be found in [2]. Definitions and previous works concerning RFSAs and DeLeTe2 algorithm can be found in [1] and in some other previous works of the same authors.

The RPNI (Regular Positive and Negative Inference) algorithm [2] is used for inference of regular languages. It receives a sample of the target language as input and it outputs, in polynomial time, a DFA consistent with the input. This algorithm converges to the minimal automaton of the target language in the limit (i.e. when it has received a characteristic sample as input).

RPNI works merging every state of the Prefix Tree Moore Machine of the sample with the previous ones in lexicographical order and propagates the merges done to keep a deterministic automaton under the condition that it does not accept a negative sample.

Merging states can be seen as a process of enlarging the learning sample, as states that have undefined output in the tree, may now be defined if they can be merged with a state whose output belongs to $\{0,1\}$.

The main idea of the variation of RPNI that we propose in this paper and we call RPNI2 is the following: If two states p and q can not be merged we try to establish the possible inclusion relation between them (We say that $q \prec q'$ if no word w exists such that $\delta(q, w)$ is a final state whereas $\delta(q', w)$ is not), which will sometimes permit us to define the output associated to some states that were previously undefined (if $q \prec q'$, then if q is final and q' is undefined, q' can be set as final, otherwise if q' is not final and q is undefined, q can be set as final). Except for this variation, RPNI2 works exactly as previous RPNI does and it converges to the minimal DFA of the target language.

J. Farré, I. Litovsky, and S. Schmitz (Eds.): CIAA 2005, LNCS 3845, pp. 343–344, 2006.
© Springer-Verlag Berlin Heidelberg 2006

2   Results

The aim of the experiments is to compare RPNI2 with DeLeTe2. We have used the samples provided in http://www.grappa.univlille3.fr/~lemay/. These samples are generated from 20 state (on average) NFAs, which correspond to 120 state (on average) DFAs.

The table shown below reports the recognition rate and the average size (the number of states of the hypothesis). The error rate of the new algorithm RPNI2 is better than the former RPNI but slightly worse than DeLeTe2. The opposite happens with the description complexity (i.e. number of states) of the output hypothesis. The results obtained by RPNI2 are then better than those of DeLeTe2.

Iden.	RPNI		RPNI2		DeLeTe2	
	Recognition rate	Average size	Recognition rate	Average size	Recognition rate	Average size
er_50	76.36%	9.63	80.03%	16.32	81.68%	32.43
er_100	80.61%	14.16	88.68%	19.24	91.72%	30.73
er_150	84.46%	15.43	90.61%	26.16	92.29%	60.96
er_200	91.06%	13.3	93.38%	27.37	95.71%	47.73
nfa_50	64.8%	14.3	66.43%	30.64	69.80%	71.26
nfa_100	68.25%	21.83	72.79%	53.14	74.82%	149.13
nfa_150	71.21%	28.13	75.69%	71.87	77.14%	218.26
nfa_200	71.74%	33.43	77.25%	88.95	79.42%	271.3

3   Conclusions

Although the experiments are still preliminary, it seems that the slightly better results obtained by DeLeTe2 with respect to RPNI2 do not compensate the fact that the size of the representations obtained by RPNI2 are clearly smaller. A more exhaustive set of experiments should be done in future works.

References

1. Denis, F. Lemay, A., Terlutte, A.: Learning regular languages using rfsas. Theoretical Computer Science **313** (2004) 267–294
2. Oncina, J., García, P.: Inferring regular languages in polynomial updated time. In Pattern Recognition and Image Analysys (1992)

Learning Stochastic Finite Automata for Musical Style Recognition*

Colin de la Higuera, Frédéric Piat, and Frédéric Tantini

EURISE, Université de Saint-Etienne, 23 rue du Docteur Paul Michelon,
42023 Saint-Etienne, France
{cdlh, piat, tantini}@univ-st-etienne.fr

Abstract. We use stochastic deterministic finite automata to model musical styles: a same automaton can be used to classify new melodies but also to generate them. Through grammatical inference these automata are learned and new pieces of music can be parsed. We show that this works by proposing promising classification results.

In music, notes are grouped (played sequentially or simultaneously in the case of chords) to instantiate classes (e.g. the sequence of notes C-E-G-C instantiates the C Major scale because it contains its more important notes, a scale being an ordered subset of the 12 notes used in western music). Further, there exists rules of well-formedness and typical sequences in the structure of musical passages, which vary according to musical styles, just like a verb can be in the middle or at the end of a sentence depending on the language. This suggests that tools used for language modeling such as formal language theory and grammatical inference could be of great help for the analysis and understanding of music [1, 2].

Grammatical inference is concerned with finding grammars or automata corresponding to strings, sentences or other structured data. The inferred grammar is supposed to generate the language from which the data has been extracted. Techniques can be empirical or provable. There is a variety of problems depending on whether the data is clean or noisy, or if there is additional knowledge about the distribution of the strings, about some partial rules or if we are given counter-examples [3, 4].

We have followed in this work the lines of previous work by Cruz and Vidal [2]: music can be encoded in a simple way through the pitch and the length of the notes of a melody. Obviously this encoding does not take into account polyphony or even the characteristics of the instruments. A melody will therefore be a string and from a set of melodies/strings it will be possible to infer a grammatical representation of the language corresponding to the musical style. Because of the characteristics of the task and the good performances obtained in other settings (speech for example) we have chosen to represent the languages by stochastic deterministic finite automata (SDFA). We used algorithm MDI [5] to learn these automata, and ideas from grammatical inference [6] to adapt the algorithm.

---

* This work was supported in part by the IST Programme of the European Community, under the PASCAL Network of Excellence, IST-2002-506778. This publication only reflects the authors' views.

J. Farré, I. Litovsky, and S. Schmitz (Eds.): CIAA 2005, LNCS 3845, pp. 345–346, 2006.

We used a dataset by [2] made up of 100 pieces for each of the 4 styles "Gregorian","Jig","Reel" and "Scarlatti". These are clearly different from each other except for jigs and reels which are subtypes of Celtic folklore, and share a lot of tonal and melodic patterns in spite of different rhythmic structures. This should give us insight about the capacity of automata to differentiate classes on the basis of principally one dimension (durations) and on the nature of confusions (between remote vs. styles related on one dimension).

Melody lengths range from 61 to 1825 notes (mean= 550). We used a 10-fold cross-validation to generate the confusion matrices presented in Table 1, allowing direct comparison between typed and non-typed automata performances.

Table 1. Confusion matrix of musical style classification by non-typed and typed automata

	reel	scarlat	jig	greg	recall	reel	scarlat	jig	greg	recall
Reel	98	0	1	1	98	95	0	1	4	95
Scarlatti	6	90	4	0	90	5	93	2	0	93
Gig	0	1	99	0	99	0	1	99	0	99
Gregorian	2	0	0	98	98	2	0	0	98	98
Total	106	91	104	99	**96.25**	102	94	102	102	**96.25**
Precision	92.45	98.90	95.19	98.99	**96.38**	93.14	98.94	97.06	96.08	**96.30**

Acknowledgement. The authors are grateful to Pedro Cruz for his benchmarks and for many ideas used in this work. They also thank Thierry Murgue and Franck Thollard for help with MDI and parsers.

References

1. Narmour, E.: The analysis and cognition of melodic complexity: The implication-realization model. Chicago: University of Chicago Press (1992)
2. Cruz, P., Vidal, E.: Learning regular grammars to model musical style: Comparing different coding schemes. In Honavar, V., Slutski, G., eds.: Grammatical Inference, Proceedings of ICGI '98. Number 1433 in LNAI, Berlin, Heidelberg, Springer-Verlag (1998) 211–222
3. Sakakibara, Y.: Recent advances of grammatical inference. Theoretical Computer Science **185** (1997) 15–45
4. de la Higuera, C.: A bibliographical study of grammatical inference. Pattern Recognition (2005) To appear.
5. Thollard, F., Dupont, P., de la Higuera, C.: Probabilistic DFA inference using Kullback-Leibler divergence and minimality. In: Proc. 17th International Conf. on Machine Learning, Morgan Kaufmann, San Francisco, CA (2000) 975–982
6. Kermorvant, C., de la Higuera, C.: Learning languages with help. In Adriaans, P., Fernau, H., van Zaannen, M., eds.: Grammatical Inference: Algorithms and Applications, Proceedings of ICGI '02. Volume 2484 of LNAI., Berlin, Heidelberg, Springer-Verlag (2002) 161–173

Simulation of Soliton Circuits

Miklós Krész

Department of Computer Science, Juhász Gyula Teacher Training College,
University of Szeged, Szeged, Hungary
kresz@jgytf.u-szeged.hu

Soliton circuits are among the most promising alternatives for molecular electronic devices based on the design of molecular level conventional digital circuits. In order to capture the logical and computational aspects of these circuits, a mathematical model called soliton automaton was introduced by Dassow and Jürgensen in 1990.

The underlying object of a soliton automaton is a so called soliton graph, which is a finite undirected graph allowed to have loops and multiple edges. In order for the graph to act as an automaton, it must have a *perfect internal matching*, which is a matching covering all vertices with degree at least 2. Such vertices are called *internal*, while *external* vertices are ones with degree 1.

Let G be a soliton graph, fixed for our present discussion. The graph G defines an automaton $\mathcal{A}(G)$, the states of which are the perfect internal matchings of G. With a slight ambiguity, we shall also say that "M is a state of G", rather than "M is a state of $\mathcal{A}(G)$". Inputs to $\mathcal{A}(G)$ are pairs of external vertices of G. In state M, a possible transition on input (v_1, v_2) is carried out by switching along an alternating walk – called *soliton walk* – connecting v_1 with v_2. In that case the above transition is expressed by $M' \in \delta(M, (v_1, v_2))$, where M' denotes the induced state and δ denotes the transition function of $\mathcal{A}(G)$.

From practical point of view it is a fundamental question to develop a simulation method for soliton circuits. Translating the above problem to the language of soliton automata, we consider the following task.

Automaton Construction Problem (ACP): *Given a soliton graph G. Construct the automaton $\mathcal{A}(G)$ associated with G.*

In order to give a solution for ACP, first we must design a method determining the set $S(G)$ of states of G, then an algorithm for constructing the transition function is needed.

The first problem can be solved by adopting an extension of the method suggested by Itai, Rodeh and Tanimoto for bipartite graphs with perfect matchings. Working out the technical details of this method, after a careful complexity analysis the following result is obtained.

Theorem 1. *Let G be a soliton graph, $m = |E(G)|$ and $k = |S(G)|$. Then $S(G)$ can be constructed in $\mathcal{O}(k \cdot m)$ time.*

Now we are left to provide a method constructing the transition function of $\mathcal{A}(G)$. The basic step solving this problem is to determine the set of input pairs (v, w) for any states $M_1, M_2 \in S(G)$ such that $M_2 \in \delta(M_1, (v, w))$.

J. Farré, I. Litovsky, and S. Schmitz (Eds.): CIAA 2005, LNCS 3845, pp. 347–348, 2006.
© Springer-Verlag Berlin Heidelberg 2006

First consider the case of $M_1 \neq M_2$. In that situation we can capitalize the characterization of the structure of the symmetric difference $N(M_1, M_2)$ of M_1 and M_2. Making use this result, our problem can be reduced to testing the accessibility of alternating cycles in $N(M_1, M_2)$ by M_1-alternating paths starting from v. Therefore, applying an efficient alternating path procedure, we obtain the following.

Theorem 2. *Let M_1 and M_2 be distinct states of $\mathcal{A}(G)$, $m = |E(G)|$ and let l denote the number of external vertices. Then the set of input pairs (v, w) for which $M_2 \in \delta(M_1, (v, w))$ can be constructed in $\mathcal{O}(l \cdot m)$ time.*

Having solved the problem of transitions between distinct states, now we turn to *self-transitions*, i.e. transitions from a state to itself. Self-transitions can be characterized with the help of the so-called *soliton trails*, i.e. external alternating walks returning to themselves only in the last step. A trail is a *c-trail* (*l-trail*) if it closes up an even-length (respectively, odd-length) cycle. An *M-alternating double soliton c-trail* from external vertex v is a pair of M-alternating soliton c-trails (α^1, α^2) from v such that the cycles of α^1 and α^2 are either the same or disjoint.

Now for an arbitrary external vertex v and state M of G, construct the graph $G[M, v]$ determined by the edges traversed by an M-alternating path or an M-alternating soliton trail starting from v. Then the key point for our algorithm is the following result.

Theorem 3. *For any state M of soliton automaton $\mathcal{A}(G)$ and for any external vertex v of G, $M \in \delta(M, (v, v))$ iff one of the following conditions holds:*

(a) $G[M, v]$ is a non-bipartite graph.

(b) $G[M, v]$ is a bipartite graph containing an M-alternating double soliton c-trail from v.

(c) $G[M, v]$ is a bipartite graph not containing an M-alternating even-length cycle.

Now making use of the above theorem we can give a method deciding for any state M and external vertex v of G if $M \in \delta(M, (v, v))$ holds. For this goal we need to design efficient procedures for constructing $G[M, v]$ and for searching alternating cycles with certain properties in $G[M, v]$. Using standard algorithmic techniques such as depth-first search and breadth-first search with respect to alternating paths, an algorithm is worked out with a complexity proportional to the number of vertices and edges.

Our closing result summarizes the preceding observations.

Theorem 4. *Let G be a soliton graph with $n = |V(G)|$, $m = |E(G)|$, $k = |S(G)|$ and l denoting the number of external vertices. Then ACP can be solved in $\mathcal{O}((k + n) \cdot (k \cdot l \cdot m))$ time.*

Acyclic Automata with Easy-to-Find Short Regular Expressions*

José João Morais, Nelma Moreira, and Rogério Reis

DCC-FC & LIACC, Universidade do Porto,
R. do Campo Alegre 823, 4150 Porto, Portugal
jjoao@netcabo.pt, {nam, rvr}@ncc.up.pt

Abstract. Computing short regular expressions equivalent to a given
finite automaton is a hard task. We present a class of acyclic automata for
which it is easy-to-find a regular expression that has linear size. We call
those automata UDR. A UDR automaton is characterized by properties
of its underlying digraph. We give a characterisation theorem and an
efficient algorithm to determine if an acyclic automaton is UDR, that
can be adapted to compute an equivalent short regular expression.

Computing a regular expression from a given finite automaton can be achieved
by well-known algorithms based on Kleene's theorem. However the resulting
regular expression depends on the order in which the automaton's states are
considered in the conversion. In particular, this is the case if the algorithm is
based on the *state elimination technique*. Consider the following automaton:

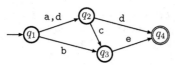

If we remove the state q_2 and then the state q_3, we obtain the regular expression
$(a + d)d + ((a + d)c + b)e$. But if we remove first q_3 and then q_2, we obtain the
regular expression $be + (a + d)(ce + d)$. If our goal is to obtain a short regular
expression, the order in which we consider the automaton states is of great importance. Moreover, obtaining a minimal regular expression equivalent to a given automaton is PSPACE-complete, and remains NP-complete for acyclic automata.
In this work we present a characterisation of acyclic automata for which it is easy
to find an order of state removal such that the resulting regular expressions have
size linear in the number of the automata transitions. Given a *nondeterministic finite automaton* (NFA) $A = (Q, \Sigma, \delta, q_0, F)$, its *underlying digraph* is $D =
(Q, E)$ such that $E = \{(q, q') \mid q, q' \in Q$ and $\exists a \in \Sigma \cup \{\epsilon\}$ such that $(q, a, q') \in
\delta\}$. An automaton is *useful* if in its underlying digraph, every state is in a path
from the initial state to a final state. An automaton is *acyclic* if its underlying
digraph is acyclic. We will consider only useful acyclic automata with one final
state. We say that two digraphs are homeomorphic if both can be obtained from
the same digraph by a sequence of subdivisions of arcs. Let consider the di-
graph $R^{\rightarrow} = (\{q_1, q_2, q_3, q_4\}, \{(q_1, q_2), (q_1, q_3), (q_2, q_3), (q_2, q_4), (q_3, q_4)\})$. A useful

* Work partially funded by Fundação para a Ciência e Tecnologia and Program POSI.

J. Farré, I. Litovsky, and S. Schmitz (Eds.): CIAA 2005, LNCS 3845, pp. 349–350, 2006.

acyclic NFA with one final state is *UDR* (*Unique for the Distributivity Rule*) if its underlying digraph does not contain a subgraph homeomorphic to $R^{\rightarrow}$. The underlying digraph is a *UDR digraph*. The NFA represented above is not UDR, as its underlying digraph is $R^{\rightarrow}$. If an automaton is not UDR, there are at least two states such that the order chosen to eliminate them leads to two different regular expressions, one that results from the application of a distributivity rule to the other. This is not the case for UDR automata. We have:[1]

Theorem 1. *Let $D = (Q, E, i, f)$ be a UDR digraph and $|Q| > 2$. Then D has at least a vertex q such that its indegree and its outdegree are 1 (i.e. $q(1;1)$).*

Theorem 2. *Let $A = (Q, \Sigma, i, \delta, f)$ be a useful acyclic NFA. We can obtain a regular expression equivalent to A using the state elimination algorithm in such way that in each step we remove a state q with $q(1;1)$ if and only if A is UDR. Moreover, that regular expression has size linear in the size of A.*

The following algorithm determines if an acyclic digraph is UDR in $O(n^2 \log n)$. If an automaton is UDR, the algorithm udrp can be adapted to compute an equivalent regular expression with size linear in the size of the automaton.

```
udrp {
  %AdjT(v):list of vertices adjacent to v
  %AdjF(v):list of vertices adjacent from v
  %label(u,v):for each edge (u,v), a list of vertices vn with
  %           |AdjF(vn)|> 1 that precedes v in a path from i
  % ← assignment
  % == strictly identical (\== not identical)
  % ?= unifiable, = unification a la Prolog
  for v1 in Q topological order do
      nf ← |AdjF(v1)|
      while nf > 1 do
          max ← max{|label(v,v1)|:v ∈ AdjF(v1)}
          lmax ← {v ∈ AdjF(v1):|label(v,v1)| = max}
          vi ← first(lmax)
          if v in lmax-{vi} and (label(v,v1) \== label(vi,v1))
             and (label(v,v1) ?= label(vi,v1)) then
                  vp ← last(label(vi,v1))
                  outdegree(vp) ← outdegree(vp) - 1
                  label(v,v1) = label(vi,v1)
                  if outdegree(vp) == 1 then
                      label(v,v1) ← butlast(label(v,v1))
                  nf ← nf - 1
          else return 0 % is not UDR
      if v1 == i then lp ← nil
      else lp = label(first(AdjF(v1)),v1)
      for v2 in AdjT(v1) do
          if outdegree(v1) ≠ 1 then label(v1,v2) ← lp.v1
          else label(v1,v2) = lp
  return 1 % is UDR }
```

---

[1] For the proofs see http://www.dcc.fc.up.pt/Pubs/TR05/dcc-2005-03.ps.gz.

On the Equivalence Problem for Programs with Mode Switching

Rimma I. Podlovchenko, Dmitry M. Rusakov, and Vladimir A. Zakharov

Lomonosov Moscow State University,
Moscow State University, Vorobyovy Gory, Moscow, 119992, Russia
rip@vvv.srcc.msu.su, zakh@cs.msu.su

Abstract. We study a formal model of imperative sequential programs and focus on the equivalence problem for some class of programs with mode switching whose runs can be divided into two stages. In the first stage a program selects an appropriate mode of computation. Several modes may be tried (switched) in turn before making the ultimate choice. Every time when the next mode is put to a test, the program brings data to some predefined state. In the second stage of the run, once a definite mode is fixed, the final result of computation is produced. We develop a new technique for simulating the behavior of such programs by means of finite automata and demonstrate that the equivalence problem for programs with mode switching is decidable within a polynomial space. By revealing a close relationships between the equivalence problem for this class of programs and the intersection emptiness problem for deterministic finite automata we show that the the former is *PSPACE*-complete.

We give a complete solution to the equivalence problem for propositional sequential programs (PSPs for short) with mode switching. PSPs provide a model of computation which is particularly adapted to the analysis of imperative sequential programs. PSPs with mode switching are used to simulate a behavior of some programs whose runs can be divided into two stages. In the first stage a program selects an appropriate mode of computation. Several modes may be tried in turn before the ultimate choice will be fixed. Every time when the next mode is put to a test, the program brings the data back to some predefined state corresponding to this mode. In the second stage, once a definitive mode is fixed, the final result of computation is generated.

PSPs with mode switching may be thought of as finite automata operating on free semigroups with right zeros [1]. In [1, 2] the equivalence problem for such automata was proved to be decidable, but the decision techniques used in both papers are very much sophisticated and does not enable to estimate the complexity of the problem. By revealing close relationships between the equivalence problem for PSPs with mode switching and the Intersection Emptiness Problem [3] for deterministic finite state automata we introduce a straightforward equivalence-checking procedure and demonstrate that the equivalence problem for PSPs with mode switching is *PSPACE*-complete. This result was obtained in the framework of our research aimed at developing efficient equivalence-checking procedures for abstract models of programs [4, 5].

J. Farré, I. Litovsky, and S. Schmitz (Eds.): CIAA 2005, LNCS 3845, pp. 351–352, 2006.
© Springer-Verlag Berlin Heidelberg 2006

The syntax of PSPs is defined as follows. Let $\mathcal{A}$ and $\mathcal{P}$ be two finite alphabets whose elements are called *basic statements* and *basic predicates* respectively. Basic statements stand for assignment statements in imperative programs. We assume that the set $\mathcal{A}$ is partitioned into two subsets $\mathcal{A}_0$ (*ordinary actions*) and $\mathcal{A}_1$ (*mode switches*). Basic predicates stand for elementary built-in relations on program data; they may be evaluated by 0 (false) or 1 (true). A tuple $\langle \delta_1, \ldots, \delta_k \rangle$ of truth-values of all basic predicates is called a *condition*. The set of all conditions is denoted by $\mathcal{C}$.

A PSP is a finite transition system $\pi = \langle V, \mathbf{entry}, \mathbf{exit}, T, B \rangle$, where

- V is a set of *program points*;
- **entry** and **exit** are the *initial* and the *terminal* points respectively;
- $T: (V - \{\mathbf{exit}\}) \times \mathcal{C} \to V$ is a (total) *transition function*;
- $B: (V - \{\mathbf{exit}\}) \to \mathcal{A}$ is a (total) *binding function*.

The semantics of PSPs with mode switching is defined as follows. Let $\mu : \mathcal{A}^* \to \mathcal{C}$ be an *evaluation function* which gives an interpretation of basic predicates. A *run* of π on μ is a sequence of pairs $r(\pi, \mu) = (v_0, s_0), (v_1, s_1), \ldots, (v_i, s_i), \ldots$, where v_i, $i \geq 0$, are program points and s_i are words from $\mathcal{A}^*$ such that

1. $v_0 = \mathbf{entry}$, $s_0 = \lambda$ (empty word);
2. for every i, $i \geq 0$, we have $v_{i+1} = T(v_i, \mu(s_i))$, and s_{i+1} is either a word $s_i B(v_i)$ in case of $B(v_i) \in \mathcal{A}_0$ (this means that an ordinary action facilitates a progress of program computation), or a single letter $B(v_i)$ in case of $B(v_i) \in \mathcal{A}_1$ (this means that a mode switch abandons any previous intermediate result of computation and brings data into some distinguished state);
3. the sequence $r(\pi, \mu)$ either is infinite (the run *loops* and yields no results), or ends with a pair $(\mathbf{exit}, s_n)$ (the run *terminates* and gives a result s_n).

We denote by $[r(\pi, \mu)]$ the result of the run $r(\pi, \mu)$ assuming that the result is undefined when $r(\pi, \mu)$ loops. PSPs π_1 and π_2 are said to be *equivalent* ($\pi_1 \sim \pi_2$ in symbols) iff $[r(\pi_1, \mu)] = [r(\pi_2, \mu)]$ holds for every evaluation function μ. The *equivalence problem* for PSPs is to check, given a pair of PSPs π_1 and π_2, whether $\pi_1 \sim \pi_2$ holds.

Theorem 1. *The equivalence problem for PSPs with mode switching is PSPACE-complete.*

References

1. Letichevsky, A.A.: Functional equivalence of discrete transducers. Cybernetics (1970) 14–28.
2. Lisovik, L.P.: Hard sets and semilinear reservoir method with applications. Lecture Notes in Computer Science, **1099** (1996) 219–231.
3. Kozen, D.: Lower bounds for natural proof systems. In: 18th Annual Symposium on Foundation of Computer Science (FOCS), IEEE, (1977) 254–266.
4. Podlovchenko, R.I., Zakharov, V.A.: On the polynomial-time algorithm deciding the commutative equivalence of program schemes. Reports of the Russian Academy of Science, **362** (1998)
5. Zakharov, V.A.: The equivalence problem for computational models: decidable and undecidable cases. Lecture Notes in Computer Science, **2055** (2001) 133–153.

Automata and AB-Categorial Grammars

Isabelle Tellier

GRAppA & Inria Futurs, Lille (MOSTRARE project),
Université Charles de Gaulle- Lille 3, 59653 Villeneuve d'Ascq, France
isabelle.tellier@univ-lille3.fr

1 Introduction

AB-categorial grammars (CGs in the following) is a lexicalized formalism having the expressive power of ϵ-free context-free languages [1]. It has a long common history with natural language [2]. Here, we first relate unidirectional CGs to a special case of recursive transition networks [3]. We then illustrate how the structures produced by a CG can be generated by a *pair of recursive automata*.

2 Automata for Unidirectional Categorial Grammars

Definition 1. *Let $\mathcal{B}$ be a set of basic categories among which is the axiom $S \in \mathcal{B}$. $Cat(\mathcal{B})$ is the smallest set including $\mathcal{B}$ and every A/B and $B\backslash A$, for any A, B in $Cat(\mathcal{B})$. A CG $G \subset \Sigma \times Cat(\mathcal{B})$ is a finite relation between a vocabulary Σ and $Cat(\mathcal{B})$. In CGs, the syntactic rules are reduces to two rewriting schemes: FA (Forward Application): $A/B \ B \rightarrow A$ and BA (Backward Application): $B \ B\backslash A \rightarrow A$. The language generated by a CG is the set of strings in Σ^* corresponding to a string in $(Cat(\mathcal{B}))^*$ which reduces to S. Unidirectional CGs make an exclusive use of $/$ (or of $\backslash$). They can produce every ϵ-free CF language.*

Example 1. The classical unidirectional CGs recognizing $a^n b^n$, $n \geq 1$ are: $G_{FA} = \{\langle a, S/B \rangle, \langle a, (S/B)/S \rangle, \langle b, B \rangle\}$ and $G_{BA} = \{\langle a, A \rangle, \langle b, A\backslash S \rangle, \langle b, S\backslash(A\backslash S) \rangle\}$. They can respectively be represented by the "recursive automata" given in Figure 1.

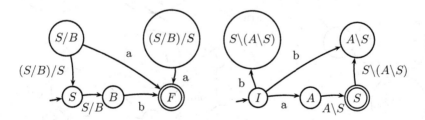

Fig. 1. Two recusive automata both recognizing $a^n b^n$, $n \geq 1$

In these automata (seee [4] for details), the transitions labelled by a state refer to *state languages*: for unidirectional CGs making only use of $/$ (resp. of $\backslash$),

J. Farré, I. Litovsky, and S. Schmitz (Eds.): CIAA 2005, LNCS 3845, pp. 353–355, 2006.
© Springer-Verlag Berlin Heidelberg 2006

the language $L_{FA}(Q)$ (resp. $L_{BA}(Q)$) is the set of strings produced by starting in Q and reaching the state F (resp. by starting in I and reaching the state Q).

3 Automata for AB-Categorial Grammars

Now, to produce the same *structures* as a CG, it is enough to consider two mutually recursive automata: one for *FA* rules, the other for *BA* rules. $\forall Q \in Cat(\mathcal{B})$: $L(Q) = L_{FA}(Q) \cup L_{BA}(Q)$. This generative model improves the readability of a CG. A promising application domain is grammatical inference [4].

Example 2. Let $\mathcal{B} = \{S, T, CN\}$ (where T stands for "term" and CN for "common noun"), $\Sigma = \{John, runs, loves, a, cat\}$ and $G = \{\langle John, T \rangle, \langle loves, (T\backslash S)/T \rangle, \langle loves, T\backslash(S/T) \rangle, \langle runs, T\backslash S \rangle, \langle cat, CN \rangle, \langle a, (S/(T\backslash S))/CN \rangle, \langle a, ((S/T)\backslash S)/CN \rangle\}$.

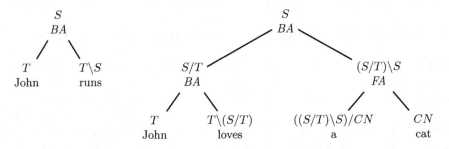

Fig. 2. Syntactic Parse Trees Produced by the Categorial Grammar G

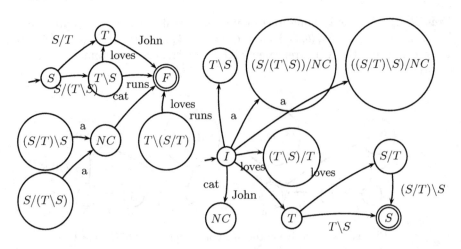

Fig. 3. A Pair of Mutually Recursive Automata Representing G

References

1. Bar Hillel, Y., Gaifman, C., Shamir, E.: On Categorial and Phrase Structure Grammars. Bulletin of the Research Council of Israel **9F** (1960)
2. Oehrle, R.T., Bach, E., Wheeler, D.: Categorial Grammars and Natural Language Structures. D. Reidel Publishing Company, Dordrecht (1988)
3. Woods, W.A.: Transition network grammars for natural language analysis. Communication of the ACM **13 10** (1970) 591–606
4. Tellier, I.: When Categorial Grammars meet Regular Grammatical Inference. In: proceedings of LACL 2005. LNAI **3492** (2005) 317–332

On a Class of Bijective Binary Transducers with Finitary Description Despite Infinite State Set*

Michael Vielhaber and Mónica del Pilar Canales Ch.

Instituto de Matemáticas, Universidad Austral de Chile Casilla 567,Valdivia
{monicadelpilar, vielhaber}@gmail.com

Abstract. We show that an infinite isometry f on $\{0,1\}^\omega$, *i.e.* computable by an infinite transducer $\mathcal{T}_f$, can be represented finitarily, provided the isometry $[\sigma, f] := \sigma^{-1} \circ f^{-1} \circ \sigma \circ f$, the shift commutator of f, is finite, *i.e.* has a finite transducer $\mathcal{T}_{[\sigma,f]}$. We can describe all states of $\mathcal{T}_f$ as words over $Q_{[\sigma,f]}$ and, using the nextstate and output functions of $\mathcal{T}_{[\sigma,f]}$, obtain linear time algorithms for $\mathcal{T}_f$ (in the length of the word in $Q_{[\sigma,f]}^*$ describing the state in Q_f). The task of determining state equivalence within the first n input symbols or $N = 2^{n+1} - 1$ states is *polynomial* in the number N of states, if the shift commutator is finite.

Definitions. Let $A = \{0,1\}$, $a,b \in A^\omega$ with $a = (a_1, a_2, \ldots)$. Let the 2–*adic distance* be $d(a,a) = 0$ and otherwise $d(a,b) = 2^{-k}$, if $a_i = b_i$ for $i < k, a_k \neq b_k$.

A selfmap f on A^ω is called an *isometry* if $\forall a,b \in A^\omega$: $d(a,b) = d(f(a), f(b))$.

A *synchronous invertible binary transducer* is a 5–tuple $\mathcal{T} = (Q, A, i, \rho, \tau)$ (state set, alphabet, initial state, transition, and output) where $\tau: Q \to A$, $\tau(q) = \tau'(q,0)$ with $\tau': Q \times A \to A$, $b_i = \tau'(q, a_i)$, and $\tau'_q := \tau'(q, \cdot) : A \to A$ is bijective, hence $b_i = \tau(q) + a_i \bmod 2$. If $|Q_f| < \infty$, $\mathcal{T}_f$ and f are called finite.

Let $\sigma(a) = (a_2, a_3, \ldots)$ be the *one–sided shift* on A^ω, and for $\alpha \in A$, $\sigma_\alpha^{-1}(a) = (\alpha, a_1, a_2, \ldots)$. Let the *shift commutator* of an isometry f on A^ω be $[\sigma, f](a) = \sigma_\alpha^{-1} \circ f^{-1} \circ \sigma \circ f(a)$, where $\alpha := f(a)_1$ is the symbol shifted out by σ.

(References and more details in [1])

Proposition 1. *Let F be some isometry with $f = [\sigma, F]$. Then we can compute F by iterating f: $F(a)_n = \left(F \circ (\sigma \circ f)^{n-1}\right)(a)_1 = \left(f \circ (\sigma \circ f)^{n-1}\right)(a)_1$.*

Proof. $F \circ (\sigma \circ f)^{n-1} = F \circ (F^{-1} \circ \sigma \circ F)^{n-1} = \sigma^{n-1} \circ F$ and $F(b)_1 = \alpha = f(b)_1$. $\square$

Algorithm. Let f be an isometry computable by $\mathcal{T}_f = (Q_f, A, i_f, \rho_f, \tau_f)$ with $|Q_f| < \infty$. We construct a transducer $\mathcal{T}_F$ as follows:

(*i*) State space Q_F: the hull of i_F under ρ_F, a subset of Q_f^*.

(*ii*) Initial state $i_F := i_f$ (as a one letter word in Q_f^*).

(*iii*) Nextstate function $\rho_F: Q_F \times A \to Q_F$, $\rho_F(w_1 w_2 \ldots w_n, \alpha_1) := z_1 z_2 \ldots z_n z_{n+1}$, where $w_i, z_i \in Q_f$, $w_1 w_2 \ldots w_n \in Q_F \subset Q_f^*, \alpha_1 \in \{0,1\}$ and iteratively $z_i := \rho_f(w_i, \alpha_i), \alpha_{i+1} := \alpha_i + \tau_f(w_i), i = 1, \ldots, n$, $z_{n+1} := i_f$.

We extend ρ_F to $Q_F \times A^*$ by $\rho_F(q, a_1 \ldots a_n) := \rho_F(\rho_F(q, a_1), a_2 \ldots a_n)$.

(*iv*) Output function $\tau_F: Q_F \to A$, $\tau_F(w_1 \ldots w_n) := \sum_{i=1}^n \tau_f(w_i) \bmod 2$.

---

* Supported by FONDECYT 1040975, CONICYT. Partly supported by DID–UACh.

J. Farré, I. Litovsky, and S. Schmitz (Eds.): CIAA 2005, LNCS 3845, pp. 356–357, 2006.
© Springer-Verlag Berlin Heidelberg 2006

Theorem 2. (i) *The isometries f and F computed by the transducers in the Algorithm are related by $f = [\sigma, F]$ that is $\mathcal{T}_F$ computes $F = [\sigma, \bullet]^{-1}(f)$.*

(ii) *An input word $s \in A^*$ goes to a state $\rho_f(i_f, s)$ with $|\rho_f(i_f, s)| \leq |s| + 1$.*

(iii) *The nextstate and output functions ρ_F and τ_F are computable in $O(|w|)$ bit operations, where $|w|$ is the length of the word $w \in Q_f^*$ describing the state.*

Proof. (i) We simulate F by running $n = 1, 2, \ldots$ copies of f, starting a new transducer $\mathcal{T}_f$ for every input symbol. From Proposition 1, we have $F(a)_n = (f^{(n)} \circ \sigma \circ f^{(n-1)} \ldots \circ \sigma \circ f^{(1)})(a)_1$, where superscripts distinguish the copies of $\mathcal{T}_f$. Comparing with the definition of ρ_F, the symbol $w_i \in Q_f$ stores the state of the transducer for $f^{(i)}$, which is updated to $z_i = \rho_f(w_i, \alpha_i)$. The σ are accounted for by starting each copy of f one step later. Hence $z_1 z_2 \ldots z_{n+1}$ is the updated state after all n copies have advanced and a new $f^{(n+1)}$ just started in $z_{n+1} = i_f$.

We obtain α_i from the input symbol $a_n = \alpha_1$ and the copies 1 to $i - 1$ of $\mathcal{T}_f$ according to $\alpha_i = \alpha_1 + \tau_f(w_1) + \ldots + \tau_f(w_{i-1})$. Thus, the output at position n is $\alpha_{n+1} = \alpha_1 + \sum_{i=1}^{n} \tau_f(w_i) = a_n + \tau_F(w_1 \ldots w_n)$ as required.

(ii) By definition, $\rho_F(i_f, s_1 s_2 \ldots s_n)$ is an $(n + 1)$–letter word over Q_f.

(iii) For each symbol in w, a constant time is needed for ρ_f and τ_f, hence $\mathcal{T}_F$ proceeds in $O(|w|)$ time with calculating ρ_F, τ_F. □

State Equivalence. Let two states $v, w \in Q_F \subset Q_f^*$ be equivalent, if and only if for all $s \in A^*$, $\tau_F(\rho_F(v, s)) = \tau_F(\rho_F(w, s))$.

Theorem 3. (i) *State equivalence can be determined in $O(q^{|v|+|w|})$ bit operations, where v, w are the words defining the two states.*

(ii) *For inputs up to length n, $\mathcal{T}_F$ uses $N := 2^{n+1} - 1$ states, and their reduced set of inequivalent states can be determined in $O(N^{2+2 \cdot \log_2 q})$ bit operations.*

(For related work in Model Checking compare with [2])

Proof. (i) For all $s \in A^*$, let $q^{(s)} = \rho_F(v, s)$, $r^{(s)} = \rho_F(w, s)$, let $\alpha_1^{(s)} = \beta_1^{(s)} = s_1$, $\alpha_{i+1}^{(s)} = \alpha_i^{(s)} + \tau_f(q_i^{(s)})$, $\beta_{i+1}^{(s)} = \beta_i^{(s)} + \tau_f(r_i^{(s)})$, and $k = |v| + 1, l = |w| + 1$.

Let s^* be a shortest word with $\tau_F(q^{(s^*)}) \neq \tau_F(r^{(s^*)})$. For all s with $|s| < |s^*|$, the suffixes of $q^{(s)}, r^{(s)}$ satisfy $q_{k \ldots k+|s|}^{(s)} = r_{l \ldots l+|s|}^{(s)} = \rho(i_f, t)$ for a t with $|t| = |s|$, $t_i = \alpha_k^{(s_1 \ldots s_i)} = \beta_l^{(s_1 \ldots s_i)}, 1 \leq i \leq |s|$. These α_k and β_l are the same since otherwise some $\alpha_{k+i}^{(s_1 \ldots s_i)} \neq \beta_{l+i}^{(s_1 \ldots s_i)}$, contradicting the minimality of $|s^*|$.

Hence for s^*, τ_F already differs on the first k, resp. l symbols, and it suffices to compare τ_F on the hulls of v and w in at most $q^{|v|+|w|}$ steps.

(ii) By Theorem 2(ii), $|v|, |w| \leq n + 1$. Checking $\binom{N}{2}$ stateword pairs needs $\binom{N}{2} \cdot O(q^{|v|+|w|}) \leq N^2 \cdot O(q^{2 \log_2 N}) = O(N^{2+2 \log_2 q})$ steps. □

References

1. del P. Canales, M., Vielhaber, M.: Isometries of binary formal power series and their shift commutators. Electronic Colloq. on Comput. Compl **TR04–057** (2004)
2. Bouajjani, A., Jonsson, B., Nilsson, M., Touili, T.: Regular model checking. Proc. 12th CAV, LNCS **1855** (2000)

Author Index

Lecture Notes in Computer Science

For information about Vols. 1–3780

please contact your bookseller or Springer

Vol. 3826: B. Benatallah, F. Casati, P. Traverso (Eds.), Service-Oriented Computing - ICSOC 2005. XVIII, 597 pages. 2005.

Vol. 3824: L.T. Yang, M. Amamiya, Z. Liu, M. Guo, F.J. Rammig (Eds.), Embedded and Ubiquitous Computing – EUC 2005. XXIII, 1204 pages. 2005.

Vol. 3823: T. Enokido, L. Yan, B. Xiao, D. Kim, Y. Dai, L.T. Yang (Eds.), Embedded and Ubiquitous Computing – EUC 2005 Workshops. XXXII, 1317 pages. 2005.

Vol. 3822: D. Feng, D. Lin, M. Yung (Eds.), Information Security and Cryptology. XII, 420 pages. 2005.

Vol. 3821: R. Ramanujam, S. Sen (Eds.), FSTTCS 2005: Foundations of Software Technology and Theoretical Computer Science. XIV, 566 pages. 2005.

Vol. 3820: L.T. Yang, X.-s. Zhou, W. Zhao, Z. Wu, Y. Zhu, M. Lin (Eds.), Embedded Software and Systems. XXVIII, 779 pages. 2005.

Vol. 3819: P. Van Hentenryck (Ed.), Practical Aspects of Declarative Languages. X, 231 pages. 2005.

Vol. 3818: S. Grumbach, L. Sui, V. Vianu (Eds.), Advances in Computer Science – ASIAN 2005. XIII, 294 pages. 2005.

Vol. 3817: M. Faundez-Zanuy, L. Janer, A. Esposito, A. Satue-Villar, J. Roure, V. Espinosa-Duro (Eds.), Nonlinear Analyses and Algorithms for Speech Processing. XII, 380 pages. 2006. (Sublibrary LNAI).

Vol. 3816: G. Chakraborty (Ed.), Distributed Computing and Internet Technology. XXI, 606 pages. 2005.

Vol. 3815: E.A. Fox, E.J. Neuhold, P. Premsmit, V. Wuwongse (Eds.), Digital Libraries: Implementing Strategies and Sharing Experiences. XVII, 529 pages. 2005.

Vol. 3814: M. Maybury, O. Stock, W. Wahlster (Eds.), Intelligent Technologies for Interactive Entertainment. XV, 342 pages. 2005. (Sublibrary LNAI).

Vol. 3813: R. Molva, G. Tsudik, D. Westhoff (Eds.), Security and Privacy in Ad-hoc and Sensor Networks. VIII, 219 pages. 2005.

Vol. 3811: C. Bussler, M.-C. Shan (Eds.), Technologies for E-Services. VIII, 127 pages. 2006.

Vol. 3810: Y.G. Desmedt, H. Wang, Y. Mu, Y. Li (Eds.), Cryptology and Network Security. XI, 349 pages. 2005.

Vol. 3809: S. Zhang, R. Jarvis (Eds.), AI 2005: Advances in Artificial Intelligence. XXVII, 1344 pages. 2005. (Sublibrary LNAI).

Vol. 3808: C. Bento, A. Cardoso, G. Dias (Eds.), Progress in Artificial Intelligence. XVIII, 704 pages. 2005. (Sublibrary LNAI).

Vol. 3807: M. Dean, Y. Guo, W. Jun, R. Kaschek, S. Krishnaswamy, Z. Pan, Q.Z. Sheng (Eds.), Web Information Systems Engineering – WISE 2005 Workshops. XV, 275 pages. 2005.

Vol. 3806: A.H. H. Ngu, M. Kitsuregawa, E.J. Neuhold, J.-Y. Chung, Q.Z. Sheng (Eds.), Web Information Systems Engineering – WISE 2005. XXI, 771 pages. 2005.

Vol. 3805: G. Subsol (Ed.), Virtual Storytelling. XII, 289 pages. 2005.

Vol. 3804: G. Bebis, R. Boyle, D. Koracin, B. Parvin (Eds.), Advances in Visual Computing. XX, 755 pages. 2005.

Vol. 3803: S. Jajodia, C. Mazumdar (Eds.), Information Systems Security. XI, 342 pages. 2005.

Vol. 3802: Y. Hao, J. Liu, Y.-P. Wang, Y.-m. Cheung, H. Yin, L. Jiao, J. Ma, Y.-C. Jiao (Eds.), Computational Intelligence and Security, Part II. XLII, 1166 pages. 2005. (Sublibrary LNAI).

Vol. 3801: Y. Hao, J. Liu, Y.-P. Wang, Y.-m. Cheung, H. Yin, L. Jiao, J. Ma, Y.-C. Jiao (Eds.), Computational Intelligence and Security, Part I. XLI, 1122 pages. 2005. (Sublibrary LNAI).

Vol. 3799: M. A. Rodríguez, I.F. Cruz, S. Levashkin, M.J. Egenhofer (Eds.), GeoSpatial Semantics. X, 259 pages. 2005.

Vol. 3798: A. Dearle, S. Eisenbach (Eds.), Component Deployment. X, 197 pages. 2005.

Vol. 3797: S. Maitra, C. E. V. Madhavan, R. Venkatesan (Eds.), Progress in Cryptology - INDOCRYPT 2005. XIV, 417 pages. 2005.

Vol. 3796: N.P. Smart (Ed.), Cryptography and Coding. XI, 461 pages. 2005.

Vol. 3795: H. Zhuge, G.C. Fox (Eds.), Grid and Cooperative Computing - GCC 2005. XXI, 1203 pages. 2005.

Vol. 3794: X. Jia, J. Wu, Y. He (Eds.), Mobile Ad-hoc and Sensor Networks. XX, 1136 pages. 2005.

Vol. 3793: T. Conte, N. Navarro, W.-m.W. Hwu, M. Valero, T. Ungerer (Eds.), High Performance Embedded Architectures and Compilers. XIII, 317 pages. 2005.

Vol. 3792: I. Richardson, P. Abrahamsson, R. Messnarz (Eds.), Software Process Improvement. VIII, 215 pages. 2005.

Vol. 3791: A. Adi, S. Stoutenburg, S. Tabet (Eds.), Rules and Rule Markup Languages for the Semantic Web. X, 225 pages. 2005.

Vol. 3790: G. Alonso (Ed.), Middleware 2005. XIII, 443 pages. 2005.

Vol. 3789: A. Gelbukh, Á. de Albornoz, H. Terashima-Marín (Eds.), MICAI 2005: Advances in Artificial Intelligence. XXVI, 1198 pages. 2005. (Sublibrary LNAI).

Vol. 3788: B. Roy (Ed.), Advances in Cryptology - ASIACRYPT 2005. XIV, 703 pages. 2005.

Vol. 3787: D. Kratsch (Ed.), Graph-Theoretic Concepts in Computer Science. XIV, 470 pages. 2005.

Vol. 3786: J. Song, T. Kwon, M. Yung (Eds.), Information Security Applications. XI, 378 pages. 2006.

Vol. 3785: K.-K. Lau, R. Banach (Eds.), Formal Methods and Software Engineering. XIV, 496 pages. 2005.

Vol. 3784: J. Tao, T. Tan, R.W. Picard (Eds.), Affective Computing and Intelligent Interaction. XIX, 1008 pages. 2005.

Vol. 3783: S. Qing, W. Mao, J. Lopez, G. Wang (Eds.), Information and Communications Security. XIV, 492 pages. 2005.

Vol. 3782: K.-D. Althoff, A. Dengel, R. Bergmann, M. Nick, T.R. Roth-Berghofer (Eds.), Professional Knowledge Management. XXIII, 739 pages. 2005. (Sublibrary LNAI).

Vol. 3781: S.Z. Li, Z. Sun, T. Tan, S. Pankanti, G. Chollet, D. Zhang (Eds.), Advances in Biometric Person Authentication. XI, 250 pages. 2005.